Advances in Computer Vision and Pattern Recognition

More information about this series at http://www.springer.com/series/4205

Gabriela Csurka
Editor

Domain Adaptation in Computer Vision Applications

Springer

Editor
Gabriela Csurka
Naver Labs Europe
Meylan
France

ISSN 2191-6586 ISSN 2191-6594 (electronic)
Advances in Computer Vision and Pattern Recognition
ISBN 978-3-319-58346-4 ISBN 978-3-319-58347-1 (eBook)
DOI 10.1007/978-3-319-58347-1

Library of Congress Control Number: 2017939548

Printed on acid-free paper

This Springer imprint is published by Springer Nature
The registered company is Springer International Publishing AG
The registered company address is: Gewerbestrasse 11, 6330 Cham, Switzerland

To Gabriel, Elisabeth and Mikhaël

Preface

While the proliferation of sensors being deployed in cell phones, vehicles, buildings, roadways, and computers allows for larger and more diverse information to be collected, the cost of acquiring labels for all these data remains extremely high. To overcome the burden of annotation, alternative solutions have been proposed in the literature to learn decision making models by exploiting unlabeled data from the same domain (data acquired in similar conditions as the targeted data) or also data from related but different domains (different datasets due to different conditions or provided by different customers). In many real-world machine learning scenarios, using only the data from the same domain might be insufficient and data or models borrowed from similar domains can significantly improve the learning process. Such a process, referred to as *domain adaptation*, aims to leverage labeled data in one or more related domains (sources), in order to build models for a target domain.

Domain adaptation is particularly critical for service companies, where all machine learning components deployed in a given service solution should be customized for a new customer either by annotating new data or, preferably, by calibrating the models in order to achieve a contractual performance in the new environment. While adaptation across domains is a challenging task for many applications, in this book, we focus on solutions for *visual applications*.

The aim of the book is to give a relatively broad view of the field by selecting a diverse set of methods which made different advances in the field. The book begins with a comprehensive survey of domain adaptation and transfer learning, including historical shallow methods, more recent methods using deep architectures, and methods addressing computer vision tasks beyond image categorization, such as detection, segmentation or visual attributes. Then, Chap. 2 gives a deeper look at dataset bias in existing datasets when different representations including features extracted from deep architectures are used. The rest of the book is divided into four main parts, following the same structure as the survey presented in Chap. 1.

Part I is dedicated to shallow domain adaptation methods, beginning with the widely used Geodesic Flow Kernel (Chap. 3) and Subspace Alignment (Chap. 4). Both chapters propose solutions for selecting landmark samples in the source dataset. Chapter 5 presents domain-invariant embedding methods and Chap. 6

describes the Transductive Transfer Machine, a method that combines local feature space transformation with classifier selection and parameter adaptation. The first part ends with Chap. 7 that addresses domain adaptation cases where the access to the source data is constrained.

Part II is dedicated to deep adversarial discriminative domain adaptation methods. The first two methods presented use a confusion loss as an adversarial objective to adapt the source network towards the target data. The deep CORAL (Chap. 8) learns a nonlinear transformation that aligns correlations of activation layers of the deep model. The Deep Domain Confusion network (Chap. 9) uses a Maximum Mean Discrepancy based domain confusion loss to induce domain invariant representations. In contrast, Chap. 10 presents the domain-adversarial neural network that integrates a Gradient Reversal Layer to promote the emergence of features discriminative for the main learning task and non-discriminate with respect to the domain shift.

Part III is a collection of contributions addressing domain adaptation problems different from classical image categorization. As such, Chap. 11 focuses on Fisher vector based patch encoding adaptation in the context of vehicle re-identification. Chapter 12 explores the adaptation of semantic segmentation models trained on synthetic images to correctly operate in real scenarios. Chapter 13 addresses the challenge of pedestrian detection by adapting a Deformable Part-Based Model trained on virtual-world data to real world data using structure-aware adaptive structural SVMs. Finally, Chap. 14 proposes a method to generalize semantic part detectors across domains.

Part IV concludes the book with unifying perspectives. On the one hand, Chap. 15 proposes to use multi-source domain generalization techniques for the purpose of learning cross-category generalizable attribute detectors. On the other hand, Chap. 16 proposes a common framework that unifies multi-domain and multi-task learning which can be flexibly applied also to zero-shot learning and zero-shot domain adaptation.

Overall, this comprehensive volume, designed to form and inform professionals, young researchers, and graduate students, is the first collection dedicated to domain adaptation for visual applications. In this book I wanted not only to address historically shallow and recent deep domain adaptation methods, but also contributions focused on object or object part detection, re-identification, image segmentation, attribute detection as well to present generic frameworks that unify domain adaptation with multi-domain, multi-task and zero-shot learning.

To give such a broad view, I brought together leading experts in the field to showcase their techniques. I would like to thank them specially for accepting my invitation and for their dedicated effort to share in this book their valuable experiences in the various chapters. Finally, I would also like to thank our Springer editors, Wayne Wheeler and Simon Rees, for their advice and their help in guiding me through the book production process.

Meylan, France Gabriela Csurka
February 2017

Contents

Chapter 1
A Comprehensive Survey on Domain Adaptation for Visual Applications

Gabriela Csurka

Abstract The aim of this chapter is to give an overview of domain adaptation and transfer learning with a specific view to visual applications. After a general motivation, we first position domain adaptation in the more general transfer learning problem. Second, we try to address and analyze briefly the state-of-the-art methods for different types of scenarios, first describing the historical shallow methods, addressing both the homogeneous and heterogeneous domain adaptation methods. Third, we discuss the effect of the success of deep convolutional architectures which led to the new type of domain adaptation methods that integrate the adaptation within the deep architecture. Fourth, we review DA methods that go beyond image categorization, such as object detection, image segmentation, video analyses or learning visual attributes. We conclude the chapter with a section where we relate domain adaptation to other machine learning solutions.

1.1 Introduction

While huge volumes of unlabeled data are generated and made available in many domains, the cost of acquiring data labels remains high. To overcome the burden of annotation, alternative solutions have been proposed in the literature in order to exploit the unlabeled data (referred to as semi-supervised learning), or data and/or models available in similar domains (referred to as transfer learning). Domain adaptation (DA) is a particular case of transfer learning (TL) that leverages labeled data in one or more related *source* domains, to learn a classifier for unseen or unlabeled data in a *target* domain. In general it is assumed that the task is the same, i.e. class labels are shared between domains. The source domains are assumed to be related to the target domain, but not identical, in which case, it becomes a standard machine learning (ML) problem where we assume that the test data is drawn from the same distribution as the training data. When this assumption is not verified, i.e. the

G. Csurka (✉)
Naver Labs Europe, Meylan, France
e-mail: gabriela.csurka@naverlabs.com

G. Csurka (ed.), *Domain Adaptation in Computer Vision Applications*,
Advances in Computer Vision and Pattern Recognition,
DOI 10.1007/978-3-319-58347-1_1

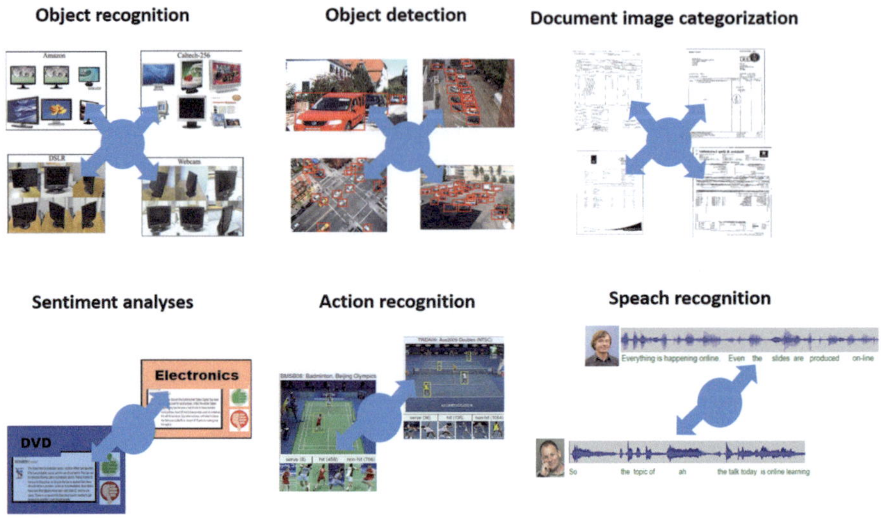

Fig. 1.1 Example scenarios with domain adaptation needs

distributions of training and test sets do not match, the performance at test time can be significantly degraded.

In visual applications, such distribution difference, called domain shift, are common in real-life applications. They can be consequences of changing conditions, i.e. background, location, pose changes, but the domain mismatch might be more severe when, for example, the source and target domains contain images of different types, such as photos, NIR images, paintings or sketches [63, 102, 271, 412]. Service provider companies are especially concerned since, for the same service (task), the distribution of the data may vary a lot from one customer to another. In general, machine learning components of service solutions that are re-deployed from a given customer or location to a new customer or location require specific customization to accommodate the new conditions. For example, in brand sentiment management it is critical to tune the models to the way users talk about their experience when given different products. In surveillance and urban traffic understanding, pretrained models on previous locations might need adjustment to the new environment. All these entail either acquisition of annotated data in the new field or the calibration of the pretrained models to achieve the contractual performance in the new situation. However, the former solution, i.e. data labeling, is expensive and time consuming due to the significant amount of human effort involved. Therefore, the second option is preferred when possible. This can be achieved either by adapting the pretrained models taking advantage of the unlabeled (and if available labeled) target set or, to build the target model, by exploiting both previously acquired labeled source data and the new unlabeled target data together.

Numerous approaches have been proposed in the last years to address adaptation needs that arise in different application scenarios (see a few examples in Fig. 1.1).

Examples include DA and TL solutions for named entity recognition and opinion extraction across different text corpora [42, 118, 356, 589], multilingual text classification [372, 587, 588], sentiment analysis [77, 194], WiFi-based localization [354], speech recognition across different speakers [292, 385], object recognition in images acquired in different conditions [164, 200, 312, 407, 465], video concept detection [555], video event recognition [137], activity recognition [155, 590], human motion parsing from videos [430], face recognition [424, 429, 557], facial landmark localization [446], facial action unit detection [91], 3D pose estimation [551], document categorization across different customer datasets [85, 105, 109], etc.

In this chapter, we mainly focus on *domain adaptation* methods applied to *visual tasks*. For a broader review of the transfer learning literature as well as for approaches specifically designed to solve non-visual tasks, e.g. text or speech, please refer to [535].

The rest of the chapter is organized as follows. In Sect. 1.2 we define more formally transfer learning and domain adaptation. In Sect. 1.3 we review shallow DA methods that can be applied on visual features extracted from the images, both in the homogeneous and heterogeneous case. Section 1.4 addresses more recent deep DA methods and Sect. 1.5 describes DA solutions proposed for computer vision applications beyond image classification. In Sect. 1.6 we relate DA to other transfer learning and standard machine learning approaches and in Sect. 1.7 we conclude the chapter.

1.2 Transfer Learning and Domain Adaptation

In this section, we follow the definitions and notation of [355, 535]. Accordingly, a domain $\mathcal{D}$ is composed of a d-dimensional feature space $\mathcal{X} \subset R^d$ with a marginal probability distribution $P(\mathbf{X})$, and a task $\mathcal{T}$ defined by a label space $\mathcal{Y}$ and the conditional probability distribution $P(\mathbf{Y}|\mathbf{X})$, where $\mathbf{X}$ and $\mathbf{Y}$ are random variables. Given a particular sample set $\mathbf{X} = \{\mathbf{x}_1, \dots \mathbf{x}_n\}$ of $\mathcal{X}$, with corresponding labels $\mathbf{Y} = \{y_1, \dots y_n\}$ from $\mathcal{Y}$, $P(\mathbf{Y}|\mathbf{X})$ can in general be learned in a supervised manner from these feature-label pairs $\{\mathbf{x}_i, y_i\}$.

Let us assume that we have two domains with their related tasks: a *source* domain $\mathcal{D}^s = \{\mathcal{X}^s, P(\mathbf{X}^s)\}$ with $\mathcal{T}^s = \{\mathcal{Y}^s, P(\mathbf{Y}^s|\mathbf{X}^s)\}$ and a *target* domain $\mathcal{D}^t = \{\mathcal{X}^t, P(\mathbf{X}^t)\}$ with $\mathcal{T}^t = \{\mathcal{Y}^t, P(\mathbf{Y}^t|\mathbf{X}^t)\}$. If the two domains correspond, i.e. $\mathcal{D}^s = \mathcal{D}^t$ and $\mathcal{T}^s = \mathcal{T}^t$, traditional ML methods can be used to solve the problem, where $\mathcal{D}^s$ becomes the training set and $\mathcal{D}^t$ the test set.

When this assumption does not hold, i.e. $\mathcal{D}^t \neq \mathcal{D}^s$ or $\mathcal{T}^t \neq \mathcal{T}^s$, the models trained on $\mathcal{D}^s$ might perform poorly on $\mathcal{D}^t$, or they are not applicable directly if $\mathcal{T}^t \neq \mathcal{T}^s$. When the source domain is somewhat related to the target, it is possible to exploit the related information from $\{\mathcal{D}^s, \mathcal{T}^s\}$ to learn $P(\mathbf{Y}^t|\mathbf{X}^t)$. This process is known as *transfer learning* (TL).

We distinguish between *homogeneous TL*, where the source and target are represented in the same the feature space, $\mathcal{X}^t = \mathcal{X}^s$, with $P(\mathbf{X}^t) \neq P(\mathbf{X}^s)$ due to domain

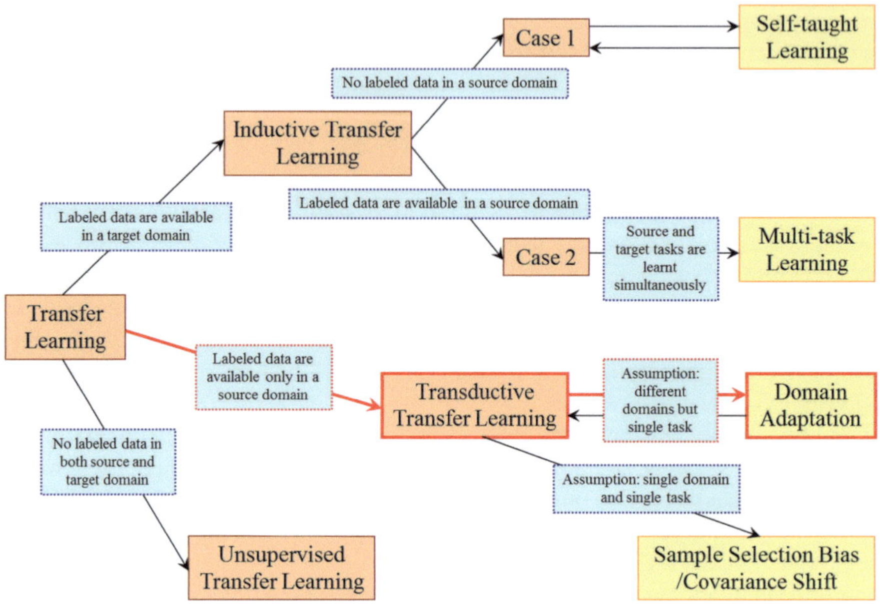

Fig. 1.2 An overview of different transfer learning approaches. (Courtesy to S.J. Pan [355])

shift, and *heterogeneous TL* where the source and target data can have different representations, $\mathcal{X}^t \neq \mathcal{X}^s$ (or they can even be of different modalities such as image versus text).

Based on these definitions, [355] categorizes the TL approaches into three main groups depending on the different situations concerning source and target domains and the corresponding tasks. These are the inductive TL, transductive TL and unsupervised TL (see Fig. 1.2). The *inductive TL* is the case where the target task is different but related to the source task, no matter whether the source and target domains are the same or not. It requires at least some labeled target instances to induce a predictive model for the target data. In the case of the *transductive TL*, the source and target tasks are the same, and either the source and target data representations are different ($\mathcal{X}^t \neq \mathcal{X}^s$) or the source and target distributions are different due to selection bias or distribution mismatch. Finally, the *unsupervised TL* refers to the case where both the domains and the tasks are different but somewhat related. In general, labels are not available neither for the source nor for the target, and the focus is on exploiting the (unlabeled) information in the source domain to solve unsupervised learning task in the target domain. These tasks include clustering, dimensionality reduction and density estimation [113, 537].

According to this classification, DA methods are transductive TL solutions, where it is assumed that the tasks are the same, i.e. $\mathcal{T}^t = \mathcal{T}^s$. In general they refer to a categorization task, where both the set of labels and the conditional distributions are assumed to be shared between the two domains, i.e. $\mathcal{Y}^s = \mathcal{Y}^t$ and $P(\mathbf{Y}|\mathbf{X}^t) = P(\mathbf{Y}|\mathbf{X}^s)$. However, the second assumption is rather strong and does not always hold in real-life applications. Therefore, the definition of domain adaptation is relaxed to the case where only the first assumption is required, i.e. $\mathcal{Y}^s = \mathcal{Y}^t = \mathcal{Y}$.

In the DA community, we further distinguish between the *unsupervised*[1] (US) case where the labels are available only for the source domain and the *semi-supervised* (SS) case where a small set of target examples are labeled.

1.3 Shallow Domain Adaptation Methods

In this section, we review shallow DA methods that can be applied on vectorial visual features extracted from images.[2] First, in Sect. 1.3.1 we survey homogeneous DA methods, where the feature representation for the source and target domains is the same, $\mathcal{X}^t = \mathcal{X}^s$ with $P(\mathbf{X}^t) \neq P(\mathbf{X}^s)$, and the tasks shared, $\mathcal{Y}^s = \mathcal{Y}^t$. Then, in Sect. 1.3.2 we discuss methods that can exploit efficiently several source domains. Finally, in Sect. 1.3.3, we discuss the heterogeneous case, where the source and target data have different representations.

1.3.1 Homogeneous Domain Adaptation Methods

Instance re-weighting methods. The DA case when we assume that the conditional distributions are shared between the two domains, i.e. $P(\mathbf{Y}|\mathbf{X}^s) = P(\mathbf{Y}|\mathbf{X}^t)$, is often referred to as *dataset bias* or *covariate shift* [434]. In this case, one could simply apply the model learned on the source to estimate $P(\mathbf{Y}|\mathbf{X}^t)$. However, as $P(\mathbf{X}^s) \neq P(\mathbf{X}^t)$, the source model might yield a poor performance when applied on the target set despite the underlying $P(\mathbf{Y}|\mathbf{X}^s) = P(\mathbf{Y}|\mathbf{X}^t)$ assumption. The most popular early solutions proposed to overcome this to happen are based on instance reweighting (see Fig. 1.3 for an illustration).

To compute the weight of an instance, early methods proposed to estimate the ratio between the likelihoods of being a source or target example. This can be done either by estimating the likelihoods independently using a domain classifier [570] or by approximating directly the ratio between the densities with a Kullback–Leibler Importance Estimation Procedure [261, 463]. However, one of the most popular measures used to weight data instances, used for example in [214, 243, 354], is the Maximum Mean Discrepancy (MMD) [45] computed between the data distributions in the two domains.

[1]Note also that the unsupervised DA is not related to the unsupervised TL, for which no source labels are available and in general the task to be solved is unsupervised.

[2]Chapters 3–7 in Part I, as individual contributions, propose a detailed analysis of several popular shallow methods.

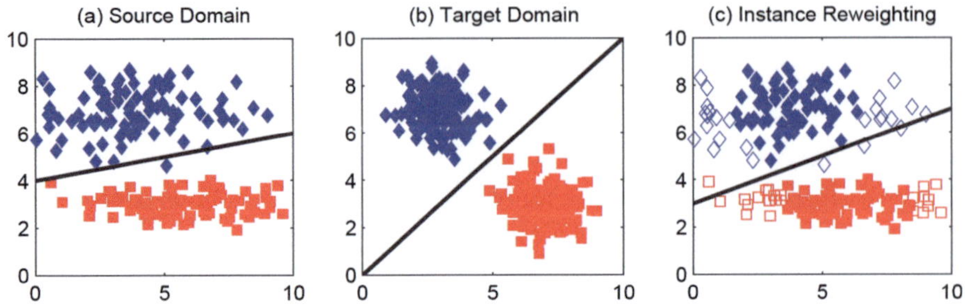

Fig. 1.3 Instance re-weighting on the source classifier. (Courtesy to M. Long [313])

The method proposed in [142] infers re-sampling weights through maximum entropy density estimation. [434] improves predictive inference under covariate shift by weighting the log-likelihood function. The importance weighted twin Gaussian processes [551] directly learns the importance weight function, without going through density estimation, by using the relative unconstrained least-squares importance fitting. The Selective Transfer Machine [91] jointly optimizes the weights as well as the classifier's parameters to preserve the discriminative power of the new decision boundary.

The Transfer Adaptive Boosting (TrAdaBoost) [112], is an extension to AdaBoost [168] that iteratively re-weights both source and target examples during the learning of a target classifier. This is done by increasing the weights of miss-classified target instances as in the traditional AdaBoost, but decreasing the weights of miss-classified source samples in order to diminish their importance during the training process. The TrAdaBoost was further extended by integrating dynamic updates in [9, 86].

Parameter adaptation methods. Another set of early DA methods, which does not necessarily assume $P(\mathbf{Y}|\mathbf{X}^s) = P(\mathbf{Y}|\mathbf{X}^t)$, investigates different options to adapt the parameters of the classifier, in general an SVM, trained on the source domain to perform better on the target set. Note that these methods in general require at least a small amount of labeled target examples per class, hence they can only be applied in the semi-supervised DA scenario. Such methods are the followings. The Transductive SVM [257] aims at decreasing the generalization error of the classification by incorporating knowledge about the target data into the SVM optimization process. The Adaptive SVM (A-SVM) [554] progressively adjusts the decision boundaries of the source classifiers using a set of perturbation functions built with the available labeled target examples (see Fig. 1.4). The Domain Transfer SVM (DT-SVM) [136] simultaneously reduces the distribution mismatch (MMD) between two domains and learns the target decision function. The Adaptive Multiple Kernel Learning (A-MKL) [137] generalizes the latter by learning an adapted classifier based on multiple base kernels and the pretrained average classifier. The model minimizes jointly the structural risk functional and the MMD between the two domains.

The Domain Adaptation SVM [55] exploits within the semi-supervised DA scenario both the Transductive SVM [257] and its extension, the progressive transduc-

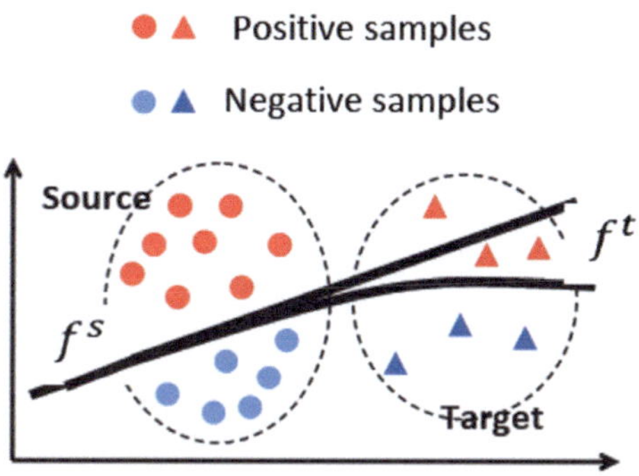

Fig. 1.4 Illustration of the Adaptive SVM [554], where a set of so-called perturbation functions Δ_f are added to the source classifier f^s to progressively adjusts the decision boundaries of f^s for the target domain. (Courtesy to D. Xu)

tive SVM [83]. The Cross-Domain SVM proposed in [256] constrains the impact of source data to the k-nearest neighbors (similarly to the spirit of the Localized SVM [84]). This is done by down-weighting support vectors from the source data that are far from the target samples.

Feature augmentation. One of the simplest methods for DA was proposed in [116], where the original representation $\mathbf{x}$ is augmented with itself and a vector of the same size filled with zeros as follows: the source features become $\begin{bmatrix}\mathbf{x}^s\\ \mathbf{x}^s\\ \mathbf{0}\end{bmatrix}$ and target features $\begin{bmatrix}\mathbf{x}^t\\ \mathbf{0}\\ \mathbf{x}^t\end{bmatrix}$. Then, an SVM is trained on these augmented features to figure out which parts of the representation is shared between the domains and which are the domain-specific ones.

The idea of feature augmentation is also behind the Geodesic Flow Sampling (GFS) [206, 207] and the Geodesic Flow Kernel (GFK) [196, 200]. These methods represent the domains, embedded in d-dimensional linear subspaces, as points on the Grassman manifold corresponding to the collection of all d-dimensional subspaces. In the case of GFS [206, 207], following the geodesic path between the source and target domains, representations, intermediate domains are sampled gradually and concatenated (see illustration in Fig. 1.5). Instead of sampling, GFK [196, 200], described in Chap. 3, extends GFS to the infinite case, proposing a kernel that makes the solution equivalent to integrating over all common subspaces lying on the geodesic path.

A more generic framework, proposed in [207], accommodates domain representations in high-dimensional Reproducing Kernel Hilbert Space (RKHS) using kernel methods and low-dimensional manifold representations corresponding to Laplacian Eigenmaps. The approach described in [344] was inspired by the manifold-based incremental learning framework in [206]. It generates a set of intermediate dictionaries which smoothly connect the source and target domains. This is done by decomposing the target data with the current intermediate domain dictionary updated with

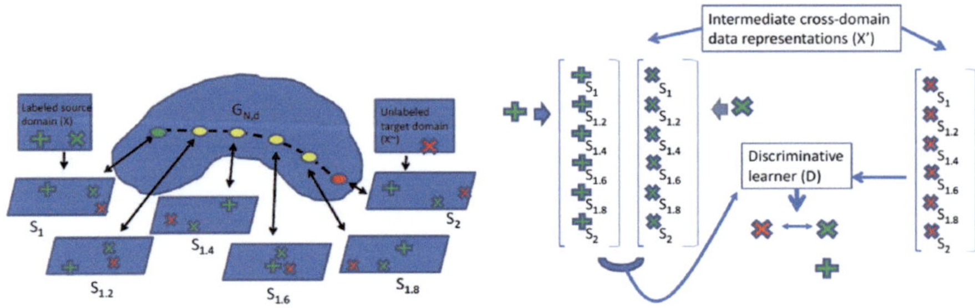

Fig. 1.5 The GFS samples between source S_1 and target S_2 on the geodesic path intermediate domains $S_{1,i}$ that can be seen as cross-domain data representations. (Courtesy to R. Gopalan [206])

a reconstruction residue estimated on the target. Concatenating these intermediate representations enables learning a better cross-domain classifier.

These methods exploit *intermediate cross-domain* representations that are built without the use of class labels. Hence, they can be applied to both, the US and SS, scenarios. These cross-domain representations are then used either to train a discriminative classifier [207] using the available labeled set, or to label the target instances using nearest neighbor search in the kernel space [196, 200].

Feature space alignment. Instead of augmenting the features, another set of methods attempts the alignment of the source features with the target ones. As such, the Subspace Alignment (SA) [164] aligns the source subspace obtained by PCA with the target PCA subspace, where the PCA dimensions are selected by minimizing the Bregman divergence between the subspaces. The Correlation Alignment (CORAL) [465] minimizes the domain shift by using second-order statistics of the source and target distributions. This is achieved by a whitening of the source data using its covariance followed by a "*re-coloring*" using the target covariance matrix.[3]

As an alternative to feature alignment, a large set of feature transformation methods were proposed with the objective to find a projection of the data into a latent space such that the discrepancy between the source and target distributions is decreased (see Fig. 1.6). Note that the projections can be shared between the domains or they can be domain-specific projections. In the latter case we talk about asymmetric feature transformation. Furthermore, when learning the transformation requires no class labels, the method is called *unsupervised* feature transformation and when the transformation is learned by exploiting class labels (only from the source or also from the target when available) it is referred to as *supervised* feature transformation.

Unsupervised feature transformation. One of the first such DA methods is the Transfer Component Analysis[4] (TCA) [354] that proposes to discover common latent features having the same marginal distribution across the source and target domains,

[3]More details on SA can be found in Chap. 4 and on CORAL in Chap. 8.

[4]Details about TCA can be found in Chap. 5.

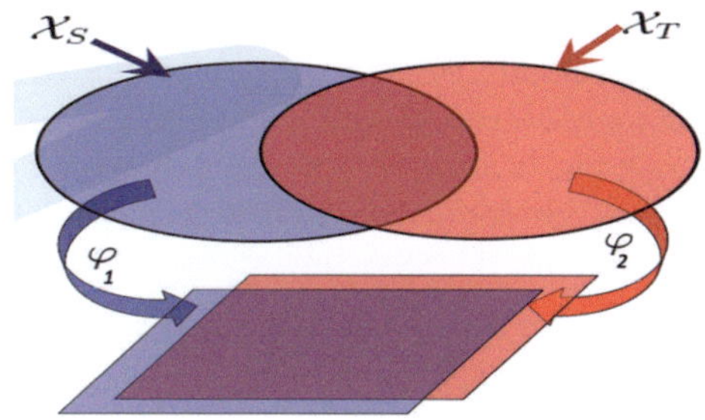

Fig. 1.6 Feature transformation based approaches aim in finding a projection $\phi_1 = \phi_2$ in general into a lower dimensional space where the domains shift is decreased (Courtesy to D. Xu.)

while maintaining the intrinsic structure (local geometry of the data manifold) of the original domain by a smoothness term.

Instead of restricting the discrepancy to a simple distance between the sample means in the lower dimensional space, the domain invariant projection (DIP) [25] compares directly the distributions in the RKHS while constraining the transformation to be orthogonal. The Statistically Invariant Embedding (SIE) [26], based on the fact that probability distributions lie on a Riemannian manifold, uses the Hellinger distance on this manifold to compare kernel density estimates between the domains.[5] Both, DIP and SIE, involve non-linear optimization solved with the conjugate gradient algorithm [143].

The Transfer Sparse Coding [310] learns robust sparse representations for classifying cross-domain data accurately. To bring the domains closer, the distances between the source and target sample means along each dimension is incorporated into the objective function to be minimized. The Transfer Joint Matching [313] learns a non-linear transformation between the two domains by minimizing the distance between the empirical expectations of source and target data distributions integrated within a kernel embedding. In addition, to put less emphasis on the source instances that are irrelevant to classify the target data, instance re-weighing is employed.

The feature transformation proposed by in [77] exploits the correlation between the source and target set to learn a robust representation by reconstructing the original features from their noised counterparts. The method, called Marginalized Denoising Autoencoder[6] (MDA), is based on a quadratic loss and a drop-out noise level that factorizes over all feature dimensions. This allows the method to avoid explicit data corruption by marginalizing out the noise and having a closed-form solution for the feature transformation. Note that it is straightforward to stack together several layers with optional non-linearities between layers to obtain a multi-layer network with the parameters for each layer obtained in a single forward pass.

In general, the above-mentioned methods learn the transformation without using any class label. After projecting the data in the new space, any classifier trained on the source set can be used to predict labels for the target data. The model often works even better if in addition a small set of the target examples are hand-labeled

[5]Chapter 5 describes several invariant embedding approaches considering both the RKHS space and the Riemannian manifold.

[6]More details about MDA can be found in Chap. 7.

(SS adaptation). The class labels can also be used to learn a better transformation. Such methods, called supervised feature transformation based DA methods, to learn the transformation exploit class labels, either only from the source or also from the target (when available). When only the source class labels are exploited, the method can still be applied to the US scenario, while methods using also target labels are designed for the SS case.

Supervised feature transformation. Several unsupervised feature transformation methods, cited above, have been extended to capitalize on class labels to learn a better transformation. Among these extensions, we can mention the semi-supervised TCA [327, 354] where the objective function that is minimized contains a label dependency term in addition to the distance between the domains and the manifold regularization term. The label dependency term has the role of maximizing the alignment of the projections with the source labels and, when available, target labels.

Similarly, in [106] a quadratic regularization term, relying on the pretrained source classifier, is added into the MDA framework [77], in order to keep the denoised source data well classified. Moreover, the domain denoising and cross-domain classifier can be learned jointly by iteratively solving a Sylvester linear system to estimate the transformation and a linear system to get the classifier in closed form.

To take advantage of class labels, the distance between each source sample and its corresponding class means is added as regularizer into the DIP [25] respectively SIE model [26]. This term encourages the source samples from the same class to be clustered in the latent space. The Adaptation Regularization Based Transfer Learning [311] performs DA by optimizing simultaneously the structural risk functional, the joint distribution matching between domains and the manifold consistency. The Max-Margin Domain Transform [239] optimizes both the transformation and classifier parameters jointly, by introducing an efficient cost function based on the misclassification loss.

Another set of methods extends marginal distribution discrepancy minimization to conditional distribution involving data labels from the source and class predictions from the target. Thus, [586] proposes an adaptive kernel approach that maps the marginal distribution of the target and source sets into a common kernel space, and use a sample selection strategy to draw conditional probabilities between the two domains closer. The Joint Distribution Adaptation [312] jointly adapts the marginal distribution through a principled (PCA based) dimensionality reduction procedure and the conditional distribution between the domains.

Metric learning based feature transformation. These methods are particular supervised feature transformation methods that involve that at least a limited set of target labels are available, and they use metric learning techniques to bridge the relatedness between the source and target domains. Thus, [575] proposes distance metric learning with either log-determinant or manifold regularization to adapt face recognition models between subjects. [407] uses the Information-theoretic Metric Learning from [119] to define a common distance metric across different domains. This method was further extended in [278] by incorporating non-linear kernels, which enable the

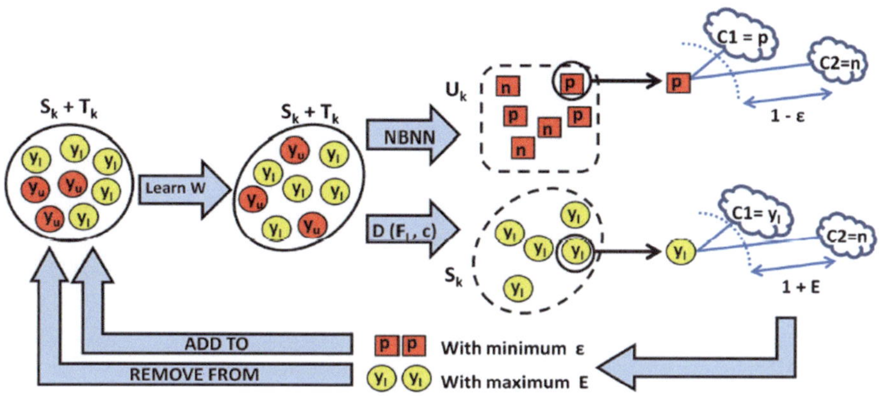

Fig. 1.7 The NBNN-DA adjusts the image-to-class distances by tuning per class metrics and progressively making it more suitable for the target. (Courtesy to T. Tommasi [206])

model to be applicable to the heterogeneous case (i.e. different source and target representations).

The metric learning for domain-specific class means (DSCM) [107] learns a transformation of the feature space which, for each instance minimizes the weighted soft-max distances to the corresponding domain-specific class means. This allows the projected space to decrease the intraclass and to increase the interclass distances (see also Fig. 1.9). This was extended with an active learning component by the self-adaptive metric learning domain adaptation (SaML-DA) [107] framework, where the target training set is iteratively increased with labels predicted with DSCM and used to refine the current metric. SaML-DA was inspired by the Naive Bayes Nearest Neighbor based domain adaptation (NBNN-DA) [483] framework, which combines metric learning and NBNN classifier to adjust the instance-to-class distances by progressively making the metric more suitable for the target domain (see Fig. 1.7). The main idea behind both methods, SaML-DA and NBNN-DA, is to replace at each iteration the most ambiguous source example of each class by the target example for which the classifier (DSCM respectively NNBA) is the most confident for the given class.

Local feature transformation. The previous methods learn a global transformation to be applied to the whole source and target sets. In contrast, the Adaptive Transductive Transfer Machines [152], described in Chap. 6, complements the global transformation with a sample-based transformation to refine the probability density function of the source instances assuming that the transformation from the source to the target domain is locally linear. This is achieved by representing the target set by a Gaussian Mixture Models (GMM) and learning an optimal translation parameter that maximizes the likelihood of the translated source as a posterior.

Similarly, the Optimal Transport for Domain Adaptation [101], considers a local transportation plan for each source example. The model can be seen as a graph

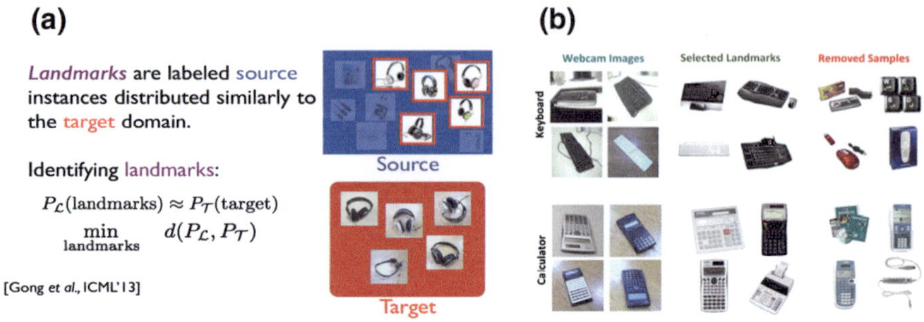

Fig. 1.8 Landmarks selected for the task *Amazon versus Webcam* of the Office 31 dataset [407] using **a** MMD [196] or **b** the Hellinger distance on the statistical manifold [26]

matching problem, where the final coordinates of each sample are found by mapping the source samples to the target ones, while respecting the marginal distribution of the target domain. To exploit class labels, a regularization term with group-lasso is added inducing, on one hand, group sparsity and, on another hand, constraining source samples of the same class to remain close during the transport.

Landmark selection. In order to improve the feature learning process, several methods have been proposed with the aim of selecting the most relevant instances from the source, so-called landmark examples, to be used to train the adaptation model (see examples in Fig. 1.8). Thus, [196] proposes to minimize a variant of the MMD to identify good landmarks by creating a set of auxiliary tasks that offer multiple views of the original problem (detailed in Chap. 3). The Statistically Invariant Sample Selection method [26], uses the Hellinger distance on the statistical manifold instead of MMD. The selection is forced to keep the proportions of the source samples per class the same as in the original data. Contrariwise to these approaches, the multi-scale landmark selection [10] (described in Chap. 4) does not require any class labels. It takes each instance independently and considers it as a good candidate if the Gaussian distributions of the source examples and of the target points centered on the instance are similar over a set of different scales (Gaussian variances).

Note that the landmark selection process, although strongly related to instance re-weighting methods with binary weights, can be rather seen as data preprocessing and hence complementary to the adaptation process.

1.3.2 Multi-source Domain Adaptation

Most of the above-mentioned methods were designed for a single source vs. target case. When multiple sources are available, they can be concatenated to form a *single* source set, but because the possible shift between the different source domains, this might not be always a good option. Alternatively, the models built for each *source-*

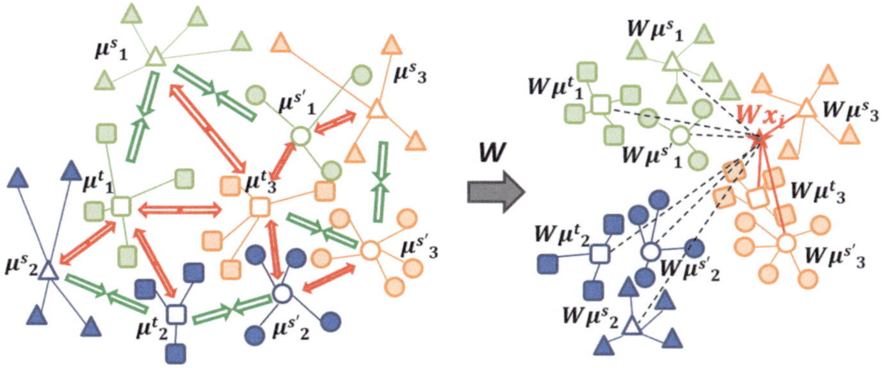

Fig. 1.9 Metric learning for the DSCM classifier, where $\mu^s_{c_i}$ and $\mu^{s'}_{c_i}$ represent source-specific class means and $\mu^t_{c_i}$ class means in the target domain. The feature transformation **W** is learned by minimizing for each sample the weighted soft-max distances to the corresponding domain-specific class means in the projected space

target pair (or their results) can be combined to make a final decision. However, a better option might be to build multi-source DA models which, relying only on the a priori *known* domain labels, are able to exploit the specificity of each source domain.

Such methods are the Feature Augmentation (FA) [116] and the A-SVM [554], already mentioned in Sect. 1.3.1, both exploiting naturally the multi-source aspect of the dataset. Indeed in the case of FA, extra feature sets, one for each source domain, concatenated to the representations, allow learning source-specific properties shared between a given source and the target. The A-SVM uses an ensemble of source-specific auxiliary classifiers to adjust the parameters of the target classifier.

Similarly, the Domain Adaptation Machine [138] l leverages a set of source classifiers by the integration of domain-dependent regularizer term which is based on a smoothness assumption. The model forces the target classifier to share similar decision values with the relevant source classifiers on the unlabeled target instances. The conditional probability based multi-source domain adaptation (CP-MDA) approach [68] extends the above idea by adding weight values for each source classifier based on conditional distributions. The DSCM proposed in [107] relies on domain-specific class means both to learn the metric but also to predict the target class labels (see illustration in Fig. 1.9). The domain regularization and classifier based regularization terms of the extended MDA [106] are both sums of source-specific components.

The Robust DA via Low-Rank Reconstruction (RDALRR) [252] transforms each source domain into an intermediate representation such that the transformed samples can be linearly reconstructed from the target ones. Within each source domain, the intrinsic relatedness of the reconstructed samples is imposed by using a low-rank structure where the outliers are identified using sparsity constraints. By enforcing different source domains to have jointly low ranks, a compact source sample set is formed with a distribution close to the target domain (see Fig. 1.10).

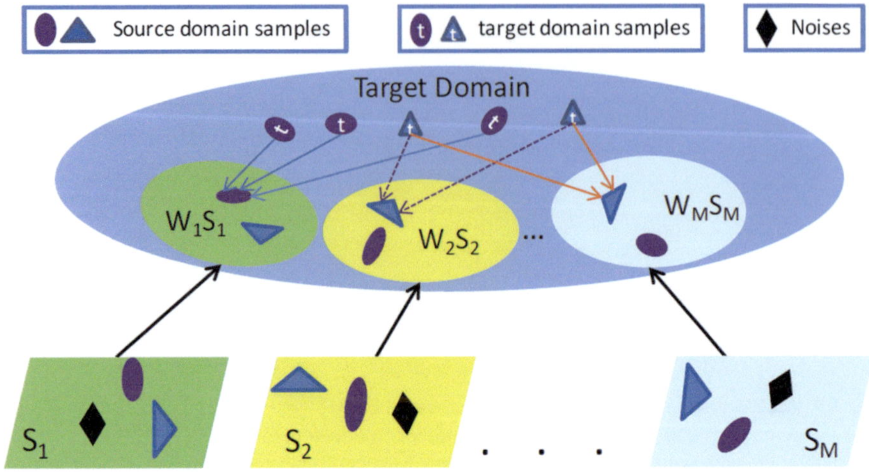

Fig. 1.10 The RDALRR [252] transforms each source domain into an intermediate representation such that they can be linearly reconstructed from the target samples. (Courtesy to I. H. Jhuo)

To better take advantage of having multiple source domains, extensions to methods previously designed for a single source vs. target case were proposed in [62, 207, 238, 565]. Thus, [207] describes a multi-source version of the GFS [206], which was further extended in [62] to the subspaces by sampling spline flow approach. The latter uses smooth polynomial functions determined by splines on the manifold to interpolate between different source and the target domain. [238] combines constrained clustering algorithm, used to identify automatically source domains in a large data set, with a multi-source extension of the asymmetric kernel transform [278]. [565] efficiently extends the TrAdaBoost [112] to multiple source domains.

Source domain weighting. When multiple sources are available, it is desired to select those domains that provide the best information transfer and to remove the ones that have more likely negatively impact on the final model. Thus, to down-weight the effect of less related source domains, in [185] first the available labels are propagated within clusters obtained by spectral clustering and then to each source cluster a supervised local weight (SLW) is assigned based on the percentage of label matches between predictions made by a source model and those made by label propagation.

In the Locally Weighted Ensemble Framework [185], the model weights are computed as a similarity between the local neighborhood graphs centered on source and target instances. The CP-MDA [68], mentioned above, uses a weighted combination of source learners, where the weights are estimated as a function of conditional probability differences between the source and target domains. The rank of domain value defined in [200] measures the relatedness between each source and target domain as the KL divergences between data distributions once the data is projected into the latent subspace. The Multi-Model Knowledge Transfer [482] minimizes the negative transfer by giving higher weights to the most related linear SVM source classifiers. These weights are determined through a leave one out learning process.

1.3.3 Heterogeneous Domain Adaptation

Heterogeneous transfer learning (HTL) refers to the setting where the representation spaces are different for the source and target domains ($\mathcal{X}^t \neq \mathcal{X}^s$ as defined in Sect. 1.2). As a particular case, when the tasks are assumed to be the same, i.e. $\mathcal{Y}^s = \mathcal{Y}^t$, we refer to it as *heterogeneous domain adaptation* (HDA).

Both HDAand HTL are strongly related to multi-view learning [525, 543], where the presence of multiple information sources gives an opportunity to learn better representations (features) by analyzing the views simultaneously. This makes possible to solve the task when not all the views are available. Such situations appear when processing simultaneously audio and video [69], documents containing both image and text (e.g. web pages or photos with tags or comments) [223, 450, 552], images acquired with depth information [237], etc. We can also have multi-view settings when the views have the same modalities (textual, visual, audio), such as in the case of parallel text corpora in different languages [158, 515], photos of the same person taken across different poses, illuminations and expressions [377, 424, 425, 557].

Multi-view learning assumes that at training time for the same data instance multiple views from complementary information sources are available (e.g. a person is identified by photograph, fingerprint, signature or iris). Instead, in the case of HTL and HDA, the challenge comes from the fact that we have one view at training and another one at test time. Therefore, one set of methods proposed to solve HDA relies on some multi-view auxiliary data[7] to bridge the gap between the domains (see Fig. 1.11).

Methods relying on auxiliary domains. These methods principally exploit feature co-occurrences (e.g. between words and visual features) in the multi-view auxiliary domain. As such, the Transitive Transfer Learning [473] selects an appropriate domain from a large data set guided by domain complexity and, the distribution differences between the original domains (source and target) and the selected one (auxiliary). Then, using non-negative matrix tri-factorization [122], feature clustering and label propagation are performed simultaneously through the intermediate domain.

The Mixed-Transfer approach [474] builds a joint transition probability graph of mixed instances and features, considering the data in the source, target and intermediate domains. The label propagation on the graph is done by a random walk process to overcome the data sparsity. In [593] the representations of the target images are

[7] When the bridge is to be done between visual and textual representations, a common practice is to crawl the web for pages containing both text and images in order to build such intermediate multi-view data.

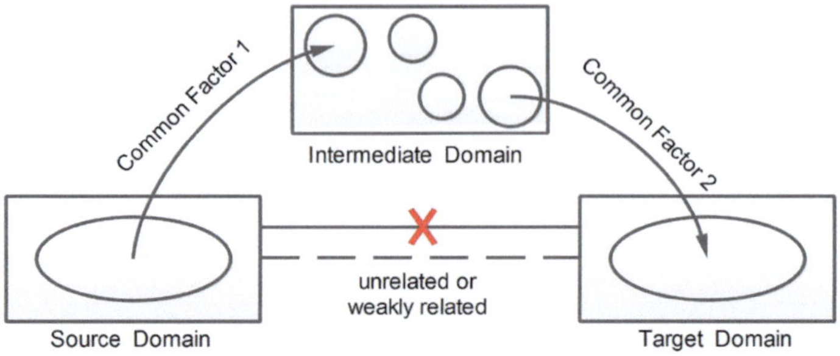

Fig. 1.11 Heterogeneous DA through an intermediate domain allowing to bridge the gap between features representing the two domains. For example, when the source domain contains text and the target images, the intermediate domain can be built from a set of crawled Web pages containing both text and images. (Image courtesy B. Tan [473])

enriched with semantic concepts extracted from the intermediate data through a collective matrix factorization [444].

[374] proposes to build a translator function between the source and target domain by learning directly the product of the two transformation matrices that map each domain into a common (hypothetical) latent topic built on the co-occurrence data. Following the principle of parsimony, they encode as few topics as possible in order to be able to match text and images. The semantic labels are propagated from the labeled text corpus to unlabeled new images by a cross-domain label propagation mechanism using the built translator. In [556] the co-occurrence data is represented by the principal components computed in each feature space and a Markov chain Monte Carlo [14] is employed to construct a directed cyclic network where each node is a domain and each edge weight represents the conditional dependence between the corresponding domains defined by the transfer weights.

[553] studies online HDA, where offline labeled data from a source domain is transferred to enhance the online classification performance for the target domain. The main idea is to build an offline classifier based on heterogeneous similarity using labeled data from a source domain and unlabeled co-occurrence data collected from web pages and social networks (see Fig. 1.12). The online target classifier is combined with the offline source classifier using Hedge weighting strategy, used in Adaboost [168], to update their weights for ensemble prediction.

Instead of relying on external data to bridge the data representation gap, several HDA methods exploit directly the data distribution in the source and target domains willing to remove simultaneously the gap between the feature representations and minimizing the data distribution shift. This is done by learning either a projection for each domain into a domain-invariant common latent space, referred to as *symmetric transformation* based HDA,[8] or a transformation from the source space towards

[8]These methods can be used even if the source and target data are represented in the same feature space, i.e. $\mathcal{X}^t = \mathcal{X}^s$. Therefore, it is not surprising that several methods are direct extensions of homogeneous DA methods described in Sect. 1.3.1.

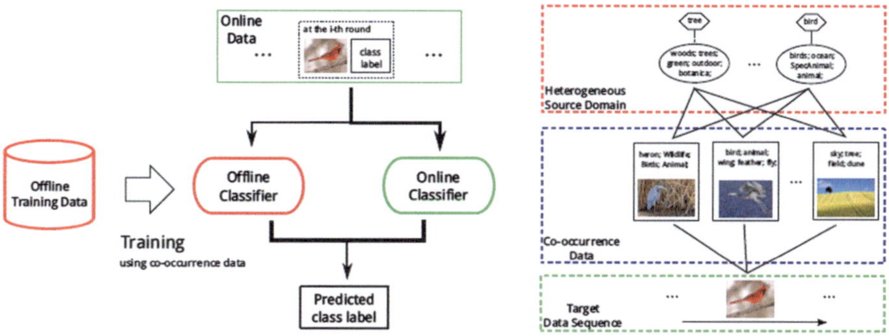

Fig. 1.12 Combining the online and offline classifiers (*right*) and transfer the knowledge through co-occurrences data in the heterogeneous intermediate domain (*left*). (Courtesy to Y. Yan [553])

the target space, called *asymmetric transformation* based HDA. These approaches require at least a limited amount of labeled target examples (semi-supervised DA).

Symmetric feature transformation. The aim of symmetric transformation based HDA approaches is to learn projections for both the source and target spaces into a common latent (embedding) feature space better suited to learn the task for the target. These methods are related, on the one hand, to the feature transformation based homogeneous DA methods described in Sect. 1.3.1 and, on the other hand, to multi-view embedding [59, 202, 223, 343, 425, 523], where different views are embedded in a common latent space. Therefore, several DA methods originally designed for the homogeneous case, have been inspired by the multi-view embedding approaches and extended to heterogeneous data.

As such, the Heterogeneous Feature Augmentation (HFA) [139], prior to data augmentation, embeds the source and target into a common latent space (see Fig. 1.13). In order to avoid the explicit projections, the transformation metrics are computed by the minimization of the structural risk functional of SVM expressed as a function of these projection matrices. The final target prediction function is computed by an alternating optimization algorithm to simultaneously solve the dual SVM and to find the optimal transformations. This model was further extended in [299], where each projection matrix is decomposed into a linear combination of a set of rank-one positive semi-definite matrices and they are combined within a multiple kernel learning approach.

The Heterogeneous Spectral Mapping [432] unifies different feature spaces using spectral embedding where the similarity between the domains in the latent space is maximized with the constraint to preserve the original structure of the data. Combined with a source sample selection strategy, a Bayesian-based approach is applied to model the relationship between the different output spaces.

[542] presents a semi-supervised subspace co-projection method, which addresses heterogeneous multi-class DA. It is based on discriminative subspace learning and exploits unlabeled data to enforce an MMD criterion across domains in the projected

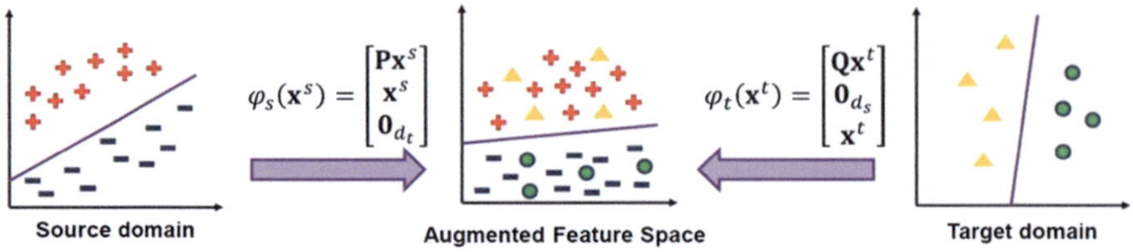

Fig. 1.13 The HFA [139] is seeking for an optimal common space while simultaneously learning a discriminative SVM classifier. (Courtesy to D. Xu)

subspace. It uses error correcting output codes (ECOC) to address the multi-class aspect and to enhance the discriminative informativeness of the projected subspace. The Semi-supervised Domain Adaptation with Subspace Learning [564] jointly explores invariant low-dimensional structures across domains to correct data distribution mismatch and leverages available unlabeled target examples to exploit the underlying intrinsic information in the target domain.

To deal with both domain shift and heterogeneous data, the Shared Domain-Adapted Dictionary Learning (SDDL) [429] learns a class-wise discriminative dictionary in the latent projected space (see Fig. 1.14). This is done by jointly learning the dictionary and the projections of the data from both domains onto a common low-dimensional space, while maintaining the manifold structure of data represented by sparse linear combinations of dictionary atoms.

The Domain Adaptation Manifold Alignment (DAMA) [520] models each domain as a manifold and creates a separate mapping function to transform the heterogeneous input space into a common latent space while preserving the underlying structure of each domain. This is done by representing each domain with a Laplacian that captures the closeness of the instances sharing the same label. The RDALRR [252], mentioned above, transforms each source domain into an intermediate representation such that the source samples linearly reconstructed from the target samples are enforced to be related to each other under a low-rank structure. Note that both DAMA and RDALRR are multi-source HDA approaches.

Asymmetric feature transformation. In contrast to symmetric transformation based HDA, these methods aim to learn a projection of the source features into the target space such that the distribution mismatch within each class is minimized. Such method is the Asymmetric Regularized Cross-Domain Transformation [278] that utilizes an objective function responsible for the domain-invariant transformation learned in a nonlinear Gaussian RBF kernel space. The Multiple Outlook MAPping algorithm [224] finds the transformation matrix by singular value decomposition process that encourages the marginal distributions within the classes to be aligned while maintaining the structure of the data. It requires a limited amount of labeled target data for each class to be paired with the corresponding source classes.

[588] proposes a sparse and class-invariant feature mapping that leverages the weight vectors of the binary classifiers learned in the source and target domains. This is done by considering the learning task as a Compressed Sensing [129] problem and

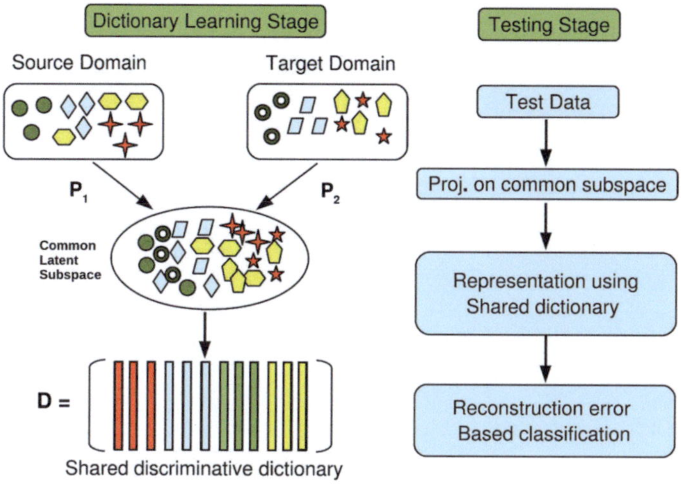

Fig. 1.14 The SDDL proposes to learn a dictionary in a latent common subspace while maintaining the manifold structure of the data. (Courtesy to S. Shekhar [429])

using the ECOC scheme to generate a sufficient number of binary classifiers given the set of classes.

1.4 Deep Domain Adaptation methods

With the recent progress in image categorization due to deep convolutional architectures—trained in a fully supervised fashion on large scale annotated datasets, in particular on part of ImageNet [404]—allowed a significant improvement in the categorization accuracy over previous state-of-the art solutions. Furthermore, it was shown that features extracted from the activation layers of these deep convolutional networks can be re-purposed to novel tasks [128] even when the new tasks differ significantly from the task originally used to train the model.

Concerning domain adaptation, baseline methods without adaptation obtained using features generated by deep models[9] on the two most popular benchmark datasets Office (OFF31) [407] and Office+Caltech (OC10) [200] outperform by a large margin the shallow DA methods using the SURFBOV features originally provided with these datasets. Indeed, the results obtained with such features even without any adaptation to the target are significantly better that the results obtained with any DA method based on SURFBOV [88, 106, 128, 465]. As shown also in [32, 567], this suggests that deep neural networks learn more abstract and robust repre-

[9]Activation layers extracted from popular CNN models, such as AlexNet [275], VGGNET [443], ResNet [230] or GoogleNet [472].

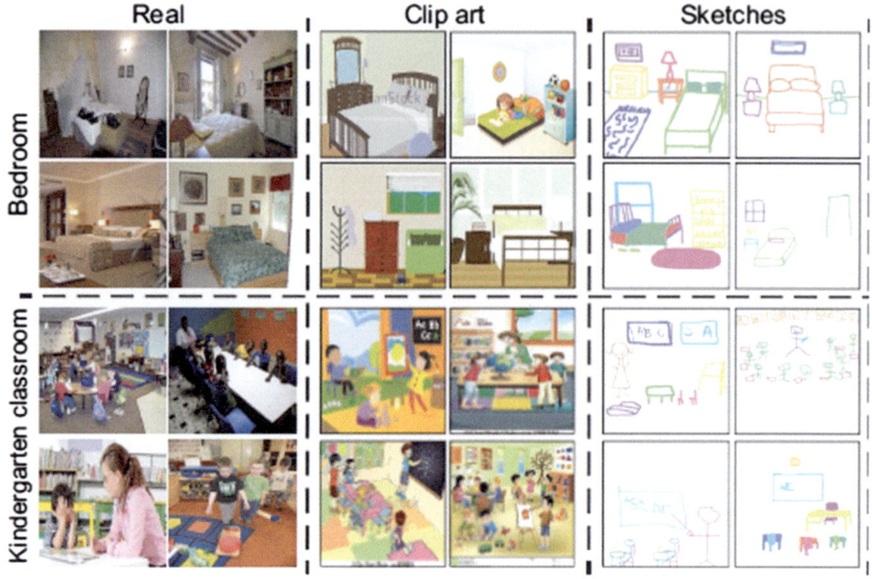

Fig. 1.15 Examples from the Cross-Modal Place dataset [63]. (Courtesy to L. Castrejón)

sentations, encode category-level information and remove, to a certain measure, the domain bias [106, 128, 412, 465].

Note however that in OFF31 and OC10 datasets the images remain relatively similar to the images used to train these models (usually datasets from the ImageNet Large-Scale Visual Recognition Challenge [404]). In contrast, if we consider category models between e.g. images and paintings, drawings, clip art or sketches (see e.g. Fig. 1.15), the models have more difficulties to handle the domain differences [63, 102, 103, 271] and alternative solutions are necessary.

Solutions proposed in the literature to exploit deep models can be grouped into three main categories. The first group considers the CNN models to extract vectorial features to be used by the shallow DA methods. The second solution is to train or fine-tune the deep network on the source domain, adjust it to the new task, and use the model to predict class labels for target instances. Finally, the most promising methods are based on deep learning architectures designed for DA.

Shallow methods with deep features. The first, naive solution is to consider the deep network as feature extractor, where the activation of a layer or several layers of the deep architecture is considered as a representation of the input image. These deep convolutional activation features (DeCAF) [128] extracted from both source and target examples can then be used within any shallow DA method described in Sect. 1.3. For example, Feature Augmentation [116], Max- Margin Domain Transform [239] and Geodesic Flow Kernel [200] were applied to DECAF features in [128], Subspace Alignment [164] and Correlation Alignment in [465]. [106] experiments with

DeCAF features within the extended MDA framework, while [412] explores various metric learning approaches to align deep features extracted from RGB face images (source) and NIR or sketches (target).

In general, these DA methods allow to further improve the classification accuracy compared to the baseline classifiers trained only on the source data with these DeCAF features [106, 128, 412, 465]. Note however that the gain is often relatively small and significantly lower than the gain obtained with the same methods when used with the SURFBOV features.

Fine-tuning deep CNN architectures. The second and most used solution is to fine-tune the deep network model on the new type of data and for the new task [23, 90, 349, 572]. But fine-tuning requires in general a relatively large amount of annotated data which is not available for the target domain, or it is very limited. Therefore, the model is in general fine-tuned on the source—augmented with, when available, the few labeled target instances—which allows in a first place to adjust the deep model to the new task,[10] common between the source and target in the case of DA. This is fundamental if the targeted classes do not belong to the classes used to pretrain the deep model. However, if the domain difference between the source and target is important, fine-tuning the model on the source might over-fit the model for the source. In this case the performance of the fine-tuned model on the target data can be worse than just training the class prediction layer or as above, using the model as feature extractor and training a classifier[11] with the corresponding DeCAF features [88, 465].

1.4.1 DeepDA Architectures

Finally, the most promising are the deep domain adaptation (deepDA) methods that are based on deep learning architectures designed for domain adaptation.[12] One of the first deep model used for DA is the Stacked Denoising Autoencoders [514] proposed to adapt sentiment classification between reviews of different products [194]. This model aims at finding common features between the source and target collections relying on denoising autoencoders. This is done by training a multi-layer neural network to reconstruct input data from partial random corruptions with backpropagation. The Stacked Marginalized Denoising Autoencoders [77] (see also in Sect. 1.3.1) is a variant of the SDA, where the random corruption is marginalized out and hence yields a unique optimal solution (feature transformation) computed in closed form between layers.

[10]This is done by replacing the class prediction layer to correspond to the new set of classes.

[11]Note that the two approaches are equivalent when the layer preceding the class prediction layer are extracted.

[12]In Chaps. 8–10 (Part II) of this book several deepDA methods are described and analyzed in detail as individual contributions.

The Domain Adaptive Neural Network [190] uses such denoising autoencoder as a pretraining stage. To ensure that the model pretrained on the source continue to adapt to the target, the MMD is embedded as a regularization in the supervised backpropagation process (added to the cross-entropy based classification loss of the labels source examples).

The Deep Learning for Domain Adaptation [88], inspired by the intermediate representations on the geodesic path [200, 207], proposes a deep model based interpolation between domains. This is achieved by a deep nonlinear feature extractor trained in an unsupervised manner using the Predictive Sparse Decomposition [267] on intermediate datasets, where the amount of source data is gradually replaced by target samples.

[11] proposes a light-weight domain adaptation method, which, by using only a few target samples, analyzes and reconstructs the output of the filters that were found affected by the domain shift. The aim of the reconstruction is to make the filter responses, given a target image resembles the response map of a source image. This is done by simultaneously selecting and reconstructing the response maps of the bad filters using a lasso based optimization with a KL-divergence measure that guides the filter selection process.

Most DeedDA methods follow a Siamese architectures [52] with two streams, representing the source and target models (see for example Fig. 1.16), and are trained with a combination of a *classification loss* and a *discrepancy loss* [190, 309, 314, 468, 499] or an *adversarial loss*. The classification loss depends on the labeled source data. The discrepancy loss aims to diminish the shift between the two domains while the adversarial loss tries to encourage a common feature space through an adversarial objective with respect to a domain discriminator.

Discrepancy-based methods. These methods, inspired by the shallow feature space transformation approaches described in Sect. 1.3.1, use in general a discrepancy defined between corresponding activation layers of the two streams of the Siamese architecture. One of the first such methods is the Deep Domain Confusion (DDC) [499] where the layer to be considered for the discrepancy and its dimension is automatically selected among a set of fine-tuned networks based on linear MMD between the source and the target. Instead of using a single layer and linear MMD, the Deep Adaptation Network (DAN) [309] considers the sum of MMDs defined between several layers, including the soft prediction layer too. Furthermore, DAN explores multiple kernels for adapting these deep representations, which substantially enhance adaptation effectiveness compared to a single kernel method used in [499]. This was further improved by the Joint Adaptation Networks [314], which unlike the sum of marginal distributions (MMD) defined between different layers, consider the joint distribution discrepancies of these features.

The deep CORAL [468] extends the shallow CORAL [465] method described in Sect. 1.3 to deep architectures.[13] The main idea is to learn a nonlinear transformation that aligns correlations of activation layers between the two streams. This idea is sim-

[13]Both the shallow CORAL and the Deep CORAL are described in details in Chap. 8.

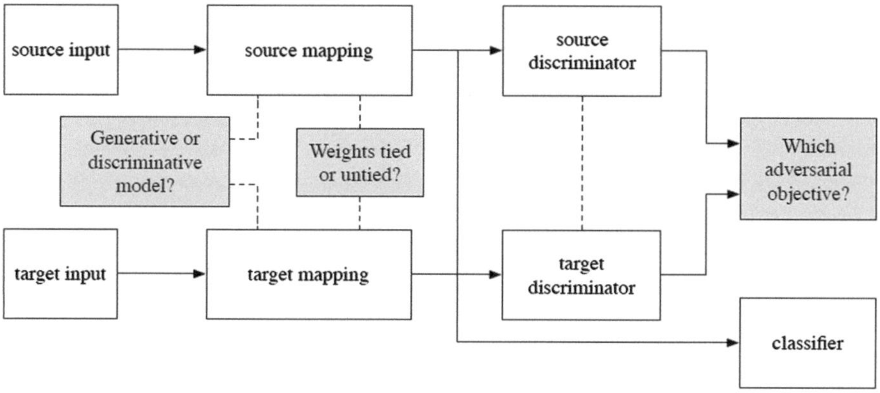

Fig. 1.16 Adversarial adaptation methods can be viewed as instantiations of the same framework with different choices regarding their properties [498] (Image courtesy E. Tzeng)

ilarly to DDC and DAN except that, instead of MMD, the CORAL loss[14] (expressed by the distance between the covariances) is used to minimize discrepancybetween the domains.

In contrast to the above methods, [402] considers the MMD between the weights of the source respectively target models of different layers, where an extra regularizer term ensures that the weights in the two models remain linearly related.

Adversarial discriminative models. The aim of these models is to encourage domain confusion through an adversarial objective with respect to a domain discriminator. [498] proposes a unified view of existing adversarial DA methods by comparing them depending on the loss type, the weight sharing strategy between the two streams and, on whether they are discriminative or generative (see illustration in Fig. 1.16). Among the discriminative models we have the model proposed in [497] using a confusion loss, the Adversarial Discriminative Domain Adaptation [498] that considers an inverted label GAN loss [204] and the Domain-Adversarial Neural Networks [183] with a minimax loss. The generative methods, additionally to thediscriminator, rely on a generator, which, in general, is a Generative Adversarial Network (GAN) [204].

The domain confusion based model proposed in [497] considers a domain confusion objective, under which the mapping is trained with both unlabeled and sparsely labeled target data using a cross-entropy loss function against a uniform distribution. The model simultaneously optimizes the domain invariance to facilitate domain transfer and uses a soft label distribution matching loss to transfer information between tasks.

The Domain-Adversarial Neural Networks [183] (see Chap. 10), integrates a gradient reversal layer into the standard architecture to promote the emergence of fea-

[14]Note that this loss can be seen as minimizing the MMD with a polynomial kernel.

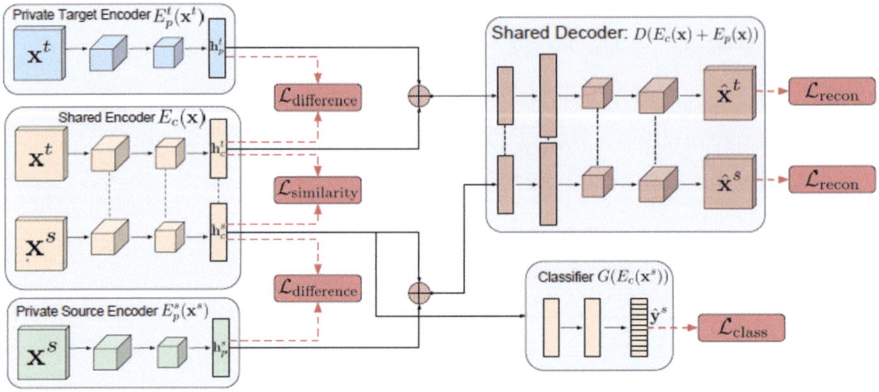

Fig. 1.17 The DSN architecture combines shared and domain-specific encoders, which learns common and domain-specific representation components respectively with a shared decoder that learns to reconstruct the input samples. (Image courtesy K. Bousmalis [49])

tures that are discriminative for the main learning task on the source domain and indiscriminate with respect to the shift between the domains. This layer is left unchanged during the forward propagation and its gradient reversed during backpropagation.

The adversarial Discriminative Domain Adaptation [498] uses an inverted label GAN loss to split the optimization into two independent objectives, one for the generator and another for the discriminator. In contrast to the above methods, this model considers independent source and target mappings (unshared weights between the two streams) allowing domain- specific feature extraction to be learned, where the target weights are initialized by the network pretrained on the source.

Adversarial generative models. These models combine the discriminative model with a generative component in general based on GANs [204]. As such, the coupled Generative Adversarial Networks [304] consists of a tuple of GANs each corresponding to one of the domains. It learns a joint distribution of multi-domain images and enforces a weight sharing constraint to limit the network capacity.

The model proposed in [48] also exploit GANs with the aim to generate source-domain images such that they appear as if they were drawn from the target domain. Prior knowledge regarding the low-level image adaptation process, such as foreground-background segmentation mask, can be integrated into the model through content-similarity loss defined by a masked pairwise mean squared error [144] between the unmasked pixels of the source and generated images. As the model decouples the process of domain adaptation from the task-specific architecture, it is able to generalize also to object classes unseen during the training phase.

Data reconstruction (encoder-decoder) based methods. In contrast to the above methods, the Deep Reconstruction Classification Network [191] combines the standard convolutional network for source label prediction with a deconvolutional network [574] for target data reconstruction. To jointly learn source label predictions and unsupervised target data reconstruction, the model alternates between unsupervised and supervised training. The parameters of the encoding are shared across both tasks, while the decoding parameters are separated. The data reconstruction can be viewed as an auxiliary task to support the adaptation of the label prediction.

The Domain Separation Networks (DSN) [49] introduce the notion of a private subspace for each domain, which captures domain-specific properties, such as background and low- level image statistics. A shared subspace, enforced through the use of autoencoders and explicit loss functions, captures common features between the domains. The model integrates a reconstruction loss using a shared decoder, which learns to reconstruct the input sample by using both the private (domain specific) and source representations (see Fig. 1.17).

Heterogeneous deep DA methods. Concerning heterogeneous or multi-modal deep domain adaptation, we can mention the Transfer Neural Trees [80] proposed to relate heterogeneous cross-domain data. It is a two stream network, one stream for each modality, where the weights in the latter stages of the network are shared. As the prediction layer, a Transfer Neural Decision Forest (Transfer-NDF) is used that performs jointly adaptation and classification.

The weakly shared deep transfer networks for heterogeneous-domain knowledge propagation [437] learns a domain translator function from multi-modal source data that can be used to predict class labels in the target even if only one of the modality is present. The proposed structure has the advantage to be flexible enough to represent both domain-specific features and shared features across domains.

1.5 Beyond Image Classification

In the previous sections, we attempted to provide an overview of visual DA methods with emphasis on image categorization. Compared to this vast literature focused on object recognition, relatively few papers go beyond image classification and address domain adaptation related to other computer vision problems such as object detection, semantic segmentation, pose estimation, video event or action detection. One of the main reasons is probably due to the fact that these problems are more complex and have often additional challenges and requirements (e.g. precision related to the localization in the case of detection, pixel level accuracy required for image segmentation, increased amount of annotation burden needed for videos, etc.) Moreover, adapting visual representations such as contours, deformable and articulated 2D or 3D models, graphs, random fields or visual dynamics, is less obvious with classical *vectorial DA* techniques.

Therefore, when these tasks are addressed in the context of domain adaptation, the problem is generally rewritten as a classification problem with vectorial feature representations and a set of predefined class labels. In this case the main challenge becomes finding the best vectorial representation for the given the task. When this is possible, shallow DA methods, described in the Sect. 1.3, can be applied to the problem. Thereupon, we can find in the literature DA solutions such as Adaptive SVM [554], DT-SVM [136], A-MKL [137] or Selective Transfer Machine [91] applied to video concept detection [555], video event recognition [137], activity recognition [155, 590], facial action unit detection [91], and 3D pose estimation [551].

When rewriting the problem into classification of vectorial representation is less obvious, as in the case of image segmentation, where the output is a structured output, or detection where the output is a set of bounding boxes, most often the target training set is simply augmented with the source data and traditional—segmentation, detection, etc.—methods are used. To overcome the lack of labels in the target domain, source data is often gathered by crawling the web (webly supervised) [82, 104, 123] or the target set is enriched with synthetically generated data. The usage of the synthetic data became even more popular since the massive adoption of deep CNNs to perform computer vision tasks requiring a large amount of annotated data.

Synthetic data based adaptation. Early methods use 3D CAD models to improve solutions for pose and viewpoint estimation [4, 357, 435, 460], object and object part detection [44, 229, 326, 364, 365, 401, 458, 467], segmentation and scene understanding [73, 358, 411]. The recent progress in computer graphics and modern high-level generic graphics platforms such as game engines enables to generate photo-realistic virtual worlds with diverse, realistic, and physically plausible events and actions. Such virtually generated and controlled environments come with different levels of labeling for free and therefore have great promise for deep learning across a variety of computer vision problems, including optical flow [56, 328, 329, 348], object trackers [175, 477], depth estimation from RGB [421], object detection [325, 503, 546] semantic segmentation [222, 387, 396] or human actions recognition [452].

In most cases, the synthetic data is used to enrich the real data for building the models (see examples in Chap. 12). However, DA techniques can further help to adjust the model trained with virtual data (source) to real data (target) especially when no or few labeled examples are available in the real domain [396, 452, 496, 545]. As such, [496] propose a deep spatial feature point architecture for visuomotor representation which, using synthetic examples and a few supervised examples, transfer the pretrained model to real imagery. This is done by combining a pose estimation loss, a domain confusion loss that aligns the synthetic and real domains, and a contrastive loss that aligns specific pairs in the feature space. Altogether these three losses ensure that the representation is suitable to the pose estimation task while remaining robust to the synthetic-real domain shift.

The Cool Temporal Segment Network [452] is an end-to-end action recognition model for real-world target categories that combines a few examples of labeled real-world videos with a large number of procedurally generated synthetic videos. The model uses a deep multi-task representation learning architecture, able to mix synthetic and real videos even if the action categories differ between the real and synthetic sets.

1.5.1 Object Detection

Concerning visual applications, after the image level categorization task, object detection received the most attention from the visual DA/TL community. Object detection models, until recently, were composed of a window selection mechanism and appearance based classifiers trained on the features extracted from labeled bounding boxes. At test time, the classifier was used to decide if a region of interest obtained by sliding windows or generic window selection models [500, 528, 595] contains the object or not.

Therefore, considering the window selection mechanism as being domain independent, standard DA methods can be integrated with the appearance based classifiers to adapt to the target domain the models trained on the source domain. The Projective Model Transfer SVM (PMT-SVM) and the Deformable Adaptive SVM (DA-SVM) proposed in [21] are such methods, which adapt HOG deformable source templates [114, 162] with labeled target bounding boxes (SS scenario), and the adapted template is used at test time to detect the presence or absence of an object class in sliding windows. In [126] the PMT-SVM was further combined with MMDT [239] to handle complex domain shifts. The detector is further improved by a smoothness constraints imposed on the classifier scores utilizing instance correspondences (e.g. the same object observed simultaneously from multiple views or tracked between video frames).

[334] uses the TCA [354] to adapt image level HOG representation between source and target domains for object detection. [577] proposes a Taylor Expansion Based Classifier Adaptation for either boosting or logistic regression to adapt person detection between videos acquired in different meeting rooms.

Online adaptation of the detector. Most early works related to object detector adaptation concern online adaptation of a generic detector trained on strongly labeled images (bounding boxes) to detect objects (in general cars or pedestrians) in videos. These methods exploit redundancies in videos to obtain prospective positive target examples (windows) either by background modeling/subtraction [399, 456], or by a combination of object tracking with regions proposed by the generic detector [174, 176, 427, 475] (see the main idea in Fig. 1.18). Using these designated target samples in the new frame the model is updated involving semi-supervised approaches such as self-training [398, 540] or co-training [249, 294].

For instance, [527] proposes a non-parametric detector adaptation algorithm, which adjusts an offline frame-based object detector to the visual characteristic of a new video clip. The Structure-Aware Adaptive Structural SVM [544] adapts online the Deformable Part-Based Model [124] for pedestrian detection (see details in Chap. 13). To handle the case when no target label is available, a strategy inspired by self-paced learning and supported by a Gaussian Process Regression is used to automatically label samples in the target domains. The temporal structure of the video is exploited through similarity constraints imposed on the adapted detector.

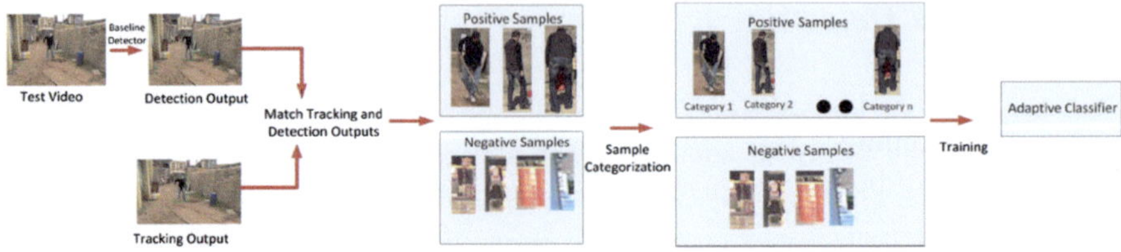

Fig. 1.18 Online adaptation of the generic detector using new target samples for example obtained by tracking. (Image courtesy P. Sharma [427])

Multi-object tracking. Multi-object tracking aims at automatically detecting and tracking individual object (e.g. car or pedestrian) instances [174, 176, 426]. These methods generally capitalize on multi-task and multi-instance learning to perform category-to-instance adaptation. For instance, [426] introduces a Multiple Instance Learning (MIL) loss function for real Adaboost, which is used within a tracking based unsupervised online sample collection mechanism to incrementally adjust the pretrained detector.

[176] proposes an unsupervised, online and self-tuning learning algorithm to optimize a multi-task learningbased convex objective involving a high-precision/low-recall off-the-shelf generic detector. The method exploits the data structure to jointly learn an ensemble of instance-level trackers, from which adapted category-level object detectors are derived. The main idea in [174] is to jointly learn all detectors (the target instance models and the generic one) using an online adaptation via Bayesian filtering coupled with multi-task learning to efficiently share parameters and reduce drift, while gradually improving recall.

The transductive approach in [475] re-trains the detector with automatically discovered target domain examples starting with the easiest first, and iteratively re-weighting labeled source samples by scoring trajectory tracks. [427] introduces a multi-class random fern adaptive classifier where different categories of the positive samples (corresponding to different video tracks) are considered as different target classes, and all negative online samples are considered as a single negative target class. [51] proposes a particle filtering framework for multi-person tracking-by-detection to predict the target locations.

Deep neural architectures. More recently, end-to-end deep learning object detection models were proposed that integrate and learn simultaneously the region proposals and the object appearance. In general, these models are initialized by deep models pretrained with image level annotations (often on the ILSVRC datasets [404]). In fact, the pretrained deep model, combined with class-agnostic region of interest proposal, can already be used to predict the presence or absence of the target object in the proposed local regions [192, 236, 349, 418]. When strongly labeled target data is available, the model can further be fine-tuned using the labeled bounding boxes to improve both the recognition and the object localization. Thus, the Large-Scale Detection through Adaptation [236] learns to transform an image classifier into an object detector by fine-tuning the CNN model, pretrained on images, with a set of labeled bounding boxes. The advantage of this model is that it generalizes well even for localization of classes for which there were no bounding box annotations during the training phase.

Instead fine-tuning, [381] uses Subspace Alignment [164] to adjust class-specific representations of bounding boxes (BB) between the source and target domain. The source BBs are extracted from the strongly annotated training set, while the target BBs are obtained with the RCNN-detector [192] trained on the source set. The detector is then re-trained with the target aligned source features and used to classify the target data projected into the target subspace.

1.6 Beyond Domain Adaptation: Unifying Perspectives

The aim of this section is to relate domain adaptation to other machine learning solutions. First in Sect. 1.6.1 we discuss how DA is related to other transfer learning (TL) techniques. Then, in Sect. 1.6.2 we connect DA to several classical machine learning approaches illustrating how these methods are exploited in various DA solutions. Finally, in Sect. 1.6.3 we examine the relationship between heterogeneous DA and multi-view/multi-modal learning.

1.6.1 DA Within Transfer Learning

As shown in Sect. 1.2, DA is a particular case of the transductive transfer learning aimed to solve a classification task common to the source and target, by simultaneously exploiting labeled source and unlabeled target examples (see also Fig. 1.2). As such, DA is opposite to unsupervised TL, where both domains and tasks are different with labels available neither for source nor for target.

DA is also different from self-taught learning [380], which exploits a limited labeled target data for a classification task together with a large amount of unlabeled source data mildly related to the task. The main idea behind self-taught learning is to explore the unlabeled source data and to discover repetitive patterns that could be used for the supervised learning task.

On the other hand, DA is more closely related to domain generalization [179, 190, 339, 347, 549], multi-task learning [61, 149, 394] or few-shot learning [159, 333] discussed below.

Domain generalization. Similar to multi-source DA [68, 138, 252], domain generalization methods [179, 190, 339, 347, 549] aim to average knowledge from several related source domains, in order to learn a model for a new target domain. But, in contrast to DA where unlabeled target instances are available to adapt the model, in domain generalization, no target example is accessible at training time.[15]

Multi-task learning. In multi-task learning [61, 149, 394] different tasks (e.g. sets of the labels) are learned at the same time using a shared representation such that what is learned for each task can help in learning the other tasks. If we consider the tasks in DA as domain source and target) specific tasks, a semi-supervised DA method can be seen as a sort of two-task learning problem where, in particular, learning the source-specific task helps learning the target-specific task. Furthermore, in the case of multi-source domain adaptation [107, 135, 197, 207, 238, 323, 429, 471, 482, 565] different source-specific tasks are jointly exploited in the interest of the target task.

On the other hand, as we have seen in Sect. 1.5.1, multi-task learning techniques can be beneficial for online DA, in particular for multi-object tracking and detection [174, 176], where the generic object detector (trained on source data) is adapted for each individual object instance.

Few-shot learning. Few-shot learning [159, 333, 481, 482] aims to learn information about object categories when only a few training images are available for training. This is done by making use of prior knowledge of related categories for which larger amount of annotated data is available. Existing solutions are the knowledge transfer through the reuse of model parameters [167], methods sharing parts or features [28] or approaches relying on contextual information [340].

An extreme case of few-shot learning is the *zero-shot learning* [166, 287], where the new task is deduced from previous tasks without using any training data for the current task. To address zero-shot learning, the methods rely either on nameable image characteristics and semantic concepts [166, 170, 287, 353], or on latent topics discovered by the system directly from the data [171, 290, 428]. In both cases, detecting these attributes can be seen as the common tasks between the training classes (source domains) and the new classes (target domains).

Unified DA and TL models. We have seen that the particularity of DA is the shared label space, in contrast to more generic TL approaches where the focus is on the task transfer between classes. However, in [362] it is claimed that task transfer and domain shift can be seen as different declinations of *learning to learn* paradigm, i.e. the ability to leverage prior knowledge when attempting to solve a new task. Based on this observation, a common framework is proposed to leverage source data regardless of the origin of the distribution mismatch. Considering prior models as experts, the original features are augmented with the output confidence values of the source models and target classifiers are then learned with these features.

Similarly, the Transductive Prediction Adaptation (TPA) [94] (see also Chap. 7) augments the target features with class predictions from source experts, before applying the MDA framework [77] on these augmented features. It is shown that MDA, exploiting the correlations between the target features and source predictions, can

[15] An example of domain generalization methods applied to visual attribute detection can be found in Chap. 15 and applied to semantic part detectors in Chap. 14.

denoise the class predictions and improve classification accuracy. In contrast to the method in [362], TPA works also in the case when no label is available in the target domain (US scenario).

The Cross-Domain Transformation [407] learns a regularized nonlinear transformation using supervised data from both domains to map source examples closer to the target ones. It is shown that the models built in this new space generalize well not only new samples from categories used to train the transformation (DA) but also new categories that were not present at training time (task transfer). The Unifying Multi-Domain Multi-Task Learning [560], described in Chap. 16, is a Neural Network framework that can be flexibly applied to multi-task, multi-domain and zero-shot learning and even to zero-shot domain adaptation.

1.6.2 Connection Between DA and Traditional ML Methods

Semi-supervised learning. DA can be seen as a particular case of the semi-supervised learning [65, 592], where, similarly to the majority of DA approaches, unlabeled data is exploited to remedy the lack of labeled data. Hence, ignoring the domain shift, traditional semi-supervised learning can be used as a solution for DA, where the source instances form the supervised part, and the target domain provides the unlabeled data. For this reason, DA methods often exploit or extend semi-supervised learning techniques such as transductive SVM [55], self-training [107, 398, 483, 540], or co-training [249, 294]. When the domain shift is small, traditional semi-supervised methods can already bring a significant improvement over baseline methods obtained with the pretrained source model [55].

Active learning. Instance selection based DA methods exploit ideas from active learning [419] to select instances with best potentials to help the training process. Thus, the Migratory-Logit algorithm [302] explore, both the target and source data to actively select unlabeled target samples to be added to the training sets. [431] describes an active learning method for relevant target data selection and labeling, which combines TrAdaBoost [112] with standard SVM. [347], (see also Chap. 15), uses active learning and DA techniques to generalize semantic object parts (e.g. animal eyes or legs) to unseen classes (animals). The methods described in [64, 107, 379, 408, 483, 530] combine transfer learning and domain adaptation with the target sample selection and automatic sample labeling, based on the classifier confidence. These new samples are then used to iteratively update the target models.

Online learning. Online or sequential learning [46, 422, 423] is strongly related to active learning; in both cases the model is iteratively and continuously updated using new data. However, while in active learning the data to be used for the update is actively selected, in online learning generally the new data is acquired sequentially. Domain adaptation can be combined with online learning too. As an example, we presented in Sect. 1.5.1 the online adaptation for incoming video frames of a generic object detector trained offline on labeled image sets [51, 544]. [553] proposes online adaptation of image classifier to user generated content in social computing applications.

Furthermore, as discussed in Sect. 1.4, fine-tuning a deep model [23, 88, 90, 349, 465, 572], pretrained on ImageNet (source), for a new dataset (target), can be seen as sort of semi-supervised domain adaptation. Both, fine-tuning as well as training deep DA models [183, 191, 309], use sequential learning where data batches are used to perform the stochastic gradient updates. If we assume that these batches contain the target data acquired sequentially, the model learning process can be directly used for online DA adaptation of the original model.

Metric learning. In Sect. 1.3 we presented several metric learning based DA methods [107, 278, 407, 575, 581]. where class labels from both domains are exploited to bridge the relatedness between the source and target. Thus, [575] proposes a new distance metric for the target domain by using the existing distance metrics learned on the source domain. [407] uses Information-theoretic Metric Learning [119] as a distance metric across different domains, which was extended to nonlinear kernels in [278]. [107] proposes a metric learning adapted to the DSCM classifier, while [581] defines a multi-task metric learning framework to learn relationships between source and target tasks. [412] explores various metric learning approaches to align deep features extracted from RGB and NIR face images.

Classifier ensembles. Well studied in ML, classifier ensembles have also been considered for DA and TL. As such, [260] applies a bagging approach for transferring the learning capabilities of a model to different domains where a high number of trees is learned on both source and target data in order to build a pruned version of the final ensemble to avoid a negative transfer. [388] uses random decision forests to transfer relevant features between domains. The optimization framework in [3] takes as input several classifiers learned on the source domain as well as the results of a cluster ensemble operating solely on the target domain, yielding a consensus labeling of the data in the target domain. Boosting was extended to DA and TL in [9, 86, 112, 565, 577].

1.6.3 HDA Related to Multi-view/Multi-modal Learning

In many data intensive applications, such as video surveillance, social computing, medical health records or environmental sciences, data collected from diverse domains or obtained from various feature extractors exhibit heterogeneity. For example, a person can be identified by different facets, e.g. face, fingerprint, signature or iris, or in video surveillance, an action or event can be recognized using multiple cameras. When working with such heterogeneous or multi-view data most, methods try to exploit simultaneously different modalities to build better final models.

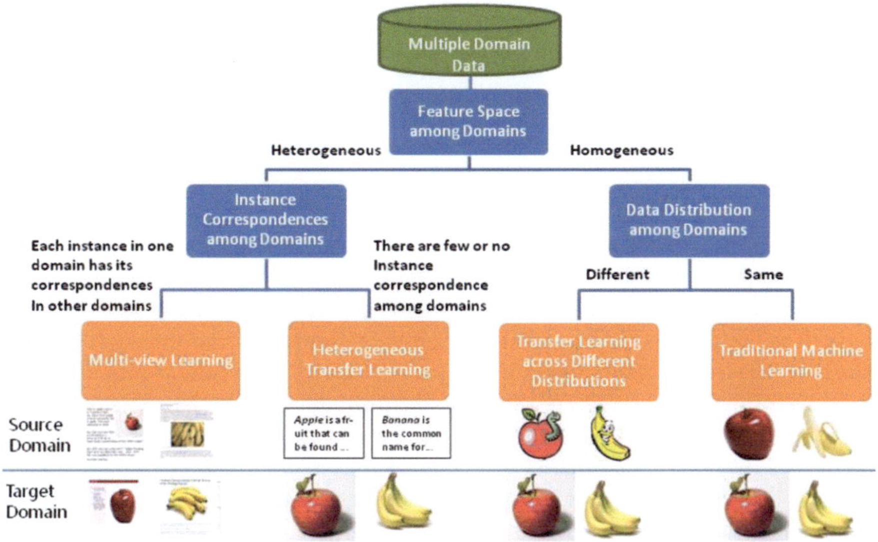

Fig. 1.19 Illustrating through an example the difference between TL to ML in the case of homogeneous data and between multi-view and HTL/HDA when working with heterogeneous data. Image courtesy Q. Yang [558]

As such, multi-view learning methods are related to HDA/HTL as discussed also in Sect. 1.3.3. Nevertheless, while multi-view learning [525, 543] assumes that multi-view examples are available during training, in the case of HDA [252, 429, 432, 520, 564], this assumption rarely holds (see illustration in Fig. 1.19). On contrary, the aim of HDA is to transfer information from the source domain represented with one type of data (e.g. text) to the target domain represented with another type of data (e.g. images). While this assumption essentially differentiates the multi-view learning from HDA, we have seen in Sect. 1.3.3 that HDA methods often rely on an auxiliary intermediate multi-view domain [374, 473, 474, 553, 556, 593]. Hence, HDA/HTL can strongly benefit from multi-view learning techniques such as canonical correlation analysis [223], co-training [76], spectral embedding [432] and multiple kernel learning [139].

Similarly to HDA/HTL relying on intermediate domains, cross-modal image retrieval methods depend on multi-view auxiliary data to define cross-modal similarities [6, 254], or to perform semantic [169, 382, 536, 552] or multi-view embedding [59, 202, 223, 343, 425, 523]. Hence, HDA/HTL can strongly benefit from such cross-modal data representations.

In the same spirit, *webly supervised* approaches [36, 82, 123, 163, 178, 417, 529] are also related to DA and HDA as is these approaches rely on collected web data (source) data used to refine the target model. As such, [140] uses multiple kernel learning to adapt visual events learned from the web data for video clips. [470] and [178] propose domain transfer approaches from weakly-labeled web images for action localization and event recognition tasks.

1.7 Conclusion

In this chapter we tried to provide an overview of different solutions for visual domain adaptation, including both shallow and deep methods. We grouped the methods both by their similarity concerning the problem (homogeneous vs. heterogeneous data, unsupervised vs. semi-supervised scenario) and by the solutions proposed (feature transformation, instance reweighing, deep models, online learning, etc.). We also reviewed methods that solve DA in the case of heterogeneous data as well as approaches that address computer vision problems beyond the image classification, such as object detection or multi-object tracking. Finally, we positioned domain adaptation within a larger context by linking it to other transfer learning techniques as well as to traditional machine learning approaches.

Due to the lack of the space and the large amount of methods mentioned, we could only briefly depict each method; the interested reader can follow the reference for deeper reading. We also decided not to provide any comparative experimental results between these methods for the following reasons: (1) Even if many DA methods were tested on the benchmark OFF31 [407] and OC10 [200] datasets, papers use often different experimental protocols (sampling the source vs. using the whole data, unsupervised vs. supervised) and different parameter tuning strategies (fix parameter sets, tuning on the source, cross- validation or unknown). (2) Results reported in different papers given the same methods (e.g. GFK, TCA, SA) vary also a lot between different re-implementations. For all these reasons, making a fair comparison between all the methods based only on the literature review is rather difficult. (3) These datasets are rather small, some methods have published results only with the outdated SURFBOV features and relying only on these results is not sufficient to derive general conclusions about the methods. For a fair comparison, deep methods should be compared to shallow methods using deep features extracted from similar architectures, but both features extracted from the latest deep models and deep DA architectures build on these models perform extremely well on OFF31 and OC10 even without adaptation.

Most DA solutions in the literature are tested on these relatively small datasets (both in terms of number of classes and number of images). However, with the proliferation of sensors, a large amount of heterogeneous data is collected, and hence there is a real need for solutions being able to efficiently exploit them. This shows a real need for more challenging datasets to evaluate and compare the performance of different methods. The few new DA datasets, such as the testbed cross-dataset (TB) [486] described in Chap. 2, or datasets built for model adaptation between photos, paintings and sketches [63, 102, 271, 412] while more challenging than the popular

OFF31 [407], OC10 [200] or MNIST [291] vs. SVHN [342], they are only sparsely used. Moreover, except the cross-modal place dataset [63], they are still small scale and single modality datasets.

We have also seen that only relatively few papers address adaptation beyond recognition and detection. Image and video understanding, semantic and instance-level segmentation, human pose, event and action recognition, motion and 3D scene understanding, where trying to simply describe the problem with a vectorial representation and classical domain adaptation, even when it is possible, has serious limitations. Recently, these challenging problems are addressed with deep methods requiring a large amount of labeled data. How to adapt these new models between domains with no or very limited amount of data is probably one of the main challenges that should be addressed by the visual domain adaptation and transfer learning community in the next few years.

Acknowledgements This work has been supported by Xerox Research Center Europe.

Chapter 2
A Deeper Look at Dataset Bias

Tatiana Tommasi, Novi Patricia, Barbara Caputo and Tinne Tuytelaars

Abstract The presence of a bias in each image data collection has recently attracted a lot of attention in the computer vision community showing the limits in generalization of any learning method trained on a specific dataset. At the same time, with the rapid development of deep learning architectures, the activation values of Convolutional Neural Networks (CNN) are emerging as reliable and robust image descriptors. In this chapter we propose to verify the potential of the CNN features when facing the dataset bias problem. With this purpose we introduce a large testbed for cross-dataset analysis and we discuss the challenges faced to create two comprehensive experimental setups by aligning twelve existing image databases. We conduct a series of analyses looking at how the datasets differ among each other and verifying the performance of existing debiasing methods under different representations. We learn important lessons on which part of the dataset bias problem can be considered solved and which open questions still need to be tackled.

T. Tommasi (✉) · N. Patricia · B. Caputo
University of Rome La Sapienza, Rome, Italy
e-mail: tommasi@dis.uniroma1.it

N. Patricia
e-mail: novi.patricia@idiap.ch

B. Caputo
e-mail: caputo@dis.uniroma1.it

N. Patricia
EPL Lausanne, CH, Lausanne, Switzerland

T. Tuytelaars
KU Leuven, ESAT, PSI, IMEC, Leuven, Belgium
e-mail: Tinne.Tuytelaars@esat.kuleuven.be

G. Csurka (ed.), *Domain Adaptation in Computer Vision Applications*,
Advances in Computer Vision and Pattern Recognition,
DOI 10.1007/978-3-319-58347-1_2

2.1 Introduction

Since its spectacular success in the 2012 edition of the Imagenet Large Scale Visual Recognition Challenge (ILSVRC, [404]), deep learning has dramatically changed the research landscape in visual recognition [275]. By training a Convolutional Neural Network (CNN) over millions of data it is possible to get impressively high quality object annotations [5] and detections [579]. A large number of studies have recently proposed improvements over the CNN architecture of Krizhevsky et al. [275] with the aim to better suit an ever increasing typology of visual applications [88, 236, 579]. At the same time, the activation values of the final hidden layers have quickly gained the status of off-the-shelf state of the art features [384]. Indeed, several works demonstrated that DeCAF (as well as Caffe [128], Overfeat [418], VGG-CNN [66], etc.) can be used as powerful image descriptors [66, 203]. The improvements obtained by previous methods are so impressive that one might wonder whether they can be considered as a sort of "universal features", i.e. image descriptors that can be helpful in any possible visual recognition problem.

The aim of this work is to contribute to answering this question when focusing on the bias of existing image collections. The *dataset bias* problem was presented ad discussed for the first time in [489]. The *capture bias* is related to how the images are acquired both in terms of the used device and of the collector preferences for point of view, lighting conditions, etc. The *category or label bias* is due to a poor definition of the visual semantic categories and to the in-class variability: similar images may be annotated with different names and the same name can be assigned to visually different images. Finally, each collection may contain a distinct set of categories and this causes the *negative bias*. If we focus only on the classes shared among them, the rest of the world will be defined differently depending on the collection.

All these aspects induce a generalization issue when training and testing a learning algorithm on images extracted from different collections. Previous work seemed to imply that this issue was solved, or on the way to be solved, by using CNN features [128, 573]. However, the evaluation is generally restricted to controlled cases where the data variability is limited to specific visual domain shift [128, 241] or some images extracted from the testing collection are available at training time [349, 573]. Here we revisit and scale up the analysis, making three contributions:

1. We introduce a large-scale testbed for cross-dataset analysis and discuss the challenges faced when aligning twelve existing image datasets (see Fig. 2.1).
2. We define two comprehensive experimental setups and we assess on them the performance of the CNN features for dataset bias.
3. We propose a new measure to evaluate quantitatively the ability of a given algorithm to address the dataset bias. As opposed to what proposed previously in the literature [489], our measure takes into account both the performance obtained on the in-dataset task and the percentage drop in performance across datasets.

Our experiments evaluate the suitability of CNN features for attacking the dataset bias problem, pointing out that: (1) the capture bias is class-dependent and can be

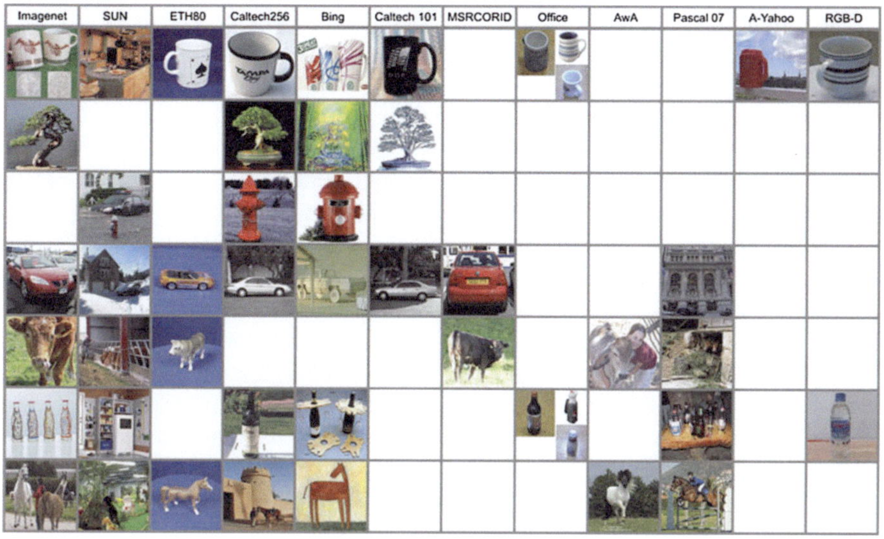

Fig. 2.1 We show here one image example extracted from each of the 12 datasets (*columns*) for 7 object categories (*rows*): mug, bonsai, fire-hydrant, car, cow, bottle, horse. The empty positions indicate that the corresponding dataset is not annotated for the considered class

enhanced by the CNN representation due to the influence of the classes on which the neural network was originally trained; (2) the negative bias persists regardless of the representation; (3) attempts of undoing the dataset bias with existing ad-hoc learning algorithms do not help, while some previously discarded adaptive strategies appear effective; (4) fine-tuning the CNN network cannot be applied in the dataset bias setting and if naïvely forced does not seem beneficial.

The picture emerging from these findings is that of a problem open for research and in need of new directions, able to accommodate at the same time the potential of deep learning and the difficulties of large-scale cross-database generalization.

Related Work. The existence of several data related issues in any area of automatic classification technology was first discussed by Hand in [220]. The first sign of peril in image collections was indicated in presenting the Caltech256 dataset [215] where the authors recognized the danger of learning ancillary cues of the image collection (e.g. characteristic image size) instead of intrinsic features of the object categories. However, only recently this topic has been really put under the spotlight for computer vision tasks by Torralba and Efros [489]. Their work pointed out the idiosyncrasies of existing image datasets: the evaluation of cross-dataset performance revealed that standard detection and classification methods fail because the uniformity of training and test data is not guaranteed.

This initial analysis of the *dataset bias* problem gave rise to a series of works focusing on how to overcome the specific image collection differences and learn robust classifiers with good generalization properties. The proposed methods have been mainly tested on binary tasks (object versus rest) where the attention is focused on categories like *car* or *person* which are common among six popular datasets: SUN, LabelMe, PascalVOC, Caltech101, Imagenet, and MSRC [489]. A further group of three classes was soon added to the original set (*bird*, *chair* and *dog*) defining a total of five object categories over the first four datasets listed before [151, 268]. A larger scale analysis in terms of categories was proposed in [389] by focusing on 84 classes of Imagenet and SUN, while a study on how to use weakly labeled Bing images to classify Caltech256 samples was proposed in [36]. Finally the problem of partially overlapping label sets among different datasets was considered in [485].

Together with the growing awareness about the characteristic signature of each existing image set, the related problem of *domain shift* has also emerged. Given a source and target image set with different marginal probability distributions, any learning method trained on the first will present lower performance on the second. In real life settings it is often impossible to have full control on how the test images will differ from the original training data and an adaptation procedure to remove the domain shift is necessary. An efficient (and possibly unsupervised) solution is to learn a shared representation that eliminates the original distribution mismatch. Different methods based on subspace data embedding [164, 200], metric [407, 483] and vocabulary learning [377] have been presented. As already mentioned above, several works have also demonstrated that deep learning architectures may produce domain invariant descriptors through highly nonlinear transformation of the original features [128]. Domain adaptation (DA) algorithms have been mostly evaluated on the Office (OFF31) dataset [407] and Office-Caltech (OC10) [200] containing office-related object categories from three respectively 4 domains.

Despite their close relation, visual domain and dataset bias are not the same. Domain adaptation solutions have been used to tackle the dataset bias problem, but domain discovery approaches have shown that a single dataset may contain several domains [238] while a single domain may be shared across several datasets [197]. Moreover, the domain shift problem is generally considered under the covariate shift assumption with a fixed set of classes shared by the domains and analogous conditional distributions. On the other hand, different image datasets may contain different object classes.

Here we make up the lack of a standard testbed for large-scale cross-dataset analysis and we evaluate the effect of the CNN features for this task. We believe that widening the attention from few shared classes to the whole dataset structures can reveal much about the nature of the biases and on the effectiveness of the proposed representations and algorithmic solutions.

2.2 A Large-Scale Cross-Dataset Testbed

In this section we first give a brief description of the considered image datasets, created and used before for object categorization:

ETH80 [293] was created to facilitate the transition from object identification (recognize a specific object instance) to categorization (assign the correct class label to an object instance never seen before). It contains 8 categories and 10 toy objects each represented by 41 images captured against a blue background from viewpoints spaced equally over the upper viewing hemisphere.

Caltech101 [160] contains 101 object categories and was the first large-scale collection proposed as a testbed for object recognition algorithms. Each category contains a different number of samples between 31 and 800 images. The images have little or no clutter with the objects centered and presented in a stereotypical pose.

Caltech256 [215]. Differently from the previous case the images in this dataset were not manually aligned, thus the objects appear in several different poses. This collection contains 256 categories with between 80 and 827 images per class.

Bing [36] contains images downloaded from the Internet for the same set of 256 object categories of the previous collection. Text queries give as output several noisy images which are not removed, resulting in a weakly labeled collection. The number of samples per class goes from a minimum of 197 to a maximum of 593.

Animals with Attributes (AwA) [287] presents a total of 30475 images of 50 animal categories. Each class is associated to an 85-element vector of numeric attribute values that indicate general characteristics shared between different classes. The animals appear in different pose and at different scales in the images.

a-Yahoo [157]. As the previous one, this dataset was collected to explore attribute descriptions. It contains 12 object categories with a minimum of 48 and a maximum of 366 samples per class.

MSRCORID [331]. The Microsoft Research Cambridge Object Recognition Image Database contains a set of digital photographs grouped into 22 categories spanning over objects (19 classes) and scenes (3 classes).

PascalVOC2007 [148]. The Pascal Visual Object Classes dataset contain 20 object categories and a total of 9963 images. Each image depicts objects in realistic scenes and may contain instances of more than one category. This dataset was used as testbed for the Pascal object recognition and detection challenges in 2007.

SUN [541] contains a total of 142165 pictures[1] and it was created as a comprehensive collection of annotated images covering a large variety of environmental scenes, places and objects. Here the objects appear at different scales and positions in the

---

[1]Version available on December 2013 at http://labelme.csail.mit.edu/Release3.0/Images/users/antonio/static_sun_database/ and the list of objects reported at http://groups.csail.mit.edu/vision/SUN/.

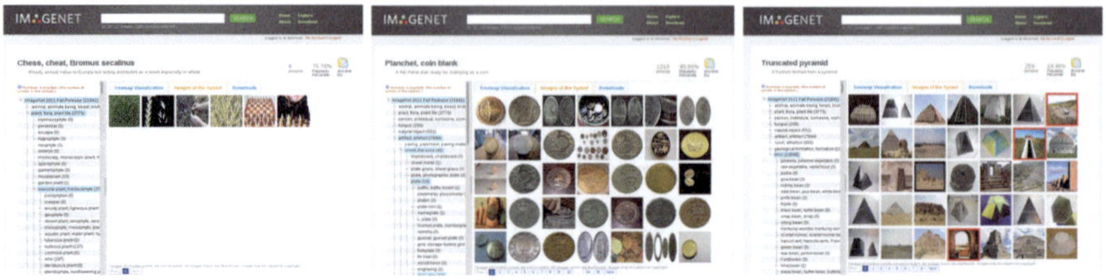

Fig. 2.2 Three cases of Imagenet categories. *Left* some images in class *chess* are wrongly labeled. Middle: the class *planchet* or coin blank contains images that can be more easily labeled as *coin*. *Right* the images highlighted with a *red square* in the class *truncated pyramid* do not contain a pyramid (best viewed in color and with magnification)

images and many of the instances are partially occluded making object recognition and categorization very challenging.

Office [407]. This dataset contains images of 31 object classes over three domains: the images are either obtained from the Amazon website, or acquired with a high-resolution digital camera (DSLR), or taken with a low resolution webcam. The collection contains a total of 4110 images with a minimum of 7 and a maximum of 100 samples per domain and category.

RGB-D [284] is similar in spirit to ETH80 but it was collected with a Kinect camera, thus each RGB image is associated to a depth map. It contains images of 300 objects acquired under multiple views and organized into 51 categories.

Imagenet [120]. At the moment this collection contains around 21800 object classes organized according to the Wordnet hierarchy.

2.2.1 Merging Challenges

There are two main challenges that must be faced when organizing and using at once all the data collections listed before. One is related to the alignment of the object classes and the other is the need for a shared feature representation.

Composing the datasets in a single corpus turned out to be quite difficult. Even if each image is labeled with an object category name, the class alignment is tricky due to the use of different words to indicate the very same object, for instance *bike* versus *bicycle* and *mobilephone* versus *cellphone*. Sometimes the different nuance of meaning of each word is not respected: *cup* and *mug* should indicate two different objects, but the images are often mixed; *people* is the plural of *person*, but images of this last class often contain more than one subject. Moreover, the choice of different ontology hierarchical levels (*dog* versus *dalmatian* versus *greyhound*, *bottle* versus *water-bottle* versus *wine-bottle*) complicates the combination. Psychological studies demonstrated that humans prefer entry-level categories when naming visual objects [350], thus when combining the datasets we chose "natural" labels that correspond to

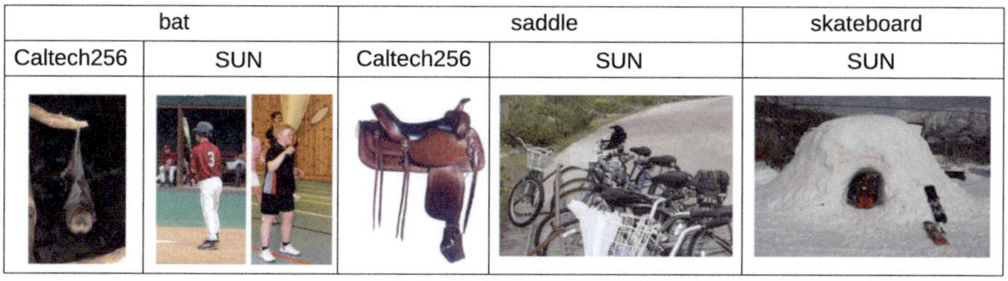

Fig. 2.3 Three categories with labeling issues. The class *bat* has different meanings both across datasets and within a dataset. A *saddle* can be a seat to ride a horse or a part of a bicycle. A *skateboard* and a *snowboard* may be visually similar, but they are not the same object

intermediate nodes in the Wordnet hierarchy. For instance, we used *bird* to associate humming bird, pigeon, ibis, flamingo, rooster, cormorant, ostrich and owl, while *boat* covers kayak, ketch, schooner, speed boat, canoe and ferry. In the cases in which we combine only two classes we keep both their names, e.g. *cup and mug*.

In the alignment process we came across a few peculiar cases. Figure 2.2 shows samples of three classes in Imagenet. The category *chess board* does not exist at the moment, but there are three classes related to the word *chess*: chess master, chessman or chess piece, chess or cheat or bromus secalinus (we use "or" here to indicate different labels associated to the same synset). This last category contains only a few images but some of them are not correctly annotated. The categories *coin* and *pyramid* are still not present in Imagenet. For the first, the most closely related class is *planchet* or *coin blank*, which contains many examples of what would be commonly named as a coin. For the second, the most similar *truncated pyramid* contains images of some non-truncated pyramids as well as images not containing any pyramids at all. In general, it is important to keep in mind that several of the Imagenet pictures are weakly labeled, thus they cannot be considered as much more reliable than the corresponding Bing images. Imagenet users are asked to clean and refine the data collection by indicating whether an image is a typical or wrong example.

We noticed that the word *bat* usually indicates the flying mammal except in SUN where it refers to the baseball and badminton bat. A *saddle* in Caltech256 is the supportive structure for a horse rider, while in SUN it is a bicycle seat. Tennis shoes and sneakers are two synonyms associated to the same synset in Imagenet, while they correspond to two different classes in Caltech256. In SUN, there are two objects annotated as skateboards, but they are in fact two snowboards. Some examples are shown in Fig. 2.3. We disregarded all these ambiguous cases and we do not consider them in the final combined setups.

Although many descriptors have been extracted and evaluated separately on each image collection, the considered features usually differ across datasets. Public repositories with pre-calculated features exist for Caltech101 and Caltech256, Bing and

Caltech256, and for a set of five classes out of four datasets.[2] Here we consider the group of twelve datasets listed in the previous section and extracted the same features from all of them defining a homogeneous reference representation for cross-dataset analysis.

2.2.2 Data Setups and Feature Descriptor

Dense set. Among the considered datasets, the ones with the highest number of categories are Caltech256, Bing, SUN and Imagenet. In fact the last two are open collections progressively growing in time. Overall they share 114 categories: some of the 256 object categories are missing at the moment in Imagenet but they are present in SUN (e.g. desk-globe, fire-hydrant) and vice versa (e.g. butterfly, pram). Out of this shared group, 40 classes (see Fig. 2.4) contain more than 20 images per dataset and we selected them to define a dense cross-dataset setup. We remark that each image in SUN is annotated with the list of objects visible in the depicted scene: we consider an image as a sample of a category if the category name is in the mentioned list.

Sparse set. A second setup is obtained by searching over all the datasets for the categories which are shared at least by four collections and that contain a minimum of 20 samples. We allow a lower number of samples only for the classes shared by more than four datasets (i.e. from the fifth dataset on the images per category may be less than 20). These conditions are satisfied by 105 object categories in Imagenet overlapping with 95 categories of Caltech256 and Bing, 89 categories of SUN, 34 categories of Caltech101, 17 categories of Office, 18 categories of RGB-D, 16 categories of AwA and PascalVOC07, 13 categories of MSRCORID, 7 categories of ETH80 and 4 categories of a-Yahoo. The histogram in Fig. 2.5 shows the defined sparse set and the number of images per class: the category *cup and mug* is shared across nine datasets, making it the most popular one.

Representation. We release the cross-dataset with three feature representations:

• **BOWsift:** dense SIFTs have been among the most widely used handcrafted features in several computer vision tasks before the advent of the CNN representations, thus we decided to use this descriptor as reference and we adopted the same extraction protocol proposed in the Imagenet development kit[3] by running their code over the twelve considered datasets. Each image is resized to have a max size length of no more than 300 pixels and SIFT descriptors [315] are computed on 20×20 overlapping patches with a spacing of 10 pixels. Images are further downsized (to 1/2 and 1/4 of the side length) and more descriptors are computed. We used the visual vocab-

[2]Available respectively at http://files.is.tue.mpg.de/pgehler/projects/iccv09/, http://vlg.cs.dartmouth.edu/projects/domainadapt/, http://undoingbias.csail.mit.edu/.

[3]www.image-net.org/download-features.

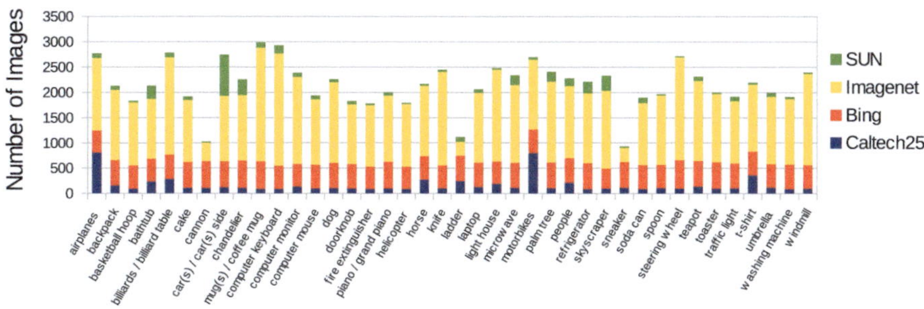

Fig. 2.4 Stack histogram showing the number of images per class of our cross-dataset dense setup

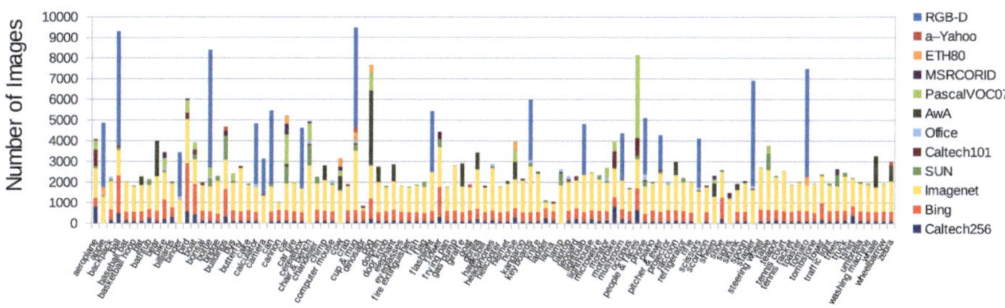

Fig. 2.5 Stack histogram showing the number of images per class of our cross-dataset sparse setup (best viewed in color and with magnification)

ulary of 1000 words provided with the mentioned kit to obtain the Bag of Words (BOW) representation [108, 445]: it was built over the images of the 1000 classes of the ILSVRC2010 challenge [404] by clustering a random subset of 10 million SIFT vectors.

• **DeCAF6, DeCAF7:** the mean-centered raw RGB pixel intensity values of all the collection images (warped to 256×256) are given as input to the CNN architecture of Krizhevsky et al. [275] by using the DeCAF implementation.[4] The activation values of the 4096 neurons in the 6-th and 7-th layers of the network are considered as image descriptors [128].

In our experiments we use the L2-normalized version of the feature vectors and adopt the z-score normalization for the BOWsift features when testing DA methods. We mostly focus on the results obtained with the DeCAF features and use the BOWsift representation as a reference baseline.

Evaluation Protocol. Our basic experimental setup considers both in-dataset and cross-dataset evaluations. With *in-dataset* we mean training and testing on samples extracted from the same dataset, while with *cross-dataset* we indicate experiments where training and testing samples belong to different collections. We use *Self* to

[4]https://github.com/UCB-ICSI-Vision-Group/decaf-release/.

specify the in-dataset performance and $Mean\ Other$ for the average cross-dataset performance over multiple test collections.

One way to quantitatively evaluate the cross dataset generalization was previously proposed in [489]. It consists of measuring the percentage drop ($\%\ Drop$) between $Self$ and $Mean\ Others$. However, being a relative measure, it loses the information on the value of $Self$ which is important if we want to compare the effect of different learning methods or different representations. For instance a 75% drop w.r.t a 100% self average precision has a different meaning than a 75% drop w.r.t. a 25% self average precision. To overcome this drawback, we propose here a different *Cross-Dataset (CD)* measure defined as $CD = (1 + exp^{-\{(Self-Mean\ Others)/100\}})^{-1}$. It uses directly the difference $(Self - Mean\ Others)$ while the sigmoid function rescales this value between 0 and 1. This allows for the comparison among the results of experiments with different setups. Specifically CD values over 0.5 indicate a presence of a bias, which becomes more significant as CD gets close to 1. On the other hand, CD values below 0.5 correspond to cases where either $Mean\ Other \geq Self$ or the $Self$ result is very low. Both these conditions indicate that the learned model is not reliable on the data of its own collection and it is difficult to draw any conclusion from its cross-dataset performance.

2.3 Studying the Sparse Set

Dataset Recognition. One of the effects of the capture bias is that it makes any dataset easily recognizable. We want to evaluate whether this effect is enhanced or decreased by the use of the CNN features. To do it we run the *name the dataset* test [489] on the sparse data setup. We extract randomly 1000 images from each of the 12 collections and we train a 12-way linear SVM classifier that we then test on a disjoint set of 300 images. The experiment is repeated 10 times with different data splits and we report the obtained average results in Fig. 2.6. The plot on the left indicates that DeCAF allows for a much better separation among the collections than what is obtained with BOWsift. In particular DeCAF7 shows an advantage over DeCAF6 for a large number of training samples. From the confusion matrices (middle and right in Fig. 2.6) we see that it is easy to distinguish ETH80, Office and RGB-D datasets from all the others regardless of the used representation, given the specific lab-nature of these collections. DeCAF captures better than BOWsift the characteristics of A-Yahoo, MSRCORID, Pascal VOC07 and SUN, improving the recognition results on them. Finally, Bing, Caltech256 and Imagenet are the datasets with the highest confusion level, an effect mainly due to the large number of classes and images per class. Still, this confusion decreases when using DeCAF.

These experiments show that the idiosyncrasies of each data collection become more evident when using a highly accurate representation. However, the dataset recognition performance does not provide an insight on how the classes in each collection are related to each other, nor how a specific class model will generalize to other datasets. We look into this problem in the following paragraph.

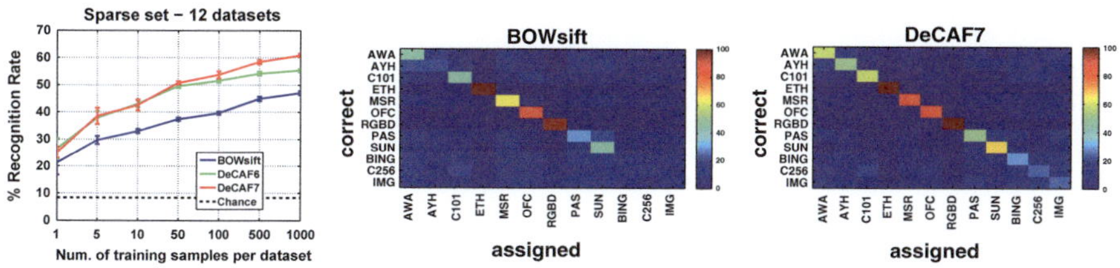

Fig. 2.6 Name the dataset experiment over the sparse setup with 12 datasets. The title of each confusion matrix indicates the feature used for the corresponding experiments

Class-Specific cross-dataset generalization test. We study the effect of the CNN features on the cross-dataset performance of two object class models: *car* and *cow*. Four collections of the sparse set contain images labeled with these object classes: PascalVOC07 (P), SUN (S), ETH80 (E), and MSRCORID (M). For the class car we selected randomly from each dataset two groups of 50 positive/1000 negative examples respectively for training and testing. For the class cow we considered 30 positive/1000 negative examples in training and 18 positive/1000 negative examples in testing (limited by the number of cow images in SUN). We repeat the sample selection 10 times and the average precision results obtained by linear SVM classification are presented in the matrices of Table 2.1.

Coherently with what deduced over all the classes from the *name the dataset* experiment, scene-centric (P,S) and object-centric (E,M) collections appear separated from each other. For the first ones, the low in-dataset results are mainly due to their multi-label nature: an image labeled as people may still contain a car and this creates confusion both at training and at test time. The final effect is a cross-dataset performance higher than the respective in-dataset one. This behavior becomes even more evident when using DeCAF than with BOWsift.

Although the *name the dataset* experiment indicated almost no overall confusion between E and M, the per-class results on car and cow show different trends. Learning a *car* model from images of toys (E) or of real objects (M) does not seem so different in terms of the final testing performance when using DeCAF. The diagonal matrix values prominent with BOWsift are surrounded by high average precision results for DeCAF. On the other hand, recognizing a living non-rigid object like a *cow* is more challenging. An important factor that may influence these results is the high level nature of the DeCAF representation: they are obtained as a byproduct of a training process over 1000 object classes [128] which cover several vehicles and animal categories. The class *car* is in this set, but *cow* is not. This intrinsically induces a category-specific bias effect, which may augment the image collection differences. Overall the DeCAF features provide a high performance inside each collection, but the difference between the in-dataset and cross-dataset results remains large almost as with BOWsift.

We also re-run the experiments on the class cow by using a fixed negative set in the test always extracted from the training collection. The visible increase in the

Table 2.1 Binary cross-dataset generalization for two example categories, car and cow. Each matrix contains the object classification performance (AP) when training on one dataset (rows) and testing on another (columns). The diagonal elements correspond to the self results, i.e. training and testing on the same dataset. We report in bold the CD values higher than 0.5. P,S,E,M stand respectively for the datasets Pascal VOC07, SUN, ETH80, MSRCORID

	train \ test	BOWsift P	S	E	M	% Drop	CD	DeCAF6 P	S	E	M	% Drop	CD	DeCAF7 P	S	E	M	% Drop	CD
Car	P	28.6	26.4	26.7	29.2	3.9	0.50	26.2	19.2	44.3	42.6	-35.1	0.47	14.5	11.8	28.9	28.3	-59.1	0.47
	S	25.4	26.8	25.7	25.7	4.3	0.50	15.4	15.6	19.9	17.9	-13.9	0.49	27.1	27.4	32.8	28.1	-6.8	0.49
	E	14.7	9.1	98.5	25.2	83.4	**0.69**	27.3	18.7	100.0	93.5	53.5	**0.63**	31.0	24.0	100.0	90.9	51.3	**0.62**
	M	17.4	8.7	9.7	90.5	86.8	**0.69**	41.6	12.8	95.8	99.7	49.8	**0.62**	43.8	14.9	93.8	99.7	49.0	**0.62**
Cow	P	14.1	18.8	11.9	17.9	-15.1	0.49	35.3	34.4	20.2	39.1	11.4	**0.51**	46.6	44.0	31.3	47.3	12.3	**0.51**
	S	16.1	38.3	12.5	27.1	51.4	**0.54**	18.6	62.7	10.7	33.5	66.7	**0.60**	12.8	40.1	12.1	23.6	59.7	**0.56**
	E	2.3	2.3	29.8	2.0	92.6	**0.57**	4.4	8.3	91.9	4.1	93.9	**0.70**	7.2	7.7	90.1	5.3	92.5	**0.70**
	M	8.6	17.4	2.4	52.5	82.0	**0.61**	13.8	46.7	9.3	97.2	76.0	**0.68**	14.1	39.4	10.4	97.7	78.2	**0.68**
Cow - fixed negatives	P	14.1	16.2	12.0	18.6	-10.7	0.49	35.3	32.7	16.9	46.6	9.1	0.50	46.6	39.1	26.4	48.9	18.2	**0.52**
	S	18.7	38.3	17.0	35.8	-37.8	**0.53**	38.5	62.7	21.0	69.5	31.4	**0.54**	25.7	40.1	12.8	43.3	31.9	**0.53**
	E	23.5	22.2	29.8	14.0	33.3	**0.52**	6.1	7.9	91.9	4.6	93.2	**0.70**	11.2	9.0	90.1	11.0	88.4	**0.69**
	M	8.9	9.4	2.0	52.5	87.1	**0.61**	65.2	62.0	51.5	97.2	38.5	**0.59**	69.4	55.1	47.4	97.7	41.3	**0.59**

cross-dataset results indicates that the negative set bias maintains its effect regardless of the used representation.

From the values of $\%Drop$ and CD we see that these two measures may have a different behavior: for the class cow with BOWsift, the $\%Drop$ value for E (92.6) is higher than the corresponding value for M (82.0), but the opposite happens for CD (respectively 0.57 and 0.61). The reason is that CD integrates the information on the in-dataset recognition which is higher and more reliable for M. Passing from BOWsift to DeCAF the CD value increases in some cases indicating a more significant bias.

On the basis of the presented results we can state that the DeCAF features are not fully solving the dataset bias. Although similar conclusions have been mentioned in a previous publication [241], our more extensive analysis provides a reliable measure to evaluate the bias and explicitly indicate some of the main causes of the observed effect: (1) the capture bias appears class-dependent and may be influenced by the original classes on which the CNN features have been trained; (2) the negative bias persists regardless of the feature used to represent the data.

Undoing the Dataset Bias. We focus here on the method proposed in [268] to overcome the dataset bias and verify its effect when using the DeCAF features. The *Unbias* approach has a formulation similar to multi-task learning: the available images of multiple datasets are kept separated as belonging to different tasks and a max-margin model is learned from the information shared over all of them.

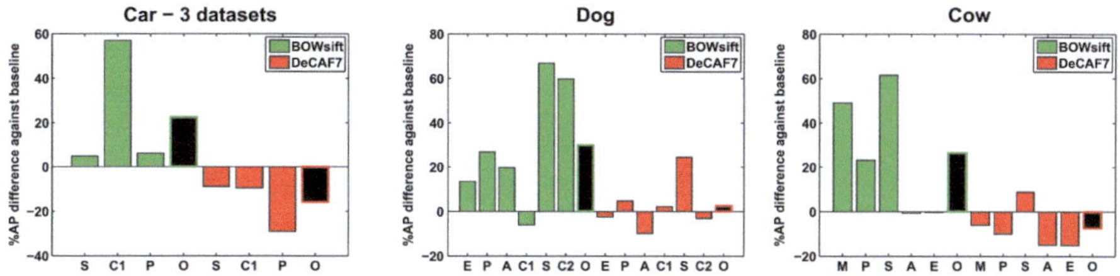

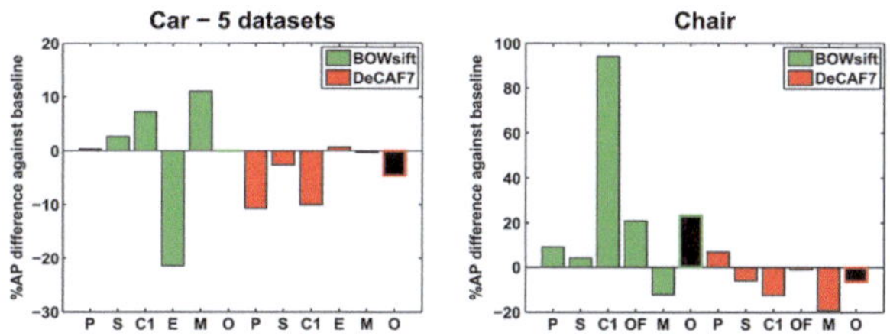

Cow	*Self*	*Other*
M	98.97	86.56
P	53.67	34.29
S	40.89	29.20
A	44.76	25.94
E	99.40	86.56

Fig. 2.7 Percentage difference in average precision between the results of *Unbias* and the baseline *All* over each target dataset. P,S,E,M,A,C1,C2,OF stand respectively for the datasets Pascal VOC07, SUN, ETH80, MSRCORID, AwA, Caltech101, Caltech256 and Office. O indicates the overall value, i.e. the average of the percentage difference over all considered datasets (*shown in black*)

We run the experiments focusing on the classes *car*, *cow*, *dog* and *chair* and reproducing a similar setup to what previously used in [268]. For the class car we consider two settings with three and five datasets, while we use five datasets for cow and chair and six datasets for dog. One of the datasets is left out in the round for testing while all the others are used as sources of training samples.

We compare the obtained results against those produced by a linear SVM when *All* the training images of the source datasets are considered together. We show the percentage relative difference in terms of average precision for these two learning strategies in Fig. 2.7. The results indicate that, in most cases when using BOWsift the *Unbias* method improves over the plain *All* SVM, while the opposite happens when using DeCAF7. As already suggested by the results of the cross-dataset generalization test, the DeCAF features, by capturing the image details, may enhance the differences among the same object category in different collections. As a consequence, the amount of shared information among the collections decrease, together with the effectiveness of the methods that leverage over it. On the other hand, removing the dataset separation and considering all the images together provides a better coverage of the object variability and allows for a higher cross-dataset performance.

In the last column of Fig. 2.7 we present the results obtained with the class *cow* together with the average precision per dataset when using DeCAF7. Specifically, the table allows to compare the performance of training and testing on the same dataset ($Self$) against the best result between *Unbias* and *All* (indicated as $Other$). Despite the good performance obtained by directly learning on other datasets, the obtained results are still lower than what can be expected having access to trained samples of each collection. This suggests that an adaptation process from generic to specific is still necessary to close the gap. Similar trends can be observed for the other categories.

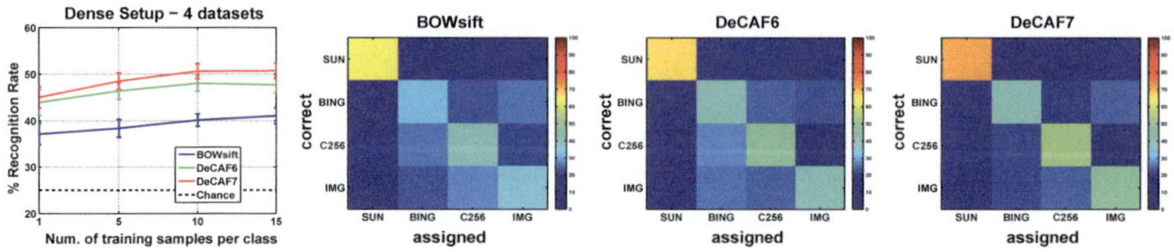

Fig. 2.8 Name the dataset experiment over the dense setup with 4 datasets. The title of each confusion matrix indicates the feature used for the corresponding experiments

Fig. 2.9 *Left* Imagenet images annotated as Caltech256 data with BOWsift but correctly recognized with decaf7. *Right* Caltech256 images annotated as Imagenet by BOWsift but correctly recognized with DeCAF7

2.4 Studying the Dense Set

Dataset Recognition. The second group of experiments on the dense setup allows us to analyze the differences among the datasets avoiding the negative set bias. We run again the *name the dataset* test maintaining the balance among the 40 classes shared by Caltech256, Bing, SUN and Imagenet. We consider a set of 5 samples per object class in testing and an increasing amount of training samples per class from 1 to 15. The results in Fig. 2.8 indicate again the better performance of DeCAF7 over DeCAF6 and BOWsift.

From the confusion matrices it is clear that the separation between object- (Bing, Caltech256, Imagenet) and scene-centric (SUN) datasets is quite easy regardless of the representation, while the differences among the object-centric collections become more evident when passing from BOW to DeCAF. We can get a more concrete idea of the DeCAF performance by looking at Fig. 2.9. Here images on the left present Imagenet images that have been assigned to Caltech256 with BOWsift but which are correctly recognized with DeCAF7. Images on the right contain instead Caltech256 images wrongly annotated as Imagenet samples by BOWsift but correctly labeled with DeCAF7. Considering the white background and standard pose that characterize Caltech256 images, together with the less stereotypical content of Imagenet data, the mistakes of BOWsift can be visually justified, nevertheless the DeCAF features overcome them.

Table 2.2 Multi-class cross-dataset generalization performance (recognition rate). The percentage difference between the self results and the average of the other results per row correspond to the value indicated in the column $\% \ Drop$. CD is our newly proposed cross-dataset measure

BOWsift

train \ test	C256	IMG	SUN	% Drop	CD
C256	25.15	15.05	9.35	51.5	0.53
IMG	14.50	17.85	9.05	34.0	0.52
SUN	7.70	8.00	13.55	42.1	0.51

DeCAF7

train \ test	C256	IMG	SUN	% Drop	CD
C256	73.15	56.05	20.20	47.9	0.58
IMG	64.10	64.90	22.65	33.2	0.55
SUN	21.35	23.15	30.05	25.9	0.52

Since all the datasets contain the same object classes, we are in fact reproducing a setup generally adopted for DA [164, 200]. By identifying each dataset with a domain, we can interpret the results of this experiment as an indication of the domain divergence [31] and deduce that a model trained on SUN will perform poorly on the object-centric collections and vice versa. On the other hand, a better cross-dataset generalization should be observed among Imagenet, Caltech256 and Bing. We verify it in the following sections.

Cross-dataset generalization test. We consider the same setup used before with 15 samples per class from each collection in training and 5 samples per class in test. However, now we train a one-vs-all multi-class SVM per dataset. Due to its noisy nature we exclude Bing here and we dedicate more attention to it in the next paragraph.

The average recognition rate results over 10 data splits are reported in Table 2.2. By comparing the values of $\%Drop$ and CD we observe that they provide opposite messages. The first suggests that we get a better generalization when passing from BOWsift to DeCAF7. However, considering the higher $Self$ result, CD evaluates the dataset bias as more significant when using DeCAF7. The expectation indicated before on the cross-dataset performance are confirmed here: the classification models learned on Caltech256 and Imagenet have low recognition rate on SUN. Generalizing between Caltech256 and Imagenet, instead, appears easier and the results show a particular behavior: although the classifier on Caltech256 tends to fail more on Imagenet than on itself, when training on Imagenet the in-dataset and cross-dataset performance are almost the same. Of course we have to remind that the DeCAF features where defined over Imagenet samples and this can be part of the cause of the observed asymmetric results.

To visualize the effect of the dataset-bias per class we present the separate recognition rate in Fig. 2.10. Specifically we consider the case of training on Caltech256. From the top plot we can see that *motorcycle*, *aeroplane* and *car* are the objects better recognized when testing on Caltech256 with BOWsift and they are also the classes that mostly contribute to the recognition drop when testing on ImageNet and SUN. On the other hand, the classes *steering-wheel*, *windmill*, *bathtub*, *lighthouse* and

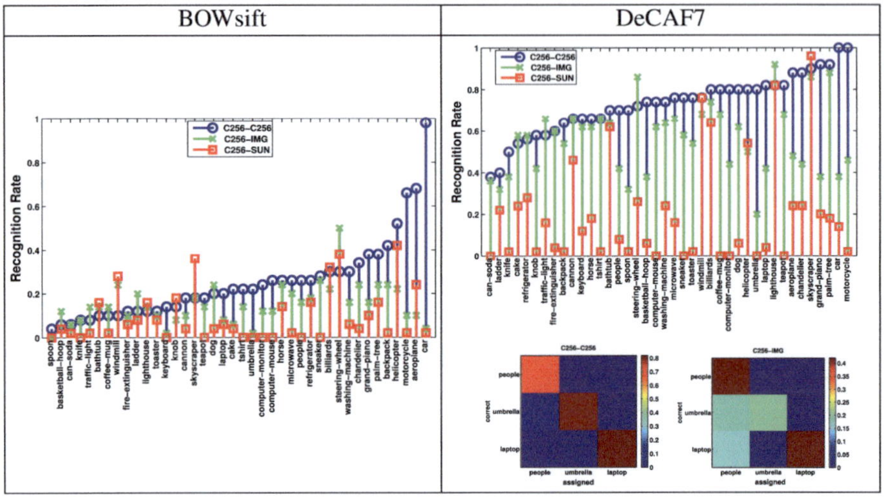

Fig. 2.10 Recognition rate per class from the multi-class cross-dataset generalization test. C256, IMG and SUN stand respectively for Caltech256, ImageNet and SUN datasets. We indicate with "train-test" the pair of datasets used in training and testing

skyscraper are better recognized on SUN and/or Imagenet than on Caltech256. All these last objects occupy most part of the image in all the collections and present less dataset-specific characteristics. When looking at the results with DeCAF7, *motorcycle* and *car* are still among the classes with the highest cross-dataset recognition difference, together with *people*, *spoon*, *umbrella*, *basketball-hoop* and *laptop*.

As already indicated by the binary experiments, even these results confirm that the dataset bias is in fact class dependent and that using DeCAF does not automatically solve the problem. A further remark can be done here about Imagenet. Although often considered as one of the less biased collections it actually presents a specific characteristic: the images are annotated with a single label but in fact may contain more than one visual category. In particular, its images often depict people even when they are labeled with a different class name. As a demonstration we report at the bottom of Fig. 2.10 a sub-part of the confusion matrix when training on Caltech256 and testing both on itself and on Imagenet. The results show that people are recognized in the class umbrella and laptop with relevant influence on the overall annotation errors.

Noisy Source Data and Domain Adaptation. Until now we have discussed and demonstrated empirically that the difference among two data collections can actually originate from multiple and often co-occurring causes. However the standard assumption is that the label assigned to each image is correct. In some practical cases this condition does not hold, as in learning from web data [66]. Some DA strategies seem perfectly suited for this task (see Fig. 2.11 top part) and we use them here to evaluate the cross-dataset generalization performance when training on Bing (noisy

	The *landmark* method [196] samples the source training images that are more relevant for the target test data and train a model only on them.
	The *reshape* approach [238] identifies latent sub-domains. The obtained sub-groups of data present different noise levels. *Subspace Alignment* (SA) [164] is used to adapt only the best source to the target.
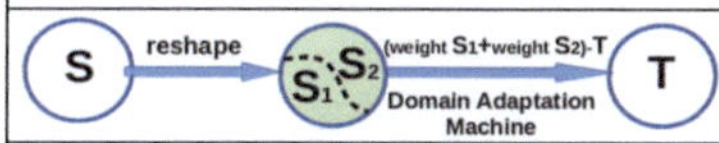	Domain Adaptation Machine (DAM [135]) recombines the two sub-domains with different weights.
	*Self-labeling* [486] learns a model over the full set of source data and progressively selects target samples to augment the training set.

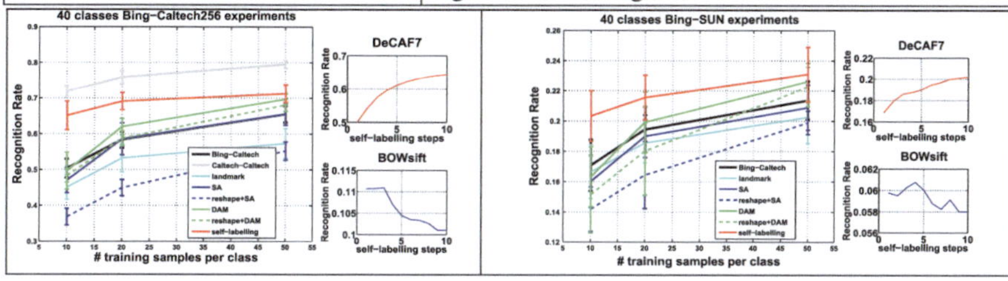

Fig. 2.11 *Top* schematic description of the used DA methods. *Bottom* Results of the Bing-Caltech256 and Bing-SUN experiments with DeCAF7. We report the performance of different DA methods (big plots) together with the recognition rate obtained in 10 subsequent steps of the self-labeling procedure (small plots). For the last ones we show the performance obtained both with DeCAF7 and with BOWsift when having originally 10 samples per class from Bing

object-centric source domain) and testing on Caltech256 and SUN (respectively an object-centric and a scene-centric target domain). We consider an increasing number of training images per class from 10 to 50 and we test on 30 images per class on Caltech256 and 20 images per class on SUN. The experiments are repeated for 10 random data splits.

The obtained results are shown in Fig. 2.11—bottom part, go in the same direction of what observed previously with the *Unbias* method. Despite the presence of noisy data, selecting them (landmark) or grouping the samples (reshape+SA, reshape+DAM) do not seem to work better than just using all the source data at once. On the other hand, keeping all the source data together and augmenting them with target samples by *self-labeling* [486] consistently improves the original results with a significant gain in performance especially when only a reduced set of training images per class is available. One well known drawback of this strategy is that progressively accumulated errors in the target annotations may lead to significant drift from the correct solution. However, when working with DeCAF features this risk appears highly reduced: this can be appreciated by looking at the recognition rate obtained over ten iterations of the target selection procedure, considering in particular the comparison against the corresponding performance obtained when using BOWsift (see the small plots in Fig. 2.11).

Fine-Tuning. As indicated in Sect. 2.2.2 the CNN features used for our analysis were obtained from pre-trained network whose parameters remain untouched. Previous work showed that modifying the network by fine-tuning before using it for recognition on a new task can be useful [349, 573]. We clarify here that this standard fine-tuning process does not fit in the dataset bias setting used for our study.

A network pre-trained on a dataset D is generally fine-tuned on a new dataset D' when the final task is also tested on D'. Thus the scheme (train,fine-tune,test) is (D, D', D'). In our analysis we have instead a different condition: (D, D', D'') where D' consists in a reduced amount of labeled data, while D'' is the test set extracted from a collection different from D'. It has been demonstrated that fine-tuning on a small amount of samples provides bad results [241] and it makes the features dataset-specific [66], which can only increase the bias. By using the Caffe CNN implementation we fine-tuned the Imagenet pre-trained network on the dense set, specifically on Caltech256 (5046 train images, 40 classes) and SUN (3015 train images, 40 classes), reserving respectively 1500 and 1300 images from these two datasets as test data. The in-dataset and cross-dataset experimental results are: $(Imagenet, Caltech256, Caltech256) = 86.4\%$; $(Imagenet, SUN, SUN) = 41.1\%$. $(Imagenet, SUN, Caltech256) = 37.5\%$; $(Imagenet, Caltech256, SUN) = 25.7\%$. Compared with what presented in Table 2.2 these results show the advantage of the fine-tuning in terms of overall recognition rate. However they also confirm that the fine-tuning process does not remove the bias (86.4 $>$ 25.7%; 41.1 $>$ 37.5%) and that using the wrong dataset to refine the network can be detrimental (86.4 $>$ 37.5%; 41.1 $>$ 25.7%).

2.5 Conclusion

In this paper we attempted at positioning the dataset bias problem in the CNN-based features arena with an extensive experimental evaluation. At the same time, we pushed the envelope in terms of the scale and complexity of the evaluation protocol, so to be able to analyze all the different nuances of the problem. We proposed a large-scale cross-dataset testbed defined over 12 existing datasets organized into two setups, and we focused on DeCAF features for the impressive results obtained so far in several visual recognition domains.

A first main result of our analysis is that DeCAF not only does not solve the dataset bias problem in general, but in some cases (both class- and dataset-dependent) they capture specific information that, although otherwise useful, induce a low performance in the cross-dataset object categorization task. The high level nature of the CNN features adds a further hidden bias that needs to be considered when comparing the experimental results against standard hand-crafted representations. Moreover, the negative bias remains, as it cannot intrinsically be removed (or alleviated) by changing feature representation. A second result concerns the effectiveness of learning methods applied over the chosen features: nor a method specifically designed to undo the dataset bias, neither algorithms successfully used in the domain adaptation setting seem to work when applied over DeCAF features. It appears as if the highly descriptive power of the features, that determined much of their successes so far, in the particular dataset-bias setting backfires, as it makes the task of learning how to extract general information across different data collection more difficult. Interestingly, a simple selection procedure based on target self-labeling leads to a significant increase in performance. This questions whether methods effectively used in DA should be considered automatically as suitable for dataset bias, and vice versa.

How to leverage over the power of deep learning methods to attack this problem in all its complexity, well represented by our proposed experimental setup, is open for research in future work. We consider this work as the first step of a wider project (the official webpage https://sites.google.com/site/crossdataset/): we already calculated and released new versions of the CNN features obtained with different architectures and by using different pre-training datasets on which we are planning an even larger experimental evaluation.

Part I
Shallow Domain Adaptation Methods

Chapter 3
Geodesic Flow Kernel and Landmarks: Kernel Methods for Unsupervised Domain Adaptation

Boqing Gong, Kristen Grauman and Fei Sha

Abstract Domain Adaptation (DA) aims to correct the mismatch in statistical properties between the source domain on which a classifier is trained and the target domain to which the classifier is to be applied. In this chapter, we address the challenging scenario of *unsupervised domain adaptation*, where the target domain does not provide any annotated data to assist in adapting the classifier. Our strategy is to learn robust features which are resilient to the mismatch across domains allowing to construct classifiers that will perform well on the target domain. To this end, we propose novel kernel learning approaches to inferring such features for adaptation. Concretely, we explore two closely related directions. On one hand, we propose *unsupervised learning* of a Geodesic Flow Kernel (GFK) which summarizes the inner products in an infinite sequence of feature subspaces that smoothly interpolate between the source and target domains. On the other hand, we propose *supervised learning* of a kernel that discriminatively combines multiple base GFKs to model the source and the target domains at fine-grained granularities. In particular, each base kernel pivots on a different set of landmarks—the most useful data instances that reveal the similarity between the source and target domains, thus bridging them to achieve adaptation. The proposed approaches are computationally convenient and capable of learning features/kernels and classifiers discriminatively without the need of labeled target data. We show through extensive empirical studies, using standard benchmark object recognition datasets, that our approaches outperform a variety of competing methods.

B. Gong (✉)
University of Central Florida, Orlando, FL 32816, USA
e-mail: boqinggong@gmail.com

K. Grauman
University of Texas at Austin, Austin, TX 78712, USA
e-mail: grauman@cs.utexas.edu

F. Sha
University of Southern California, Los Angeles, CA 90089, USA
e-mail: feisha@usc.edu

G. Csurka (ed.), *Domain Adaptation in Computer Vision Applications*,
Advances in Computer Vision and Pattern Recognition,
DOI 10.1007/978-3-319-58347-1_3

3.1 Introduction

Statistical machine learning algorithms often rely on the assumption that data used for training and testing are drawn from the same distribution. However, the validity of this assumption is frequently challenged in real-world applications. Figure 3.1 gives an illustrative example. Imagine that we are to deploy an APP to recognize images captured by mobile phone cameras. Instead of demanding that users provide labels to our learning algorithms, can we train classifiers with existing tagged Flickr images, and hope the classifiers will still work well on mobile camera test images? Our intuition says no. We suspect that the strong distinction between the Flickr images and the typical mobile phone images will cripple the classifiers.

Indeed, a stream of studies has shown that when the classifiers for object recognition are evaluated outside of their training datasets, the performance degrades significantly [124, 368, 489]. The culprit is clear: the visual appearance of even the same object varies across different datasets as a result of many factors, such as imaging devices, photographers' preferences, and background. These idiosyncrasies often cause a substantial mismatch between the training and testing data. In addition to object recognition, the mismatch is also abundant in other computer vision tasks [136, 140, 248, 524], speech recognition [292], and text analysis [40, 43].

In all these pattern recognition tasks, there is a common theme. There are two distinct types of datasets: one from a **source** domain and the other from a **target** domain. The source domain contains a large amount of labeled data such that a classifier can be reliably built. The target domain refers broadly to a related dataset that has different characteristics from the source domain. In other words, the underlying distributions of the datasets are different. Note that we assume the set of possible labels remains the same across domains.

How to build classifiers that are robust to the mismatched distributions?
Techniques for addressing this challenge have been investigated under the names of domain adaptation, covariate shift, or transfer learning [118, 214, 355, 434]. When there is no labeled data from the target domain to help learning, the problem, illustrated in Fig. 3.1, is called **unsupervised DA** [40, 43, 76, 200, 206]. When some labeled data from the target domain is accessible (but insufficient for constructing a good classifier), the problem is similar to semi-supervised learning and is named semi-supervised DA [36, 117, 407]. In either case, how to effectively leverage *unlabeled* target data is key to domain adaptation.

Discovering domain-invariant feature spaces that enable the adaptation of classifiers or regressors has been an extensively studied paradigm [31, 40, 43, 116, 354]. The feature representation can be derived by using auxiliary tasks that predict "pivot features" [13, 43], augmenting the feature space [116, 117, 205, 297], co-training with multi-view representations [76], or matching probabilistic distributions [354] (see more details in Chap. 1 of this book). In such a space, the source and target domains have the same (or similar) marginal distributions over the input data, and the posterior distributions of the labels are often assumed to be the same across domains too. Hence, a conventional classifier trained on the labeled source would

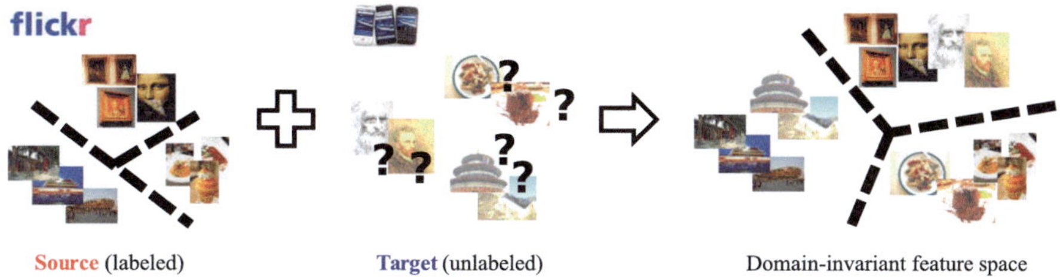

Fig. 3.1 Illustrative example of unsupervised domain adaptation, where the goal is to classify unlabeled data from the target domain that has different characteristics from the labeled source domain. The central idea behind our approaches is to use the data from both domains to infer a domain-invariant feature/kernel space such that, in this space, the classifier learned using the labels of the source domain will likely work well on the target domain

likely perform well on the target. Some theoretical analyses show that the generalization capability of the classifier on the target is indeed positively correlated with the domain-invariance, measured by different metrics, of the learned feature spaces [30, 322, 324].

Many existing feature learning methods in DA, however, are not directly applicable to *visual recognition*. For instance, the bag-of-words representations in natural language processing often contain semantic and discriminative "pivot" features that transfer across domains [40, 43, 76, 116]; to determine the sentiments (POSITIVE VS. NEGATIVE) of reviews on consumer products, words like "do not buy" transcend product categories. In computer vision tasks, this intuition no longer holds. Often, no single feature is discriminative enough for visual recognition tasks.

How can we infer an invariant feature space from visual *data?*
We therefore propose novel approaches to unsupervised DA, with applications to visual recognition in mind, as it is highly desirable in real-world applications. It taxes users minimally by automatically adapting the visual recognition systems. While appealing, unsupervised DA is especially challenging. For example, the common practice of discriminative training is generally not applicable. Without labels, it is not even clear how to define the right discriminative loss on the target domain! Similarly, it is also difficult to perform model selection.

We overcome those challenges by leveraging the conceptual connection between features and kernels, in order to better relate the source and target domains. Instead of explicitly defining which features are domain-invariant, we discover them *implicitly* by learning kernel functions that compute the inner products between data points in a (transformed) feature space. Thus, inferring domain-invariant feature spaces is equivalent to learning kernel functions that imply those features.

Learning kernels has been employed in a variety of problems in computer vision and machine learning [219, 288, 400, 507, 533]. As our ultimate goal is to build a classifier that performs well on the target, the framework of discriminatively combining multiple kernels is especially appealing [288]. To this end, we address two crucial and interdependent questions: what to use as base kernels, and how to discriminatively combine them when there is no labeled data from the target domain?

Our solution rests on two novel modeling ideas in a seamless fashion. The first leads to the development of the **Geodesic Flow Kernel** [200] that integrates an infinite number of intermediate feature spaces. Analogous to unsupervised manifold learning of kernels, GFK exploits the structures of low-dimensional subspaces in visual data. It gives rise to similarity measures that are insensitive to variations in domains. In particular, it results from aggregating the inner products defined in a sequence of infinite subspaces interpolating between the source and target domains. While each subspace may idiosyncratically favor the source or the target domain, the aggregation smooths out the idiosyncrasies. Consequently, when used in a nearest neighbor classifier as a similarity measure, GFK outperforms many competing methods for DA. The kernel function can be computed without requiring any labels from the target domain and can be plugged into any kernel-based classifier. We present the details in Sect. 3.2.

Our second modeling consideration aims to further improve GFK's discriminative power, centering around the notion of **landmarks** [196]. Concretely, we exploit the insight that *not all instances from the source domain are created equally in terms of adaptability* [196]. Existing research in modeling the discrepancy between domains has been limited to macroscopically examining their distribution similarity by tuning to statistical properties of the samples as a whole—when comparing (marginal) distributions to derive features, all the samples are used. This notion is stringent, as it requires all discrepancies to be accounted for and forces learning inefficiently (or even erroneously) from "hard" cases that might be just outliers to the target domains (c.f. examples in Fig. 3.4).

In contrast, we examine distribution similarity microscopically at the instance level. Our approach automatically plucks out and exploits the most desirable **"landmark"** instances from the source domain. The landmarks bridge the source and the target domains at a fine granularity; they are labeled instances from the source domain that are distributed similarly to the target domain. As a result, the labels of the landmarks serve as a good proxy for us to approximate the discrimintive loss on the target domain. We show how to use those landmarks to construct multiple domain-invariant features (i.e., multiple GFKs) and how those kernels can be discriminatively combined to learn a new domain-invariant feature space such that the adapted classifier performs the best on the target domain (c.f. Sect. 3.3).

We conduct extensive empirical studies in Sect. 3.4 to validate our approaches on the task of visual object recognition, where we train classifiers on one dataset and then apply them to others. Section 3.5 concludes this chapter.

3.2 The Base Geodesic Flow Kernel (GFK)

The main idea behind GFK is to *implicitly* construct a feature space that aggregates information on the source domain $\mathcal{D}_S$, the target $\mathcal{D}_T$, and "phantom" domains interpolating between those two. In particular, the phantom domains represent incremental changes in the geometric and statistical properties between the two domains.

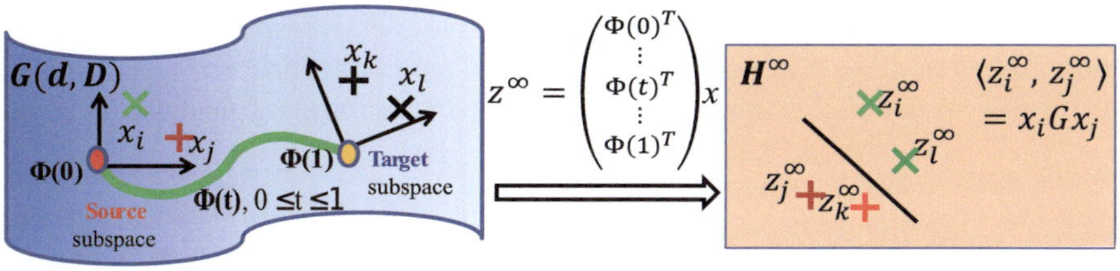

Fig. 3.2 The main idea of our GFK. The source and target domains are embedded in a Grassmann manifold, which is a collection of all d-dimensional subspaces of $\mathbb{R}^D$. The two subspaces of the two domains, respectively, are connected on the manifold by a continuous geodesic flow $\boldsymbol{\Phi}(t)$. After projecting a data point $\boldsymbol{x}$ to this flow, we arrive at an infinitely dimensional feature vector $z^\infty \in \mathcal{H}^\infty$ which encapsulates incremental changes from the source subspace to the target subspace. As a result, the inner product between two such vectors "averages out" the domains' idiosyncrasies and can be analytically computed in a closed form. (Best viewed in color)

While each of the domains is represented with a subspace, the inner products in $\mathcal{H}^\infty$ are defined to integrate over an infinite number of such subspaces. Intuitively, this integration averages out domain-specific idiosyncrasies and computes similarity measures that are insensitive to domain mismatch. Equivalently, the inner products give rise to a kernel function that defines the kernel mapping from the original feature space to a domain-invariant feature space. Figure 3.2 sketches the main idea.

3.2.1 Modeling Domains on Grassmann Manifold

In statistical modeling, we often assume data can be embedded in a low-dimensional linear subspace. For example, principal component analysis (PCA) identifies the subspace where the variances of the embedded data are maximized. It is convenient to refer to a subspace with its basis $\mathbf{P} \in \mathbb{R}^{D \times d}$, where D and d are the dimensions of the data and subspace, respectively. The collection of all d-dimensional subspaces form the Grassmannian $\mathbb{G}(d, D)$, a smooth Riemannian manifold on which we can define geometric, differential, and probabilistic structures.

As an intuitive example of how manifolds can help us tackle domain adaptation, imagine that we compute the subspaces of the datasets for the $\mathcal{D}_S$ and $\mathcal{D}_T$ domains and map them to two points on a Grassmannian. Intuitively, if these two points are close by, then the two domains could be similar in the distribution of their data. Thus, a source $\mathcal{D}_S$-trained classifier is likely to work well on the target $\mathcal{D}_T$.

However, *what if these two domains are far apart on the manifold?* For example, suppose two datasets of car images with large differences in poses are placed far apart on the manifold. We aim to use intermediate subspaces to learn domain-invariant features for adaptation. Specifically, the intermediate subspaces would capture statistics of car images under poses interpolated between the source and the target domains. Being informed of all these different subspaces from the same category, the learning algorithms might be able to extract features that are less sensitive to variations in pose. To this end, we will use the geodesic flow path to connect the two domains, where every point on this flow path is an intermediate subspace (phantom domain).

3.2.2 Defining the Geodesic Flow Kernel

Our approach consists of the following steps:

(1) determine the optimal dimensionality of the subspaces to embed domains;
(2) construct the geodesic flow;
(3) compute the geodesic flow kernel;
(4) use the kernel to construct a classifier with the labeled source data.

We defer describing step (1) to the next section and focus on steps (2) and (3). For step (2), we state only the main computational steps; the detailed derivation can be found in [206] and references therein. Step (4) is omitted for brevity, as it is the same as constructing any other kernel-based classifiers.

Construct the geodesic flow. Let $\mathbf{P}_S, \mathbf{P}_T \in \mathbb{R}^{\mathsf{D}\times\mathsf{d}}$ denote the two sets of basis of the subspaces for the source and target domains, respectively. Let $\mathbf{R}_S \in \mathbb{R}^{\mathsf{D}\times(\mathsf{D}-\mathsf{d})}$ denote the orthogonal complement to $\mathbf{P}_S$, namely $\mathbf{R}_S^\top \mathbf{P}_S = \mathbf{0}$. Using the canonical Euclidean metric for the Riemannian manifold, the geodesic flow is parameterized as $\boldsymbol{\Phi} : t \in [0, 1] \to \boldsymbol{\Phi}(t) \in G(\mathsf{d}, \mathsf{D})$ under the constraints that $\boldsymbol{\Phi}(0)$ is the subspace of the source domain and $\boldsymbol{\Phi}(1)$ is the subspace of the target. For other t, we have

$$\boldsymbol{\Phi}(t) = \mathbf{P}_S \mathbf{U}_1 \boldsymbol{\Gamma}(t) - \mathbf{R}_S \mathbf{U}_2 \boldsymbol{\Sigma}(t), \tag{3.1}$$

where $\mathbf{U}_1 \in \mathbb{R}^{\mathsf{d}\times\mathsf{d}}$ and $\mathbf{U}_2 \in \mathbb{R}^{(\mathsf{D}-\mathsf{d})\times\mathsf{d}}$ are orthonormal matrices. They are given by the following pair of (generalized) SVDs

$$\mathbf{P}_S^\top \mathbf{P}_T = \mathbf{U}_1 \boldsymbol{\Gamma} \mathbf{V}^\top, \quad \text{and} \quad \mathbf{R}_S^\top \mathbf{P}_T = -\mathbf{U}_2 \boldsymbol{\Sigma} \mathbf{V}^\top. \tag{3.2}$$

$\boldsymbol{\Gamma}$ and $\boldsymbol{\Sigma}$ are $\mathsf{d} \times \mathsf{d}$ diagonal matrices with the diagonal elements being $\cos\theta_i$ and $\sin\theta_i$, respectively. In particular, θ_i are called the principal angles between $\mathbf{P}_S$ and $\mathbf{P}_T$, measuring the degree by which subspaces "overlap". Moreover, $\boldsymbol{\Gamma}(t)$ and $\boldsymbol{\Sigma}(t)$ are diagonal matrices whose elements are $\cos(t\theta_i)$ and $\sin(t\theta_i)$ respectively.

Compute the geodesic flow kernel. The geodesic flow parameterizes how the source domain smoothly changes to the target domain. Consider the subspace $\boldsymbol{\Phi}(t)$ for $t \in (0, 1)$ and compute $\boldsymbol{\Phi}(t)^\top \mathbf{x}$, i.e., the projection of a feature vector $\boldsymbol{x}$ into this subspace. If $\boldsymbol{x}$ is from the source domain and t is close to 1, then the projection will appear as if it is likely coming from the target domain, and conversely for t close to 0. Thus, using the projections to the subspaces ($\boldsymbol{\Phi}(t), t \in [0, 1]$) to build a classifier would result in a model using a set of features that are characteristic of both domains. Hence, this classifier would likely perform well on the target domain.

Which values should we use for t then? Our answer is surprising at the first glance: as we suggest to use all of them! Intuitively, by expanding the original features with projections into **all** subspaces, we force a measurement of similarity (we use inner product) that is robust to any variation that leans either toward the source or towards the target or in between. In other words, the net effect is a representation that is insensitive to idiosyncrasies in either domain. While computationally this representation cannot be used explicitly, we show below that there is no need to actually compute, store, and manipulate the infinitely many projections.

Consider two original D-dimensional feature vectors $\boldsymbol{x}_i$ and $\boldsymbol{x}_j$, and their projections into $\boldsymbol{\Phi}(t)$ for a continuous t from 0 to 1. Denote the concatenation of all the projections into infinite-dimensional feature vectors z_i^∞ and z_j^∞. The inner product between them defines our Geodesic Flow Kernel (GFK):

$$\langle z_i^\infty, z_j^\infty \rangle = \int_0^1 (\boldsymbol{\Phi}(t)^\top \boldsymbol{x}_i)^\top (\boldsymbol{\Phi}(t)^\top \boldsymbol{x}_j)\, dt = \boldsymbol{x}_i^\top \mathbf{G} \boldsymbol{x}_j, \tag{3.3}$$

where $\mathbf{G} \in \mathbb{R}^{\mathsf{D}\times\mathsf{D}}$ is positive semidefinite. This is precisely the "kernel trick", where a kernel function induces inner products in an infinite-dimensional feature space. The matrix $\mathbf{G}$ can be computed in closed-form from previously defined matrices

$$\mathbf{G} = [\mathbf{P}_S\mathbf{U}_1 \;\; \mathbf{R}_S\mathbf{U}_2] \begin{bmatrix} \boldsymbol{\Lambda}_1 & \boldsymbol{\Lambda}_2 \\ \boldsymbol{\Lambda}_2 & \boldsymbol{\Lambda}_3 \end{bmatrix} \begin{bmatrix} \mathbf{U}_1^\top \mathbf{P}_S^\top \\ \mathbf{U}_2^\top \mathbf{R}_S^\top \end{bmatrix} \tag{3.4}$$

where $\boldsymbol{\Lambda}_1$ to $\boldsymbol{\Lambda}_3$ are diagonal matrices, whose diagonal elements are

$$\lambda_{1i} = 1 + \sin(2\theta_i)/(2\theta_i),\ \lambda_{2i} = (\cos(2\theta_i) - 1)/(2\theta_i),\ \lambda_{3i} = 1 - \sin(2\theta_i)/(2\theta_i).$$

Detailed derivations are given in the appendix of [198], where we provide additional details for justifying the rationale behind GFK, i.e., how GFK reduces the discrepancy across domains. At the high level, it leads to measuring *distances* between data points in a way that is insensitive to domains. The empirical studies there reveal that the subspaces induced by GFK best satisfy two desirable properties *simultaneously* for the distance measures: minimal distortions to the distances in the original source and target domains, *and* matching how distances of the two domains are distributed.

The closed-form expression of GFK is convenient to use and does not depend on user-selected parameters (e.g., the bandwidth in Gaussian RBF kernels). We only need to choose the dimension d of the subspaces, that can be inferred automatically from the data as shown in [198].

Extract domain-invariant feature space. The kernel $\mathbf{G}$ can be plugged into any kernelized classifiers (e.g., SVMs). Additionally, we can extract from it an equivalent finite-dimensional domain-invariant feature space. Let $\mathbf{L}$ be $\mathbf{G}$'s square root: $\mathbf{L}^{\top}\mathbf{L} = \mathbf{G}$. The domain-invariant feature space is given by the mapping $\boldsymbol{x} \rightarrow z = \mathbf{L}\boldsymbol{x}$, such that $z_i^{\top} z_j = \boldsymbol{x}_i^{\top}\mathbf{G}\boldsymbol{x}_j$. This explicit feature representation is convenient for constructing other types of classifiers that do not depend on inner products.

GFK as a standalone unsupervised DA approach. We note that GFK entails domain-invariant features, since it "averages out" the domain idiosyncrasies by the integration over the geodesic flow. As a result, we are able to directly use it to solve the unsupervised DA problem, in addition to employing it to build other algorithms (e.g., the landmark-based method in the next section). Concretely, we first determine the optimal dimensionality of the subspaces either by the subspace disagreement measure [198] or cross-validation. Then we compute the Geodesic Flow Kernel $\mathbf{G}$ using the subspaces Eq. (3.4). Finally, we use the kernel to construct a classifier with the labeled data, either using a kernelized classifier which requires only the inner products defined by the kernel matrix $\mathbf{G}$ or using the invariant features $\mathbf{L}\boldsymbol{x}$ in any other types of classifiers.

3.3 Landmarks for Unsupervised Domain Adaptation

One of the key challenges to unsupervised DA is that there is no labeled data in the target domain to train discriminative classifiers. We tackle this with the insight of landmarks—some labeled instances in the source domain may be regarded as a subset drawn from the target. By automatically identifying those landmarks, we can thus approximate the discriminative loss of the target domain.

As a motivating example for the landmarks, suppose the source domain contains furniture in a home environment and the target domain consists of images of office-style furniture. Conceivably, certain images from the source, e.g., those taken in home office, could also be regarded as samples from the target. Such images thus might have properties that are shared by both domains. These properties in turn can guide learning algorithms to search for invariant features or kernels.

In the following, we give an overview of the landmark-based approach, followed by details on how to identify landmarks. As the first step, our landmark-based approach plucks out and exploits the most desirable instances, i.e., *landmarks*, to facilitate adaptation. Identifying those instances requires comparing all possible subsets from the source domain to the target. We will show how this can be addressed with tractable optimization.

Leveraging the landmarks, we create a cohort of auxiliary tasks where landmarks explicitly bridge the source and target domains. Specifically, in those auxiliary tasks, the original target domain is augmented with landmarks, blurring the distinction across domains. Thus, those tasks are *easier* to solve than the original DA problem. We show this is indeed true both theoretically and empirically. The auxiliary tasks

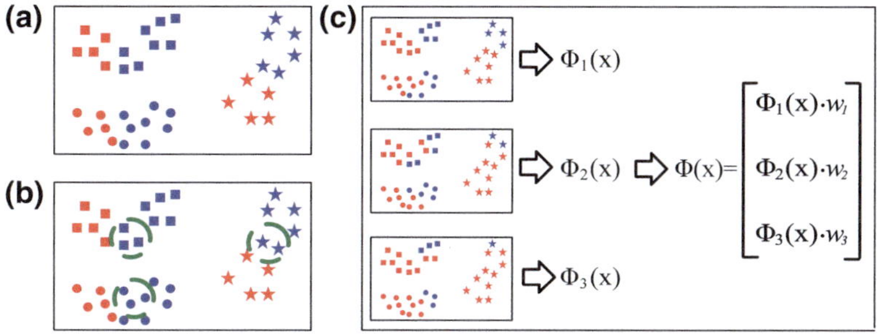

Fig. 3.3 Main idea of our landmark-based approach. **a** The original set, with target instances in *red* and source instances in *blue*. **b Landmarks** selected from the source, shown inside the *green circles*, that can be regarded as samples from the target. **c** Multiple auxiliary tasks are created by augmenting the original target with the selected landmarks, which switch their color (domain association) from *blue* to *red*. Each task gives rise to a new feature representation $\Phi_i(x)$ and these representations are combined discriminatively to form domain-invariant features $\boldsymbol{\Phi}(x)$ for the original DA problem. (Best viewed in color)

offer multiple views of the original problem; they differ by how the landmarks are selected, which in turn are determined by the data pairwise similarities. In this work, we measure similarities at multiple scales (of distances). Thus, each task provides a different perspective to the adaptation problem, by being robust to idiosyncrasies in the domains at different granularities.

The solutions of the auxiliary tasks give rise to multiple domain-invariant GFKs. We parameterize the invariant features for the original adaptation problem with those kernels. Intuitively, not all of the kernels are equally useful; to discern which are, we cast the corresponding learning problem in terms of multiple kernel learning. We learn the kernel discriminatively to minimize classification errors on the landmark data instances, which serve as a proxy to discriminative loss on the target domain. Figure 3.3 schematically illustrates the overall approach.

Step I: Landmark selection

Landmarks are data points from the source domain; however, given how they are distributed, they look like they could be samples from the target domain too (see Fig. 3.3 for a schematic illustration, and Fig. 3.4 for exemplar images identified as landmarks in vision datasets). The intuition behind our approach is to use these landmarks to bridge the source and the target domains.

How can we identify those landmarks? At first glance, it seems that we need to compare all possible subsets of training instances in the source domain to the target. We will show in the following this seemingly intractable problem can be relaxed and solved with tractable convex optimization.

Let $\mathcal{D}_S = \{(\boldsymbol{x}_m, y_m)\}_{m=1}^{\mathsf{M}}$ denote M data points and their labels from the source domain. Likewise, we use $\mathcal{D}_T = \{\boldsymbol{x}_n\}_{n=1}^{\mathsf{N}}$ for the target domain. To identify landmarks, we use M indicator variables $\boldsymbol{\alpha} = \{\alpha_m \in \{0, 1\}\}$, one for each data point in the source domain. If $\alpha_m = 1$, then $\boldsymbol{x}_m$ is regarded as a landmark. Our goal is to choose among all possible configurations of $\boldsymbol{\alpha} = \{\alpha_m\}$ such that the distribution of the ***selected*** data instances is maximally similar to that of the target domain.

To determine whether the two distributions are similar, we use a non-parametric two-sample test[1] called Maximum Mean Discrepancy (MMD) [213]. Specifically, we use a nonlinear feature mapping function $\phi(\cdot)$ to map $\boldsymbol{x}$ to a Reproducing Kernel Hilbert Space (RKHS) $\mathcal{H}$ and compare the difference in sample means. When the mapping function is a unit-ball in a universal RKHS, the difference can be conveniently calculated as follows[2]

$$\mathsf{MMD}(\boldsymbol{\alpha}) = \left\| \frac{1}{\sum_m \alpha_m} \sum_m \alpha_m \phi(\boldsymbol{x}_m) - \frac{1}{\mathsf{N}} \sum_n \phi(\boldsymbol{x}_n) \right\|_{\mathcal{H}}^2, \tag{3.5}$$

where $\sum \alpha_m$ is the number of selected landmarks, and the first term inside the norm is the mean of the selected landmarks under the mapping.

Our goal is to choose $\boldsymbol{\alpha}$ such that the difference is minimized. Furthermore, we impose the constraint that the labels are *balanced* in the selected landmarks. Concretely, we arrive at the following optimization problem

$$\min_{\alpha} \mathsf{MMD}(\boldsymbol{\alpha}) \quad \text{s.t.} \quad \frac{1}{\sum_m \alpha_m} \sum_m \alpha_m y_{mc} = \frac{1}{\mathsf{M}} \sum_m y_{mc}, \tag{3.6}$$

where y_{mc} is an indicator variable for $y_m = c$. The right-hand side of the constraint is simply the prior probability of class c, estimated from the source.

We stress that the above criterion is defined on a *subset* of the source domain called landmarks, as the sample mean is computed *only* on the selected instances (c.f. the denominator $\sum_m \alpha_m$ in Eq. (3.6)). This is very different from other approaches that have used similar non-parametric techniques for comparing distributions [214, 354]. There they make stronger assumptions that all data points in the source domain need to be collectively distributed similarly to the target domain. Furthermore, they do not impose the balance constraint of Eq. (3.6). Our experimental results show that these differences are crucial to the success of our approach.

As Eq. (3.6) is intractable due to the binary unknowns $\boldsymbol{\alpha}$, we propose to solve it efficiently by introducing new variables β_m as $\alpha_m \left(\sum_m \alpha_m\right)^{-1}$ and relaxing them to live on the simplex $\Delta = \{\beta : \beta_m \geq 0, \sum_m \beta_m = 1\}$. Substituting $\{\beta_m\}$ into Eq. (3.6) and its constraints, we arrive at the following *quadratic programming problem*

$$\min_{\beta \in \Delta} \boldsymbol{\beta}^{\top} \mathbf{A} \boldsymbol{\beta} - 2/\mathsf{N}\, \boldsymbol{\beta}^{\top} \mathbf{B} \mathbf{1} \quad \text{s.t.} \sum_m \beta_m y_{mc} = 1/\mathsf{M} \sum_m y_{mc}, \quad \forall\, c, \tag{3.7}$$

---

[1]Other approaches are also possible, including building density estimators when the dimensionality is not high.

[2]The unit-ball condition allows the difference to be represented as a metric in the form of Eq. (3.5) and the universality ensures that the means are injective such that the difference in the means is zero if and only if the two distributions are the same. For more analysis, please refer to [213].

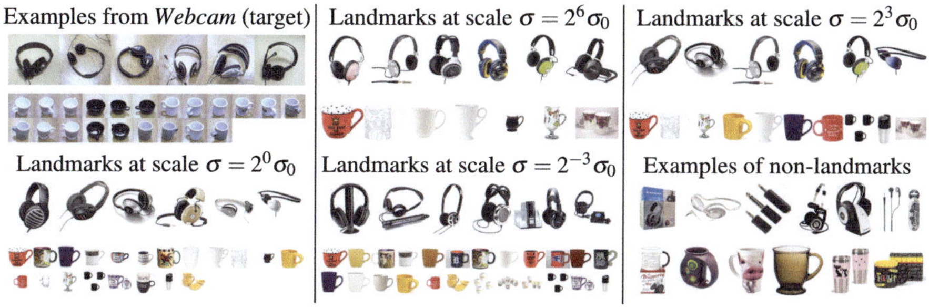

Fig. 3.4 Landmarks selected from the source domain (*Amazon*) for the target domain (*Webcam*) from the Office dataset [407], as well as instances not selected as landmarks (best viewed in color). As the scale decreases, images with greater variance in appearance are selected as expected

where $\mathbf{A} \in \mathbb{R}^{\mathsf{M}\times\mathsf{M}}$ denotes the positive semidefinite kernel matrix computed over the source domain, and $\mathbf{B} \in \mathbb{R}^{\mathsf{M}\times\mathsf{N}}$ denotes the kernel matrix computed between the source data points and target data points. We recover the binary solution for α_m by finding the support of β_m, i.e., $\alpha_m = \text{THRESHOLD}(\beta_m)$. In practice, we often obtain *sparse* solutions, supporting our modeling intuition that only a subset of instances in the source domain is needed to match the target domain.

Multi-scale analysis. The selection of landmarks depends on the kernel mapping $\phi(\boldsymbol{x})$ and its parameter(s). To satisfy the requirement of being a unit-ball in a universal RKHS, we use Gaussian RBF kernels, defined as follows

$$K(\boldsymbol{x}_i, \boldsymbol{x}_j) = \exp\{-(\boldsymbol{x}_i - \boldsymbol{x}_j)^\top \mathbf{M}(\boldsymbol{x}_i - \boldsymbol{x}_j)/\sigma^2\}, \tag{3.8}$$

where the metric $\mathbf{M}$ is positive semidefinite and we experiment with several choices.

The bandwidth σ is a scaling factor for measuring distances and similarities between data points. Since we regard landmarks as likely samples from the target domain, the bandwidth σ determines how much the source and the target are similar to each other at different granularities. A small σ will attenuate distances rapidly and regard even close points as being dissimilar. As a result, Eq. (3.6) may select a *large* number of points as landmarks in order to match the target distribution. A large σ will have the opposite effect. Figure 3.4 illustrates the effect of σ.

Instead of choosing one scale σ in the hope that it fits all, we devise a multi-scale approach. We use a set $\{\sigma_q \in [\sigma_{min}, \sigma_{max}]\}_{q=1}^{\mathsf{Q}}$. For each σ_q, we compute the kernel according to Eq. (3.8) and solve Eq. (3.7) to obtain the corresponding landmarks $\mathcal{L}^q = \{(\boldsymbol{x}_m, y_m) : \alpha_m = 1\}$. Using multiple scales adds the flexibility of modeling data where similarities cannot be measured in one homogeneous scale. For example, the category of "grizzly bear" is conceivably much closer to "grey bear" than to "polar bear", so to capture similarities among both the pairs as well as among all three, it is necessary to model them at two scales. Each set of landmarks (one set per scale) gives rise to a different perspective to the adaptation problem by suggesting which instances to explore when connecting the source and the target. We achieve this connection by creating auxiliary tasks, described below.

Step II: Constructing auxiliary tasks
Imagine we create a new source domain $\mathcal{D}_S^q = \mathcal{D}_S \setminus \mathcal{L}^q$ and a new target domain $\mathcal{D}_T^q = \mathcal{D}_T \bigcup \mathcal{L}^q$, where the landmarks $\mathcal{L}^q$ are removed from and added to the source and target domains, respectively. The landmarks' labels are not used yet at this stage.

Our auxiliary tasks are defined as Q domain adaptation problems, $\mathcal{D}_S^q \rightarrow \mathcal{D}_T^q$. The auxiliary tasks differ from the original problem $\mathcal{D}_S \rightarrow \mathcal{D}_T$ in an important aspect: the new tasks should be "easier", as the existence of landmark points ought to aid the adaptation. This is illustrated by the following theorem, stating that the discrepancy between the new domains is smaller than the original.

Let P_S and P_T denote the distributions of the original source and target domains, respectively (where we omitting the arguments X in $P(X)$ to simplify the notations). Suppose $P_S = \alpha P_N + (1-\alpha)P_L$ with $\alpha \in [0, 1)$ is a mixture model where P_L is the component corresponding to the landmark data points and P_N corresponds to the distribution of the non-landmark instances. For the auxiliary task, assume the new target distribution is modeled as a mixture distribution $Q_T = \beta P_T + (1-\beta)P_L$ where $\beta \in [0, 1)$. Furthermore, assume the source distribution remains essentially unchanged, which is easily satisfied as long as the number of instances in the source domain is significantly greater than the number of landmark instances and the landmarks are selected *i.i.d.* from $P_L(X)$.[3]

Theorem 1 *The following inequality holds,*

$$KL(P_S \| Q_T) \leq KL(P_S \| P_T)$$

where $KL(\cdot\|\cdot)$ *stands for the Kullback–Leibler divergence, if*

$$\alpha KL(P_N \| P_T) + (1-\alpha) KL(P_L \| P_T) \geq 9/8 \max\{KL(P_L \| P_N),\ KL(P_N \| P_L)\}. \tag{3.9}$$

In words, the new target distribution is closer to the source distribution, on the condition that the inter-domain difference (i.e., the left-hand side) is greater than the intra-domain discrepancy or inhomogeneity (i.e., the right-hand-side).

The proof is in the Appendix of [198]. Note that the condition in Eq. (3.9) is mild, we expect the source domain is relatively homogeneous and is distinct from the target. With the reduced discrepancy between P_S and Q_T, we can apply the analysis in [324, Lemma 1] to show that classifiers applied to Q_T attain a smaller generalization error bound than those applied to P_T.

These insights motivate our design of auxiliary tasks: they conceivably give rise to low accuracy if we build a binary classifier to classify data into either the source

[3]Note that we do not require the landmarks to be *i.i.d* samples from $P_S(X)$; they only need to be representative samples of $P_L(X)$.

or the target domain, as the landmarks blend the two domains and discourage the use of domain-specific features. We describe next how to extract domain-invariant kernels/features using the solutions of those easy problems as a *basis*.

Learning basis from auxiliary tasks. For every pair of auxiliary domains, we use the Geodesic Flow Kernel to compute domain-invariant features. The GFK is particularly adept at measuring domain-invariant distances among data points, as exemplified by its superior performance in nearest-neighbor classifiers (c.f. Sect. 3.4.1). Thus, it is especially suitable for the final stage of our approach when we compose complex domain-invariant features extracted as the mapping $\Phi_q(\boldsymbol{x}) = \mathbf{L}_q\boldsymbol{x}$, where $\mathbf{G}_q = \mathbf{L}_q^\top\mathbf{L}_q$ is the GFK for the q-th auxiliary task. In the following, we describe how to integrate the spaces, one for each auxiliary task, *discriminatively* so that the final feature space is optimal for the target.

Step III: Discriminative learning of kernels and classifiers
In this final step, we reveal the second use of landmarks beyond constructing auxiliary tasks, i.e., we use their labels to learn *discriminative* domain-invariant features for the target domain.

Concretely, we compose the features for the original adaptation problem with the auxiliary tasks' features as a basis. We scale and concatenate those features $\{\sqrt{w_q}\Phi_q(\boldsymbol{x})\}_{q=1}^{\mathsf{Q}}$ into a "super" vector $\boldsymbol{f}$. Learning $\{w_q\}$ is cast as learning a convex combination of all kernels $\mathbf{G}_q$ [288],

$$\mathbf{F} = \sum_q w_q\mathbf{G}_q, \qquad \text{s.t.} \;\; w_q \geq 0 \text{ and } \sum_q w_q = 1. \tag{3.10}$$

Finally, we use the kernel $\mathbf{F}$ in training an SVM classifier and the labels of the landmarks $\{\mathcal{L}^q\}$, i.e., $\mathcal{D}_{\text{TRAIN}} = \sum_q \mathcal{L}^q$ to optimize $\{w_q\}$ discriminatively. We use $\mathcal{D}_{\text{DEV}} = \mathcal{D}_S \setminus \mathcal{D}_{\text{TRAIN}}$ as the validation dataset for model selection. Since $\mathcal{D}_{\text{TRAIN}}$ consists of landmarks that are distributed similarly to the target, we expect the classification error on $\mathcal{D}_{\text{TRAIN}}$ to be a good proxy to that of the target.

3.4 Experiments

We evaluate our methods in the context of visual object recognition; more results for other tasks (e.g., text analyses) are shown in a prior conference paper [196]. We describe the general experimental setup first, and then report the results of our GFK and landmark-based approaches to DA.

The Office-Caltech (OC10) Dataset. We use the three domains from the Office (OFF31) dataset [407] in our experiments: Amazon (images downloaded from online merchants), Webcam (low-resolution images by a web camera), and DSLR (high-resolution images by a digital SLR camera). Additionally, we added Caltech-256 [215] as the fourth domain. We extract 10 classes common to all domains:

Fig. 3.5 Example images from Caltech-256, Amazon, DSLR, and Webcam. Caltech and Amazon images are mostly from online merchants, while DSLR and Webcam images are from offices

backpack, touring-bike, calculator, head-phones, computer-keyboard, laptop-101, computer-monitor, computer-mouse, video-projector and *coffee-mug*. There are 8 to 151 samples per category per domain, and 2533 images in total. Figure 3.5 highlights the differences among these domains with example images from the MONITOR class. We report our results on adapting 10-way classification between the four domains.[4] We obtain the results of the competing methods by rerunning publicly available code or our implementation if the code is unavailable.

Features. We follow similar feature extraction and experiment protocols used in previous work. Briefly, we use SURF features [29] and encode the images with 800-bin histograms with the visual codebook [108, 445] trained from a subset of Amazon images. The histograms are normalized first and then z-scored to have zero mean and unit standard deviation in each dimension. We share our SURFBOV features (and code) publicly to promote direct reproducibility of our results.[5]

Training settings. For experiments using GFK for adaptation, we conduct experiments in 20 random trials for each pair of source and target domains. In each trial, we randomly sample labeled data in the source domain as training examples, and unlabeled data in the target domain as testing examples. This setting is in accordance with prior work [206, 278, 407] and provides the maximal comparability to those methods. More details on the data split are provided in the next section. We report averaged accuracies on target domains as well as standard errors. For GFK results, 1-NN is used as our classifier as it does not require cross-validating parameters. For our algorithms, the dimensionalities of subspaces are selected according to the subspace disagreement measure in [200]. For the hyper-parameters of the methods we compare to, we use what are recommended in the published work.

For experiments using our landmark-based approach for adaptation, we use all training instances from the source domains. Except for this difference, other training setups are the same as for the experiments using GFK.

[4]The results on the OFF31 dataset [407] reported in the supplementary material of [200], similarly outperform the competing approaches.

[5]Features and code of our methods: http://www-scf.usc.edu/~boqinggo/da.html.

3.4.1 Adaptation via GFK

We compare our methods with various baseline and competing approaches: (1) NO ADAPT where we use the original features, i.e., without learning any new representations for domain adaptation; (2) PCA_S where we project the original features into the PCA subspace learned from the *source* domain; (3) PCA_T where we project the original features into the PCA subspace learned from the *target* domain; (4) PCA_{S+T} where the PCA subspace is learned from the *combined* data of both the source and target domains; (5) PLS_S where we project the original features into the Partial Least Squares (PLS) [228] subspace computed using the source domain's labels.

We also implement the method in [206]. We refer to it as the geodesic flow sampling approach (GFS). While it also uses geodesic flows to model domain mismatch, the approach *samples* a finite number of subspaces and uses them to construct high-dimensional features, followed by dimensionality reduction and classification. As the authors of this method suggest, we use PCA subspaces for both domains. We report results on two variants: (i) our implementation using the recommended parameters reported in [206], such as the number of sampled subspaces and the reduced dimensionality (denoted GFS (impl.)), and (ii) our implementation using the optimal dimensionality automatically selected by our algorithm (GFS (opti.)).

For our approach, we use two types of subspaces for the source data: PCA_S and PLS_S. For the target domains, we use only PCA_T as there are no labels. Thus, there are two variants of our method: GFK(PCA_S, PCA_T) and GFK(PLS_S, PCA_T).

Table 3.1 summarizes the classification accuracies (see [198] for standard errors) of all the above methods for different pairings of the source and target domains. Note that, to fit the table within the width of the page, we have shortened GFK(PCA_S, PCA_T) to GFK(A,A), and GFK(PLS_S, PCA_T) to GFK(S,A). The best group (differences up to one standard error) in each column is in bold font and the second best group (differences up to one standard error) is in italics and underlined.

All DA methods improve the accuracies over the baseline NO ADAPT. Further, our GFK based methods in general outperform GFS. Moreover, GFK(PLS_S, PCA_T) performs the best. Two key factors may contribute to the superiority of our method: (i) the kernel integrates all the subspaces along the flow, and is hence able to model better the domain shift between the source and the target; (ii) this method uses a discriminative subspace (by PLS) in the source domain to incorporate the label information. This has the benefit of avoiding projection directions that contain noise and very little useful discriminative information. PCA, on the other hand, does not always yield subspaces that contain discriminative information.

It is also interesting to note that the PCA-based baselines, especially PCA_{S+T} and PCA_T, perform quite well. They are often in the second-best performing group, and are even better than the GFS methods on D $\rightarrow$ W and W $\rightarrow$ D. We suspect that because the domain difference between DSLR and Webcam is small, either PCA_T or PCA_{S+T} is already able to capture the commonness of the two domains well. For instance, both DSLR and Webcam contain similar office images though with different resolutions (see Fig. 3.5 for an example).

Table 3.1 Recognition accuracies on target domains with *unsupervised* adaptation via GFK. (C: Caltech, A: Amazon, W: Webcam, and D: DSLR)

Method	C→A	C→W	C→D	A→C	A→W	A→D
NO ADAPT	20.8	19.4	22.0	22.6	23.5	22.2
PCA$_S$	34.7	_31.3_	33.6	34.0	31.3	29.4
PCA$_T$	_37.5_	**33.9**	_37.8_	_35.4_	**34.9**	_33.3_
PCA$_{S+T}$	_36.6_	_32.1_	34.9	_35.8_	_32.8_	31.5
PLS$_S$	26.7	26.0	28.2	31.1	29.3	28.0
GFS (impl.)	_36.8_	_30.6_	32.6	_35.3_	31.0	30.7
GFS (opti.)	_36.9_	**33.9**	35.2	_35.6_	**34.4**	**34.9**
GFK (A,A)	_36.9_	**33.7**	35.2	_35.6_	**34.4**	**35.2**
GFK (S,A)	**40.4**	**35.8**	**41.1**	**37.9**	**35.7**	**35.1**
Method	W→C	W→A	W→D	D→C	D→A	D→W
NO ADAPT	16.1	20.7	37.3	24.8	27.7	53.1
PCA$_S$	23.4	28.0	68.2	26.8	28.1	61.7
PCA$_T$	**29.6**	_32.5_	67.4	_31.2_	_34.4_	**79.4**
PCA$_{S+T}$	_28.1_	_31.6_	**74.1**	_30.8_	33.3	**79.7**
PLS$_S$	18.3	21.1	42.8	21.4	26.5	41.9
GFS (impl.)	21.7	27.5	54.3	29.4	32.0	66.0
GFS (opti.)	_27.3_	_31.3_	_70.7_	30.0	32.6	_74.9_
GFK (A,A)	_27.2_	_31.1_	_70.6_	29.8	32.5	_74.9_
GFK (S,A)	**29.3**	**35.5**	_71.2_	**32.7**	**36.2**	**79.1**

Table 3.2 Recognition accuracies with *unsupervised* adaptation via GFK using "deep" DECAF features [127]

Method	C→D	C→W	C→A	A→C	A→W	A→D
GFK (S,A)	89.5	79.5	85.3	81.4	77.3	84.5
Method	W→C	W→A	W→D	D→C	D→A	D→W
GFK (S,A)	74.7	84.2	99.5	76.6	76.9	97.3

GFK with "deep" features. Deep learning has been shown very effective for a variety of computer vision tasks. Table 3.2 are the results of GFK with the deep DECAF features [127]. The experiment setup remains the same as before except that, in each of the 20 random rounds, we use the remaining source data as the validation set to choose the subspace dimension—since the DECAF features are very high dimensional, the subspace disagreement measure [200] is always below the threshold 1. The selected subspace dimensions are between 10 and 40. Comparing Tables 3.1 and 3.2, we can see that the deep features significantly outperform the handcrafted SURF features for the unsupervised DA.

Table 3.3 Recognition accuracies of unsupervised DA via the landmark-based approach

%	A→C	A→D	A→W	C→A	C→D	C→W	W→A	W→C	W→D
NO ADAPT	41.7	41.4	34.2	51.8	54.1	46.8	31.1	31.5	70.7
TCA [354]	35.0	36.3	27.8	41.4	45.2	32.5	24.2	22.5	80.2
GFS [206]	39.2	36.3	33.6	43.6	40.8	36.3	33.5	30.9	75.7
GFK+1NN (ours)	42.2	42.7	40.7	44.5	43.3	44.7	31.8	30.8	75.6
GFK+SVM (ours)	38.8	43.3	37.3	50.2	40.1	45.1	39.1	34.5	67.5
SCL [43]	42.3	36.9	34.9	49.3	42.0	39.3	34.7	32.5	83.4
KMM [243]	42.2	42.7	42.4	48.3	53.5	45.8	31.9	29.0	72.0
METRIC [407]	42.4	42.9	**49.8**	46.6	47.6	42.8	38.6	33.0	**87.1**
GFK + LANDMARK (ours)	**45.5**	**47.1**	46.1	**56.7**	**57.3**	**49.5**	**40.2**	**35.4**	75.2

3.4.2 *Adaptation via the Landmark-Based Approach*

Next we test our landmark adaptation approach. For the hyper-parameters, we set the threshold of β_m in Eq. (3.7) to be a small number (10^{-8}–10^{-10}) due to floating point arithmetics. The RBF kernel bandwidths in Eq. (3.8) are $\sigma_q = 2^q \sigma_0$ with $q \in \{-6, -5, \ldots, 5, 6\}$, where σ_0 is the median of pairwise distances between all training instances. This ensures we select at least one instance per category and we do not select all instances from the source domains as landmarks. The SVM trade-off parameters are tuned on the validation data, c.f. Sect. 3.3.

Recognition accuracies. Table 3.3 reports object recognition accuracies on the *target* under nine pairs of source and target domains—we did not use DSLR as the source domain as it is too small to select landmarks. We contrast the proposed approach (LANDMARK) to the methods of Transfer Component Analysis (TCA) [354], Geodesic Flow Sampling (GFS) [206], our GFK approaches respectively with 1-NN and linear SVM (GFK + 1NN and GFK + SUM), Structural Correspondence Learning (SCL) [43], Kernel Mean Matching (KMM) [243], and a metric learning method (METRIC) [407]. Note METRIC is for *semi-supervised* DA, so we reveal the labels of one instance per category from the target domains. We also report the baseline results of NO ADAPT described in Sect. 3.4.1.

Our approach LANDMARK clearly performs the best on almost all pairs, even when compared to the METRIC method which has access to labels from the target. The only significant exception is on the pair W→D. Error analysis reveals that the two domains are very similar, containing images of the same object instances with different imaging resolutions. As such, many data points in *Webcam* are selected as landmarks, leaving very few instances for model selection.

Detailed analysis on landmarks. Next, we further examine the utility of landmarks in DA to better understand why they are working well. We first study whether *auto-*

Table 3.4 Contrasting landmark selection algorithm to several variants

%	A→C	A→D	A→W	C→A	C→D	C→W	W→A	W→C	W→D
GFK + LANDMARK (ours)	**45.5**	47.1	**46.1**	**56.7**	**57.3**	49.5	**40.2**	**35.4**	**75.2**
RAND. SEL.	44.5	44.5	41.9	53.8	49.9	49.5	39.8	34.1	74.2
SWAP	41.3	**47.8**	37.6	46.2	42.0	46.1	38.2	32.2	70.1
UNBALANCED	37.0	36.9	38.3	55.3	49.0	**50.1**	39.4	34.9	73.9
EUC + LANDMARK	44.5	44.0	41.0	50.2	40.1	45.1	39.1	34.5	67.5

matically selected landmarks coincide with our modeling intuition, i.e., that they look like samples from the target domain.

Figure 3.4 confirms our intuition. It displays several landmarks selected from the source domain *Amazon* when the target domain is *Webcam*. The top-left panel shows representative images from the *headphone* and *mug* categories from *Webcam*, and the remaining panels display images from *Amazon*, including both landmarks and those which are not. When the scale σ is large, the selected landmarks are very similar in visual appearance to the images of the target. As the scale decreases, landmarks with greater variance show up. This is particularly pronounced at $2^{-3}\sigma_0$. Nonetheless, they still look far more likely to be from the target *Webcam* domain than non-landmark images (see the bottom-right panel)—the non-landmarks for the *headphone* category contain images such as earphones and packaging boxes. Similarly, non-landmarks for the *mug* category are more unusually shaped ones.

In Table 3.4, we contrast our method to some of its variants, illustrating quantitatively the novelty and significance of using landmarks to facilitate adaptation. First, we study the adverse effect of selecting incorrect images as landmarks. The row of RAND. SEL. displays results of randomly selecting landmarks, as opposed to using the algorithm proposed in Sect. 3.3. (The number of random landmarks is the average number of "true" landmarks chosen in LANDMARK.) The averaged accuracies over 10 rounds are reported. GFK+LANDMARK outperforms the random strategy, often by a significant margin, validating the automatic selection algorithm.

The SWAP row in Table 3.4 gives yet another strong indication of how landmarks could be viewed as samples from the target. Recall that landmarks are used as *training* data in the final stage of our learning algorithm (c.f. Sect. 3.3), while non-landmarks in the source are used for model selection. This setup follows the intuition that as landmarks are mostly similar to the target, they are a better proxy than non-landmarks for optimizing discriminative loss for the target. When we swap the setup, the accuracies drop significantly, except on the pair $A \rightarrow D$ (compare the rows SWAP and GFK+LANDMARK). This once again establishes the unique and extremely valuable role of the landmarks automatically selected by our algorithm.

We also study the class balancing constraint in Eq. (3.6), which enforces that the selected landmarks obey the class prior distribution. Without it, some classes dominate and result in poor classification results. This is clearly evidenced in the row of UNBALANCED where accuracies drop significantly after we remove the constraint.

Finally, we study the effect of using GFK to measure distribution similarity, as in Eq. (3.8). The row of EUC. + LANDMARK reports the results of using the conventional Euclidean distance, illustrating the striking benefit of using GFK (in the row of GFK+LANDMARK). While using non-parametric two-sample tests to measure distribution similarity has been previously used for DA (e.g., kernel mean matching, c.f. the row of KMM in Table 3.3), selecting a proper kernel has received little attention, despite its vital importance. Our comparison to EUC. SEL. indicates that measuring distribution similarity *across* domains is greatly enhanced with a kernel revealing domain-invariant features.

Value of auxiliary tasks and multi-scale analysis. The auxiliary tasks are DA problems over the new pairs of source and target domains $\mathcal{D}_S^q \rightarrow \mathcal{D}_T^q$, c.f. Sect. 3.3. As indicated by Theorem 1, by incorporating landmarks in the augmented target domain, the auxiliary adaptation problems become easier to solve. Figure 3.6 provides strong empirical evidence supporting the theorem. In the figure, we show the object recognition accuracies on the original target domain as a result of solving those auxiliary tasks individually. Specifically, for each scale σ_q, we use the method of GFK to compute $\mathbf{G}_q$ for the pair $\mathcal{D}_S^q \rightarrow \mathcal{D}_T^q$ to extract invariant features and then train an SVM classifier using the landmarks (and their labels). We contrast to GFK+SVM reported in Table 3.3, where the only difference from the experiments here is to solve the original adaptation problem. Clearly, the auxiliary tasks are easier to solve, resulting in more effective adaptations such that the accuracies on the target domains are in general much better than GFK+SVM. This asserts firmly that landmarks bridge between the source and the target, and thus are an important adaptation mechanism to exploit.

In Fig. 3.6, we also contrast results of individual tasks to the proposed method LANDMARK where the solutions of multiple auxiliary tasks are *combined* discriminatively. Combination clearly improves on individual tasks, verifying the effectiveness of combination and our hypothesis that the data is modeled better at multiple scales. We mark in red color those individual tasks whose kernels have contributed to the final solution in Eq. (3.10).

3.5 Conclusion

Unsupervised DA is an important yet very challenging problem. Our work has shown that it is very effective to address it by leveraging and modeling intrinsic structures such as subspaces and landmarks in the data. The key insight behind our approaches is to learn kernel functions that correspond to (implicitly defined) feature spaces that are robust to the mismatch between the source and the target domains.

Our first approach, the Geodesic Flow Kernel (GFK), exploits the low-dimensional subspace structures in the visual data and measures similarity between data points in a way that is insensitive to each domain's idiosyncrasies. It is simple to implement, free of hyper-parmeter tuning, and performs very well in benchmark tasks. Our second

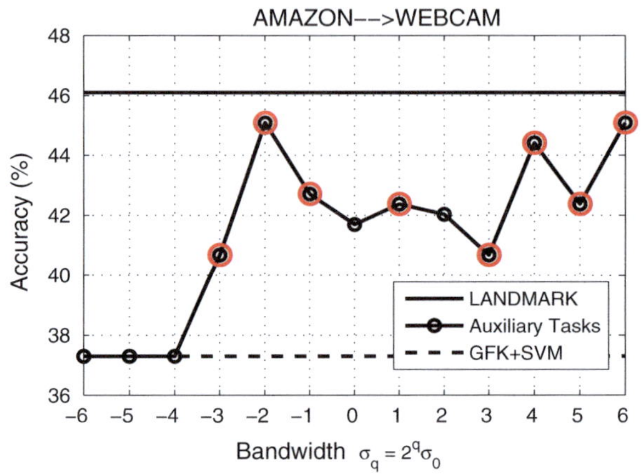

Fig. 3.6 Performance of individual auxiliary tasks. Each circle point on the curves shows recognition accuracy on the original target domain $\mathcal{D}_T$, by using the kernel computed from the auxiliary task. All the *circle* points are above GFK + SVM except when the scale is very small and results in that almost all source domain data are selected as landmarks. The *red circles* denote the auxiliary tasks whose kernels contribute to the final kernel **F** (cf. Eq. (3.10) and the corresponding result shown as the *solid horizontal line*) after discriminative learning

approach builds on the success of GFK and exploits the landmark structures between two domains. Essentially, the landmarks are data points from the source domain but also serve as a bridge to the target domain. The landmarks enable analyzing distribution similarity on multiple scales, hypothesizing a basis for invariant features, and discriminatively learning features/kernels. On benchmark tasks for visual recognition, this approach consistently outperforms others (including the approach of GFK), often by large margins. Furthermore, we show that the landmark approach is strongest when using the GFK as its component kernel.

This chapter has just scratched the surface of the domain adaptation problem in visual recognition. While we have shown that learning kernels is powerful in discovering feature spaces where the two domains are similar, learning kernels is potentially useful for answering more challenging problems: what is a domain? and how can we characterize the difference between domains? Our paper [197] sheds some light on these questions. We challenge the conventional wisdom and practice that equates a dataset to a domain. Instead, we argue that vision datasets are likely a mélange of multiple latent and heterogeneous domains. We propose new learning algorithms that identify the latent domains in a vision dataset. We then show that using the resulting domains to adapt is more effective than using the original dataset.

Overall, the kernel learning framework opens the door for future research towards DA. For instance, GFK is just one possibility of averaging inner products from multiple subspaces interpolating between the source and target domains. It would be interesting to explore other choices. The auxiliary tasks in the landmark-based approach can be regarded as multiple sources, and multiple-source DA algorithms could be explored [130, 138] jointly with the landmarks.

Acknowledgements This work is partially supported by DARPA D11-AP00278 and NSF IIS-1065243 (B. G. and F. S.), and ONR ATL #N00014-11-1-0105 (K. G.). The Flickr images in Fig. 3.1 are under a CC Attribution 2.0 Generic license, courtesy of berzowska, IvanWalsh.com, warrantedarrest, HerryLawford, yuichi.sakuraba, zimaowuyu, GrahamAndDairne, Bernt Rostad, Keith Roper, flavorrelish, and deflam.

Chapter 4
Unsupervised Domain Adaptation Based on Subspace Alignment

Basura Fernando, Rahaf Aljundi, Rémi Emonet, Amaury Habrard, Marc Sebban and Tinne Tuytelaars

Abstract Subspace-based domain adaptation methods have been very successful in the context of image recognition. In this chapter, we discuss methods using Subspace Alignment (SA). They are based on a mapping function which aligns the source subspace with the target one, so as to obtain a domain invariant feature space. The solution of the corresponding optimization problem can be obtained in closed form, leading to a simple to implement and fast algorithm. The only hyperparameter involved corresponds to the dimension of the subspaces. We give two methods, SA and SA-MLE, for setting this variable. SA is a purely linear method. As a nonlinear extension, Landmarks-based Kernelized Subspace Alignment (LSSA) first projects the data nonlinearly based on a set of landmarks, which have been selected so as to reduce the discrepancy between the domains.

B. Fernando
The ANU, Canberra, Australia
e-mail: basura.fernando@anu.edu.au

R. Aljundi · T. Tuytelaars
KU Leuven, SAT-PSI, IMEC, Leuven, Belgium
e-mail: Rahaf.Aljundi@kuleuven.be

T. Tuytelaars
e-mail: Tinne.Tuytelaars@kuleuven.be

R. Emonet (✉) · A. Habrard · M. Sebban
Univ. Lyon, JM-Saint-Etienne, CNRS,
Institut D'Optique Graduate School Laboratoire Hubert Curien UMR 5516,
St-Etienne, France
e-mail: Remi.Emonet@univ-st-etienne.fr

A. Habrard
e-mail: Amaury.Habrard@univ-st-etienne.fr

M. Sebban
e-mail: Marc.Sebban@univ-st-etienne.fr

G. Csurka (ed.), *Domain Adaptation in Computer Vision Applications*,
Advances in Computer Vision and Pattern Recognition,
DOI 10.1007/978-3-319-58347-1_4

4.1 Introduction

In the case of unsupervised domain adaptation (DA), no labeled target data is available. To overcome the issue of domain shift, the global statistics of the data, i.e.the differences in data distribution, then seem one of the few cues left. This is what subspace-based domain adaptation methods try to exploit: *If source and target data span different subspaces in feature space, then how can we exploit this observation to overcome the domain shift?* First (see also Chap. 1 of this book), it was proposed to use a set of intermediate subspaces to model the shift between the two domains. Gopalan et al. [207] proposed to generate intermediate representations in the form of subspaces along the geodesic path connecting the source subspace and the target subspace on the Grassmann manifold. Gong et al. [200] built on this work and introduced a Geodesic Flow Kernel which models incremental changes between the source and target domains. But do we really need these intermediate subspaces? Subspace Alignment [164, 165] directly reduces the discrepancy between the two domains by moving the source and target subspaces closer (in terms of Bregman divergence). This is achieved by optimizing a mapping function that transforms a point from the source subspace to a "corresponding" point on the target subspace. By transforming all the data points of the source domain, we bring them closer to the target data. A classifier learned on such target-aligned source data, will then yield better results on the target data then a classifier learned on the original source data.

The set of transformations we consider for mapping the source subspace onto the target subspace is the set of linear transformations. So the transformation takes the form of multiplication with a matrix M. One can show that the optimal solution corresponds to the covariance matrix between the top d source and target eigenvectors, where d represents the subspace dimensionality. From this transformation matrix, a similarity function $Sim(\mathbf{y_S}, \mathbf{y_T})$ is derived comparing a source data point $\mathbf{y_S}$ with a target example $\mathbf{y_T}$. The similarity function $Sim(\mathbf{y_S}, \mathbf{y_T})$ can be used directly in a nearest neighbor classifier. Alternatively, we can also learn a global classifier such as a support vector machine on the source data after mapping the data onto the target-aligned source subspace.

The advantages of Subspace Alignment are numerous: (1) By adapting the bases of the subspaces, our approach is *global* as it manipulates the global covariance matrices. This allows us to induce robust classifiers that are not sensitive to local perturbations (in contrast to metric learning-based domain adaptation approaches that need to consider pairwise or triplet-based constraints for inducing the metric). (2) By aligning the source and target subspaces, the method is *intrinsically regularized*. Unlike most optimization-based DA methods, we do not need to tune regularization parameters in the objective function. (3) SA is efficient and intuitive. (4) Above all, SA turns out to be quite effective, reaching state-of-the-art results.

Of course SA also has some drawbacks: (1) A linear transformation for aligning source and target subspaces may be insufficient in practice, and (2) adapting all the source data to the target domain may not be optimal, given that in many cases only a subset of source and target examples are similarly distributed. To overcome these limitations, we propose a nonlinear landmarks-based extension, which we refer to as LSSA [10].

In this chapter, we discuss in detail the standard Subspace Alignment (SA) method in Sect. 4.2 as well as its nonlinear extension LSSA in Sect. 4.3. After that, we perform a more in-depth analysis and report experimental results in Sect. 4.4 and conclude the chapter in Sect. 4.5.

4.2 Subspace Alignment

We assume that we have a set S of labeled source data (resp. a set T of unlabeled target data), both lying in the same D-dimensional space and drawn *i.i.d.* according to a fixed but unknown source distribution $P(\chi_S;\theta_S)$ (resp. target distribution $P(\chi_T;\theta_T)$) where $P(\chi_S;\theta_S) \neq P(\chi_T;\theta_T)$. We assume that the source labeling function is more or less similar to the target labeling function. We denote the transpose operation by $'$. We denote vectors by lowercase bold fonts such as $\mathbf{y_i}$ and the class label by notation L_i. Matrices are represented by uppercase letters such as M.

Subspace generation. Even though both the source and target data lie in the same D-dimensional space, they have been drawn according to different distributions and span different manifolds in this D-dimensional space. Consequently, rather than working on the original data, we suggest to handle more robust representations of the source and target domains and to learn the shift between these two domains. First, we transform all source and target data to a D-dimensional z-normalized vector (i.e.of zero mean and unit standard deviation). Note that z-normalization is an important step in most of the subspace-based DA methods such as GFK [200] and GFS [206]. Then, using PCA, we select for each domain the d eigenvectors corresponding to the d largest eigenvalues. These eigenvectors are used as bases of the source and target subspaces, respectively denoted by X_S and X_T ($X_S, X_T \in \mathbb{R}^{D\times d}$). Note that X'_S and X'_T are orthonormal (thus, $X'_S X_S = I_d$ and $X'_T X_T = I_d$ where I_d is the identity matrix of size d). In the following, X_S and X_T are used to learn the shift between the two domains. Sometimes, we refer to X_S and X_T as subspaces, although they are actually the basis vectors of the subspaces.

Domain Adaptation with Subspace Alignment. The first step of SA consists of projecting each source ($\mathbf{y_S}$) and target ($\mathbf{y_T}$) data point (with $\mathbf{y_S}, \mathbf{y_T} \in \mathbb{R}^{1\times D}$) to its respective subspace X_S and X_T by the operations $\mathbf{y_S}X_S$ and $\mathbf{y_T}X_T$, respectively. Then, we use a linear transformation M to map (or *align*) the source subspace to the target one. This step allows us to directly compare source and target samples in their respective subspaces. The linear transformation is modeled by a transformation matrix M ($M \in \mathbb{R}^{d\times d}$) with those of X_T. We find the optimal M by minimizing the Bregman matrix divergence

$$M^* = \arg\min_M \|X_S M - X_T\|_F^2 \tag{4.1}$$

Algorithm 1: Subspace alignment in the lower d-dimensional space

Input: Source data S, Target data T, Source labels L_S, Subspace dimension d
1: $X_S \leftarrow PCA(S, d)$;
2: $X_T \leftarrow PCA(T, d)$;
3: $X_a \leftarrow X_S X_S' X_T$;
4: $S_a = S X_a$;
5: $T_T = T X_T$;
6: $L_T \leftarrow NN - Classifier(S_a, T_T, L_S)$;
Output: Predicted target labels L_T

where $\|.\|_F^2$ is the Frobenius norm. Since X_S and X_T are generated from the first d eigenvectors, they tend to be intrinsically regularized.[1] Therefore, we suggest not to add a regularization term in the Eq. (4.1). It is thus possible to obtain a simple solution of Eq. (4.1) in closed form. Because the Frobenius norm is invariant to orthonormal operations, we can rewrite the objective function in Eq. (4.1) as follows

$$M^* = \arg\min_M \left\| X_S' X_S M - X_S' X_T \right\|_F^2 = \arg\min_M \left\| M - X_S' X_T \right\|_F^2 = X_S' X_T. \quad (4.2)$$

where we used the orthonormality of the source subspace X_S. In words: the optimal transformation corresponds to the covariance matrix of the basis vectors of the two subspaces. This implies a new coordinate system $X_a = X_S M = X_S X_S' X_T$. We call X_a the *target-aligned source coordinate system*. It is worth noting that if the source and target domains are the same, then $X_S = X_T$ and M^* is the identity matrix.

In order to compare a source data point $\mathbf{y_S}$ with a target data point $\mathbf{y_T}$, one needs a similarity function $Sim(\mathbf{y_S}, \mathbf{y_T})$. Projecting $\mathbf{y_S}$ and $\mathbf{y_T}$ in their respective subspace X_S and X_T and applying the optimal transformation matrix M^*, we can define $Sim(\mathbf{y_S}, \mathbf{y_T})$ using cosine similarity as follows

$$Sim(\mathbf{y_S}, \mathbf{y_T}) = \left(\mathbf{y_S} X_S M^*\right)\left(\mathbf{y_T} X_T\right)' = \mathbf{y_S} X_S M^* X_T' \mathbf{y_T}' = \mathbf{y_S} A \mathbf{y_T}', \quad (4.3)$$

where $A = X_S X_S' X_T X_T'$ and $A \in \mathbb{R}^{D \times D}$. Note that Eq. (4.3) looks like a generalized dot product or Mahalanobis distance (even though A is not necessarily positive semi-definite). A encodes the relative contributions of the different components of the vectors in their original space.

We use the matrix A to construct the kernel matrices via $Sim(\mathbf{y_S}, \mathbf{y_T})$ and perform SVM-based classification. Alternatively, one can use a nearest neighbor classifier. To this end, we project the source data via X_a into the target-aligned source subspace and the target data into the target subspace (using X_T), and perform the classification in this d-dimensional space. The pseudo-code of this algorithm is presented in Algorithm 1. From now on, we will simply use M to refer to M^*.

[1]We experimented with several regularization methods on the transformation matrix M such as 2-norm, trace norm, and Frobenius norm regularization. None of these regularization strategies improved over using no regularization.

Geometric Interpretation. While the above algebraic derivation perfectly explains the SA algorithm, it is useful to interpret the equations in a geometric fashion, to get a better understanding of the algorithm.

A common misinterpretation of SA is that the transformation M aligns the source and target subspaces by mapping the k-th principal component of X_S onto the k-th principal component of X_T, for $k \leq d$. This interpretation, however, is incorrect. Instead, matrix M in Eq. (4.2) aims at approximating, as accurately as possible, each of the first d target principal components (i.e., the basis vectors of the target subspace) using a linear combination of the first d source principal components (i.e., the basis vectors of the source subspace). From a geometric point of view, it is clear that this corresponds to finding, for each of the target subspace basis vectors, the closest point on the source subspace. This point, in turn, can be found by *projecting the target basis vector onto the source subspace*. The k-th column of M can thus be interpreted as the d-dimensional coordinates of the k-th target basis vector after projection onto the source subspace, expressed relative to the source subspace basis. Additionally, note how $M' = (X_S' X_T)' = X_T' X_S$, so likewise the rows of M can be interpreted as the projection of the source basis vectors onto the target subspace, expressed relative to the target subspace basis.

From this, it follows that a mode of variation present in the source but absent in the target data, represented by a source principal component with eigenvector orthogonal to the target subspace, will be ignored by SA: the target-aligned source subspace is spanned by the projections of the target eigenvectors onto the source subspace. Since this particular source eigenvector is orthogonal to all target eigenvectors, it is not used for the target-aligned source subspace and the classifier learned in that subspace will not exploit such information. Likewise, a mode of variation present in the target data but absent in the source, will not play a role either. On the other hand, correlations, both in source and target data, are optimally exploited: a feature (dimension) that is only observed in target data and never in source data can still contribute to the classification, if it's strongly correlated with another feature that does appear both in source and target, as it will impact the same principal component after projection on the target subspace.

4.2.1 Setting the Subspace Dimensionality d

The algorithm given above describes the whole subspace alignment process. Given the data, computing the matrix M and projecting the data onto the corresponding subspaces is easy. The only remaining issue is how to set the one hyperparameter involved: the subspace dimensionality d. Since we are working in an unsupervised setting (no labels available for the target data), it is not possible to determine the optimal value for d through cross-validation on the target data. Instead, we developed two alternative methods, as described below.

For the first method, we present a theoretical result on the stability of the solution and then use this result to tune d. For the second method we use maximum likelihood estimation to find the intrinsic subspace dimensionalities of the source domain (d_s) and the target domain (d_t). We refer to this second method as *SA-MLE*. Note how *SA-MLE* does not necessarily need to have the same dimensionality for both the source subspace X_S and the target subspace X_T.

SA: Using a consistency theorem on $Sim(\mathbf{y_S}, \mathbf{y_T})$

Inspired from concentration inequalities on eigenvectors [597], an upper bound on the similarity function $Sim(\mathbf{y_S}, \mathbf{y_T})$ can be derived to tune d. Basically, the eigenvectors of X_S and X_T are estimated based on n_S (resp. n_T) data points sampled from the full distribution. It can be shown that, to keep these estimates sufficiently close to their real values (say below a predefined threshold γ), only the first d_{max} eigenvectors are to be used, with d_{max} a complex function of the number of samples (n_S and n_T), the threshold γ, and the required confidence δ. For each $d \in \{1 \ldots d_{max}\}$, we can then prove that $\|X_S^d M X_T^{d\,\prime} - X_{S_n}^d M_n X_{T_n}^{d\,\prime}\| \leq \gamma$, with the superscript d referring to the subspace dimensionality used and the subscript n referring to the samples-based estimates. In other words, as long as we select a subspace dimension d such that $d \leq d_{max}$, the solution M is stable and not prone to over-fitting.

Now, we use this theoretical result to obtain the subspace dimensionality for our method. To find a suitable subspace dimensionality ($d^* \leq d_{max}$), we consider all the subspaces of size $d = 1$ to d_{max} and select the value for d that minimizes the classification error using a two fold cross-validation over the labeled source data. Consequently, we assume that the source and the target subspaces have the same dimensionality. For the full derivation of the consistency theorem and further details, we refer to [165].

SA-MLE: Using maximum likelihood estimation

This section presents an alternative more efficient method for estimating the subspace dimensionality. It uses maximum likelihood estimation and is especially well suited for high-dimensional data and in combination with a nearest neighbor classifier. This method is called *SA-MLE*. It addresses two problems that arise when applying subspace alignment on high-dimensional data (for example, Fisher Vectors [369]). First, the cross-validation procedure as explained above becomes computationally expensive. Second, the size of the similarity metric A is $D \times D$ which is not memory efficient for high-dimensional data.

A key insight is that, after obtaining the domain transformation matrix M, any classification learning problem can be formulated in the *target-aligned source subspace* (i.e.$X_S M$) which has smaller dimensionality than the original space $\mathbb{R}^D$. To reduce the computational effort, we evaluate the sample dissimilarity $D_{SA-MLE}(\mathbf{y_s}, \mathbf{y_t})$ after projection, i.e.between the target-aligned source samples and the target subspace projected target samples, using Euclidean distance in $\mathbb{R}^d$

$$D_{SA-MLE}(\mathbf{y_s}, \mathbf{y_t}) = \|\mathbf{y_s} X_S M - \mathbf{y_t} X_T\|_2 \,. \tag{4.4}$$

The source and target subspaces X_s and X_t are obtained by PCA as before. But now the size of the subspaces can be different: we denote them as d_s and d_t, respectively. We estimate d_s and d_t independently, using the intrinsic dimensionality method of [295]. This method aims at retaining the local neighborhood information after dimensionality reduction. To this end, it uses the Maximum Likelihood Estimator (MLE) of the dimension d from *i.i.d.* observations.

The MLE estimator assumes that the observations represent an embedding of a lower dimensional sample. For instance, we can write $\mathbf{y} = \phi(\mathbf{z})$ where ϕ is a continuous and sufficiently smooth mapping, and $\mathbf{z}$ are sampled from a smooth density function f on $\mathbb{R}^d$, with unknown dimensionality d with $d < D$. In this setting, close neighbors in $\mathbf{R}^d$ are mapped to close neighbors in the embedding $\mathbb{R}^D$. Let us fix a point $\mathbf{y}$ and assume $f(\mathbf{y}) \approx const$ in a small sphere $S_{\mathbf{y}}(R)$ of radius R around $\mathbf{y}$. The binomial process $\{N(t, \mathbf{y}); 0 \leq t \leq R\}$ which counts the observations within distance t from $\mathbf{y}$ is

$$N(t, \mathbf{y}) = \sum_{i=1}^{n} \mathbf{1}\{\mathbf{y}_i \in S_{\mathbf{y}}(t)\}\,, \tag{4.5}$$

where $\mathbf{1}\{\cdot\}$ is the indicator function. By approximating Eq. (4.5) with a Poisson process it can be shown that the maximum likelihood estimate of the intrinsic dimensionality for the data point $\mathbf{y}$ is

$$\widehat{d}(\mathbf{y}) = \left[\frac{1}{N(R, \mathbf{y})} \sum_{j=1}^{N(R,\mathbf{y})} \log \frac{R}{\Theta_j(\mathbf{y})}\right]^{-1} \tag{4.6}$$

where $\Theta_j(\mathbf{y})$ is the distance from sample $\mathbf{y}$ to its jth nearest neighbor [295].

It is recommended to set R to the mean pairwise distance among the samples. The intrinsic dimensionality of a domain is then obtained by the average $\widehat{d} = \frac{1}{n}\sum_{i=1}^{n} \widehat{d}(\mathbf{y}_i)$ over all its instances. The two domains are considered separately, which implies $d_S \neq d_T$.

4.3 Landmarks-Based Kernelized Subspace Alignment

Landmarks-based Kernelized Subspace Alignment (LSSA) tackles two limitations of SA: it aligns the source and target subspaces but goes *beyond a linear transformation*, and, it is able to *ignore points from the source domain that are irrelevant* to the adaptation task. LSSA introduces a landmark selection (LS) process followed by a subspace alignment (SA) step, which is carried out exactly as presented before.

As SA uses a PCA on each domain, it is tempting to nonlinearly extend SA by using kernel PCA [67]. This, however, does not work at all, as shown in the experiments. The geometric interpretation of SA makes it easier to understand why. The two kernel PCA extract a kernelized subspace for each domain but these two subspaces have no semantic link, while, in the linear case, the PCA basis vectors of the domains are both expressed in the common original space. Having no link

Algorithm 2: Landmarks based subspace alignment DA algorithm.

Input: Source data S, Target data T, Source labels L_S, Threshold th, Subspace dimension d.
1: $A \leftarrow choose\_landmarks(S, T, th)$
2: $P \leftarrow S \cup T$
3: $\sigma \leftarrow median(\{\|a - b\|, (a, b) \in P^2\})$
4: $K_S \leftarrow project\_using\_kernel(S, A, \sigma)$
5: $K_T \leftarrow project\_using\_kernel(T, A, \sigma)$
6: $X_S \leftarrow PCA(K_S, d)$
7: $X_T \leftarrow PCA(K_T, d)$
8: $X_a \leftarrow X_S X_S' X_T$
9: $S_a = K_S X_a$
10: $T_T = K_T X_T$
11: $L_T \leftarrow classifier(S_a, T_T, L_S)$
Output: Target labels L_T.

between the subspaces, learning an optimal projection of one onto the other does not make sense.

To be able to make a meaningful projection of one nonlinear subspace onto the other, LSSA selects a single set of points, from both the source and target domains. These points, or landmarks, are selected so as to decrease the discrepancy between the domains. This unique set of landmarks is used together with a Gaussian kernel to project all points from both domains. Experiments show that this approach for making SA nonlinear is effective and that the proposed landmark selection strategy is also the most suited.

Landmark selection overview. Intuitively, a good set of landmarks is a set of points which can be used to project the source and target data onto a shared space in which their distributions are more similar. Our method chooses the landmarks among $S \cup T$ (all points from the source and target domains) and does not use any label. The final output of the landmark selection procedure is a set of landmarks $A = \{\alpha_1, \alpha_2, ...\}$, $A \subset S \cup T$.

To avoid any computationally expensive iterative optimization method, we propose a direct method for asserting whether a point should be kept as a landmark or not. The method considers a set of candidate landmarks (all source and target points, or a randomized subsample if the domains are dense), extracts a quality measure for each point at different scales, and keeps as landmarks all candidates which quality exceeds a threshold.

Once the set of landmarks A has been selected, we use a Gaussian kernel to achieve a nonlinear mapping of all points into a common space defined by these landmarks. The subspaces from the source and the target domains are then aligned using a linear transformation. Algorithms 2 and 3 summarize the overall LSSA approach and its landmarks selection process.

Multiscale landmark selection. LSSA's landmark selection approach considers each point c from $S \cup T$ as a candidate landmark. Each candidate is considered independently from the others: a quality measure is computed and if this measure is above a threshold, the candidate is kept as a landmark.

Algorithm 3: Landmarks selection, the *choose_landmarks* function.

Input: Source data S, Target data T, Threshold th.

```
A ← {}
P ← S ∪ T
distances ← { ||a − b|| , (a, b) ∈ P² }
for s in percentiles(distances) do
    for c in S ∪ T do
        KV_S ← { exp(−||c−p||²/(2s²)) , p ∈ S }
        KV_T ← { exp(−||c−p||²/(2s²)) , p ∈ T }
        if overlap(KV_S, KV_T) > th then
            A = A ∪ {c}
```

Output: Set of selected landmarks A.

To assess the quality of the candidate c, its similarity with each point $p \in S \cup T$ is first computed, using a Gaussian kernel with standard deviation s

$$K(c, p) = \exp\left(\frac{-\|c - p\|^2}{2s^2}\right) \tag{4.7}$$

The quality measure for the candidate c is computed as an overlap between the distribution of the $K(c, .)$-values for the source points, and the one for the target points, as explained below.

The value of the kernel radius s from Eq. (4.7) is important as it defines the size of the neighborhood that the candidate landmark considers. Choosing the right s for a given landmark will allow us to capture the local phenomena at the proper scale and to better align the source and target distributions. Extreme values for s must be avoided as they lead to a perfect match between the distributions of source and target points: all values of $K(c, .)$ become 0 (when s is close to 0) or 1 (when s is very big).

When calculating the quality of a candidate landmark, we actually perform a multiscale analysis: we select the best scale s to capture the local properties of the data, at the same time avoiding extreme values for s. To do so, we compute the distribution of Euclidean distances between all pairs of points and try every percentile value of this distribution. With this percentile-based approach, we consider a range of values for the scale s which are all plausible. For each considered scale s, we compute an overlap measure between the source and target distributions, keeping the greatest one as the quality measure for the candidate landmark.

Distribution overlap criteria. For a candidate landmark c and a scale s, we want to compute a degree of overlap between two sets of $K(c, .)$-values: the one for the source points KV_S and the one for the target points KV_T. To lower the computational cost, the two distributions are approximated as normal distributions and thus summarized by their means and standard deviations $\mu_S, \sigma_S, \mu_T, \sigma_T$. To be able to use a fixed threshold and give some semantics to it, we use a normalized overlap measure, explained below and computed as follows

$$overlap(\mu_S, \sigma_S; \mu_T, \sigma_T) = \frac{\mathcal{N}(\mu_S - \mu_T \mid 0, \sigma_{sum}^2)}{\mathcal{N}(0 \mid 0, \sigma_{sum}^2)} \tag{4.8}$$

where $\sigma_{sum}^2 = \sigma_S^2 + \sigma_T^2$ and $\mathcal{N}(. \mid 0, \sigma_{sum}^2)$ is the centered 1D normal distribution.

To compute the overlap of two probability densities f and g, we can integrate their product: $\int f(x)g(x)dx$. Intuitively, the more overlap there is between the densities, the bigger their product. This overlap measure follows similar principles as the Bhattacharyya coefficient. By analytically integrating the product of two normal distributions, we obtain the numerator of Eq. (4.8)

$$\int \mathcal{N}(x \mid \mu_S, \sigma_S^2)\mathcal{N}(x \mid \mu_T, \sigma_T^2)dx = \mathcal{N}(\mu_S - \mu_T \mid 0, \sigma_{sum}^2) \tag{4.9}$$

The denominator in Eq. (4.8) corresponds to the maximum value of the numerator for a given σ_{sum} (obtained when $\mu_S = \mu_T$). The denominator acts as a normalization factor: it sets the overlap to 1 when the distributions are perfectly matching and gives an easier interpretation, helping in the choice of the threshold th.

Projection on the selected landmarks. Each point p from $S \cup T$ is projected onto each landmark $\alpha_j \in A$ using a Gaussian kernel with standard deviation σ

$$K(p, \alpha_j) = \exp\left(\frac{-\left\|p - \alpha_j\right\|^2}{2\sigma^2}\right) \tag{4.10}$$

Overall, the points from both S and T are projected in a common space that has as many dimensions as there are landmarks. Following other nonlinear methods we set σ to the median distance between any pair of points drawn randomly from $S \cup T$. After projection, we obtain new representations for the source and target, respectively denoted by K_S and K_T. Using these new set of points K_S and K_T, we then apply the SA method.

4.4 Experimental Results

For most of our experiments, we use the Office (OFF31) dataset [407], extended with Caltech [215]—this has become a standard benchmark in the domain adaptation literature called Office+Caltech (OC10) and detailed in [200] and Chap. 3. These datasets have 10 common classes. The OFF31 dataset contains 3 domains, with images acquired with web cameras (denoted as W in most articles), images taken with a digital SLR camera (D) and images collected from the Amazon website (A). Caltech (C) is considered a separate domain. Combining these domains, we obtain 12 different domain adaptation problems. Unless noted otherwise, we use the provided SURFBOV features encoded with a visual dictionary of 800 words.

Table 4.1 Recognition accuracy using NN classifier (OC10)

Method	C→A	D→A	W→A	A→C	D→C	W→C	A→D	C→D	W→D	A→W	C→W	D→W	AVG.
NA	21.5	26.9	20.8	22.8	24.8	16.4	22.4	21.7	40.5	23.3	20.0	53.0	26.2
Baseline-S	38.0	29.8	35.5	30.9	29.6	31.3	34.6	37.4	71.8	35.1	33.5	74.0	40.1
Baseline-T	**40.5**	33.0	**38.0**	33.3	31.2	31.9	34.7	36.4	72.9	36.8	34.4	78.4	41.8
SA	39.0	**38.0**	37.4	**35.3**	**32.4**	**32.3**	**37.6**	**39.6**	**80.3**	**38.6**	**36.8**	**83.6**	**44.2**

Insights about SA. For detailed experimental evaluations of the (linear) Subspace Alignment method, we refer to the original conference paper [164] as well as an extended version thereof available on ArXiv [165]. Here, we only summarize the most important findings. By default, we use the linear SA method, with the dimension estimation method based on the consistency theorem and cross-validation.

Comparison against baselines. In a first experiment, we compare our Subspace Alignment with a couple of baselines. `Baseline-S` projects both the source and target data onto the source subspace X_S. Similarly, `Baseline-T` uses the projection defined by the PCA subspace X_T built from the target domain. Finally, we compare against no adaptation `NA` where no projection is made, i.e.using the original input space without learning a new representation.

The results for the 12 DA problems in the unsupervised setting using a nearest neighbor classifier are shown in Table 4.1. It is interesting to see that simply projecting to the target domain (Baseline-T) already works quite well for most DA problems—actually outperforming various other more complex subspace-based DA methods. A possible explanation for this is, that by projecting onto the target subspace, the source data is brought closer to the target distribution. Modes of variation not present in the target domain get ignored as part of this process. In 10 out of 12 DA problems the full SA algorithm (first projecting the source data onto the source subspace, before projecting them onto the target subspace) brings a further improvement. The improvement over No Adaptation is remarkable. Similar results obtained with an SVM classifier are shown in Table 4.2. Our SA method outperforms all the other methods in 11 DA problems. These results indicate that our method works better than other DA methods not only for NN-like local classifiers but also with more global SVM classifiers.

Importance of z-normalization. As we mentioned before, z-normalization has a big impact on subspace-based Domain Adaptation methods such as GFK, TCA and SA. To evaluate this, we perform an experiment using the OC10 dataset. We report mean accuracy over 12 domain adaptation problems in Fig. 4.1, both with and without z-normalization for all considered DA methods.

It is clear that all DA methods, including the methods such as projecting to the source (*Baseline-S*) and target domain (*Baseline-T*), hugely benefited by the z-normalization.

Table 4.2 Recognition accuracy using SVM classifier (OC10)

Method	C→A	D→A	W→A	A→C	D→C	W→C	A→D	C→D	W→D	A→W	C→W	D→W	AVG.
NA	44.0	34.6	30.7	35.7	30.6	23.4	34.5	36.0	67.4	26.1	29.1	70.9	38.6
Baseline-S	44.3	36.8	32.9	36.8	29.6	24.9	36.1	38.9	73.6	**42.5**	34.6	75.4	42.2
Baseline-T	44.5	38.6	34.2	37.3	31.6	28.4	32.5	35.3	73.6	37.3	34.2	80.5	42.3
SA	**46.1**	**42.0**	**39.3**	**39.9**	**35.0**	**31.8**	**38.8**	**39.4**	**77.9**	39.6	**38.9**	**82.3**	**45.9**

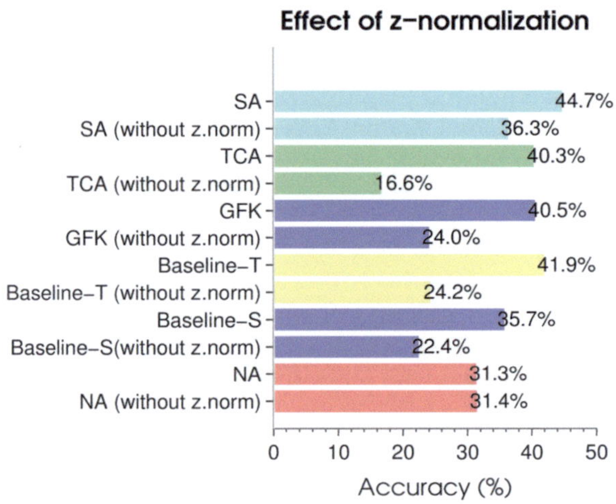

Fig. 4.1 The effect of z-normalization on subspace-based DA methods. Mean classification accuracy on 12 DA problems on OC10 dataset with and without z-normalization

Comparison of subspace dimensionality estimation methods. Next, we compare the two different methods for estimating the subspace dimensionality. Since the SA-MLE method is especially useful when working with high-dimensional features, we use *Fisher Vectors* [369] for this experiment. Fisher Vectors have proven to be a robust image representation for image classification task, albeit at the cost of a high-dimensional representation.

We start from SURF [29] features to create a Gaussian Mixture Model (GMM) of 64 components and encode images using Fisher encoding [369]. The GMM is created from Amazon images from the OFF31 dataset.

In Table 4.3 results for the 12 DA problems of OC10 are reported. These results indicate the effectiveness of SA-MLE method considering the fact that it can estimate the subspace dimensionality almost 100 times faster than SA method when used with Fisher vectors. On all DA problems, SA-MLE outperforms no adaptation (NA) results.

Note that SA-MLE is fast and operates in the low-dimensional target subspace. The computational complexity of SA-MLE is equal to $\mathcal{O}(\hat{d}^2)$ where d is the target

Table 4.3 Recognition accuracy obtained on the OC10 dataset when images are encoded with SURF features and Fisher vectors of 64 GMM components

Method	C→A	D→A	W→A	A→C	D→C	W→C	A→D	C→D	W→D	A→W	C→W	D→W	AVG
NA	44.3	35.7	34.2	36.9	33.9	30.8	37.4	42.1	76.7	35.2	32.2	82.7	43.5
SA	**48.2**	**44.6**	**43.1**	**40.3**	**38.4**	**35.9**	**45.0**	**51.6**	**87.6**	**44.8**	**44.4**	**90.1**	**51.2**
SA-MLE	48.0	39.0	40.0	39.9	37.5	33.0	43.9	50.8	86.3	40.7	40.5	88.7	49.0

subspace dimensionality. On the other hand, an estimate of the computational complexity of SA is $\mathcal{O}(D^2 \times d_{max})$ due to the cross-validation procedure necessary to establish the optimal subspace dimensionality. Given the fact that SA-MLE is way faster than SA method and obtains reasonable results, we recommend SA-MLE for real time DA methods. Also we recommend to use SA-MLE method if the dimensionality of the data is large and when computational time is an issue.

Limitations and assumptions. Our method assumes that both the source and the target data lie in the same space and that the joint distributions are correlated. Indeed subspace alignment exploits this correlation, if there is any, to do the adaptation. If both joint distributions are completely independent, then it is impossible for our method to learn any meaningful adaptation.

Further, the Subspace Alignment method assumes both source and target domain have similar class prior probability distributions. When there is significant change in class prior probability (as discussed in the work on target shifts [578]), the subspace alignment method may fail.

4.4.1 Evaluation of LSSA

The original article [10] gives detailed results about LSSA, applied on the 12 unsupervised DA subproblems of the OC10 dataset [200]. In this section, we summarize and comment over the results obtained in the article.

Quality and diversity of the selected landmarks. The proposed landmark selection process has been evaluated in itself (without SA) by comparing it to different baselines. The principle is to select landmarks and use them to nonlinearly transform all the points from both domains in a common space, performing no further adaptation. By doing nothing (keeping the original space) an average accuracy of 42.2% is achieved. Both the previous state of the art [196] (only its landmark selection) and a random selection of 150 landmarks from each domain, achieve an average accuracy of 45.6%. By taking all points as landmarks, a better average accuracy of 46.5% is reached, at the cost of computing more similarities. The proposed LSSA method significantly outperforms any other method, with an accuracy of 48.1%. If the multi-scale selection is disabled, the method performs badly, with 45.1% accuracy. These results show how important it is to both filter the landmarks (we can do better than taking all points) and to have a multiscale reasoning for evaluating the landmark quality.

While certain landmark selection methods explicitly optimize the diversity of landmarks, LSSA does not use class information when selecting landmarks. The class information is used in [196] and the landmark selection process ensures that classes are balanced among the landmarks. Experiments have shown that, even without class information, LSSA is able to make a balanced selection among the classes.

Performance of the overall LSSA. LSSA has been compared to the previous state-of-the-art methods, showing an absolute gain of average accuracy of over 2%. The very baseline that does not perform any adaptation reaches an accuracy of 42.2%. The tempting but inadequate idea of using Kernel PCA followed by SA results in an accuracy 8.7% (close to random). This shows how meaningless it is to try to project Kernel PCAs dimensions from one domain into another.

Compared to state-of-the-art complete methods for domain adaptation, we show again that linear SA achieves an accuracy of 49.3%, significantly above the more complicated GFK method [200] with 45.9%. The previous state of the art, Transfer Joint Matching [313], also involves more computation but reaches 50.5% of accuracy. Finally, LSSA outperforms all other methods with an accuracy of 52.6%.

4.5 Conclusion

We have presented a new visual domain adaptation method using subspace alignment. In this method, we create subspaces for both source and target domains and learn a linear mapping that aligns the source subspace with the target subspace. This allows us to compare the source domain data directly with the target domain data and to build classifiers on source data and apply them on the target domain. As a further extension, we have proposed LSSA, where a set of landmarks are selected and used to perform a nonlinear mapping, prior to the actual application of the subspace alignment method. This further improves the results.

Due to its simplicity and theoretically founded stability, our method has the potential to be applied on large datasets and in combination with high-dimensional features.

Acknowledgements The authors gratefully acknowledge support from the FP7 ERC Starting Grant 240530 COGNIMUND, and the ANR projects SOLSTICE (ANR-13-BS02-01) and LIVES (ANR-15-CE23-0026-03).

Chapter 5
Learning Domain Invariant Embeddings by Matching Distributions

Mahsa Baktashmotlagh, Mehrtash Harandi and Mathieu Salzmann

Abstract One of the characteristics of the domain shift problem is that the source and target data have been drawn from different distributions. A natural approach to addressing this problem therefore consists of learning an embedding of the source and target data such that they have similar distributions in the new space. In this chapter, we study several methods that follow this approach. At the core of these methods lies the notion of distance between two distributions. We first discuss domain adaptation (DA) techniques that rely on the Maximum Mean Discrepancy to measure such a distance. We then study the use of alternative distribution distance measures within one specific Domain Adaptation framework. In this context, we focus on f-divergences, and in particular on the KL divergence and the Hellinger distance. Throughout the chapter, we evaluate the different methods and distance measures on the task of visual object recognition and compare them against related baselines on a standard DA benchmark dataset.

5.1 Introduction

The domain shift problem occurs in scenarios where the test (target) data is acquired under different conditions from the training (source) data. As a consequence, the source and target distributions are different, and a classifier trained on the source domain will perform poorly on the target one.

M. Baktashmotlagh (✉)
Queensland University of Technology, Brisbane, Australia
e-mail: m.baktashmotlagh@qut.edu

M. Harandi
Australian National University and Data 61, CSIRO, Canberra, Australia
e-mail: mehrtash.harandi@data61.csiro.au

M. Salzmann
CVLab, EPFL, Lausanne, Switzerland
e-mail: mathieu.salzmann@epfl.ch

G. Csurka (ed.), *Domain Adaptation in Computer Vision Applications*,
Advances in Computer Vision and Pattern Recognition,
DOI 10.1007/978-3-319-58347-1_5

A natural idea to address this issue consists of explicitly accounting for the difference between the source and target distributions. For example, in [138], this has been achieved by encouraging the target SVM classifier to share similar decision values to the source SVM classifier. To this end, the Maximum Mean Discrepancy (MMD) [212], a popular distance measure between empirical distributions, was employed to determine the values of parameters controlling the spread of the source and target distributions. By contrast, sample re-weighting [243] or selection [196] approaches work independently of a classifier and have relied on the MMD to find the source samples whose distribution is similar to the target ones. The main drawback of these approaches is that they directly compare the source and target distributions in the original input space. This space, however, might be ill-suited to this task, since the features have typically been distorted by the domain shift.

In this chapter, we study a different approach to accounting for the source and target distribution mismatch that consists of learning a transformation of the data to a low-dimensional space where the distributions are similar. Learning such an embedding, and measuring distribution distances in the resulting space, explicitly addresses the drawback that the original features have been distorted by the domain shift. Throughout the chapter, we discuss different methods that follow this approach, as well as different distribution distance measures. While we focus on the unsupervised scenario, where no labeled target data is available, the resulting algorithms can easily be adapted to incorporate labeled target samples.

In the first part of the chapter, we discuss several domain adaptation (DA) methods that rely on the MMD to learn a domain-invariant embedding. In particular, we first study Transfer Component Analysis (TCA) [354] that learns a subspace projection after having mapped the samples to a high-dimensional Reproducing Kernel Hilbert Space (RKHS). We then discuss Domain-Invariant Component Analysis (DICA) [339], which can be thought of as an extension of TCA that can account for multiple source domains. As discussed in Sect. 5.3, while inspired by the MMD, both these works can be interpreted as directly comparing the means of the source and target samples in the resulting subspace, without the usual RKHS mapping of the MMD, after a nonlinear transformation of the data. We then present our Distribution Matching Embedding (DME) approach [25, 27], which, by contrast, learns a linear subspace projection from the original input space, without RKHS mapping, but compares the source and target distributions using the MMD with an RKHS mapping.

In the second part of the chapter, we study the use of alternating distribution distances within our DME framework. In particular, we focus on two f-divergences: the Kullback–Leibler (KL) divergence and the Hellinger distance. A nice property of these distances is their relation with the Riemannian metric on the statistical manifold, i.e. the Riemannian manifoldof probability distributions. The resulting algorithms can therefore be thought of as the first attempts to exploit the Riemannian structure of the space of probability distributions for DA.

The approaches discussed in this chapter all learn a subspace projection of the data. Note that, while other subspace-based DA methods have been proposed, they significantly differ from the techniques discussed here. For example, in [200], the data is directly represented as a collection of subspaces. In [164], pre-computed source and target subspaces are aligned via a linear transformation. In short, none of these works explicitly models the distribution differences between the source and target samples, which is the topic of this chapter.

We evaluate the methods presented throughout the chapter on the task of visual object recognitionusing the Office-Caltech (OC10) benchmark [200] detailed in Chap. 3. We split our evaluation into comparisons of (i) the different MMD-based approaches; (ii) the different distribution distances within our DME framework; and (iii) the transformation-learning methods with other approaches relying on distribution distances.

5.2 Background: Distances Between Distributions

In this chapter, we study the problem of learning embeddings that minimize the dissimilarity between the source distribution s and the target one t. Before discussing the domain adaptation algorithms that tackle this problem, we briefly review the distribution distance measures that will be used in the following sections. In particular, we focus on the MMD and two f-divergences, i.e. the KL divergence and the Hellinger distance. As discussed below, these distances allow us to make use of non-parametric representations of the data distributions, which are particularly well-suited to visual data that typically exhibits complex probability distributions in high-dimensional spaces.

5.2.1 Maximum Mean Discrepancy

The MMD [212] is an effective non-parametric criterion that compares the distributions of two sets of data by mapping the data to RKHS. Given two distributions s and t, the MMD between s and t is defined as

$$D'_{MMD}(\mathfrak{F}, s, t) = \sup_{f \in \mathfrak{F}} \left(E_{\mathbf{x}_s \sim s}[f(\mathbf{x}_s)] - E_{\mathbf{x}_t \sim t}[f(\mathbf{x}_t)] \right) ,$$

where $E_{\mathbf{x} \sim s}[\cdot]$ is the expectation under distribution s. By defining $\mathfrak{F}$ as the set of functions in the unit ball in a universal RKHS $\mathcal{H}$, it was shown that $D'(\mathfrak{F}, s, t) = 0$ if and only if $s = t$ [212].

Let $\mathbf{X}_s = \{\mathbf{x}_s^1, \cdots, \mathbf{x}_s^n\}$ and $\mathbf{X}_t = \{\mathbf{x}_t^1, \cdots, \mathbf{x}_t^m\}$ be two sets of observations drawn *i.i.d.* from s and t, respectively. An empirical estimate of the MMD can be computed as

$$D_{MMD}(\mathbf{X}_s, \mathbf{X}_t) = \left\| \frac{1}{n} \sum_{i=1}^{n} \phi(\mathbf{x}_s^i) - \frac{1}{m} \sum_{j=1}^{m} \phi(\mathbf{x}_t^j) \right\|_{\mathcal{H}} \tag{5.1}$$

$$= \left(\sum_{i,j=1}^{n} \frac{k(\mathbf{x}_s^i, \mathbf{x}_s^j)}{n^2} + \sum_{i,j=1}^{m} \frac{k(\mathbf{x}_t^i, \mathbf{x}_t^j)}{m^2} - 2 \sum_{i,j=1}^{n,m} \frac{k(\mathbf{x}_s^i, \mathbf{x}_t^j)}{nm} \right)^{\frac{1}{2}},$$

where $\phi(\cdot)$ is the mapping to the RKHS $\mathcal{H}$, and $k(\cdot, \cdot) = \langle \phi(\cdot), \phi(\cdot) \rangle$ is the universal kernel associated with this mapping. In short, the MMD between the distributions of two sets of observations is equivalent to the distance between the sample means in a high-dimensional feature space.

5.2.2 *f*-Divergences

Another way to think of probability distributions is as elements of a Riemannian manifold, named the statistical manifold [12]. Loosely speaking, given a non-empty set $\mathcal{X}$ and a family of probability density functions $p(x|\boldsymbol{\theta})$ parameterized by $\boldsymbol{\theta}$ on $\mathcal{X}$, the space $\mathcal{M} = \{p(x|\boldsymbol{\theta})|\boldsymbol{\theta} \in \mathbb{R}^d\}$ forms a Riemannian manifold. The Fisher-Rao Riemannian metric on $\mathcal{M}$ is a function of $\boldsymbol{\theta}$ and induces geodesics, i.e. curves with minimum length on $\mathcal{M}$.

In general, the parametrization of the PDFs of the data at hand is unknown, and choosing a specific distribution may not reflect the reality. This makes the Fisher-Rao metric ill-suited to measure the similarity between probability distributions in practical scenarios.[1] Therefore, several studies have opted for approximations of the Fisher-Rao metric. An important class of such approximations is the f-divergences, which can be expressed as

$$D_f(s\|t) = \int f\left(\frac{s(x)}{t(x)}\right) t(x) dx \ .$$

Defining the distributions s and t in a non-parametric manner, such as by Kernel Density Estimation (KDE), makes measuring the similarity between two distributions practical. Below, we discuss two special cases of f-divergences: the KL divergence and the Hellinger distance. The non-parametric estimates of these distances will be discussed in Sect. 5.4 within the derivation of the algorithms.

---

[1]Note that, even with known parameters, computing the Fisher-Rao metric may not be feasible in closed-form.

Kullback–Leibler Divergence. The KL divergence is perhaps the best-known example of an f-divergence. It is obtained by setting $f(q) = q \log q$ in the definition of the f-divergence. This results in the relative entropy of one probability distribution function to the other, which is expressed as

$$KL(s||t) = \int s(x) \log \frac{s(x)}{t(x)} dx \ . \tag{5.2}$$

The KL divergence is related to the Fisher information distance $D_F(s, t)$ by the property $\sqrt{2KL(s||t)} \to D_F(s, t)$ as $s \to t$.

A drawback of the KL divergence is that it does not satisfy symmetry, i.e. $KL(s||t) \neq KL(s||t)$. This yields the undesirable property that an algorithm would not give the same result if the two distributions are swapped. To address this issue, one can rely on the symmetric KL divergence

$$D_{KL}(s, t) = KL(s||t) + KL(s||t) \ . \tag{5.3}$$

As for the asymmetric case, the symmetric KL divergence approximates the Fisher information distance as $\sqrt{D_{KL}(s, t)} \to D_F(s, t)$ as $s \to t$. Note, however, that the symmetric KL divergence is still not a distance metric because it does not satisfy the triangle inequality. In practice, in this chapter, we will make use of the symmetric KL divergence.

Hellinger Distance. The Hellinger distance is another special case of an f-divergence, obtained by taking $f(q) = (\sqrt{q} - 1)^2$. The (squared) Hellinger distance can thus be written as

$$D_H^2(s\|t) = \int \left(\sqrt{s(x)} - \sqrt{t(x)}\right)^2 dx \ , \tag{5.4}$$

and is symmetric, satisfies the triangle inequality and is bounded from above by 2.

More importantly,

Theorem 5.1 *The length of any curve γ is the same under the Fisher-Rao metric D_{FR} and the Hellinger distance D_H up to a scale of 2.*

Proof We start with the definition of intrinsic metric and curve length. Without any assumption on differentiability, let (M, d) be a metric space. A curve in M is a continuous function $\gamma : [0, 1] \to M$ and joins the starting point $\gamma(0) = s$ to the end point $\gamma(1) = t$. Our proof then relies on two theorems from [227] stated below. Let us first define the following according to [227]

Defnition 5.1 The length of a curve γ is the supremum of $L(\gamma; m_i)$ over all possible partitions m_i with m_i being $0 = m_0 < m_1 < ... < m_n = 1$ and $L(\gamma; m_i) = \sum_i d(\gamma(m_i), \gamma(m_{i-1}))$.

Defnition 5.2 The intrinsic metric $\hat{\delta}$ is defined as the infimum of the lengths of all paths from x to y.

Theorem 5.2 *([227]) If the intrinsic metrics induced by two metrics d_1 and d_2 are identical to scale ξ, then the length of any given curve is the same under both metrics up to ξ.*

Proof We refer the reader to [227] for the proof of this theorem.

Theorem 5.3 *([227]) If $d_1(s,t)$ and $d_2(s,t)$ are two metrics defined on a space M such that*

$$\lim_{d_1(s,t)\to 0} \frac{d_2(s,t)}{d_1(s,t)} = 1 \tag{5.5}$$

uniformly (with respect to s and t), then their intrinsic metrics are identical.

Proof We refer the reader to [227] for the proof of this theorem.

In [266], it was shown that $\lim_{s\to t} D_H(s\|t) = 0.5D_{FR}(s\|t)$. The asymptotic behavior of the Hellinger distance and the Fisher-Rao metric can be expressed as $D_H(s,t) = 0.5 * D_{FR}(s,t) + O(D_{FR}(s,t)^3)$ as $s \to t$. This guarantees uniform convergence since the higher order terms are bounded and vanish rapidly independently of the path between s and t. It therefore directly follows from Theorems 5.3 and 5.2 that the length of a curve under D_H and D_{FR} is the same up to a scale of 2, which concludes the proof.

5.3 MMD-Based Transformation Learning

In this section, we discuss several algorithms that rely on the MMD to learn a transformation matrix $\mathbf{W}$ that yields a domain invariant embedding of the source and target data. In particular, we focus on TCA [354], DICA [339], and DME-MMD [25, 27].

In the following, we define $\mathbf{X}_s = \left[\mathbf{x}_s^1, \cdots, \mathbf{x}_s^n\right]$ to be the $D \times n$ matrix containing n samples from the source domain, and $\mathbf{X}_t = \left[\mathbf{x}_t^1, \cdots, \mathbf{x}_t^m\right]$ to be the $D \times m$ matrix containing m samples from the target domain. Using this notation, the MMD introduced in Eq. (5.1) can be computed in matrix form as

$$D^2_{MMD}(\mathbf{X}_s, \mathbf{X}_t) = Tr(\mathbf{KL}) , \tag{5.6}$$

where

$$\mathbf{K} = \begin{bmatrix} \mathbf{K}_{s,s} & \mathbf{K}_{s,t} \\ \mathbf{K}_{t,s} & \mathbf{K}_{t,t} \end{bmatrix} \in \mathbb{R}^{(n+m)\times(n+m)} , \text{ and} \tag{5.7}$$

$$L_{ij} = \begin{cases} 1/n^2 & i,j \in \mathcal{S} \\ 1/m^2 & i,j \in \mathcal{T} \\ -1/(nm) & \text{otherwise} \end{cases} , \tag{5.8}$$

with, e.g. $\mathbf{K}_{s,s}$ the kernel matrix computed between the source samples, and $\mathcal{S}$ and $\mathcal{T}$ the sets of source and target indices, respectively.

5.3.1 *Transfer Component Analysis (TCA)*

The motivation behind TCA is to find a mapping $\phi(\cdot)$ such that the distributions $s(\phi(\mathbf{X}_s))$ and $t(\phi(\mathbf{X}_t))$ are similar. Minimizing the MMD directly using such a non-linear mapping yields a semi-definite program (SDP) in terms of a kernel matrix $\mathbf{K}$. To avoid the high computational cost of solving an SPD, TCA relies on a projection $\tilde{\mathbf{W}} \in \mathbb{R}^{(n+m)\times d}$ of the empirical kernel map to a d-dimensional space, with typically $d \ll D$. This projection yields a new kernel matrix

$$\tilde{\mathbf{K}} = \mathbf{K}\mathbf{W}\mathbf{W}^\top\mathbf{K} ,$$

where $\mathbf{W} = \mathbf{K}^{-1/2}\tilde{\mathbf{W}}$. Using this new kernel matrix, the MMD can be expressed as

$$D^2_{MMD}(\mathbf{X}_s, \mathbf{X}_t) = Tr((\mathbf{K}\mathbf{W}\mathbf{W}^\top\mathbf{K})\mathbf{L}) = Tr(\mathbf{W}^\top\mathbf{K}\mathbf{L}\mathbf{K}\mathbf{W}) . \tag{5.9}$$

TCA then aims at finding the projection $\mathbf{W}$ that minimizes this MMD.

To better constrain the projection $\mathbf{W}$, TCA makes use of two additional regularizers. The first one simply controls the complexity of $\mathbf{W}$ and can thus be written as $Tr(\mathbf{W}^\top\mathbf{W})$. Inspired by PCA, the second regularizer aims at preserving the variance of the data. After projection to the subspace, the covariance matrix of the data can be written as

$$\tilde{\mathbf{\Sigma}} = \mathbf{W}^\top\mathbf{K}\mathbf{H}\mathbf{K}\mathbf{W} , \tag{5.10}$$

where $\mathbf{H} = \mathbf{I} - (1/(n+m)\mathbf{1}\mathbf{1}^\top) \in \mathbb{R}^{(n+m)\times(n+m)}$ is the centering matrix.

The final optimization problem solved by TCA can then be written as

$$\min_{\mathbf{W}} \quad Tr(\mathbf{W}^\top\mathbf{K}\mathbf{L}\mathbf{K}\mathbf{W}) + \mu Tr(\mathbf{W}^\top\mathbf{W}) \quad \text{s.t. } \tilde{\mathbf{\Sigma}} = \mathbf{I}_d$$

where $\mathbf{I}_d \in \mathbb{R}^{d\times d}$ is the identity matrix and μ is a parameter setting the influence of the first regularizer. The solution to this problem can be obtained by retaining the d eigenvectors of the matrix $\mathbf{M} = (\mathbf{K}\mathbf{L}\mathbf{K} + \mu\mathbf{I})^{-1}\mathbf{K}\mathbf{H}\mathbf{K}$ with largest eigenvalues. Given $\mathbf{W}$, the data can be embedded as $\mathbf{X}^* = \mathbf{K}\mathbf{W}$, and a classifier learned from the source data in this new space.

TCA can also be interpreted as mapping the samples to an RKHS via the mapping $\phi(\mathbf{x})$, projecting the resulting data to a d-dimensional space as $\hat{\mathbf{W}}^\top\phi(\mathbf{x})$ and then simply computing the distance between the source and target means in this d-dimensional space. To see this, one can rely on the Representer theorem and express $\hat{\mathbf{W}}$ as a linear combination of the samples in Hilbert space, that is, $\hat{\mathbf{W}} = \mathbf{W}\Phi([\mathbf{X}_s, \mathbf{X}_t])$. In other words, while inspired by the MMD, TCA does not compare the source and target means in RKHS, but rather in a low-dimensional space obtained after a nonlinear transformation of the data.

5.3.2 Domain Invariant Component Analysis (DICA)

DICA can be thought of as a generalization of TCA to the scenario where we have more than two domains. Let $\mathbf{X} = \{\mathbf{X}_i\}_{i=1}^N$ be the set of all domains, including the target one, with $\mathbf{X}_i = \{\mathbf{x}_k\}_{k=1}^{n_i}$ containing all samples from domain i. By relying on a probability distribution $\mathcal{P}$ on an RKHS $\mathcal{H}$, DICA introduces the notion of distributional variance, defined as

$$V_{\mathcal{H}}(\mathcal{P}) = \frac{1}{N} Tr(\boldsymbol{\Sigma}) = \frac{1}{N} Tr(\mathbf{G}) - \frac{1}{N^2} \sum_{i,j=1}^{N} \mathbf{G_{i,j}} \,, \tag{5.11}$$

where $\boldsymbol{\Sigma}$ is the covariance operator of $\mathcal{P}$ and $\mathbf{G}$ is the $N \times N$ Gram matrix such that

$$\mathbf{G}_{i,j} = \langle \mu_{p_i}, \mu_{p_j} \rangle_{\mathcal{H}} \,, \tag{5.12}$$

with μ_{p_i} the mean operator of distribution p_i in RKHS. In [339], it is shown that, if the kernel k associated with the RKHS $\mathcal{H}$ is characteristic, then

$$V_{\mathcal{H}}(\mathcal{P}) = \frac{1}{N} \sum_{i=1}^{N} \|\mu_{p_i} - \mu_{\bar{p}}\|_{\mathcal{H}}^2 \,, \tag{5.13}$$

where $\bar{p}$ is an average distribution. This shows a strong connection between the distributional variance and the MMD, that both compare means in an RKHS, with the distributional variance dealing with more than two sets of samples.

Let the block kernel matrix and coefficient matrix

$$\mathbf{K} = \begin{bmatrix} \mathbf{K}_{1,1} & \cdots & \mathbf{K}_{1,N} \\ \vdots & \ddots & \vdots \\ \mathbf{K}_{N,1} & \cdots & \mathbf{K}_{N,N} \end{bmatrix}, \quad \mathbf{Q} = \begin{bmatrix} \mathbf{Q}_{1,1} & \cdots & \mathbf{Q}_{1,N} \\ \vdots & \ddots & \vdots \\ \mathbf{Q}_{N,1} & \cdots & \mathbf{Q}_{N,N} \end{bmatrix},$$

with, following Eq. (5.11), $\mathbf{Q}_{i,j}$ containing coefficients $(N-1)/(N^2 n_i^2)$ if $i = j$ and $-1/(N^2 n_i n_j)$ otherwise. The empirical distributional variance can then be expressed as $\hat{V}_{\mathcal{H}}(\mathbf{X}) = Tr(\mathbf{KQ})$.

Similarly to TCA, DICA then replaces the kernel matrix $\mathbf{K}$ with a kernel obtained after projection to a low-dimensional space. The goal then becomes that of finding a projection $\mathbf{W}$ that minimizes the empirical distributional variance $Tr(\mathbf{W}^\top \mathbf{KQKW})$.

In the unsupervised scenario, which we focus on here, this is achieved by jointly minimizing the complexity of the mapping, encoded via the regularizer $Tr(\mathbf{W}^\top \mathbf{K}\mathbf{W})$, and maximizing the variance of the data in the subspace $Tr(\mathbf{W}^\top \mathbf{K}^2 \mathbf{W})/n$, where n is the total number of samples.

Altogether, Unsupervised DICA (UDICA) can be formulated as the optimization problem

$$\max_{\mathbf{W}} \frac{Tr(\mathbf{W}^\top \mathbf{K}^2 \mathbf{W})/n}{Tr(\mathbf{W}^\top \mathbf{K}\mathbf{Q}\mathbf{K}\mathbf{W} + \mathbf{W}^\top \mathbf{K}\mathbf{W})} . \tag{5.14}$$

The solution of this problem can be obtained by solving a generalized eigenvalue problem. Similarly to TCA, the data can then be mapped to the low-dimensional space, and a classifier trained on the source samples, potentially coming from multiple source domains.

5.3.3 *Distribution Matching Embedding—MMD (DME-MMD)*

As mentioned above, TCA and DICA can be thought of as directly computing the distance between the means of the source and target data in the low-dimensional embedding after a nonlinear transformation of the data. In other words, this can be thought of as not using any mapping to an RKHS in the MMD. Here, we discuss our DME-MMD algorithm that follows a different strategy: We learn a linear transformation of the data, but compare the distributions of the source and target samples in the resulting space using the MMD with an RKHS mapping.

More specifically, given the $D \times n$ and $D \times m$ matrices $\mathbf{X}_s$ and $\mathbf{X}_t$ containing the source and target samples, respectively, we search for a $D \times d$ projection matrix $\mathbf{W}$, such that the distributions of the source and target samples in the resulting d-dimensional subspace are as similar as possible. By making use of the MMD, this distance can be expressed as

$$D_{MMD}(\mathbf{W}^\top \mathbf{X}_s, \mathbf{W}^\top \mathbf{X}_t) = \left\| \frac{1}{n} \sum_{i=1}^{n} \phi(\mathbf{W}^\top \mathbf{x}_s^i) - \frac{1}{m} \sum_{j=1}^{m} \phi(\mathbf{W}^\top \mathbf{x}_t^j) \right\|_{\mathcal{H}} , \tag{5.15}$$

with $\phi(\cdot)$ the mapping from $\mathbb{R}^D$ to the high-dimensional RKHS $\mathcal{H}$. Note that, here, $\mathbf{W}$ appears inside $\phi(\cdot)$ in order to measure the MMD of the projected samples. This is in contrast with TCA and UDICA where the projection appears outside the mapping $\phi(\cdot)$. This also differs from sample re-weighting, or selection methods [196, 243] that place weights outside $\phi(\cdot)$ and thus compare the distributions in the original image feature space, which has typically been distorted by the domain shift.

Learning $\mathbf{W}$ can then be expressed as the optimization problem

$$\mathbf{W}^* = \underset{\mathbf{W}}{\operatorname{argmin}} \quad D^2_{MMD}(\mathbf{W}^\top \mathbf{X}_s, \mathbf{W}^\top \mathbf{X}_t)$$
$$\text{s.t.} \quad \mathbf{W}^\top \mathbf{W} = \mathbf{I}_d \ , \tag{5.16}$$

where the constraints enforce $\mathbf{W}$ to be orthogonal. Such constraints prevent our model from wrongly matching the two distributions by distorting the data, and make it very unlikely that the resulting subspace only contains the noise of both domains. Orthogonality constraints have proven effective in many subspace methods, such as PCA or CCA, and are also employed in TCA and UDICA presented above.

As discussed in Sect. 5.2.1, the MMD can be expressed in terms of a kernel function $k(\cdot, \cdot)$. In particular here, we exploit the Gaussian kernel function, which is known to be universal [459]. This lets us rewrite our objective function as

$$\begin{aligned} D^2_{MMD}(\mathbf{W}^\top \mathbf{X_s}, \mathbf{W}^\top \mathbf{X_t}) = & \\ \frac{1}{n^2} \sum_{i,j=1}^{n} \exp\left(-\frac{(\mathbf{x}_s^i - \mathbf{x}_s^j)^\top \mathbf{W}\mathbf{W}^\top (\mathbf{x}_s^i - \mathbf{x}_s^j)}{\sigma} \right) & \\ + \frac{1}{m^2} \sum_{i,j=1}^{m} \exp\left(-\frac{(\mathbf{x}_t^i - \mathbf{x}_t^j)^\top \mathbf{W}\mathbf{W}^\top (\mathbf{x}_t^i - \mathbf{x}_t^j)}{\sigma} \right) & \\ - \frac{2}{mn} \sum_{i,j=1}^{n,m} \exp\left(-\frac{(\mathbf{x}_s^i - \mathbf{x}_t^j)^\top \mathbf{W}\mathbf{W}^\top (\mathbf{x}_s^i - \mathbf{x}_t^j)}{\sigma} \right) & . \end{aligned} \tag{5.17}$$

In practice, we set σ to the median squared distance between all source examples.

Since the Gaussian kernel satisfies the universality condition of the MMD, it is a natural choice for our approach. However, it was shown that, in practice, choices of non-universal kernels may be more appropriate to measure the MMD [45]. In particular, the more general class of characteristic kernels can also be employed. This class incorporates all strictly positive definite kernels, such as the well-known polynomial kernel.

Following Eq. (5.6), the MMD can be expressed as $Tr(\mathbf{K_W}\mathbf{L})$, where the subscript $\cdot_\mathbf{W}$ indicates the dependency of the kernel on the transformation, that is, each element in $\mathbf{K_W}$ is computed using the kernel function, and thus depends on $\mathbf{W}$. Note, however, that, with the Gaussian kernel, $\mathbf{K_W}$ can be computed efficiently in matrix form (i.e. without looping over its elements).

Altogether, DME-MMD can then be expressed as the optimization problem

$$\mathbf{W}^* = \underset{\mathbf{W}}{\operatorname{argmin}} \quad Tr\,(\mathbf{K_W}\mathbf{L})$$
$$\text{s.t.} \quad \mathbf{W}^\top \mathbf{W} = \mathbf{I}_d \ , \tag{5.18}$$

which is a nonlinear, constrained problem. To tackle this challenging scenario, we note that the constraints on **W** make it a point on a Grassmann manifold. This lets us rewrite our constrained optimization problem as an unconstrained problem on the manifold $\mathcal{G}(d, D)$. Optimization on Grassmann manifolds has proven effective at avoiding bad local minima [2]. More specifically, manifold optimization methods often have better convergence behavior than iterative projection methods, which can be crucial with a nonlinear objective function [2]. In particular, we make use of the conjugate gradient method on the manifold of the manopt toolbox. Note that other Grassmannian optimization techniques have been proposed [305, 403, 454], such as stochastic-gradient flow, acceptance-rejection methods and simulated annealing. However, a full review and comparison of these methods is beyond the scope of this chapter.

As in TCA and UDICA, given **W**, the samples can be projected to the low-dimensional space, and a classifier trained using the projected source data.

5.3.4 Empirical Comparison

We evaluated the MMD-based approaches discussed above on the task of visual object recognition using the OC10 dataset originally introduced in [407] and complemented with Caltech by [200]. This dataset contains images from four different domains: Amazon, DSLR, Webcam, and Caltech. The Amazon domain consists of images acquired in a highly-controlled environment with studio lighting conditions. These images capture the large intra-class variations of 31 classes, but typically show the objects only from one canonical viewpoint. The DSLR domain consists of high resolution images of 31 categories acquired in an office environment under natural lighting. The Webcam images were acquired in a similar environment as the DSLR ones, but have much lower resolution and contain significant noise, as well as color and white balance artifacts. The last domain, Caltech [215], consists of images of 256 object classes downloaded from Google images. Following [200], we use the 10 object classes common to all four datasets. This yields 2533 images in total, with 8 to 151 images per category per domain.

For our evaluation, we used two different types of image features. First, we employed the SURFBOV features provided by [200], which were obtained using the protocol described in [407] and described also in Chap. 3. They are 800-bin normalized histograms obtained with a visual codebook built with SURF descriptors [29] using k-means on a subset of the Amazon dataset.

As a second feature type, we used the deep learning features of [127], which have shown promising results for object recognition. Specifically, we used the outputs of the 7th layer of a deep convolutional network (CNN) with weights trained on the ImageNet dataset [120], leading to 4096-dimensional $DeCAF7$ features [486].

We used the conventional evaluation protocol introduced in [407], which consists of splitting the data into multiple partitions. For each source/target pair, we report the average recognition accuracy and standard deviation over the 20 partitions

Table 5.1 Recognition accuracies on 6 pairs of source/target domains using the evaluation protocol of [407] and using SURFBOV features with Linear SVM

Method	$A \to C$	$A \to D$	$A \to W$	$C \to A$	$C \to D$	$C \to W$
TCA	37.0 ± 2.5	36.6 ± 3.2	33.2 ± 4.4	42.9 ± 2.7	39.5 ± 3.2	36.03 ± 4.3
UDICA	32.7 ± 1.7	36.4 ± 3.4	31.0 ± 2.0	39.0 ± 3.2	36.7 ± 3.5	30.3 ± 4.2
DME-MMD	**43.1 ± 1.9**	**39.9 ± 4.0**	**41.7 ± 3.2**	**45.9 ± 3.1**	**43.7 ± 3.8**	**45.7 ± 3.6**

Table 5.2 Recognition accuracies on the remaining 6 pairs of source/target domains using the evaluation protocol of [407] and using SURFBOV features with Linear SVM

Method	$D \to A$	$D \to C$	$D \to W$	$W \to A$	$W \to C$	$W \to D$	Avg.
TCA	34.4 ± 1.9	**33.2 ± 1.7**	**76.4 ± 2.3**	38.3 ± 2.2	33.8 ± 1.6	57.8 ± 5.2	41.6
UDICA	30.4 ± 3.1	26.9 ± 3.2	49.1 ± 5.7	31.7 ± 1.6	25.9 ± 1.2	70.5 ± 3.2	36.7
DME-MMD	**38.1 ± 2.7**	32.8 ± 1.1	74.9 ± 1.9	**42.3 ± 2.8**	**35.2 ± 1.2**	**74.5 ± 2.1**	**46.4**

Table 5.3 Recognition accuracies on 6 pairs of source/target domains using the evaluation protocol of [407] and using DeCAF7 features with Linear SVM

Method	$A \to C$	$A \to D$	$A \to W$	$C \to A$	$C \to D$	$C \to W$
TCA	**86.5 ± 0.8**	**90.1 ± 3.0**	**80.5 ± 3.0**	91.7 ± 0.5	86.3 ± 3.8	**84.6 ± 2.9**
UDICA	85.7 ± 1.2	88.1 ± 1.8	79.5 ± 3.1	**92.0 ± 0.6**	87.8 ± 1.9	83.0 ± 1.7
DME-MMD	85.6 ± 0.8	89.2 ± 2.9	78.1 ± 3.2	91.1 ± 0.8	**88.2 ± 2.3**	82.5 ± 2.9

Table 5.4 Recognition accuracies on the remaining 6 pairs of source/target domains using the evaluation protocol of [407] and using DeCAF7 features with Linear SVM

Method	$D \to A$	$D \to C$	$D \to W$	$W \to A$	$W \to C$	$W \to D$	Avg.
TCA	**91.7 ± 0.4**	**84.0 ± 0.9**	**97.0 ± 0.9**	**90.6 ± 1.6**	**81.1 ± 0.8**	**98.6 ± 0.9**	**88.5**
UDICA	88.2 ± 0.8	79.8 ± 1.6	95.9 ± 1.0	80.0 ± 3.2	76.8 ± 0.6	98.3 ± 0.8	86.3
DME-MMD	88.5 ± 1.1	83.1 ± 2.6	96.6 ± 1.6	86.1 ± 3.1	79.3 ± 0.9	98.3 ± 0.9	87.2

provided with the GFK implementation.[2] With this protocol, we evaluated all possible combinations of source and target domains. For all the methods, we used the dimensionalities provided in the GFK code. In our experiments, we first applied PCA to the concatenated source and target data, kept all the data variance, and initialized $\mathbf{W}$ to the truncated identity matrix. For recognition, we employed a linear SVM classifier trained on the projected source samples. The only parameter of such a classifier is the regularizer weight C. For each method, we tested with $C = 10^p$, where $p \in \{-5, -4, \cdots, 4, 5\}$, and report the best result.

In Tables 5.1 and 5.2, we compare the results of TCA [354], UDICA [339] and DME-MMD using the SURFBOV features. As can be observed by the average accu-

[2] www-scf.usc.edu/~boqinggo/domainadaptation.html.

Table 5.5 Recognition accuracies of UDICA on 12 triplets of domains (2 sources, 1 target using the evaluation protocol of [407] and using SURFBOV features with Linear SVM

$A, D \to C$	$A, W \to D$	$A, C \to W$	$C, D \to A$	$C, W \to D$	$C, D \to W$
37.8 ± 2.8	64.9 ± 5.4	35.4 ± 2.5	41.8 ± 2.2	69.2 ± 6.2	48.2 ± 5.0
$A, W \to C$	$D, W \to C$	$D, A \to W$	$W, C \to A$	$A, C \to D$	$D, W \to A$
36.1 ± 1.9	31.8 ± 1.4	70.4 ± 4.9	41.9 ± 1.9	40.1 ± 4.6	46.5 ± 0.6

Table 5.6 Recognition accuracies of UDICA on 12 triplets of domains (2 sources, 1 target) using the evaluation protocol of [407] and using DeCAF7 features with Linear SVM

$A, D \to C$	$A, W \to D$	$A, C \to W$	$C, D \to A$	$C, W \to D$	$C, D \to W$
87.1 ± 0.9	96.6 ± 0.9	84.2 ± 1.6	92.0 ± 0.5	95.9 ± 1.8	92.4 ± 1.4
$A, W \to C$	$D, W \to C$	$D, A \to W$	$W, C \to A$	$A, C \to D$	$D, W \to A$
85.8 ± 1.2	79.3 ± 2.0	89.5 ± 1.2	90.9 ± 1.1	88.4 ± 1.5	83.8 ± 1.1

racy over all domain pairs reported in the last column of the second table, DME-MMD performs best on this data. In Tables 5.3 and 5.4, we present the results obtained with the DeCAF7 features. Here, TCA performs best. Note, however, that the gap between all methods is much smaller, indicating the better representational power of the deep learning features. Nevertheless, the methods still yield better accuracy than not performing any adaptation (85.2%). We further provide the results of UDICA using 2 source domains in Tables 5.5 and 5.6, and using 3 source domains in Table 5.7. Note that, typically, adding a source domain helps for the target domain.

5.4 Transformation Learning with f-Divergences

In this section, we study the use of other distribution distance measures to learn an embedding for DA. In particular, we discuss two different f-divergences: the KL divergence and the Hellinger distance. We introduce the use of these distances within the DME framework discussed in Sect. 5.3.3, which can easily adapt to alternative measures.

As opposed to the MMD, the two f-divergences that we study below require having an explicit representation of the data distributions. To avoid having to rely on parametric representations that may not reflect the given data well, we make use of non-parametric estimates. In particular, we rely on Kernel Density Estimation (KDE) with a Gaussian kernel. Given n training samples $\{\mathbf{x}^i\}_{i=1}^n$, either source or target ones, this lets us write the probability of a sample $\mathbf{x}$ as

Table 5.7 Recognition accuracies on 6 quadruplets of domains (3 sources, 1 target) using the evaluation protocol of [407] and using SURFBOV and DeCAF7 features with Linear SVM

SURFBOV				DECAF7			
$A, D, C \to W$	$A, C, W \to D$	$D, C, W \to A$	$D, W, A \to C$	$A, D, C \to W$	$A, C, W \to D$	$D, C, W \to A$	$D, W, A \to C$
44.8 ± 3.3	63.8 ± 5.6	41.2 ± 1.8	37.2 ± 1.8	89.6 ± 1.6	96.4 ± 1.0	91.1 ± 0.9	85.9 ± 0.8

$$\hat{p}(x) = \frac{1}{n} \sum_{i=1}^{n} \frac{1}{\sqrt{|2\pi \mathbf{H}|}} \exp\left(-\frac{(\mathbf{x} - \mathbf{x}^i)^\top \mathbf{H}^{-1} (\mathbf{x} - \mathbf{x}^i)}{2}\right), \tag{5.19}$$

where $\mathbf{H}$ is a diagonal matrix which can be computed, e.g. from the standard deviation of the data using the maximal smoothing principle [479].

Let $s(\mathbf{x})$ and $t(\mathbf{x})$ be the source and target distributions, respectively, with $\hat{s}(\mathbf{x})$ and $\hat{t}(\mathbf{x})$ their KDE estimates. In the remainder of this section, to derive reliable empirical estimates of our two f-divergences, we will rely on the quantity

$$T(\mathbf{x}) = \frac{s(\mathbf{x})}{s(\mathbf{x}) + t(\mathbf{x})}, \tag{5.20}$$

and its corresponding empirical estimate $\hat{T}(\mathbf{x}) = \hat{s}(\mathbf{x})/(\hat{s}(\mathbf{x}) + \hat{t}(\mathbf{x}))$.

We now turn to the derivation of the domain adaptation algorithms using the KL divergence and the Hellinger distance, respectively.

5.4.1 DME with KL Divergence (DME-KL)

To derive an algorithm similar to the DME-MMD method of Sect. 5.3.3, but using the KL divergence, we need to be able to compute an empirical estimate of the KL divergence. Since, according to Eq. (5.2), the KL divergence can be thought of as an expectation under $s(\mathbf{x})$, the most straightforward estimate would consist of relying on the strong law of large numbers to compute an average over the source samples. As noted in [60], however, such an estimate would not be guaranteed to be non-negative, thus violating a property of the KL divergence.

Instead, following [60], we make use of the following equivalence

$$
\begin{aligned}
KL(s||t) &= \int s(x)\log\frac{s(x)}{t(x)}dx \\
&= \int \frac{s(x)}{s(x)+t(x)}\log\left(\frac{s(x)}{s(x)+t(x)}/\frac{t(x)}{s(x)+t(x)}\right)(s(x)+t(x))dx \\
&= \int T(x)\log\frac{T(x)}{1-T(x)}s(x)dx + \int T(x)\log\frac{T(x)}{1-T(x)}t(x)dx\ .
\end{aligned}
$$

Thus, the KL divergence can be expressed as a sum of two expectations, one under s and the other under t. Following the strong law of large numbers, this yields the empirical estimate

$$
\hat{KL}(s||t) = \frac{1}{n}\sum_{i=1}^{n}\hat{T}(x_s^i)\log\frac{\hat{T}(x_s^i)}{1-\hat{T}(x_s^i)} + \frac{1}{m}\sum_{i=1}^{m}\hat{T}(x_t^i)\log\frac{\hat{T}(x_t^i)}{1-\hat{T}(x_t^i)}\ , \tag{5.21}
$$

which is guaranteed to be non-negative. An empirical estimate of the symmetric KL divergence can then directly be obtained by making use of the definition of Eq. (5.3) and of the empirical estimate above.

DME-KL can then be formulated as the problem of finding a projection $\mathbf{W}$ that minimizes the symmetric KL divergence between the projected source and target data. This can be expressed as the optimization problem

$$
\begin{aligned}
\min_{\mathbf{W}}\quad & \frac{1}{n}\sum_{i=1}^{n}(2\hat{T}(\mathbf{W}^\top x_s^i)-1)\log\frac{\hat{T}(\mathbf{W}^\top x_s^i)}{1-\hat{T}(\mathbf{W}^\top x_s^i)} \\
& + \frac{1}{m}\sum_{i=1}^{m}(2\hat{T}(\mathbf{W}^\top x_t^i)-1)\log\frac{\hat{T}(\mathbf{W}^\top x_t^i)}{1-\hat{T}(\mathbf{W}^\top x_t^i)} \\
\text{s.t.}\quad & \mathbf{W}^\top\mathbf{W} = \mathbf{I}\ .
\end{aligned} \tag{5.22}
$$

Note that, since we compute the matrices $\mathbf{H}_s$ and $\mathbf{H}_t$ in the KDE of the source and target distributions (c.f. Eq. (5.19)) using the standard deviations of the data, these matrices become functions of $\mathbf{W}$ to measure these deviations in the latent space. As in the MMD case, this optimization problem can be solve using conjugate gradient descent on a Grassmann manifold.

5.4.2 DME with Hellinger Distance (DME-H)

Similarly to the case of the KL divergence, to derive A Hellinger distance based DME algorithm, we need to be able to compute an empirical estimate of this distance. Following a similar idea as before, we seek to transform the Hellinger distance into a sum of two expectations. To this end, as noted in [60], we can write

$$
\begin{aligned}
D_H^2(s\|t) &= \int \left(\sqrt{s(x)} - \sqrt{t(x)}\right)^2 dx \\
&= \int \left(\sqrt{\frac{s(x)}{s(x)+t(x)}} - \sqrt{\frac{t(x)}{s(x)+t(x)}}\right)^2 (s(x)+t(x))dx \\
&= \int (\sqrt{T(x)} - \sqrt{1-T(x)})^2 s(x)dx + \int (\sqrt{T(x)} - \sqrt{1-T(x)})^2 t(x)dx \,.
\end{aligned}
$$

Having now a sum of two expectations, we can write the empirical estimate of the Hellinger distance as

$$
\begin{aligned}
\hat{D}_H^2(s\|t) = &\frac{1}{n}\sum_{i=1}^{n}\left(\sqrt{\hat{T}(x_s^i)} - \sqrt{1-\hat{T}(x_s^i)}\right)^2 \\
&+ \frac{1}{m}\sum_{i=1}^{m}\left(\sqrt{\hat{T}(x_t^i)} - \sqrt{1-\hat{T}(x_t^i)}\right)^2 \,.
\end{aligned} \tag{5.23}
$$

Importantly, as noted in [60], this numerical approximation respects some of the properties of the true Hellinger distance, such as the fact that it is symmetric and bounded from above by 2.

DME-H then aims at learning an embedding where the empirical Hellinger distance between the source and target samples is minimized. This can be expressed as the optimization problem [26]

$$
\begin{aligned}
\min_{\mathbf{W}} \quad & \frac{1}{n}\sum_{i=1}^{n}\left(\sqrt{\hat{T}(\mathbf{W}^\top x_s^i)} - \sqrt{1-\hat{T}(\mathbf{W}^\top x_s^i)}\right)^2 \\
&+ \frac{1}{m}\sum_{i=1}^{m}\left(\sqrt{\hat{T}(\mathbf{W}^\top x_t^i)} - \sqrt{1-\hat{T}(\mathbf{W}^\top x_t^i)}\right)^2 \\
\text{s.t.} \quad & \mathbf{W}^\top\mathbf{W} = \mathbf{I} \,.
\end{aligned} \tag{5.24}
$$

As before, the matrices $\mathbf{H}_s$ and $\mathbf{H}_t$ in the KDE of the source and target distributions (see Eq. (5.19)) are functions of $\mathbf{W}$, and we use conjugate gradient descent on a Grassmann manifold to solve our optimization problem.

5.4.3 Empirical Comparison

We compare the Hellinger distance based (DME-H) and KL Divergence based (DME-KL) approaches discussed above against the MMD-based approach (DME-MMD)

Table 5.8 Recognition accuracies on 6 pairs of source/target domains using the evaluation protocol of [407] and using SURFBOV features with Linear SVM

Method	$A \to C$	$A \to D$	$A \to W$	$C \to A$	$C \to D$	$C \to W$
DME-MMD	**43.1 ± 1.9**	39.9 ± 4.0	41.7 ± 3.2	45.9 ± 3.1	43.7 ± 3.8	**45.7 ± 3.6**
DME-KL	40.0 ± 1.7	35.8 ± 3.3	**43.2 ± 2.4**	45.3 ± 3.1	42.7 ± 2.8	43.5 ± 3.1
DME-H	42.7 ± 1.9	**40.3 ± 3.8**	42.0 ± 2.7	**46.7 ± 2.4**	**44.1 ± 2.6**	45.2 ± 3.1

Table 5.9 Recognition accuracies on the remaining 6 pairs of source/target domains using the evaluation protocol of [407] and using SURFBOV features with Linear SVM

Method	$D \to A$	$D \to C$	$D \to W$	$W \to A$	$W \to C$	$W \to D$	Avg.
DME-MMD	**38.1 ± 2.7**	32.8 ± 1.1	74.9 ± 1.9	**42.3 ± 2.8**	35.2 ± 1.2	74.5 ± 2.1	46.4
DME-KL	36.4 ± 3.6	31.1 ± 5.0	**76.5 ± 1.9**	**42.3 ± 0.8**	**36.8 ± 1.7**	**76.6 ± 0.6**	45.9
DME-H	37.4 ± 1.9	**34.6 ± 1.7**	74.3 ± 1.4	41.3 ± 0.9	35.0 ± 1.4	73.9 ± 2.2	**46.5**

Table 5.10 Recognition accuracies on 6 pairs of source/target domains using the evaluation protocol of [407] and using DeCAF7 features with Linear SVM

Method	$A \to C$	$A \to D$	$A \to W$	$C \to A$	$C \to D$	$C \to W$
DME-MMD	85.6 ± 0.8	**89.2 ± 2.9**	78.1 ± 3.2	91.1 ± 0.8	88.2 ± 2.3	**82.5 ± 2.9**
DME-KL	85.7 ± 0.5	**89.2 ± 2.5**	78.3 ± 3.8	91.3 ± 0.9	88.1 ± 2.1	81.7 ± 3.8
DME-H	**86.1 ± 1.1**	88.5 ± 2.0	**78.9 ± 4.3**	**92.2 ± 0.5**	**88.6 ± 2.9**	82.0 ± 3.4

Table 5.11 Recognition accuracies on the remaining 6 pairs of source/target domains using the evaluation protocol of [407] and using DeCAF7 features with Linear SVM

Method	$D \to A$	$D \to C$	$D \to W$	$W \to A$	$W \to C$	$W \to D$	Avg.
DME-MMD	88.5 ± 1.1	**83.1 ± 2.6**	96.6 ± 1.6	86.1 ± 3.1	79.3 ± 0.9	**98.3 ± 0.9**	87.2
DME-KL	88.7 ± 0.8	82.7 ± 2.9	**97.2 ± 1.3**	87.1 ± 2.1	79.2 ± 1.0	98.0 ± 0.8	87.3
DME-H	**89.0 ± 1.1**	82.4 ± 2.4	96.8 ± 1.0	**89.7 ± 3.1**	**79.5 ± 2.0**	98.1 ± 1.0	**87.7**

of Sect. 5.3.3 on the OC10 dataset introduced in Sect. 5.3.4. We report the results of these three approaches on all source and target pairs in Tables 5.8 and 5.9 for the SURFBOV features, and in Tables 5.10 and 5.11 for the DeCAF7 features. In both cases, according to the average accuracies computed over all pairs, the DME-H algorithm slightly outperforms the other two. This suggests the Hellinger distance as a somewhat preferable measure to compare the distributions.

Table 5.12 Recognition accuracies on 6 pairs of source/target domains using the evaluation protocol of [407] and using SURFBOV features with Linear SVM

Method	$A \rightarrow C$	$A \rightarrow D$	$A \rightarrow W$	$C \rightarrow A$	$C \rightarrow D$	$C \rightarrow W$
SVM (no adapt)	38.3 ± 1.8	35.9 ± 2.6	38.1 ± 2.4	44.7 ± 2.1	40.7 ± 3.3	37.4 ± 1.9
SVMA [138]	34.8 ± 1.4	34.1 ± 3.7	32.5 ± 2.9	39.1 ± 2.0	34.5 ± 3.5	32.9 ± 2.3
DAM [138]	34.9 ± 1.5	34.3 ± 3.6	32.5 ± 2.7	39.2 ± 2.1	34.7 ± 3.5	33.1 ± 2.3
KMM [243]	38.3 ± 1.8	36.0 ± 2.6	38.1 ± 2.4	44.7 ± 2.1	40.7 ± 3.3	37.4 ± 1.9
TCA [354]	37.0 ± 2.5	36.6 ± 3.2	33.2 ± 4.4	42.9 ± 2.7	39.5 ± 3.2	36.3 ± 4.3
UDICA [339]	32.7 ± 1.7	36.4 ± 3.4	31.0 ± 2.0	39.0 ± 3.2	36.7 ± 3.5	30.3 ± 4.2
DME-MMD	$\mathbf{43.1 \pm 1.9}$	39.9 ± 4.0	41.7 ± 3.2	45.9 ± 3.1	43.7 ± 3.8	$\mathbf{45.7 \pm 3.6}$
DME-KL	40.0 ± 1.7	35.8 ± 3.3	$\mathbf{43.2 \pm 2.4}$	45.3 ± 3.1	42.7 ± 2.8	43.5 ± 3.1
DME-H	42.7 ± 1.9	$\mathbf{40.3 \pm 3.8}$	42.0 ± 2.7	$\mathbf{46.7 \pm 2.4}$	$\mathbf{44.1 \pm 2.6}$	45.2 ± 3.1

Table 5.13 Recognition accuracies on the remaining 6 pairs of source/target domains using the evaluation protocol of [407] and using SURFBOV features with Linear SVM

Method	$D \rightarrow A$	$D \rightarrow C$	$D \rightarrow W$	$W \rightarrow A$	$W \rightarrow C$	$W \rightarrow D$	Avg.
SVM (no adapt)	33.8 ± 2.0	31.4 ± 1.3	75.5 ± 2.2	36.6 ± 1.1	32 ± 1.1	$\mathbf{80.5 \pm 1.4}$	43.7
SVMA [138]	33.4 ± 1.2	31.4 ± 0.9	74.4 ± 2.2	36.6 ± 1.1	33.5 ± 0.8	74.9 ± 2.7	41.1
DAM [138]	33.5 ± 1.3	31.5 ± 0.9	74.6 ± 2.1	34.7 ± 1.1	31.1 ± 1.3	68.3 ± 3.2	40.2
KMM [243]	33.8 ± 2.0	31.4 ± 1.3	75.5 ± 2.2	36.6 ± 1.1	32.1 ± 1.1	$\mathbf{80.5 \pm 1.4}$	43.8
TCA [354]	34.4 ± 1.9	33.2 ± 1.7	76.4 ± 2.3	38.3 ± 2.2	33.8 ± 1.6	57.8 ± 5.2	41.6
UDICA [339]	30.4 ± 3.1	26.9 ± 3.2	49.1 ± 5.7	31.7 ± 1.6	25.9 ± 1.2	70.5 ± 3.2	36.7
DME-MMD	$\mathbf{38.1 \pm 2.7}$	32.8 ± 1.1	74.9 ± 1.9	$\mathbf{42.3 \pm 2.8}$	35.2 ± 1.2	74.5 ± 2.1	46.4
DME-KL	36.4 ± 3.6	31.1 ± 5.0	$\mathbf{76.5 \pm 1.9}$	$\mathbf{42.3 \pm 0.8}$	$\mathbf{36.8 \pm 1.7}$	76.6 ± 0.6	45.9
DME-H	37.4 ± 1.9	$\mathbf{34.6 \pm 1.7}$	74.3 ± 1.4	41.3 ± 0.9	35.0 ± 1.4	73.9 ± 2.2	**46.5**

5.5 Comparison with Related Baselines

Finally, we compare the results of the methods studied in this chapter with several baselines that also make use of the notion of distance between the source and target distributions, but not within a subspace learning framework. In particular, we evaluated the SVMA and DAM methods of [138], both of which make use of the MMD to adapt the parameters of a classifier. We also evaluated the KMM algorithm of [243], which re-weighs the source samples so as to minimize the MMD between the (re-weighted) source and target data. We also report the results obtained by not performing any adaptation. The results of all methods are reported in Tables 5.12, 5.13, 5.14 and 5.15 for the SURFBOV and DeCAF7 features. In both cases, the DME approaches perform, on average, better than the baselines. The performance of TCA and UDICA depend on the features; while their results with SURFBOV features are not spectacular, they perform quite well with DeCAF7 features, particularly TCA. As observed before, the difference between the methods becomes

Table 5.14 Recognition accuracies on 6 pairs of source/target domains using the evaluation protocol of [407] and using DeCAF7 features with Linear SVM

Method	$A \to C$	$A \to D$	$A \to W$	$C \to A$	$C \to D$	$C \to W$
SVM (no adapt)	85.4 ± 0.8	87.3 ± 1.6	76.8 ± 3.2	90.9 ± 0.9	86.1 ± 3.2	77.5 ± 4.3
SVMA [138]	84.5 ± 1.3	84.9 ± 3.2	74.8 ± 4.4	91.8 ± 0.7	83.5 ± 2.3	78.5 ± 4.0
DAM [138]	85.5 ± 1.2	84.0 ± 5.0	77.4 ± 4.6	**92.2 ± 0.6**	83.5 ± 2.7	81.1 ± 3.9
KMM [243]	85.5 ± 0.7	87.1 ± 2.4	76.5 ± 4.1	91.4 ± 0.7	86.3 ± 2.7	78.2 ± 4.9
TCA [354]	**86.5 ± 0.8**	**90.1 ± 3.0**	**80.5 ± 3.0**	91.7 ± 0.5	86.3 ± 3.8	**84.6 ± 2.9**
UDICA [339]	85.7 ± 1.2	88.1 ± 1.8	79.5 ± 3.1	**92.0 ± 0.6**	87.8 ± 1.9	83.0 ± 1.7
DME-MMD	85.6 ± 0.8	89.2 ± 2.9	78.1 ± 3.2	91.1 ± 0.8	88.2 ± 2.3	82.5 ± 2.9
DME-KL	85.7 ± 0.5	89.2 ± 2.5	78.3 ± 3.8	91.3 ± 0.9	88.1 ± 2.1	81.7 ± 3.8
DME-H	86.1 ± 1.1	88.5 ± 2.0	78.9 ± 4.3	92.2 ± 0.5	**88.6 ± 2.9**	82.0 ± 3.4

Table 5.15 Recognition accuracies on the remaining 6 pairs of source/target domains using the evaluation protocol of [407] and using DeCAF7 features with Linear SVM

Method	$D \to A$	$D \to C$	$D \to W$	$W \to A$	$W \to C$	$W \to D$	Avg.
SVM (no adapt)	88.3 ± 1.2	80.4 ± 1.0	**97.3 ± 1.2**	82.1 ± 1.1	76.1 ± 0.6	95.2 ± 0.9	85.2
SVMA [138]	87.6 ± 1.1	80.8 ± 0.9	96.0 ± 1.5	81.0 ± 1.6	77.0 ± 0.7	98.4 ± 1.0	84.9
DAM [138]	90.1 ± 1.1	83.1 ± 1.2	95.3 ± 1.3	81.7 ± 3.4	77.8 ± 2.4	95.6 ± 2.2	85.6
KMM [243]	87.9 ± 1.4	80.3 ± 0.8	97.0 ± 1.4	82.4 ± 1.9	77.5 ± 1.4	98.5 ± 0.9	85.7
TCA [354]	**91.7 ± 0.4**	**84.0 ± 0.9**	97.0 ± 0.9	**90.6 ± 1.6**	**81.1 ± 0.8**	**98.6 ± 0.9**	**88.5**
UDICA [339]	88.2 ± 0.8	79.8 ± 1.6	95.9 ± 1.0	80.0 ± 3.2	76.8 ± 0.6	98.3 ± 0.8	86.3
DME-MMD	88.5 ± 1.1	83.1 ± 2.6	96.6 ± 1.6	86.1 ± 3.1	79.3 ± 0.9	98.3 ± 0.9	87.2
DME-KL	88.7 ± 0.8	82.7 ± 2.9	97.2 ± 1.3	87.1 ± 2.1	79.2 ± 1.0	98.0 ± 0.8	87.3
DME-H	89.0 ± 1.1	82.4 ± 2.4	96.8 ± 1.0	89.7 ± 3.1	79.5 ± 2.0	98.1 ± 1.0	87.7

smaller when using DeCAF7 features. Note, however, that, in this setting, only the transformation learning methods still yield significantly higher accuracies than not performing any domain adaptation.

5.6 Discussion

In this chapter, we have studied several approaches to unsupervised DA that focus on learning a domain invariant representation of the data by matching the source and target distributions in a low-dimensional space. We have first discussed several methods based on the MMD, and then investigated the use of f-divergences within one of the previous frameworks. Our experiments have shown that the DME approach works generally well, and, for DeCAF7 features, so does TCA. Within the DME framework, a slight preference goes to the Hellinger distance, that accounts for the Riemannian structure of the statistical manifold. Our results have also shown that the transformation learning approach discussed here typically outperforms other methods that rely on distribution distances for DA.

As discussed in [27], however, the accuracy of the techniques discussed here is not quite comparable to that of the more recent end-to-end Deep Learning frameworks, which will be studied in Part II of this book. Nevertheless, we believe that several ideas that have been discussed here can be used in the Deep Learning context. As a matter of fact, most existing Deep Learning based methods [181, 499] aim at finding a domain invariant representation, and some have already used the MMD [499]. We believe that exploring the use of other distribution distance measures, such as the f-divergences discussed here, but also others, would be an interesting direction for future research.

Chapter 6
Adaptive Transductive Transfer Machines: A Pipeline for Unsupervised Domain Adaptation

Nazli Farajidavar, Teofilo de Campos and Josef Kittler

Abstract This chapter addresses the problem of transfer learning by unsupervised domain adaptation. We introduce a pipeline which is designed for the case where the joint distribution of samples and labels $P(\mathbf{X}^{src}, \mathbf{Y}^{src})$ in the source domain is assumed to be different, but related to that of a target domain $P(\mathbf{X}^{trg}, \mathbf{Y}^{trg})$, but labels $\mathbf{Y}^{trg}$ are not available for the target set. This is a problem of Transductive Transfer Learning. In contrast to other methodologies in this book, our method combines steps that adapt both the marginal and the conditional distributions of the data.

6.1 Introduction

The transfer learning (TL) taxonomy presented by Pan and Yang [355] and described also in Chap. 1 classifies TL approaches into three main categories: Inductive TL, when labeled samples are available in both source and target domains; Transductive TL, when labels are only available in the source set, and Unsupervised TL, when labeled data is not present. They also categorized the methods based on *instance re-weighting* (e.g., [91, 111]), *feature space transformation* (e.g., [45, 312]) and *learning parameters transformation* (e.g., [21, 55]).

The work presented in this chapter has its focus on Transductive TL, also known as Domain Adaptation (DA) problems. While different methods can potentially be combined to achieve a successful transductive transfer, in this work we have mainly

N. Farajidavar (✉)
Institute of Biomedical Engineering, University of Oxford, Guildford, UK
e-mail: nazli.farajidavar@eng.ox.ac.uk

J. Kittler
CVSSP, University of Surrey, Guildford, UK
e-mail: j.kittler@surrey.ac.uk

T. de Campos (✉)
Department of Computer Science (CIC), University of Brasilia, DF, Brazil
e-mail: t.decampos@st-annes.oxon.org

G. Csurka (ed.), *Domain Adaptation in Computer Vision Applications*,
Advances in Computer Vision and Pattern Recognition,
DOI 10.1007/978-3-319-58347-1_6

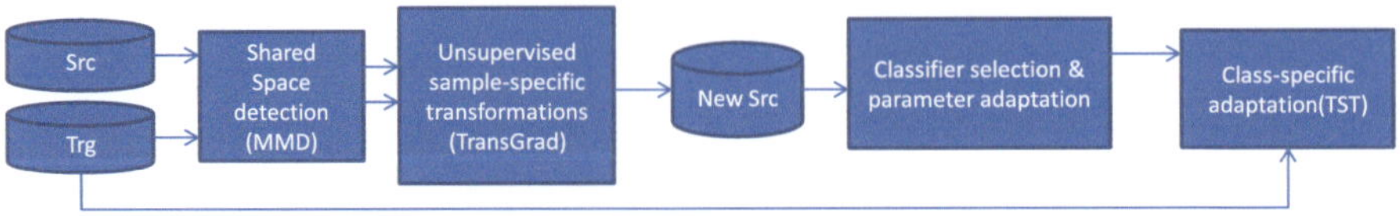

Fig. 6.1 The Adaptive Transductive Transfer Machine (ATTM)

restricted our attention to methods which focus on *feature space transformation*, *learning parameters transformation* and their combination.

Among the researchers following a similar line of work, Long et al. [312] proposed to do Joint Distribution Adaptation (JDA) by iteratively adapting both the marginal and conditional distributions modified Maximum Mean Discrepancy (MMD) algorithm [45]. JDA uses the pseudo target labels to define a shared subspace between the two domains. At each iteration, this method requires the construction and eigen decomposition of an $n \times n$ matrix whose complexity can be up to $O(n^3)$ where $n = n_{src} + n_{trg}$ is the total number of samples. Similarly, Gong et al. in [200] proposed a kernel-based domain adaptation method that exploits intrinsic low-dimensional structures in the datasets.

In this chapter[1] we propose a Transductive Transfer Machine (TTM) algorithm which combines methods that adapt the marginal and the conditional distribution of the samples, so that the source and target datasets become more similar. After adaptation, the transformed source domain data can be used to design a classifier for the target domain's samples. The TTM approaches this problem by combining four types of adaptation: (a) solving the task in a lower dimensional space that is shared between the two domains, (b) a set of local transformations to further increase the domain similarity, and (c) a set of class-conditional transformations aiming to increase the similarity between the posterior probability of samples in the source and target sets, (d) and finally we introduce the Adaptive TTM (ATTM), which uses two unsupervised dissimilarity measures before step (c) to perform classifier selection and automatic kernel parameter tuning.

Section 6.2 presents the core TTM components of our method and discusses the relation with previous works. This is followed in Sect. 6.3 by a description of our ATTMframework. In Sect. 6.4, the proposed pipeline is compared against other state-of-the-art methods and showing performance boost in cross-domain image classification, using various datasets. Section 6.5 concludes the paper.

[1]This chapter is an amalgamation of the works published in [152–154] with additional analysis taking into account the works of other authors which were developed concurrently to our work.

6.2 Marginal and Conditional Distribution Adaptation

In order to introduce the ATTM, depicted in Fig. 6.1, we will first present its core component, *feature space transformation*, referred to as Transductive Transfer Machines (TTM), summarized in the steps below:

1. A global linear transformation G' is applied to $\mathbf{X}^{src}$ and $\mathbf{X}^{trg}$ such that the marginal distribution of the source samples, $P(G'(\mathbf{X}^{src}))$ becomes more similar to that of target's, $P(G'(\mathbf{X}^{trg}))$. This is done by minimizing the MMD between the sets as described in Sect. 6.2.1.
2. Aiming to minimize the difference between the marginal distributions, a local transformation is applied to each transformed source domain sample $G''_i(G'(\mathbf{x}_i^{src}))$. This transformation, dubbed TransGrad, uses the gradient of the target data log-likelihood at each source sample. Details are in Sect. 6.2.2.
3. Finally, aiming to reduce the difference between the conditional distributions in source and target spaces, a class-based transformation is applied to each class of the transformed source samples $G'''_{y_i}(G''_i(G'(\mathbf{x}_i^{src})))$. While the first two steps are unsupervised transfer learning methods, this step is transductive, as it uses source labels. The transformation applies translation and scale transformations (TST) to each training set, as described in Sect. 6.2.3.

Fig. 6.2 illustrates these steps using a dataset composed of digits 1 and 2 from MNIST and USPS datasets. The first two principal components of the source data are used to project the data into a two dimensional space for a better visualization.

6.2.1 *Shared Space Detection with MMD*

In the first step of TTM pipeline, we look for a shared space projection that reduces dimensionality of the data whilst minimizing the reconstruction error. As explained in [312], one possibility for that is to search for an orthogonal transformation matrix $\mathbf{W} \in \mathbb{R}^{f \times f'}$ such that the embedded data variance is maximized,

$$\max_{\mathbf{W}^\top \mathbf{W}=I} Tr(\mathbf{W}^\top \mathbf{X}\mathbf{H}\mathbf{X}^\top \mathbf{W}) , \tag{6.1}$$

where $\mathbf{X} = [\mathbf{X}^{src}; \mathbf{X}^{trg}] \in \mathbb{R}^{f \times n_{src}+n_{trg}}$ is the input data matrix that combines source and target samples, $Tr(\cdot)$ is the trace of a matrix, $\mathbf{H} = I - \frac{1}{n_{src}+n_{trg}} \mathbb{1}$ is a centering matrix where I is the identity matrix, $\mathbb{1}$ is a $(n_{src} + n_{trg}) \times (n_{src} + n_{trg})$ matrix of ones and f' is the dimensionality after the projection where $f' \leq f$.

The optimization problem can be efficiently solved by eigen decomposition. However, the above PCA-based representation may not reduce the difference between source and target domains, hence the need for a more appropriate transformation remains.

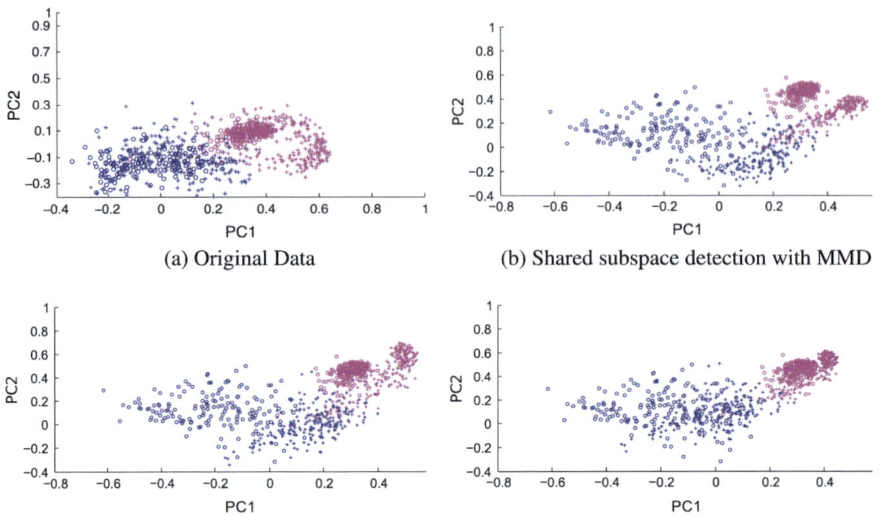

(a) Original Data

(b) Shared subspace detection with MMD

(c) Marginal adaptation with TransGrad

(d) Conditional adaptation with TST

Fig. 6.2 The effect of different steps of the pipeline on digits 1 and 2 of the MNIST → USPS datasets, visualized in 2D through PCA. Source samples (MNIST) are indicated by stars, target ones (USPS) by circles, *red* indicates samples of digit 1 and *blue* indicates digit 2

Following [213, 312, 354, 471] the empirical MMD measure, proposed in [354], is used as the distance measure to compare different distributions. This algorithm searches for a projection matrix, $\mathbf{W} \in \mathbb{R}^{f \times f'}$ which minimizes the distance between the means of the two distributions:

$$\left\| \frac{1}{n_{src}} \sum_{i=1}^{n_{src}} \mathbf{W}^\top \mathbf{x}_i - \frac{1}{n_{trg}} \sum_{j=n_{src}+1}^{n_{src}+n_{trg}} \mathbf{W}^\top \mathbf{x}_j \right\|^2 = Tr(\mathbf{W}^\top \mathbf{X} \mathbf{M} \mathbf{X}^\top \mathbf{W}) \tag{6.2}$$

where $\mathbf{M}$ is the MMD matrix and is computed as follows:

$$\mathbf{M}_{ij} = \begin{cases} \frac{1}{n_{src} n_{src}}, & \mathbf{x}_i, \mathbf{x}_j \in \mathbf{X}^{src} \\ \frac{1}{n_{trg} n_{trg}}, & \mathbf{x}_i, \mathbf{x}_j \in \mathbf{X}^{trg} \\ \frac{-1}{n_{src} n_{trg}}, & \text{otherwise.} \end{cases} \tag{6.3}$$

The constraint optimization problem then is to minimize Eq. (6.2) such that Eq. (6.1) is maximized, i.e., solve the following eigen-decomposition problem: $(\mathbf{X}\mathbf{M}\mathbf{X}^\top + \varepsilon\mathbb{I})\mathbf{W} = \mathbf{X}\mathbf{H}\mathbf{X}^\top\mathbf{W}\mathbf{D}$, giving the eigenvectors $\mathbf{W}$ and the associated eigenvalues in the form of the diagonal matrix $\mathbf{D}$. The effect is to obtain a lower dimensional shared space between the two domains. Consequently, under the new representation $G'(\mathbf{x}) = \mathbf{W}^\top \mathbf{X}$, the marginal distributions of the two domains are drawn closer to each other, as the distance between their means is minimized. The effect of this transformation is shown[2] in Fig. 6.2b.

6.2.2 *Sample-Based Adaptation with TransGrad*

In the next step of the pipeline, we propose a sample-based transformation that shifts the source probability density function toward target clusters. Via the TransGrad step a set of local translations is applied to the source samples, making their distribution more similar to that of the target samples.

In general, target data may, but does not have to, lie in the same observation space. However, for the sake of simplicity, we shall assume that the transformation of the source to the target domain is locally linear, i.e., a sample's feature vector **x** from the source domain is shifted to the target space by

$$G''(\mathbf{x}) = \mathbf{x} + \gamma \mathbf{b_x} \ , \qquad (6.4)$$

where the f dimensional vector $\mathbf{b_x}$ represents a local offset in the target domain and γ is a translation regulator. In order to impose as few assumptions as possible, we shall model the unlabeled target data, $\mathbf{X}^{trg}$ by a mixture of Gaussian probability density functions, $p(\mathbf{x}|\lambda) = \sum_{k=1}^{K} w_k p(\mathbf{x}|\lambda_k)$, whose parameters are denoted by $\lambda = \{w_k, \boldsymbol{\mu}_k, \boldsymbol{\Sigma}_k, k = 1, \cdots, K\}$ where w_k, $\boldsymbol{\mu}_k$ and $\boldsymbol{\Sigma}_k$ denote the weight, mean vector and covariance matrix of Gaussian component k, respectively, and K denotes the number of components $p(\mathbf{x}|\lambda_k) = \mathcal{N}(\boldsymbol{\mu}_k, \boldsymbol{\Sigma}_k)$.

The problem of finding an optimal translation parameter $\mathbf{b_x}$ can then be formulated as one of moving the source point **x** to a new location $G''(\mathbf{x}) = \mathbf{x} + \gamma \mathbf{b_x}$ to increase its likelihood as measured using $p(G''(\mathbf{x})|\lambda^{trg})$. Using the Taylor expansion, in the vicinity of **x**, the likelihood of $p(\mathbf{x} + \gamma \mathbf{b_x})$ can be expressed as:

$$p(\mathbf{x} + \gamma \mathbf{b_x}|\lambda) = p(\mathbf{x}|\lambda) + \gamma (\nabla_{\mathbf{x}} p(\mathbf{x}|\lambda))^{\top} . \mathbf{b_x} \ . \qquad (6.5)$$

We wish to maximize the $p(\mathbf{x} + \gamma \mathbf{b_x}|\lambda)$ with respect to the unknown parameter, $\mathbf{b_x}$. The learning problem then can be formulated as:

$$\max_{\mathbf{b_x}} \left(p(\mathbf{x}|\lambda) + \gamma (\nabla_{\mathbf{x}} p(\mathbf{x}|\lambda))^{\top} . \mathbf{b_x} \right) \quad \text{s.t. } \mathbf{b_x}^{\top} . \mathbf{b_x} = 1 \ . \qquad (6.6)$$

The Lagrangian of Eq. (6.6) is $p(\mathbf{x}|\lambda) + \gamma (\nabla_{\mathbf{x}} p(\mathbf{x}|\lambda))^{\top} . \mathbf{b_x} - \gamma' (\mathbf{b_x}^{\top} . \mathbf{b_x} - 1)$. Setting its gradient with respect to $\mathbf{b_x}$ to zero

[2]Note however that in Fig. 6.2b a 2D view of feature space was generated using PCA and only two out of ten classes of digits in MNIST/USPS dataset are shown, while the MMD computation was (Footnote 2 continued)
done in a higher dimensional space with samples from all ten classes. For these reasons it may not be easy to see that the means of the source and target samples became closer after MMD.

$$\nabla_{\mathbf{x}} p(\mathbf{x}|\lambda) - \gamma'' \mathbf{b}_{\mathbf{x}} = 0 \,, \qquad (6.7)$$

where γ'' is considered as TransGrad's step size parameter and is equal to $\frac{2\gamma'}{\gamma}$, we find that the source data-point $\mathbf{x}$ should be moved in the direction of maximum gradient of the function $p(\mathbf{x}|\lambda)$. Accordingly, $\mathbf{b}_{\mathbf{x}}$ is defined as

$$\mathbf{b}_{\mathbf{x}} = \nabla_{\mathbf{x}} p(\mathbf{x}|\lambda) = \sum_{k=1}^{K} w_k p(\mathbf{x}^{src}|\lambda_k).\boldsymbol{\Sigma}_k^{-1}(\mathbf{x} - \boldsymbol{\mu}_k) \,. \qquad (6.8)$$

In practice, Eq. (6.4) translates $\mathbf{x}^{src}$ using the combination of the translations between $\mathbf{x}^{src}$ and $\boldsymbol{\mu}_k$, weighted by the likelihood of $G''(\mathbf{x}^{src})$ given λ_k. Up to our knowledge, this is the first time a sample-based transformation is proposed for transfer learning. The effect of this transformation can be seen in Fig. 6.2c.

6.2.3 Conditional Distribution Adaptation with TST

In order to reduce the class-conditional distribution mismatch between the corresponding clusters of the two domains, we used a set of linear class-specific transformations which we refer to as translation and scaling transformation, or TST. To achieve this, we assume that a Gaussian Mixture Model (GMM) fitted to the source classes can be adapted in a way that it matches to target classes. We follow Reynolds et al. [385] and use only diagonal covariance matrices in the GMM, making the complexity of the estimation system linear in f. In our experiments, we further simplify the model for this step of the pipeline by using only one Gaussian distribution per class, which is not unrealistic considering the fact that what we are eventually interested in are compact and dense classes.

In order to adapt the class-conditional distributions, one can start with an attempt to match the joint distribution of the features and labels between the corresponding clusters of the two domains. However, in Transductive Transfer application scenarios, labeled samples are not available in the target domain. We thus use posterior probability of the target instances to build class-based models in the target domain. This relates to JDA [312], which uses pseudo-labels to iteratively update a supervised version of MMD. In our case, class-based adaptations are simplified to translation and scaling transformations, making the computational cost very attractive.

The proposed transformation adjusts the mean and standard deviation of the corresponding clusters from the source domain, i.e., each feature j of each sample $\mathbf{x}^i$ is adapted as follows:

$$G_{y^i}(x_j^i) = \frac{x_j^i - E^{src}[x_j, y^i]}{\sigma_{j,y_i}^{src}} \sigma_{j,y^i}^{trg} + E_{\Lambda_{src}}^{trg}[x_j, y^i] \,, \forall i = 1 : n_{src} \,, \qquad (6.9)$$

where σ_{j,y^i}^{src} is the standard deviation of feature x_j of the source samples labeled as y^i and $E^{src}[x_j, y^i]$ is the joint expectation of the feature x_j and labels y^i defined by

$$E^{src}[x_j, y^i] = \frac{\sum_{i=1}^{n_{src}} x_j^i \mathbb{1}_{[y]}(y^i)}{\sum_{i=1}^{n_{src}} \mathbb{1}_{[y]}(y^i)} . \tag{6.10}$$

In Eq. (6.10) $\mathbb{1}_{[y]}(y^i)$ is an indicator function.[3]

An estimation of the target joint expectation is thus formulated as

$$E^{trg}[x_j, y] \approx E_{\Lambda_{src}}^{trg}[x_j, y] = \frac{\sum_{i=1}^{n_{trg}} x_j^i P_{\Lambda_{src}}(y|\mathbf{x}_i)}{\sum_{i=1}^{n_{trg}} P_{\Lambda_{src}}(y|\mathbf{x}_i)} \tag{6.11}$$

We propose to estimate the standard deviation per feature and per class using

$$\sigma_{j,y^i}^{trg} = \sqrt{\frac{\sum_{n=1}^{n_{trg}} (x_j^n - E_{\Lambda_{src}}^{trg}[x_j, y^i])^2 P_{\Lambda_{src}}(y^i|\mathbf{x}_n)}{\sum_{n=1}^{n_{trg}} P_{\Lambda_{src}}(y^i|\mathbf{x}_n)}} . \tag{6.12}$$

In summary, in a common DA problem, the joint expectation of the features and labels over source distribution, $E^{src}[x_j, y^i]$, is not necessarily equal to $E^{trg}[x_j, y^i]$. Therefore, one can argue that if the expectations in the source and target domains are induced to be similar, then the model Λ learned on the source data will generalize well to the target data. Consequently, the less these distributions differ, the better the trained model will perform.

Since the target expectation $E_{\Lambda_{src}}^{trg}[x_j, y^i]$ is only an approximation based on the target's posterior probabilities, rather than the ground-truth labels (which are not available in the target set), there is a danger that samples that would be miss-classified could lead to negative transfer, i.e., negative impact. To alleviate this, we follow Arnold et al.'s [18] suggestion and smooth out the transformation by applying the following mapping

$$G_{y^i}'''(x_j^i) = (1 - \theta)x_j^i + \theta G_{y^i}(x_j^i) , \tag{6.13}$$

where $\theta \in [0, 1]$ is the transfer rate parameter. As it can be inferred from the MMD and TST equations, the effect of the first transformation is that it tries to find a shared subspace between the two domains to reduce the distributional mismatch at a global level second one is actually a class-specific transformation aiming to reduce the class-conditional mismatch among the clusters from one domain to another.

Iterative refinement of the conditional distribution. Matching the marginal distributions does not guarantee that the conditional distribution of the target can be approximated to that of the source. To our knowledge, most of the recent works related to this issue [55, 76, 378, 586] are Inductive Transfer Learning methods and

[3]Our method uses insights from Arnold et al. [18], but Eqs. (6.10) and (6.11) rectify those from [18], as discussed in [154].

they have access to some labeled data in the target domain which in practice makes the posteriors' estimations easier.

Instead, our class-specific transformation method (TST), reduces the difference between the likelihoods $P(G_y'''(\mathbf{x}^{src})|y = c)$ and $P(\mathbf{x}|y = c)$ by using the target posteriors estimated from a model trained on gradually modified source domain Eq. (6.13). Hence, these likelihood approximations will not be reliable unless we iterate over the whole distribution adaptation process and retrain the classifier model using $G_y'''(\mathbf{x}^{src})$.

Global dissimilarity as stopping criterion. In order to automatically control the number of the iterations in our pipeline, we introduce a domain dissimilarity measure inspired by sample selection bias correction techniques [99, 434]. Many of those techniques are based on weighting samples $\mathbf{x}_i^{src}$ using the ratio $w(\mathbf{x}) = \frac{P(\mathbf{x}|trg)}{P(\mathbf{x}|src)}$. This ratio can be estimated using a classifier that is trained to distinguish between source and target domains, i.e., samples are labeled as either belonging to class src or trg. Based on this idea, we use this classification performance as a measure of dissimilarity between two domains, i.e., if it is easy to distinguish between source and target samples, it means they are dissimilar. We coin this measure as Global Dissimilarity, $D^{\text{global}}(\mathbf{X}^{src}, \mathbf{X}^{trg})$ which is defined by the accuracy of a nearest neighbor domain classifier using a random split of training and test samples, each containing 50% of the data. If the domain dissimilarity is high, then more iterations are needed to achieve a better match between the domains.

Note that other methods could be used as stopping criteria. For instance by checking the incremental change in the transformation between two consecutive iterations we could stop the iterations in case that this measure is below a specific threshold, e.g., using the Frobenius norm between the covariances of the transformed source matrices of two consecutive iterative steps. However, we use $D^{\text{global}}(\mathbf{X}^{src}, \mathbf{X}^{trg})$ because this same measure is also engaged for selecting classifiers.

6.3 ATTM via Classifier Selection and Parameter Adaptation

We do not assume that source and target domain samples follow the same distribution, so the best performing learner for the source set may not be the best for the target set. We propose to use dissimilarity measures between source and target sets in order to select the classifier and adjust its kernel parameters. The empirical results showed that the optimization of SVM using grid search in the parameter space with cross-validation on the source led to over-fitting. We therefore prefer to use Kernel LDA (KDA) [57] and PCA+NN classifiers as the main learners.

To select between these classifiers and to adapt the KDA kernel length-scale parameter, we propose to use two measures. The first is the **Global Dissimilarity** between the source and target distributions, described in Sect. 6.2.3. The second measure, coined **Clusters Dissimilarity** ($D^{\text{clusters}}(\mathbf{X}^{src}, \mathbf{X}^{trg})$), is proportional to the average dissimilarity between the source and target clusters, computed using the average of the distances between the source class centers and their nearest target cluster center. The target clusters centers are obtained using K-means on the target data, initialized using source class centers. We therefore assume that there is no shuffling in the placement of the clusters from one domain to another.

The proposed **Clusters Dissimilarity** is similar to the cross-domain sparse-shot similarity of Xu et al. [548] which is used for multi-source motion tracking. Xu et al. proposed to use object motion tracking data in each domain and compared tracks across domains using the Kullback-Leibler Divergence between GMMs that represent them.[4]

When both dissimilarity measures indicate that the cross-domain datasets are very different, the choice of a nonparametric classifier such as Nearest Neighbor (NN) is preferred, requiring no optimization during training. When the two domains are similar at the global level, the choice of a parametric classifier such as KDA is more sensible, however, with care taken, to avoid over-fitting on the training set. So if the local dissimilarity is high, the kernel parameters must be adapted.

Following the common practice in the vision community (e.g., [521]), we initially set σ parameter of the Radial Basis Function (RBF) kernel in KDA to

$$\sigma = \frac{1}{n_{src}^2} \sum_{i,j}^{n_{src}} |\mathbf{x}_i - \mathbf{x}_j|_1, \forall \mathbf{x}_i, \mathbf{x}_j \in \mathbf{X}^{src} \tag{6.14}$$

where ℓ^1 norm is used in the kernel function. This is then adapted using a linear function of the cluster dissimilarity measure

$$\sigma' = \sigma \gamma''' D^{\text{clusters}}(\mathbf{X}^{src}, \mathbf{X}^{trg}) , \tag{6.15}$$

where γ''' is a constant value which is empirically set to be the average cluster dissimilarity obtained in a set of cross-domain comparisons. This was devised based on the fact that the credibility of a classifier is inversely proportional to the dissimilarity between training and test samples. In the case of KDA, the best way to tune its generalization ability is via the kernel length-scale.

Note that the cluster dissimilarity measure can only be computed if enough samples are available in both source and target sets or if they are not too unbalanced. When these conditions are not satisfied, our algorithm avoids kernel-based method and selects the NN classifier. The parameter selection and model adaptation mechanism is summarized in Table 6.1, where the arrows pointing up ($\Uparrow$) indicate high dissimilarity and arrows pointing down ($\Downarrow$) indicate low dissimilarity.[5]

In conclusion, our ATTM pipeline will use a PCA+NN classifier as its main learner model if the global dissimilarity between the two domains is high or there are not enough source samples and consequently not enough cluster-wise samples to train a highly reliable learner model or to further adjust the classifier parameters.

---

[4]Table 6.3 shows these two measures computed on all datasets, discussed later.

[5]The measures were judged as high or low based on a subset of values observed in Table 6.3.

Table 6.1 Classifier selection and length-scale adaptation

D^{global}	$D^{clusters}$	Classifier	How to set σ'
$\Uparrow$	$\Uparrow$	NN	—
$\Downarrow$	$\Downarrow$	KDA	$\sigma' = \sigma^{src}$ Eq. (6.14)
$\Downarrow$	$\Uparrow$	KDA	$\sigma' = \sigma^{src}\gamma''' D^{\text{clusters}}(\mathbf{X}^{src}, \mathbf{X}^{trg})$

In any other circumstances, the model will use the KDA classifier and adjusts the kernel length-scale if required.

Computational complexity. The proposed TTM method for feature space adaptation has computational cost as follows:

1. MMD: $O(n^2)$ for constructing the MMD matrix, $O(nf^2)$ for covariance computation and $O(f^3)$ for eigen decomposition.
2. TransGrad: $O(nK)$ for Expectation step of GMM computation, $O(nKf)$ for the computation of covariance matrices and $O(K)$ for the Maximization step of the GMM computation. Once the GMM is built, the TransGrad transformation itself is $O(nKf)$.
3. TST: $O(Cnf)$ for class-specific TST transformations where C is the number of classes.
4. NN classifier: zero for training and $O(n^2 f)$ for reapplying the classifier.

For each of the T iterations, the classifier is re-applied and TST is computed. Therefore, the overall complexity of our training algorithm is dominated by the cost of training a GMM (which is low by using diagonal covariances) and iteratively applying a classifier. The core transformations proposed in this pipeline, TransGrad and TST are $O(nKf)$ and $O(Cnf)$, respectively,i.e., much cheaper than most methods in the literature. MMD is the only component whose complexity is greater than linear on n, but it is executed only once and its main cost comes from eigen decomposition, for which there is a wide range of optimized libraries available.

By adding the classifier selection step and kernel adaptation to TTM, we obtain ATTM, shown in algorithm 4. The classifier selection step uses the computation of the $D^{\text{clusters}}(\mathbf{X}^{src}, \mathbf{X}^{trg})$, which costs $O(n^2)$, as it uses K-means clustering, but this is executed only once. TST, which has linear cost, is the main part of the algorithm. As it uses source labels, it is iterated. The most expensive part of the loop is the re-training and application of classifiers.

6.4 Experimental Evaluation

In the experiments of this chapter, we used three public benchmark datasets: the USPS/MNIST [110], COIL20 [341] and Caltech+office (OC10) [407]. These are

Algorithm 4: ATTM: Adaptive Transductive Transfer Machine

Input: $\mathbf{X}^{src}, \mathbf{Y}^{src}, \mathbf{X}^{trg}$

1. Search for the shared subspace between the two domains (MMD, Sect. 6.2.1)
2. TransGrad: apply local adjustments to the source marginal distribution (Sect. 6.2.2)
3. Select the appropriate classifier (Sect. 6.3), if it is kernel-based, tune σ using Eq. (6.15)

while $T < 10$ *and* $|D^{global}(G^t(\mathbf{X}^{src}), \mathbf{X}^{trg})| >$ *threshold* **do**

4. Find the feature-wise TST transformation Eqs. (6.9), (6.11), 6.12)
5. Transform the source domain clusters Eq. (6.13)
6. Retrain the classifier using the transformed source

Output: $\mathbf{Y}^{trg}$

widely used to evaluate computer vision and transfer learning algorithms, enabling us to compare our results with other state-of-the-art methods. In most of our experiments, we used their standard features, available from their website: raw images for USPS, MNIST and COIL20; and SURFBOV for OC10. In Sect. 6.4.1, we show results using DeCAF [128] features.

Preliminary evaluations. In a preliminary evaluation of the characteristics of the domains and classifiers, we evaluated a set of widely used classifiers on all the datasets using a fivefold cross-validation, reporting mean accuracy measure in Table 6.2. In the case of the NN classifier, we further projected our full space into its principal components (PCA), retaining 90% of the energy. As one can note in most of the experiments KDA is the winning classifier. SVM is also a strong learner but it requires optimization of parameters C and σ, which can make it optimal for the source domain, but not necessarily for the target. It is worth noting that PCA+NN's performance is remarkably close to that of KDA on the first two datasets and it is significantly superior on the DSLR dataset.

The two cross-domain dissimilarity measures are shown in Table 6.3. These results justify the design options shown in Table 6.1 so NN is used for the digits datasets (MNIST$\leftrightarrow$USPS) and where the number of source samples was not adequate for an accurate parameter adaptation (D$\leftrightarrow$W), and KDA is used for the remaining transfer tasks, with kernel parameters set based on $D^{\text{clusters}}(\mathbf{X}^{src}, \mathbf{X}^{trg})$.

Probing and benchmark results. We performed probing experiments to evaluate the relevance of each component of the proposed system. The simplest design, labeled TTM0 refers to an iterative version of TST [154]; TTM1 is the combination of the MMD and TST; and finally TTM2 adds to TTM1 the samplewise marginal

Table 6.2 Evaluation of four classifiers using fivefold cross-validation on individual domains

Classifier	MNIST	USPS	COIL1	COIL2	Caltech	Amazon	Webcam	DSLR
PCA+NN	91.97	93.64	99.02	98.91	38.80	60.59	79.58	**76.95**
LR	86.15	89.22	92.36	92.22	56.27	72.46	80.01	67.49
KDA	**94.05**	94.84	**100.00**	**99.71**	**58.16**	**78.73**	**89.54**	63.94
SVM	91.80	**95.28**	99.72	99.44	57.17	74.86	86.44	75.80

Table 6.3 Cross-domain dissimilarities between domains ($src \rightarrow trg$), with datasets abbreviated as M: MNIST, U: USPS, CO1: COIL1, CO2: COIL2, C: Caltech, A: Amazon, W: Webcam, and D: DSLR

src	M	U	CO1	CO2	C	C	C	A	A	A	W	W	W	D	D	D
trg	U	M	CO2	CO1	A	W	D	C	W	D	C	A	D	C	A	W
D^{clusters} (%)	3.4	3.2	2.6	2.5	3.2	3.3	3.1	3.1	3.5	3.6	3.7	3.5	3.7	3.5	3.4	3.3
D^{global} (%)	9.8	9.8	6.3	5.6	5.5	7.8	7.9	6.1	7.4	0.8	7.5	7.2	5.1	7.8	7.9	4.7

adaptation (TransGrad) applied before TST (see Fig. 6.1). We have also carried out experiments to show that our proposed classifier selection and model adaptation techniques (ATTM) improve the performance of both TTM and JDA algorithms significantly. We compared our methods with four state-of-the-art approaches [200, 312, 354, 438] using the same public datasets and the same settings as those of [200, 312]. The results are in Table 6.4. Further comparisons with other DA methods such

Table 6.4 Recognition accuracies on DA tasks with datasets abbreviated as in Table 6.3. Comparisons in column two start with the baseline accuracy obtained using NN and PCA followed by the results of the algorithms discussed. The last two columns show the effect of the classifier selection and model adaptation techniques (6.3) on JDA andTTM algorithms

Transfer task	NN base-line	PCA base-line	TCA [354]	TSL [438]	GFK (PLS, PCA) [200]	JDA (1NN) [312]
M → U	65.94	66.22	56.28	66.06	67.22	67.28
U → M	44.70	44.95	51.05	53.75	46.45	59.65
CO1 → 2	83.61	84.72	88.47	88.06	72.50	89.31
CO2 → 1	82.78	84.03	85.83	87.92	74.17	88.47
C → A	23.70	36.95	38.20	44.47	41.4	44.78
C → W	25.76	32.54	38.64	34.24	40.68	41.69
C → D	25.48	38.22	41.40	43.31	41.1	45.22
A → C	26.00	34.73	27.76	37.58	37.9	39.36
A → W	29.83	35.59	37.63	33.90	35.7	37.97
A → D	25.48	27.39	33.12	26.11	36.31	39.49
W → C	19.86	26.36	29.30	29.83	29.3	31.17
W → A	22.96	31.00	30.06	30.27	35.5	32.78
W → D	59.24	77.07	87.26	87.26	80.89	89.17
D → C	26.27	29.65	31.70	28.50	30.28	31.52
D → A	28.50	32.05	32.15	27.56	36.1	33.09
D → W	63.39	75.93	86.10	85.42	79.1	89.49
Average	43.06	49.23	50.35	52.34	50.00	54.88

(continued)

Table 6.4 (continued)

Transfer task	TTM0 (TST, 1NN)	TTM1 (MMD + TTM0)	TTM2 (TransGrad + TTM1)	AJDA (Adapt.JDA)	ATTM (Adapt.TTM2)
M → U	75.94	76.61	77.94	67.28	**77.94**
U → M	59.79	59.41	61.15	59.65	**61.15**
CO1 → 2	88.89	88.75	93.19	**94.31**	92.64
CO2 → 1	88.89	88.61	88.75	**92.36**	91.11
C → A	39.87	44.25	46.76	58.56	**60.85**
C → W	41.02	39.66	41.02	48.81	**62.03**
C → D	50.31	44.58	47.13	45.86	**50.32**
A → C	36.24	35.53	39.62	40.43	**42.92**
A → W	37.63	42.37	39.32	49.83	**50.51**
A → D	33.75	29.30	29.94	38.21	**39.49**
W → C	26.99	29.83	30.36	**35.80**	34.02
W → A	29.12	30.69	31.11	38.94	**39.67**
W → D	85.98	89.17	89.81	89.17	**89.81**
D → C	29.65	31.25	32.06	28.31	**32.41**
D → A	31.21	29.75	30.27	37.47	**38.73**
D → W	85.08	**90.84**	88.81	89.49	88.81
Average	54.12	55.10	56.20	59.17	**60.72**

as Sampling Geodesic Flow (SGF) using the Grassmann manifolds [206] are reported in [200].

As one can note, all the DA methods improve the accuracy over the baseline. Furthermore, our ATTM method generally outperforms all the other methods. The main reason for that is that our method combines three different feature adaptation techniques with a further classifier parameter adaptation step.

In most of the tasks, both TTM1, 2 algorithms show comparative performance with respect to the JDA [312]. The average performance accuracy of the TTM1 and TTM2 on 16 transfer tasks is **55.10** and **56.20%**, respectively, where the performance improved by **0.22** and **1.32%** compared to the best performing baseline method JDA [200]. Moreover in almost all datasets, TTM2 wins over TTM1 due to its initial domain dissimilarity adjustments using the TransGrad. On average, our methods (TTM1, TTM2 and ATTM) give better results than JDA [312] (and AJDA) because the MMD-based transformation of JDA is coarser than ours. Furthermore, in JDA [312] the number of iterations is a predefined constant, in our algorithm we based this number on a sensible measure of domain dissimilarity described earlier. Moreover, the proposed TTM guarantees an acceptable level of performance about five times faster than the best performing state-of-the-art approach. GFK performs well on some of the OC10 experiments but poorly on the others. The reason is that the subspace dimension should be small enough to ensure that different sub-spaces transit smoothly along the geodesic flow, which may not be an accurate representation of the input data. JDA and TTM perform much better by learning a more accurate shared space.

We also evaluated the proposed classifier selection and model adaptation techniques on JDA [312] and TTM [153]. The results are indicated by AJDA and ATTM in Table 6.4. Their performance shows that the model adaptation significantly enhances the final classifier. One should note that in the cases where our model adaptation technique selects the NN classifier as the main learner of the algorithm, the results remain steady. The performance gains of **4.59** and **4.29%** in ATTM and AJDA, respectively, validate the proposed dissimilarity measures for model selection and adaptation. The proposed model adaptation step of the pipeline selected the NN classifier for MNIST↔USPS and for DSLR→Webcam. For all other transfer problems, KDA was chosen and σ adaptation was used.

Shared subspace projection methods. After developing our MMD-based algorithm, we came across alternative subspace projection methods [25, 164]. In [25] the author proposes the Domain Invariant Projection (DIP) where a Grassmann manifold latent subspace is used to project the data and the MMD measure is subsequently applied for evaluating the source and target domains dissimilarity. The aim is to find a representation of the data that is invariant across different domains. Alternatively, they propose a second projection, DIP-CC, that not only minimizes the distance between the distribution of the projected source and target, but also yields better classification performance. The algorithm searches for a projection that encourages samples with the same labels to form a more compact cluster which is achieved by minimizing the distance between the projected samples of each class and their mean.

In contrast to the manifold alignment methods that use local statistical structure of the data [519, 520, 576], the authors of [164] exploit the global covariance statistical structure of the two domains during the adaptation process. The source data is projected onto the source subspace and the target data onto the target subspace in contrast to most domain adaptation methods in the literature. This method, called Subspace Alignment (SA), is totally unsupervised and does not require any target labels. SA makes use of the correlated features in both domains where some of these features can be specific to one domain yet correlated to some other features in the other one allowing the method to use both shared and domain specific features.

In Table 6.5 we compare these state-of-the-art latent subspace detection methods (DIP, DIP-CC, and SA) with the MMD-PCA-based method which we used in our TTM framework. As one can note, some of these methods outperform MMD-based subspace projection at the cost of a higher computational complexity. All these subspace detection methods could replace the first step of our pipeline and potentially improve the final classification performance. However, given that MMD is the step with the highest asymptotic cost of our pipeline (see Sect. 6.3), we advocate that it is important to use the simplest unsupervised subspace transformation method and focus on the transductive part of the algorithm to improve performance.

Table 6.5 Recognition accuracies obtained with 1NN classifiers on target domains using different shared subspace projection methods, compared to MMD, i.e., the first step of our TTM

DA experiment	DIP [25]	DIP-CC [25]	SA [164]	MMD
C → A	50.0	**51.8**	39.0	46.1
C → W	47.6	**47.7**	36.8	38.0
C → D	49.0	**51.4**	39.6	45.9
A → C	**43.3**	43.2	35.3	40.6
A → W	46.7	**47.8**	38.6	40.0
A → D	42.8	**43.3**	37.6	31.9
W → C	37.0	**37.1**	32.3	31.3
W → A	**42.5**	41.1	37.4	31.9
W → D	86.4	85.3	80.3	**89.2**
D → C	**39.0**	35.8	32.4	33.4
D → A	40.5	**41.0**	38.0	31.2
D → W	86.7	84.0	83.6	**87.5**
average	**51.0**	50.8	44.2	45.6

6.4.1 Using Stronger Features (DeCAF)

Following the same experimental setting, we present further results for OC10 dataset. The previous sections show the results obtained using the original standard feature extraction method for these datasets (bags of SURF features). Owing to the success of deep CNN methods, a newer feature extraction method has become standard, known as Deep Convolutional Activation Features (DeCAF) [127]. State-of-the-art method [275] Following [275], we used the output from the sixth layer as the visual features, leading to 4,096-dim DeCAF6 features. In this set of experiments we compare our TTM and ATTM methods with the methods that aim to solve the DA task by adapting the classifiers hyperplanes or by means of auxiliary classifiers, namely; the Adaptive SVM (A-SVM) [554], Domain Adaptation Machine (DAM) [135] and DA-M2S [74].

In [135], the author proposed a multiple source domain adaptation method referred to as DAM by leveraging a set of pre-learned classifiers independently trained with the labeled patterns from multiple source domains. More specifically, DAM was introduced as a data dependent regulator constrained by Least-Squares SVM (LS-SVM), which forces the target classifier to share similar decision values with auxiliary classifiers from the relevant source domains on the unlabeled patterns of the target domain. For a single source domain scenario, the experiments were repeated 10 times by using randomly generated subsets of source and target domain samples and the mean performance is reported in Table 6.6.

The DA-M2s method of [74] is an extension of the DAM method where from each RGB image data two nonlinear features are extracted, one describing the depth information and the other containing visual information. Using the Kernel Canonical

Table 6.6 Results obtained on the OC10 dataset using DeCAF features. The Baseline, JDA and TTM columns show the results achieved using the 1-NN classifier

Transfer task	Baseline DeCAF	SVM-A [554]	DAM [135]	DA-M2S [74]	JDA [312]	TTM (1NN)	ATTM
C → A	85.70	83.54	84.73	84.27	89.77	89.98	**92.17**
C → W	66.10	81.72	82.48	82.87	83.73	86.78	**90.84**
C → D	74.52	74.58	78.14	75.83	86.62	89.17	**92.99**
A → C	70.35	74.36	76.60	78.11	82.28	83.70	**86.55**
A → W	64.97	70.58	74.32	71.04	78.64	**89.81**	89.15
A → D	57.29	96.56	93.82	**96.62**	80.25	81.36	90.45
W → C	60.37	85.37	**87.88**	86.38	83.53	80.41	83.44
W → A	62.53	96.71	96.31	**97.12**	90.19	88.52	92.27
W → D	98.73	78.14	81.27	77.60	100	100	**100**
D → C	52.09	91.00	**91.75**	91.37	85.13	82.90	82.28
D → A	62.73	76.61	79.39	78.14	91.44	90.81	**91.65**
D → W	89.15	83.89	84.59	83.31	98.98	98.98	**98.98**
Avg	70.33	83.95	84.06	84.97	87.55	87.87	**90.90**

Correlation Analysis (KCCA), the correlation between these two types of features is maximized. For the OC10 dataset (which have no depth maps), the method DA-M2s w/o depth represents source and target domains as two views of the same object classes. DA-M2s and LS-SVM are built on top of Adaptive SVM (SVM-A) [554], which is a general framework to adapt one or more existing classifiers of any type to a new target dataset.

Note that in Table 6.6 the baseline without any transformation using the DeCAF features and NN classifier is significantly better than the results of Table 6.4, simply because the DeCAF features are better than SURF. As one can see our TTM and ATTM methods both outperform the other state-of-the-art approaches in most of the cases gaining 2.9 and 5.96% average performance enhancements over the best performing state-of-the-art method of DA-M2S (w/o depth), respectively. One should note that in both state-of-the-art approaches, DAM [135] and DA-M2S [74], the model has access to a small number of labeled samples from the target domain while our model does not benefit from that.

Sensitivity of TransGrad parameters. To evaluate sensitivity of TransGrad parameters, we ran TTM varying values of the regulator γ'' of the TransGrad step Eq. (6.7), and the results are in Fig. 6.3a. For all datasets, the performance improved as γ'' grows but it plateau for $\gamma'' \geq 5$. For this reason we used $\gamma'' = 5$ in all experiments of this chapter.

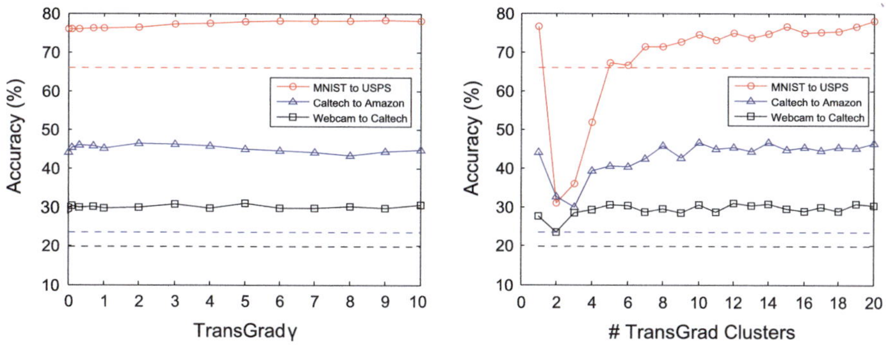

(a) TransGrad γ'' (b) TransGrad GMM components' size

Fig. 6.3 The effect of different γ'' values and number of GMM clusters in the TransGrad step of our framework on the final performance of the pipeline for three cross-domain experiments. Constant lines show the baseline accuracy for each experiment

We also ran TTM with varying number Gaussian components K in the TransGrad step for the target GMM. Theoretically as the number of GMM components increases the translations get more accurate and the performance becomes more stable. We plot the classification accuracy w.r.t. K in Fig. 6.3b. Note that for $K = 1$, TransGrad contributes to an improvement over the baseline, as it induces a global shift toward the target set. But in general, for values of K smaller than the number of classes, we do not actually expect TransGrad to help, as it will shift samples from different classes toward the same clusters. This explains why the performance increases with K for $K > 2$. Based on this result, we adopted $K = 20$ in all other experiments of this chapter.

Timing comparison. We have compared the execution time of our TTM algorithm against JDA [312] in the transfer task from the MNIST digits dataset to the USPS digits dataset. Both algorithms were implemented in Matlab and were evaluated on a Intel Core2 64bit, 3 GHz machine running Linux. We averaged the time measured over five experiments. The JDA algorithm took 21.38 ± 0.26 s and our full TTM framework took 4.42 ± 0.12 s, broken down as: 0.40 ± 0.01 seconds to find the appropriate shared space using the MMD, 1.90 ± 0.06 to perform the sample-wise marginal distribution adaptations using TransGrad and finally 2.42 ± 0.12 s to apply the iterative conditional distribution adaptations (TST). The time complexity obviously will grow for both AJDA and ATTM due to kernel computation of the KDA classifier.

6.5 Conclusion and Discussion

In this chapter, we introduced Transductive Transfer Machine (TTM), which aim to adapt both the marginal and conditional distributions of the source samples so that they become more similar to those of target samples, leading to an improvement in the classification results in DA scenarios. The proposed TTM pipeline consists of the following steps: first, a global linear transformation is applied to both source and target domain samples, so that their expected values match. In the next step, a novel method applies a sample-based transformation to source samples. This leads to a finer adaptation of their marginal distribution, taking into account the likelihood of each source sample given the target PDF. Finally, we proposed to iteratively adapt the class-based posterior distribution of source samples using an efficient linear transformation whose complexity only depends on the number of features. In addition, we proposed the use of two unsupervised comparison measures, Global and Clusters Dissimilarities. The former is used both to automatically determine the number of iterations needed and also to select the pipeline's main learner model. The latter measure, Clusters Dissimilarity, is used for adjusting the classifier's parameters for the new target domain. Our approach was shown to outperform state-of-the-art methods on various datasets, with a lower computational cost.

Our work [153] was one of the first to show that although DeCAF features lead to a step change in both discrimination power and generalization of image descriptors, they actually do not "undo the domain bias," as argued in [127]. DeCAF features can in fact be improved by applying feature space transformation using DA methods, and our method (ATTM) delivers improvement in performance, outperforming all the methods published prior to [152].

Acknowledgements N. FarajiDavar and T. deCampos were both at the CVSSP, University of Surrey when the experiments reported in this chapter were developed. This work was supported by the Engineering and Physical Sciences Research Council (EPSRC) Grant number EP/K014307/2 and the MOD University Defence Research Collaboration in Signal Processing.

Chapter 7
What to Do When the Access to the Source Data Is Constrained?

Gabriela Csurka, Boris Chidlovskii and Stéphane Clinchant

Abstract A large majority of existing domain adaptation methods makes an assumption of freely available labeled source and unlabeled target data. They exploit the discrepancy between their distributions and build representations common to both target and source domains. In reality, such a simplifying assumption rarely holds, since source data are routinely a subject of legal and contractual constraints between data owners and data customers. Despite a limited access to source domain data, decision-making procedures might be available in the form of, e.g., classification rules trained on the source and made ready for a direct deployment and later reuse. In other cases, the owner of a source data is allowed to share a few representative examples such as class means. The aim of this chapter is therefore to address the domain adaptation problem in such constrained real world applications, i.e. where the reuse of source domain data is *limited to classification rules or a few representative examples*. As a solution, we extend recent techniques based on *feature corruption* and their *marginalization*, both considering supervised and unsupervised domain adaptation settings. The proposed models are tested and compared on private and publicly available source datasets showing significant performance gains despite the absence of the whole source data and shortage of labeled target data.

7.1 Introduction

Numerous approaches have been proposed to address textual and visual domain adaptation, as described at the beginning of this book. The majority of these methods makes an assumption of freely available source domain data. An equal access to both

G. Csurka (✉)
Naver Labs Europe, Meylan, France
e-mail: gabriela.csurka@naverlabs.com

B. Chidlovskii
e-mail: boris.chidlovskii@naverlabs.com

S. Clinchant
e-mail: Stephane.Clinchant@naverlabs.com

G. Csurka (ed.), *Domain Adaptation in Computer Vision Applications*,
Advances in Computer Vision and Pattern Recognition,
DOI 10.1007/978-3-319-58347-1_7

source and target data allows to measure the discrepancy between their distributions and either to build representations common to both target and sources, or to directly reuse the source instances for a better target classification [550].

But in reality, such a simplifying assumption rarely holds, especially in the case of service companies operating in health care, customer care, human resource, and finance. The data of previous customers, which can be a good source of data for a new customer, are often subject of legal, technical and contractual constraints between data owners and data customers. Moreover, beyond privacy and disclosure obligations, customers are often simply reluctant to share their data.

It is more common in these cases that instead some *decision-making procedures* are available from a customer, allowing for adaptation. These procedures are often presented in the form of classification, identification, ranking, etc., rules trained on source data and made ready for a direct deployment and later reuse. In other cases, the owner of a source data is not allowed to share the entire dataset, but is ready to share some representative source examples, such as class means.

In this chapter, we address the domain adaptation problem in applications, i.e. where the reuse of source domain data is *limited to classification rules or a few representative examples*. As a solution to this problem, we adopt the recent techniques of *feature corruption* and their *marginalization*, both in the supervised Marginalized Corrupted Features [319] and the unsupervised Marginalized Denoising Autoencoder [77] frameworks. We propose several extensions to these methods in order to be able to address the adaptation needs without accessing the whole source data.

We cope with four typical cases of what is available from the source domain for adaptation, namely: (a) the classical case, when we can access the *full source dataset* (*FSD*); (b) the source classifiers case (*SCL*), where the (linear) classifiers trained on the source data are available; (c) the class mean case (*CM*), where class representatives (means) are available from the source and (d) the black box predictions case (*BBP*), when only class predictions for the target data can be obtained with the help of the source. In this case, the classifiers pre-trained on the source data can only be accessed as black boxes (e.g. through an API) to make predictions for the target inputs.

In the target domain, we may have access to both labeled and unlabeled instances, denoted by $\mathbf{X}_l^t$ and $\mathbf{X}_u^t$ accordingly. The labeled target set $\mathbf{X}_l^t$, when available, is rather small, as otherwise a conventional supervised learning routine can be applied. Depending on what is available from the target domain, we distinguish three domain adaptation scenarios: (a) the supervised scenario (**SUP**), when only $\mathbf{X}_l^t$ is available; (b) the unsupervised scenario (**US**), when only $\mathbf{X}_u^t$ is available and (c) the semi-supervised scenario (**SS**), when both $\mathbf{X}_l^t$ and $\mathbf{X}_u^t$ are available.

In what follows, we address all these scenarios and discuss four adaptation cases listed above. Each time we start with the case of full source access (*FSD*), and then discuss three cases of limited accessibility, *SCL*, *CM*, and *BBP*.

7.2 Supervised Domain Adaptation

In the supervised DA scenario, only a small labeled target set $\mathbf{X}_l^t$ is available and the adaptation task assumes no access to unlabeled target data. To address this scenario, we consider and adapt the Marginalized Corrupted Features framework [319].

Marginalized Corrupted Features (MCF). To marginalize the corrupted features in the MCF, a corrupting distribution is first defined to transform observations $\mathbf{x}$ into corrupted versions $\tilde{\mathbf{x}}$. The corrupting distribution is assumed to factorize over all feature dimensions and, each individual distribution is assumed to be a member of the natural exponential family, $p(\tilde{\mathbf{x}}_n|\mathbf{x}_n) = \prod_{d=1}^{D} p(\tilde{x}_{nd}|x_{nd}; \theta_d)$, where $\mathbf{x}_n = [x_{n1}, \ldots, x_{nD}]$ and $\theta_d, d = 1, \ldots, D$ are a parameter of the corrupting distribution on dimension d. Some known examples of distribution P that factorizes over dimensions are the dropout [514], Gaussian, Laplace, and Poisson noise [319].

The direct approach to learn a classifier with corrupted features is to consider the training set, that in our case is $\mathcal{D}^t = \{(\mathbf{x}_n, y_n)\}, n = 1, \ldots, N, \mathbf{x}_n \in \mathbf{X}_l^t, y_n \in \mathcal{Y}$, where $\mathcal{Y}$ is the set of C class labels. Then each dimension of any instance $\mathbf{x}_n$ is randomly corrupted and the process is repeated M times. This extended data set denoted by $\tilde{\mathcal{D}}^t$ can be used for training the model by minimizing the following empirical risk

$$\mathcal{L}(\tilde{\mathcal{D}}^t; \boldsymbol{\Omega}) = \sum_{n=1}^{N} \frac{1}{M} \sum_{m=1}^{M} \mathcal{L}(\tilde{\mathbf{x}}_{nm}, y_n; \boldsymbol{\Omega}), \tag{7.1}$$

where $\tilde{\mathbf{x}}_{nm} \sim p(\tilde{\mathbf{x}}_{nm}|\mathbf{x}_n)$ denotes the m-th corrupted observation of $\mathbf{x}_n$ and $\boldsymbol{\Omega}$ is the set of model parameters.

As explicit corruption comes at a high computational cost, Maaten et al. in [319] proposed to *marginalize out* the noise by considering the limiting case when $M \to \infty$. In this case, they show that the weak law of large numbers can be applied to rewrite Eq. (7.1) as its expectation. Using quadratic, exponential, logistic [319] or hinge loss [78], such model can be trained efficiently by marginalizing out the noise and generalizes better than the model trained only on the uncorrupted data.

In this chapter, we focus on the model obtained with the quadratic loss. It yields reasonably good performance on most datasets [319], and in addition allows a closed form solution.[1] The expected value of the quadratic loss under corrupting distribution $p(\tilde{\mathbf{x}}|\mathbf{x})$ is given by

$$\begin{aligned}\mathcal{L}(\mathcal{D}^t; \boldsymbol{\Omega}) &= \sum_n \mathbb{E}[\|\mathbf{y}_n - \tilde{\mathbf{x}}_n \boldsymbol{\Omega}\|^2] \qquad (7.2)\\ &= \sum_n Tr\left(\mathbb{E}[\mathbf{y}_n^\top \mathbf{y}_n] - \boldsymbol{\Omega}^\top \mathbb{E}[\tilde{\mathbf{x}}_n]^\top \mathbf{y}_n - \mathbf{y}_n^\top \mathbb{E}[\tilde{\mathbf{x}}_n]\boldsymbol{\Omega} + \boldsymbol{\Omega}^\top \mathbb{E}[\tilde{\mathbf{x}}_n^\top \tilde{\mathbf{x}}_n]\boldsymbol{\Omega}\right),\end{aligned}$$

[1] The minimization with the exponential loss requires a gradient descent technique, the logistic and hinge losses can be approximated by the upper bounds.

where $\mathbf{y}_n$ is a label vector of size $1 \times C$, with the component c corresponding to the class label y_n of $\mathbf{x}_n$ set to 1, and all others set to 0; $\boldsymbol{\Omega}$ is a $D \times C$ parameter matrix where the column c can be seen as a linear classifier corresponding to the class c, and $Tr(\cdot)$ denotes the matrix trace.

As the quadratic loss is convex under any corruption model, the optimal solution for $\boldsymbol{\Omega}^*$ can be given in a closed form [319] even when we add a regularization term $\lambda\|\boldsymbol{\Omega}\|^2$ to Eq. (7.2)

$$\boldsymbol{\Omega}^* = \left(\sum_{n=1}^{N} \mathbb{E}[\tilde{\mathbf{x}}_n^\top \tilde{\mathbf{x}}_n] + \lambda \mathbf{I}_d\right)^{-1} \left(\sum_{n=1}^{N} \mathbb{E}[\tilde{\mathbf{x}}_n]^\top \mathbf{y}_n\right). \quad (7.3)$$

As a corruption model, we consider the *biased dropout noise*,[2] with the noise level p; it means that the probability to set the feature to 0 is $p(\tilde{x}_{nd} = 0) = p$ and the probability to keep it unchanged is and $p(\tilde{x}_{nd} = x_{nd}) = 1 - p$. The expected value of $\tilde{x}_{nd}$ is $\mathbb{E}[\tilde{x}_{nd}] = (1-p)x_{nd}$ and its variance $Var[\tilde{x}_{nd}] = p(1-p)x_{nd}^2$. As the corruption distribution factorizes over all dimensions, we have $Cov(\tilde{x}_{nd}, \tilde{x}_{nd'}) = 0$ and hence $\boldsymbol{\Omega}^*$ in Eq. (7.3) depends on the original features and p only

$$\mathbb{E}[\tilde{\mathbf{x}}_n] = \mathbf{x}_n \quad \text{and} \quad \mathbb{E}[\tilde{\mathbf{x}}_n^\top \tilde{\mathbf{x}}_n] = (1-p)^2(\mathbf{x}_n^\top \mathbf{x}_n) + p(1-p)diag(\mathbf{x}_n^\top \mathbf{x}_n), \quad (7.4)$$

where $diag(\mathbf{M})$ denotes a diagonal matrix where all nondiagonal elements are set to zero. If we denote the $N \times D$ matrix formed with the elements of $\mathbf{x}_n$ by $\mathbf{X}$, the $N \times C$ matrix formed with the elements of $\mathbf{y}_n$ by $\mathbf{Y}$, and the covariance matrix $\mathbf{X}^\top\mathbf{X}$ by $\mathbf{S}$, then we can rewrite Eq. (7.3) as $\boldsymbol{\Omega}^* = (\mathbf{Q} + \lambda \mathbf{I}_D)^{-1}\mathbf{R}$, where

$$\mathbf{Q} = (1-p)^2\mathbf{S} + p(1-p)diag(\mathbf{S}) \quad \text{and} \quad \mathbf{R} = (1-p)\mathbf{X}^\top\mathbf{Y}. \quad (7.5)$$

MCF Applied to Domain Adaptation. To integrate in this framework the *FSD* case when all source instances are available, it is sufficient to consider both the labeled source $\mathbf{X}^s$, $\mathbf{Y}^s$ and target $\mathbf{X}_l^t$, $\mathbf{Y}_l^t$ instances forming the data matrix $\mathbf{X}$ and the label matrix $\mathbf{Y}$. Similarly, in the *CM* case when the source class means or representatives are only available, we can form $\mathbf{X}$ and $\mathbf{Y}$ as the union of the labeled target set with the available source class means or representatives and apply directly the framework. When the source classifiers (*SCL case*) or black box classifier outputs (*BBP case*) are available, we propose to adapt the framework as follows.

7.2.1 Integrating Source Classifiers in the MCF

In this section, we assume that a set of source classifiers $f_s \in \mathcal{F}$ is trained on source domains $\mathcal{S}_s$, and they can be exploited when learning a classifier for a target set $\mathcal{T}$,

[2]The framework can be easily generalized to Gaussian, Laplace and Poisson noise [319].

Algorithm 5: Marginalized Corrupted Features and Source Classifiers.

Input: Labeled target dataset $\mathbf{X}_l^t \in \mathbb{R}^{N_l \times D}$ with labels $\mathbf{Y}^t$.
Input: Unlabeled target dataset $\mathbf{X}_u^t \in \mathbb{R}^{N_u \times D}$.
Input: Source classifiers $f_s \in \mathbb{R}^D \to \mathbb{R}^C$.
Input: Dropout noise level p and parameter λ.
1: Generate the source outputs $\mathbf{f}(\mathbf{x}_n^t)$ for labeled $\mathbf{x}_n^t \in \mathbf{X}_l^t$.
2: **If** f_s are known linear functions represented by **A**, **then**
3: Estimate $\boldsymbol{\Omega}_{\mathcal{F}}^* = (\mathbf{Q}_{\mathcal{F}} + \lambda \mathbf{I}_{D+SC})^{-1}\mathbf{R}_{\mathcal{F}}$ with Eq. (7.8).
4: **Else**
5: Build $\mathbf{X}_{\mathcal{F}}$ with the augmented features $\mathbf{v}_n^t = [\mathbf{x}_n^t; \mathbf{f}(\mathbf{x}_n^t)]$.
6: Estimate $\boldsymbol{\Omega}_{\mathcal{F}}^* = (\mathbf{Q}_{\mathcal{F}} + \lambda \mathbf{I}_{D+SC})^{-1}\mathbf{R}_{\mathcal{F}}$ using Eq. (7.5) with $\mathbf{X}_{\mathcal{F}}$ and $\mathbf{S}_{\mathcal{F}}$.
7: Generate source classifier outputs $\mathbf{f}(\mathbf{x}_u^t)$ for unlabeled $\mathbf{x}_u^t \in X_u^t$.
8: Estimate class predictions as $\mathbf{y}^t = [\mathbf{x}_u^t, \mathbf{f}(\mathbf{x}_u^t)]\boldsymbol{\Omega}_{\mathcal{F}}^*$.
9: Label each $\mathbf{x}_u^t$ with $c^* = \arg\max_c \{y_c^t | \mathbf{y}^t\}$.
Output: Labels for $\mathbf{X}_u^t$.

instead of unavailable source data instances. To address this domain adaptation case, we adapt MCF [319] by extending the features $\mathbf{x}_n$ with the outputs of the source classifiers $f_s(\mathbf{x}_n)$. This yields the augmented representation $\mathbf{v}_n = [\mathbf{x}_n, \mathbf{f}(\mathbf{x}_n)]$, where $\mathbf{f}(\mathbf{x}_n) = [f_1(\mathbf{x}_n), \ldots, f_S(\mathbf{x}_n)]$. The empirical loss $\mathcal{L}(\tilde{\mathbf{v}}_{nm}, y_n, \mathcal{F}; \boldsymbol{\Omega}, \boldsymbol{\Gamma})$ to minimize becomes

$$\mathcal{L}(\mathcal{D}^t, \mathcal{F}; \boldsymbol{\Omega}_{\mathcal{F}}) = \sum_{n=1}^{N} \frac{1}{M} \sum_{m=1}^{M} [\mathcal{L}(\tilde{\mathbf{v}}_{nm}, y_{nm}, \mathcal{F}; \boldsymbol{\Omega}_{\mathcal{F}})], \tag{7.6}$$

where the corrupting distribution $p(\tilde{\mathbf{x}}_n|\mathbf{x}_n)$ factorizes over the d dimensions of $\mathbf{x}_n$. The explicit corruption comes at a high computational cost, as the minimization of Eq. (7.6) scales up linearly with the number of corrupted observations and we have to compute $f_s(\tilde{\mathbf{x}}_{nm})$ for each function f_s explicitly. Therefore, we consider again the expected quadratic loss

$$\mathcal{L}(\mathcal{D}^t, \mathcal{F}; \boldsymbol{\Omega}_{\mathcal{F}}) = \sum_{n=1}^{N} \mathbb{E}\left[\|\mathbf{y}_n^\top - \tilde{\mathbf{v}}_n \boldsymbol{\Omega}_{\mathcal{F}}\|^2\right], \tag{7.7}$$

whose closed form solution is $\boldsymbol{\Omega}_{\mathcal{F}}^* = (\mathbf{Q}_{\mathcal{F}} + \lambda \mathbf{I}_{D+SC})^{-1}\mathbf{R}_{\mathcal{F}}$, where

$$\mathbf{Q}_{\mathcal{F}} = \sum_n \begin{bmatrix} \mathbb{E}[\tilde{\mathbf{x}}_n^\top \tilde{\mathbf{x}}_n] & \mathbb{E}[\tilde{\mathbf{x}}_n^\top \mathbf{f}(\tilde{\mathbf{x}}_n)] \\ \mathbb{E}[\mathbf{f}(\tilde{\mathbf{x}}_n)^\top \tilde{\mathbf{x}}_n] & \mathbb{E}[\mathbf{f}(\tilde{\mathbf{x}}_n)^\top \mathbf{f}(\tilde{\mathbf{x}}_n)] \end{bmatrix} \quad \text{and} \quad \mathbf{R}_{\mathcal{F}} = \sum_n \begin{bmatrix} \mathbb{E}[\tilde{\mathbf{x}}_n]^\top \\ \mathbb{E}[\mathbf{f}(\tilde{\mathbf{x}}_n)]^\top \end{bmatrix} \mathbf{y}_n.$$

This extended version of the MCF is called *Marginalized Corrupted Features and Source Classifiers* (see also [85]) and denoted by MCFSC.

As described in the previous section, the corruption in MCF factorizes over all dimensions, this yields covariance matrix $Cov(\tilde{x}_{nd}, \tilde{x}_{nd'}) = 0$ and results in Eq. (7.4). When $\mathbf{x}_{nd}$ is corrupted, the corruption of $f_s(\mathbf{x}_n)$ is dependent on the corruption of $\mathbf{x}_{nd}$ and the covariance matrix cannot be reduced to the diagonal matrix of individual variances. This makes the computation of the expectations more complex, especially if the functions in $\mathcal{F}$ are also complex. Here we consider two particular cases, represented in Algorithm 5. First, we assume that $\mathbf{f}(\mathbf{x}_n)$ is a linear classifier, $\mathbf{f}(\mathbf{x}_n) = \mathbf{x}_n\mathbf{A}$. Second, instead of corrupting $\mathbf{x}_n$ and computing $\mathbf{f}(\tilde{\mathbf{x}}_n)$, we consider the elements of $\mathbf{v}_n$ as "independent" features, and the corruption can be factorized over all $D + SC$ dimensions of $\mathbf{v}_n$. In such a case, we need only the outputs of f_s on the target instances $\mathbf{x}_n$, hence it can be applied when the classifiers are available as black boxes (*BBP case*).

Linear Source Classifiers. If $\mathbf{f}(\mathbf{x}_n) = \mathbf{x}_n\mathbf{A}$ is linear, we have $\mathbb{E}[\mathbf{f}(\tilde{\mathbf{x}}_n)] = \mathbb{E}[\tilde{\mathbf{x}}_n]\mathbf{A}$, and the terms in $\mathbf{Q}_{\mathcal{F}}$ becomes

$$\begin{bmatrix} \mathbb{E}[\tilde{\mathbf{x}}_n^\top \tilde{\mathbf{x}}_n] & \mathbb{E}[\tilde{\mathbf{x}}_n^\top \tilde{\mathbf{x}}_n]\mathbf{A} \\ \mathbf{A}^\top \mathbb{E}[\tilde{\mathbf{x}}_n^\top \tilde{\mathbf{x}}_n] & \mathbf{A}^\top \mathbb{E}[\tilde{\mathbf{x}}_n^\top \tilde{\mathbf{x}}_n]\mathbf{A} \end{bmatrix} = \begin{bmatrix} \mathbf{I}_D \\ \mathbf{A}^\top \end{bmatrix} \mathbb{E}[\tilde{\mathbf{x}}_n \tilde{\mathbf{x}}_n^\top]\, [\mathbf{I}_D,\ \mathbf{A}]$$

and by denoting $[\mathbf{I}_D,\ \mathbf{A}]$ by $\mathbf{B}$, we can easily derive that

$$\mathbf{Q}_{\mathcal{F}} = \sum_n \mathbf{B}^\top \mathbb{E}[\tilde{\mathbf{x}}_n \tilde{\mathbf{x}}_n^\top]\mathbf{B} = \mathbf{B}^\top \mathbf{Q}\mathbf{B}, \quad \text{and} \quad \mathbf{R}_{\mathcal{F}} = \mathbf{B}^\top \mathbf{R}, \tag{7.8}$$

where $\mathbf{Q}$ and $\mathbf{R}$ are defined in Eq. (7.5).

Classifiers as a Black Box. If the classifier parameters are unknown (*BBP case*) or they are complex nonlinear functions, it is hard to directly estimate their expectation and variance, but we can consider directly the outputs generated by the source classifiers for the target instances. In these cases, we consider $\mathbf{v}_n$ as a feature vector with the dropout corruption factorized over all $D + SC$ dimensions. Hence we have $p(\tilde{\mathbf{v}}|\mathbf{v}) = \prod_{d=1}^{D+SC} p(\tilde{v}_d|v_d)$, and can compute $\boldsymbol{\Omega}_{\mathcal{F}}$ using Eq. (7.5), with $\mathbf{X}_{\mathcal{F}}$ and $\mathbf{S}_{\mathcal{F}}$ formed with the augmented features $\mathbf{v}_n$.

7.3 Unsupervised and Semi-supervised Domain Adaptation

The supervised domain adaptation presented in the previous section has two main drawbacks. First, it requires target labeled instances which are not always easy to obtain, and second, it does not exploit the unlabeled target instances $\mathbf{X}_u^t$, which are often easier to obtain than $\mathbf{X}_l^t$. In this section, we address the unsupervised DA scenario where we have $\mathbf{X}_u^t$ but $\mathbf{X}_l^t$ is empty, and the semi-supervised scenario where we have both. In both scenarios, we extend the Marginalized Denoising Autoencoder [77] to address DA task under the limited access to the source data.

Marginalized Denoising Autoencoder (MDA). The MDA loss can be written as

$$\mathcal{L}(\mathbf{W}, \mathbf{X}) = \frac{1}{M} \sum_{m=1}^{M} \|\mathbf{X} - \tilde{\mathbf{x}}_m \mathbf{W}\|^2 + \omega \|\mathbf{W}\|^2, \tag{7.9}$$

Algorithm 6: Marginalized Denoising Autoencoder with Source Classifiers.

Input: Target dataset $\mathbf{X}_u^t \in \mathbb{R}^{N\times D}$ without labels.
Input: Source classifiers $f_s \in \mathbb{R}^D \rightarrow \mathbb{R}^C$.
Input: Dropout noise level p, the number of stacked layer k and ω.
1: Generate class predictions $\mathbf{f}(\mathbf{x}_n^t)$ for all $\mathbf{x}_n^t \in \mathbf{X}_u^t$.
2: Compose augmented features $\mathbf{v}_n^t = [\mathbf{x}_n^t; \mathbf{f}(\mathbf{x}_n^t)]$ to compose $\mathbf{X}_{\mathcal{F}}^t$.
3: Estimate $\mathbf{W}_{\mathcal{F}}^1 = (\mathbf{Q}_{\mathcal{F}} + \omega\mathbf{I}_{D+SC})^{-1}\mathbf{P}_{\mathcal{F}}$, where $\mathbf{P}_{\mathcal{F}} = (1-p)\mathbf{S}_{\mathcal{F}}$ and $\mathbf{Q}_{\mathcal{F}} = (1-p)^2\mathbf{S}_{\mathcal{F}} + p(1-p)diag(\mathbf{S}_{\mathcal{F}})$.
4: (Optionally), stack K layers with $\hat{\mathbf{h}}_n^k = \tanh(\mathbf{h}_n^{k-1}\mathbf{W}_{\mathcal{F}}^k)$, $\mathbf{h}_n^0 = \mathbf{v}_n^t$.
5: Denote the elements of the final "reconstructed" augmented features by $\nu_1^{tn} \ldots, \nu_{D+SC}^{tn}$.
6: Label $\mathbf{x}_n^t$ with $c^* = \arg\max_c \sum_{s=1}^S \nu_{D+c+(s-1)C}^{tn}$.
Output: Labels for $\mathbf{X}_u^t$.

where $\tilde{\mathbf{x}}_m \in \mathbb{R}^N \times \mathbb{R}^d$ is the m-th corrupted version of $\mathbf{X}$ by random feature dropout with a probability p and $\omega\|\mathbf{W}\|^2$ is a regularization term. In order to avoid the explicit feature corruption and an iterative optimization, Chen et al. [77] showed that considering the limiting case $M \rightarrow \infty$, the weak law of large numbers allows rewriting $\mathcal{L}(\mathbf{W}, \mathbf{X})$ as its expectation, and the optimal $\mathbf{W}^*$ can be written as the closed form solution $\mathbf{W}^* = (\mathbf{Q} + \omega\mathbf{I}_D)^{-1}\mathbf{P}$. The matrices $\mathbf{Q}$ given in Eq. (7.5) and $\mathbf{P} = (1-p)\mathbf{S}$ depend only on $\mathbf{S} = \mathbf{X}^\top\mathbf{X}$ and p.

This closed form solution allows stacking together several MDA layers which are computed only in one forward pass. They create a *deep architecture* where the representations of the $(k-1)^{th}$ denoising layer are fed as input to the kth layer yielding the transformation $\mathbf{W}^k$ to reconstruct the previous layer from its corrupted equivalent. Optionally, to extend the mapping beyond a linear transformation, nonlinear functions, like the hyperbolic tangent $\mathbf{h}_k = \mathtt{tanh}(\mathbf{h}_{k-1}\mathbf{W}^k)$ or rectified linear units $\mathbf{h}_k = max(\mathbf{h}_{k-1}\mathbf{W}^k, 0)$ can be added between the layers. The final output $\mathbf{h}_k$ corresponding to the input $\mathbf{x}_n$ will be denoted by $\hat{\mathbf{x}}_n$. In the literature [77, 183], the final classifier is often learned on a feature vector concatenating the original features with the output of all layers.

MDA Applied to Domain Adaptation. The main advantage of the MDA is that it does not require any label; hence we can take advantage of the unlabeled target data and apply the MDA for unsupervised domain adaptation [77]. The main idea is to consider the union of the source and target instances (*FSD case*) to form the input matrix $\mathbf{X} = [\mathbf{X}^s, \mathbf{X}_u^t]$ and let the MDA to exploit the correlation between the source and the target features and to learn a common denoising representation. In this case, the reconstructed features aim to describe what is common between the source and the target sets.

As the source data is unavailable in our case, $\mathbf{X}^s = \emptyset$, we only have an access to the source classifiers $\mathcal{F}$ (*SCL case*), to their outputs (*BBP case*) or to a set of class representatives for each domain X_s (*CM case*). In the first case, we can build, similarly to the MCFSC, a Marginalized Denoising Autoencoder with Source Classifiers (MDASC) by applying the MDA to the concatenated features $\mathbf{v}_n = [\mathbf{x}_n, \mathbf{f}(\mathbf{x}_n)]$. As in the case of MCFSC, we can compute the denoising matrix in closed form, $\mathbf{W}^*_{\mathcal{F}} = (\mathbf{Q}_{\mathcal{F}} + \omega\mathbf{I}_{D+SC})^{-1}\mathbf{P}_{\mathcal{F}}$, where if functions in $\mathcal{F}$ are linear, we have $\mathbf{Q}_{\mathcal{F}} = \mathbf{B}^\top\mathbf{Q}\mathbf{B}$ and $\mathbf{P}_{\mathcal{F}} = \mathbf{B}^\top\mathbf{P}$; otherwise, we apply the dropout corruption independently over all $D + SC$ dimensions of $\mathbf{v}_n$, and compute $\mathbf{W}^*_{\mathcal{F}} = (\mathbf{Q}_{\mathcal{F}} + \omega\mathbf{I}_{D+SC})^{-1}\mathbf{P}_{\mathcal{F}}$, where $\mathbf{Q}_{\mathcal{F}}$ and $\mathbf{P}_{\mathcal{F}}$ depend on $\mathbf{S}_{\mathcal{F}} = \mathbf{X}_{\mathcal{F}}^\top\mathbf{X}_{\mathcal{F}}$ and p. We summarize this MDASC framework, called Transductive Domain Adaptation in [85, 94], in Algorithm 6.

Similarly to the MDA, we can stack several MDASC layers with nonlinearities applied between the layers. Let us denote the output of the final layer by $^{\circ tn} = [\nu_1^{tn}, \ldots, \nu_{D+SC}^{tn}]$. In order to learn a classifier using these features we need labeled examples. In the semi-supervised scenario (**SS**), we can indeed train a classifier using either the "reconstructed" augmented features $^{\circ tn}$ or considering only their first d dimensions corresponding to the original features $\mathbf{x}_n^t \in \mathbf{X}_l^t$, where nevertheless the source classifier scores contributed to the computations of the reconstruction matrices $\mathbf{W}_{\mathcal{F}}^K$.

In the unsupervised adaptation scenario (**US**), where neither labeled source instances nor labeled target instances are available, instead of learning a new classifier in the new space, we can directly use the latter to assign class labels to the target. Indeed, we claim that the system, exploiting the correlation between the target data $\mathbf{X}^t$ and source predictions $\mathbf{f}(\mathbf{x}_n^t)$, "denoises" both the target data and the class predictions. The latter values, $\nu_{D+1}^{tn}, \ldots, \nu_{D+SC}^{tn}$, can be used to assign the class label to the target $\mathbf{x}_n^t$ by $c^* = \arg\max_c \sum_{s=1}^{S} \nu_{D+c+(s-1)C}^{tn}$.

7.3.1 Adaptation with Class Means

In the previous section, we used the source classifier predictions to augment the features; the reconstructed scores were then used to assign labels to target instances. In the *CM case*, where class means from the source domains are only available, first we can use the class means with the Domain-Specific Class Means (DSCM) framework [107] to obtain softmax class predictions for the target instances and feed them into the MDASC framework.

When class means are available, they can be used either as classifiers or as data instances. Therefore here we discuss an alternative solution where we apply the MDA framework to the target instances and source class means and then apply the DSCM to the denoised data.

Used as classifiers, the class means can directly predict labels with a weighted softmax distance [107]. Indeed, the DSCM [107] classifier considers the class means for each domain

$$\boldsymbol{\mu}_c^d = \frac{1}{N_d^c} \sum_{\mathbf{x}_i^d \in \mathcal{D}_d, y_i^d = c} \mathbf{x}_i^d, \tag{7.10}$$

Algorithm 7: Adapting Domain Specific Class Means.

Input: A large set of unlabeled target dataset $\mathbf{X}_u^t$ and optionally a small set of labeled $\mathbf{X}_l^t$
Input: A set of source class means $\mu_1^{s_1}, \ldots \mu_C^{s_1}, \mu_1^{s_2}, \ldots \mu_C^{S}$
Input: Dropout noise level p and the number of stacked layer k.
1: Compute $\mathbf{W}^* = (\mathbf{Q} + \omega \mathbf{I}_D)^{-1}\mathbf{P}$ with $\mathbf{X} = [\mu_1^{s_1}, \ldots \mu_C^{S}, \mathbf{x}_1^t, \ldots, \mathbf{x}_N^t]$ and the noise level p.
2: (Optionally) repeat k times, while alternating with $\mathbf{h}_k = \texttt{tanh}(\mathbf{h}_{k-1}\mathbf{W}^k)$.
3: Decompose $\mathbf{h}_k$ into reconstructed class means $\hat{\mu}_c^s$ and reconstructed targets $\hat{\mathbf{x}}_n^t$.
4: (Optionally) concatenate $\hat{\mathbf{x}}_n^t$ with the original features $\mathbf{x}_n^t$, and $\hat{\mu}_c^s$ with μ_c^s)
5: (Optionally) if $\mathbf{X}_l^t \neq \emptyset$, compute target class means $\hat{\mu}_c^t$ from $\{\hat{\mathbf{x}}_n^t | \mathbf{x}_n^t \in \mathbf{X}_l^t$.
6: $p(c|\mathbf{x}_n^t) = \dfrac{\sum_d w_d e^{(-\|\hat{\mathbf{x}}_n^t - \hat{\mu}_c^d\|)}}{\sum_{c'}\sum_d w_d \left(e^{(-\|\hat{\mathbf{x}}_n^t - \hat{\mu}_{c'}^d\|)}\right)}$ where $d \in \{s_1, \ldots S, t\}$ if $\mathbf{X}_l^t \neq \emptyset$ and $d \in \{s_1, \ldots S\}$ otherwise.
7: Label $\mathbf{x}_n^t$ with $c^* = \arg\max_c p(c|\mathbf{x}_n^t)$
Output: Labels for X_u^t.

where N_d^c is the number of instances of class c in domain $\mathcal{D}_d$. To predict the class label for an unlabeled target instance, a weighted softmax distance to these domain-specific class means is used, as follows:

$$p(c|\mathbf{x}_i) = \frac{\sum_d w_d e^{(-\|\mathbf{x}_i - \boldsymbol{\mu}_c^d\|)}}{\sum_{c'}\sum_d w_d e^{(-\|\mathbf{x}_i - \boldsymbol{\mu}_{c'}^d\|)}}, \tag{7.11}$$

where w_d is the domain weight. In the unsupervised scenario, the DSCM makes predictions only with the source class means μ_c^s. If labeled target instances are also available (the **SS** scenario), the classifier can additionally consider the target domain with the corresponding class means μ_c^t. Note that when we have one source domain only, this corresponds to the Nearest Class Mean (NCM) classifier.

Used as representatives of source data, the class means can be concatenated with the target data and fed to MDA for a joint denoising. The denoised class means can then used to classify the denoised target instances [105]. This approach called the Adapted Class Means (ACM) [105] classifier can be hence seen as an extension of the DSCM, where first, the MDA is used to jointly denoise the target instances and the source class means. To do this, the source class means $[\mu_1^{s_1}, \ldots, \mu_C^{S}]$ are considered as the source data $\mathbf{X}^s$ and concatenated with the unlabeled target data $\mathbf{X}_u^t$ to form the data matrix $\mathbf{X}$. By optimizing the expected loss of Eq. (7.9) on $\mathbf{X}$, the MDA can obtain the denoising transformation matrix $\mathbf{W}$ (or a set of stacked transformation matrices $\mathbf{W}^k$). The denoised source class means $\hat{\boldsymbol{\mu}}_c^s = \boldsymbol{\mu}_c^s\mathbf{W}$ can be used as the new classifiers in the DSCM framework Eq. (7.11) to predict labels for the denoised target instances $\hat{\mathbf{x}}_n^t = \mathbf{x}_n^t\mathbf{W}$. Algorithm 7 describes all steps of this approach.

7.4 Experimental Results

In this section, we evaluate the proposed frameworks in three domain adaptation scenarios: supervised (**SUP**), unsupervised (**US**), and semi-supervised (**SS**). In each scenario, we first evaluate the models in the ideal, full source dataset (*FSD*) case. We then evaluate the models in three limited access cases, i.e., with linear classifiers (*SCL*), with source class means only (*CM*) or with the source classifiers (black box) predictions (*BBP*). In our experiments we used five different datasets:

The Office 31 (OFF31) [200] and the Office+Caltech (OC10) [407] datasets are the most popular datasets used for comparing visual domain adaptation methods and are described in Chap. 3. In addition to the provided and widely used SURF-BOV features, we used the publicly available AlexNet [275], VGGNET (16 layers), CNN models [443], and the ResNet50 [230] models trained on ImageNet to build DeCAF [127] features. We experimented with the FC6 activation layer of the AlexNet[3] (AN-FC6) and the VGGNET (VG-FC6) and with the activation of the last feature layer (before the class prediction layer) of the ResNet50 (RNET).

The LandMark Domain Adaptation (LMDA) is a dataset[4] created to assess how DA techniques can cope with image modality changes between photos, paintings, and drawings (see a few examples in Fig. 7.1). The dataset contains 4606 images with around 1500 images for each modalities (Photos, Paintings, and Drawings) containing 25 different touristic landmark places (classes) such as The Eiffel Tower, Golden Gate, The Statue of Liberty, Taj Mahal, etc. As features extraction, we use again the activation features AN-FC6. In addition, we consider the Regional Maximum Activations of Convolutions (RMAC) model proposed in [480] where the information is extracted from image regions and aggregated to yield a compact global representation of images and the Region Proposal Network (RPN) model proposed in [208] that extends RMAC by integrating region proposals into the network and learning the model parameters with a Three-stream Siamese network using a triplet loss. The latter model was trained on a large landmark dataset proposed in [23] using ranking loss where given a query only images of the same landmark are considered relevant. Therefore, we think it is interesting to test these features (RMAC and RPN) on this dataset.

The Testbed Cross-Dataset (TB) dataset proposed in [486] and detailed in Chap. 2 contains images from 40 common classes of the Bing [36], Caltech256 [215], ImageNet [120], and SUN [541] dataset. In our experiments, we made experiments with the provided BOWsift and DeCAF7 features, denoted by SIFTBOV and AN-FC7 in our case.

The last collection called XC3 we experimented with is a part of the Xerox's Smart Document Management data. It contains printed/scanned documents from three Xerox customers considered as domains. Documents for each customer are grouped into 21 classes. These classes are related to different document types, such as invoices, contracts, IDs and filled forms (see examples in Fig. 7.2). Some classes

[3]It corresponds to the DeCAF6 used in the previous chapters and several papers.

[4]We will make the dataset with several set of features available soon.

Fig. 7.1 Examples from the LandMarkDA datasets. Each line corresponds to one image modality (domain) and each column refers to one Landmark (class)

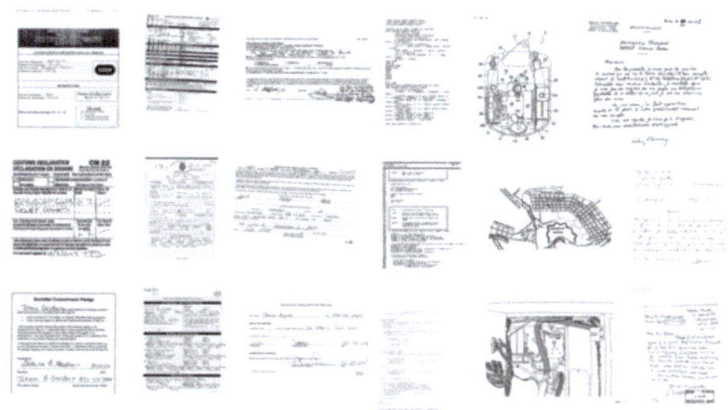

Fig. 7.2 Examples from the XC3 datasets. Each line corresponds to one domain and each column refers to one document class (documents are intentionally blurred for privacy reasons)

refer to generic concepts, such as printed emails, computer programs, drawings, handwritten letters; Other classes represent more fine-grained categories, such as different (*contract types* and *filled forms*). The number of documents per class and per domain varies from 24 to 859; in total, we have around 2.5 K documents per domain. These documents were represented by deep convolutional activation features [127] obtained using the AlexNet model [275] trained on the 1000 classes of ImageNet [404] and fine-tuned on the RVL-CDIP document image dataset [226]. We have seen in [109] that best features with reasonable size that performed well when transferred to new task were the fully connected activation layer corresponding to the AlexNet pool5 layer denoted by AN-P5 ($d = 9216$) and the Fisher Vector followed by PCA ($d = 4096$). Therefore we used these features in our experiments and added the AN-FC6 from the fine-tuned model as it is one of the most used layer in DA (see OC10 and OC31).

Experimental Setup. In each dataset, any domain can be considered as a *target*, with the other domains being considered as *sources*. All source-target configurations are taken into account, including multi-source ones; e.g. for OFF31 we define nine adaptation tasks: D→A, W→A, D,W→A, A→D, W→D, A,W→D, A→W, D→W, and A,D→W. When one domain is chosen as a target, we select randomly three instances per class to form the labeled target set, all other instances from the unlabeled target set. In most cases, results are averaged over all configurations for a dataset and shown for different feature types.

In all experiments, the source classifier is either the source class means or a linear ridge classifier; both are trained on the full source dataset. The source data is then discarded, and either the class means or the classifiers are used to evaluate a model on the target domain. The ridge classifier was selected for its simplicity, as a previous study [85] showed that the choice of source classifier has a little impact on the performance of the domain adaptation methods. In addition, the linear classifier is easy to integrate with the if branch of the Algorithm 5 denoted by **MCFSCa** in which follows.

When we evaluate the performance of the *FSD* case, we do cross-validation[5] on the source and the small target set if any. However, in the cases of limited access to the source data, and we have no or very few labeled target making the cross-validation impossible. Therefore, in all our experiments we decided to use a fixed parameter for the dropout noise level setting to $p = 0.5$ and for the regularization term of the MDA[6] setting to $\omega = 0.01$. The DSCM domain-specific weights are set to $w_s = 1$ for source domains and $w_t = 2$ for the target used in the **SS** scenario as suggested in [107]. We observed, that varying the regularizer term λ of the MCF and MCFSC classifiers has a more important effect and best values often depends on the feature type used. Therefore, we set this parameter to the norm of the target domain centroid which seemed a reasonable choice.

Finally, to make MDA comparable to MCF, we used only the output of a single layer with the tangent hyperbolic nonlinearity but without stacking or concatenating with the original features. This might explain why the improvement obtained with MDA over the baseline is in general weaker compared to the experiments shown in the literature where in general as in [77] the outputs of several layers are used and concatenated with the original features before any classifier is applied.

The Supervised Scenario (SUP). We begin with the supervised scenario, where we only have as input a few labeled target instances $\mathbf{X}_l^t$, without any access to the unlabeled target instances at training time. We evaluate the performance of both **MCFSCa** (if branch) and **MCFSCb** (else branch) of the Algorithm 5 and compare them to three baselines: (a) **MCFtt**, which consists in training MCF with the quadratic loss on the set of labeled target instances without using any knowledge from the source. It can be computed in closed form by Eq. (7.5), (b) **RDGsc** corresponds to the accuracy obtained from the source classifiers scores (directly or as output of an API) when applied to predict the class labels for the target test data[7]; and finally (c) **LateF** is a simple unweighted late fusion of the previous two cases, i.e. using score averaging of the source classifier **RDGsc** and the target classifier **MCFtt**.

---

[5]Note however, that the parameters obtained by cross-validation on the source are in general sub-optimal when applied to the target.

[6]It performs well in general with small impact when we vary it between 10e-3 and 10e-1.

[7] Note that this latter is obtained without using the labeled target set and hence will be used also as baseline in the **US** scenario.

Table 7.1 Supervised adaptation accuracies (averaged over all single and multi-source configurations) using three labeled target instances per class. Underline indicates improvement over both baselines and *red bold* indicates the best performance per task, except the ideal (*FSD*) case that is denoted by italic

Dataset	Feature	MCFtt	RDGsc	LateF	MCFSCa	MCFSCb	MCFfsd
OC10	SURFBOV	48.6	46.9	**53.0**	47.8	49.2	*51.6*
OC10	AN-FC6	84.5	67.8	83.6	**84.9**	**84.9**	*84.9*
OC10	VG-FC6	92.8	92.7	95.3	92.1	**95.4**	*94.7*
OFF31	SURFBOV	42.7	26.7	**44.3**	42.7	43.4	*34.1*
OFF31	AN-FC6	74.1	70.3	**81.6**	72.5	76.8	*77.5*
OFF31	VG-FC6	80.9	77.6	**85.5**	80.7	83.7	*82.8*
LMDA	AN-FC6	48.6	69.5	**72.1**	45.6	52.2	*73*
LMDA	RMAC	54.4	80.4	**83.8**	54.5	61.2	*84.5*
LMDA	RPN	86.8	91.6	**93.9**	84.4	89.2	*94.4*
XS3	AN-FC6	87.9	43.8	81.9	85.1	**89.0**	*80.6*
XS3	AN-P5	91.6	41.6	86.5	89.6	**93.1**	*76.3*
XS3	FV-PCA	91.8	47.3	83.7	91.2	**92.5**	*77.4*
TB	SIFTBOV	12.5	19.0	**20.4**	12.1	12.9	*20.2*
TB	AN-FC7	39.6	49.8	**52.5**	38.2	45.1	49.0

We also compare the results to "the ideal *FSD* case" where the union of the source set $\mathbf{X}^s$ and labeled target set $\mathbf{X}_l^t$ is used by the MCF classifier. This case will be denoted by **MCF**fsd and the results are shown in italic.

In Table 7.1, we show averaged results over all the tasks given a dataset and a feature type. From this table, we can deduce the following observations. If **MCFSCa** can yield improvements over both baselines, in average it performs poorly. Furthermore even if the parameters of the linear classifier are available, it seems more interesting to apply **MCFSCb** that exploit directly the scores instead, (considering them as independent features corrupted by MCF).

The **MCFSCb** brings always an improvement over the target baseline **MCFtt**, but when the latter performs significantly worse than the source baseline **RDGsc**, the performance of **MCFSCb** in average is below the performance of the **RDGsc** (see LMDA dataset). The reason is that even with the augmented representation, the small target dataset might remain too poor to allow learning the classes. In some cases, the performance of **MCFSCb** is close to the performance of the "ideal" **MCF**fsd and when **RDGsc** performs poorly on the target compared to **MCFtt**, it can even significantly outperform **MCF**fsd (see XS3 dataset).

Finally, surprisingly the best strategy seems to be **LateF**, except when **MCFtt** significantly outperforms **RDGsc**. In the latter case, MCFSC can still take advantage of these poor scores to improve over **MCFtt** in contrast to **LateF**, where averaging the **MCFtt** and **RDGsc** scores causes a significant performance drop (see XS3 dataset). Note that while **MCFSC** and **MCF**fsd with parameters validated on the test set can

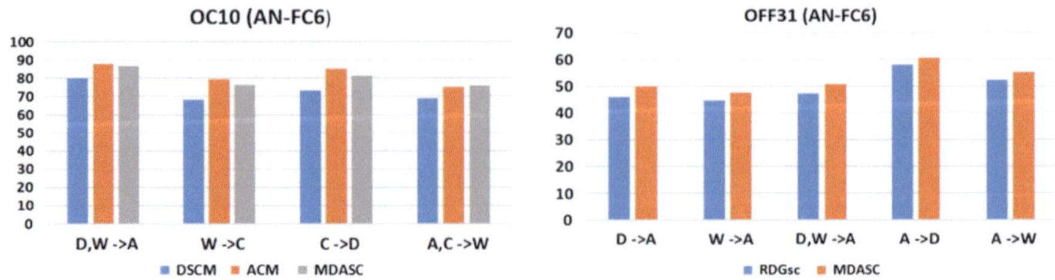

Fig. 7.3 Comparative plots for the unsupervised DA considering different source(s)-target configurations.

easily outperform **LateF** on the individual source-target configurations, it is difficult to "guess" these winning parameters without using the test set. The labeled target set is too small to allow cross-validation[8] and the results of **MCF** fsd in Table 7.1, often bellow the **LateF** results, suggest that cross-validation on the source is in general sub-optimal for the target set.

Unsupervised Setting. In this section, we compare the unsupervised **ACM** (Algorithm 6) used in the *CM case* and the **MDASC** (Algorithm 6) used in the *BBP case* with their corresponding baselines. Our experimental results are summarized in Table 7.2 and in Fig. 7.3, we show a few comparative plots for different source(s)-target configurations both from the OC10 and OFF31 datasets using the AN-FC6 features.

In order to have a comparison between these two methods, the class predictions are computed using the softmax distances of target samples to the source class means (NCM) and the classification scores can be integrated in the **MDASC** framework. Therefore, in Table 7.2 (left) we show the performance of both **ACM** and **MDASC**, where the source classifier is NCM. In the right part of the table, we show results of the **MDASC** using the RDG classifier outputs.

We will consider as baseline the results obtained directly from the source classifier scores, denoted by **NCMsc** and **RDGsc** respectively. Note that when have several sources, we simply average the predictions of the corresponding classifiers. In the *CM case*, instead we can also apply DSCM using Eq. (7.11) considering the class means from all sources. However, we observed no significant difference between the results off this two options. The average results in the average for **NCMsc** in the Table 7.2 were obtained with the former option (averaging NCM scores when multi-source configurations were considered), while in Fig. 7.3 (left) we show DSCM results for D,W$\rightarrow$A and A,C$\rightarrow$W.

As above, we also consider the "ideal *FSD* case," denoted by **MDA** fsd meaning here that we apply first a standard MDA to the union of sources and target data, then predict the target labels with the DSCM (at left) respectively the RDG (at right) classifier using the denoised data. These results are shown in italic in the Table 7.2.

[8]If we assume large labeled target set, there is no more need to use the source data.

Table 7.2 Unsupervised adaptation accuracies (averaged over all single and multi-source configurations). Underline indicates improvement over the corresponding baseline and *red bold* indicates the best performance per line not considering the *FSD cases* whose results are shown in italic

Source classifier		NCM (*CM* and *BBP* case)				RDG (*BBP* case)		
Dataset	Feature	NCMsc	ACM	MDASC	MDAfsd	RDGsc	MDASC	MDAfsd
OC10	SURFBOV	49.6	51.0	51.9	*50.4*	50.5	**52.2**	*50.6*
OC10	AN-FC6	83.2	**88.1**	87.2	*84.4*	86.8	**88.1**	*85.8*
OC10	VG-FC6	91.3	93.1	92.8	*91.7*	92.6	**93.2**	*91.7*
OFF31	SURFBOV	27.6	26.2	27.3	*26.4*	30.5	**31.5**	*29.1*
OFF31	AN-FC6	64.5	68.3	67.5	*64.7*	70.3	**72.4**	*68.3*
OFF31	VG-FC6	75.7	78.0	77.3	*76.4*	77.6	**79.1**	*75.9*
LMDA	AN-FC6	58.5	62.0	62.1	*58.2*	69.8	**71.2**	*70.8*
LMDA	RMAC	67.4	**83**	77.5	*69.8*	80.4	82.9	*82.4*
LMDA	RPN	84.6	90.2	89.4	*86.2*	91.9	**92.5**	*93.4*
XS3	AN-FC6	40.0	**49.1**	43.8	*42.5*	44.6	46.4	*45.9*
XS3	AN-P5	36.7	**44.9**	41.9	*38.8*	41.6	43.2	*41.7*
XS3	FV-PCA	35.1	**52.2**	44.3	*38.4*	47.4	49.1	*47.8*
TB	SIFTBOV	16.9	15.9	16.1	*15.7*	19.0	**19.3**	*20.5*
TB	AN-FC7	46.8	47.6	46.2	*46.7*	**49.8**	49.0	*50.8*

From this table we can deduce the following observations. Except a few cases both **ACM** and **MDASC** yield in general significant improvements over the corresponding baselines. Even more surprisingly, they often outperform the results obtained with the corresponding "ideal *FSD* case" (**MDA**fsd).

When we compute class means, **ACM** performs in general better than **MDASC** using the NCM scores, meaning that if a choice has to be made, exploiting directly the class representatives is more interesting than considering only the NCM scores. The main advantage of the **MDASC** however is that it works with any classifier and we rarely observe decreased performance compared to the corresponding baselines. We can also see that the better the performance of the original classifier is (see comparison between RDG versus NCM), the better the denoising **MDASC** results are.

Semi-supervised Setting. Finally, we consider the transductive semi-supervised setting, where we assume that in addition to the unlabeled target set $\mathbf{X}^{\mathbf{t}}_{\mathbf{u}}$, a small set of labeled target set $\mathbf{X}^{\mathbf{t}}_{\mathbf{l}}$ is available. When we consider the *CM case*, the semi-supervised version of ACM is compared to the DSCM baseline and **MDA**fsd corresponds as above to MDA applied to the union of all source and target data followed by the DSCM. These results are shown in Table 7.3 (left).

For the *BBP case*, shown in Table 7.3 (right). we consider as baseline the late fusion of the results **MCFtt** and **RDGsc** scores (already shown in Table 7.1) as it is in general better than both baselines. Using the **RDGsc** scores we apply **MDASC** to denoise both the target data and the scores as in the **US** scenario, but here we further combine these scores with the **MCFtt** scores. Alternatively, we also tested

Table 7.3 Semi-supervised adaptation accuracies (averaged over all single and multi-source configurations) using three labeled target instances per class. Underline indicates improvement over both baselines and *red bold* indicates the best performance per task, not considering the ideal (*FSD*), that is denoted by italic.

Source classifier		NCM (*CM*)			RDG (*BBP* case)			
Dataset	Feature	DSCM	ACM	MDA fsd	Late	MDASC	MCFSCc	MDA fsd
OC10	SURFBOV	57.6	59.3	*59.8*	**53.0**	56.3	53.3	*53.1*
OC10	AN-FC6	90.6	92.1	*91.1*	83.6	**92.3**	91.1	*91.7*
OC10	VG-FC6	95.3	95.6	*95.4*	95.3	95.3	**95.7**	*94.9*
OFF31	SURFBOV	**46.8**	46.3	*46.1*	44.3	45.7	44.5	*35.9*
OFF31	AN-FC6	76.6	**78.3**	*77.1*	**81.6**	81.1	77.5	*81.0*
OFF31	VG-FC6	83.8	84.3	*93.9*	**85.5**	**85.5**	84.2	*86.0*
LMDA	AN-FC6	56.5	57.5	*56.3*	72.1	**72.8**	53.2	*74.6*
LMDA	RMAC	66.3	75.9	*71.7*	83.8	**84.4**	61.9	*85.3*
LMDA	RPN	89.0	90.7	*89.7*	93.9	**94.3**	89.7	*95.2*
XS3	AN-FC6	86.9	**90.9**	*89.6*	81.9	82.4	90.2	*82.3*
XS3	AN-P5	90.1	**94.2**	*92.4*	86.5	85.9	93.2	*85.7*
XS3	FV-PCA	89.7	**94.4**	*92.6*	83.7	82.1	**93.8**	*85.8*
TB	SIFTBOV	17.5	19.1	*17.3*	20.4	**21.2**	11.9	*20.7*
TB	AN-FC7	49.6	50.5	*49.6*	**52.5**	51.6	43.2	*52.1*

the MCFSC (branch else) framework considering outputs denoised by **MDASC**. We denote the latter with **MCFSCc**. Here **MDA** fsd corresponds to the case when MDA is applied to the union of all source and target data followed by the RDG classifier learned with all the denoised source and denoised labeled target data.

From the Table 7.3 we can deduce the followings. Except a single case, the semi-supervised ACM outperforms the DSCM and in most cases even the corresponding **MDA** fsd using the whole source and target dataset. The reason might be that using all source examples brings more noise and hence makes more difficult to the MDA finding a denoised space where the source and the target is better correlated, while the means are less perturbed by the outliers.

Merging the target scores with the **MDASC** denoised **RDGsc** scores (column 5) in general outperforms the late fusion of **MCFtt** and **RDGsc** (column 4). Furthermore, the result is often above the corresponding **MDA** fsd obtained by training RDG on the union of the denoised source and target data (*FSD* case).

Finally, the strategy **MCFSCc** when we apply MCFSC to the denoised target data concatenated with the denoised scores seems to work well only for the OC10 and XS3 dataset (as in the **SUP** scenario). The reason might be again that the randomly selected small labeled target dataset even with the denoised features and concatenated scores is not sufficient to learn a good multi-class linear classifier.

7.5 Conclusion

In this paper, we addressed the problem of domain adaptation in real world applications, where the reuse of source data is limited, due to legal and contractual obligations, to classification rules or a few representative examples. We adapted recent techniques such as *feature corruption* and their *marginalization* developed for the supervised (MCF) and unsupervised (sMDA) settings. We proposed several extensions in order to address cases when the access to the source is limited to prediction scores or class representatives. We conducted a series of experiments on three public and two in-house datasets; for each dataset we extracted different types of features and evaluate the methods within supervised, unsupervised and semi-supervised scenarios. We observe that in the supervised case, the proposed methods outperform the source only or target only baselines, but a simple late fusion of these classification scores can achieve similarly good or sometimes even better performance. On the other hand, when no labeled target examples (unsupervised scenario) are available the method allows significant performance gains despite the absence of source data. Concerning the semi-supervised scenario, when we only have class representatives, ACM outperforms the baseline and most often even DSCM used after MDA applied to the whole source and target dataset. When only classifier scores are available, the best to be used is less obvious and varies between datasets.

Acknowledgements This work has been supported by Xerox Research Center Europe.

Part II
Deep Domain Adaptation Methods

Chapter 8
Correlation Alignment for Unsupervised Domain Adaptation

Baochen Sun, Jiashi Feng and Kate Saenko

Abstract In this chapter, we present CORrelation ALignment (CORAL), a simple yet effective method for unsupervised domain adaptation. CORAL minimizes domain shift by aligning the second-order statistics of source and target distributions, without requiring any target labels. In contrast to subspace manifold methods, it aligns the original feature distributions of the source and target domains, rather than the bases of lower-dimensional subspaces. It is also much simpler than other distribution matching methods. CORAL performs remarkably well in extensive evaluations on standard benchmark datasets. We first describe a solution that applies a linear transformation to source features to align them with target features before classifier training. For linear classifiers, we propose to equivalently apply CORAL to the classifier weights, leading to added efficiency when the number of classifiers is small but the number and dimensionality of target examples are very high. The resulting CORAL Linear Discriminant Analysis (CORAL-LDA) outperforms LDA by a large margin on standard domain adaptation benchmarks. Finally, we extend CORAL to learn a nonlinear transformation that aligns correlations of layer activations in deep neural networks (DNNs). The resulting Deep CORAL approach works seamlessly with DNNs and achieves state-of-the-art performance on standard benchmark datasets. Our code is available at: https://github.com/VisionLearningGroup/CORAL.

B. Sun (✉)
University of Massachusetts Lowell, Lowell, MA, USA
e-mail: bsun@cs.uml.edu; baochens@gmail.com

J. Feng
National University of Singapore, Singapore, Singapore
e-mail: elefjia@nus.edu.sg

K. Saenko
Boston University, Boston, MA, USA
e-mail: saenko@bu.edu

G. Csurka (ed.), *Domain Adaptation in Computer Vision Applications*,
Advances in Computer Vision and Pattern Recognition,
DOI 10.1007/978-3-319-58347-1_8

8.1 Introduction

Machine learning is very different from human learning. Humans are able to learn from very few labeled examples and apply the learned knowledge to new examples in novel conditions. In contrast, traditional machine learning algorithms assume that the training and test data are independent and identically distributed (*i.i.d.*) and supervised machine learning methods only perform well when the given extensive labeled data are from the same distribution as the test distribution. However, this assumption rarely holds in practice, as the data are likely to change over time and space. To compensate for the degradation in performance due to domain shift, *domain adaptation* [115, 164, 200, 313, 407, 465, 467, 499] tries to *transfer* knowledge from source (training) domain to target (test) domain. Our approach is in line with most existing unsupervised domain adaptation approaches in that we first transform the source data to be as close to the target data as possible. Then a classifier trained on the transformed source domain is applied to the target data.

In this chapter, we mainly focus on the unsupervised scenario as we believe that leveraging the unlabeled target data is key to the success of domain adaptation. In real world applications, unlabeled target data are often much more abundant and easier to obtain. On the other side, labeled examples are very limited and require human annotation. So the question of how to utilize the unlabeled target data is more important for practical visual domain adaptation. For example, it would be more convenient and applicable to have a pedestrian detector automatically adapt to the changing visual appearance of pedestrians rather than having a human annotator label every frame that has a different visual appearance.

Our goal is to propose a simple yet effective approach for domain adaptation that researchers with little knowledge of domain adaptation or machine learning could easily integrate into their application. In this chapter, we describe a "frustratingly easy" (to borrow a phrase from [115]) *unsupervised* domain adaptation method called CORrelation ALignment or CORAL [465] in short. CORAL aligns the input feature distributions of the source and target domains by minimizing the difference between their second-order statistics. The intuition is that we want to capture the structure of the domain using feature correlations. As an example, imagine a target domain of Western movies where most people wear hats; then the "head" feature may be positively correlated with the "hat" feature. Our goal is to transfer such correlations to the source domain by transforming the source features.

In Sect. 8.2, we describe a linear solution to CORAL, where the distributions are aligned by re-coloring whitened source features with the covariance of the target data distribution. This solution is simple yet efficient, as the only computations it needs are (1) computing covariance statistics in each domain and (2) applying the whitening and re-coloring linear transformation to the source features. Then, supervised learning proceeds as usual—training a classifier on the transformed source features.

For linear classifiers, we can equivalently apply the CORAL transformation to the classifier weights, leading to better efficiency when the number of classifiers is small but the number and dimensionality of the target examples are very high. We present the resulting CORAL—Linear Discriminant Analysis (CORAL-LDA) [467] in Sect. 8.3, and show that it outperforms standard Linear Discriminant Analysis (LDA) by a large margin on cross domain applications. We also extend CORAL to work seamlessly with deep neural networks by designing a layer that consists of a differentiable CORAL loss [468], detailed in Sect. 8.4. On the contrary to the linear CORAL, Deep CORAL learns a nonlinear transformation and also provides end-to-end adaptation. Section 8.5 describes extensive quantitative experiments on several benchmarks, and Sect. 8.6 concludes the chapter.

8.2 Linear Correlation Alignment

In this section, we present CORrelation ALignment (CORAL) for unsupervised domain adaptation and derive a linear solution. We first describe the formulation and derivation, followed by the main linear CORAL algorithm and its relationship to existing approaches. In this section and Sect. 8.3, we constrain the transformation to be linear. Section 8.4 extends CORAL to learn a nonlinear transformation that aligns correlations of layer activations in deep neural networks (Deep CORAL).

Formulation and Derivation. We describe our method by taking a multi-class classification problem as the running example. Suppose we are given source-domain training examples $\mathbf{D}_S = \{\mathbf{x}_i\}, \mathbf{x} \in \mathbb{R}^d$ with labels $L_S = \{y_i\}, y \in \{1, ..., L\}$, and target data $\mathbf{D}_T = \{\mathbf{u}_i\}, \mathbf{u} \in \mathbb{R}^d$. Here both $\mathbf{x}$ and $\mathbf{u}$ are the d-dimensional feature representations $\phi(I)$ of input I. Suppose μ_s, μ_t and $\mathbf{C}_S, \mathbf{C}_T$ are the feature vector means and covariance matrices. Assuming that all features are normalized to have zero mean and unit variance, $\mu_t = \mu_s = 0$ after the normalization step, while $\mathbf{C}_S \neq \mathbf{C}_T$.

To minimize the distance between the second-order statistics (covariance) of the source and target features, we apply a linear transformation A to the original source features and use the Frobenius norm as the matrix distance metric

$$\min_A \|\mathbf{C}_{\hat{S}} - \mathbf{C}_T\|_F^2 = \min_{\mathbf{A}} \|\mathbf{A}^\top \mathbf{C}_S \mathbf{A} - \mathbf{C}_T\|_F^2 \tag{8.1}$$

where $\mathbf{C}_{\hat{S}}$ is covariance of the transformed source features $\mathbf{D}_s\mathbf{A}$ and $\|\cdot\|_F^2$ denotes the squared matrix Frobenius norm.

If $\text{rank}(\mathbf{C}_S) \geq \text{rank}(\mathbf{C}_T)$, then an analytical solution can be obtained by choosing A such that $\mathbf{C}_{\hat{S}} = \mathbf{C}_T$. However, the data typically lie on a lower-dimensional manifold [164, 200, 224], and so the covariance matrices are likely to be low rank [225]. We derive a solution for this general case, using the following lemma.

Lemma 8.1 *Let* $\mathbf{Y}$ *be a real matrix of rank* r_Y *and* X *a real matrix of rank at most* r, *where* $r \leqslant r_Y$; *let* $\mathbf{Y} = \mathbf{U}_Y \boldsymbol{\Sigma}_Y \mathbf{V}_\mathbf{Y}$ *be the SVD of* $\mathbf{Y}$, *and* $\boldsymbol{\Sigma}_{Y[1:r]}, \mathbf{U}_{Y[1:r]}, \mathbf{V}_{Y[1:r]}$ *be the largest* r *singular values and the corresponding left and right singular vectors of* $\mathbf{Y}$, *respectively. Then,* $\mathbf{X}^* = \mathbf{U}_{Y[1:r]} \boldsymbol{\Sigma}_{Y[1:r]} \mathbf{V}_{Y[1:r]}^\top$ *is the optimal solution to the problem of* $\min_{\mathbf{X}} \|\mathbf{X} - \mathbf{Y}\|_F^2$. *[58]*

Theorem 8.1 *Let $\boldsymbol{\Sigma}^{+}$ be the Moore–Penrose pseudoinverse of $\boldsymbol{\Sigma}$, $r_{\mathbf{C}_S}$ and $r_{\mathbf{C}_T}$ denote the rank of $\mathbf{C}_S$ and $\mathbf{C}_T$, respectively. Then, $\mathbf{A}^* = \mathbf{U}_S \boldsymbol{\Sigma}_S^{+\frac{1}{2}} {\mathbf{U}_S}^\top \mathbf{U}_{T[1:r]} \boldsymbol{\Sigma}_{T[1:r]}^{\frac{1}{2}} {\mathbf{U}_{T[1:r]}}^\top$ is the optimal solution to the problem in Eq. (8.1) with $r = \min(r_{\mathbf{C}_S}, r_{\mathbf{C}_T})$.*

Proof Since $\mathbf{A}$ is a linear transformation, $\mathbf{A}^\top \mathbf{C}_S \mathbf{A}$ does not increase the rank of $\mathbf{C}_S$. Thus, $r_{\mathbf{C}_{\hat{S}}} \leqslant r_{\mathbf{C}_S}$. Since $\mathbf{C}_S$ and $\mathbf{C}_T$ are symmetric matrices, conducting SVD on $\mathbf{C}_S$ and $\mathbf{C}_T$ gives $\mathbf{C}_S = \mathbf{U}_S \boldsymbol{\Sigma}_S {\mathbf{U}_S}^\top$ and $\mathbf{C}_T = \mathbf{U}_T \boldsymbol{\Sigma}_T \mathbf{U}_T^\top$, respectively. We first find the optimal value of $\mathbf{C}_{\hat{S}}$ through considering the following two cases:

Case 8.1 $r_{\mathbf{C}_S} > r_{\mathbf{C}_T}$. The optimal solution is $\mathbf{C}_{\hat{S}} = \mathbf{C}_T$. Thus, $\mathbf{C}_{\hat{S}} = \mathbf{U}_T \boldsymbol{\Sigma}_T {\mathbf{U}_T}^\top = \mathbf{U}_{T[1:r]} \boldsymbol{\Sigma}_{T[1:r]} {\mathbf{U}_{T[1:r]}}^\top$ is the optimal solution to Eq. (8.1) where $r = r_{\mathbf{C}_T}$.

Case 8.2 $r_{\mathbf{C}_S} \leqslant r_{\mathbf{C}_T}$. Then, according to Lemma 8.1, $\mathbf{C}_{\hat{S}} = \mathbf{U}_{T[1:r]} \boldsymbol{\Sigma}_{T[1:r]} {\mathbf{U}_{T[1:r]}}^\top$ is the optimal solution to Eq. (8.1) where $r = r_{\mathbf{C}_S}$.

Combining the results in the above two cases yields that $\mathbf{C}_{\hat{S}} = \mathbf{U}_{T[1:r]} \boldsymbol{\Sigma}_{T[1:r]} {\mathbf{U}_{T[1:r]}}^\top$ is the optimal solution to Eq. (8.1) with $r = \min(r_{\mathbf{C}_S}, r_{\mathbf{C}_T})$. We then proceed to solve for $\mathbf{A}$ based on the above result. Letting $\mathbf{C}_{\hat{S}} = \mathbf{A}^\top \mathbf{C}_S \mathbf{A}$, we can write

$$\mathbf{A}^\top \mathbf{C}_S \mathbf{A} = \mathbf{U}_{T[1:r]} \boldsymbol{\Sigma}_{T[1:r]} {\mathbf{U}_{T[1:r]}}^\top .$$

Since $\mathbf{C}_S = \mathbf{U}_S \boldsymbol{\Sigma}_S {\mathbf{U}_S}^\top$, we have

$$\mathbf{A}^\top \mathbf{U}_S \boldsymbol{\Sigma}_S {\mathbf{U}_S}^\top \mathbf{A} = \mathbf{U}_{T[1:r]} \boldsymbol{\Sigma}_{T[1:r]} {\mathbf{U}_{T[1:r]}}^\top .$$

This gives

$$({\mathbf{U}_S}^\top \mathbf{A})^\top \boldsymbol{\Sigma}_S ({\mathbf{U}_S}^\top \mathbf{A}) = \mathbf{U}_{T[1:r]} \boldsymbol{\Sigma}_{T[1:r]} {\mathbf{U}_{T[1:r]}}^\top .$$

Let $\mathbf{E} = \boldsymbol{\Sigma}_S^{+\frac{1}{2}} {\mathbf{U}_S}^\top \mathbf{U}_{T[1:r]} \boldsymbol{\Sigma}_{T[1:r]}^{\frac{1}{2}} {\mathbf{U}_{T[1:r]}}^\top$, then the right hand side of the above equation can be re-written as $\mathbf{E}^\top \boldsymbol{\Sigma}_S \mathbf{E}$. This gives

$$({\mathbf{U}_S}^\top \mathbf{A})^\top \boldsymbol{\Sigma}_S ({\mathbf{U}_S}^\top \mathbf{A}) = \mathbf{E}^\top \boldsymbol{\Sigma}_S \mathbf{E} .$$

By setting ${\mathbf{U}_S}^\top \mathbf{A}$ to $\mathbf{E}$, we obtain the optimal solution of $\mathbf{A}$ as

$$\mathbf{A}^* = \mathbf{U}_S \mathbf{E} = (\mathbf{U}_S \boldsymbol{\Sigma}_S^{+\frac{1}{2}} {\mathbf{U}_S}^\top)(\mathbf{U}_{T[1:r]} \boldsymbol{\Sigma}_{T[1:r]}^{\frac{1}{2}} {\mathbf{U}_{T[1:r]}}^\top). \tag{8.2}$$

Correlation Alignment (CORAL). Figure 8.1a–c illustrate the linear CORAL approach. Figure 8.1a shows example original source and target data distributions. We can think of the transformation A intuitively as follows: the first part $\mathbf{U}_S \boldsymbol{\Sigma}_S^{+\frac{1}{2}} {\mathbf{U}_S}^\top$ whitens the source data, while the second part $\mathbf{U}_{T[1:r]} \boldsymbol{\Sigma}_{T[1:r]}^{\frac{1}{2}} {\mathbf{U}_{T[1:r]}}^\top$ re-colors it with the target covariance. This is illustrated in Fig. 8.1b and c, respectively.

In practice, for the sake of efficiency and stability, we can avoid the expensive SVD steps and perform traditional data whitening and coloring. Traditional whitening

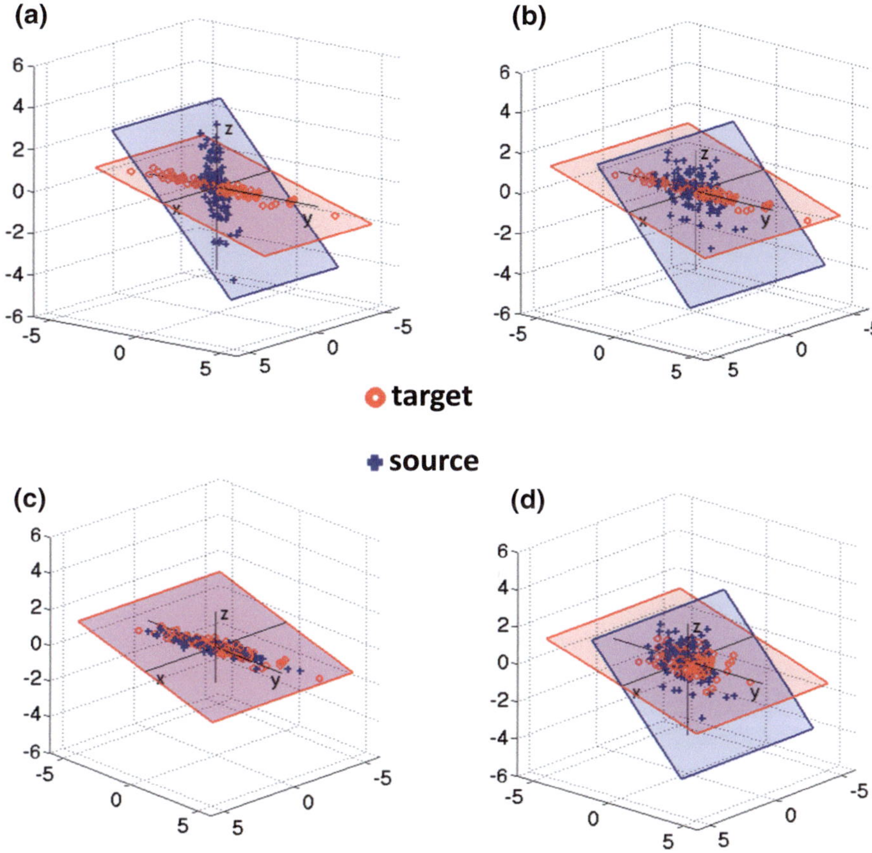

Fig. 8.1 **a–c** Illustration of CORrelation ALignment (CORAL) for Domain Adaptation: **a** The original source and target domains have different distribution covariances, despite the features being normalized to zero mean and unit standard deviation. This presents a problem for transferring classifiers trained on source to target. **b** The same two domains after source decorrelation,i.e., removing the feature correlations of the source domain. **c** Target re-correlation, adding the correlation of the target domain to the source features. After this step, the source and target distributions are well aligned and the classifier trained on the adjusted source domain is expected to work well in the target domain. **d** One might instead attempt to align the distributions by whitening both source and target. However, this will fail since the source and target data are likely to lie on different subspaces due to domain shift. (Best viewed in color)

adds a small regularization parameter λ to the diagonal elements of the covariance matrix to explicitly make it full rank and then multiplies the original features by its inverse square root (or square root for coloring.) This is advantageous because: (1) it is faster[1] and more stable, as SVD on the original covariance matrices might not be

[1]The entire CORAL transformation takes less than one minute on a regular laptop for dimensions as large as $\mathbf{D}_S \in \mathbb{R}^{795\times 4096}$ and $\mathbf{D}_T \in \mathbb{R}^{2817\times 4096}$.

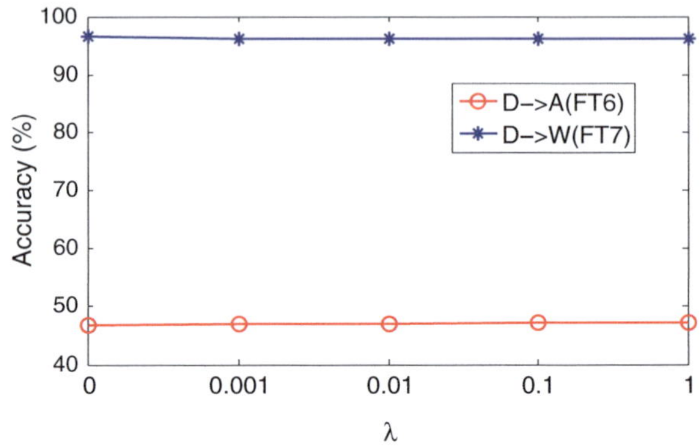

Fig. 8.2 Sensitivity of CORAL to the covariance regularization parameter λ with $\lambda \in \{0, 0.001, 0.01, 0.1, 1\}$. The plots show classification accuracy on target data for two domain shifts (*blue* and *red*). When $\lambda = 0$, there is no regularization and we use the analytical solution in Eq. (8.2). Please refer to Sect. 8.5.1 for details of the experiment

stable and might be slow to converge; (2) as illustrated in Fig. 8.2, the performance is similar to the analytical solution in Eq. (8.2) and very stable with respect to λ.[2] The final algorithm can be written in four lines of MATLAB code as illustrated in Algorithm 8.

One might instead attempt to align the distributions by whitening both source and target. As shown in Fig. 8.1d, this will fail as the source and target data are likely to lie on different subspaces due to domain shift. An alternative approach would be whitening the target and then re-coloring it with the source covariance. However, as demonstrated in [164, 224] and our experiments, transforming data from source to target space gives better performance. This might be due to the fact that by transforming the source to target space the classifier is trained using both the label information from the source and the unlabeled structure from the target.

After CORAL transforms the source features to the target space, a classifier $f_{\mathbf{w}}$ parametrized by $\mathbf{w}$ can be trained on the adjusted source features and directly applied to target features. For a linear classifier $f_{\mathbf{w}}(I) = \mathbf{w}^{\top}\phi(I)$, we can apply an equivalent transformation to the parameter vector $\mathbf{w}$ (e.g., $f_{\mathbf{w}}(I) = (\mathbf{w}^{\top}A)\phi(I))$ instead of the features (e.g., $f_{\mathbf{w}}(I) = \mathbf{w}^{\top}(A\phi(I)))$. This results in added efficiency when the number of classifiers is small but the number and dimensionality of target examples is very high. For linear SVM, this extension is straightforward. In Sect. 8.3, we apply the idea of CORAL to another commonly used linear classifier–Linear Discriminant Analysis (LDA). LDA is special in the sense that its weights also use the covariance of the data. It is also extremely efficient for training a large number of classifiers [225].

Relationship to Existing Methods. It has long been known that input feature normalization improves many machine learning methods,e.g., [247]. However, CORAL does not simply perform feature normalization, but rather aligns two different distributions. Batch Normalization [247] tries to compensate for *internal* covariate shift by normalizing each mini-batch to be zero mean and unit variance. However, as illustrated in Fig. 8.1a, such normalization might not be enough. Even if used with full whitening, Batch Normalization may not compensate for *external* covariate shift:

---

[2]In the experiments provided at the end of this chapter we set λ to 1.

Algorithm 8 CORAL for Unsupervised Domain Adaptation

Input: Source Data $\mathbf{D}_S$, Target Data $\mathbf{D}_T$

1: $\mathbf{C}_S = cov(\mathbf{D}_S) + eye(size(\mathbf{D}_S, 2))$

2: $\mathbf{C}_T = cov(\mathbf{D}_T) + eye(size(\mathbf{D}_T, 2))$

3: $\mathbf{D}_S = \mathbf{D}_S * \mathbf{C}_S^{\frac{-1}{2}}$ % whitening source

4: $\mathbf{D}_S^* = \mathbf{D}_S * \mathbf{C}_T^{\frac{1}{2}}$ % re-coloring with target covariance

Output: Adjusted Source Data $\mathbf{D}_s^*$

the layer activations will be decorrelated for a source point but not for a target point. What's more, as mentioned in Sect. 8.2, whitening both domains is not a successful strategy.

Recent state-of-the-art unsupervised approaches project the source and target distributions into a lower-dimensional manifold and find a transformation that brings the subspaces closer together [164, 200, 206, 224]. CORAL avoids subspace projection, which can be costly and requires selecting the hyper-parameter that controls the dimensionality of the subspace, k. We note that subspace-mapping approaches [164, 224] only align the top k eigenvectors of the source and target covariance matrices. On the contrary, CORAL aligns the covariance matrices, which can only be re-constructed using all eigenvectors and eigenvalues. Even though the eigenvectors can be aligned well, the distributions can still differ a lot due to the difference of eigenvalues between the corresponding eigenvectors of the source and target data. CORAL is a more general and much simpler method than the above two as it takes into account *both* eigenvectors *and* eigenvalues of the covariance matrix without the burden of subspace dimensionality selection.

Maximum Mean Discrepancy (MMD) based methods such as TCA [354] or DAN [309] can be interpreted as "moment matching" and can express arbitrary statistics of the data. Minimizing MMD with a polynomial kernel ($k(\mathbf{x}, \mathbf{y}) = (1 + \mathbf{x}^\top \mathbf{y})^q$ with $q = 2$) is similar to the CORAL objective, however, no previous work has used this kernel for domain adaptation nor proposed a closed form solution to the best of our knowledge. The other difference is that MMD based approaches usually apply the *same* transformation to both the source and target domain. As demonstrated in [164, 224, 278], asymmetric transformations are more flexible and often yield better performance for domain adaptation tasks. Intuitively, symmetric transformations find a space that "ignores" the differences between the source and target domain while asymmetric transformations try to "bridge" the two domains.

8.3 CORAL Linear Discriminant Analysis

In this section, we introduce how CORAL can be applied for aligning multiple linear classifiers. In particular, we take LDA as the example for illustration, considering LDA is a commonly used and effective linear classifier. Combining CORAL and

LDA gives a new efficient adpative learning approach CORAL-LDA. We use the task of object detection as a running example to explain CORAL-LDA.

We begin by describing the decorrelation-based approach to detection proposed in [225]. Given an image I, it follows the sliding-window paradigm, extracting a d-dimensional feature vector $\phi(I, b)$ at each window b across all locations and at multiple scales. It then scores the windows using a scoring function $f_{\mathbf{w}}(I, b) = \mathbf{w}^{\top}\phi(I, b)$. In practice, all windows with values of $f_{\mathbf{w}}$ above a predetermined threshold are considered positive detections.

In recent years, use of the linear SVM as the scoring function $f_{\mathbf{w}}$, usually with Histogram of Gradients (HOG) as the features ϕ, has emerged as the predominant object detection paradigm. Yet, as observed by Hariharan et al. [225], training SVMs can be expensive, especially because it usually involves costly rounds of hard negative mining. Furthermore, the training must be repeated for each object category, which makes it scale poorly with the number of categories.

Hariharan et al. [225] proposed a much more efficient alternative, learning $f_{\mathbf{w}}$ with Linear Discriminant Analysis (LDA). LDA is a well-known linear classifier that models the training set of examples $\mathbf{x}$ with labels $y \in \{0, 1\}$ as being generated by $p(\mathbf{x}, y) = p(\mathbf{x}|y)p(y)$. $p(y)$ is the prior on class labels and the class-conditional densities are normal distributions

$$p(\mathbf{x}|y) = \mathcal{N}(\mathbf{x}; \mu^{y}, \mathbf{C_S}), \tag{8.3}$$

where the feature vector covariance $\mathbf{C_S}$ is assumed to be the same for both positive and negative (background) classes. In our case, the feature is represented by $\mathbf{x} = \phi(I, b)$. The resulting classifier is given by

$$\mathbf{w} = \mathbf{C_S}^{-1}(\mu_{\mathbf{1}} - \mu_{\mathbf{0}}) \tag{8.4}$$

The innovation in [225] was to re-use $\mathbf{C_S}$ and $\mu_{\mathbf{0}}$, the background mean, for all categories, reducing the task of learning a new category model to computing the average positive feature, $\mu_{\mathbf{1}}$. This was accomplished by calculating $\mathbf{C_S}$ and $\mu_{\mathbf{0}}$ for the largest possible window and sub-sampling to estimate all other smaller window sizes. Also, $\mathbf{C_S}$ was shown to have a sparse local structure, with correlation falling off sharply beyond a few nearby image locations.

Like other classifiers, LDA learns to suppress nondiscriminative structures and enhance the contours of the object. However it does so by learning the global covariance statistics once for all natural images, and then using the inverse covariance matrix to remove the nondiscriminative correlations, and the negative mean to remove the average feature. LDA was shown in [225] to have competitive performance to SVM, and can be implemented both as an exemplar-based [321] or as deformable parts model (DPM) [162].

We observe that estimating global statistics $\mathbf{C_S}$ and $\mu_{\mathbf{0}}$ once and re-using them for all tasks may work when training and testing in the same domain, but in our case, the source training data is likely to have different statistics from the target data. Figure 8.4 illustrates the effect of centering and decorrelating a positive mean using

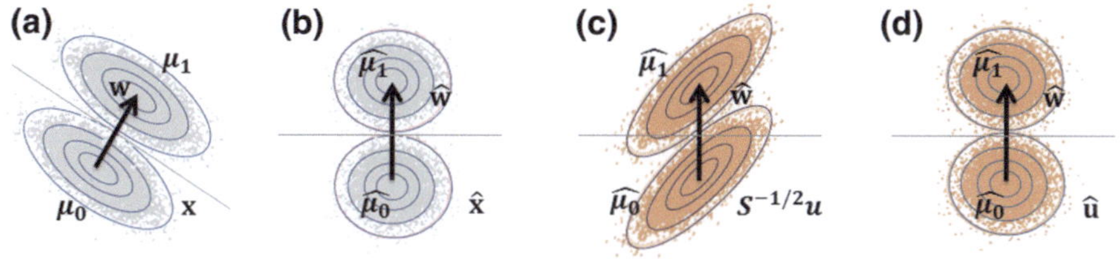

Fig. 8.3 **a** Applying a linear classifier $\mathbf{w}$ learned by LDA to source data $\mathbf{x}$ is equivalent to **b** applying classifier $\hat{\mathbf{w}} = \mathbf{C_S}^{-1/2}\mathbf{w}$ to decorrelated points $\mathbf{C_S}^{-1/2}\mathbf{x}$. **c** However, target points $\mathbf{u}$ may still be correlated after $\mathbf{C_S}^{-1/2}\mathbf{u}$, hurting performance. **d** Our method uses target-specific covariance to obtain properly decorrelated $\hat{\mathbf{u}}$

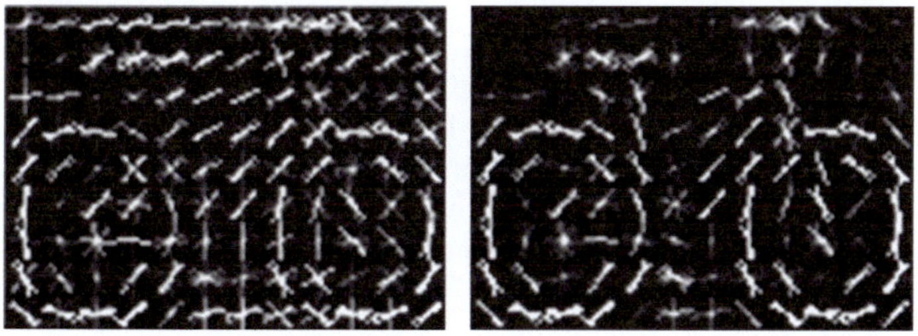

Fig. 8.4 Visualization of classifier weights of bicycle (decorrelated with mismatched-domain covariance (*left*) v.s. with same-domain covariance (*right*))

global statistics from the wrong domain. The effect is clear: important discriminative information is removed while irrelevant structures are not.

Based on this observation, we propose an adaptive decorrelation approach to detection. Assume that we are given labeled training data $\{\mathbf{x}, y\}$ in the source domain (e.g., virtual images rendered from 3D models), and unlabeled examples $\mathbf{u}$ in the target domain (e.g., real images collected in an c.f.environment). Evaluating the scoring function $f_{\mathbf{w}}(\mathbf{x})$ in the source domain is equivalent to first decorrelating the training features $\hat{\mathbf{x}} = \mathbf{C_S}^{-1/2}\mathbf{x}$, computing their positive and negative class means $\hat{\mu_1} = \mathbf{C_S}^{-1/2}\mu_1$ and $\hat{\mu_0} = \mathbf{C_S}^{-1/2}\mu_0$ and then projecting the decorrelated feature onto the decorrelated difference between means, $f_{\mathbf{w}}(\mathbf{x}) = \hat{\mathbf{w}}^{\top}\hat{\mathbf{x}}$, where $\hat{\mathbf{w}} = (\hat{\mu_1} - \hat{\mu_0})$. This is illustrated in Fig. 8.3a–b.

However, as we saw in Fig. 8.4, the assumption that the input is properly decorrelated does not hold if the input comes from a target domain with a different covariance structure. Figure 8.3c illustrates this case, showing that $\mathbf{C_S}^{-1/2}\mathbf{u}$ does not have isotropic covariance. Therefore, $\mathbf{w}$ cannot be used directly.

We may be able to compute the covariance of the target domain on the unlabeled target points $\mathbf{u}$, but not the positive class mean. Therefore, we would like to re-use the decorrelated mean difference $\hat{\mathbf{w}}$, but adapt to the covariance of the target domain. In the rest of the chapter, we make the assumption that the difference between positive and negative means is the same in the source and target. This may or may not hold in practice, and we discuss this further in Sect. 8.5.

Let the estimated target covariance be $\mathbf{C_T}$. We first decorrelate the target input feature with its inverse square root, and then apply ($\hat{\mathbf{w}}$ directly $\hat{\mathbf{w}}^\top \hat{\mathbf{u}}$), as shown in Fig. 8.3d. The resulting scoring function is

$$\begin{aligned} f_{\hat{\mathbf{w}}}(\mathbf{u}) &= \left(\mathbf{C_S}^{-1/2}(\mu_1 - \mu_0)\right)^\top (\mathbf{C_T}^{-1/2}\mathbf{u}) \\ &= \left((\mathbf{C_T}^{-1/2})^\top \mathbf{C_S}^{-1/2}(\mu_1 - \mu_0)\right)^\top \mathbf{u} \end{aligned} \tag{8.5}$$

This corresponds to a transformation $(\mathbf{C_T}^{-1/2})^\top(\mathbf{C_S}^{-1/2})$ instead of the original whitening $\mathbf{C_S}^{-1}$ being applied to the difference between means to compute $\mathbf{w}$. Note that if source and target domains are the same, then $(\mathbf{C_T}^{-1/2})^\top(\mathbf{C_S}^{-1/2})$ equals to $\mathbf{C_S}^{-1}$ since both $\mathbf{C_T}$ and $\mathbf{C_S}$ are symmetric. In this case, Eq. (8.5) ends up the same as Eq. (8.4).

In practice, either the source or the target component of the above transformation may also work, or even statistics from similar domains. However, as we will see in Sect. 8.5.2, dissimilar domain statistics can significantly hurt performance. Furthermore, if either source or target has only images of the positive category available, and cannot be used to properly compute background statistics, the other domain can still be used.

CORAL-LDA works in a purely unsupervised way. Here, we extend it to semi-supervised adaptation when a few labeled examples are available in the target domain. Following [195], a simple adaptation method is used whereby the template learned on source positives is combined with a template learned on target positives, using a weighted combination. The key difference with our approach is that the target template uses target-specific statistics.

In [195], the author uses the same background statistics as [225] which were estimated on 10,000 natural images from the PASCAL VOC 2010 dataset. Based on our analysis above, even though these background statistics were estimated from a very large amount of real image data, it will not work for all domains. In Sect. 8.5.2, our results confirm this claim.

8.4 Deep CORAL

In this section, we extend CORAL to work seamlessly with deep neural networks by designing a differentiable CORAL loss. Deep CORAL enables end-to-end adaptation and also learns more a powerful nonlinear transformation. It can be easily integrated into different layers or network architectures. Figure 8.5 shows a sample Deep CORAL architecture using our proposed correlation alignment layer for deep domain adaptation. We refer to Deep CORAL as any deep network incorporating the CORAL loss for domain adaptation.

We first describe the CORAL loss between two domains for a single feature layer. Suppose the numbers of source and target data are n_S and n_T, respectively. Here both $\mathbf{x}$ and $\mathbf{u}$ are the d-dimensional deep layer activations $\phi(I)$ of input I that we

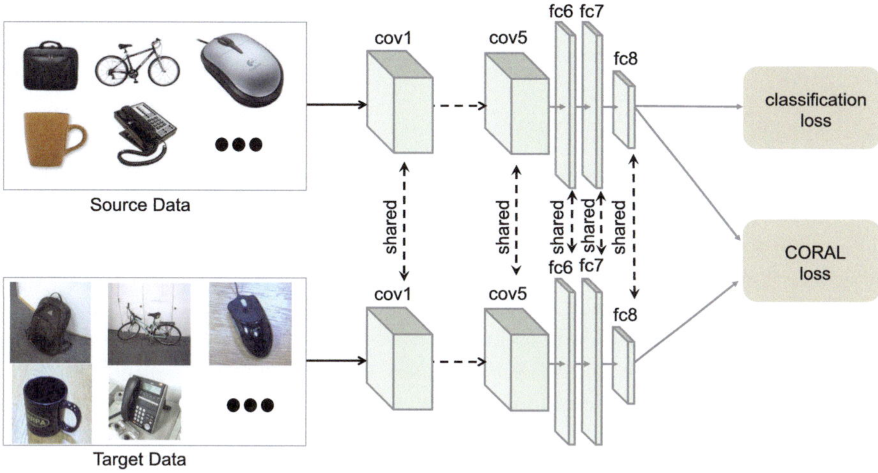

Fig. 8.5 Sample Deep CORAL architecture based on a CNN with a classifier layer. For generalization and simplicity, here we apply the CORAL loss to the $fc8$ layer of AlexNet [275]. Integrating it into other layers or network architectures is also possible

are trying to learn. Suppose D_S^{ij} (D_T^{ij}) indicates the j-th dimension of the i-th source (target) data example and $\mathbf{C}_S$ ($\mathbf{C}_T$) denote the feature covariance matrices.

We define the CORAL loss as the distance between the second-order statistics (covariances) of the source and target features

$$\mathcal{L}_{CORAL} = \frac{1}{4d^2} \|\mathbf{C}_S - \mathbf{C}_T\|_F^2 \tag{8.6}$$

where $\|\cdot\|_F^2$ denotes the squared matrix Frobenius norm. The covariance matrices of the source and target data are given by

$$\mathbf{C}_S = \frac{1}{n_S - 1}(\mathbf{D}_S^\top \mathbf{D}_S - \frac{1}{n_S}(\mathbf{1}^\top \mathbf{D}_S)^\top (\mathbf{1}^\top \mathbf{D}_S)) \tag{8.7}$$

$$\mathbf{C}_T = \frac{1}{n_T - 1}(\mathbf{D}_T^\top \mathbf{D}_T - \frac{1}{n_T}(\mathbf{1}^\top \mathbf{D}_T)^\top (\mathbf{1}^\top \mathbf{D}_T)) \tag{8.8}$$

where $\mathbf{1}$ is a column vector with all elements equal to 1.

The gradient with respect to the input features can be calculated using the chain rule

$$\frac{\partial \mathcal{L}_{CORAL}}{\partial D_S^{ij}} = \frac{1}{d^2(n_S - 1)}((\mathbf{D}_S^\top - \frac{1}{n_S}(\mathbf{1}^\top \mathbf{D}_S)^\top \mathbf{1}^\top)^\top (\mathbf{C}_S - \mathbf{C}_T))^{ij} \tag{8.9}$$

$$\frac{\partial \mathcal{L}_{CORAL}}{\partial D_T^{ij}} = -\frac{1}{d^2(n_T - 1)}((\mathbf{D}_T^\top - \frac{1}{n_T}(\mathbf{1}^\top \mathbf{D}_T)^\top \mathbf{1}^\top)^\top (\mathbf{C}_S - \mathbf{C}_T))^{ij} \tag{8.10}$$

In our experiments, we use batch covariances and the network parameters are shared between the two networks, but other settings are also possible.

To see how this loss can be used to adapt an existing neural network, let us return to the multi-class classification problem. Suppose we start with a network with a final classification layer, such as the ConvNet shown in Fig. 8.5. As mentioned before, the final deep features need to be both discriminative enough to train a strong classifier and invariant to the difference between source and target domains. Minimizing the classification loss itself is likely to lead to over-fitting to the source domain, causing reduced performance on the target domain. On the other hand, minimizing the CORAL loss alone might lead to degenerated features. For example, the network could project all of the source and target data to a single point, making the CORAL loss trivially zero. However, no strong classifier can be constructed on these features. Joint training with both the classification loss and CORAL loss is likely to learn features that work well on the target domain

$$\mathcal{L} = \mathcal{L}_{CLASS} + \sum_{i=1}^{t} \lambda_i \mathcal{L}_{CORAL_i} \tag{8.11}$$

where t denotes the number of CORAL loss layers in a deep network and λ_i is a weight that trades off the adaptation with classification accuracy on the source domain. As we show below, these two losses play counterparts and reach an *equilibrium* at the end of training, where the final features are discriminative and generalize well to the target domain.

8.5 Experiments

We evaluate CORAL and Deep CORAL on object recognition [407] using standard benchmarks and protocols. In all experiments we assume the target domain is unlabeled. For CORAL, we follow the standard procedure [128, 164] and use a linear SVM as the base classifier. The model selection approach of [164] is used to set the C parameter for the SVM by doing cross-validation on the source domain. For CORAL-LDA, as efficiency is the main concern, we evaluate it on the more time constrained task–object detection. We follow the protocol of [195] and use HOG features. To have a fair comparison, we use accuracies reported by other authors with exactly the same setting or conduct experiments using the source code provided by the authors.

Table 8.1 Object recognition accuracies of all 12 domain shifts on the OC10 dataset [200] with SURF features, following the protocol of [164, 200, 206, 278, 407]

	A → C	A → D	A → W	C → A	C → D	C → W	D → A	D → C	D → W	W → A	W → C	W→ D	AVG
NA	35.8	33.1	24.9	43.7	39.4	30.0	26.4	27.1	56.4	32.3	25.7	78.9	37.8
SVMA	34.8	34.1	32.5	39.1	34.5	32.9	33.4	31.4	74.4	36.6	33.5	75.0	41.0
DAM	34.9	34.3	32.5	39.2	34.7	33.1	33.5	31.5	74.7	34.7	31.2	68.3	40.2
GFK	38.3	37.9	39.8	44.8	36.1	34.9	37.9	31.4	79.1	37.1	29.1	74.6	43.4
TCA	40.0	**39.1**	**40.1**	46.7	**41.4**	36.2	39.6	34.0	80.4	**40.2**	33.7	77.5	45.7
SA	39.9	38.8	39.6	46.1	39.4	38.9	**42.0**	**35.0**	82.3	39.3	31.8	77.9	45.9
CORAL	**40.3**	38.3	38.7	**47.2**	40.7	**39.2**	38.1	34.2	**85.9**	37.8	**34.6**	**84.9**	**46.7**

8.5.1 Object Recognition

In this set of experiments, domain adaptation is used to improve the accuracy of an object classifier on novel image domains. Both the standard Office (OFF31) [407] and the extended Office-Caltech10 (OC10) [200] datasets described in Chap. 3 are used as benchmarks in this work. OC10 contains 10 object categories in 4 image domains: $Webcam$, $DSLR$, $Amazon$, and $Caltech256$ while OFF31 31 classes in three domains: $Webcam$, $DSLR$, and $Amazon$.

Shallow Features. We follow the standard protocol of [164, 200, 206, 278, 407] and conduct experiments on the OC10 dataset with shallow features (SURF). The SURF features were encoded with 800-bin bag-of-words histograms and normalized to have zero mean and unit standard deviation in each dimension. Since there are four domains, there are 12 experiment settings, namely, A → C (train on (A)mazon, test on (C)altech), A → D, A → W, and so on. We follow the standard protocol [164, 200, 206, 278, 407] described in Chap. 3.

In Table 8.1, we compare our method to: SVMA [134], DAM [135], GFK [200], SA [164], and TCA [354] as well as the no adaptation baseline (NA). GFK, SA, and TCA are manifold based methods that project the source and target distributions into a lower-dimensional manifold. GFK integrates over an infinite number of subspaces along the subspace manifold using the kernel trick. SA aligns the source and target subspaces by computing a linear map that minimizes the Frobenius norm of their difference. TCA performs domain adaptation via a new parametric kernel using feature extraction methods by projecting data onto the learned transfer components. DAMintroduces smoothness assumption to enforce the target classifier share similar decision values with the source classifiers. Even though these methods are far more complicated than ours and require tuning of hyperparameters (e.g., subspace dimensionality), our method achieves the best average performance across all the

Table 8.2 Object recognition accuracies for all six domain shifts on the standard OFF31 dataset with deep features, following the standard unsupervised adaptation protocol

	A → D	A → W	D → A	D → W	W → A	W → D	AVG
GFK	52.4±0.0	54.7±0.0	43.2±0.0	92.1±0.0	41.8±0.0	96.2±0.0	63.4
SA	50.6±0.0	47.4±0.0	39.5±0.0	89.1±0.0	37.6±0.0	93.8±0.0	59.7
TCA	46.8±0.0	45.5±0.0	36.4±0.0	81.1±0.0	39.5±0.0	92.2±0.0	56.9
CORAL	65.7±0.0	64.3±0.0	48.5±0.0	**96.1 ±0.0**	48.2±0.0	**99.8 ±0.0**	70.4
CNN	63.8±0.5	61.6±0.5	51.1±0.6	95.4±0.3	49.8±0.4	99.0±0.2	70.1
DDC	64.4±0.3	61.8±0.4	52.1±0.8	95.0±0.5	**52.2 ±0.4**	98.5±0.4	70.6
DAN	65.8±0.4	63.8±0.4	**52.8 ±0.4**	94.6±0.5	51.9±0.5	98.8±0.6	71.3
D-CORAL	**66.8 ±0.6**	**66.4±0.4**	**52.8±0.2**	95.7±0.3	51.5±0.3	99.2±0.1	**72.1**

12 domain shifts. Our method also improves on the no adaptation baseline (NA), in some cases increasing accuracy significantly (from 56 to 86% for D → W).

Deep Features. For visual domain adaptation with deep features, we follow the standard protocol of [128, 182, 200, 309, 499] and use all the labeled source data and all the target data without labels on the standard OFF31 dataset [407]. Since there are three domains, we conduct experiments on all 6 shifts (5 runs per shift), taking one domain as the source and another as the target.

In this experiment, we apply the CORAL loss to the last classification layer as it is the most general case–most deep classifier architectures (e.g., convolutional neural networks, recurrent neural networks) contain a fully connected layer for classification. Applying the CORAL loss to other layers or other network architectures is also possible. The dimension of the last fully connected layer ($fc8$) was set to the number of categories (31) and initialized with $\mathcal{N}(0, 0.005)$. The learning rate of $fc8$ was set to 10 times the other layers as it was training from scratch. We initialized the other layers with the parameters pre-trained on ImageNet [120] and kept the original layerwise parameter settings. In the training phase, we set the batch size to 128, base learning rate to 10^{-3}, weight decay to 5×10^{-4}, and momentum to 0.9. The weight of the CORAL loss (λ) is set in such way that at the end of training the classification loss and CORAL loss are roughly the same. It seems be a reasonable choice as we want to have a feature representation that is both discriminative and also minimizes the distance between the source and target domains. We used Caffe [255] and BVLC Reference CaffeNet for all of our experiments.

We compare to 7 recently published methods: CNN [275] (with no adaptation), GFK [200], SA [164], TCA [354], CORAL [465], DDC [499], DAN [309]. GFK, SA, and TCA are manifold based methods that project the source and target distributions into a lower-dimensional manifold and are not end-to-end deep methods. DDC adds a domain confusion loss to AlexNet [275] and fine-tunes it on both the source and target domain. DAN is similar to DDC but utilizes a multi-kernel selection method for better mean embedding matching and adapts in multiple layers. For direct comparison, DAN in this paper uses the hidden layer $fc8$. For GFK, SA, TCA, and CORAL, we use the $fc7$ feature fine-tuned on the source domain ($FT7$ in [465]) as it achieves better performance than generic pre-trained features, and train a linear SVM [164, 465]. To have a fair comparison, we use accuracies reported by other authors with exactly the same setting or conduct experiments using the source code provided by the authors.

From Table 8.2 we can see that Deep CORAL (D-CORAL) achieves better average performance than CORAL and the other 6 baseline methods. In 3 out of 6 shifts, it achieves the highest accuracy. For the other 3 shifts, the margin between D-CORAL and the best baseline method is very small ($\leqslant 0.7$).

Domain Adaptation Equilibrium. To get a better understanding of Deep CORAL, we generate three plots for domain shift A $\rightarrow$ W. In Fig. 8.6a we show the training (source) and testing (target) accuracies for training with v.s. without CORAL loss. We can clearly see that adding the CORAL loss helps achieve much better performance on the target domain while maintaining strong classification accuracy on the source domain.

In Fig. 8.6b we visualize both the classification loss and the CORAL loss for training w/ CORAL loss. As the last fully connected layer is randomly initialized with $\mathcal{N}(0, 0.005)$, in the beginning the CORAL loss is very small while the classification loss is very large. After training for a few hundred iterations, these two losses are about the same and reach an *equilibrium*. In Fig. 8.6c we show the CORAL distance between the domains for training w/o CORAL loss (setting the weight to 0). We can see that the distance is getting much larger ($\geqslant 100$ times larger compared to training w/ CORAL loss). Comparing Fig. 8.6b and c, we can see that even though the CORAL loss is not always decreasing during training, if we set its weight to 0, the distance between source and target domains becomes much larger. This is reasonable as fine-tuning without domain adaptation is likely to overfit the features to the source domain. Our CORAL loss constrains the distance between source and target domain during the fine-tuning process and helps to maintain an *equilibrium* where the final features work well on the target domain.

8.5.2 *Object Detection*

Following protocol of [195], we conduct object detection experiment on the OFF31 dataset [407] with HOG features. We use the same setting as [195], performing detection on the *Webcam* domain as the target (test) domain, and evaluating on the same 783 image test set of 20 categories (out of 31). As source (training) domains, we use: the two remaining real-image domains in OFF31, *Amazon* and *DSLR*, and two domains that contain virtual images only, *Virtual* and *Virtual-Gray*, generated from 3d CAD models. The inclusion of the two virtual domains is to reduce human effort in annotation and facilitate future research [464]. Examples of *Virtual* and *Virtual-Gray* are shown in Fig. 8.7. Please refer to [466] for detailed explanation of the data generation process. We also compare to [195] who use corresponding ImageNet [120]

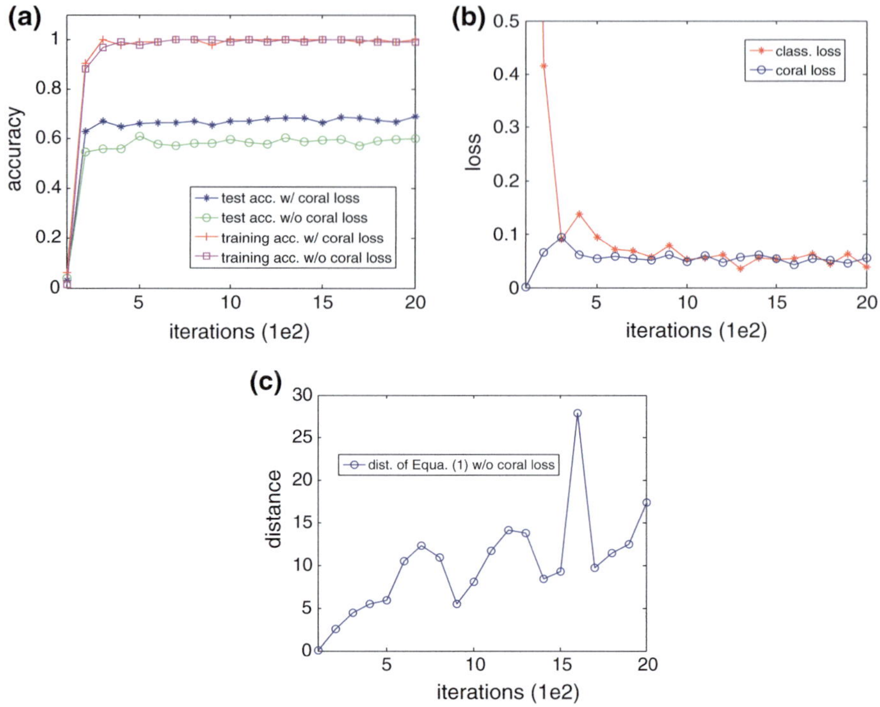

Fig. 8.6 Detailed analysis of shift A $\rightarrow$ W for training w/ v.s. w/o CORAL loss. **a**: training and test accuracies for training w/ v.s. w/o CORAL loss. We can see that adding CORAL loss helps achieve much better performance on the target domain while maintaining strong classification accuracy on the source domain. **b**: classification loss and CORAL loss for training w/ CORAL loss. As the last fully connected layer is randomly initialized, CORAL loss is very small while classification loss is very large at the beginning. After training for a few hundred iterations, these two losses are about the same. **c**: CORAL distance for training w/o CORAL loss (setting the weight to 0). The distance is getting much larger ($\geqslant$ 100 times larger compared to training w/ CORAL loss)

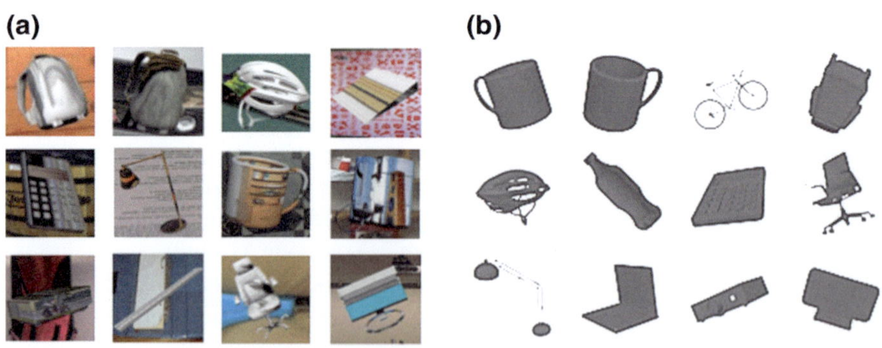

Fig. 8.7 Two sets of virtual images used in this section: **a** *Virtual*: background and texture-map from a random real ImageNet image; **b** *Virtual-Gray*: uniform gray texture-map and white background. Please refer to [466] for detailed explanation of the data generation process

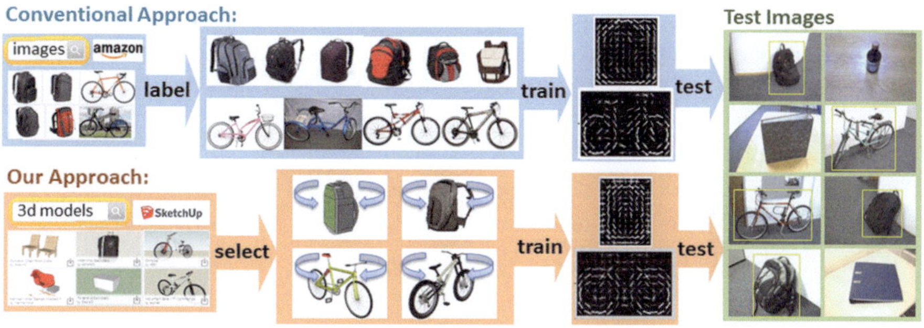

Fig. 8.8 Overview of our evaluation on object detection. With CORAL Linear Discriminant Analysis (LDA), we show that a strong object detector can be trained from virtual data only

synsets as the source. Thus, there are four potential source domains (two synthetic and three real) and one (real) target domain.[3] Figure 8.8 shows an overview of our evaluation.

Effect of Mismatched Image Statistics. First, we explore the effect of mismatched precomputed image statistics on detection performance. For each source domain, we train CORAL-LDA detectors using the positive mean from the source, and pair it with the covariance and negative mean of other domains. The virtual and the OFF31 domains are used as sources, and the test domain is always Webcam. The statistics for each of the four domains were calculated using all of the training data, following the same approach as [225]. The precomputed statistics of 10,000 real images from PASCAL, as proposed in [195, 225], are also evaluated.

Detection performance, measured in Mean Average Precision (MAP), is shown in Table 8.3. We also calculate the normalized Euclidean distance between pairs of domains as $(\|\mathbf{C^1} - \mathbf{C^2}\|)/(\|\mathbf{C^1}\| + \|\mathbf{C^2}\|) + (\|\mu_0^1 - \mu_0^2\|)/(\|\mu_0^1\| + \|\mu_0^2\|)$, and show the average distance between source and target in parentheses in Table 8.3.

From these results we can see a trend that larger domain difference leads to poorer performance. Note that larger difference to the target domain also leads to lower performance, confirming our hypothesis that both source and target statistics matter. Some of the variation could also stem from our assumption about the difference of means being the same not quite holding true. Finally, the PASCAL statistics from [225] perform the worst. Thus, in practice, statistics from either source or target domain or domains close to them could be used. However, unrelated statistics will not work even though they might be estimated from a very large amount of data [225].

Unsupervised and Semi-supervised Adaptation. Next, we report the results of our unsupervised and semi-supervised adaptation technique. We use the same setting as [195], in which three positive and nine negative labeled images per category were

[3]The number of positive training images per category in each domain are: Amazon (20), DSLR (8), Virtual(30) and Virtual-Gray (39) and ImageNet (150-2000).

Table 8.3 MAP of CORAL-LDA trained on positive examples from each row's source domain and background statistics from each column's domain. The average distance between each set of background statistics and the true source and target statistics is shown in parentheses

	Virtual	Virtual-Gray	Amazon	DSLR	PASCAL
Virtual	30.8 (*0.1*)	16.5 (*1.0*)	24.1 (*0.6*)	28.3 (*0.2*)	10.7(*0.5*)
Virtual-Gray	32.3 (*0.6*)	32.3 (*0.5*)	27.3 (*0.8*)	32.7 (*0.6*)	17.9 (*0.7*)
Amazon	39.9 (*0.4*)	30.0 (*1.0*)	39.2 (*0.4*)	37.9 (*0.4*)	18.6 (*0.6*)
DSLR	68.2 (*0.2*)	62.1 (*1.0*)	68.1 (*0.6*)	66.5 (*0.1*)	37.7 (*0.5*)

Table 8.4 *Top*: Comparison of the source-only [225] and semi-supervised adapted model of [195] with our unsupervised-adapted and semi-supervised adapted models. Target domain is $Webcam$. Mean AP across categories is reported on the $Webcam$ test data, using different source domains for training. *Bottom*: Sample detections of the DSLR-UnsupAdapt-Ours detectors

Source	Source-only [225]	Unsup-Ours	SemiSup [195]	SemiSup-Ours
Virtual	10.7	27.9	30.7	45.2
Virtual-Gray	17.9	33.0	35.0	54.7
Amazon	18.6	38.9	35.8	53.0
DSLR	37.7	67.1	42.9	71.4

used for semi-supervised adaptation. Target covariance in Eq. (8.5) is estimated from 305 unlabeled training examples. We also followed the same approach to learn a linear combination between the unsupervised and supervised model via cross-validation. The results are presented in Table 8.4. Please note that our target-only MAP is 52.9 compared to 36.6 in [195]. This also confirms our conclusion that the statistics should come from a related domain. It is clear that both of our unsupervised and semi-supervised adaptation techniques outperform the method in [195]. Furthermore, *Virtual-Gray* data outperforms *Virtual*, and *DSLR* does best, as it is very close to the target domain (the main difference between $DLSR$ and $Webcam$ domains is in the camera used to capture images).

Finally, we compare our method trained on *Virtual-Gray* to the results of adapting from ImageNet reported by [195], in Fig. 8.9. While their unsupervised models are learned from 150–2000 real ImageNet images per category and the background statistics are estimated from 10,000 PASCAL images, we only have 30 virtual images per category and the background statistics is learned from about 1,000 images. What's more, all the virtual images used are with uniform gray texture-map and white background. This clearly demonstrates the importance of domain-specific decorrelation, and shows that the there is no need to collect a large amount of real images to train a good classifier.

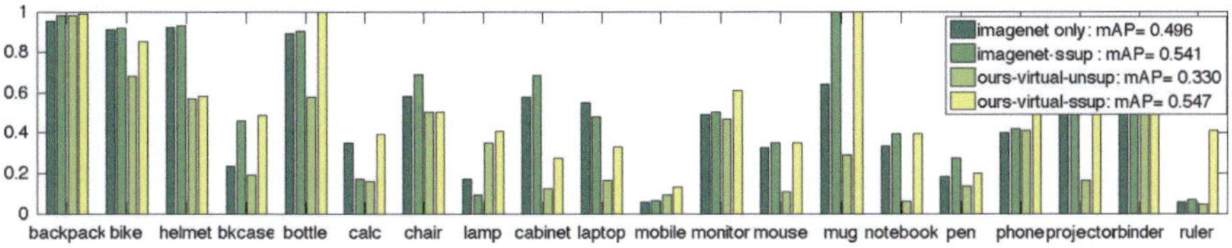

Fig. 8.9 Comparison of unsupervised and semi-supervised adaptation of virtual detectors using our method with the results of training on ImageNet and supervised adaptation from ImageNet reported in [195]. Our semi-supervised adapted detectors achieve comparable performance despite not using any real source training data, and using only three positive images for adaptation, and even outperform ImageNet significantly for several categories (e.g., *ruler*)

8.6 Conclusion

In this chapter, we described a simple, effective, and efficient method for unsupervised domain adaptation called CORrelation ALignment (CORAL). CORAL minimizes domain shift by aligning the second-order statistics of source and target distributions, without requiring any target labels. We also developed novel domain adaptation algorithms by applying the idea of CORAL to three different scenarios. In the first scenario, we applied a linear transformation that minimizes the CORAL objective to source features prior to training the classifier. In the case of linear classifiers, we equivalently applied the linear CORAL transform to the classifier weights, significantly improving efficiency and classification accuracy over standard LDA on several domain adaptation benchmarks. We further extended CORAL to learn a nonlinear transformation that aligns correlations of layer activations in deep neural networks. The resulting Deep CORAL approach works seamlessly with deep networks and can be integrated into any arbitrary network architecture to enable end-to-end unsupervised adaptation. One limitation of CORAL is that it captures second-order statistics only and may not preserve higher-order structure in the data. However, as demonstrated in this chapter, it works fairly well in practice, and can also potentially be combined with other domain-alignment loss functions.

Chapter 9
Simultaneous Deep Transfer Across Domains and Tasks

Judy Hoffman, Eric Tzeng, Trevor Darrell and Kate Saenko

Abstract Recent reports suggest that a generic supervised deep CNN model trained on a large-scale dataset reduces, but does not remove, dataset bias. Fine-tuning deep models in a new domain can require a significant amount of labeled data, which for many applications is simply not available. We propose a new CNN architecture to exploit unlabeled and sparsely labeled target domain data. Our approach simultaneously optimizes for domain invariance to facilitate domain transfer and uses a soft label distribution matching loss to transfer information between tasks. Our proposed adaptation method offers empirical performance which exceeds previously published results on two standard benchmark visual domain adaptation tasks, evaluated across supervised and semi-supervised adaptation settings.

9.1 Introduction

Consider a group of robots trained by the manufacturer to recognize thousands of common objects using standard image databases, then shipped to households around the country. As each robot starts to operate in its own unique environment, it is likely to have degraded performance due to the shift in domain. It is clear that, given enough extra supervised data from the new environment, the original perfor-

J. Hoffman and E. Tzeng—Contributed equally.

J. Hoffman (✉) · E. Tzeng · T. Darrell
UC Berkeley, Berkeley, USA
e-mail: jhoffman@eecs.berkeley.edu; jhoffman@cs.stanford.edu

E. Tzeng
e-mail: etzeng@eecs.berkeley.edu

T. Darrell
e-mail: trevor@eecs.berkeley.edu

K. Saenko
UMass Lowell, Lowell, USA
e-mail: saenko@cs.uml.edu

G. Csurka (ed.), *Domain Adaptation in Computer Vision Applications*,
Advances in Computer Vision and Pattern Recognition,
DOI 10.1007/978-3-319-58347-1_9

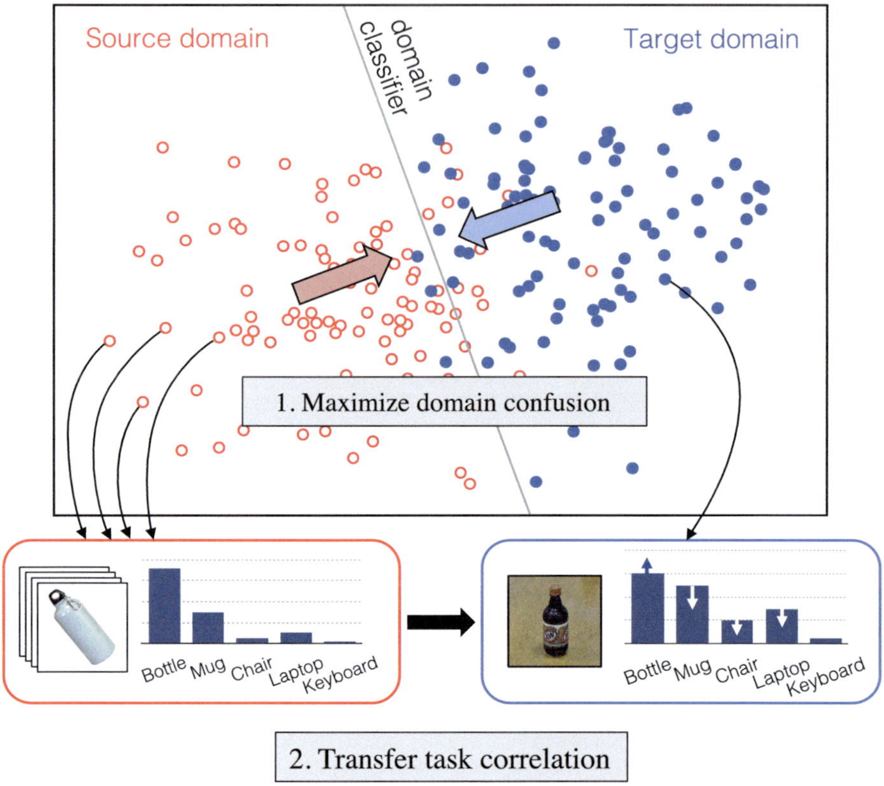

Fig. 9.1 We transfer discriminative category information from a source to a target domain via two methods. *1*. We maximize domain confusion by making the marginal distributions of the two domains as similar as possible. *2*. We transfer correlations between classes learned on the source examples directly to the target examples, thereby preserving the relationships between classes

mance could be recovered. However, state-of-the-art recognition algorithms rely on high-capacity convolutional neural network (CNN) models that require millions of supervised images for initial training. Even the traditional approach for adapting deep models, fine-tuning [192, 418], may require hundreds or thousands of labeled examples for each object category that needs to be adapted.

It is reasonable to assume that the robot's new owner will label a handful of examples for a few types of objects, but completely unrealistic to presume full supervision in the new environment. Therefore, we propose an algorithm that effectively adapts between the training (source) and test (target) environments by utilizing both generic statistics from unlabeled data collected in the new environment as well as a few human labeled examples from a subset of the categories of interest. Our approach performs transfer learning both across domains and across tasks (see Fig. 9.1). Intuitively, domain transfer is accomplished by making the marginal feature distributions of source and target as similar to each other as possible. Task transfer is enabled by transferring empirical category correlations learned on the source to the target domain. This helps to preserve relationships between categories, e.g., *bottle* is similar to *mug* but different from *keyboard*. Previous work proposed techniques for domain transfer with CNN models [182, 309] but did not utilize the learned source semantic structure for task transfer.

To enable domain transfer, we use the unlabeled target data to compute an estimated marginal distribution over the new environment and explicitly optimize a feature representation that minimizes the distance between the source and target domain distributions. Dataset bias was classically illustrated in computer vision by the "name the dataset" game of Torralba and Efros [489], which trained a classifier to predict which dataset an image originates from, thereby showing that visual datasets are biased samples of the visual world. Indeed, this turns out to be formally connected to measures of domain discrepancy [45, 269]. Optimizing for domain invariance, therefore, can be considered equivalent to the task of learning to predict the class labels while simultaneously finding a representation that makes the domains appear as similar as possible. This principle forms the domain transfer component of our proposed approach. We learn deep representations by optimizing over a loss which includes both classification error on the labeled data as well as a *domain confusion* (DC) loss which seeks to make the domains indistinguishable.

However, while maximizing domain confusion pulls the marginal distributions of the domains together, it does not necessarily align the classes in the target with those in the source. Thus, we also explicitly transfer the similarity structure amongst categories from the source to the target and further optimize our representation to produce the same structure in the target domain using the few target labeled examples as reference points. We are inspired by prior work on distilling deep models [22, 232] and extend the ideas presented in these works to a domain adaptation setting. We first compute the average output probability distribution, or "soft label," over the source training examples in each category. Then, for each target labeled example, we directly optimize our model to match the distribution over classes to the soft label. In this way we are able to perform task adaptation by transferring information to categories with no explicit labels in the target domain.

We solve the two problems jointly using a new CNN architecture, outlined in Fig. 9.2. We combine a DC and softmax cross-entropy losses to train the network with the target data. Our architecture can be used to solve *supervised adaptation*, when a small amount of target labeled data is available from each category, and *semi-supervised adaptation*, when a small amount of target labeled data is available from a subset of the categories. We provide a comprehensive evaluation on the popular Office benchmark (OFF31) [407] and the recently introduced cross-dataset collection [486] for classification across visually distinct domains. We demonstrate that by jointly optimizing for DC and matching soft labels, we are able to outperform the current state-of-the-art visual DA results.

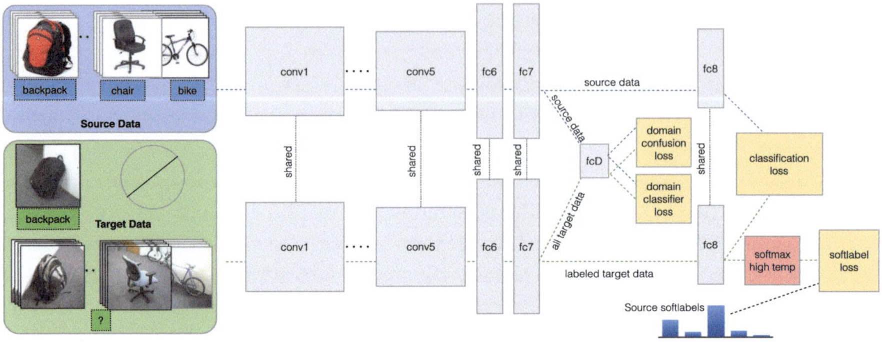

Fig. 9.2 Our overall CNN architecture for domain and task transfer. We use a DC loss over all source and target (both labeled and unlabeled) data to learn a domain invariant representation. We simultaneously transfer the learned source semantic structure to the target domain by optimizing the network to produce activation distributions that match those learned for source data in the source-only CNN. (*Best viewed in color*)

Related work. There have been many approaches proposed in recent years to solve the visual DA problem (see Chap. 1), which is also commonly framed as the visual dataset bias problem [489]. All recognize that there is a shift in the distribution of the source and target data representations. In fact, the size of a domain shift is often measured by the distance between the source and target subspace representations [45, 164, 269, 322, 354].

Recently, supervised CNN-based feature representations have been shown to be extremely effective for a variety of visual recognition tasks [128, 192, 275, 418]. In particular, using deep representations dramatically reduces the effect of resolution and lighting on domain shifts [128, 239]. Parallel CNN architectures such as Siamese networks have been shown to be effective for learning invariant representations [52, 89]. However, training these networks requires labels for each training instance, so it is unclear how to extend these methods to unsupervised or semi-supervised settings.

Training a joint source and target CNN architecture was proposed by [88], but was limited to two layers and so was significantly outperformed by the methods with a deeper architecture [275], (pretrained on ImageNet [404]). Reference [189] proposed pretraining with a denoising autoencoder, then training a two-layer network simultaneously with the MMD domain confusion loss. This effectively learns a domain invariant representation, but again, because the learned network is relatively shallow, it lacks the strong semantic representation that is learned by directly optimizing a classification objective with a supervised deep CNN.

Other works have contemporaneously explored the idea of directly optimizing a representation for domain invariance [182, 309]. However, they either use weaker measures of domain invariance or make use of optimization methods that are less robust than our proposed method, and they do not attempt to solve the task transfer problem in the semi-supervised setting.

9.2 Joint CNN Architecture for Domain and Task Transfer

We first give an overview of our convolutional network (CNN) architecture, depicted in Fig. 9.2, that learns a representation which both aligns visual domains and transfers the semantic structure from a well-labeled source domain to the sparsely labeled target domain. We assume access to a limited amount of labeled target data, potentially from only a subset of the categories of interest. With limited labels on a subset of the categories, the traditional domain transfer approach of fine-tuning on the available target data [192, 236, 418] is not effective. Instead, since the source labeled data shares the label space of our target domain, we use the source data to guide training of the corresponding classifiers.

Our method takes as input the labeled source data $\{\mathbf{x}_S, y_S\}$ (blue box in Fig. 9.2) and the target data $\{\mathbf{x}_T, y_T\}$ (green box in Fig. 9.2), where the labels y_T are only provided for a subset of the target examples. Our goal is to produce a category classifier θ_C that operates on an image feature representation $f(\mathbf{x}; \theta_{\text{repr}})$ parameterized by representation parameters θ_{repr} and can correctly classify target examples at test time.

For a setting with K categories, let our desired classification objective be defined as the standard softmax loss

$$\mathcal{L}_C(\mathbf{x}, y; \theta_{\text{repr}}, \theta_C) = -\sum_k \mathbb{1}[y = k] \log p_k, \tag{9.1}$$

where p is the softmax of the classifier activations, $p = \text{softmax}(\theta_C^T f(\mathbf{x}; \theta_{\text{repr}}))$.

We could use the available source labeled data to train our representation and classifier parameters according to Eq. (9.1), but this often leads to overfitting to the source distribution, causing reduced performance at test time when recognizing in the target domain. However, if the source and target domains are very similar under the learned representation, θ_{repr} then the classifier trained on the source will perform well on the target.

Inspired by the "name the dataset" game of Torralba and Efros [489], we can directly train a domain classifier θ_D to identify whether a training example originates from the source or target domain given its feature representation. Intuitively, if our choice of representation suffers from domain shift, then they will lie in distinct parts of the feature space, and a classifier will be able to easily separate the domains. We use this notion to add a new *domain confusion* (DC) loss $\mathcal{L}_{\text{conf}}(\mathbf{x}_S, \mathbf{x}_T, \theta_D; \theta_{\text{repr}})$ to our objective and directly optimize our representation so as to minimize the discrepancy between the source and target distributions (see Sect. 9.2.1).

Domain confusion can be applied to learn a representation that aligns source and target data without any target labeled data. However, we also presume a handful of sparse labels in the target domain, y_T. In this setting, a simple approach is to incorporate the target labeled data along with the source labeled data into the classification objective of Eq. (9.1).[1] However, fine-tuning with hard category labels limits

[1] We present this approach as one of our baselines.

the impact of a single training example, making it hard for the network to learn to generalize from the limited labeled data. Additionally, fine-tuning with hard labels is ineffective when labeled data is available for only a subset of the categories.

For our approach, we draw inspiration from recent network distillation works [22, 232], which demonstrate that a large network can be "distilled" into a simpler model by replacing the hard labels with the softmax activations from the original large model. This modification proves to be critical, as the distribution holds key information about the relationships between categories and imposes additional structure during the training process. In essence, because each training example is paired with an output distribution, it provides valuable information about not only the category it belongs to, but also each other category the classifier is trained to recognize.

Thus, we propose using the labeled target data to optimize the network parameters through a *soft label* (SL) loss, $\mathcal{L}_{\text{soft}}(\mathbf{x}_T, y_T; \theta_{\text{repr}}, \theta_C)$. This loss, detailed in Sect. 9.2.2, will train the network parameters to produce a "soft label" activation that matches the average output distribution of source examples on a network trained to classify source data. By training the network to match the expected source output distributions on target data, we transfer the learned interclass correlations from the source domain to examples in the target domain. This directly transfers useful information from source to target, such as the fact that *bookshelves* appear more similar to *filing cabinets* than to *bicycles*.

Our full method then minimizes the joint loss function

$$\begin{aligned}\mathcal{L}(\mathbf{x}_S, y_S, \mathbf{x}_T, y_T, \theta_D; \theta_{\text{repr}}, \theta_C) = \; & \mathcal{L}_C(\mathbf{x}_S, y_S, \mathbf{x}_T, y_T; \theta_{\text{repr}}, \theta_C) \\ & + \lambda \mathcal{L}_{\text{conf}}(\mathbf{x}_S, \mathbf{x}_T, \theta_D; \theta_{\text{repr}}) \\ & + \nu \mathcal{L}_{\text{soft}}(\mathbf{x}_T, y_T; \theta_{\text{repr}}, \theta_C),\end{aligned}$$

where λ and ν determine how strongly DC and SL influence the optimization.

Our ideas of domain confusion and soft label loss for task transfer are generic and can be applied to any CNN classification architecture. For our experiments and for the detailed discussion in this paper we modify the standard Krizhevsky architecture [275], which has five convolutional layers (conv1–conv5) and three fully connected layers (fc6–fc8). The representation parameter θ_{repr} corresponds to layers 1–7 of the network, and the classification parameter θ_C corresponds to layer 8. For the remainder of this section, we provide further details on our novel loss definitions and the implementation of our model.

9.2.1 Aligning Domains via Domain Confusion (DC)

In this section we describe in detail our proposed *domain confusion* (DC) loss objective. Recall that we introduce the domain confusion loss as a means to learn a representation that is domain invariant, and thus will allow us to better utilize a classifier trained using the labeled source data. We consider a representation to be domain invariant if a classifier trained using that representation cannot distinguish examples from the two domains.

To this end, we add an additional domain classification layer, denoted as fcD in Fig. 9.2, with parameters θ_D. This layer simply performs binary classification using the domain corresponding to an image as its label. For a particular feature representation, θ_{repr}, we evaluate its domain invariance by learning the best domain classifier on the representation. This can be learned by optimizing the following objective, where y_D denotes the domain that the example is drawn from:

$$\mathcal{L}_D(\mathbf{x}_S, \mathbf{x}_T, \theta_{\text{repr}}; \theta_D) = -\sum_d \mathbb{1}[y_D = d] \log q_d \tag{9.2}$$

with the softmax of the domain classifier activation $q = \text{softmax}(\theta_D^T f(\mathbf{x}; \theta_{\text{repr}}))$.

For a particular domain classifier, θ_D, we can now introduce our loss which seeks to "maximally confuse" the two domains by computing the cross entropy between the output predicted domain labels and a uniform distribution over domain labels:

$$\mathcal{L}_{\text{conf}}(\mathbf{x}_S, \mathbf{x}_T, \theta_D; \theta_{\text{repr}}) = -\sum_d \frac{1}{D} \log q_d. \tag{9.3}$$

This domain confusion (DC) loss seeks to learn domain invariance by finding a representation in which the best domain classifier performs poorly.

Ideally, we want to simultaneously minimize Eqs. (9.2) and (9.3) for the representation and the domain classifier parameters. However, the two losses stand in direct opposition to one another: learning a fully domain invariant representation means the domain classifier must do poorly, and learning an effective domain classifier means that the representation is not domain invariant. invariant image representation, θ_{repr} because an ideal domain invariant representation will result in a perfectly confused domain classifier. Rather than globally optimizing θ_D and θ_{repr}, we instead perform and introduce a separate loss function to optimize the image representation. This amounts to performing iterative updates for the following two objectives given the fixed parameters from the previous iteration:

$$\min_{\theta_D} \mathcal{L}_D(\mathbf{x}_S, \mathbf{x}_T, \theta_{\text{repr}}; \theta_D) \tag{9.4}$$

$$\min_{\theta_{\text{repr}}} \mathcal{L}_{\text{conf}}(\mathbf{x}_S, \mathbf{x}_T, \theta_D; \theta_{\text{repr}}). \tag{9.5}$$

These losses are readily implemented in standard deep learning frameworks, and after setting learning rates properly so that Eq. (9.4) only updates θ_D and Eq. (9.5) only updates θ_{repr}, the updates can be performed via standard backpropagation. Together, these updates ensure that we learn a representation that is domain invariant.

9.2.2 Aligning Source and Target Classes via Soft Labels (SL)

While training the network to confuse the domains acts to align their marginal distributions, there are no guarantees about the alignment of classes between each domain. To ensure that the relationships between classes are preserved across source and target, we fine-tune the network against "soft labels" rather than the image category hard label.

We define a soft label for category k as the average over the softmax of all activations of source examples in category k, depicted graphically in Fig. 9.3, and denote this average as $l^{(k)}$. Note that, since the source network was trained purely to optimize a classification objective, a simple softmax over each z_S^i will hide much of the useful information by producing a very peaked distribution. Instead, we use a softmax with a high temperature τ so that the related classes have enough probability mass to have an effect during fine-tuning. With our computed per-category soft labels we can now define our soft label loss:

$$\mathcal{L}_{\text{soft}}(\mathbf{x}_T, y_T; \theta_{\text{repr}}, \theta_C) = -\sum_i l_i^{(y_T)} \log p_i, \tag{9.6}$$

where q denotes the soft activation of the target image: $p = \text{softmax}(\theta_C^T f(\mathbf{x}_T; \theta_{\text{repr}})/\tau)$. The loss above corresponds to the cross-entropy loss between the soft activation of a particular target image and the soft label corresponding to the category of that image, as shown in Fig. 9.4.

To see why this will help, consider the soft label for a particular category, such as *bottle*. The soft label $l^{(\text{bottle})}$ is a K-dimensional vector, where each dimension indicates the similarity of bottles to each of the K categories. In this example, the bottle soft label will have a higher weight on *mug* than on *keyboard*, since bottles and mugs are more visually similar. Thus, soft label training with this particular soft label directly enforces the relationship that bottles and mugs should be closer in feature space than bottles and keyboards.

One important benefit of using this soft label loss is that we ensure that the parameters for categories without any labeled target data are still updated to output nonzero probabilities. We explore this benefit in Sect. 9.3, where we train a network using labels from a subset of the target categories and find significant performance improvement even when evaluating only on the unlabeled categories.

9.3 Evaluation

To analyze the effectiveness of our method, we evaluate it on the OFF31 dataset [407], and on a new large-scale cross-dataset DA challenge [486].

Adaptation on the OFF31 dataset. The OFF31 dataset [407] is a collection of images from three distinct domains, $(A)mazon$, $(D)SLR$, and $(W)ebcam$, of 31

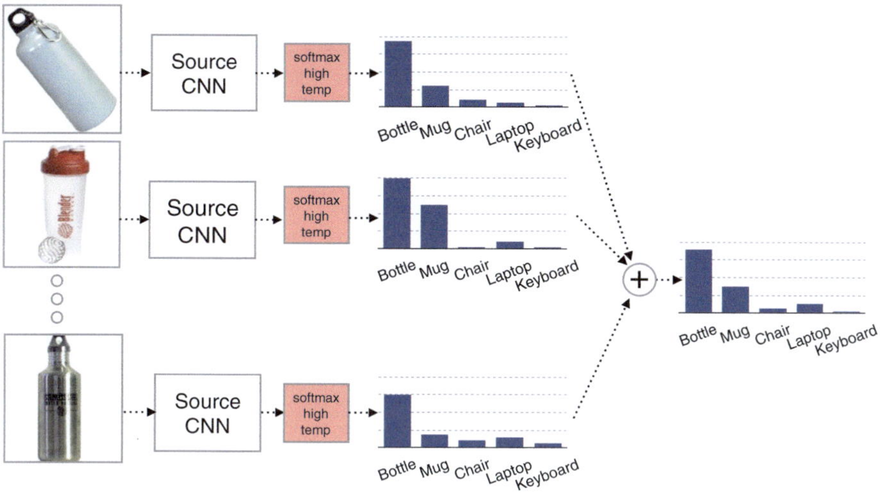

Fig. 9.3 Soft label distributions are learned by averaging the per-category activations of source training examples using the source model. An example, with 5 categories, depicted here to demonstrate the final soft activation for the bottle category will be primarily dominated by bottle and mug with very little mass on chair, laptop, and keyboard

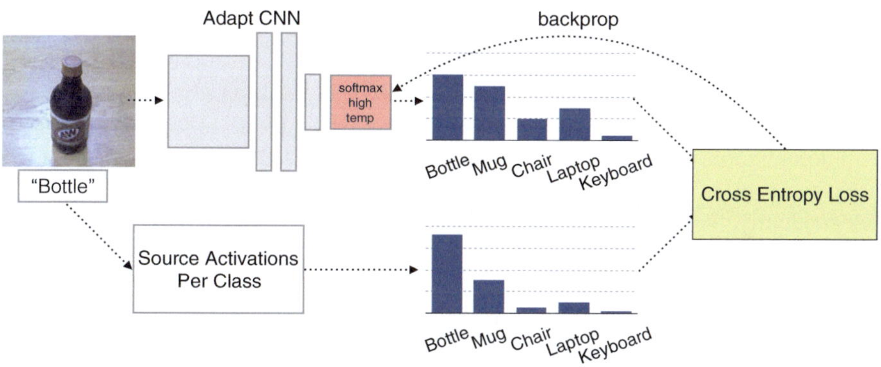

Fig. 9.4 Depiction of the use of source per-category soft activations with the cross entropy loss function over the current target activations

common categories in the dataset consist of objects commonly encountered in office settings (see details in Chap. 2). We evaluate our method in two different settings: (1) **Supervised adaptation** where labeled training data for all categories is available in source and sparsely in target; (2) **Semi-supervised adaptation (task adaptation)** where labeled training data is available in source and sparsely for a subset of the target categories.

For all experiments we initialize the parameters of conv1–fc7 using the released CaffeNet [255] weights. We then further fine-tune the network using the source labeled data in order to produce the soft label distributions and use the learned source CNN weights as the initial parameters for training our method. All implementations

Table 9.1 Multi-class accuracy evaluation on the OFF31 dataset using the standard experimental protocol from [407]. Here, we compare against three state-of-the-art DA methods as well as a CNN trained using only source data, only target data, or both source and target data together

	$A \rightarrow W$	$A \rightarrow D$	$W \rightarrow A$	$W \rightarrow D$	$D \rightarrow A$	$D \rightarrow W$	Average
DLID [88]	51.9	–	–	89.9	–	78.2	–
DeCAF_6 [128]	80.7 ± 2.3	–	–	–	–	94.8 ± 1.2	–
DaNN [189]	53.6 ± 0.2	–	–	83.5 ± 0.0	–	71.2 ± 0.0	–
Source CNN	56.5 ± 0.3	64.6 ± 0.4	42.7 ± 0.1	93.6 ± 0.2	47.6 ± 0.1	92.4 ± 0.3	66.22
Target CNN	80.5 ± 0.5	81.8 ± 1.0	59.9 ± 0.3	81.8 ± 1.0	59.9 ± 0.3	80.5 ± 0.5	74.05
S+T CNN	82.5 ± 0.9	85.2 ± 1.1	$\mathbf{65.2 \pm 0.7}$	96.3 ± 0.5	65.8 ± 0.5	93.9 ± 0.5	81.50
Ours: DC only	$\mathbf{82.8 \pm 0.9}$	85.9 ± 1.1	64.9 ± 0.5	97.5 ± 0.2	$\mathbf{66.2 \pm 0.4}$	95.6 ± 0.4	82.13
Ours: SL only	82.7 ± 0.7	84.9 ± 1.2	$\mathbf{65.2 \pm 0.6}$	$\mathbf{98.3 \pm 0.3}$	66.0 ± 0.5	$\mathbf{95.9 \pm 0.6}$	82.17
Ours: DC+SL	82.7 ± 0.8	$\mathbf{86.1 \pm 1.2}$	65.0 ± 0.5	97.6 ± 0.2	$\mathbf{66.2 \pm 0.3}$	95.7 ± 0.5	**82.22**

are produced using the open source Caffe [255] framework, and the network definition files and cross-entropy loss layer needed for training will be released upon acceptance. We optimize the network using a learning rate of 0.001 and set the hyperparameters to $\lambda = 0.01$ (confusion) and $\nu = 0.1$ (soft).

For each of the six domain shifts, we evaluate across five train/test splits, which are generated by sampling[2] examples from the full set of images per domain. We first present results for the supervised setting, where 3 labeled examples are provided for each category in the target domain. We report accuracies on the remaining unlabeled images, following the protocol in [407]. In addition to a variety of baselines, we report numbers for both soft label fine-tuning alone as well as soft labels with domain confusion in Table 9.1. Because the OFF31 dataset is imbalanced, we report multi-class accuracies, which are obtained by computing per-class accuracies independently, then averaging over all 31 categories.

We see that fine-tuning with soft labels or domain confusion provides a consistent improvement over hard label training in 5 of 6 shifts. Combining soft labels with domain confusion produces marginally higher performance on average. This result follows the intuitive notion that when enough target labeled examples are present, directly optimizing for the joint source and target classification objective (S+T CNN) is a strong baseline and so using either of our new losses adds enough regularization to improve performance.

Next, we experiment with the semi-supervised adaptation setting. We consider the case in which training data and labels are available for some, but not all of the categories in the target domain. We are interested in seeing whether we can transfer information learned from the labeled classes to the unlabeled classes. To do this, we consider having 10 target labeled examples per category from only 15 of the 31 total categories, following the standard protocol introduced with the *OFF31* dataset [407]. We then evaluate our classification performance on the remaining 16 categories for which no data was available at training time.

[2]In the source domain, we follow the protocol in [407] and generate splits by sampling 20 examples per category for the *Amazon*, and 8 for the *DSLR* and *Webcam* domains.

Table 9.2 Multi-class accuracy evaluation on the standard semi-supervised adaptation setting with the OFF31 dataset. We evaluate on 16 held-out categories for which we have no access to target labeled data. We show results on these unsupervised categories for domain confusion (DC), our model trained using only soft labels (SL) for the 15 auxiliary categories, and finally using domain confusion together with soft labels on the 15 auxiliary categories (DC+SL)

	$A \to W$	$A \to D$	$W \to A$	$W \to D$	$D \to A$	$D \to W$	Average
MMDT [239]	–	44.6 ± 0.3	–	58.3 ± 0.5	–	–	–
Source CNN	54.2 ± 0.6	63.2 ± 0.4	34.7 ± 0.1	94.5 ± 0.2	36.4 ± 0.1	89.3 ± 0.5	62.0
Ours: DC only	55.2 ± 0.6	63.7 ± 0.9	$\mathbf{41.1 \pm 0.0}$	96.5 ± 0.1	41.2 ± 0.1	$\mathbf{91.3 \pm 0.4}$	64.8
Ours: SL only	56.8 ± 0.4	65.2 ± 0.9	38.8 ± 0.4	96.5 ± 0.2	41.7 ± 0.3	89.6 ± 0.1	64.8
Ours: DC+SL	$\mathbf{59.3 \pm 0.6}$	$\mathbf{68.0 \pm 0.5}$	40.5 ± 0.2	$\mathbf{97.5 \pm 0.1}$	$\mathbf{43.1 \pm 0.2}$	90.0 ± 0.2	**66.4**

In Table 9.2 we present multi-class accuracies over the 16 held-out categories and compare our method to a previous domain adaptation method [239] as well as a source-only trained CNN. Note that, since the performance here is computed over only a subset of the categories in the dataset, the numbers in this table should not be directly compared to the supervised setting in Table 9.1.

We find that all variations of our method (SL only, DC only, and both together) outperform the baselines. Contrary to the fully supervised case, here we note that both domain confusion and soft labels contribute significantly to the overall performance improvement of our method. This stems from the fact that we are now evaluating on categories which lack labeled target data, and thus the network can not implicitly enforce domain invariance through the classification objective alone. Separately, the fact that we get improvement from the soft label training on related tasks indicates that information is being effectively transferred between tasks.

In Fig. 9.5, we show examples for the A→W shift where our method correctly classifies images from held-out object categories and the baseline does not. We find that our method is able to consistently overcome error cases, such as the notebooks that were previously confused with letter trays, or the black mugs that were confused with black computer mice.

Adaptation between diverse domains. For an evaluation with larger, more distinct domains, we test on the recent testbed for cross-dataset analysis [486], detailed in Chap. 2, which collects images from classes shared in common among computer vision datasets. We use the dense version of this testbed, which consists of 40 categories shared between the ImageNet, Caltech-256, SUN, and Bing datasets, and evaluate specifically with ImageNet as source and Caltech-256 as target.

We follow the protocol outlined in [486] and generate 5 splits by selecting 5534 images from ImageNet and 4366 images from Caltech-256 across the 40 shared categories. Each split is then equally divided into a train and test set. Since we are most interested in evaluating in the setting with limited target data, we further subsample the target training set into smaller sets with only 1, 3, and 5 labeled examples per category.

Results from this evaluation are shown in Fig. 9.6. We compare our method to both CNNs fine-tuned only on source or on source and target labeled data. Contrary to the

Fig. 9.5 Examples from the A→W shift in the semi-supervised DA setting, where our method (*bottom*, *turquoise label*) correctly classifies images while the baseline (*top*, *purple label*) does not

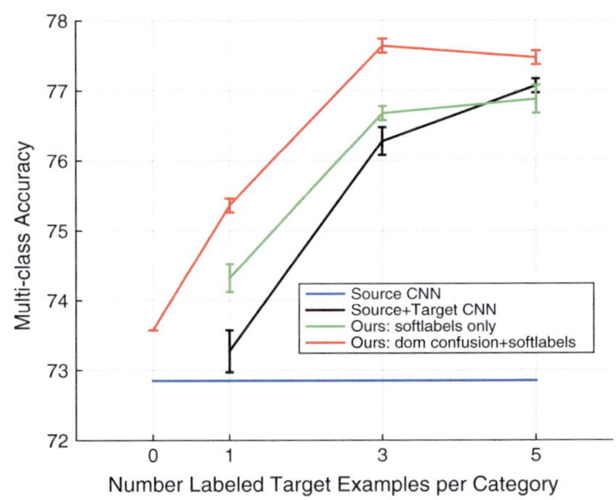

Fig. 9.6 ImageNet→Caltech supervised adaptation from the Cross-dataset [486] testbed with varying numbers of labeled target examples per category. We find that our method using soft label loss (with and without DC) outperforms the baselines of training on source data alone or using a standard fine-tuning strategy to train with the source and target data. (*Best viewed in color*).

previous supervised adaptation experiment, our method significantly outperforms both baselines. We see that our full architecture, combining DC with the SL loss, performs the best overall and is able to operate in the regime of no labeled examples in the target (corresponding to the red line at point 0 on the x-axis).

We find that the most benefit of our method arises when there are few labeled training examples per category in the target domain. As we increase the number of labeled examples in the target, the standard fine-tuning strategy begins to approach the performance of the adaptation approach. This indicates that direct joint source

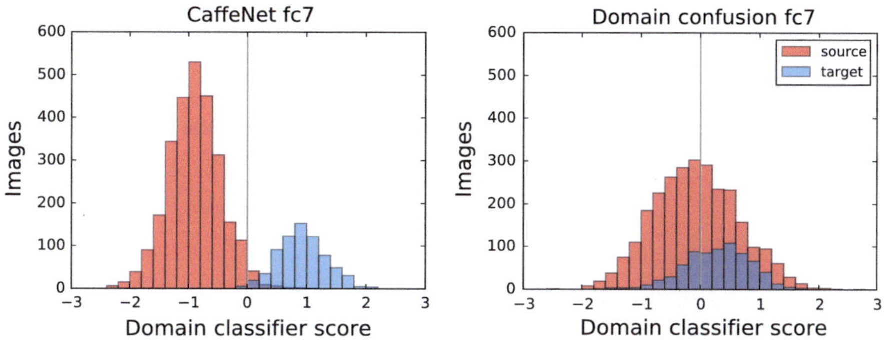

Fig. 9.7 We compare the baseline CaffeNet representation to our representation learned with domain confusion by training an SVM to predict the domains (*Amazon* and *Webcam*). For each representation, we plot a histogram of the classifier decision scores of the test images. In the baseline representation, the classifier is able to separate the two domains with 99% accuracy. In contrast, the representation learned with DC is domain invariant, and the classifier can do no better than 56%

and target fine-tuning is a viable adaptation approach when you have a reasonable number of training examples per category. In comparison, fine-tuning on the target examples alone yields accuracies of 36.6 ± 0.6, 60.9 ± 0.5, and 67.7 ± 0.5 for the cases of 1, 3, and 5 labeled examples per category, respectively. All of these numbers under perform the source-only model, indicating that adaptation is crucial in the setting of limited training data.

Finally, we note that our results are significantly higher than the 24.8% result reported in [486], despite the use of much less training data. This difference is explained by their use of SURFBOV features, indicating that CNN features are a much stronger feature for use in adaptation tasks.

Domain confusion enforces domain invariance. We begin by evaluating the effectiveness of domain confusion at learning a domain invariant representation. As previously explained, we consider a representation to be domain invariant if an optimal classifier has difficulty predicting which domain an image originates from. Thus, for our representation learned with a domain confusion loss, we expect a trained domain classifier to perform poorly.

We train two SVMs to classify images into domains: one using the baseline CaffeNet fc7 representation, and the other using our fc7 learned with domain confusion. These SVMs are trained using 80 images from *Amazon* and 80 from *Webcam*, then tested on the remaining images from those domains. We plot the classifier scores for each test image in Fig. 9.7. It is obvious that the domain confusion representation is domain invariant, making it much harder to separate the two domains—the test accuracy on the domain confusion representation is only 56%, not much better than random. In contrast, on the baseline CaffeNet representation, the domain classifier achieves 99% test accuracy.

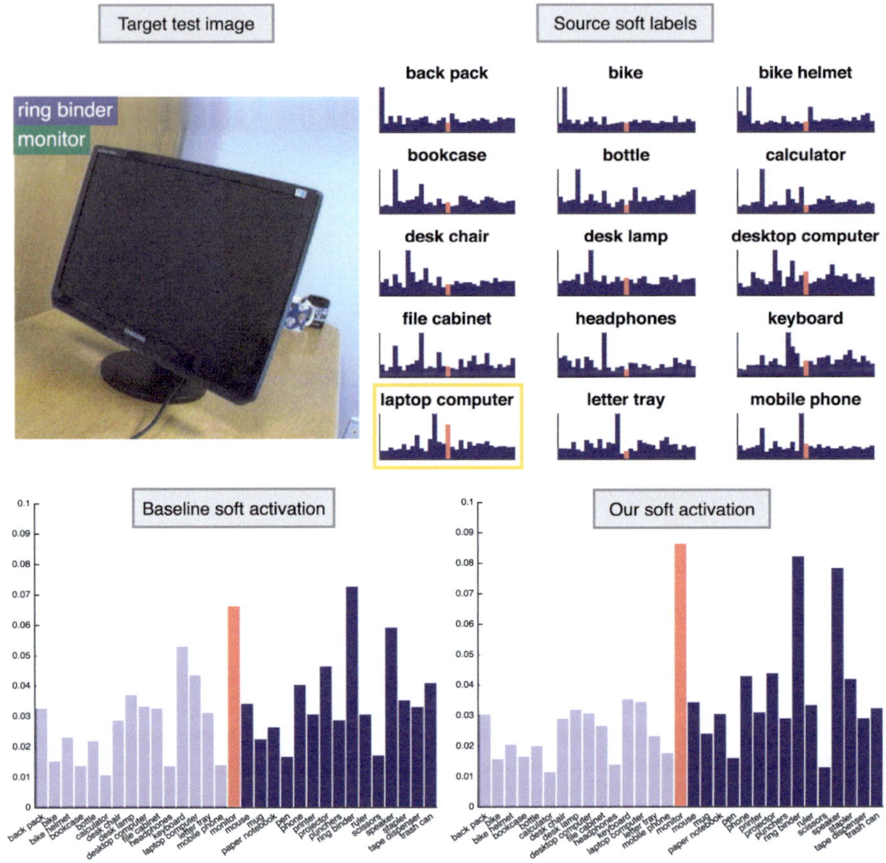

Fig. 9.8 Our method (*bottom turquoise label*) correctly predicts the category of this image, whereas the baseline (*top purple label*) does not. The source per-category soft labels for the 15 categories with labeled target data are shown in the *upper right corner*, where the x-axis represents the 31 categories and the y-axis the output probability. We highlight the index corresponding to the *monitor* category in *red*. In our method the related category of *laptop computer* (outlined with *yellow box*) transfers information to the *monitor* category. As a result, after training, our method places the highest weight on the correct category. Probability score per category for the baseline and our method are shown in the *bottom left* and *right*, respectively, training categories are opaque and correct test category is shown in *red*

Soft labels for task transfer. We now examine the effect of soft labels in transferring information between categories. We consider the A$\rightarrow$W shift from the semi-supervised adaptation experiment in the previous section. Recall that in this setting, we have access to target labeled data for only half of our categories. We use soft label information from the source domain to provide information about the held-out categories which lack labeled target examples. Figure 9.8 examines one target example from the held-out category *monitor*. No labeled target monitors were available during training; however, as shown in the upper right corner of Fig. 9.8, the soft labels for *laptop computer* was present during training and assigns a relatively high weight to the *monitor* class. Soft label fine-tuning thus allows to exploit the fact that these categories are similar. We see that the baseline model misclassifies this image as a *ring binder*, while our SL model correctly assigns the *monitor* label.

9.4 Conclusion

We have presented a CNN architecture that effectively adapts to a new domain with limited or no labeled data per target category. We accomplish this through a novel CNN architecture which simultaneously optimizes for domain invariance, to facilitate domain transfer, while transferring task information between domains in the form of a cross entropy soft label loss. We demonstrate the ability of our architecture to improve adaptation performance in the *supervised* and *semi-supervised* settings by experimenting with two standard domain adaptation benchmark datasets. In the semi-supervised adaptation setting, we see an average relative improvement of 13% over the baselines on the four most challenging shifts in the OFF31 dataset. Overall, our method can be easily implemented as an alternative fine-tuning strategy when limited or no labeled data is available per category in the target domain.

Acknowledgements This work was supported by DARPA; AFRL; NSF awards 113629, IIS-1427425, and IIS-1212798; DoD MURI award N000141110688; and the Berkeley Vision and Learning Center.

Chapter 10
Domain-Adversarial Training of Neural Networks

Yaroslav Ganin, Evgeniya Ustinova, Hana Ajakan, Pascal Germain, Hugo Larochelle, François Laviolette, Mario Marchand and Victor Lempitsky

Abstract We introduce a representation learning approach for domain adaptation, in which data at training and test time come from similar but different distributions. Our approach is directly inspired by the theory on domain adaptation suggesting that, for effective domain transfer to be achieved, predictions must be made based on features that cannot discriminate between the training (source) and test (target) domains. The approach implements this idea in the context of neural network architectures that are trained on labeled data from the source domain and unlabeled data from the target domain (no labeled target-domain data is necessary). As the training progresses, the approach promotes the emergence of features that are (i) discriminative for the main learning task on the source domain and (ii) indiscriminate with respect to the shift

Y. Ganin (✉) · E. Ustinova · V. Lempitsky
Skolkovo Institute of Science and Technology, Skolkovo, Moscow Region, Russia
e-mail: ganin@skoltech.ru; yaroslav.ganin@gmail.com

E. Ustinova
e-mail: evgeniya.ustinova@skoltech.ru

V. Lempitsky
e-mail: lempitsky@skoltech.ru

H. Ajakan · F. Laviolette · M. Marchand
Département d'informatique et de génie logiciel, Université Laval, Québec, QC, Canada
e-mail: hana.ajakan.1@ulaval.ca

F. Laviolette
e-mail: francois.laviolette@ift.ulaval.ca

M. Marchand
e-mail: mario.marchand@ift.ulaval.ca

P. Germain
INRIA Paris - École Normale Supérieure, Paris, France
e-mail: pascal.germain@inria.fr

H. Larochelle
Twitter, Cambridge, MA, USA
e-mail: hugo.larochelle@usherbrooke.ca

H. Larochelle
Université de Sherbrooke, Québec, QC, Canada

G. Csurka (ed.), *Domain Adaptation in Computer Vision Applications*,
Advances in Computer Vision and Pattern Recognition,
DOI 10.1007/978-3-319-58347-1_10

between the domains. We show that this adaptation behavior can be achieved in almost any feed-forward model by augmenting it with few standard layers and a new *Gradient Reversal* Layer. The resulting augmented architecture can be trained using standard backpropagation, and can thus be implemented with little effort using any of the deep learning packages. We demonstrate the success of our approach for image classification, where state-of-the-art domain adaptation performance on standard benchmarks is achieved. We also validate the approach for descriptor learning task in the context of person re-identification application.

10.1 Introduction

The cost of generating labeled data for a new prediction task is often an obstacle for applying machine learning methods. In particular, this is a limiting factor for the further progress of deep neural network architectures. Another common problem is that, even when the training sets are big enough for training large-scale deep models, they may that suffer from the *shift* in data distribution from the actual data encountered at "test time." One important example is training an image classifier on synthetic or semi-synthetic images, which may come in abundance and be fully labeled, but which inevitably have a distribution that is different from real images. Learning a predictor in the presence of a *shift* between training and test distributions is known as *domain adaptation* (DA). The appeal of the DA approaches is the ability to learn a mapping between domains in the situation when the target domain data are either fully unlabeled (*unsupervised domain annotation*) or have few labeled samples (*semi-supervised DA*). Below, we focus on the harder unsupervised case, although the proposed approach (*domain-adversarial learning*) can be generalized to the semi-supervised case rather straightforwardly.

Unlike many DA methods that work with fixed feature representations, we focus on combining domain adaptation and deep feature learning within one training process. Our goal is to embed domain adaptation into the process of learning representation, so that the final classification decisions are made based on features that are both discriminative and invariant to the change of domains, i.e., have the same or very similar distributions in the source and the target domains. In this way, the obtained feed-forward network can be applicable to the target domain without being hindered by the shift between the two domains. Our approach is motivated by the theory on domain adaptation [30, 31], that suggests that a good representation for cross-domain transfer is one for which an algorithm cannot learn to identify the domain of origin of the input observation.

We thus focus on learning features that combine (i) discriminativeness and (ii) domain-invariance. This is achieved by jointly optimizing the underlying features as well as two discriminative classifiers operating on these features: (i) the *label predictor* that predicts class labels and is used both during training and at test time and (ii) the *domain classifier* that discriminates between the source and the target domains during training. While the parameters of the classifiers are optimized in order to minimize their error on the training set, the parameters of the underlying deep feature mapping are optimized in order to *minimize* the loss of the label classifier and to *maximize* the loss of the domain classifier. The latter update thus works *adversarially* to the domain classifier, and it encourages domain-invariant features to emerge in the course of the optimization.

Crucially, we show that all three training processes can be embedded into an appropriately composed deep feed-forward network, called *domain-adversarial neural network* (DANN) (illustrated by Fig. 10.1) that uses standard layers and loss functions, and can be trained using standard backpropagation algorithms based on stochastic gradient descent or its modifications (e.g., SGD with momentum). The approach is generic as a DANN version can be created for almost any existing feed-forward architecture that is trainable by backpropagation. In practice, the only nonstandard component of the proposed architecture is a rather trivial *gradient reversal* layer that leaves the input unchanged during forward propagation and reverses the gradient by multiplying it by a negative scalar during the backpropagation.

We provide an experimental evaluation of the proposed domain-adversarial learning idea over a range of deep architectures and applications. We first consider the simplest DANN architecture where the three parts (label predictor, domain classifier and feature extractor) are linear, and study its behavior on a toy dataset. We further evaluate the approach extensively for an image classification task, and present results on traditional deep learning image data sets. Finally, we evaluate domain-adversarial *descriptor* learning in the context of person re-identification application [201], where the task is to obtain good pedestrian image descriptors that are suitable for retrieval and verification.

Related Work This book chapter is strongly based on a recent journal paper [183]. We focus here on the theoretical foundation of our method and the applications in computer vision. Please refer to [183] for an in-depth discussion about previous related literature and application of our method to a text sentiment analysis benchmark. For a DA survey see Chap. 1.

10.2 Domain Adaptation

We consider classification tasks where X is the input space and $Y = \{0, 1, \ldots, L-1\}$ is the set of L possible labels. Moreover, we have two different distributions over $X \times Y$, called the *source domain* $\mathcal{D}_S$ and the *target domain* $\mathcal{D}_T$. An *unsupervised domain adaptation* learning algorithm is then provided with a *labeled source sample* S drawn *i.i.d.* from $\mathcal{D}_S$, and an *unlabeled target sample* T drawn *i.i.d.* from $\mathcal{D}_T^X$, where $\mathcal{D}_T^X$ is the marginal distribution of $\mathcal{D}_T$ over X.

$$S = \{(\mathbf{x}_i, y_i)\}_{i=1}^{n} \sim (\mathcal{D}_S)^n \,; \quad T = \{\mathbf{x}_i\}_{i=n+1}^{N} \sim (\mathcal{D}_T^X)^{n'},$$

with $N = n + n'$ being the total number of samples. The goal of the learning algorithm is to build a classifier $\eta : X \to Y$ with a low *target risk*

$$R_{\mathcal{D}_\mathrm{T}}(\eta) = \Pr_{(\mathbf{x},y)\sim\mathcal{D}_\mathrm{T}} \Big(\eta(\mathbf{x}) \neq y\Big),$$

while having no information about the labels of $\mathcal{D}_\mathrm{T}$.

Domain Divergence To tackle the challenging domain adaptation task, many approaches bound the target error by the sum of the source error and a notion of distance between the source and the target distributions. These methods are intuitively justified by a simple assumption: the source risk is expected to be a good indicator of the target risk when both distributions are similar. Several notions of distance have been proposed for domain adaptation [30, 31, 188, 322, 324]. In this paper, we focus on the $\mathcal{H}$-divergence used in [30, 31], and based on the earlier work of Kifer et al. [269]. Note that we assume in Definition 10.1 below that the hypothesis class $\mathcal{H}$ is a (discrete or continuous) set of binary classifiers $\eta : X \to \{0, 1\}$.[1]

Definition 10.1 (c.f. [30, 31, 269]) Given two domain distributions $\mathcal{D}_\mathrm{S}^X$ and $\mathcal{D}_\mathrm{T}^X$ over X, and a hypothesis class $\mathcal{H}$, the *$\mathcal{H}$-divergence* between $\mathcal{D}_\mathrm{S}^X$ and $\mathcal{D}_\mathrm{T}^X$ is

$$d_\mathcal{H}(\mathcal{D}_\mathrm{S}^X, \mathcal{D}_\mathrm{T}^X) = 2 \sup_{\eta\in\mathcal{H}} \left| \Pr_{\mathbf{x}\sim\mathcal{D}_\mathrm{S}^X} \big[\eta(\mathbf{x}) = 1\big] - \Pr_{\mathbf{x}\sim\mathcal{D}_\mathrm{T}^X} \big[\eta(\mathbf{x}) = 1\big] \right|.$$

That is, the $\mathcal{H}$-divergence relies on the capacity of the hypothesis class $\mathcal{H}$ to distinguish between examples generated by $\mathcal{D}_\mathrm{S}^X$ from examples generated by $\mathcal{D}_\mathrm{T}^X$. BenDavid et al.in [30, 31] proved that, for a symmetric hypothesis class $\mathcal{H}$, one can compute the *empirical $\mathcal{H}$-divergence* between two samples $S \sim (\mathcal{D}_\mathrm{S}^X)^n$ and $T \sim (\mathcal{D}_\mathrm{T}^X)^{n'}$ by computing

$$\hat{d}_\mathcal{H}(S, T) = 2\left(1 - \min_{\eta\in\mathcal{H}} \left[\frac{1}{n}\sum_{i=1}^{n} I[\eta(\mathbf{x}_i){=}0] + \frac{1}{n'}\sum_{i=n+1}^{N} I[\eta(\mathbf{x}_i){=}1]\right]\right), \tag{10.1}$$

where $I[a]$ is the indicator function which is 1 if predicate a is true, and 0 otherwise.

Proxy Distance (c.f. [31]) suggested that, even if it is generally hard to compute $\hat{d}_\mathcal{H}(S, T)$ exactly (e.g., when $\mathcal{H}$ is the space of linear classifiers on X), we can easily approximate it by running a learning algorithm on the problem of discriminating between source and target examples. To do so, we construct a new data set $U = \{(\mathbf{x}_i, 0)\}_{i=1}^n \cup \{(\mathbf{x}_i, 1)\}_{i=n+1}^N$, where the examples of the source sample are labeled 0 and the examples of the target sample are labeled 1. Then, the risk of the classifier trained on the new data set U approximates the "min" part of Eq. (10.1). Given a

[1] As mentioned in [31], the same analysis holds for multi-class setting. However, to obtain the same results when $|Y| > 2$, one should assume that $\mathcal{H}$ is a symmetrical hypothesis class. That is, for all $h \in \mathcal{H}$ and any permutation of labels $c : Y \to Y$, we have $c(h) \in \mathcal{H}$. Note that this is the case for most commonly used neural network architectures.

generalization error ϵ on the problem of discriminating between source and target examples, the $\mathcal{H}$-divergence is then approximated by $\hat{d}_{\mathcal{A}} = 2(1-2\epsilon)$. In [31], the value $\hat{d}_{\mathcal{A}}$ is called the *Proxy $\mathcal{A}$-distance* (PAD). The *$\mathcal{A}$-distance* being defined as $d_{\mathcal{A}}(\mathcal{D}_S^X, \mathcal{D}_T^X) = 2\sup_{A\in\mathcal{A}} \mid \Pr_{\mathcal{D}_S^X}(A) - \Pr_{\mathcal{D}_T^X}(A) \mid$, where $\mathcal{A}$ is a subset of X. Note that, by choosing $\mathcal{A} = \{A_\eta | \eta \in \mathcal{H}\}$, with A_η the set represented by the characteristic function η, the $\mathcal{A}$-distance and the $\mathcal{H}$-divergence of Definition 10.1 are identical.

Generalization Bound on the Target Risk BenDavid et al. in [30, 31] also showed that the $\mathcal{H}$-divergence $d_{\mathcal{H}}(\mathcal{D}_S^X, \mathcal{D}_T^X)$ is upper bounded by its empirical estimate $\hat{d}_{\mathcal{H}}(S, T)$ plus a constant complexity term that depends on the *VC dimension* of $\mathcal{H}$ and the size of samples S and T. By combining this result with a similar bound on the source risk, the following theorem is obtained.

Theorem 10.1 ([31]) *Let $\mathcal{H}$ be a hypothesis class of VC dimension d. With probability $1-\delta$ over the choice of samples $S \sim (\mathcal{D}_S)^n$ and $T \sim (\mathcal{D}_T^X)^n$, for every $\eta \in \mathcal{H}$:*

$$R_{\mathcal{D}_T}(\eta) \le \widehat{R}_S(\eta) + \sqrt{\tfrac{4}{n}\left(d\log\tfrac{2e\,n}{d} + \log\tfrac{4}{\delta}\right)} + \hat{d}_{\mathcal{H}}(S,T) + 4\sqrt{\tfrac{1}{n}\left(d\log\tfrac{2n}{d} + \log\tfrac{4}{\delta}\right)} + \beta,$$

with $\beta \ge \inf_{\eta^*\in\mathcal{H}} \left[R_{\mathcal{D}_S}(\eta^*) + R_{\mathcal{D}_T}(\eta^*)\right]$, and $\widehat{R}_S(\eta) = \frac{1}{n}\sum_{(\mathbf{x},y)\in S} I[\eta(\mathbf{x})\neq y]$ is the empirical source risk.

The previous result tells us that $R_{\mathcal{D}_T}(\eta)$ can be low only when the β term is low, i.e., only when there exists a classifier that can achieve a low risk on both distributions. It also tells us that, to find a classifier with a small $R_{\mathcal{D}_T}(\eta)$ in a given class of fixed VC dimension, the learning algorithm should minimize (in that class) a trade-off between the source risk $\widehat{R}_S(\eta)$ and the empirical $\mathcal{H}$-divergence $\hat{d}_{\mathcal{H}}(S, T)$. As pointed out in [31], a strategy to control the $\mathcal{H}$-divergence is to find a representation of the examples where both the source and the target domain are as indistinguishable as possible. Under such a representation, a hypothesis with a low source risk will, according to Theorem 10.1, perform well on the target data.

10.3 Domain-Adversarial Neural Networks (DANN)

An original aspect of our approach is to explicitly implement the idea exhibited by Theorem 10.1 into a neural network classifier. That is, to learn a model that can generalize well from one domain to another, we ensure that the internal representation of the neural network contains no discriminative information about the origin of the input (source or target), while preserving a low risk on the source (labeled) examples. In this section, we detail the proposed approach for incorporating a "domain adaptation component" to neural networks. We start by developing the idea for the simplest possible case, i.e., a single hidden layer, fully connected neural network. We then describe how to generalize the approach to arbitrary (deep) architectures.

Shallow Neural Network Let us first consider a standard neural network architecture with a single hidden layer. For simplicity, we suppose that the input space is formed by m-dimensional real vectors. Thus, $X = \mathbb{R}^m$. The hidden layer G_f learns a function $G_f : X \to \mathbb{R}^D$ that maps an example into a new D-dimensional representation,[2] and is parametrized by a matrix-vector pair $(\mathbf{W}, \mathbf{b}) \in \mathbb{R}^{D\times m} \times \mathbb{R}^D$:

$$G_f(\mathbf{x}; \mathbf{W}, \mathbf{b}) = \operatorname{sigm}\big(\mathbf{W}\mathbf{x} + \mathbf{b}\big), \quad \text{with } \operatorname{sigm}(\mathbf{a}) = \left[\frac{1}{1+\exp(-a_i)}\right]_{i=1}^{|\mathbf{a}|}. \tag{10.2}$$

Similarly, the prediction layer G_y learns a function $G_y : \mathbb{R}^D \to [0, 1]^L$ parametrized by a pair $(\mathbf{V}, \mathbf{c}) \in \mathbb{R}^{L\times D} \times \mathbb{R}^L$:

$$G_y(G_f(\mathbf{x}); \mathbf{V}, \mathbf{c}) = \operatorname{softmax}\big(\mathbf{V}G_f(\mathbf{x}) + \mathbf{c}\big), \quad \text{with } \operatorname{softmax}(\mathbf{a}) = \left[\frac{\exp(a_i)}{\sum_{j=1}^{|\mathbf{a}|}\exp(a_j)}\right]_{i=1}^{|\mathbf{a}|}.$$

Here we have $L = |Y|$. By using the softmax function, each component of vector $G_y(G_f(\mathbf{x}))$ denotes the conditional probability that the neural network assigns $\mathbf{x}$ to the class in Y represented by that component. Given a source example $(\mathbf{x}_i, y_i)$, the natural classification loss to use is the negative log-probability of the correct label: $\mathcal{L}_y\big(G_y(G_f(\mathbf{x}_i)), y_i\big) = -\log\big[G_y(G_f(\mathbf{x}))_{y_i}\big]$. Training the neural network then leads to the following optimization problem on the source domain:

$$\min_{\mathbf{W},\mathbf{b},\mathbf{V},\mathbf{c}} \left[\frac{1}{n}\sum_{i=1}^{n} \mathcal{L}_y^i(\mathbf{W}, \mathbf{b}, \mathbf{V}, \mathbf{c}) + \lambda \cdot R(\mathbf{W}, \mathbf{b})\right], \tag{10.3}$$

where $\mathcal{L}_y^i(\mathbf{W}, \mathbf{b}, \mathbf{V}, \mathbf{c}) = \mathcal{L}_y\big(G_y(G_f(\mathbf{x}_i; \mathbf{W}, \mathbf{b}); \mathbf{V}, \mathbf{c}), y_i\big)$ is a shorthand notation for the prediction loss on the i-th example, and $R(\mathbf{W}, \mathbf{b})$ is an optional regularizer that is weighted by hyperparameter λ.

The heart of our approach is to design a *domain regularizer* directly derived from the $\mathcal{H}$-divergence of Definition 10.1. To this end, we view the output of the hidden layer G_f (Eq. (10.2)) as the internal representation of the neural network. Thus, we denote the source sample representations as $S(G_f) = \big\{G_f(\mathbf{x}) \,\big|\, \mathbf{x} \in S\big\}$. Similarly, given an unlabeled sample from the target domain we denote the corresponding representations $T(G_f) = \big\{G_f(\mathbf{x}) \,\big|\, \mathbf{x} \in T\big\}$. Based on Eq. (10.1), $\hat{d}_{\mathcal{H}}\big(S(G_f), T(G_f)\big)$, i.e., the empirical $\mathcal{H}$-divergence of a symmetric hypothesis class $\mathcal{H}$ between samples $S(G_f)$ and $T(G_f)$, is given by:

$$2\left(1 - \min_{\eta\in\mathcal{H}}\left[\frac{1}{n}\sum_{i=1}^{n} I\big[\eta(G_f(\mathbf{x}_i))=0\big] + \frac{1}{n'}\sum_{i=n+1}^{N} I\big[\eta(G_f(\mathbf{x}_i))=1\big]\right]\right). \tag{10.4}$$

[2]For brevity of notation, we will sometimes drop the dependence of G_f on its parameters $(\mathbf{W}, \mathbf{b})$ and shorten $G_f(\mathbf{x}; \mathbf{W}, \mathbf{b})$ to $G_f(\mathbf{x})$.

Let us consider $\mathcal{H}$ as the class of hyperplanes in the representation space. Inspired by the Proxy $\mathcal{A}$-distance (see Sect. 10.2), we suggest estimating the "min" part of Eq. (10.4) by a *domain classification layer* G_d that learns a logistic regressor $G_d : \mathbb{R}^D \to [0, 1]$, parametrized by a vector-scalar pair $(\mathbf{u}, z) \in \mathbb{R}^D \times \mathbb{R}$, that models the probability that a given input is from the source domain $\mathcal{D}_S^X$ or the target domain $\mathcal{D}_T^X$. Thus,

$$G_d(G_f(\mathbf{x}); \mathbf{u}, z) = \operatorname{sigm}\big(\mathbf{u}^\top G_f(\mathbf{x}) + z\big). \tag{10.5}$$

Hence, the function $G_d(\cdot)$ is a *domain regressor*. We define its loss by:

$$\mathcal{L}_d\big(G_d(G_f(\mathbf{x}_i)), d_i\big) = -d_i \log\big[\mathbf{d}(\mathbf{f}(\mathbf{x}_i))\big] - (1-d_i)\log\big[1-\mathbf{d}(\mathbf{f}(\mathbf{x}_i))\big].$$

where d_i denotes the binary variable (*domain label*) for the i-th example, which indicates whether $\mathbf{x}_i$ come from the source distribution ($\mathbf{x}_i \sim \mathcal{D}_S^X$ if $d_i=0$) or from the target distribution ($\mathbf{x}_i \sim \mathcal{D}_T^X$ if $d_i=1$).

Recall that for the examples from the source distribution ($d_i=0$), the corresponding labels $y_i \in Y$ are known at training time. For the examples from the target domains, we do not know the labels at training time, and we want to predict such labels at test time. This enables us to add a domain adaptation term to the objective of Eq. (10.3), giving the following regularizer:

$$R(\mathbf{W}, \mathbf{b}) = \max_{\mathbf{u}, z}\left[-\frac{1}{n}\sum_{i=1}^{n} \mathcal{L}_d^i(\mathbf{W}, \mathbf{b}, \mathbf{u}, z) - \frac{1}{n'}\sum_{i=n+1}^{N} \mathcal{L}_d^i(\mathbf{W}, \mathbf{b}, \mathbf{u}, z)\right], \tag{10.6}$$

where $\mathcal{L}_d^i(\mathbf{W}, \mathbf{b}, \mathbf{u}, z) = \mathcal{L}_d\big(G_d(G_f(\mathbf{x}_i; \mathbf{W}, \mathbf{b}); \mathbf{u}, z), d_i\big)$. This regularizer seeks to approximate the $\mathcal{H}$-divergence of Eq. (10.4), as $2(1 - R(\mathbf{W}, \mathbf{b}))$ is a surrogate for $\hat{d}_{\mathcal{H}}\big(S(G_f), T(G_f)\big)$. In line with Theorem 10.1, the optimization problem given by Eqs. (10.3) and (10.6) implements a trade-off between the minimization of the source risk $\widehat{R}_S(\cdot)$ and the divergence $\hat{d}_{\mathcal{H}}(\cdot, \cdot)$. The hyperparameter λ is then used to tune the trade-off between these two quantities during the learning process.

For learning, we first note that we can rewrite the complete optimization objective of Eq. (10.3) as follows:

$$\begin{aligned} &E(\mathbf{W}, \mathbf{V}, \mathbf{b}, \mathbf{c}, \mathbf{u}, z) \\ &= \frac{1}{n}\sum_{i=1}^{n} \mathcal{L}_y^i(\mathbf{W}, \mathbf{b}, \mathbf{V}, \mathbf{c}) - \lambda\Big(\frac{1}{n}\sum_{i=1}^{n} \mathcal{L}_d^i(\mathbf{W}, \mathbf{b}, \mathbf{u}, z) + \frac{1}{n'}\sum_{i=n+1}^{N} \mathcal{L}_d^i(\mathbf{W}, \mathbf{b}, \mathbf{u}, z)\Big). \end{aligned} \tag{10.7}$$

We are seeking the parameters $\hat{\mathbf{W}}, \hat{\mathbf{V}}, \hat{\mathbf{b}}, \hat{\mathbf{c}}, \hat{\mathbf{u}}, \hat{z}$ that deliver a saddle point given by

$$(\hat{\mathbf{W}}, \hat{\mathbf{V}}, \hat{\mathbf{b}}, \hat{\mathbf{c}}) = \operatorname*{arg\,min}_{\mathbf{W}, \mathbf{V}, \mathbf{b}, \mathbf{c}} E(\mathbf{W}, \mathbf{V}, \mathbf{b}, \mathbf{c}, \hat{\mathbf{u}}, \hat{z}), \text{ with } (\hat{\mathbf{u}}, \hat{z}) = \operatorname*{arg\,max}_{\mathbf{u}, z} E(\hat{\mathbf{W}}, \hat{\mathbf{V}}, \hat{\mathbf{b}}, \hat{\mathbf{c}}, \mathbf{u}, z).$$

Thus, the optimization problem involves a minimization with respect to some parameters, as well as a maximization with respect to the others.

We propose to tackle this problem with a simple stochastic gradient procedure, in which updates are made in the opposite direction of the gradient of Eq. (10.7) for the minimizing parameters, and in the direction of the gradient for the maximizing parameters. Stochastic estimates of the gradient are made, using a subset of the training samples to compute the averages.

During training, the neural network (parametrized by $\mathbf{W}, \mathbf{b}, \mathbf{V}, \mathbf{c}$) and the domain regressor (parametrized by $\mathbf{u}$, z) are competing against each other, in an adversarial way, over the objective of Eq. (10.7). For this reason, we refer to networks trained according to this objective as Domain-Adversarial Neural Networks (DANN). It will effectively attempt to learn a hidden layer $G_f(\cdot)$ that maps an example (either source or target) into a representation allowing the output layer $G_y(\cdot)$ to accurately classify source samples, but crippling the ability of the domain regressor $G_d(\cdot)$ to detect whether each example belongs to the source or target domains.

Generalization to Arbitrary Architectures It is straightforward to generalize the single hidden layer DANN, presented above, to other sophisticated architectures, which might be more appropriate for the data at hand. To do so, let us now use a more general notation for the different components of DANN. Namely, let $G_f(\cdot; \theta_f)$ be the D-dimensional neural network feature extractor, with parameters θ_f. Also, let $G_y(\cdot; \theta_y)$ be the part of DANN that computes the network's label prediction output layer, with parameters θ_y, while $G_d(\cdot; \theta_d)$ now corresponds to the computation of the domain prediction output of the network, with parameters θ_d. Note that for preserving the theoretical guarantees of Theorem 10.1, the hypothesis class $\mathcal{H}_d$ generated by the domain prediction component G_d should include the hypothesis class $\mathcal{H}_y$ generated by the label prediction component G_y. Thus, $\mathcal{H}_y \subseteq \mathcal{H}_d$. We will note the prediction loss and the domain loss respectively by

$$\mathcal{L}_y^i(\theta_f, \theta_y) = \mathcal{L}_y\big(G_y(G_f(\mathbf{x}_i; \theta_f); \theta_y), y_i\big)\,; \quad \mathcal{L}_d^i(\theta_f, \theta_d) = \mathcal{L}_d\big(G_d(G_f(\mathbf{x}_i; \theta_f); \theta_d), d_i\big).$$

Training DANN then parallels the single layer case and consists in optimizing

$$E(\theta_f, \theta_y, \theta_d) = \frac{1}{n}\sum_{i=1}^{n} \mathcal{L}_y^i(\theta_f, \theta_y) - \lambda\Big(\frac{1}{n}\sum_{i=1}^{n} \mathcal{L}_d^i(\theta_f, \theta_d) + \frac{1}{n'}\sum_{i=n+1}^{N} \mathcal{L}_d^i(\theta_f, \theta_d)\Big) \quad (10.8)$$

by finding the saddle point $\hat{\theta}_f, \hat{\theta}_y, \hat{\theta}_d$ such that

$$(\hat{\theta}_f, \hat{\theta}_y) = \operatorname*{arg\,min}_{\theta_f, \theta_y} E(\theta_f, \theta_y, \hat{\theta}_d)\,, \quad \text{with } \hat{\theta}_d = \operatorname*{arg\,max}_{\theta_d} E(\hat{\theta}_f, \hat{\theta}_y, \theta_d)\,. \quad (10.9)$$

As suggested previously, a saddle point defined by Eq. (10.9) can be found as a stationary point of the following gradient updates:

$$\theta_f \longleftarrow \theta_f - \mu \left(\frac{\partial \mathcal{L}_y^i}{\partial \theta_f} - \lambda \frac{\partial \mathcal{L}_d^i}{\partial \theta_f} \right), \tag{10.10}$$

$$\theta_y \longleftarrow \theta_y - \mu \frac{\partial \mathcal{L}_y^i}{\partial \theta_y}, \quad \text{and} \quad \theta_d \longleftarrow \theta_d - \mu\lambda \frac{\partial \mathcal{L}_d^i}{\partial \theta_d}, \tag{10.11}$$

where μ is the learning rate. We use stochastic estimates of these gradients, by sampling examples from the data set.

The updates of Eqs. (10.10) and (10.11) are very similar to stochastic gradient descent (SGD) updates for a feed-forward deep model that comprises feature extractor fed into the label predictor and into the domain classifier (with loss weighted by λ). The only difference is that in Eq. (10.10), the gradients from the class and domain predictors are subtracted, instead of being summed (the difference is important, as otherwise SGD would try to make features dissimilar across domains in order to minimize the domain classification loss). Since SGD—and its many variants, such as ADAGRAD [141] or ADADELTA [571]—is the main learning algorithm implemented in most libraries for deep learning, it would be convenient to frame an implementation of our stochastic saddle point procedure as SGD.

Fortunately, such a reduction can be accomplished by introducing a special *Gradient Reversal Layer* (GRL), defined as follows. The Gradient Reversal Layer has no parameters associated with it. During the forward propagation, the GRL acts as an identity transformation. During the backpropagation however, the GRL takes the gradient from the subsequent level and changes its sign, i.e. multiplies it by -1, before passing it to the preceding layer. Implementing such a layer using existing object-oriented packages for deep learning is simple, requiring only to define procedures for the forward propagation (identity transformation), and backpropagation (multiplying by -1). The layer requires no parameter update.

The GRL as defined above is inserted between the feature extractor G_f and the domain classifier G_d, resulting in the architecture depicted in Fig. 10.1. As the backpropagation process passes through the GRL, the partial derivatives of the loss that is downstream the GRL (i.e., $\mathcal{L}_d$) w.r.t. the layer parameters that are upstream the GRL (i.e., θ_f) get multiplied by -1, i.e., $\frac{\partial \mathcal{L}_d}{\partial \theta_f}$ is effectively replaced with $-\frac{\partial \mathcal{L}_d}{\partial \theta_f}$. Therefore, running SGD in the resulting model implements the updates of Eqs. (10.10) and (10.11) and converges to a saddle point of Eq. (10.8).

Mathematically, we can formally treat the Gradient Reversal Layer as a "pseudo-function" $\mathcal{R}(\mathbf{x})$ defined by two (incompatible) equations describing its forward and backpropagation behavior:

$$\mathcal{R}(\mathbf{x}) = \mathbf{x}, \quad \text{and} \quad \frac{d\mathcal{R}}{d\mathbf{x}} = -\mathbf{I},$$

where $\mathbf{I}$ is an identity matrix. Then, we define the objective "pseudofunction" of $(\theta_f, \theta_y, \theta_d)$ that is being optimized by the gradient descent within our method:

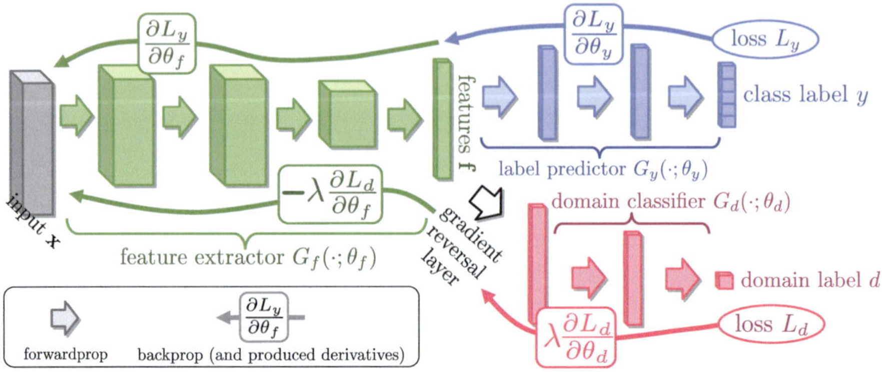

Fig. 10.1 The **proposed architecture** includes a *feature extractor* (*green*) and a *label predictor* (*blue*), which together form a standard feed-forward architecture. Unsupervised DA is achieved by adding a *domain classifier* (*red*) connected to the feature extractor via a *Gradient Reversal Layer* (GRL) that multiplies the gradient by a certain negative constant during the backpropagation-based training. The GRL ensures that the feature distributions over the two domains are made similar (as indistinguishable as possible for the domain classifier)

$$\tilde{E}(\theta_f,\theta_y,\theta_d) = \frac{1}{n}\sum_{i=1}^{n}\mathcal{L}_y\left(G_y(G_f(\mathbf{x}_i;\theta_f);\theta_y), y_i\right)$$
$$-\lambda\Big(\frac{1}{n}\sum_{i=1}^{n}\mathcal{L}_d\left(G_d(\mathcal{R}(G_f(\mathbf{x}_i;\theta_f));\theta_d), d_i\right) + \frac{1}{n'}\sum_{i=n+1}^{N}\mathcal{L}_d\left(G_d(\mathcal{R}(G_f(\mathbf{x}_i;\theta_f));\theta_d), d_i\right)\Big). \quad (10.12)$$

Running updates Eqs. (10.10)–(10.11) can then be implemented as doing SGD for Eq. (10.12) and leads to the emergence of features that are domain-invariant and discriminative at the same time. After the learning, the label predictor $G_y(G_f(\mathbf{x};\theta_f);\theta_y)$ can be used to predict labels for both target and source samples.

10.4 Experiments

10.4.1 Toy Experiment with Shallow Neural Networks

In this first experiment section, we evaluate the adaptation capability of the simple version of DANN described by Eq. (10.7). To do so, we compare its decision boundary and internal representation to the ones of a standard neural network (NN), on a variant of the *intertwinning moons* 2D problem.[3] In these toy experiments, both algorithms share the same network architecture, with a hidden layer size of 15 neurons. The

[3]To create the source sample S, we generate a lower moon and an upper moon labeled 0 and 1 respectively, each of which containing 150 examples. The target sample T is obtained by (1) generating a sample S' the same way S has been generated; (2) rotating each example by 35°; and (3) removing all the labels. Thus, T contains 300 unlabeled examples.

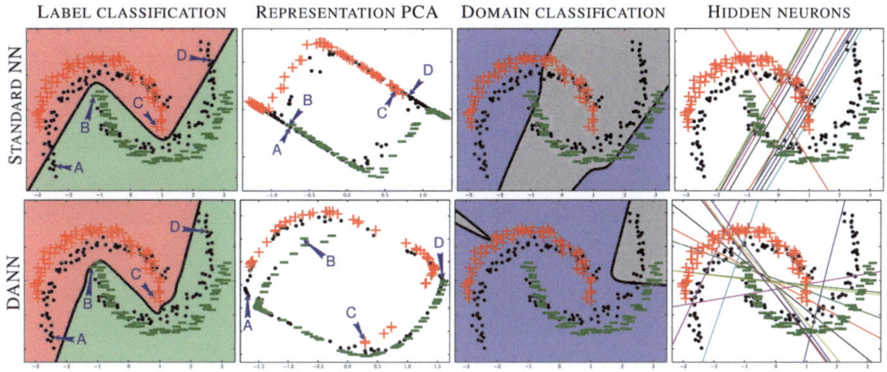

Fig. 10.2 The *intertwinning moons* toy problem. Examples from the source sample are represented as a "+" (label 1) and a "−" (label 0), while examples from the unlabeled target sample are represented as *black dots*. See text for the figure discussion

stochastic gradient descent approach here consists of sampling a pair of source and target examples and performing a gradient step update of all network parameters. Crucially, while the update of the regular parameters follows as usual the opposite direction of the gradient, for the adversarial parameters the of the DANN step must the gradient's direction. We train the NN using a very similar procedure. That is, we even keep updating the domain regressor component using target sample T (with a hyperparameter $\lambda = 6$; the same value is used for DANN), but we disable the *adversarial* backpropagation into the hidden layer. This allows recovering the NN learning algorithm—based on the source risk minimization of Eq. (10.3) without any regularizer—and simultaneously train the domain regressor of Eq. (10.5) to discriminate between source and target domains.

The analysis of the experiment appears in Fig. 10.2, where we compare standard NN (upper graphs) and DANN (lower graphs) from four different perspectives, described in details below.

Label Classification As expected, NN accurately classifies the two classes of the source sample S, but is *not fully adapted* to the target sample T. On the contrary, the decision boundary of DANN perfectly classifies examples from both source and target samples. In the studied task, DANN clearly adapts to the target distribution.

Representation PCA The graphs are obtained by applying a Principal component analysis (PCA) on the set of all representation of source and target data points, i.e., $S(G_f) \cup T(G_f)$. Thus, given the trained network (NN or DANN), every point from S and T is mapped into a 15-dimensional feature space through the hidden layer, and projected back into a two-dimensional plane by the PCA transformation. In the DANN-PCA representation, we observe that target points are homogeneously spread out among source points; In the NN-PCA representation, many target points belong to clusters containing no source points. Hence, labeling the target points seems an easier task given the DANN-PCA representation. To highlight that the representation promoted by DANN is better suited to the adaptation problem, the "Label classification" and "PCA representation" graphs tag four data points (denoted A, B, C, D) that correspond to the moon extremities in the original space. Points A and B are very close to each other in the NN-PCA representation, while they clearly belong to different classes. The same happens to points C and D. Conversely, these four points are at the opposite four corners in the DANN-PCA representation. Also, the target point A (resp. D)—that is difficult to classify in the original space—is located in the "+" cluster (resp. "−" cluster) in the DANN-PCA representation.

Domain Classification We show the decision boundary on the domain classification problem, which is given by the domain regressor G_d of Eq. (10.5). More precisely, an example $\mathbf{x}$ is classified as a source example when $G_d(G_f(\mathbf{x})) \geq 0.5$, and is classified as a target example otherwise. As explained above, we trained a domain regressor during the learning process of NN, but without allowing it to influence the learned representation $G_f(\cdot)$. On one hand, the DANN domain regressor clearly fails to generalize source and target distribution topologies. On the other hand, the NN domain regressor shows a better (although imperfect) generalization capability, as it roughly capture the rotation angle of the target distribution.

Hidden Neurons We show the configuration of hidden layer neurons (by Eq. (10.2), we have that each neuron is indeed a linear regressor). In other words, each of the 15 plot line corresponds to the coordinates $\mathbf{x} \in \mathbb{R}^2$ for which the ith component of $G_f(\mathbf{x})$ equals $\frac{1}{2}$, for $i \in \{1, \ldots, 15\}$. We observe that the standard NN neurons are grouped in three clusters, each one allowing to generate a straight line of the *zigzag* decision boundary for the label classification problem. However, most of these neurons are also able to (roughly) capture the rotation angle of the domain classification problem. Hence, we observe that the adaptation regularizer of DANN prevents these kinds of neurons to be produced. It is indeed striking to see that the two predominant patterns in the NN neurons (i.e., the two parallel lines crossing the plane from lower left to upper right) are vanishing in the DANN neurons.

10.4.2 Deep Networks on Image Classification

We now perform extensive evaluation of a deep version of DANN (see Eq. (10.12)) on a number of popular image data sets and their modifications. These include large-scale data sets of small images popular with deep learning methods (see examples in Fig. 10.3), and the OFF31 dataset [407], which are a *de facto* standard for DA in computer vision, but have much fewer images.

Baselines The following baselines are evaluated in the experiments of this subsection. The *source-only* model is trained without consideration for target-domain data (no domain classifier branch included into the network). The *train-on-target* model is trained on the target domain with class labels revealed. This model serves as an upper bound on DA methods, assuming that target data are abundant and the shift

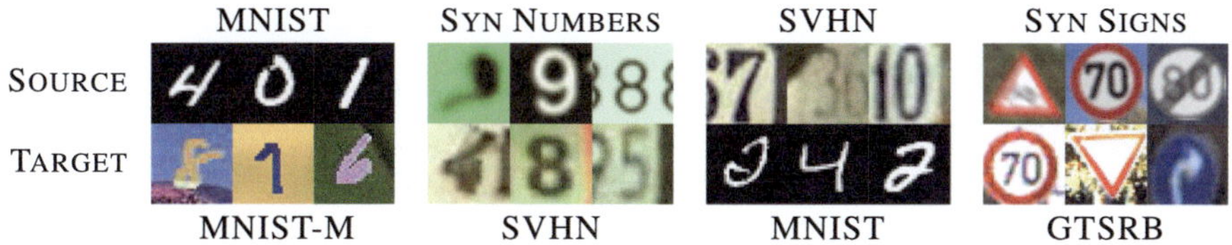

Fig. 10.3 Examples of domain pairs used in the experiments of Sect. 10.4.2

between the domains is considerable. In addition, we compare our approach against the recently proposed unsupervised DA method based on *Subspace Alignment (SA)* [164], which is simple to setup and test on new data sets, but has also been shown to perform very well in experimental comparisons with other "shallow" DA methods. To boost the performance of this baseline, we pick its most important free parameter (the number of principal components) from the range $\{2, \ldots, 60\}$, so that the test performance on the target domain is maximized. To apply SA in our setting, we train a source-only model and then consider the activations of the last hidden layer in the label predictor (before the final linear classifier) as descriptors/features, and learn the mapping between the source and the target domains [164]. Since the SA baseline requires training a new classifier after adapting the features, and in order to put all the compared settings on an equal footing, we retrain the last layer of the label predictor using a standard linear SVM [150] for all four considered methods (including ours; the performance on the target domain remains approximately the same after the retraining). For the Office (OFF31) dataset [407], we directly compare the performance of our full network (feature extractor and label predictor) against recent DA approaches using previously published results.

CNN Architectures and Training Procedure In general, we compose feature extractor from two or three convolutional layers, picking their exact configurations from previous works. More precisely, four different architectures were used in our experiments. The first three are shown in Fig. 10.4. For the OFF31 domains, we use pretrained `AlexNet` from the `Caffe`-package [255]. The adaptation architecture is identical to [499].[4]

For the domain adaption component, we use three $(x \to 1024 \to 1024 \to 2)$ fully connected layers, except for MNIST where we used a simpler $(x \to 100 \to 2)$ architecture to speed up the experiments. Admittedly these choices for domain classifier are arbitrary, and better adaptation performance might be attained if this part of the architecture is tuned. For the loss functions, we set $\mathcal{L}_y$ and $\mathcal{L}_d$ to be the logistic regression loss and the binomial cross-entropy respectively. Following [455] we also use dropout and ℓ_2-norm restriction when we train the SVHN architecture. The learning rate is adjusted during the stochastic gradient descent using the formula $\mu_p = \frac{\mu_0}{(1+\alpha \cdot p)^\beta}$, where p is the training progress linearly changing from 0 to 1, $\mu_0 = 0.01$, $\alpha = 10$ and $\beta = 0.75$ (the schedule was optimized to promote convergence and low error

[4]A 2-layer domain classifier $(x \to 1024 \to 1024 \to 2)$ is attached to the 256-dimensional bottleneck of `fc7`.

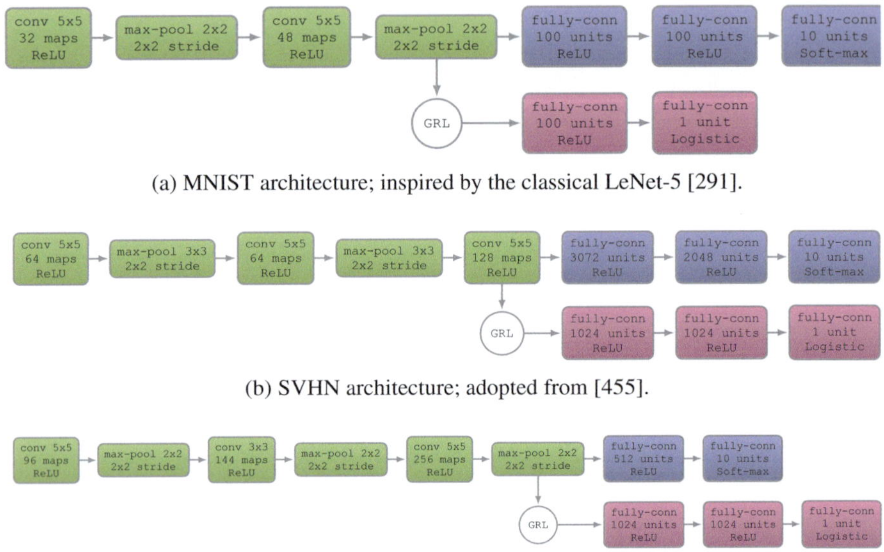

(a) MNIST architecture; inspired by the classical LeNet-5 [291].

(b) SVHN architecture; adopted from [455].

(c) GTSRB architecture; we used the single-CNN baseline from [93] as our starting point.

Fig. 10.4 CNN architectures used in the experiments. *Boxes* correspond to transformations applied to the data. Color-coding is the same as in Fig. 10.1

on the *source* domain). A momentum term of 0.9 is also used. The domain adaptation parameter λ is initiated at 0 and is gradually changed to 1 using the schedule $\lambda_p = \frac{2}{1+\exp(-\gamma \cdot p)} - 1$, where γ was set to 10 in all experiments (the schedule was not optimized/tweaked). This strategy allows the domain classifier to be less sensitive to noisy signal at the early stages of the training procedure. Note however that these λ_p were used only for updating the *feature extractor* component G_f. For updating the *domain classification* component, we used a fixed $\lambda = 1$, to ensure that the latter trains as fast as the *label predictor* G_y.[5]

Finally, note that the model is trained on 128-sized batches (images are pre-processed by the mean subtraction). A half of each batch is populated by the samples from the source domain (with known labels), the rest constitutes the target domain (with labels not revealed to the algorithms except for the train-on-target baseline).

Visualizations We use t-SNE [501] projection to visualize feature distributions at different points of the network, while color-coding the domains (Fig. 10.5). As we already observed with the shallow version of DANN (see Fig. 10.2), there is a strong correspondence between the success of the adaptation in terms of the classification accuracy for the target domain, and the overlap between the domain distributions in such visualizations.

[5]Equivalently, one can use the same λ_p for both feature extractor and domain classification components, but use a learning rate of μ/λ_p for the latter.

MNIST → MNIST-M: top feature extractor layer | SYN NUMBERS → SVHN: last hidden layer of the label predictor

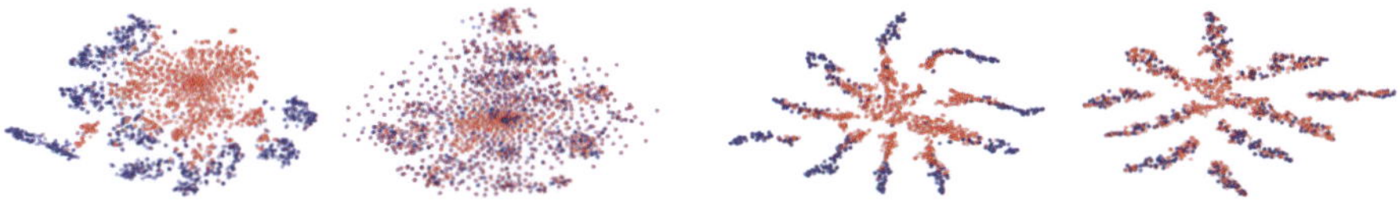

(a) Non-adapted (b) Adapted (a) Non-adapted (b) Adapted

Fig. 10.5 The effect of adaptation on the distribution of the extracted features (*best viewed in color*). The figure shows t-SNE [501] visualizations of the CNN's activations (**a**) when no adaptation was performed and (**b**) when our adaptation procedure was incorporated into training. *Blue* points correspond to the source domain examples, while *red* ones correspond to the target domain

Table 10.1 Digit image classifications accuracies. The first row corresponds to the lower performance bound (no adaptation). The last row corresponds to training on the target data with known labels (upper bound on the DA performance). For SA and DANN we show how much of the gap between the lower and the upper bounds was covered (in brackets)

METHOD	SOURCE	MNIST	SYN NUMBERS	SVHN	SYN SIGNS
	TARGET	MNIST-M	SVHN	MNIST	GTSRB
SOURCE ONLY		0.5225	0.8674	0.5490	0.7900
SA [164]		0.5690 (4.1%)	0.8644 (−5.5%)	0.5932 (9.9%)	0.8165 (12.7%)
DANN		**0.7666** (52.9%)	**0.9109** (79.7%)	**0.7385** (42.6%)	**0.8865** (46.4%)
TRAIN ON TARGET		0.9596	0.9220	0.9942	0.9980

Results On Image Data Sets We now discuss the experimental settings and the results. In each case, we train on the source data set and test on a different target domain data set, with considerable shifts between domains (see Fig. 10.3). The results are summarized in Tables 10.1 and 10.2.

MNIST → MNIST-M Our first experiment deals with the MNIST data set [291] (source). In order to obtain the target domain (MNIST- M) we blend digits from the original set over patches randomly extracted from color photos from BSDS500 [16]. This operation is formally defined for two images I^1, I^2 as $I^{out}_{ijk} = |I^1_{ijk} - I^2_{ijk}|$, where i, j are the coordinates of a pixel and k is a channel index. In other words, an output sample is produced by taking a patch from a photo and inverting its pixels at positions corresponding to the pixels of a digit. For a human the classification task becomes only slightly harder compared to the original data set (the digits are still clearly distinguishable) whereas for a CNN trained on MNIST this domain is quite distinct, as the background and the strokes are no longer constant. Consequently, the source-only model performs poorly. Our approach succeeded at aligning feature distributions (Fig. 10.5), which led to successful adaptation results (considering that the adaptation is unsupervised). At the same time, the improvement over source-only model achieved by SA [164] is quite modest, thus highlighting the difficulty of the adaptation task.

Table 10.2 Accuracy evaluation of different DA approaches on the standard OFF31 [407] data set. All methods (except SA) are evaluated in the "fully transductive" protocol (some results are reproduced from [309])

METHOD S → T	GFK [200]	SA* [164]	DLID [88]	DDC [499]	DAN [309]	SOURCE ONLY	DANN
A → W	0.197	0.450	0.519	0.618	0.685	0.642	**0.730**
D → W	0.497	0.648	0.782	0.950	0.960	0.961	**0.964**
W → D	0.663	0.699	0.899	0.985	0.990	0.978	**0.992**

Synthetic numbers → SVHN To address a common scenario of training on synthetic data and testing on real data, we use Street-View House Number data set SVHN [342] as the target domain and synthetic digits as the source. The latter (SYN NUMBERS) consists of ≈500,000 images generated by ourselves from Windows™ fonts by varying the text (that includes different one-, two-, and three-digit numbers), positioning, orientation, background and stroke colors, and the amount of blur. The degrees of variation were chosen manually to simulate SVHN, however the two data sets are still rather distinct, the biggest difference being the structured clutter in the background of SVHN images.

The proposed backpropagation-based technique works well covering almost 80% of the gap between training with source data only and training on target domain data with known target labels. In contrast, SA [164] results in a slight classification accuracy drop (probably due to the information loss during the dimensionality reduction), indicating that the adaptation task is even more challenging than in the case of the MNIST experiment.

MNIST ↔ SVHN In this experiment, we further increase the gap between distributions, and test on MNIST and SVHN, which are significantly different in appearance. Training on SVHN even without adaptation is challenging—classification error stays high during the first 150 epochs. In order to avoid ending up in a poor local minimum we, therefore, do not use learning rate annealing here. Obviously, the two directions (MNIST → SVHN and SVHN → MNIST) are not equally difficult. As SVHN is more diverse, a model trained on SVHN is expected to be more generic and to perform reasonably on the MNIST data set. This, indeed, turns out to be the case and is supported by the appearance of the feature distributions. We observe a quite strong separation between the domains when we feed them into the CNN trained solely on MNIST, whereas for the SVHN-trained network the features are much more intermixed. This difference probably explains why our method succeeded in improving the performance by adaptation in the SVHN → MNIST scenario (see Table 10.1) but not in the opposite direction (SA is not able to perform adaptation in this case either). Unsupervised adaptation from MNIST to SVHN gives a failure example for our approach: it doesn't manage to improve upon the performance of the non-adapted model which achieves ≈0.25 accuracy (we are unaware of any unsupervised DA methods capable of performing such adaptation).

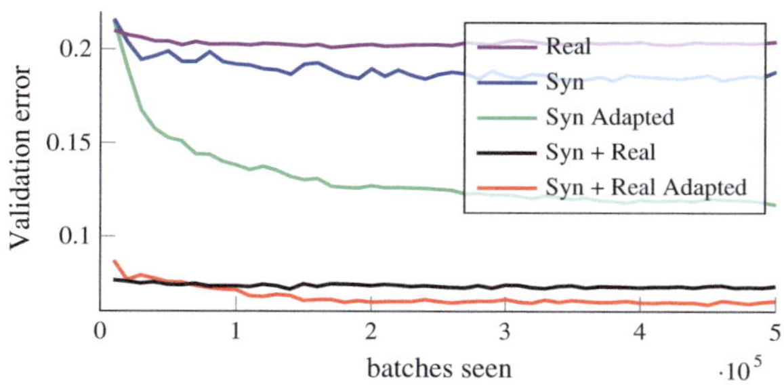

Fig. 10.6 Results for the traffic signs classification in the semi-supervised setting. *Syn* and *Real* denote available labeled images (100,000 synthetic and 430 real respectively); *Adapted* means that ≈31,000 unlabeled target domain images were used for adaptation. The best performance is achieved by employing both the labeled samples and the unlabeled corpus in the target domain

Synthetic Signs → GTSRB Overall, this setting is similar to the SYN NUMBERS → SVHN experiment, except the distribution of the features is more complex due to the significantly larger number of classes (43 instead of 10). For the source domain we obtained 100,000 synthetic images (which we call SYN SIGNS) simulating various imaging conditions. In the target domain, we use 31,367 random training samples for unsupervised adaptation and the rest for evaluation. Once again, our method achieves a sensible increase in performance proving its suitability for the synthetic-to-real data adaptation.

As an additional experiment, we also evaluate the proposed algorithm for semi-supervised DA, i.e., when one is additionally provided with a small amount of labeled target data. Here, we reveal 430 labeled examples (10 samples per class) and add them to the training set for the label predictor. Figure 10.6 shows the change of the validation error throughout the training. While the graph clearly suggests that our method can be beneficial in the semi-supervised setting, thorough verification of semi-supervised setting is left for future work.

OFF31 Dataset We finally evaluate our method on OFF31 data set, which is a collection of three distinct domains: (A)MAZON, (D)SLR, and (W)EBCAM. Unlike previously discussed data sets, OFF31 is rather small-scale with only 2817 labeled images spread across 31 different categories in the largest domain. The amount of available data is crucial for a successful training of a deep model, hence we opted for the fine-tuning of the CNN pretrained on the ImageNet (`AlexNet` from the `Caffe` package [255]) as it is done in some recent DA works [127, 240, 309, 499]. We make our approach comparable with [499] by using exactly the same network architecture replacing domain mean-based regularization with the domain classifier.

Following previous works, we assess the performance of our method across three transfer tasks most commonly used for evaluation. Our training protocol is adopted from [88, 196, 309] as during adaptation we use all available labeled source examples and unlabeled target examples (the premise of our method is the abundance of unlabeled data in the target domain). Also, all source domain data are used for training. Under this "fully transductive" setting, our method is able to improve previously reported state-of-the-art accuracy for unsupervised adaptation very considerably (Table 10.2), especially in the most challenging AMAZON → WEBCAM scenario (the two domains with the largest domain shift). Interestingly, in all three experiments we observe a slight overfitting (performance on the target domain degrades while accuracy on the source continues to improve) as training progresses, however, it does not ruin the validation accuracy. Moreover, switching off the domain classifier branch makes this effect far more apparent, from which we conclude that our technique serves as a regularizer.

10.4.3 Deep Image Descriptors for Re-identification

In this section we discuss the application of the described adaptation method to person re-identification *(re-id)* problem. The task of person re-identification is to match pedestrian images coming from multiple cameras. Unlike classification problems that are discussed above, re-identification problem implies that each image is mapped to a vector descriptor. The distance between descriptors is then used to match images. To evaluate results of re-id methods the *Cumulative Match Characteristic* (CMC) curve is commonly used. It is a plot of the probability of correct identification for different sizes of candidate list returned.

Most existing works train descriptor mappings and evaluate them within the same data set containing images from a certain camera network with similar imaging conditions. Several papers, however, observed that the performance of the resulting re-identification systems drops considerably when descriptors trained on one data set and tested on another. It is therefore natural to handle such cross-domain evaluation as a domain adaptation problem, where each camera network (data set) constitutes a domain. Recently, several papers with significantly improved re-identification performance [352, 583, 584] have been presented, with [317] reporting good results in cross-data-set evaluation scenario. At the moment, deep learning methods [566] do not achieve state-of-the-art results probably because of the limited size of the training sets. Domain adaptation thus represents a viable direction for improving deep re-identification descriptors.

Data Sets and Protocols Following [317], we use PRID [233], VIPeR [211], CUHK [298] as target data sets for our experiments (see examples in Fig. 10.7). The *PRID* data set exists in two versions, and as in [317] we use a single-shot variant. It contains images of 385 persons viewed from camera A and images of 749 persons viewed from camera B, 200 persons appear in both cameras. The *VIPeR* data set also contains images taken with two cameras, and in total 632 persons are captured, for every person there is one image for each of the two camera views. The *CUHK* data set consists of images from five pairs of cameras, two images for each person for each camera inthe pair. We refer to the subset of this data set that includes the first pair of cameras only as *CUHK/p1* (as most papers use this subset).

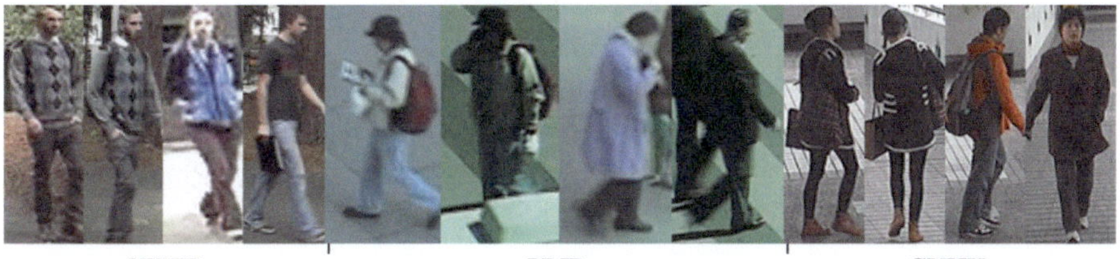

Fig. 10.7 Matching and non-matching pairs of probe-gallery images from different person re-identification data sets. The three data sets are treated as different domains in our experiments

We perform extensive experiments for various pairs of data sets, where one data set serves as a source domain, i.e., it is used to train a descriptor mapping in a supervised way. The second data set is used as a target domain (the labeling is not used). In more detail, CUHK/p1 is used for experiments when CUHK serves as a target domain and two settings ("whole CUHK" and CUHK/p1) are used for experiments when CUHK serves as a source domain. Given PRID as a target data set, we randomly choose 100 persons appearing in both camera views as training set. The images of the other 100 persons from camera A are used as probe, all images from camera B excluding those used in training (649 in total) are used as gallery at test time. For VIPeR, we use random 316 persons for training and all others for testing. For CUHK, 971 persons are split into 485 for training and 486 for testing.

Following [566], we augmented our data with mirror images, and during test time we calculate similarity score between two images as the mean of the four scores corresponding to different flips of the two compared images. In case of CUHK, where there are 4 images (including mirror images) for each of the two camera views for each person, all 16 combinations' scores are averaged.

CNN architectures and Training Procedure In our experiments, we use siamese architecture proposed in [566] for learning deep image descriptors on the source data set. This architecture incorporates two convolution layers (with 7×7 and 5×5 filter banks), followed by ReLU and max pooling, and one fully connected layer, which gives 500-dimensional descriptors as an output. There are three parallel flows within the CNN for processing three part of an image: the upper, the middle, and the lower one. The first convolution layer shares parameters between three parts, and the outputs of the second convolution layers are concatenated. During training, we follow [566] and calculate pairwise cosine similarities between 500-dimensional features within each batch and backpropagate the loss for all pairs within batch.

To perform domain-adversarial training, we construct a DANN architecture. The feature extractor includes the two convolutional layers followed by max pooling and ReLU. The label predictor in this case is replaced with *descriptor predictor* that includes one fully connected layer. The domain classifier includes two fully connected layers with 500 units in the intermediate representation ($x \rightarrow 500 \rightarrow 1$). For the verification loss function in the descriptor predictor we used Binomial Deviance loss, defined in [566] with similar parameters: $\alpha = 2$, $\beta = 0.5$, $c = 2$. The domain

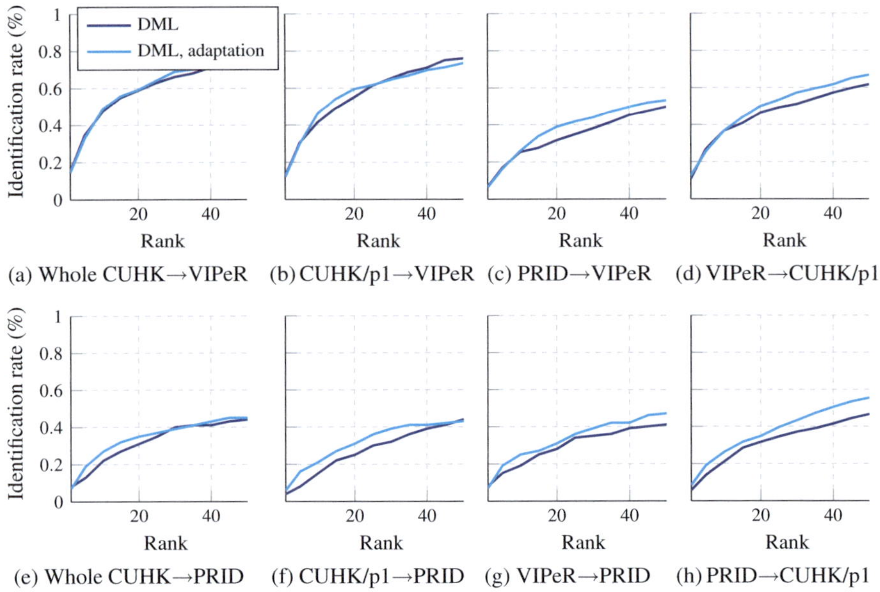

Fig. 10.8 Results on VIPeR, PRID and CUHK/p1 with and without domain-adversarial learning. Across the eight domain pairs DANN improves re-identification accuracy. For some domain pairs the improvement is considerable

classifier is trained with logistic loss as in Sect. 10.4.2. We used learning rate fixed to 0.001 and momentum of 0.9. The schedule of adaptation similar to the one described in Sect. 10.4.2 was used. We also inserted dropout layer with rate 0.5 after the concatenation of outputs of the second max pooling layer. 128-sized batches were used for source data and 128-sized batches for target data.

Results on Re-identification data sets Figure 10.8 shows results in the form of CMC curves for eight pairs of data sets. Depending on the hardness of the annotation problem we trained either for 50,000 iterations (CUHK/p1 → VIPeR, VIPeR → CUHK/p1, PRID → VIPeR) or for 20,000 iterations (the other five pairs). After the sufficient number of iterations, domain-adversarial training consistently improves the performance of re-identification. For the pairs that involve PRID data set, which is more dissimilar to the other two data sets, the improvement is considerable. Overall, this demonstrates the applicability of the domain-adversarial learning beyond classification problems.

10.5 Conclusion

The paper proposes a new approach to DA of feed-forward neural networks, which allows large-scale training based on large amount of annotated data in the source domain and large amount of unannotated data in the target domain. Similarly to many previous shallow and deep DA techniques, the adaptation is achieved through aligning the distributions of features across the two domains. However, unlike previous approaches, the alignment is accomplished through standard backpropagation training. Moreover, our approach is motivated and supported by the domain adaptation theory of [30, 31]. The main idea behind DANN is to enjoin the network hidden layer to learn a representation which is predictive of the source example labels, but uninformative about the domain of the input (source or target). We have shown that our approach is flexible and achieves state-of-the-art results on a variety of benchmark in DA.

A convenient aspect of our approach is that the DA component can be added to almost any neural network architecture that is trainable with backpropagation, allowing simple implementation within virtually any deep learning package through the introduction of a simple Gradient Reversal Layer. Toward this end, we have demonstrated experimentally that the approach is not confined to classification tasks but can be used in other feed-forward architectures, e.g., for descriptor learning for person re-identification.

Acknowledgements This work has been supported by National Science and Engineering Research Council (NSERC) Discovery grants 262067 and 0122405 as well, as the Russian Ministry of Science and Education grant RFMEFI57914X0071. We also thank the Graphics & Media Lab, Faculty of Computational Mathematics and Cybernetics, Lomonosov Moscow State University for providing the synthetic road signs data set. Most of the work of this paper was carried out while P. Germain was affiliated with Département d'informatique et de génie logiciel, Université Laval, Québec, Canada.

Part III
Beyond Image Classification

Chapter 11
Unsupervised Fisher Vector Adaptation for Re-identification

Usman Tariq, Jose A. Rodriguez-Serrano and Florent Perronnin

Abstract Matching and recognizing objects in images and videos, with varying imaging conditions, are a challenging problems. We are particularly interested in the unsupervised setting, i.e., when we do not have labeled data to adapt to the new conditions. Our focus in this work is on the Fisher Vector framework which has been shown to be a state-of-the-art patch encoding technique. Fisher Vectors primarily encode patch statistics by measuring first and second-order statistics with respect to an a priori learned generative model. In this work, we show that it is possible to reduce the domain impact on the Fisher Vector representation by adapting the generative model parameters to the new conditions using unsupervised model adaptation techniques borrowed from the speech community. We explain under which conditions the domain influence is canceled out and show experimentally on two in-house license plate matching databases that the proposed approach improves accuracy.

11.1 Introduction

We are interested in matching objects instances in pairs of images when the imaging conditions may vary from one image to the other. This is a practical scenario for real-world applications. As an example, we are interested in the problem of matching car images captured across a camera network where the acquisition conditions may vary significantly from one camera to another. This is known as the problem of *re-identification*. The differences in imaging conditions may arise from various reasons,

U. Tariq (✉)
Department of Electrical Engineering, American University of Sharjah, Sharjah, United Arab Emirates
e-mail: utariq@aus.edu

J.A. Rodriguez-Serrano
BBVA Data Analytics, Barcelona, Spain

F. Perronnin
Naver Labs Europe, Meylan, France
e-mail: florent.perronnin@naverlabs.com

G. Csurka (ed.), *Domain Adaptation in Computer Vision Applications*, Advances in Computer Vision and Pattern Recognition,
DOI 10.1007/978-3-319-58347-1_11

such as differences in camera models, viewing angles, illumination conditions, etc. In general, if the difference in imaging conditions is too drastic then it will have a significant impact on the representation which is extracted from the images and therefore on the end task.

In this work, our goal is to derive representations which are robust to the underlying conditions. Our focus is on the *unsupervised* setting: we consider that, when collecting data for a new "condition" (e.g., a new camera or a new domain), we are provided with no label. To be more precise, we assume that the only provided label is the camera/domain label. This is to make a clear distinction with other setting in domain adaptation (DA), which addresses classification, and where labels of object classes and of domains are available at training time.

Our focus is on the Fisher Vector (FV) image representation which is a state-of-the-art patch encoding technique [409] with excellent results on a variety of tasks such as scene/object matching [367], vehicle and person re-identification [318, 390] or fine-grained classification [209]. As other image representations, the FV is sensitive to different imaging conditions in the sense that the same object captured under substantially different conditions will lead to different representations.

In a nutshell, FVs represent an image described as a collection of local descriptors by encoding first- and second-order local statistics measured with respect to an a priori learned generative model. We propose to compensate for the differences in conditions by adapting the generic generative model to specific distributions of low-level patches observed in each condition. Generative models have extensively been used in the speech recognition community in the past. There has been strong evidence that when generative models are adapted to any particular speaker, the speech recognition improves considerably [539]. Note that images captured in different acquisition conditions are analogous to speech coming from different speakers. We propose to use the extensive literature on adapting generative models in speech, to make FVs more invariant to the image acquisition conditions.

We note that many of the techniques for DA are geared toward classification problems and would therefore be difficult to apply to a matching problem such as re-identification where there is no notion of class. We note also that these techniques are independent of the particular features which are adapted. Therefore, we believe they are orthogonal and complementary to our FV-specific technique in the sense that they could be combined. We refer the interested reader to Chap. 1 of this book for an in-depth review of the DA literature.

The remainder of this chapter is organized as follows. In Sect. 11.2 we shortly recall the problem of re-identification and we review the FV framework. Section 11.3 describes the main contribution of the chapter: we explain how to make the FV representation more independent of the conditions through the unsupervised adaptation of the underlying generative model. In Sect. 11.4 we show experimentally that the proposed approach leads to accuracy improvements on two in-house vehicle-matching databases. Finally, we conclude in Sect. 11.5.

11.2 Background

Re-identification. For the purpose of explanation we will focus on *re-identification*. Here, the problem is to match whether two images contain the same object instance. For example, whether two images are of the same car (e.g., whether the same vehicle is being observed at the entry and exit of a facility), same bicycle, same aeroplane, etc. To match two images, one may extract FVs from both the images or from some area of focus of the objects (e.g., license plate). This can then be followed by computing some sort of similarity metric between the two FVs. A threshold on the similarity metric may then be used to decide whether the two images are from the same object instance. However, if the imaging conditions are different then the extracted FVs may not be similar, despite containing the same object instance.

Suppose we want to match images from two different cameras with different imaging conditions. We start off with a generative model which is learned a priori. It has been shown that FVs essentially encode the deviations with respect to the generative model. However, a shift in the imaging conditions is reflected in the form of a corresponding shift in the model. So to counter this shift, we adapt the parameters of the generative model in an unsupervised manner using the images from each of the two cameras. This will yield two camera-specific generative models. And thus, the deviations from these models (encoded in the form of FVs) will more likely be because of image content, rather than the imaging conditions.

Fisher Vector computation. Suppose $X = \{x_1, x_2, \ldots, x_N\}$ is a set of N feature vectors extracted from image patches. Let u_Θ be the probability density function of the generative model producing such feature vectors, where Θ represents the parameters of the probability density function. Then the FV is given by [409],

$$\mathscr{G}_\Theta^X = \frac{1}{N} \sum_{i=1}^{N} \mathbf{L}_\Theta \nabla_\Theta \log u_\Theta(x_i) \tag{11.1}$$

where $\mathbf{L}_\Theta$ is the square-root of the inverse of the Fisher Information Matrix of u_Θ. Note that $\sum_{i=1}^{N} \log u_\Theta(x_i)$ is the log-likelihood of the data samples x_i with respect to u_Θ. Thus, computing its gradient (∇_Θ) gives a measure of how the parameters of the model u_Θ should be modified to better fit the data samples in X.

We choose u_Θ to be a K-component Gaussian Mixture Model (GMM) with parameters $\Theta = \{\pi_k, \mu_k, \boldsymbol{\Sigma}_k, k = 1, \ldots, K\}$, where π_k, μ_k and $\boldsymbol{\Sigma}_k$ are, respectively, the weight, mean vector and covariance matrix of the k-th mixture component. Here we require, $\forall_k : \pi_k \geq 0,\ \ \sum_{k=1}^{K} \pi_k = 1$. Thus, for any feature vector x_i we can write,

$$u_\Theta(x_i) = \sum_{k=1}^{K} \pi_k u_k(x_i) \tag{11.2}$$

where,

$$u_k(x_i) = \frac{1}{(2\pi)^{p/2}|\boldsymbol{\Sigma}|^{1/2}} \exp\left\{-\frac{1}{2}(x_i - \mu_k)^\top \boldsymbol{\Sigma}^{-1}(x_i - \mu_k)\right\} \tag{11.3}$$

Note that here p is the dimensionality of the feature vectors, x_i. Since this GMM is learned a priori and is shared across images from different classes and object instances, we will refer to it as the *Universal Background Model (UBM)* in the subsequent discussion (following the convention from speech processing [385]).

After computing $\mathbf{L}_\Theta$ under some assumptions as in [409] and considering diagonal covariance matrices $\boldsymbol{\Sigma}_k$, we arrive at the equations (derived from the Eq. (11.1)) for different parameters of GMM. However, it has been found that deriving FVs using only the means gives state-of-the-art performance in matching applications [367]. Hence, we focus on the gradient with respect to the means:

$$\mathscr{G}^X_{\mu_k} = \frac{1}{N}\frac{1}{\sqrt{\pi_k}}\sum_{i=1}^{N} p(k|x_i)\left(\frac{x_i - \mu_k}{\sigma_k}\right) \tag{11.4}$$

where

$$p(k|x_i) = \frac{\pi_k u_{\theta_k}(x_i)}{\sum_{j=1}^{K}\pi_j u_{\theta_j}(x_i)} \tag{11.5}$$

Here, σ_k are the diagonal entries of the diagonal covariance matrix for the k-th mixture component and vector division implies an *elementwise* operation. Also, $u_{\theta_k}(x_i)$ is the value of the pdf for k-th mixture component at x_i. Note that $\mathscr{G}^X_{\mu_k}$ is a $p \times 1$ vector. The final FV is the concatenation of the gradients $\mathscr{G}^X_{\mu_k}$ for all K mixture components. Hence, it is a Kp-dimensional vector. This is typically then sign-square-rooted and ℓ_2-normalized [409].

11.3 UBM Adaptation

Suppose we have cameras with differing imaging conditions. One approach to counter balance the imaging conditions may be to learn a GMM for each camera independently from scratch. However, in this way we will not have any correspondence among different mixture components from different GMMs. Thus, we will not be able to compare FVs across cameras, since FVs are constructed as a concatenation of gradient statistics for all the mixtures. Hence, as a viable alternative, we propose to adapt the model parameters of the UBM with the images from different cameras, to yield *camera-specific* GMMs. By adaptation, we expect correspondence between components of GMMs, since the adapted models can be interpreted as the updated Gaussian components of the same initial UBM. Afterwards when these camera-specific GMMs are used to compute FVs, the hope is that they will primarily encode the deviations which are specific to a particular image and not the imaging conditions.

Need for adaptation. To explain the need for adaptation further, let us consider Eq. (11.4). Here, $\mathscr{G}^X_{\mu_k}$ is a $p \times 1$ vector. The final FV is the concatenation of the gradients $\mathscr{G}^X_{\mu_k}$ for all K mixture components.

$$\begin{aligned}
\mathscr{G}^X_{\mu_k} &= \frac{1}{N}\frac{1}{\sqrt{\pi_k}}\sum_{i=1}^{N} p(k|x_i)\left(\frac{x_i-\mu_k}{\sigma_k}\right) \\
&= \frac{1}{N}\frac{1}{\sigma_k\sqrt{\pi_k}}\left(\sum_{i=1}^{N} p(k|x_i)x_i - \mu_k\sum_{i=1}^{N} p(k|x_i)\right) \\
&= \frac{1}{N}\frac{1}{\sigma_k\sqrt{\pi_k}}\left(\sum_{i=1}^{N} p(k|x_i)x_i - \mu_k\hat{n}_k\right) \\
\Rightarrow \mathscr{G}^X_{\mu_k} &= \frac{\hat{\pi}_k}{\sigma_k\sqrt{\pi_k}}\left(\hat{m}_k - \mu_k\right) \qquad (11.6)
\end{aligned}$$

where

$$\hat{n}_k = \textstyle\sum_{i=1}^{N} p(k|x_i),\ \hat{\pi}_k = \frac{\hat{n}_k}{N},\ \hat{m}_k = \frac{1}{\hat{n}_k}\sum_{i=1}^{N} p(k|x_i)x_i$$

Note that $\hat{m}_k$ and $\hat{\pi}_k$ are, respectively, the estimates of the mean and mixing weight of k-th Gaussian component given the data samples from X. Thus Eq. (11.6) defines the FV as a difference of the estimated mean ($\hat{m}_k$) and the UBM mixture component mean (μ_k).

Hence, if the change in imaging conditions can be modeled by a piecewise-constant shift δ_k over the support[1] of each Gaussian mixture component k, then the corrupted UBM mean μ_k and image-specific mean $\hat{m}_k$ become $\mu_k + \delta_k$ and $\hat{m}_k + \delta_k$, respectively.[2] But in the absence of adaptation, we will not be able to model the corruption δ_k that would impact both μ_k and $\hat{m}_k$ and would eventually cancel-out in Eq. (11.6); rather $\hat{m}_k$ would alone be impacted with the change in imaging conditions (as μ_k will remain the same without adaptation). Thus, to counter this corruption and cancel-out the effect of change in imaging condition, we need an adaptation strategy, which is what we adopted in this chapter.

Adaptation strategies. We can use various adaptation methods that are popular in the speech community as in [539]. These may include the Maximum a Posteriori (MAP) adaptation [184], the adaptation methods from the linear transformation family, e.g., Maximum Likelihood Linear Regression (MLLR) [292], techniques from the speaker clustering family, e.g., eigenvoices [277]. Each of these has its merits and demerits

[1]The support Ω_k of a Gaussian mixture component k is defined as: $\Omega_k = \{x : k = \arg\max_i p(i|x)\}$

[2]Here we made a hard assignment assumption, meaning that we assumed $p(i|x)$ to be binary, which is reasonable for high-dimensional input vectors x.

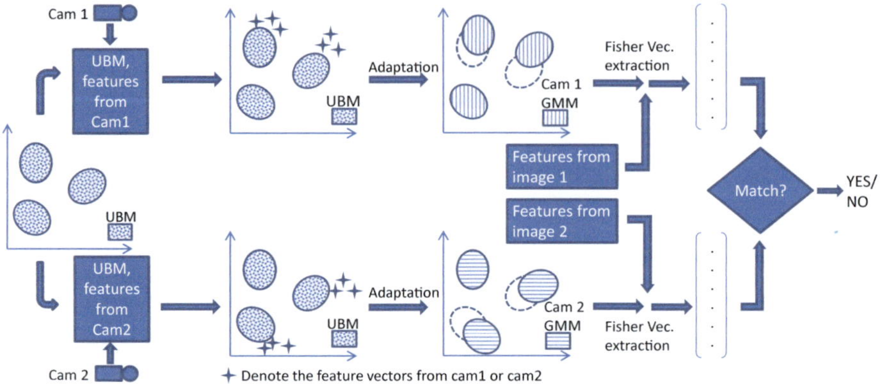

Fig. 11.1 Framework for UBM adaptation for different cameras followed by matching

and the choice may depend on the amount of adaptation data available and the intended application. We consider MAP adaptation and MLLR adaptation in our experiments. Using such techniques for the adaptation of embeddings derived from GMMs, as is the case of FVs, is novel to the best of our knowledge.

Figure 11.1 shows a general framework of UBM adaptation for different cameras. We start with a UBM learned on patches extracted from images in a subset of our data. This is then followed by unsupervised UBM adaptation with patches extracted from images captured by different cameras to yield "camera-specific" GMMs. These adapted GMMs serve for Fisher Vector computation from images that are captured by the respective cameras, which are then used for image-matching purposes.

MAP adaptation We note that our adaptation process is fully unsupervised: given a set of images associated with a camera, we do not need further information on the content of these images to adapt the camera model.

In MAP adaptation, the basic approach is to derive a domain/camera specific model, u_{Θ}^{c}, by updating the parameters in the UBM, u_{Θ}, using the features extracted from the images taken with the domain/camera c [385]. We do it in a two-step EM iterative process [38]. In the first step, we compute the estimates of the sufficient statistics of the features from the camera c (probabilistic count, first and second moments) for each mixture component in the UBM. These are then combined with the old sufficient statistics from the UBM mixture components. This combination is done through a data-dependent mixing coefficient. This coefficient puts more weight on the new sufficient statistics for the mixture components that have a higher probabilistic count from the adaptation data [385].

Suppose $X = \{x_1, x_2, \ldots, x_{N_c}\}$ is a set of N_c feature vectors extracted from the overlapping or nonoverlapping patches from the images from a camera c. For each mixture component k and feature x_i, we compute $p(k|x_i)$ in the first step from Eq. (11.5). We then use $p(k|x_i)$ and x_i to compute the probabilistic count of each mixture component k and first and second moments as in [385].

$$n_k = \sum_{i=1}^{N_c} p(k|x_i), \qquad m_k = \frac{1}{n_k} \sum_{i=1}^{N_c} p(k|x_i) x_i \tag{11.7}$$

$$S_k = \frac{1}{n_k} \sum_{i=1}^{N_c} p(k|x_i) \left[(x_i - \mu_k)(x_i - \mu_k)^\top \right] \tag{11.8}$$

In the second step, these statistics are then used to update the UBM parameters for each mixture component using the following equations [385]:

$$\hat{\pi}_k^c = \left[\tau_k^\pi \frac{n_k}{N_c} + (1 - \tau_k^\pi) \pi_k \right] \alpha \tag{11.9}$$

$$\hat{\mu}_k^c = \tau_k^\mu m_k + (1 - \tau_k^\mu) \mu_k \tag{11.10}$$

$$\hat{\boldsymbol{\Sigma}}_k^c = \tau_k^{\boldsymbol{\Sigma}} S_k + (1 - \tau_k^{\boldsymbol{\Sigma}}) \boldsymbol{\Sigma}_k. \tag{11.11}$$

The above two-step process is then repeated, with the updated UBM parameters for I iterations or till convergence. Note that α in Eq. (11.9) is computed over all mixture components to make sure that $\sum_k \pi_k^c = 1$ holds true. The adaptation parameters $\tau_k^\rho, \rho \in \{\pi, \mu, \boldsymbol{\Sigma}\}$, are given by, $\tau_k^\rho = \frac{n_k}{n_k + r^\rho}$, where r is a design parameter which controls the level of adaptation between new and old statistics. We selected r by cross-validation on a smaller subset (selected value: $r = 10$). Once r is fixed, the new statistics are emphasized more in those mixture components which have a higher probabilistic count n_k for the adaptation data. In practice we use $\tau_k^\rho = \tau$, i.e., we use the same adaptation parameter for all parameters of all Gaussians.

MLLR adaptation An alternate approach to GMM parameter adaptation is to seek an appropriate linear transformation of the model parameters. In MLLR, the Gaussian means are updated according to the following expression [539]:

$$\hat{\mu}_k^c = \mathbf{A} \mu_k + b \tag{11.12}$$

where $\mathbf{A}$ is an $p \times p$ matrix and b is an p-dimensional bias vector (as all the observations x_i are p-dimensional). Equation (11.12) can also be written as

$$\hat{\mu}_k^c = \mathbf{W} \eta_k \tag{11.13}$$

where, η_k is a $(p + 1)$-dimensional augmented mean vector $\eta_k = [1, \ \mu_k]^\top$.

In MLLR we seek the transformation $\mathbf{W}$ that maximizes the likelihood of adaptation data [292]. Similar to MAP adaptation, we can achieve it in an Expectation Maximization framework [38]. We can either learn a transformation for each Gaussian or we can choose to learn a common transformation for all Gaussians.[3] This transform sharing allows our GMM to be adapted with a relatively small amount of data [539].

In speech, a speaker-specific effect, in general, concerns primarily the Gaussian means. However, similar to the means, we can also estimate a variance transformation H. Now, if $\mathbf{L}_k$ is the Cholesky factor of the original covariance matrix $\boldsymbol{\Sigma}_k$, i.e., $\boldsymbol{\Sigma}_k = \mathbf{L}_k\mathbf{L}_k^\top$, then we can write a following expression for the transformed covariance matrix:

$$\hat{\boldsymbol{\Sigma}}_k^c = \mathbf{L}_k\mathbf{H}\mathbf{L}_k^\top. \tag{11.14}$$

Similar to **W**, we can also estimate **H** in an EM framework, where we seek to maximize the likelihood of adaptation data.

Related work. Please note that, in contrast to other DA methods, as outlined in Chap. 1, our adaptation methods are specific to FV representation. It is complementary to the other methods in the sense that they could be combined with our FV-specific technique. It is worthwhile to note that one of the only works in computer vision on feature-specific adaptation is the mean-adjustment approach for VLAD descriptors by [15]. This work is different from ours because it does not make use of a generative model of the underlying data. When applied to the FV (and extended with standard deviation adjustment), this was shown experimentally to yield worse results than a baseline system without adaptation.

The idea of applying MAP adaptation to generative models of FVs was used by [366], but our work is significantly different. In our approach, we use unsupervised adaptation to match imaging conditions, while in [366], supervised adaptation is used for each class to learn per-class GMMs.

The proposed unsupervised approach will be much advantageous in the scenarios where labeled data is either hard to get or impractical to obtain. For example, in the case of deployment for cameras in a parking lot, where the system can re-calibrate the parameters itself. And as noted earlier, the supervised approaches can be combined with the proposed method which can potentially further improve the performance, provided labeled data is available.

Apart from [366], adaptation was used for *word image* retrieval in [391]. There, images were first represented with sequences of low-level patches. These *patch sequences* were then modeled with Hidden Markov Models (HMM). And then the HMM parameters were adapted with MAP or MLLR. However, in the current work we use FV representation, which is more powerful and more discriminative than the former (confirmed by previous experiments carried beyond the scope of this work).

[3]In our experiments, we used shared transformations for all Gaussians.

11.4 Experiments

We focus on the problem of vehicle license plate matching/re-identification. Here, we have cameras on various entry-exit lanes of a parking lot. And we need to match the license plate of a vehicle exiting the parking lot to its license plate image which was captured when this vehicle entered the lot. However, the imaging conditions in both cases may be very different. The different imaging conditions may include different geometry, different camera quality, different lighting conditions, etc. As outlined earlier, this scenario is a good candidate for adaptation of the UBM to learn camera-specific (lane-specific) GMMs before FV computation to aid in matching.

Databases. We experiment with two in-house databases. The in-house vehicle re-identification databases come from two real parking facilities. We will refer to them as the *P1* and *P2* datasets. Vehicle images are captured at the entrances and exits of the parking lots. The goal is to match the plates of vehicles at entry and exit—see for instance [390]. Both datasets are pre-processed by extracting the license plates and normalizing the height to 50 pixels. P1 has 13,006 images (6503 entry-exit pairs) from 11 lanes/cameras. Five out of 11 are entry lanes while the rest are the exit lanes with varying distribution of entry-exit statistics. As for the P2 dataset, we use 9,629 images from two lanes.

Experimental setup. In the following, we present our experimental setup. We use the two in-house databases, P1 and P2, as outlined above. The P1 dataset is partitioned into three subsets. The first partition is used for unsupervised learning purposes: to learn the PCA for the dimensionality reduction of local descriptors or for the UBM training. The second is used for unsupervised UBM adaptation with images from all the lanes/cameras: we adapt the UBM to each of the different lanes/cameras to generate camera-specific GMMs. The third is used for evaluation purposes: one FV is computed per image following the setup of [409] and the entry and exit FVs are matched using the cosine similarity. During evaluation, we match the exiting license plates with the entering ones and then we report the results as a percentage of correctly matched pairs.

In another set of experiments, we replace the first partition with images from the P2 dataset to learn the UBM. This UBM is then adapted using the second partition of P1 which is followed by testing. This mimics the practical scenario where the UBM is learned on images which are not from the same dataset/parking lot.

These results are then averaged across the entry-exit pairs from 11 different cameras. We compare the results of image matching with adapted GMMs to two baselines: the system without adaptation and the system after mean and standard deviation (std.) adjustment. In the latter case for each camera, we compute the mean and standard deviation of its training samples (second partition) and standardize test vectors accordingly. We note that mean adjustment is a domain adaptation approach which was proposed for the VLAD image descriptor [15] which is closely related to the FV.[4] Mean and standard deviation adjustment is a natural extension of the

[4]Note that the VLAD does not have the probabilistic interpretation of the FV.

Table 11.1 Results for UBM learned on P1, followed by mean and mean+variance adaptation using MAP and MLLR and testing on P1. The column labeled Δ shows performance improvement over no adjustment for the respective number of mixture components

nbmix	32	Δ	64	Δ	128	Δ
No.Ad	81.6%		83.0%		84.0%	
MS	81.4%	−0.2%	82.2%	−0.8%	83.0%	−1.0%
MAP.m	**82.3%**	**0.7%**	**84.3%**	**1.3%**	**85.2%**	**1.2%**
MAP.mv	81.6%	0.0%	83.9%	**0.9%**	84.9%	**0.8%**
MLLR.dm	82.0%	0.4%	83.2%	0.2%	84.3%	0.3%
MLLR.dmdv	81.7%	0.1%	83.1%	0.1%	84.4%	0.4%
MLLR.fm	**82.3%**	**0.6%**	83.9%	**0.9%**	84.9%	**0.9%**
MLLR.fmdv	82.2%	**0.6%**	83.7%	**0.7%**	84.9%	**0.9%**

mean-adjustment approach and was found to work better than the latter alternative in preliminary experiments for our two tasks. Note that this can be understood as a diagonal approximation of the Subspace Alignment approach of [164], which is more practical when dealing with high-dimensional vectors.

There may be various options for UBM adaptation. We can adapt all the UBM parameters or select which parameters to adapt. We adapt only means and variances as weight adaptation had little additional impact.

Results and discussion. In the following we present the results of our experiments for image matching on the in-house dataset. We conducted experiments with different number of mixture components (nbmix). We report the results without adaptation (**No.Ad**), with mean and standard deviation adjustment (**MS**), with MAP adaptation and with MLLR adaptation.

We do MAP and MLLR adaptation with different settings and report the results of each. For instance, we do MAP adaptation of only the means (**MAP.m**) and MAP adaptation of both means and covariance matrices (**MAP.mv**). Similarly, we do MLLR adaptation of the means, when the transformation matrix W is diagonal (**MLLR.dm**) and full (**MLLR.fm**). While, in other experiments with MLLR, we adapt the covariance matrices in addition to the means (**MLLR.dmdv** and **MLLR.fmdv**).

Tables 11.1 and 11.2 report the results for the experiments on the in-house datasets on image matching for vehicle re-identification. Table 11.1 report the results of the experiments when the UBM is trained on part of P1 dataset, while Table 11.2 report the results of the experiments when the UBM is trained on the P2 dataset and later adapted with P1 dataset.

It can be seen from results that MAP adaptation, in general, performs better than MLLR adaptation. MAP adaptation of means alone gives better performance in general, compared to when both means and covariance matrices are adapted. This may signify that, similar to speech recognition, means are more significant. Also, we can notice from the results that MLLR adaptation of means with full transformation

Table 11.2 Results for UBM learned on P2, followed by mean and mean+variance adaptation using MAP and MLLR and testing on P1

nmix	32	Δ	64	Δ	128	Δ
No.Ad	81.1%		84.1%		84.9%	
MS	78.8%	−2.2%	83.0%	−1.1%	84.2%	−0.7%
MAP.m	**83.2%**	**2.2%**	**85.8%**	**1.7%**	85.9%	**1.0%**
MAP.mv	82.8%	**1.8%**	85.3%	**1.2%**	**86.4%**	**1.5%**
MLLR.dm	81.6%	**0.6%**	84.9%	**0.8%**	85.1%	0.2%
MLLR.dmdv	81.9%	**0.8%**	85.0%	**0.8%**	85.2%	0.3%
MLLR.fm	82.9%	**1.8%**	85.4%	**1.2%**	85.5%	**0.6%**
MLLR.fmdv	83.1%	**2.1%**	85.5%	**1.4%**	85.7%	**0.8%**

(with and without adaptation of covariance matrices), in general, outperforms the adaptation of means with diagonal transformation (with and without adaptation of covariance matrices). This may be due to the reason that a diagonal transformation may be too restrictive.

In the experiments, there is a decrease in performance with mean and standard deviation adjustment. We can see from the tables that performance increases with MAP adaptation, over no adaptation can be as high as 2.2% in the image-matching experiments with the in-house datasets. Adaptation helps in most of the cases. We underline again that all these results are obtained through unsupervised adaptation.

11.5 Further Analysis and Concluding Remarks

To further understand the need for adaptation from a different perspective, we dive into the internal mechanics of assignment of features to different mixture components in a UBM/GMM. We take, as an example, a UBM learned on the P2 dataset with 32 mixture components. Now we take adaptation data from the P1 dataset. The data from P1 dataset contains images from lanes 36 through 46. The images from each lane are then used to learn a lane/camera-specific GMM. We then compute $p(k|x_i)$ from features x_i for each mixture component k of the UBM and of each lane/camera-specific GMM through Eq. (11.5).

We then plot $p(k|x_i)$ versus k, averaged across features x_i from a particular lane in the adaptation dataset; for the UBM in Fig. 11.2a and for lane/camera-specific GMMs in Fig. 11.2b. Note that in Fig. 11.2b the GMM for each lane is different.

From Fig. 11.2a, one can notice that when the same UBM is used there is considerable spread across images from different lanes. For some lanes, some mixture components have a higher $p(k|x_i)$ while for some other lanes it may be considerably low. This shows that, although the UBM can represent the features, the representation may be different for different lanes/cameras. To counter this shift, we do adaptation

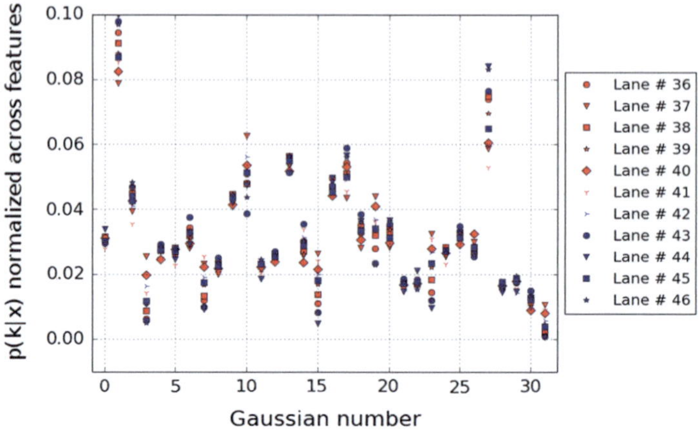

(a) Before Adaptation

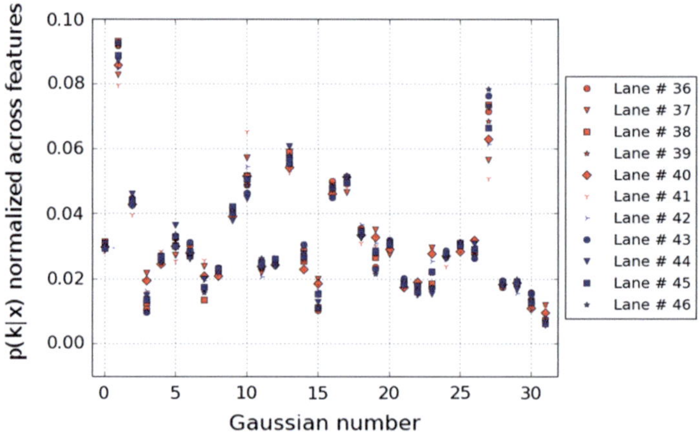

(b) After Adaptation

Fig. 11.2 The above two figures show $p(k|x_i)$, averaged across the features x_i from a particular lane in from the adaptation dataset. $p(k|x_i)$ is computed through Eq. (11.5), for each Gaussian k for a GMM with 32 mixture components. Figure 11.2a shows the spread across lanes before adaptation while Fig. 11.2b shows the spread after adaptation. (Best viewed in color)

and then use lane/camera-specific GMMs in Fig. 11.2b. As a result, the spread is considerably reduced. This shows that when these lane/camera-specific GMMs are used for FV computation, the FVs will encode the deviations which are due to a particular object in question and not due to the imaging conditions.

In the end, we conclude with the remarks that we have presented the first work on *model-level* domain adaptation geared toward image matching. We worked specifically with FVs, as this is a state-of-the-art patch encoding technique and has given excellent performance in a number of applications. Hence, any improvement that can be brought on top of FVs will have a significant impact on many applicative scenarios. And we have shown that our adaptation strategies, inspired from the works in speech recognition, are effective and produce more refined FVs that perform better, in general, compared to those without adaptation, from our experiments on the in-house datasets.

Acknowledgements The vast majority of the work was conducted while the authors were with Xerox Research Centre Europe.

Chapter 12
Semantic Segmentation of Urban Scenes via Domain Adaptation of SYNTHIA

German Ros, Laura Sellart, Gabriel Villalonga, Elias Maidanik, Francisco Molero, Marc Garcia, Adriana Cedeño, Francisco Perez, Didier Ramirez, Eduardo Escobar, Jose Luis Gomez, David Vazquez and Antonio M. Lopez

Abstract Vision-based semantic segmentation in urban scenarios is a key functionality for autonomous driving. Recent revolutionary results of deep convolutional neural networks (CNNs) foreshadow the advent of reliable classifiers to perform such visual tasks. However, CNNs require learning of many parameters from raw images; thus, having a sufficient amount of diverse images with class annotations is needed. These annotations are obtained via cumbersome, human labor which is particularly challenging for semantic segmentation since pixel-level annotations are required. In this chapter, we propose to use a combination of a virtual world to automatically generate realistic synthetic images with pixel-level annotations, and domain adaptation to transfer the models learned to correctly operate in real scenarios. We address the question of how useful synthetic data can be for semantic segmentation—in particular, when using a CNN paradigm. In order to answer this question we have generated a synthetic collection of diverse urban images, named SYNTHIA, with automatically generated class annotations and object identifiers. We use SYNTHIA in combination with publicly available real-world urban images with manually provided annotations. Then, we conduct experiments with CNNs that show that combining SYNTHIA with simple domain adaptation techniques in the training stage significantly improves performance on semantic segmentation.

12.1 Introduction

In practice, even the best visual descriptors, class models, feature encoding methods and discriminative machine learning techniques are not sufficient to produce reliable classifiers if properly annotated datasets with sufficient diversity are not

G. Ros (✉) · L. Sellart · G. Villalonga · E. Maidanik · F. Molero · M. Garcia · A. Cedeño · F. Perez · D. Ramirez · E. Escobar · J.L. Gomez · D. Vazquez · A.M. Lopez
Computer Vision Center, Campus UAB, Barcelona, Spain
e-mail: gros@cvc.uab.es

G. Csurka (ed.), *Domain Adaptation in Computer Vision Applications*,
Advances in Computer Vision and Pattern Recognition,
DOI 10.1007/978-3-319-58347-1_12

available. Indeed, this is not a minor issue since data annotation remains a cumbersome, human-based labor prone to error; even exploiting crowd-sourcing for annotation is a nontrivial task [34]. For instance, for some ADAS and for AD, semantic segmentation is a key issue [281, 395, 413] and it requires pixel-level annotations (i.e. obtained by delineating the silhouette of the different classes in urban scenarios, namely pedestrian, vehicle, road, sidewalk, vegetation, building, etc.).

Autonomous driving (AD) will be one of the most revolutionary technologies in the near future in terms of the impact on the lives of citizens of the industrialized countries [538]. Nowadays, advanced driver assistance systems (ADAS) are already improving traffic safety. The computer vision community, among others, is contributing to the development of ADAS and AD due to the rapidly increasing performance of vision-based tools such as object detection, recognition of traffic signs, road segmentation, etc.

Roughly until the end of the first decade of this century, the design of classifiers for recognizing visual phenomena was viewed as a two-fold problem. First, enormous effort was invested in research of discriminative visual descriptors to be fed as features to classifiers; as a result, descriptors such as Haar wavelets, SIFT, LBP, or HOG, were born and became widely used. Second, different machine learning methods were developed, with discriminative algorithms such as SVM, AdaBoost, or Random Forests usually reporting the best classification accuracy due to their inherent focus on searching for reliable class boundaries in feature space. Complementarily, in order to make easier the search for accurate class boundaries, methods for transforming feature space (e.g., PCA, BoW encoding, Kernel mappings) as well as more elaborate class models (e.g., DPM, superpixels) were proposed.

In order to ameliorate this problem there are paradigms such as unsupervised learning (no annotations assumed), semi-supervised learning (only a few annotated data), and active learning (to focus on annotating informative data), under the assumption that having annotated data (e.g., images) is problematic but data collection is cheap. However, for ADAS and AD such data collection is also an expensive activity since many kilometers must be traveled to obtain sufficient diversity. Moreover, it is well known that, in general terms, supervised learning (annotations assumed) tends to provide the most accurate classifiers.

Recently, the need for large amounts of accurately annotated data has become even more crucial with the massive adoption of deep convolutional neural networks (CNNs) by the computer vision community. CNNs have yielded a significant performance boost for many visual tasks [192, 275, 442, 487]. Overall, CNNs are based on highly nonlinear, end-to-end training (i.e. from the raw annotated data to the class labels) which implies the learning of millions of parameters and, accordingly, they require a relatively larger amount of annotated data than methods based on hand-crafted visual descriptors.

As we will review in Sect. 12.2, the use of visually realistic synthetic images is gaining attention in recent years (e.g., training in virtual words [19, 175, 222, 229, 325, 328, 358, 386, 435], synthesizing images with real-world backgrounds and inserted virtual objects [364, 370]) due to the possibility of having diversified samples with automatically generated annotations. In this spirit, in this chapter we address

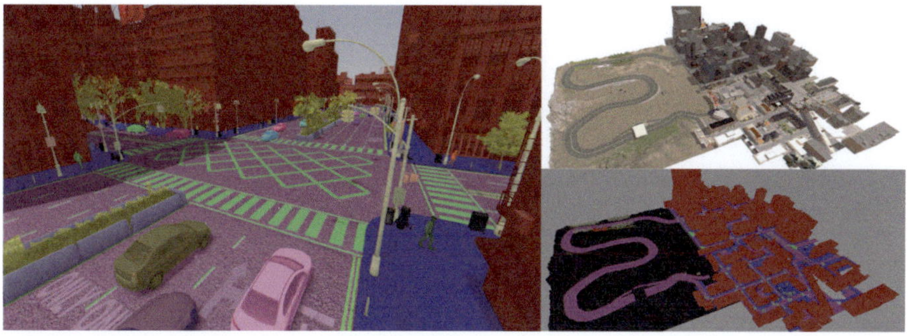

Fig. 12.1 The SYNTHIA Dataset. A sample frame with overlaid semantic labels (*Left*) and a general view of the city (*right*)

the question of *how useful can the use of realistic synthetic images of virtual-world urban scenarios be for the task of semantic segmentation—in particular, when using a CNN paradigm*. To the best of our knowledge, this analysis has not been done so far. Note that, the synthetic training data can not only come with automatically generated class annotations from multiple viewpoints and simulated lighting conditions (providing diversity), but also with ground truth for depth (e.g.,simulating stereo rigs and LIDAR), optical flow, object tracks, etc.

Moreover, in the context of ADAS/AD the interest in using virtual scenarios is already increasing for the task of validating functionalities in the Lab, i.e. to perform validation in the real world (which is very expensive) only once after extensive and well-designed simulations are passed. Therefore, these virtual worlds can be used for generating synthetic images to train the classifiers involved in environmental perception. In addition, the realism of these virtual worlds is constantly increasing thanks to the continuously growing videogames industry.

To address the above-mentioned question, we have generated *SYNTHIA*[1]: a *SYNTHetic* collection of *Imagery* and *Annotations* of urban scenarios (see Figs. 12.1, 12.2 and 12.3). In Sect. 12.3 we highlight its diversity and how we can automatically obtain a large number of images with annotations. As virtual and real-world cameras are different *sensors*, classifiers trained only with virtual images may require domain adaptation to work on real images [357, 467, 503, 545]; this is not surprising as domain adaptation is also often required when training images and testing images come from different real-world camera sensors [489, 503].

In Sect. 12.4 first we describe the CNN used to perform semantic segmentation. Then we present our domain adaptation strategy which consists of training with the synthetic data and a smaller number of real-world data simultaneously, i.e. in the same spirit than [503] for a HOG-LBP/SVM setting. In our case, the data combination is done in the generation of batches during CNN training. The experiments conducted in Sect. 12.5 show how SYNTHIA successfully complements different

[1]SYNTHIA is available at http://synthia-dataset.net.

Fig. 12.2 An example of the different areas/environments available in SYNTHIA: city center, *top-left*; town, *top-right*; highway, *bottom-left*; tunnel, *bottom-right*.)

Fig. 12.3 Dynamic objects in SYNTHIA. (*Top*) vehicles; (*middle*) cyclists; (*bottom*) pedestrians

datasets (Camvid, GeigerIJRR13Vision, RussellIJCV08labelme, Bileschi07CBCL) for the task of semantic segmentation based on CNNs, i.e. the use of the combined data significantly boosts the performance obtained when using the real-world data alone. The future work that we foresee given these results is pointed out in Sect. 12.6, together with the conclusions of the chapter.

12.2 Related Work

The generation of semantic segmentation datasets with pixel-level annotations is costly in terms of effort and money, factors that are currently slowing down the development of new large-scale collections like ImageNet [265]. Despite these factors, the community has invested great effort to create datasets such as the NYU-Depth V2

[441] (more than 1,449 images densely labeled), the PASCAL-Context Dataset [336] (10,103 images densely labeled over 540 categories), and MS COCO [303] (more than 300,000 images with annotations for 80 object categories). These datasets have definitely contributed to boost research on semantic segmentation of indoor scenes and also on common objects, but they are not suitable for more specific tasks such as those involved in autonomous navigation scenarios.

When semantic segmentation is seen in the context of autonomous vehicles, we find that the amount and variety of annotated images of urban scenarios is much lower in terms of total number of labeled pixels, number of classes and instances. A good example is the CamVid [53] dataset, which consists of a set of monocular images taken in Cambridge, UK. However, only 701 images contain pixel-level annotations over a total of 32 categories (combining objects and architectural scenes), although usually only the 11 largest categories are used. Similarly, Daimler Urban Segmentation dataset [413] contains 500 fully labeled monochrome frames for five categories. The more recent GeigerIJRR13Vision benchmark suite [186] has provided a large amount of images of urban scenes from Karlsruhe, Germany, with ground truth data for several tasks. However, it only contains a total of 430 labeled images for semantic segmentation. A common limitation of the aforementioned datasets is the bias introduced by the acquisition of images in a specific city. The RussellIJCV08labelme project [406], later refined by [397], corrects this by offering around 1,000 fully annotated images of urban environments around the world and more than 3,000 images with partial (noisy) annotations.

A larger dataset is the Bileschi07CBCL StreetScenes [37], containing 3,547 images of the streets of Chicago over nine classes with noisy annotations. This dataset has been enhanced in [397], by improving the quality of the annotations and adding extra classes. To date, the largest dataset for semantic segmentation is CordtsFDV15CityScapes [98], which consists of a collection of images acquired in 50 cities around Germany, Switzerland, and France in different seasons, and having 5,000 images with fine annotations and 20,000 with coarse annotations over a total of 30 classes. However, the cost of scaling this sort of project would require a prohibitive economic investment in order to capture images from a larger variety of countries, in different seasons and traffic conditions. For these reasons, a promising alternative proposed in this work is to use synthetic imagery that simulate real urban scenes in a vast variety of conditions and produce the appropriate annotations.

The use of synthetic data has increased considerably in recent years within the computer vision community for several problems. For instance, in [262], the authors used a virtual world to evaluate the performance of image features under certain types of changes. In the area of object detection, similar approaches have been proposed by different groups [229, 325, 364, 467], making use of CAD models, virtual worlds, and studying topics such as the impact of a realistic world on the final accuracy of detectors and the importance of domain adaptation. Synthetic data has also been used for pose estimation [19, 357] to compensate for the lack of precise pose annotations of objects. The problem of semantic segmentation has also begun to benefit from this trend, with the creation of virtual scenes to perform segmentation of indoor environments [221, 222, 358]. Recently, virtual worlds have also debuted in outdoor scenes for semantic segmentation [175, 386, 396] and related scene understanding problems, such as optical flow, scene flow, and depth estimation [328].

In this chapter, we show how state-of-the-art virtual worlds can be exploited in combination of simple DA methods to produce neural network models to operate in real environments for the task of semantic segmentation of driving scenes. We show that after adaptation these models are able to outperform state-of-the-art approaches trained on real data. To this end, we introduce a new and powerful synthetic datasets of urban scenes, which we call SYNTHIA. This dataset is a large collection of images with high variability due to simulated seasonal changes, realistic variations in illumination, textures, pose of dynamic objects, and camera viewpoints.

12.3 The SYNTHIA Dataset

The SYNTHetic collection of Imagery and Annotations (SYNTHIA) has been generated with the purpose of aiding scene understanding related problems in the context of driving scenarios, with special emphasis in semantic segmentation and instance semantic segmentation. It contains enough information to be useful in additional ADAS and AD-related tasks, such as object recognition, place identification and change detection, among others.

SYNTHIA consists of realistic frames (high fidelity with reality), rendered from a virtual city and comes with precise pixel-level semantic annotations at the level of object instances, i.e. individual object can be uniquely identified. The categories included in SYNTHIA are increasing over time due to the dynamic nature of the project, which is in continuous improvement, but the initial core contained 13 classes: sky, building, road, sidewalk, fence, vegetation, lane-marking, pole, car, traffic signs, pedestrians, cyclists, and miscellaneous (see Fig. 12.1). Frames are acquired from multiple viewpoints, and each of the frames also contains an associated depth map and information about the camera pose in global coordinates.

The Virtual World Generator. SYNTHIA has been generated by rendering a virtual city created with the Unity development platform [478]. This city includes the most important elements present on driving environments, such as street blocks, highways, rural areas, shops, parks and gardens, general vegetation, variety of pavements, lane markings, traffic signs, lamp poles, and people, among others. The virtual environment allows us to freely place any of these elements in the scene and to generate its semantic annotations without additional effort. This enables the creation of new and diverse cities as a simple combination of basic blocks. The basic properties of these blocks, such as textures, colors, and shapes can be easily changed to produce new looks and to enhance the visual variety of the data.

The city is populated with realistic models of cars, trucks, trains, vans, pedestrians, cyclists, etc. (see Fig. 12.3). In order to extend visual variability, some of these models are modified to generate new and distinctive versions.

Fig. 12.4 The same area captured in different seasons and light conditions. *Top-left*, fall; *top-right*, winter; *bottom-left*, spring; *bottom-right*, summer

We have defined suitable material coefficients for each of the surfaces of the city in order to produce realistic outcomes that look as similar as possible to real data. However, our intention is to maintain a balance between the cost of creating realistic images and the gain that this element brings to the learning process. The main point behind this work is to highlight that in terms of learning models for semantic segmentation, a cost-effective approach seems to be the one that uses just realistic enough images in combination with DA techniques. This philosophy leaves the generation of photo-realistic images as a less effective approach in terms of costs and learning gains.

Our virtual world includes four different seasons with drastic change of appearance, with snow during winter, blooming flowers during spring, etc., (see Fig. 12.4). Moreover, a dynamic illumination engine serves to produce different illumination conditions, to simulate different moments of the day, including sunny and cloudy days, rain, fog, and dusk. Shadows caused by clouds and other objects are dynamically cast on the scene, adding additional realism.

We would like to highlight the potential of this virtual world in terms of extension capabilities. New parts of the cities are constantly being extended, by adding existing blocks in different setups and additional ground truth can be produced almost effortlessly. Extending the number of classes of the city is also a simple task which consists of assigning a new id to objects. In this way, we can generate a broad variety of urban scenarios and situations, which we believe is very useful to help modern classifiers based on deep learning.

From our virtual city we have generated two complementary sets of images, referred to as SYNTHIA- RAND[2] and SYNTHIA- SEQS.

SYNTHIA-RAND. It consists of random images with no temporal consistency, created to maximize the visual variability of each image including a high density of objects. It contains 20,000 frames of the city taken from a virtual array of cameras moving randomly through the city, with its height limited to the range [1.5, 10 m] from the ground. In each of the camera poses, several frames are acquired changing the type of dynamic objects present in that part of the scene along with the illumination, season, weather conditions of the scene, and the textures of road and sidewalks. We enforce that the separation between camera positions is at least of 10 m in order to improve visual variability. This collection is oriented to serve as training data for semantic segmentation methods based on CNNs.

SYNTHIA-SEQS. It consists of video sequences, i.e. with temporal consistency, simulating different traffic situations such as traffic jams, joining a roundabout, going through a tunnel, highway traffic, etc. It is currently composed by more than eight different sequences, also referred to as "scripts." Each script captures one or various traffic situations, from regular driving to traffic jams, including very critical situations such as joining a roundabout, dealing with objects blocking transit, traffic in highways, and many others. Each script takes place in one or several of the environments present in SYNTHIA, which are highway, town, and city center. Each traffic situation is simulated under different weather and seasonal conditions, from spring to winder; from sunny days to heavy rain. Each of these frames is capture by eight cameras, forming an omni-directional stereo-rig. In total, the combination of all these factors leads to more than 300,000 frames that are available for training.

Our virtual acquisition platform consists of two omni-cameras separated by a baseline $B = 0.8$ m in the x-axis. Each of these omni-cameras consists of four monocular cameras with a common center and orientations varying every 90°, as depicted in Fig. 12.5. Since all cameras have a field of view of 100° the visual overlapping serves to create an omni-directional view on demand, as shown in Fig. 12.5. Each of these cameras also has a virtual depth sensor associated, which works in a range from 1.5 to 600 m and is perfectly aligned with the camera center, resolution and field of view (Fig. 12.5, bottom). The virtual vehicle moves through the city interacting with dynamic objects such as pedestrians and cyclists that present dynamic behavior. This interaction produces changes in the trajectory and speed of the vehicle and leads to variations of each of the individual video sequences providing data to exploit spatio-temporal constraints.

[2] Here we refer to the new SYNTHIA-RAND subset, extended after the CVPR version.

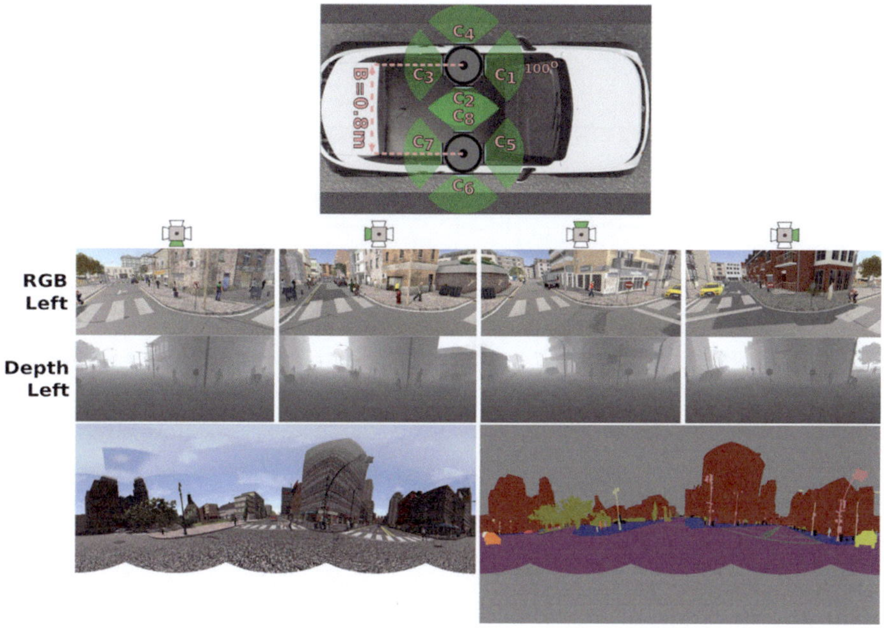

Fig. 12.5 *Top*, virtual car setup used for acquisition. Two multi-cameras with four monocular cameras are used. The baseline between the cameras is 0.8 m and the FOV of the cameras is 100 deg. *Bottom*, One shot example: the four views from the *left* multi-camera with its associated depth maps and the resulting 360 deg panorama with its semantic ground truth

12.4 Semantic Segmentation and Synthetic Images

We first define a simple but competitive deep Convolutional Neural Network (CNN) for the task of semantic segmentation of urban scenes, following the description of [397]. This architecture, referred as Target-Net (T-Net) is more suitable for its application to urban scenes due to its reduced number of parameters. As a reference, we also consider the Fully convolutional networks (FCN) [307], a state-of-the-art architecture for general semantic segmentation. Finally, we describe the strategy used to deal with the synthetic (virtual data) and the real domain during the training stage.

T-Net [397] architecture. along with its associated training procedure is drawn from [397], due to its good performance and ease of training. Similar architectures have proven to be very effective in terms of accuracy and efficiency for segmentation of general objects [346] and urban scenes [24]. Figure 12.6 shows a graphical schema of T-Net. The architecture is based on a combination of contraction, expansion blocks and a soft-max classifier. Contraction blocks consist of convolutions, batch normalization, ReLU, and max-pooling with indices storage. Expansion blocks consist of an

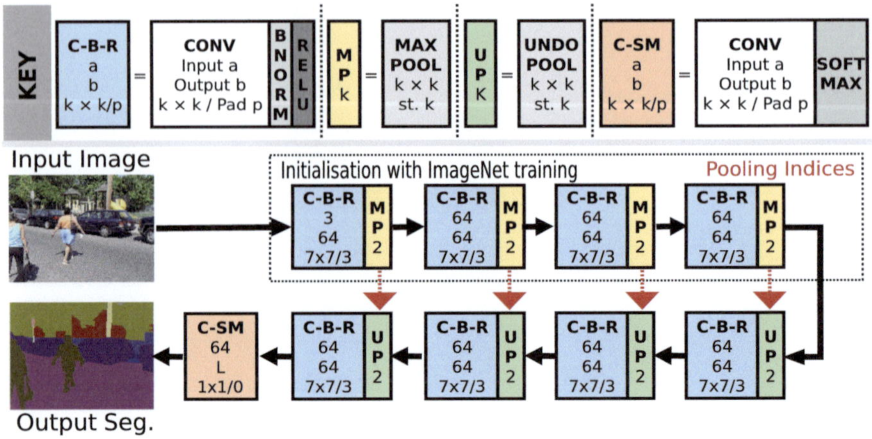

Fig. 12.6 Graphical schema of the semantic segmentation network consisting of a set of contraction (*yellow*) expansion (*green*) blocks, where a and b stand for the input and output number of channels, k is the kernel size and p the padding size, respectively. For pooling, st. stands for stride

unpooling of the blob using the pre-stored indices, convolution, batch normalization and ReLU.

FCN [307] architecture is an extension of VGG-16 [443] with deconvolution modules. Different from T-Net, FCN does not use batch normalization and its up-sampling scheme is based on deconvolutions and mixing information across layers.

We use weighted cross-entropy (WCE) as a loss function for both architectures. WCE re-scales the importance of each class, $l \in [1, \ldots, L]$, according to its inverse frequency $f^l(\mathcal{X})^{-1}$ in the training data set $\mathcal{X}$, i.e.,

$$\text{Loss}_{\text{WCE}}(x^n, y^n) = -\sum_{ijl}^{HWL} \omega(y^n_{ijl}) y^n_{ijl} \log(\mathcal{F}(x^n, \theta))_{ijl}, \tag{12.1}$$

where $\mathcal{F}$ refers to the network, x^n, y^n stand for the n-th training image and ground truth image, respectively. This helps prevent problems due to class imbalance. During training both contraction and expansion blocks are randomly initialized following the method of He et al. [231]. Input data is normalize to produce zero-mean images re-scaled in the range $[-1, 1]$ for faster convergence. Networks are trained end-to-end using KingmaICLR15Adam [270] since the learning rates are automatically adjusted. Using KingmaICLR15Adam leads the network to converge in a couple of hundred iterations, speeding up the training procedure considerably.

Training on Real and Synthetic Data. The aim of this work is to show that the use of synthetic data helps to improve semantic segmentation results on real imagery. There exist several ways to exploit synthetic data for this purpose. A trivial option would be to use the synthetic data alone for training a model and then apply it on real images. However, due to domain shift [467, 503] this approach does not usually perform well. An alternative is to train a model on the vast amount of synthetic images and afterwards fine-tuning it on a reduced set of real images. As shown later, this leads to better results, since the statistics of the real domain are considered during the second stage of training [364].

However, here we employ a more effective approach referred to as Balanced Gradient Contribution (BGC), which was first introduced in [397]. During the training stage data from both, virtual and real domain is exploited in a controlled fashion in order to maximize accuracy and generalization capabilities. The severe statistical difference between the domains usually induces a large variance in gradients for a sequence of mini-batches. Data from the virtual domain is more stable and suitable for dynamic objects, but less informative for the architectonical classes. Data from the real domain is highly informative for the architectonical classes, but usually insufficient. To deal with these aspects we propose to compute search directions in a controlled fashion, using the directions proposed by the virtual domain under a controlled perturbation given by the real domain as shown in Eq. (12.2).

$$\text{Loss}_{\text{BGC}}(\mathcal{X}, \mathcal{Y}) = \text{Loss}_{\text{WCE}}(\mathcal{X}^V, \mathcal{Y}^V) + \lambda \text{Loss}_{\text{WCE}}(\mathcal{X}^R, \mathcal{Y}^R), \tag{12.2}$$

where $\mathcal{X}, \mathcal{Y}$ stand for a subset of samples and their associated labels, drawn from the virtual (V) or real (R) domains. This procedure can be seen as the addition of a very informative regularizer controlled by the parameter λ, but an analogous effect can be achieved by generating mini-batches containing a carefully chosen proportion of images from each domain, such that $|\mathcal{X}^V| >> |\mathcal{X}^R|$. In Sect. 12.5 we show that extending real data with virtual images using this technique leads to a systematic boost in segmentation accuracy.

12.5 Experimental Evaluation

We present the evaluation of the CNNs for semantic segmentation described in Sect. 12.4, training and evaluating on several state-of-the-art datasets of driving scenes. We test how the new SYNTHIA dataset can be useful both on its own and along with real images to produce accurate segmentation results. For the following experiments, we have made use of the 20,000 images of the new SYNTHIA- RAND collection to favor visual variability while using a moderate number of images.

Validation Datasets. We selected publicly available urban datasets to study the benefits of SYNTHIA. Table 12.1 shows the different datasets along with the number of training and test images used in our experiments. It is worth highlighting the differences between these datasets. Each of them has been acquired in a different city or cities. CamVid and GeigerIJRR13Vision datasets have high quality labels and low complexity in terms of variations and atypical scenes. RussellIJCV08labelme is very challenging, since it contains images from different cities with several viewpoints. It

Table 12.1 Driving scenes sets for semantic segmentation

Dataset	# Frames	# Training	# Test
CamVid [53, 54]	701	300	401
GeigerIJRR13Vision [186, 281, 395, 397]	547	200	347
RussellIJCV08labelme [397, 406]	942	200	742
Bileschi07CBCL StreetScenes [37, 397]	3547	200	3347
SYNTHIA-RAND	20,000	20,000	0

Table 12.2 Results of training a T-Net and a FCN on SYNTHIA- RAND and evaluating it on state-of-the-art datasets of driving scenes

Method	Training	Validation	sky	building	road	sidewalk	fence	vegetat.	pole	car	sign	pedest.	cyclist	Per-class	Global
T-Net [397]	SYNTHIA- RAND	CamVid	96.2	77.8	88.4	78.2	0.4	81.8	23.4	87.0	23.1	85.2	51.1	63.0	81.6
	SYNTHIA- RAND	GeigerIJRR13Vision	89.5	72.8	49.8	56.5	0.0	83.8	35.6	46.9	14.7	66.5	24.6	49.2	66.9
	SYNTHIA- RAND	RussellIJCV08labelme	73.9	74.1	56.4	33.8	0.4	78.4	31.5	86.1	15.1	66.8	44.9	51.0	68.1
	SYNTHIA- RAND	Bileschi07CBCL	68.5	74.0	72.7	29.9	0.4	74.0	40.3	82.5	22.5	52.5	56.8	52.2	71.0
FCN [307]	SYNTHIA- RAND	CamVid	92.9	86.4	79.3	86.1	0.1	84.4	21.3	97.6	17.8	78.2	39.0	62.1	81.3
	SYNTHIA- RAND	GeigerIJRR13Vision	84.3	79.0	25.2	60.5	0.0	78.2	41.9	68.7	9.5	88.3	20.1	50.5	63.9
	SYNTHIA- RAND	RussellIJCV08labelme	64.7	82.5	37.3	63.6	0.0	90.3	30.9	79.9	15.1	74.9	24.8	51.3	69.5
	SYNTHIA- RAND	Bileschi07CBCL	71.9	72.3	71.4	39.2	0.0	86.3	45.6	79.7	19.8	57.2	56.3	54.5	72.9

has been annotated by several users and contains images with partial or noisy annotations. Bileschi07CBCL is also challenging, containing many noisy, semi-supervised annotations [397]. Each dataset is split to include a large number of validation images, keeping enough images for the training.

Analysis of Results. The following experiments have been carried out by training two types of CNNs, prioritizing a good average per-class accuracy in order to maximize recognition capabilities. All images are resized to a common resolution of 512×256. This is done to speed-up the training process and save memory. However, it has the disadvantage of decreasing the recognition of certain textures and could make harder to recognize small categories such as traffic signs and poles.

In our first experiment, we evaluate the capability of SYNTHIA- RAND in terms of the generalization of the trained models on state-of-the-art datasets. To this end, we report in Table 12.2 the accuracy (%) of T-Net and FCN for each of the 11 classes along with their average per-class and global accuracies for each of the testing sets.

The networks trained on just synthetic data produce good results recognizing roads, buildings, cars, and pedestrians in the presented datasets. Moreover, sidewalks and vegetation classes are fairly well recognized in CamVid and GeigerIJRR13Vision, probably due to their homogeneity. The high accuracy at segmenting buildings, cars, and pedestrians in RussellIJCV08labelme—one of the most challenging datasets due to the large variety of viewpoints—is a proof of the high quality of SYNTHIA. Notice also that FCN performs better than T-Net for many of the classes due to the higher capacity of the model, although in practice FCN has the

Table 12.3 Evaluation of training a T-Net and FCN on different configurations, using real and virtual images, BGC and fine-tuning. We take as references the results of each architecture when trained just with real data of a given domain (green). Then accuracy improvements are shown in **blue** if they are positive or in **red**, otherwise

Method	Training	Testing	sky	building	road	sidewalk	fence	vegetation	pole	car	sign	pedestrian	cyclist	**per-class**	**global**
T-Net [397]	Camvid	CamVid	98.1	67.0	87.8	27.3	11.3	90.8	23.7	92.1	20.6	42.8	24.5	53.3	76.0
T-Net [397]	SYNTHIA-RAND	CamVid	96.2	77.8	88.4	78.2	0.4	81.8	23.4	87.0	23.1	85.2	51.1	63.0 (9.7)	81.6 (5.6)
T-Net FT	Camvid	CamVid	91.8	67.5	79.4	64.8	0.2	85.3	25.7	89.9	27.7	93.4	45.5	61.0 (7.7)	74.6 (-1.4)
T-Net BGC	Camvid + SYNTHIA-RAND	CamVid	98.9	77.7	95.2	73.0	8.3	95.1	34.8	94.0	35.1	79.6	41.4	66.7 (13.4)	85.7 (9.7)
FCN [307]	Camvid	CamVid	99.1	80.1	97.4	64.2	18.2	95.7	49.6	94.3	41.0	72.0	35.4	67.9	86.9
FCN [307]	SYNTHIA-RAND	CamVid	92.9	86.4	79.3	86.1	0.1	84.4	21.3	97.6	17.8	78.2	39.0	62.1 (-5.8)	81.3 (-5.6)
FCN FT	Camvid	CamVid	97.9	72.9	97.0	61.2	5.2	97.1	30.6	96.2	47.7	63.1	79.9	68.1 (0.2)	84.3 (-2.6)
FCN BGC	Camvid + SYNTHIA-RAND	CamVid	97.6	86.4	96.7	85.8	19.1	98.0	35.8	96.0	45.3	76.4	90.9	75.3 (7.4)	90.2 (3.3)
T-Net [397]	GeigerIJRR13Vision	GeigerIJRR13Vision	84.1	83.0	84.1	57.4	43.8	87.1	17.1	83.3	4.0	2.3	0.8	49.7	80.2
T-Net [397]	SYNTHIA-RAND	GeigerIJRR13Vision	89.5	72.8	49.8	56.5	0.0	83.8	35.6	46.9	14.7	66.5	24.6	49.2 (-0.6)	66.9 (-13.3)
T-Net FT	GeigerIJRR13Vision	GeigerIJRR13Vision	81.4	75.6	78.6	43.8	0.7	88.1	23.2	90.6	11.4	48.5	18.2	50.9 (1.2)	76.4 (-3.8)
T-Net BGC	GeigerIJRR13Vision + SYNTHIA-RAND	GeigerIJRR13Vision	90.7	81.4	85.5	66.1	33.3	90.3	34.3	88.0	15.7	33.1	26.5	58.6 (8.9)	82.6 (2.4)
FCN [307]	GeigerIJRR13Vision	GeigerIJRR13Vision	82.7	88.6	89.1	75.0	50.5	92.7	25.9	87.8	10.2	3.3	3.4	55.4	86.0
FCN [307]	SYNTHIA-RAND	GeigerIJRR13Vision	84.3	79.0	25.2	60.5	0.0	78.2	41.9	68.7	9.5	88.3	20.1	50.5 (-4.9)	63.9 (-22.1)
FCN FT	GeigerIJRR13Vision	GeigerIJRR13Vision	86.3	79.7	86.3	42.0	5.4	85.3	20.2	89.1	8.5	52.6	18.8	52.2 (-3.2)	78.0 (-8.0)
FCN BGC	GeigerIJRR13Vision + SYNTHIA-RAND	GeigerIJRR13Vision	87.7	84.3	87.6	79.1	41.7	94.8	52.5	88.1	21.1	30.9	28.4	63.3 (7.9)	86.2 (0.2)
T-Net [397]	RussellIJCV08labelme	RussellIJCV08labelme	88.7	86.6	76.4	34.2	0.1	63.3	6.1	60.9	2.7	48.1	25.7	44.8	75.6
T-Net [397]	SYNTHIA-RAND	RussellIJCV08labelme	73.9	74.1	56.4	33.8	0.4	78.4	31.5	86.1	15.1	66.8	44.9	51.0 (6.2)	68.1 (-7.5)
T-Net FT	RussellIJCV08labelme	RussellIJCV08labelme	79.6	84.4	65.5	50.6	0.0	80.2	9.5	75.8	6.6	82.8	49.1	53.1 (8.3)	75.6 (0.0)
T-Net BGC	RussellIJCV08labelme + SYNTHIA-RAND	RussellIJCV08labelme	86.6	83.4	71.4	36.6	0.0	79.3	13.9	81.7	8.4	71.2	57.4	53.6 (8.8)	76.5 (0.9)
FCN [307]	RussellIJCV08labelme	RussellIJCV08labelme	93.6	85.6	63.2	65.9	0.2	72.8	16.9	63.0	22.3	67.5	48.4	54.5	77.2
FCN [307]	SYNTHIA-RAND	RussellIJCV08labelme	64.7	82.5	37.3	63.6	0.0	90.3	30.9	79.9	15.1	74.9	24.8	51.3 (-3.2)	69.5 (-7.7)
FCN FT	RussellIJCV08labelme	RussellIJCV08labelme	83.0	90.0	69.4	61.1	0.0	83.5	20.8	76.4	10.3	77.5	33.1	55.0 (0.5)	80.1 (2.9)
FCN BGC	RussellIJCV08labelme + SYNTHIA-RAND	RussellIJCV08labelme	87.2	90.5	67.2	69.6	0.3	86.4	21.7	82.8	10.9	82.1	38.1	57.9 (3.4)	81.9 (4.7)
T-Net [397]	Bileschi07CBCL	Bileschi07CBCL	88.5	72.7	87.9	34.3	4.9	82.4	45.5	77.9	8.5	8.5	23.2	48.6	77.3
T-Net [397]	SYNTHIA-RAND	Bileschi07CBCL	68.5	74.0	72.7	29.9	0.4	74.0	40.3	82.5	22.5	52.5	56.8	52.2 (3.6)	71.0 (-6.2)
T-Net FT	Bileschi07CBCL	Bileschi07CBCL	81.4	69.8	80.4	47.6	0.4	85.0	53.1	86.8	15.2	45.1	52.0	56.1 (7.5)	76.4 (-0.9)
T-Net BGC	Bileschi07CBCL + SYNTHIA-RAND	Bileschi07CBCL	81.6	76.5	81.7	49.4	1.4	81.5	47.4	85.2	22.8	56.9	55.7	58.2 (9.6)	78.1 (0.8)
FCN [307]	Bileschi07CBCL	Bileschi07CBCL	86.4	78.5	83.5	71.6	3.4	86.6	48.7	74.7	20.2	23.5	29.3	55.1	80.3
FCN [307]	SYNTHIA-RAND	Bileschi07CBCL	71.9	72.3	71.4	39.2	0.0	86.3	45.6	79.7	19.8	57.2	56.3	54.5 (-0.6)	72.9 (-7.4)
FCN FT	Bileschi07CBCL	Bileschi07CBCL	73.9	73.0	74.3	54.6	0.1	83.7	55.2	79.3	18.1	45.2	40.6	54.4 (-0.7)	74.5 (-5.8)
FCN BGC	Bileschi07CBCL + SYNTHIA-RAND	Bileschi07CBCL	78.7	80.2	85.8	59.0	1.1	85.0	53.1	89.1	46.4	59.3	43.7	62.0 (6.8)	81.9 (1.5)

disadvantage of being too large for embedded context such as autonomous driving. It is worth highlighting that the average per-class accuracy of the models trained with SYNTHIA is close or sometimes even higher than of the models trained on real data (see Table 12.3).

Our second experiment evaluates the true potential of SYNTHIA to boost CNN models trained on real data. To this end, we perform several tests combining data from SYNTHIA- RAND along with individual real datasets, as described in Sect. 12.4. We set our GBC method to use 10 images per batch, containing six images from the real domain and four from the synthetic one. These results are compared against using just real data coming from each respective training split and also against a fine-tuning model (i.e. taking models originally trained on SYNTHIA and fine-tune them to individual real domains). The outcome of this experiment is shown in Table 12.3. We show baselines results (training only with real data) highlighted in green. Im-

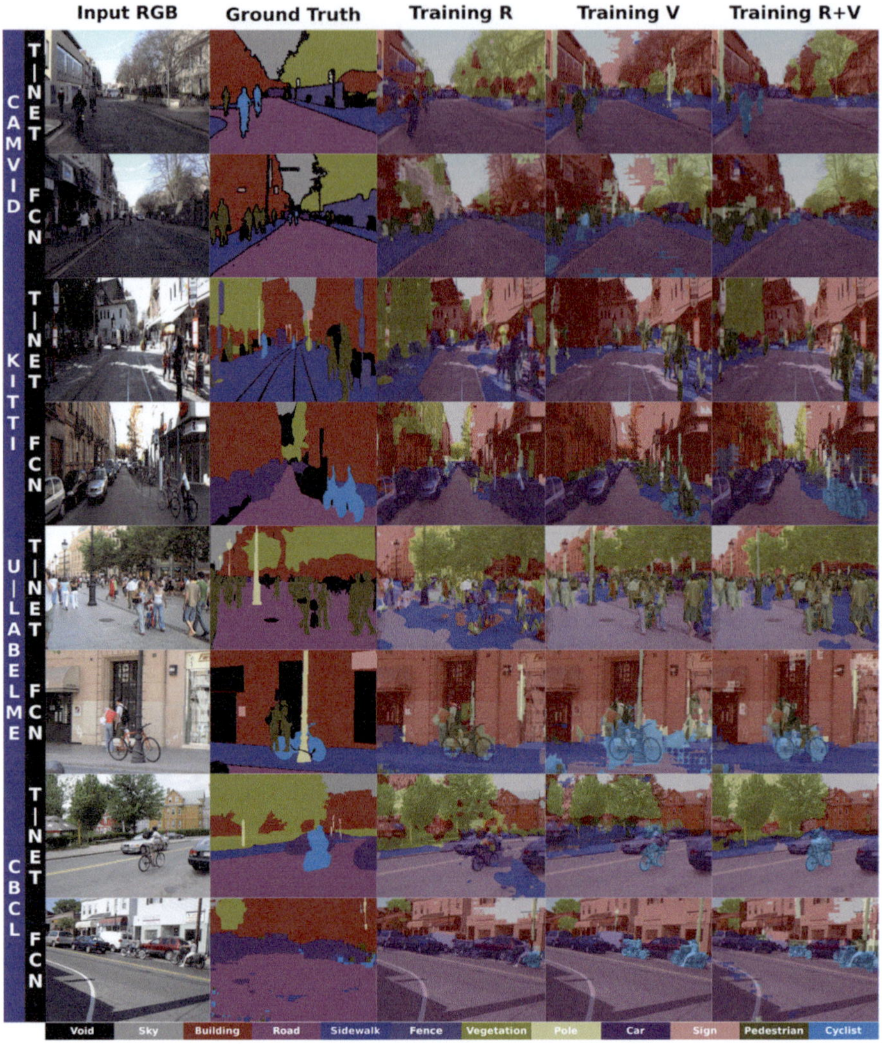

Fig. 12.7 Qualitative results for T-Net and FCN on different datasets. First column shows the **RGB** test images; second column is the **ground truth**; **Training R**, **Training V**, and **Training R+V** are results when training with the real dataset, with SYNTHIA and with the real and SYNTHIA- RAND collection, respectively. Including SYNTHIA for training considerably improves the results

provements with respect to the baselines are highlighted in blue if they are positive or in red if they are negative. Observe that, for all the datasets and architectures, the use of SYNTHIA and the proposed BGC domain adaptation method systematically outperform training just on real data and model fine-tuning for both average per-class and overall accuracy. There are improvements of more than 10 points (up to 13.4 points) in per-class accuracy. The classes that most benefit from the addition of synthetic data are pedestrian, car, and cyclist (dynamic objects), which is due to the lack of enough instances of these classes in the original datasets. On the other hand, signs and poles are very hard to segment as a consequence of the low-resolution images.

Figure 12.7 shows qualitative results of the previous experiments. Observe how the training on synthetic data is good enough to recognize pedestrians, roads, cars, and some cyclists. Then the combination of real and synthetic data (right column) produces smooth and very accurate results for both objects and architectural elements, even predicting thin objects like poles. We consider the results of these experiments an important milestone for the use of synthetic data as the main information source for semantic segmentation.

12.6 Conclusions

We empirically showed how the combination of nonphoto-realistic synthetic data and simple domain adaptation can boost a critical scene understanding problem in driving scenarios, as semantic segmentation. To this end, we presented SYNTHIA, a new dataset for scene understanding related tasks, with major focus on semantic segmentation and instance segmentation. SYNTHIA is actively growing, and currently contains more than 320,000 synthetic images, when counting both, random snapshots, and video sequences of a virtual city. Images are generated simulating different seasons, weather, and illumination conditions from multiple viewpoints. Frames include pixel-level semantic annotations and depth. Our experiments in driving semantic segmentation showed that SYNTHIA is good enough to produce good segmentations by itself on state-of-the-art real datasets, and that its combination with real data dramatically boosts the accuracy of deep learning models. We believe that further research in SYNTHIA-like approaches is a must in order to bring new advances in scene understanding for autonomous vehicles.

Acknowledgements Authors want to thank Andrew Bagdanov for his help and proofreading and the next funding bodies: the Spanish MEC Project TRA2014-57088-C2-1-R, the Spanish DGT Project SPIP2014-01352, the People Programme (Marie Curie Actions) FP7/2007-2013 REA grant agreement no. 600388, and by the Agency of Competitiveness for Companies of the Government of Catalonia, ACCIO, the Generalitat de Catalunya Project 2014-SGR-1506, and to all the members of the SYNTHIA team.

Chapter 13
From Virtual to Real World Visual Perception Using Domain Adaptation—The DPM as Example

Antonio M. López, Jiaolong Xu, José L. Gómez, David Vázquez and Germán Ros

Abstract Supervised learning tends to produce more accurate classifiers than unsupervised learning in general. This implies that training data is preferred with annotations. When addressing visual perception challenges, such as localizing certain object classes within an image, the learning of the involved classifiers turns out to be a practical bottleneck. The reason is that, at least, we have to frame object examples with bounding boxes in thousands of images. A priori, the more complex the model is regarding its number of parameters, the more annotated examples are required. This annotation task is performed by human oracles, which ends up in inaccuracies and errors in the annotations (*aka* ground truth) since the task is inherently very cumbersome and sometimes ambiguous. As an alternative, we have pioneered the use of *virtual worlds* for collecting such annotations automatically and with high precision. However, since the models learned with virtual data must operate in the real world, we still need to perform *domain adaptation* (DA). In this chapter, we revisit the DA of a *Deformable Part-Based Model* (DPM) as an exemplifying case of virtual- to real-world DA. As a use case, we address the challenge of *vehicle detection* for driver assistance, using different publicly available virtual-world data. While doing so, we investigate questions such as how does the domain gap behave due to virtual-vs-real data with respect to dominant object appearance per domain, as well as the role of photo-realism in the virtual world.

A.M. López (✉)
Computer Vision Center (CVC) and Dpt. Ciències de la Computació (DCC), Universitat Autònoma de Barcelona (UAB), Barcelona, Spain
e-mail: antonio@cvc.uab.es

J. Xu · J.L. Gómez · D. Vázquez · G. Ros
CVC and DCC, UAB, Barcelona, Spain
e-mail: jiaolong@cvc.uab.es

J.L. Gómez
e-mail: jlgomez@cvc.uab.es

D. Vázquez
e-mail: dvazquez@cvc.uab.es

G. Ros
e-mail: gros@cvc.uab.es

G. Csurka (ed.), *Domain Adaptation in Computer Vision Applications*,
Advances in Computer Vision and Pattern Recognition,
DOI 10.1007/978-3-319-58347-1_13

13.1 Need for Virtual Worlds

Since the 90s, *machine learning* has been an essential tool for solving *computer vision* tasks such as image classification, object detection, instance recognition, and (pixel-wise) semantic segmentation, among others [32, 114, 162, 409, 516]. In general terms, the best performing machine learning algorithms for these tasks are *supervised*; in other words, not only the raw data is required, but also *annotated information*, i.e., *ground truth*, must be provided to run the training protocol. Collecting the annotations has been based on human oracles and collaborative software tools such as Amazon's Mechanical Turk [373], LabelMe [406], etc. It is known, that human-based annotation is a cumbersome task, with ambiguities, and inaccuracies. Moreover, not all kinds of ground truth can be actually collected by relying on human annotators, e.g., pixel-wise optical flow and depth.

The nonexpert reader can have a feeling of the annotation effort by looking at Fig. 13.1, where we can see two typical annotation tasks, namely bounding box (BB)-based object annotations, and delineation of semantic contours between classes of interest. In the former case, the aim is to develop an object detector (e.g., a vehicle detector); in the latter, the aim is to develop a pixel-wise multi-class classifier, i.e. to perform the so-called semantic segmentation of the image.

With the new century, different datasets were created with ground truth and put publicly available for research. Providing a comprehensive list of them is out of the scope of this chapter, but we can cite some meaningful and pioneering examples related to two particular tasks in which we worked actively, namely *pedestrian detection* and *semantic segmentation*; both in road scenarios for either *advanced driver assistance systems* (ADAS) or *autonomous driving* (AD). One example is the Daimler Pedestrian dataset [146], which includeds 3,915 BB-annotated pedestrians and 6,744 pedestrian-free images (i.e., image-level annotations) for training, and 21,790 images with 56,492 BB-annotated pedestrians for testing. Another example corresponds to the pixel-wise class ground truth provided in [53] for urban scenarios; giving rise to the well-known *CamVid* dataset which considers 32 semantic classes (although only 11 are usually considered) and includes 701 annotated images, 300 normally used for training, and 401 for testing. A few years after, the KITTI Vision Benchmark Suite [186] was an enormous contribution for the research focused on ADAS/AD given the high variability of the provided synchronized data (stereo images, LIDAR, GPS) and ground truth (object bounding boxes, tracks, pixel-wise class, odometry).

In parallel to these annotation efforts and the corresponding development of new algorithms (i.e., new human-designed features, machine learning pipelines, image search schemes, etc.) for solving computer vision tasks, *deep leaning* was finding its way to become the powerful tool that is today for solving such tasks. Many researchers would point out [275] as a main breakthrough, since deep *convolutional neural networks* (CNNs) showed an astonishing performance in the data used for the *ImageNet Large-Scale Visual Recognition Challenge* (ILSVRC) [404]. ImageNet [120] contains over 15 million of human-labeled (using Mechanical Turk) high-resolution images of roughly 22,000 categories. Thus, ImageNet was a gigantic

Fig. 13.1 Ground truth obtained by human annotation: (*left*) framing the rectangular bounding box (BB) of vehicle instances; (*right*) delineating the contours (silhouettes) between the different classes of interest contained in the image, even at instance level

human annotation effort. ILSVRC uses a subset of ImageNet with about 1,000 images of 1,000 categories; overall, about 1.2M images for training, 50,000 for validation, and 150,000 for testing. Many deep CNNs developed today rely on models pre-trained on ImageNet which is modified or fine-tuned to solve a new task or operate in a new domain. The research community agrees in the fact that, in addition to powerful GPU hardware to train and test deep CNNs, having a large dataset with ground truth such as ImageNet is key for their success. In this line, more recently, it was released MS COCO dataset [303], where per-instance object segmentation is provided for 91 object types on 328,000 images, for a total of 2.5M of labeled instances.

As a matter of fact, in the field of ADAS/AD we would like to have datasets with at least the variety of information sources of KITTI and the ground truth size of ImageNet/COCO. However, when looking at the ground truth of KITTI in quantitative terms, we can see that individually they are in the same order of magnitude than other ADAS/AD-oriented publicly available datasets (e.g., see the number of pedestrians BBs of KITTI and Daimler datasets, and the number of pixel-wise annotated images of KITTI and CamVid). A proof of this need is the recently released Cityscapes dataset [97] which tries to go beyond KITTI in several aspects. For instance, it includes 5,000 pixel-wise annotated (stereo) images covering 30 classes and per-instance distinction, with GPS, odometry and ambient temperature as metadata. In addition, it includes 20,000 more images but where the annotations are coarser regarding the delineation of the instance/class contours. This kind of dataset is difficult to collect since driving through 50 cities covering several months and weather conditions was required. Moreover, providing such a ground truth can take from 30 to 90 min per image for a human oracle in case of fine-grained annotations and depending on the image content.

For the semantic segmentation task, Cityscapes goes one order of magnitude beyond KITTI and CamVid. However, it is far from the annotation numbers of ImageNet and MS COCO. The main reason is twofold. On the one hand, data collection itself, i.e., Cityscapes images are collected from on-board systems designed for ADAS/AD not just downloaded from an Internet source; moreover, metadata such as GPS and vehicle odometry is important, not to mention the possibility of obtaining depth from stereo. On the other hand, the annotations must be more precise since ultimately the main focus of ADAS/AD is on reducing traffic accidents. In any case, as we mentioned before, other interesting ground truth types are not possible or really difficult to obtain by human annotation, e.g., pixel-wise optical flow and depth (without active sensors); but eventually these are important cues for ADAS/AD based on visual perception.

In this ADAS/AD context, and due to the difficulties and relevance of having large amounts of data with ground truth for training, debugging and testing, roughly since 2008 we started to explore a different approach. In particular, the idea of using realistic virtual worlds (e.g., based on videogames) for training vision-based perception modules. The advantages were clear: (1) forcing the driving and data acquisition situations needed; (2) obtaining different types of pixel-wise ground truth (class ID, instance ID, depth, optical flow); (3) generating such data relatively fast (e.g., currently our SYNTHIA environment [396] can generate 10,000 images per hour with such ground truths, using standard consumer hardware). Of course, such a proposal also came with doubts such as *can a visual model learned in virtual worlds operate well in real-world environments?*, and *does this depend on the degree of photo-realism?*. From our pioneering paper [325], where we used pedestrian detection based on HOG/Linear-SVM as proof-of-concept, to our last work, i.e. SYNTHIA [396], where we have addressed pixel-wise semantic segmentation via deep CNNs, we have been continuously exploring the idea of learning in virtual worlds to operate in real environments.

The use of synthetic data has attracted the attention of other researchers too, and more recently specially due to the massive adoption of deep CNNs to perform computer vision tasks and their data hungry nature. 3D CAD models have been used to train visual models for pose estimation, object detection and recognition, and indoor scene understanding [4, 19, 44, 73, 210, 221, 222, 229, 326, 337, 357, 358, 364, 365, 371, 401, 411, 415, 435, 458, 460, 461, 467]; a virtual racing circuit has been used for generating different types of pixel-wise ground truth (depth, optical flow, and class ID) [218]; videogames have been used for training deep CNNs with the purpose of semantic segmentation [387] and depth estimation from RGB [421]; synthetic scenarios have been used also for evaluating the performance of different feature descriptors [20, 262, 510–512] and for training and testing optical and/or scene flow computation methods [56, 328, 329, 348], stereo algorithms [217], as well as trackers [477], even using synthetic clones of real-world areas of interest [175]; synthetic LIDAR-style data has been used for object detection too [285, 286]; finally, virtual worlds are being used for learning high-level artificial behavior such as playing Atari games [335], reproducing human behavior playing shooter games [306], and driving/navigating end-to-end [71, 594], even learning *unwritten* common sense [509, 596].

13.2 Need for Domain Adaptation

From the very beginning of our work, it was clear that there is a *domain gap* between virtual and real worlds. However, it was also clear that this was the case when using images coming from different (real) camera sensors and environments. In other words, the domain gap is not a virtual-to-real issue, but rather a more general sensor-to-sensor or environment-to-environment problem [505, 506]. Other researchers confirmed this fact too when addressing related but different visual tasks than ours [489]. Since then, training visual models in virtual worlds and applying *domain adaptation* techniques for their use in real-world scenarios come hand-by-hand for us. In fact, more authors have followed the approach of performing some explicit step of virtual- to real-world domain adaptation, without being an exhaustive list, the reader can address [286, 300, 357, 467] as illustrative examples.

We showed that virtual- to real-world DA is possible for holistic models based on the HOG+LPB/Linear-SVM paradigm [503] as well as on the Haar+EOH/AdaBoost one [504]. In the former case, proof-of-concept experiments adapting RGB-style synthetic images to far infrared ones (FIR) reported positive results too [448]. Moreover, for the *Deformable Part-based Model* (DPM) [162] we also proposed to use virtual worlds and domain adaptation [544, 546]. In most of the cases, we focused on *supervised DA*, i.e., a relatively few amount of annotated *target-domain* data (i.e., from the real world in our case) was used to adapt the model learned with *source-domain* data (from the virtual world). For the holistic models, we focused on mixing the source and target data collected via *active learning* for model adaptation, we termed the corresponding feature space as *cool world*; while for DPM we focused on using just the source-domain model together with the target-domain data, i.e., without revisiting the source-domain data. In terms of modern deep CNNs, the former case would be similar to mixing source and target data in the mini-batches while the latter case is more in the spirit of the so-called fine-tuning.

In the rest of this chapter, we are going to focus on DPM because it was the state-of-the-art for object detection before the breakthrough of deep CNNs. A priori it is a good proxy for deep CNNs regarding the specific experiments we want to address, after all deep CNNs eventually can require domain adaptation too [90, 182, 484, 497]. Obviously, being based on HOG-style features there is a point where much more data would not really translate to better accuracy [591], so we will keep training data in the order of a few thousands here. On the other hand, note that DPM can be reformulated as a deep CNN [193] for end-to-end learning. The domain adaptation techniques we proposed for DPM [544], can be used as core technology for hierarchical DA[1] [545] as well as for weakly supervised incremental DA [547].

In particular, we are going to rely on our DA method for DPM termed *Structure-aware Adaptive Structural SVM* as (SA-SSVM), which gave us the best performance in [544]. In this chapter we compliment the experiments run in [544] mainly

[1] With this technique we won the first pedestrian detection challenge of the KITTI benchmark suite, a part of the *Recognition Meets Reconstruction Challenge* held in ICCV'13.

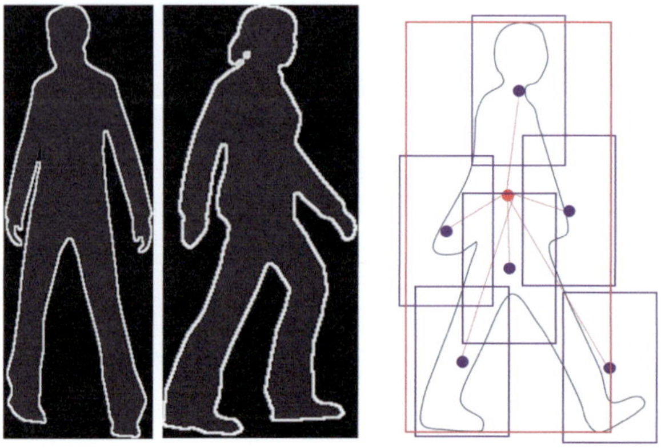

Fig. 13.2 DPM for modeling pedestrians. There are two components (*left, black background*), and each component is encoded as a root and six parts (*right*, one component)

by addressing questions such as *the role of photo-realism in the virtual world*, as well as *how does the domain gap behave in virtual-vs-real data with respect to dominant object appearance per domain*. Moreover, for the sake of analyzing new use cases, instead of focusing on pedestrian detection using virtual data from Half-Life 2 as in [544], here we focus on vehicle detection using different virtual-world datasets: Virtual-KITTI[2] [175], SYNTHIA[3] [396], and GTA [387].

13.3 Domain Adaptation for DPM in a Nutshell

DPM[4] encodes the *appearance* of objects' constituent *parts* together with a *holistic* object representation termed as *root*. In contrast to other part models, DPM allows the parts to be located at different positions with respect to the root. The plausible relative locations, known as *deformations*, are also encoded. Both appearance and deformations are learned. The appearance of the parts is learned at double the resolution than the root. The triplet root-parts-deformations are known as *component*. In order to avoid too blurred models, DPM allows to learn a mixture of components. Different components use to correspond to very different object views or poses, specially when this implies very different aspect ratios of the corresponding root BB.

In practice, a DPM is encoded as a vector $\mathbf{w}$ which has to be learned. In the domain adaptation context, we term as $\mathbf{w}^S$ the model learned with source-domain data (e.g., with virtual-world data). Our SA-SSVM domain adaptation method[5] takes $\mathbf{w}^S$ and relatively few annotated target-domain data (e.g., real-world data) to learn a new $\mathbf{w}$ model which is expected to perform better in the target domain. Let us

[2]Dataset available at http://www.xrce.xerox.com/Research-Development/Computer-Vision/Proxy-Virtual-Worlds.

[3]Dataset available at http://synthia-dataset.net.

[4]See Fig. 13.2 for a pictorial intuition.

[5]The reader is referred to [544] for the mathematical technical details.

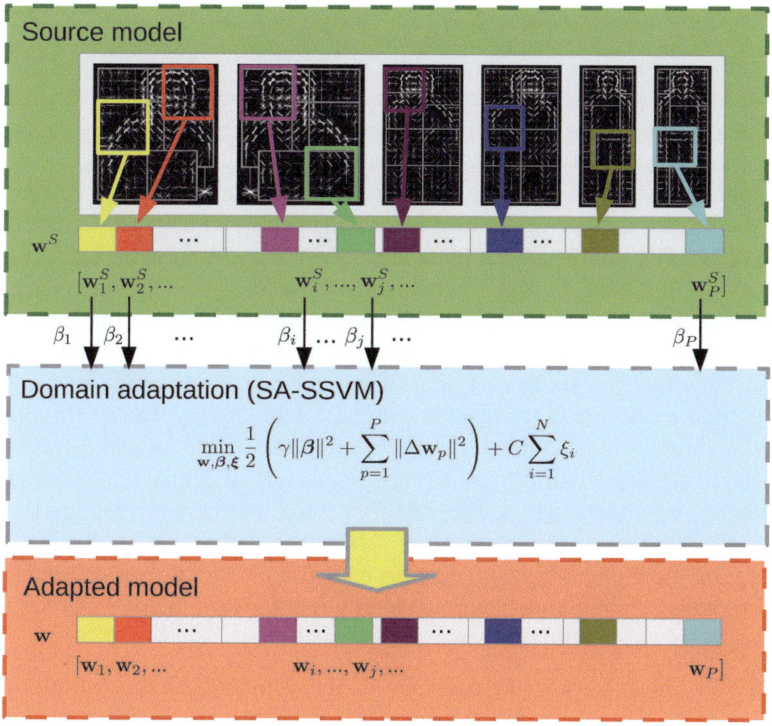

Fig. 13.3 Domain Adaptation of DPM based on SA-SSVM (see main text for details)

explain the idea with the support of the Fig. 13.3; where $\mathbf{w}^S$ consists of components: half body and full body, as well as persons seen from different viewpoints. Each component consists of root and parts (head, torso, etc.). To adapt this DPM to a target domain, we decompose it as $\mathbf{w}^S = [\mathbf{w}_1^{S'}, \ldots, \mathbf{w}_P^{S'}]'$, where P is the number of structures and u' stands for transpose of u. Note that each component, $\mathbf{w}_p^S$, may contain both appearance and deformation parameters (for roots only appearance). The decomposed model parameters are adapted to the target domain by different weights, denoted by β_p, $p \in \{1, P\}$, i.e., the SA-SSVM procedure allows domain adaptation for each of such structures separately by defining $\Delta\mathbf{w}_p = \mathbf{w}_p - \beta_p\mathbf{w}_p^S$, $p \in \{1, P\}$. In order to learn these adaptation weights, we further introduce a regularization term $\|\boldsymbol{\beta}\|^2$ in the objective function, where $\boldsymbol{\beta} = [\beta_1, \ldots, \beta_P]'$, and we use a scalar parameter γ to control its relative penalty. Finally, C and the ξ_i are just the standard terms of a SVM objective function and N the number of target-domain samples used for the adaptation. After optimizing for the objective function (mid box in Fig. 13.3), $\mathbf{w} = [\mathbf{w}_1{}', \ldots, \mathbf{w}_P{}']'$ is the domain-adapted DPM.

13.4 Experimental Results

Datasets. As we mentioned before, we are going to focus on vehicle detection for ADAS/AD applications. We use the training data of the KITTI car detection challenge [187]; which is split into two sets, one for actually training and the other for testing. Such a testing set will be the only one used here for that purpose, and we will follow the so-called *moderate* setting when considering which vehicles are mandatory to detect. For training, we will consider four more datasets in addition to the mentioned split of the KITTI car detection challenge, thus, five in total. Namely, the KITTI car tracking dataset [187], its synthesized clone Virtual KITTI [175], SYNTHIA [396], and GTA [387]. Of course, SYNTHIA is a dataset with different types of ground truth, so we selected a set of cars and images for our experiments. In the case of GTA, we semi-automatically annotated with BBs a set of cars. Table 13.1 shows the number of samples in each dataset. Figures 13.4, 13.5, show images sampled from KITTI-Det, KITTI-Track with Virtual-KITTI, respectively. Example images from SYNTHIA and GTA are shown in Figs. 13.6 and 13.7. Virtual-KITTI and SYNTHIA are based on the same development framework, i.e., Unity®Pro.[6] We can see that the images from GTA are more photo-realistic than the ones used in SYNTHIA and Virtual-KITTI. SYNTHIA images are not always corresponding to a forward facing on-board virtual camera as is the case of Virtual-KITTI and GTA.

Protocol. In order to show the accuracy of the vehicle detectors we plot curves of *false positive per image* (FPPI) versus *miss rate* (MR) according to the Caltech protocol [125], with an overlap of the 50% between detection and ground truth BBs. For training and testing we only consider *moderate* cases,[7] which according to the definition given in the KITTI car detection challenge, are those vehicles nonoccluded or just partially occluded (maximum truncation: 30%), and with a BB height $\geq$25 pixels.

Regarding DPM we use three components, each with eight parts. Part locations are initialized as 6×6 HOG-style cells (48×48 pixels) covering the root (at its double resolution version). Note that, in contrast to [544, 546], here we have not explored the use of the pixel-wise vehicle masks (available for virtual-world data) to provide a better initialization of part locations during DPM learning. Thus, real- and virtual-world training data are used equally for learning source-domain DPMs.

Regarding SA-SSVM (see Fig. 13.3) we follow the settings reported in [544] as producing the best results. Namely, the adapted structures correspond to the root and parts, i.e., not to components; and we set $\gamma = 0.08$ and $C = 0.001$. The experiments are run three times and the mean FPPI-MR curve and standard deviation-based intervals are plotted (i.e., as in [544] but with three repetitions instead of five).

Results. According to the datasets listed in Table 13.1, we define the set of source-domain datasets to be $\mathcal{S} =$ {KITTI-Track, Virtual-KITTI, SYNTHIA, SYNTHIA-Sub,

[6] See http://unity3d.com.

[7] The number of vehicles mentioned in Table 13.1 refer to moderate cases.

Table 13.1 The number of *images* and annotated *vehicles* using a bounding boxes, used for each dataset. Negative samples are selected from background areas of the same images. KITTI-Det Test and KITTI-Det Train refer to two splits of the training set of the KITTI car detection training set. KITTI-Det Test is the testing set used in all the experiments of this chapter, while the rest of datasets are used only for training. For KITTI-Track and Virtual-KITTI, we use sequences 1, 2, 6, 18, and 20 as the training datasets. SYNTHIA-Sub refers to a subset randomly sampled from SYNTHIA

	KITTI-Det Test	KITTI-Det Train	KITTI-Track	Virtual-KITTI	SYNTHIA	SYNTHIA-Sub	GTA
Images	3163	3164	2020	1880	1313	675	580
Vehicles	12894	12275	12950	6867	2052	1023	1054

Fig. 13.4 Images sampled from KITTI-Det

GTA}. The target-domain dataset is always KITTI-Det Test. KITTI-Det Train and KITTI-Det Test are coming from the same domain since they correspond to two splits we have done from the same original dataset. All the learned detectors are tested in KITTI-Det Test, and the difference among them is the data used for their training. Accordingly, the reported experiments are as follows:

- *SRC*: Training with a dataset $s \in \mathcal{S}$ (source).
- *TAR-ALL*: Training based on the full KITTI-Det Train.
- *TARX*: Training with a subset of random images from KITTI-Det Train, in particular, only using the $100X\%$ of the images.
- *SA-SSVM*: Training with a dataset $s \in \mathcal{S}$ plus the images used for the *TARX* shown in the same plot.

Following this pattern, Fig. 13.8 shows results for $X = 0.1$ (i.e., 10%), Fig. 13.9 for $X = 0.5$ (i.e., 50%), and Fig. 13.10 for $X = 1$ (i.e., *ALL*), respectively.

Discussion. The first observation comparing SRC and TAR-ALL results (constant across figures since they do not depend on X) is that there is a large domain gap. Since we would like to annotate as less real-world data as possible, let us start our analysis for $X = 0.1$ (see Fig. 13.8).

The worst case is when SRC$\in${KITTI-Track, Virtual-KITTI} since the average miss rate is ~17 points worse than for TAR-ALL. The best case is when SRC$\in${SYNTHIA, GTA}, where the gap is of ~12 points. Note that this is not related to the number of vehicle samples since GTA has ~1/6 of vehicles than Virtual-KITTI for training,

Fig. 13.5 Images sampled from KITTI-Track (*left*) and Virtual-KITTI (*right*). Note how Virtual-KITTI is a synthesized but realistic clone of KITTI-Track

Fig. 13.6 Images sampled from SYNTHIA dataset. Note that they are not always corresponding to a forward facing virtual camera on-board a car

SYNTHIA $\sim 1/3$ than Virtual KITTI, and Virtual-KITTI in turn contains $\sim 1/2$ of the vehicles in KITTI-Track and in KITTI-Det Test. An analogous behavior is seen when ranking the datasets by number of vehicle-free images. In any case, both ~ 17 and ~ 12 points are significant accuracy drops.

For going deeper in the analysis of what can be the reason for the domain gap, we can compare the results of KITTI-Track versus Virtual-KITTI. We see that they are basically equal. Since Virtual-KITTI is a synthesized clone of KITTI-Track, we think that the main reason of the accuracy drop is not the virtual-to-real nature

Fig. 13.7 Images sampled from the GTA videogame

of the training images, but the typical vehicle poses and backgrounds reflected in the training datasets, i.e., when comparing Virtual-KITTI/KITTI-Track with KITTI-Det Train. In other words, KITTI-Det Train represents better KITTI-Det Test since we built them from the same data set. Note, in addition, that KITTI-Track come from the same camera sensor as KITTI-Det Train and Test, which does not avoid the accuracy gap. Moreover, both SYNTHIA and GTA come from virtual worlds and still produce a detector that performs better than when using KITTI-Track.

We observe also that leaving out the $\sim$90% of the images in KITTI-Det Train ($X = 0.1$) causes a drop in accuracy of $\sim$6 points. In other words, in this case once we have $\sim$316 manually annotated images ($\sim$10% of KITTI-Det Train), annotating $\sim$2, 848 more is required to push the DPM to its limit, which is only $\sim$6 points better.[8] Active learning or ad hoc heuristics can be tried to alleviate such manual annotation effort. However, we observe that pre-training the DPM with automatically collected virtual-word data and using SA-SSVM for adapting the model, makes such $\sim$316 images already very valuable, since in all cases the domain-adapted vehicle detector improves both the result of TAR0.1 and SRC (only virtual-word data). We can see that the best case is for SYNTHIA, which reduces the domain gap to $\sim$2 points from $\sim$12 points, and improves the result of TAR0.1 in $\sim$4 points. An additional observation is that pre-training (SRC) the detectors with virtual-world data also allows to use active learning techniques as we did in [503] and/or ad hoc heuristics as we did in [547] for annotating more complementary images (i.e., other more informative $\sim$316 ones) or collecting more but without human intervention (i.e., self-annotation). We have not done it here for the sake of simplicity, but it is reasonable to think that this would reduce the domain gap even more.

[8] *It is a fallacy to believe that, because good datasets are big, then big datasets are good* [34].

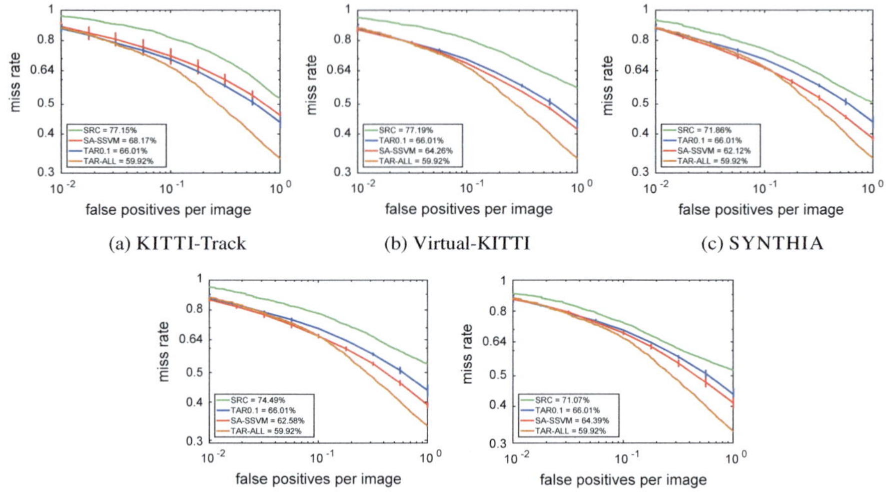

(a) KITTI-Track (b) Virtual-KITTI (c) SYNTHIA

(d) SYNTHIA-Sub (e) GTA

Fig. 13.8 Results assuming $X = 0.1$ (see main text). In the box legend it is indicated the average miss rate for each experiment. Thus, the lower the better

Figure 13.11 compares vehicle detections based only on the SYNTHIA samples we are using in this chapter, and the result of applying SA-SSVM to them with TAR0.1, in both cases setting the threshold of the model classifier to operate in the FPPI=1 regime. Note how SA-SSVM allows to obtain better results.

TAR0.5 ($X = 0.5$; see Fig. 13.9) and TAR-ALL basically show the same performance, so ~1,582 images have been annotated without a reward in DPM performance. Of course, although an annotation-training-test loop can be followed to avoid useless vehicle annotations, a priori it is difficult to know when to stop such manual annotations. On the other hand, even using TAR0.5 data, starting with a pre-trained model (SRC) on either SYNTHIA or GTA allows to improve the performance of TAR-ALL, in the case of SYNTHIA by ~2 points with respect to TAR0.5. Looking at SYNTHIA-Sub and GTA, which has a similar number of samples (see Table 13.1), we can argue that GTA could probably reach the same performance than SYNTHIA if we would have the double of GTA vehicles. In any case, what it is remarkable is that it is more effective to have DPMs pre-trained in virtual worlds than just doubling the number of manually annotated target-domain images, i.e., at least assuming a manual annotation procedure free of prior knowledge about the current vehicle detector.

Even for $X = 1$ (see Fig. 13.10), i.e., combining the data used to train TAR-ALL and SRC, pre-training in virtual worlds is able to improve the performance of TAR-ALL alone. SYNTHIA provides us ~3 points of improvement with respect to TAR-ALL, being the overall best result. Using GTA as SRC eventually can provide such improvement too (again, by extrapolation of its performance when comparing to SYNTHIA-Sub).

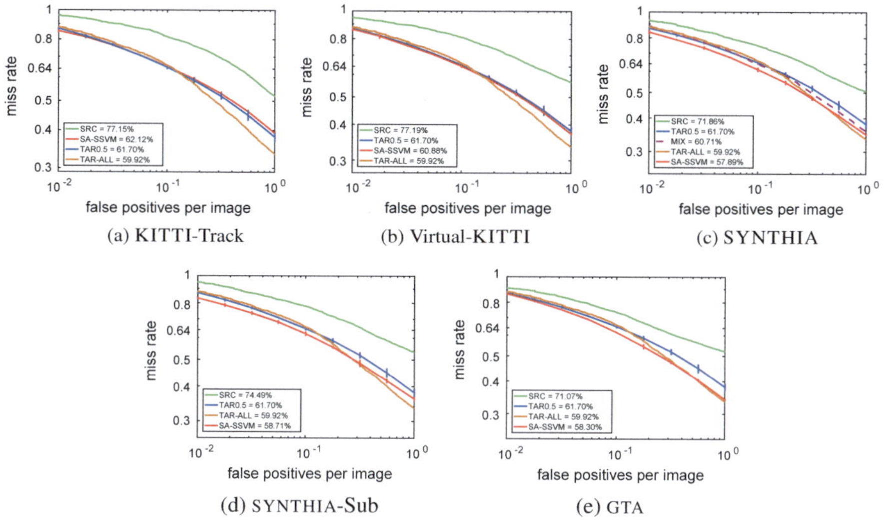

Fig. 13.9 Results assuming $X = 0.5$ (see main text). In the box legend it is indicated the average miss rate for each experiment. Thus, the lower the better

In summary, the results presented and discussed so far reinforce the take home messages we highlighted in our previous works [325, 503, 544]; namely, combining models/data pre-trained in virtual worlds with a reasonable but low amount of real-world data through domain adaptation, is a really practical paradigm worth to explore for learning different kinds of models. As a matter of fact, according to the literature reviewed in Sects. 13.1 and 13.2, nowadays this approach is being widely adopted by the computer vision community.

Another interesting question that we did not addressed before refers to the degree of photo-realism, i.e., if a higher degree would imply to learn more accurate models and eventually not even requiring domain adaptation. This is a very important question since an extreme photo-realism may require hours for rendering a few images, while the degree of photo-realism of the virtual worlds presented here is achieved in real time using a standard modern gamer PC.

In our previous works, we already saw that domain adaptation was required even when you train and test with real-world cameras. In other words, domain gap was due to sensor differences (no matter if one of the sensors operates in real or virtual worlds) and the nature of the scenario where train and test images are acquired (typical illumination, background, and pose/view of dynamic objects). Because of this, our believe was that a more photo-realistic world would be just another sensor, still different from real world, and therefore domain gaps would persists. Note that the experiments presented in this chapter reinforce this hypothesis: (1) using Virtual-KITTI and KITTI-Track gives rise to SRC and domain-adapted detectors of similar performance in all the cases, i.e., despite the fact that KITTI-Track relies on the same real-world sensor than KITTI-Det Train and Test, while Virtual-KITTI consists

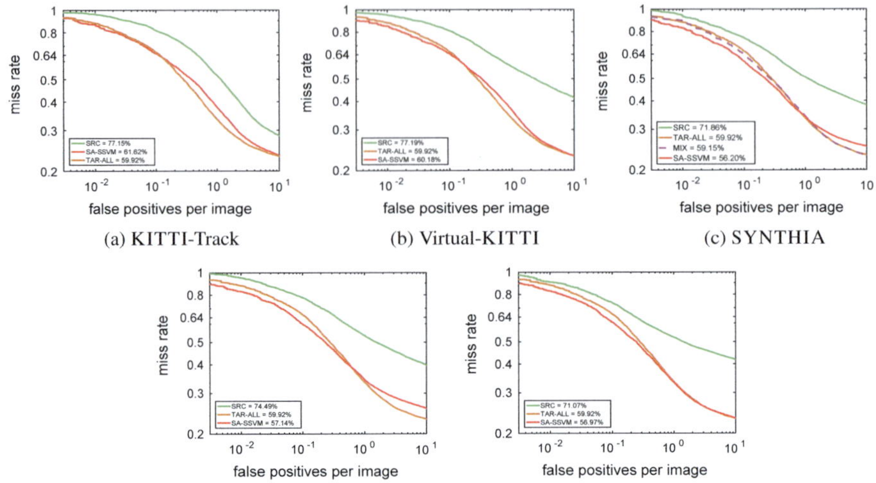

(a) KITTI-Track (b) Virtual-KITTI (c) SYNTHIA

(d) SYNTHIA-Sub (e) GTA

Fig. 13.10 Results assuming $X = 1$ (ALL; see main text). In the box legend it is indicated the average miss rate for each experiment. Thus, the lower the better

of synthesized data; (2) moreover, despite the fact that GTA contains images more photo-realistic than SYNTHIA, when using a similar number of samples (SYNTHIA-Sub) we see that the performance of the corresponding SRC and the domain-adapted detectors is basically the same.

Recent works [337, 512] reinforce the idea that once a basic photo-realism is achieved (i.e., beyond Lambertian illumination and simplistic object materials), adding more and more photo-realism do not have a relevant impact. Thus, in our opinion from the evidences collected so far, Virtual-KITTI and SYNTHIA are sufficiently photo-realistic for the tasks we are addressing (i.e., vision-based object detection and image semantic segmentation).

Another interesting point of analysis is if it is better to just mixing virtual- and real-world data or fine-tuning a pre-trained model on virtual-world data with real-world samples. The former is what we called *cool world* [503, 505], while SA-SSVM is an example of the later. Because of that we have run a *MIX* experiment with SYNTHIA and TAR-ALL, which can be seen in Fig. 13.10c. In this case, we have just mixed the data and run an standard DPM learning procedure. Note that the result is ~3 points worse than using SA-SSVM. Moreover, the training time of MIX is much longer than the one of SA-SSVM, since it uses samples from both domains and training from scratch also requires more iterations to converge. If we extrapolate these experiments to the deep CNNs paradigm, a priori we would think than fine-tuning is the proper approach. However, when working in [396, 397], i.e., in semantic segmentation based on deep CNNs, using the appropriate mini-batch scheme to weight the relevance of the samples as a function to their domain (virtual or real), we obtained better performance than with fine-tuning. Therefore, regarding

Fig. 13.11 Vehicle detections when operating in the FPPI=1 regime. *Left* DPM based on the SYNTHIA data considered in this chapter (SRC). *Middle* Using the TAR0.1 version of KITTI-Det Train. *Right* Adapting SRC by using TAR0.1 when applying SA-SSVM

this topic, we have no clear conclusions yet. Of course, the advantage of fine-tuning would be avoiding to revisit the source data; thus, this is a point to keep researching.

Overall, our research and the research presented so far by the computer vision community, led us to insist in the adoption of the paradigm where virtual worlds and domain adaptation techniques are used to train the desired models. Moreover, we think that the degree of photo-realism like the presented already in datasets such as Virtual-KITTI and SYNTHIA is sufficient for this task. In addition, although in this chapter we have focused on DPM-based vehicle detection, we think the conclusions can be extrapolated to other computer vision tasks where the visual appearance is important (e.g., object detection in general and semantic segmentation). Of course, it is worth to note that at this moment the best results on the KITTI car detection challenge are dominated by approaches based on deep CNNs, providing astonishing high performances in the moderate setting, far beyond DPM approaches. Such benchmark seems to be challenging enough for DPM, but still is a small proportion of the real world and this will be the real challenge for deep CNNs. Therefore, we also think that our conclusions will be extrapolated from DPM to other powerful models such as deep CNNs when addressing more challenging scenarios; note that in Sect. 13.2 we have mentioned already that even deep CNNs require domain adaptation. On the other hand, what is expected is that deep CNNs would require less domain adaptation than DPM since they are models with more capacity to generalize across domains.

13.5 Conclusion

In this chapter, we have shown how virtual worlds are effective for training visual models when combined with domain adaptation techniques. Although we have focused on DPM and vehicle detection as proof-of-concept, we believe that the conclusions extrapolate to other visual tasks based on more complex models such as deep CNNs. We have presented results which suggest that extreme photo-realism is not necessary, i.e., the degree of photo-realism already achieved in datasets such as Virtual-KITTI and SYNTHIA is sufficient, provided domain adaptation would be necessary even when relying on more photo-realistic datasets (here GTA).

Looking into the future, we think a best practice would be to design sets of relatively controlled virtual-world scenarios, designed to train, debug and test visual perception, and other AI capabilities (Virtual-KITTI and SYNTHIA are examples of this). In other words, with the knowledge accumulated so far, we do not bet for building a gigantic virtual world to try to avoid domain gap issues. This would be really difficult to build and handle. We prefer to pursue domain adaptation to save any existing virtual-to-real world gap. However, we think the research must go into the direction of unsupervised domain adaptation for allowing the systems trained in virtual worlds to self-adapt to real-world scenarios. An example in this line is the approach we presented in [547], where manual annotations were not required to train a domain-adapted pedestrian detector for an on-board moving camera setting. However, this approach performs the adaptation off-line, which can be perfectly right for many applications (e.g., adapting pre-trained surveillance systems to different places), but the real challenge is to do it on-line.

Acknowledgements Authors want to thank the next funding bodies: the Spanish MEC Project TRA2014-57088-C2-1-R, the People Programme (Marie Curie Actions) FP7/2007-2013 REA grant agreement no. 600388, and by the Agency of Competitiveness for Companies of the Government of Catalonia, ACCIO, the Generalitat de Catalunya Project 2014-SGR-1506 and the NVIDIA Corporation for the generous support in the form of different GPU hardware units.

Chapter 14
Generalizing Semantic Part Detectors Across Domains

David Novotny, Diane Larlus and Andrea Vedaldi

Abstract The recent success of deep learning methods is partially due to large quantities of annotated data for increasingly big variety of categories. However, indefinitely acquiring large amounts of annotations is not a sustainable process, and one can wonder if there exists a volume of annotations beyond which a task can be considered as solved or at least saturated. In this work, we study this crucial question for the task of *detecting semantic parts* which are often seen as a natural way to share knowledge between categories. To this end, on a large dataset of 15,000 images from 100 different animal classes annotated with semantic parts, we consider the two following research questions: (i) are semantic parts really visually shareable between classes? and (ii) how many annotations are required to learn a model that generalizes well enough to unseen categories? To answer these questions we thoroughly test active learning and DA techniques, and we study their generalization properties to parts from unseen classes when they are learned from a limited number of domains and example images. One of our conclusions is that, for a majority of the domains, part annotations transfer well, and that, performance of the semantic part detection task on this dataset reaches 98% of the accuracy of the fully annotated scenario by providing only a few thousand examples.

D. Novotny (✉) · A. Vedaldi
University of Oxford, Oxford, UK
e-mail: david@robots.ox.ac.uk

A. Vedaldi
e-mail: vedaldi@robots.ox.ac.uk

D. Larlus
Naver Labs Europe, Meylan, France
e-mail: diane.larlus@naverlabs.com

G. Csurka (ed.), *Domain Adaptation in Computer Vision Applications*,
Advances in Computer Vision and Pattern Recognition,
DOI 10.1007/978-3-319-58347-1_14

14.1 Introduction

Image understanding has recently progressed dramatically, primarily fueled by the availability of increasingly large quantities of labeled data. It was only with the introduction of large-scale resources such as the ImageNet dataset [120] that deep learning methods were finally able to realize their potential. However, it is unclear whether manual supervision will be able to keep up with the demands of more sophisticated and data-hungry algorithms. Recent initiatives such as the Visual Genome [274], where millions of image regions are labeled with short sentences and supporting bounding boxes, go well beyond standard datasets, such as ImageNet and offer new terrific research opportunities. At the same time, however, they raise the obvious question: *when is supervision enough?*

The idea that limitless manual supervision is impractical has motivated research in areas such as unsupervised learning or learning from off-the-shelf resources such as the Web. While these are important research directions, such approaches go to the other extreme of avoiding manual supervision altogether. In this work, we take a *pragmatic approach* and start from the assumption that explicit manual supervision is currently the most effective way of training models. However, we also ask whether there is a limit on the amount of supervision which is actually required and hence of the amount of the data that needs to be annotated.

While answering this question in full generality is difficult, we can still conduct a thorough analysis of this question in representative cases of general interest. In this paper, we focus on the problem of *recognizing and detecting semantic parts in categories*, such as animal eyes (see Fig. 14.1), because semantic parts are highly informative, and, importantly, *semantically shareable* (e.g. both monkeys and snakes have faces which, despite important differences, are broadly analogous). In fact, one of the key motivations for looking at semantic parts in computer vision is to transfer the structure of known objects to novel ones, for which no supervision is available. However, an important practical question, which is often neglected, is whether semantically shareable parts are also *visually shareable*, in the sense of being recognizable in novel objects with no or limited further supervision. This assumption has never been challenged beyond a few categories or narrow domains. In this paper, we conduct a careful investigation of *part transferability across a large target set of visually dissimilar classes*. We investigate the two key aspects of transferability under bounded supervision: (i) learning parts from a limited number of example images and (ii) applying known parts to new, unseen domains.

For the first problem, we consider an *active learning* (AL) scenario, where images are annotated with their visible semantic parts in turn, studying which images should be chosen and how many are needed to saturate performance. Working in this AL scenario, we look at part transferability as a *Domain Adaptation* (DA) problem. Differently, from the typical transductive learning scenario of DA, where algorithms leverage unlabeled data of the target domain to adapt a source predictor, our goal is to learn semantic part detectors that can be directly applied to novel classes that were never seen before, i.e. the model is expected to transfer well to new domains

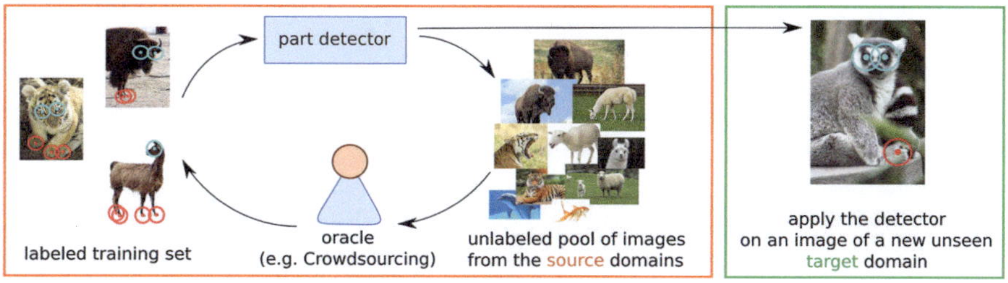

Fig. 14.1 Overview of the semantic part detector generalization problem. We investigate the ability of semantic part detectors to transfer between different domains, and study the minimal amount of supervision that is required for this task

even *without having access to samples from those domains*. This problem has been seldomly studied and is sometimes known as the *domain generalization* (DG) problem [179, 190, 339].

Another specificity of our work is that, while the majority of the existing DG methods focuses on the standard classification task, where the model predictions consist of a discrete categorical label, here we consider DG in the context of a detection task, where predictions are defined as a set of 2D part locations labeled with a real value which represents a confidence score. We thus propose extensions of existing active and transfer learning methods, which were initially designed for domain adaptive classifiers, into methods suitable for the detection task in order to make them applicable to our setting.

In this chapter, we address the DG problem of detecting semantic parts on new unseen target categories by using an efficient ensemble of detectors which is optimized for generalization to new classes and that, at the same time, can be used to guide active learning. We conduct a thorough empirical evaluation of all these research questions and provide insights on how subsets of images may be selected for labeling, and how many such labels may be required to perform well on unseen categories. We also consider several domain adaptation scenario, where a small number of annotations are available for the target classes. This chapter extends the work presented in [347].

The rest of this chapter is organized as follows. Section 14.2 provides a brief overview of related work. Section 14.3 describes the employed active and transfer learning methods. The dataset considered for our analysis is described in Sect. 14.4. Section 14.5 provides the experimental evaluation of part transferability together with a benchmark of the proposed methods. Section 14.6 concludes the work.

14.2 Related Work

Domain adaptation. DA seeks to learn predictor functions that are able to account for a shift between the distributions of the source and target data domains. Since the seminal paper of Saenko et al. [407], DA has been applied to computer vision by learning feature transformations [25, 164, 200, 206, 465], or by adapting the parameters of the predictor [239, 554]. A full survey is available in Chap. 1. Only a few papers consider DA from more than one source domain [471], and most from at most a few, while in our work we consider 50 source domains. Sometimes, the source domains are not given a priory, but discovered implicitly [238].

All these approaches formulate DA as *transductive* learning, for which they require unlabeled samples from the target domain. This is a fundamental difference from our case, where *no target samples are available*, also known as domain generalization (DG) [179, 190, 339] or predictive DA [562].

Active learning. The goal of active learning (AL) is to reduce the annotation costs by deciding which training samples should be annotated. Each annotation is associated with a cost [95] and the goal is to obtain the best performance within a budget. Many data selection strategies have been proposed, based on the uncertainty and entropy [488], used in [96, 242, 264, 376], or diversity and representativeness [259]. The work of [513] estimates a cost of different types of annotations and then modulates an expected risk function while the strategy of [405] annotates as many examples in each image as possible. [361] leverages additional information from different annotation types to improve the convergence properties of the active learner. Only few works have jointly looked at transfer learning and active learning [64, 379, 408, 530, 531] as we do here, and none of them for computer vision tasks. Moreover, the transfer learning components of these works approach the transductive DA task, whereas we focus on domain generalization.

Related transfer learning problems. Zero-shot learning, i.e. the task of recognizing a category with no training samples, is often tackled by explicitly learning classifiers that are transversal to object classes. This can be done by modeling semantic relatedness [392, 393], or by transferring other knowledge such as materials [92, 502], segments [457], parts [145, 490] or attributes [157, 287]. However, these works consider only a small number of classes and *assume* that primitives such as parts transfer visually, whereas here we explicitly question this assumption. Fewer works consider transfer learning for localization as we do; these include the works of [121, 216, 282, 338] that transfer bounding box information using the ImageNet hierarchies; the method of [236] that transfer object detectors from seed classes; and [21] which transfers detectors assuming a limited number of annotated examples in the target domain. Differently from such works, we do not transfer whole objects, but individual keypoints, and we do so between very diverse classes. Transferring keypoints was explored in [582], which detects facial landmarks using a deep multitask learning framework, while [494] induce pose for previously unseen categories.

14.3 Methods

This work tackles the semantic part detection task, and experiments focus on the dataset introduced in [347], where parts are annotated with keypoints. We first describe the keypoint detector used to locate semantic parts in images. Second, following our AL scenario, we describe how uncertainty sampling can be defined in our particular setting to sample in turn the images to be annotated. Finally, we describe how the fact that we have many source domains (i.e. source categories) to sample from can be leveraged in order to combine several detectors that are then applied to the unseen target classes.

Keypoint detector. As our baseline keypoint detector, we use the state-of-the-art method proposed by Tulsiani and Malik [495]. This architecture uses the convolutional layers from the very deep network (VGG-VD) of [443], followed by a linear regressor, that outputs a heat-map expressing the probability for a keypoint to be centered at a particular location. To improve accuracy, they linearly combine the outputs of a coarse-scale (6×6) and a fine-scale (12×12) network.

As our analysis requires frequent retraining of the model, we adapt the faster 6×6 network of [495] to output finer-scale 12×12 cell predictions. To do so, following [307], we append a bilinear upsampling layer to the final keypoint regressor convolutional layer and sum the resulting upsampled heat-map with a finer-scale convolutional heat-map derived from the pool4 VGG-VD layer. The recombined heat-map is finally followed by a sigmoid activation function. The resulting architecture allows for multi-scale end-to-end training while increasing overall training and testing speed by a factor of 3.

Active learning. The goal of AL is to select a small subset of images for annotation while maximizing the performance of the final predictor. Let U be the set of all available images. The algorithm starts with a pool $L_0 \subset U$ containing $|L_0| = 50$ randomly selected images from U and collects the corresponding annotations. Then, for every active learning round t ($t = 1, 2, \ldots$) the algorithm alternates training a CNN keypoint detector using all annotations in L_k for $k < t$, and collecting annotations for A more images in order to build L_t. For the latter, all non-annotated images in U are examined by the sampling component of the AL algorithm and the A *most informative ones* are selected for annotation.

The standard criterion to select informative images is to pick the ones which leave the current predictor uncertain, also called *uncertainty sampling*. However, while uncertainty is easily defined in classification tasks where the goal is to predict a single label per image, it is not obvious how to do so for keypoint prediction where the predictor produces a score for every image location.

We propose to do so as follows: let $p(y = +1|x, u) = \Phi(x)_u$ be the probability of finding a keypoint at location u in image x as computed by the CNN Φ (unless otherwise specified, we assume that the CNN is terminated by a sigmoid function). The uncertainty score is then given by

$$1 - 2 \times \left| \max_u p(y = +1|x, u) - \frac{1}{2} \right| \tag{14.1}$$

Intuitively, when the model is certain, either (i) there are no part keypoints in that image and $\max_u p(y = +1|x, u) \approx 0$, or (ii) there is at least one keypoint and then $\max_u p(y = +1|x, u) \approx 1$.

Transfer learning by auto-validation. Our problem differs from standard AL in that, as in DA, the target classes are *shifted* compared to the source ones. Furthermore, differently from the standard transductive learning setting in DA, our aim is to learn a "universal" part detector that *generalizes* to unseen target classes without further training. Compared to more common machine learning settings, we can leverage the fact that the source data is split in well-defined domains with a large domain shift and train a set of domain-specific detectors which are later recombined using an ensembling method, assigning higher weights to the models with better generalization capabilities. In other words, the detectors from the source domains that are more invariant to the underlying domain distributions will be given a larger impact on the final decision on the target domains.

In more detail, we do so by using an *auto-validation* procedure. Let $D = \{d_1, \ldots d_N\}$ be a set of source domains (the object categories in our case) and let $\delta \subset D$ be a subset of the source domains. For each possible δ we train a domain-specific (or group of domains specific) part predictor Φ_δ. The set of all Φ_δ, is then recombined into a single domain-invariant model by utilizing the ensembling method of Krogh et al. [276]. The recombination procedure from [276] defines the final predictor as a weighted sum of the individual domain-specific models $\sum_{\delta \subset D} \alpha_\delta \Phi_\delta$, where α_δ are the weights of the domain-specific model Φ_δ which favor a diverse set of models with good generalization capabilities. In practice, the ensemble weights are obtained by minimizing the following objective function [276]:

$$\begin{aligned} &\operatorname*{arg\,min}_{\{\alpha_\delta | \delta \subset D\}} \sum_{\delta \subset D} \alpha_\delta E_\delta + \sum_{(\delta,\delta') \subset D \times D} \alpha_\delta C_{\delta\delta'} \alpha_{\delta'} - \sum_{\delta \subset D} \alpha_\delta C_{\delta\delta} \\ &\text{s.t.: } \alpha_\delta \geq 0, \ \forall \delta \subset D, \quad \sum_{\delta \in D} \alpha_\delta = 1 \end{aligned} \tag{14.2}$$

where $C_{\delta\delta'} = E_{xuv}[\Phi_\delta(x)_{uv} \Phi_{\delta'}(x)_{uv}]$ is the the cross-correlation matrix of the response (heat-maps) of the different models and measures how much different models agree in their predictions. E_δ is the cross-validation error computed on a set of held-out samples that were unseen during the training of Φ_δ. Similar to [276], we define E_δ as the error of Φ_δ on the set of off-domain samples $D - \delta$. This process is illustrated Fig. 14.2.

It is worth mentioning that, although in [276] all the ensemble models were optimized on distinct sets of data samples, the data samples were drawn from the same data distribution. This leads to a set of models that produce similar predictions, which violates one of the main requirements of ensembling which is the fact that the ensemble members should disagree. On the contrary, our choice of creating train-test

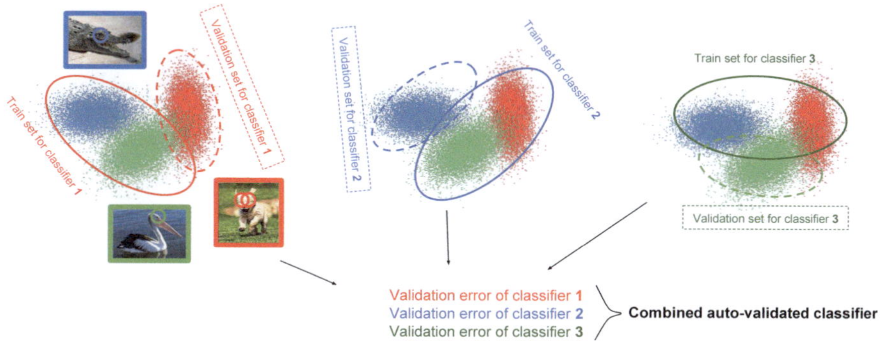

Fig. 14.2 Auto-validation of the keypoint transfer process across domains. The detectors from the source domains that are more invariant to domain shift have more impact on the final decision on the target domains. Invariance is evaluated by measuring cross-validation error on a held-out set

data splits $(\delta, D - \delta)$ which correspond to diverse animal domains leads to a set of very distinct models with a large degree of disagreement.

The original method from [276] was designed to recombine predictions of independently trained shallow neural networks. Here, we adapt the original method so the different keypoint detectors Φ_δ share weights for the early layers of the network, thus removing the costly requirement of re-optimizing a large number of CNN parameters on every training set of samples δ. In practice, we propose to decompose the CNN architecture as $\Phi_\delta = \phi_\delta \circ \phi_0$, where ϕ_0 is the same for different δ and only ϕ_δ is specific to δ. More precisely, ϕ_0 includes all learnable parameters of the original VGG-VD layers up to conv5_3 and ϕ_δ comprises the final convolutional filter terminated by the sigmoid layer that outputs part detector responses specific to the model trained with the training samples from δ.

The optimization of ϕ_δ and ϕ_0 is easily implemented using SGD: given a data sample x, for all δ in parallel, either ϕ_δ or the cross-validation error E_δ are updated, depending on whether $x \in \delta$. The cross-correlation matrix C is estimated using all samples irrespective of their origin. To ensure numerical stability we add a small constant λ to the diagonal of C ($\lambda = 0.1$ in all experiments). Once the optimization of ϕ_δ, E_δ and C completes, the coefficients α_δ are obtained by solving Eq. (14.2).

Another advantage of training an ensemble of detectors Φ_δ is that their lack of agreement on the training data can replace uncertainty sampling in guiding the AL process. We implement this query-by-committee [420] criterion (QBC) following [276]: Given, a pixel u in a test image x we assess the disagreement between pixel-wise predictors $\Phi_\delta(x)_u$ by evaluating the *ensemble ambiguity*:

$$a(x,u) = \sum_{\delta \subset D} \alpha_\delta (\Phi_\delta(x)_u - \bar{\Phi}(x)_u)^2, \quad \text{where} \quad \bar{\Phi}(x)_u = \sum_{\delta \subset D} \alpha_\delta \Phi_\delta(x)_u. \tag{14.3}$$

Similar to uncertainty sampling (Sect. 14.3) we label each image x with a disagreement score $A(x)$ by max-pooling over the pixel-wise ensemble ambiguities, i.e. $A(x) = \max_u a(x, u)$. During the labeling stage of active learning, samples with highest $A(x)$ are added first.

14.4 ImageNet Animal Parts

A thorough evaluation of the transferability of parts requires a suitable dataset with a large enough number of classes. Unfortunately, datasets that have keypoints or part-level annotations either consider a handful of classes, such as the PASCAL Parts [81], or are specialized to a narrow set of domains, focusing only on birds [517], faces [332, 582], or planes [508]. Datasets with more categories, such as the Visual Genome [274], do not contain systematic part annotations. In a preliminary version of our work, we introduce the ImageNet Animal Parts dataset[1] [347], following a procedure that we remind here.

Instead of collecting a new set of images, we build on top of the existing ImageNet dataset [120], where the classes are organized in a semantic hierarchy, induced by WordNet [161]. This provides a natural basis to study the semantic structure of this space. A very significant challenge with annotating many parts for many object categories is of course the very large cost, thus, trade-offs must be made.

Here, the singly most important aspect for experimentation is to label a sufficiently large space of categories. This space should also contain a mix of similar and dissimilar categories. Furthermore, the same parts should ideally apply to all categories. Here we select for experimentation 100 classes (see Fig. 14.3) of the 233 classes in the "vertebrate" subtree of the ImageNet ILSVRC [404]. For each class, we annotate two parts. The first one, *eyes*, exist in all selected animals. The second one, *feet*, exist in a large subset of these (mammals and reptiles but not fish). Beyond their semantic shareability (visual shareability is an assumption that we verify in our work), these parts were selected because they are easily understood by annotators from crowd sourcing platforms, and they can satisfactorily be annotated with keypoints as opposed than by drawing bounding boxes or regions. Both properties were instrumental in collecting a large dataset of part annotations in a reasonable time and budget. While limited, these annotations are sufficient to demonstrate the principles of our analysis. We collected annotations for about 150 images per class, annotating 14711 images in total.

[1]The dataset can be accessed at: http://www.robots.ox.ac.uk/~vgg/data/animal_parts/.

Fig. 14.3 ImageNet Animal Parts dataset. It contains 100 animal categories from the ImageNet dataset and selected part annotations (the figure shows one annotated example per class). We split the classes into 50 source and 50 target domains

14.5 Experiments

Experimental protocol. The set of 100 domains (i.e. animal classes) is split into 50 source domains and 50 target domains as follows. To achieve uniform coverage of the animal classes in both sets, we first cluster the 100 classes into $K = 50$ clusters using their semantic distance and spectral clustering. The semantic distance between two classes d and d' is defined as $|r \rightarrow d \cap r \rightarrow d'| / \max\{|r \rightarrow d|, |r \rightarrow d'|\}$, where $|r \rightarrow d|$ is the length of the path from the root of the hierarchy to class d. Then, each cluster representative is included in the target set and the complement is included in the source set. Furthermore, images in each class are divided into a 70/30 training-testing split, resulting in four image sets: source-train, source-testing, target-train, and target-test. As common practice [308, 559], keypoint detections are restricted to ground-truth bounding boxes for all evaluation measures.

Evaluation measures. We evaluate keypoint detection using two standard metrics [559]: PCK and APK. In **PCK**, for each ground-truth bounding box, an algorithm

Table 14.1 Validation of the keypoint detector on the AnimalParts dataset

eye $\alpha = 0.05$; foot $\alpha = 0.1$	PCK			APK		
Method	Eye	Foot	Mean	Eye	Foot	Mean
[495]—coarse-scale—6×6	37.0	73.6	55.3	17.6	58.4	38.0
[495]—fine-scale—12×12	**81.7**	73.9	**77.8**	**75.4**	64.0	**69.7**
[495]—6×6+12×12	73.6	**77.3**	75.5	55.9	**67.6**	61.8
Proposed architecture—6×6 upsample	80.2	74.1	77.2	73.1	59.2	66.2

predicts the single most confident keypoint detection. This detection is regarded as true positive if it lies within $\alpha \times \max\{w, h\}$ of the nearest ground-truth keypoint, where w, h are the box dimensions and $\alpha \in \langle 0, 1 \rangle$ controls the sensitivity of the evaluation measure to misalignments. For **APK**, keypoints are labeled as positive or negative detections using the same criterion as PCK and ranked by decreasing detection scores to compute average precision. In all of our experiments we set $\alpha = 0.05$ for the eyes, that are small and localized, and $\alpha = 0.1$ for the feet which are more difficult to annotate with a keypoint.

14.5.1 Baseline Detector

We validated our baseline keypoint detector by comparing it to the original $6 \times 6 + 12 \times 12$ model of [495]. Our implementation of the $6 \times 6 + 12 \times 12$ architecture achieves 61.1% PCK on the PASCAL VOC rigid keypoint detection task—a comparable result to 61.5% PCK reported in [495].

We also experimented on our AnimalParts dataset. Our baseline keypoint detector was compared to the 6×6, 12×12 and $6 \times 6 + 12 \times 12$ models of [495]. Each keypoint detector was trained on the *source-train* split and the mean PCK and APK over *target-test* images are reported. Table 14.1 shows that our modified 6×6 upsample architecture outperforms the low resolution 6×6 by a significant margin while being comparable to 12×12. The only case in which 6×6 performs worse is feet APK (but not PCK); however 6×6 upsample is roughly 3 times faster during both the training and test stages than 12×12. Note also that $6 \times 6 + 12 \times 12$ is not competitive for eye detection while being much heavier. In conclusion, the 6×6 upsample architecture performs on par with state-of-the-art while being much faster than alternatives.

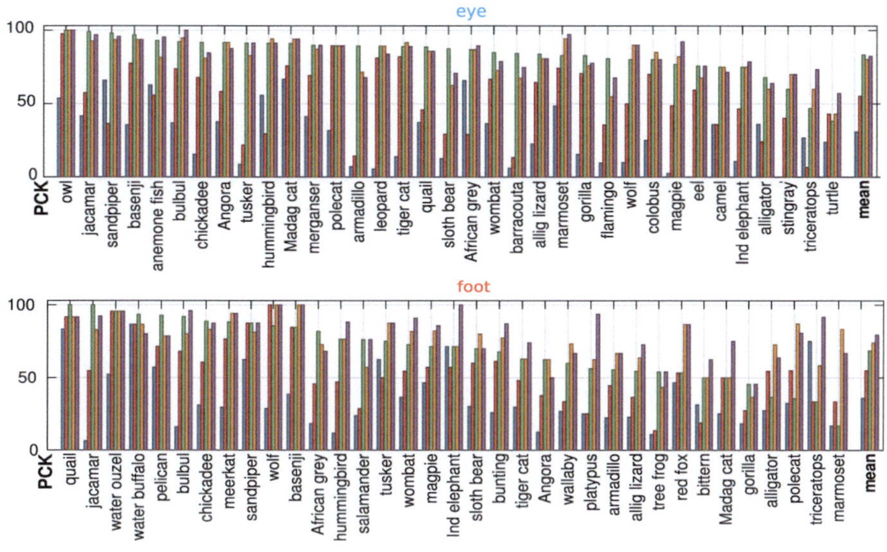

Fig. 14.4 Relative difficulty of part detection and part transfer. Part detection performance for eyes (*top*) and feet (*bottom*) for a subset of the target classes, where the detector has been trained using either: the farthest class (in semantic distance), the nearest class, the same class, the source classes, all source, and target classes. Classes are sorted by increasing difficulty

14.5.2 Visual Shareability of Parts

In this section, we challenge the idea that parts are visually shareable across different classes and that, therefore, it suffices to learn them from a limited number of classes to understand them equally well in all cases. Figure 14.4 shows part detection performance for individual classes, for different configurations that we discuss below.

Learning from a single class. We first look at the individual target class detection results when learning from annotated samples from the same class (green bar plots). We see that the difficulty of detecting a certain part strongly depends on the specific class. For example, owl's eyes have 100% PCK, whereas turtle's eyes have 38.1% PCK. We then compare with two other training sets of identical size: (i) with the nearest class (NC—red bar plot) according to the semantic measure, and (ii) with the farthest class (FC—blue bars). As expected, we verify that NC outperforms FC by 20.9% PCK in average, which translates into 39 classes out of 50 for the eyes, and 32 out of 37 for the feet. This demonstrates the relevance of the semantic distance for cross-domain transfer. In average, NC still performs 26.9% below training with the target class itself. Next, we consider transferring from more classes.

Increasing the size of the training set. We compare the performance of detectors when these are trained with larger subsets of the data: (i) using all classes available (i.e. the source and target domains, purple bar plots), and (ii) using only the source domains (that does not contain the target class, orange bars). We note several factors. First, we observe that using all classes improves performance compared to training only for the target class in average for feet, but not for eyes that perform very well already. Then, we observe that in 61% of the cases, learning a part from source classes alone or adding the target classes changes PCK by less than 7%. Hence, if parts are learned form a sufficiently diverse set of classes, they can be expected to transfer satisfactorily to novel ones as well. In average, training from the source classes only (transfer scenario) is only 2.2 PCK below training from the full set of classes for eyes, and only 5.5 PCK below for feet.

14.5.3 Active-Transfer Learning

In the previous section, we looked at how well parts transfer from known (source) classes to new (target) classes. Here, we investigate how many source images need to be annotated in the source domain. In order to answer this question, we adopt the active-transfer learning framework of Sect. 14.3 and we monitor the performance of the detector on the target classes as more annotated images for the source classes become available. The overall performance is summarized by plotting the attained mean PCK (solid lines) and APK (dashed lines) as a function of the number of labeled source images (Fig. 14.5). We compare three methods: AL by random sampling (RS), AL by uncertainty sampling (US), and network ensemble with AL by query-by-committee (ensemble+QBC).

Implementation details. The initial pool contains $|L_0| = 50$ randomly selected images and 300 additional images are added at every active learning round. For pretraining the CNN we first remove all the images of the vertebrate subtree from the original ILSVRC12 dataset and then continue according to the protocol from [443]. In each active learning round, a pretrained CNN is fine-tuned for 7 epochs, lowering the learning rate tenfold after epoch 5 (this was verified to be sufficient for convergence). Learning uses SGD with momentum and mini-batch size of 20. Mini-batches are sampled to guarantee that all the training classes are equally represented on average (rebalancing). Momentum, weight decay, and initial learning rate were set to 0.9, 0.005, and 0.0003, respectively. All parameters were validated by splitting the source domains in half. For DA by auto-validation, the set D of possible source domains was obtained by regrouping the 50 source domains into three super-domains by clustering them using their semantic similarity (hence, an ensemble of 7 CNNs is learned). All experiments are repeated 4 times and averages are reported.

Results. First, we observe that US performs slightly better than the other two algorithms on the eye, but is substantially outperformed by RS and ensemble+QBC on the foot class. We believe this because the network is typically most uncertain about images that happen to not contain any part instance, which is fairly frequent with animal feet as they tend to be occluded or truncated. On the contrary, RS is not affected by this problem. Ensemble+QBC performs as well as RS on the eye part and notice-

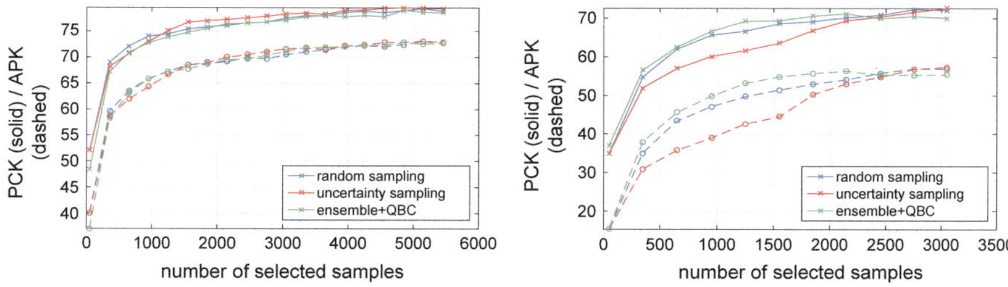

Fig. 14.5 Active-transfer learning for the eye (*left*) and foot (*right*) parts. We show PCK (*solid lines*) and APK (*dashed lines*) as a function of the number of labeled examples obtained with random sampling, uncertainty sampling, and the network ensemble with query-by-committee sampling (ensemble+QBC) methods

ably better on the foot part. This indicates that guiding active learning using the QBC criterion is more robust than US. The fact that the ensemble+QBC method performs similarly to the others on the eye class is likely due to the fact that there is less visual variability in eyes than feet and therefore all classifiers in the ensemble are similar, with poorer generalization [276]. Ensemble+QBC also benefits from improved generalization by the optimized ensemble of domain-specific models. Finally, we verified that using the ensemble of models with uncertainty sampling strategy is still not competitive. We conclude that ensemble+QBC is an effective active-transfer learning strategy.

Besides the relative merits of individual AL strategies, a main observation for our investigation is how quickly performance of different methods saturates. It can be noticed that for eyes the performance reaches 2% of the maximum with around 3,000 annotations, and for feet, the performance reaches 2% of the maximum with around 2,100 annotations. Combined with the observations in Sect. 14.5.2, this indicates that excellent performance can be achieved for part detection in most animal classes by annotating a small representative subset of classes and a small number of corresponding images. This result is somewhat remarkable and can be attributed to the excellent performance of pretrained deep neural networks as general-purpose representations. Recall that the networks were pretrained for image classification and not part detection, not using any of the source or target classes.

Sampling strategy analysis. Figure 14.6 shows the distribution of selected animal classes during individual learning rounds for the QBC strategy. The distribution is clearly nonuniform, and the method seems to select representative classes within groups such as "reptiles," "felines," etc.

14.5.4 Semi-supervised Domain Adaptation

While previous experiments focused on the DG task, where target domains are unobserved during training, here we consider a standard DA task where samples from the target domain can be accessed during training. In more detail, we assume a part

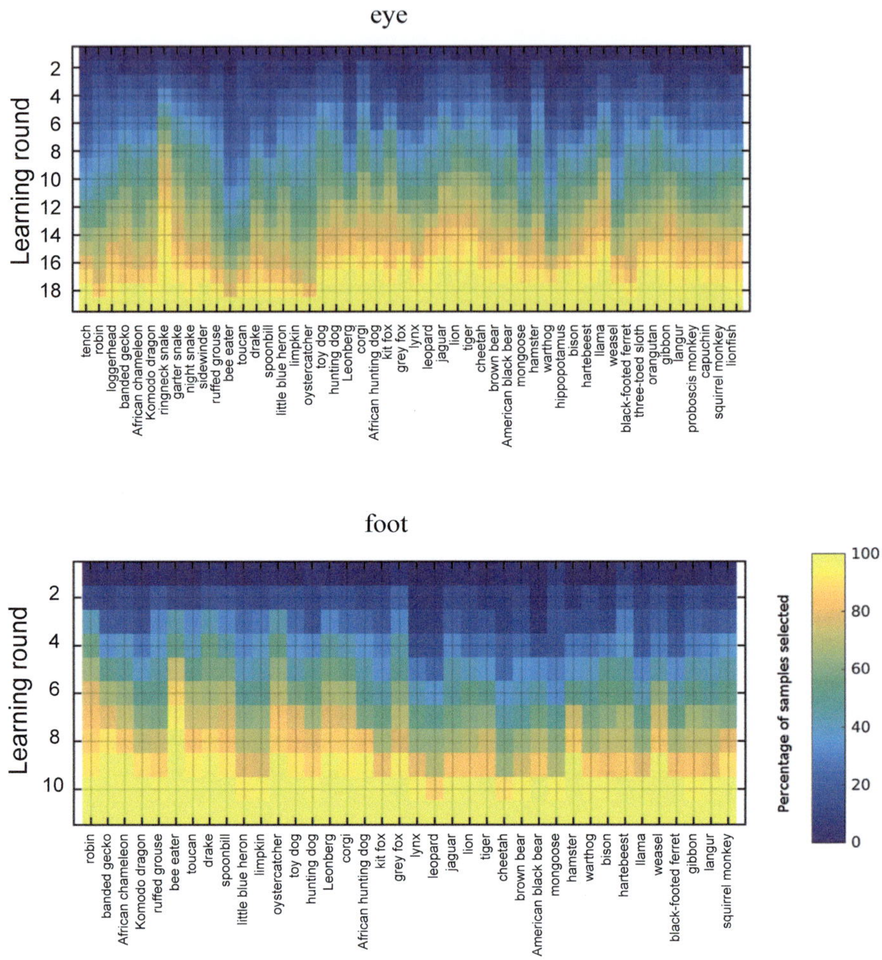

Fig. 14.6 Comparative domain importance on eye and foot detection. For each source class we show how many more images the AL selects at each round by ensemble+QBC

detector pretrained on all part annotations from a specific animal class and, given a limited number of part annotations from a specified target class, we aim to adapt the pretrained detector for this target class.

More specifically, for each class T from our pool of 50 target classes we first pretrain the baseline 6×6 upsample part detector on its T's semantically nearest animal class $N(T)$ selected from the set of all animal domains. Then, we expand the training set with the samples from T, keeping track of the evolution of the detection performance on T's testing subset as the training set increases.

This more standard semi-supervised DA scenario allows to utilize existing methods for improving the generalization properties of the part detectors. We thus attached

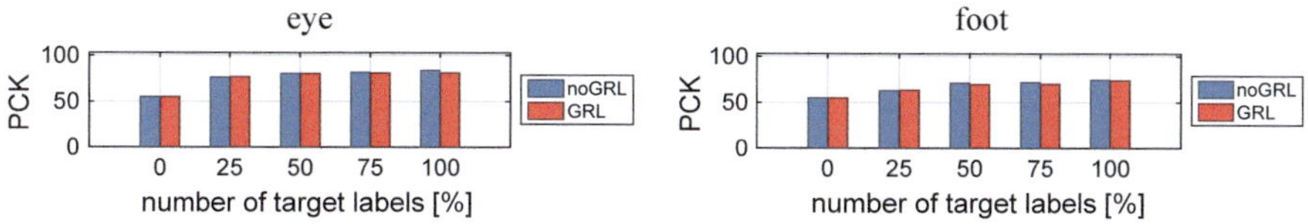

Fig. 14.7 Semi-supervised DA. For each target class, a pretrained detector is adapted from its semantically nearest class. Each bar denotes average performance (PCK) over all target classes as more target annotations are added to the training set. We compare the baseline detector (noGRL) and its extension with the Gradient Reversal Layer (GRL) for both eye and foot part detection

the Gradient Reversal Layer [182] (GRL) to the last layer before the keypoint filters (pool4 of VGG-VD) of our 6×6 upsample architecture. GRL aims to make the pool4 features invariant to the underlying domain (animal class), possibly improving the generalization capabilities of the succeeding keypoint detection layers.

The results of our experiment are reported in Fig. 14.7. Because both GRL and noGRL perform on par we conclude, in agreement with the previous sections, that, on our task, the baseline deep keypoint detector already exhibits strong domain invariance properties without the need to include additional DA components.

14.6 Conclusions

In this work, we focused on the semantic part detection task and considered the problem of the transferability of the corresponding detectors from source classes for which we have annotations, to target classes which were not seen before. We experimentally demonstrated that, as often hypothesized in previous work, semantic parts are powerful tools with good generalization properties. More precisely, we showed that parts transfer well to the majority of new classes even if trained from a limited number of examples.

These very encouraging results suggest that the pretrained deep representations have the ability to learn novel concepts quickly and effectively. We further confirmed this by showing that adding a specialized DA component to our architecture does not bring a significant boost in performance. In the future, a more systematic study of the asymptotic properties of supervised training is warranted, in order to assess if, for certain well-defined but broad problems such as the detection of certain parts in *all* animals, could be solved essentially by "exhaustion," by collecting once for all a sufficiently large pool of annotated examples.

Acknowledgements This work has been supported by Xerox Research Center Europe and ERC 677195-IDIU.

Part IV
Beyond Domain Adaptation: Unifying Perspectives

Chapter 15
A Multisource Domain Generalization Approach to Visual Attribute Detection

Chuang Gan, Tianbao Yang and Boqing Gong

Abstract Attributes possess appealing properties and benefit many computer vision problems, such as object recognition, learning with humans in the loop, and image retrieval. Whereas the existing work mainly pursues utilizing attributes for various computer vision problems, we contend that the most basic problem—how to accurately and robustly detect attributes from images—has been left underexplored. Especially, the existing work rarely explicitly tackles the need that attribute detectors should generalize well across different categories, including those previously unseen. Noting that this is analogous to the objective of multisource domain generalization, if we treat each category as a domain, we provide a novel perspective to attribute detection and propose to gear the techniques in multisource domain generalization for the purpose of learning cross-category generalizable attribute detectors. We validate our understanding and approach with extensive experiments on four challenging datasets and two different problems.

15.1 Introduction

Domain adaptation occurs in and provides an intriguing perspective to many real-world applications. In this chapter, we study a basic task in computer vision, visual attribute detection from images and videos. We show that domain generalization—a subfield of domain adaptation, leads to a novel understanding about the attribute detection problem as well as state-of-the-art performance.

C. Gan
Tsinghua University, Beijing, China
e-mail: ganchuang1990@gmail.com

T. Yang
University of Iowa, Iowa City, IA 52242, USA
e-mail: tianbao-yang@uiowa.edu

B. Gong (✉)
University of Central Florida, Orlando, FL 32816, USA
e-mail: boqinggong@gmail.com

G. Csurka (ed.), *Domain Adaptation in Computer Vision Applications*,
Advances in Computer Vision and Pattern Recognition,
DOI 10.1007/978-3-319-58347-1_15

Visual attributes are middle-level concepts which humans use to describe objects, human faces, scenes, activities, and so on (e.g., four-legged, smiley, outdoor, and crowded). A major appeal of attributes is that they are not only human-nameable but also machine-detectable, making it possible to serve as the building blocks to describe instances [157, 280, 360, 363], teach machines to recognize previously unseen classes by zero-shot learning [287, 353], or offer a natural human–computer interactions channel for image/video search [272, 439, 469, 568].

As a result of the versatileness of attributes, it is highly desired, and yet quite challenging, to accurately and robustly detect the attributes from images and videos. The visual appearance of attributes often spans a large spectrum (e.g., "furry" and "striped"). Some attributes describe local properties of an object (e.g., "smiley" and wing color), while some others are about the semantic perception of holistic scenes (e.g., "natural" and "cluttered"). In addition to tackling these challenges, a high-quality attribute detector is also expected to generalize well-across different categories, including those previously unseen ones. For instance, the attribute detector "four-legged" is expected to correctly tell a giant panda is four-legged even if it is trained from the images of horses, cows, zebras, and pigs (i.e., no pandas). Instead of attempting to tackle all the challenges, we mainly focus on learning attribute detectors that well generalize across different categories.

Most of the existing *attribute* detectors [70, 72, 75, 87, 157, 244, 245, 251, 280, 287, 508] are built using features engineered or learned for *object* recognition together with off-shelf machine learning classifiers—without tailoring them to reflect the idiosyncrasies of attributes. This is suboptimal; the successful techniques on object recognition do not necessarily apply to learning attributes mainly for two reasons. First, attributes are in a different semantic space as opposed to objects; they are in the *middle* of low-level visual cues and the high-level object labels. Second, attribute detection can even be considered as an *orthogonal* task to object recognition, in that attributes are shared by different objects (e.g., zebras, lions, and mice are all "furry") and distinctive attributes are present in the same object (e.g., a car is boxy and has wheels). As shown in Fig. 15.1, the boundaries between attributes and between object categories cross each other. Therefore, we do not expect that the features originally learned for separating elephant, sheep, and giraffe could also be optimal for detecting the attribute "bush," which is shared by them.

We reexamine the fundamental attribute detection problem and aim to develop an attribute-oriented feature representation, such that one can conveniently apply off-shelf classifiers to obtain high-quality attribute detectors. We expect that the detectors learned from our new representation are capable of breaking the boundaries of object categories and generalizing well across both seen and unseen classes. To this end, we cast **attribute detection as a multisource domain generalization problem** [339, 345, 549] by noting that the desired properties from attributes are analogous to the objective of the latter.

A domain refers to an underlying data distribution. Multisource domain generalization aims to extract knowledge from several *related* source domains such that it is applicable to different domains, especially to those unseen at the training stage.

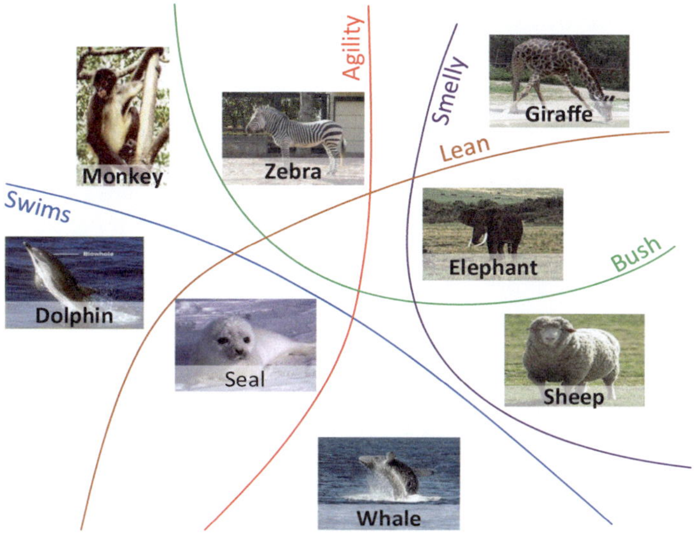

Fig. 15.1 The boundaries between middle-level attributes and high-level object classes cross each other. We thus do not expect that the features originally learned for separating elephant, sheep, and giraffe could also be optimal for detecting the attribute "bush," which is shared by them. We propose to understand attribute detection as multisource domain generalization and to explicitly break the class boundaries in order to learn high-quality attribute detectors

This is in accordance with our objective for learning cross-category generalizable attributes detectors, if we consider each category as a domain.

Motivated by this observation, we employ the Unsupervised Domain-Invariant Component Analysis (UDICA) [339] as the basic building block for our approach. The key principle of UDICA is that minimizing the distributional variance of different domains, categories in our context, can improve the cross-domain/cross-category generalization capabilities of the classifiers. A supervised extension to UDICA was introduced in [339] depending on the inverse of a covariance operator as well as some mild assumptions. However, the inverse operation is both computationally expensive and unstable in practice. We instead propose to use the alternative to account for the attribute labels; we show that the Centered Kernel Alignment (CKA) [100] can be seamlessly integrated with UDICA, enabling us to learn both category-invariant and attribute-discriminative feature representations.

We organize the rest of this chapter as follows. Section 15.2 presents our attribute learning framework, followed by the experimental settings and evaluation results (Sect. 15.3). We review some related works on attribute detection, domain generalization, and domain adaptation in Sect. 15.4. Section 15.5 concludes the chapter.

15.2 Attribute detection

This section formalizes the problem of attribute detection and shows its in-depth connection to domain generalization. Built upon this observation, we tackle attribute detection by improving upon a domain generalization algorithm. Our overall approach takes as input the features of the training images, their class (domain) labels, as well as their attribute labels. It operates upon kernels derived from the input data and learns a kernel projection to "distill" category-invariant and attribute-discriminative signals embedded in the original features. The output is a new feature vector for each image that can be readily used in many machine learning models like SVMs for training the cross-category generalizable attribute detectors.

Problem statement. Suppose that we have access to an annotated dataset of M images. They are in the form of $(\boldsymbol{x}_m, \boldsymbol{a}_m, y_m)$ where $\boldsymbol{x}_m \in \mathbb{R}^{\mathsf{D}}$ is the feature vector extracted from the mth image $I_m, m \in [\mathsf{M}] \triangleq \{1, 2, \ldots, \mathsf{M}\}$. Two types of annotations are provided for each image, the category label $y_m \in [\mathsf{C}]$ and the attribute annotations $\boldsymbol{a}_m \in \{0, 1\}^{\mathsf{A}}$. Though, we use binary attributes (e.g., the presence or absence of stripes) for clarity, it is straightforward to extend our approach to multi-way and continuous-valued attributes. Note that a particular attribute $\boldsymbol{a}_m^i$ could appear in many categories (e.g., zebras, cows, giant pandas, lions, and mice are all furry). Moreover, there may be test images from previously unseen categories $\{\mathsf{C}+1, \mathsf{C}+2, \ldots\}$ for example in zero-shot learning. Our objective is to learn accurate and robust attribute detectors $\mathcal{C}(\boldsymbol{x}_m) \in \{0, 1\}^{\mathsf{A}}$ to well generalize across different categories, especially to be able to perform well on the unseen classes.

Attribute detection as domain generalization—A new perspective. In this work, we understand attribute detection as a domain generalization problem. A domain refers to an underlying data distribution. In our context, it refers to the distribution $P_y(\boldsymbol{x}, \boldsymbol{a})$ of a category $y \in [\mathsf{C}]$ over the input $\boldsymbol{x}$ and attribute labels $\boldsymbol{a}$. As shown in Fig. 15.2, the domains/categories are assumed to be related and are sampled from a common distribution $\mathcal{P}$. This is reasonable considering that images and categories can often be organized in a hierarchy. Thanks to the relationships between different categories, we expect to learn new image representations from which the trained detectors will perform well on both seen and unseen classes.

Main idea for attribute detection. Our key idea is to find a feature transformation of the input $\boldsymbol{x}$ to eliminate the mismatches between different domains/categories in terms of their marginal distributions over the input, whereas ideally we should consider the joint distributions $P_y(\boldsymbol{x}, \boldsymbol{a})$, $y \in [\mathsf{C}]$. In particular, we use UDICA [339] and CKA [100] for this purpose. Note that modeling the marginal distributions $P_y(\boldsymbol{x})$ is common in domain generalization [190, 339, 549] and domain adaptation [200, 243, 354] and performs well in many applications. We leave investigating the joint distributions $P_y(\boldsymbol{x}, \boldsymbol{a})$ for future work. In the following, we first present some background on distributional variance. We then show how to integrate UDICA and CKA. Jointly, they give rise to new feature representations which account for both attribute-discriminativeness and cross-category generalizability.

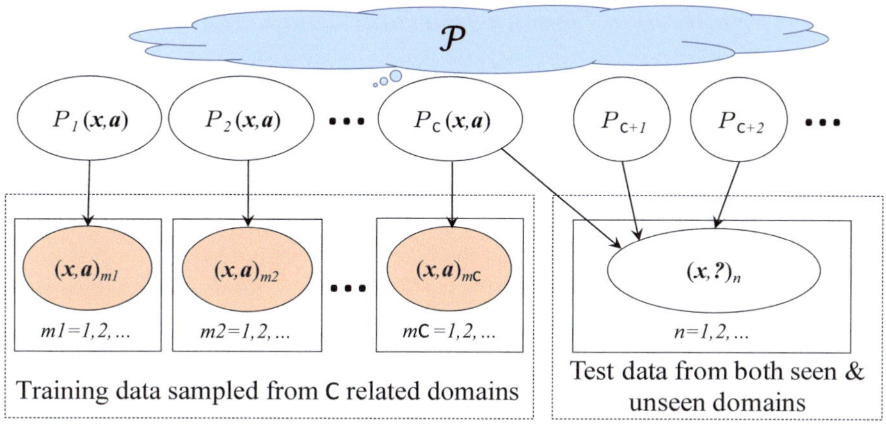

Fig. 15.2 Attribute detection as multisource domain generalization. Given labeled data sampled from several categories/domains, i.e., distributions $P_y(\boldsymbol{x}, \boldsymbol{a})$, $y \in [\mathsf{C}]$ over image representations $\boldsymbol{x}$ and attribute labels $\boldsymbol{a}$, we extract knowledge useful for attribute detection and applicable to different domains/categories, especially to previously unseen ones $P_{\mathsf{C}+1}, P_{\mathsf{C}+2}, \ldots$

15.2.1 Background on Distributional Variance

Denote by $\mathcal{H}$ and $k(\cdot,\cdot)$ respectively a Reproducing Kernel Hilbert Space and its associated kernel function. For an arbitrary distribution $P_y(\boldsymbol{x})$ indexed by $y \in \mathcal{Y}$, the following mapping,

$$\mu[P_y(\boldsymbol{x})] = \int k(\boldsymbol{x}, \cdot)\mathrm{d}P_y(\boldsymbol{x}) \triangleq \mu_y \tag{15.1}$$

is injective if k is a characteristic kernel [213, 447, 453]. In other words, the kernel mean map μ_y in the RKHS $\mathcal{H}$ preserves all the statistical information of $P_y(\boldsymbol{x})$.

The distributional variance follows naturally,

$$\mathbb{V}(\mathcal{Y}) = \frac{1}{|\mathcal{Y}|}\sum_{y\in\mathcal{Y}} \|\mu_y - \mu_0\|^2_{\mathcal{H}}, \quad \widehat{\mathbb{V}}(\mathcal{Y}) = \mathrm{Tr}(\mathbf{KQ}), \tag{15.2}$$

where μ_0 is the map of the mean of all the distributions in $\mathcal{Y}$. In practice, we do not have access to the distributions. Instead, we observe the samples S_y, $y \in \mathcal{Y}$ each drawn from a distribution $P_y(\boldsymbol{x})$ and can thus empirically estimate the distributional variance by $\widehat{\mathbb{V}}(\mathcal{Y}) = \mathrm{Tr}(\mathbf{KQ})$. Here, $\mathbf{K}$ is the (centered)[1] kernel matrix over all the samples, and $\mathbf{Q}$ collects the coefficients which depend on only the numbers of samples. We refer the readers to [339] for more details including the consistency between the distributional variance $\mathbb{V}$ and its estimate $\widehat{\mathbb{V}}$.

[1] All kernels discussed in this chapter have been centered [100].

15.2.2 Unsupervised Domain-Invariant Component Analysis

Unsupervised Domain-Invariant Component Analysis (UDICA) is an effective approach to domain generalization based on the idea of minimizing the distributional variance over different domains [339]. The projection from one RKHS to another results in the following transformation of the kernel matrices, $\mathbb{R}^{\mathsf{M}\times\mathsf{M}} \ni \mathbf{K} \mapsto \widetilde{\mathbf{K}} = \mathbf{K}\mathbf{B}\mathbf{B}^\top\mathbf{K} \in \mathbb{R}^{\mathsf{M}\times\mathsf{M}}$ [416]. As a result, one can take $(\mathbf{KB})$ as the empirical kernel map, i.e., consider the mth row of $(\mathbf{KB})$ as the new feature representations of image I_m and plug them into any linear classifiers. UDICA learns the transformation $\mathbf{B}$ by imposing the following properties.

Minimizing distributional variance. The empirical distributional variance between different domains/categories becomes the following in our context

$$\mathbb{V}_{\mathbf{B}}([\mathsf{C}]) = \mathrm{Tr}(\widetilde{\mathbf{K}}\mathbf{Q}) = \mathrm{Tr}(\mathbf{B}^\top\mathbf{KQKB}). \tag{15.3}$$

Intuitively, the domains would be perfectly matched when the variance is 0. Since there are many seen categories, each as a domain, we expect the learned projection to be generalizable and work well for the unseen classes as well.

Maximizing data variance. Starting from the empirical kernel map $(\mathbf{KB})$, it is not difficult to see that the data covariance is $(\mathbf{KB})^\top(\mathbf{KB})\,/\mathsf{M}$ and the variance is

$$\mathbb{V}_{\mathbf{B}}([\mathsf{M}]) = \mathrm{Tr}(\mathbf{B}^\top\mathbf{K}^2\mathbf{B})/\mathsf{M}. \tag{15.4}$$

Regularizing the transformation. UDICA regularizes the transformation by

$$\mathcal{R}(\mathbf{B}) = \mathrm{Tr}(\mathbf{B}^\top\mathbf{KB}). \tag{15.5}$$

Combining the above criteria, we arrive at the following problem,

$$\max_{\mathbf{B}} \quad \mathrm{Tr}(\mathbf{B}^\top K^2\mathbf{B})/\mathsf{M}/\mathrm{Tr}(\mathbf{B}^\top\mathbf{KQKB} + \mathbf{B}^\top\mathbf{KB}), \tag{15.6}$$

where the nominator corresponds to the data variance and the denominator sums up the distributional variance and the regularization over $\mathbf{B}$.

By solving the problem Eq. (15.6), we are essentially blurring the boundaries between different categories and match the classes with each other, due to the distributional variance term in the denominator. This thus eliminates the barrier for attribute detectors to generalize across various classes. Our experiments verify the effectiveness the learned new representations $(\mathbf{KB})$. Moreover, we can further improve the performance by modeling the attribute labels using CKA.

15.2.3 Centered Kernel Alignment (CKA)

Note that our training data are in the form of $(\boldsymbol{x}_m, \boldsymbol{a}_m, y_m)$, $m \in [\mathsf{M}]$. For each image there are multiple attribute labels which may be highly correlated. Besides, we would like to stick to kernel methods to be consistent with our choice of UDICA—indeed, the distributional variance is best implemented by kernel methods. These considerations lead to our decision on using kernel alignment [100] to model the multi-attribute supervised information.

Let $L_{m,m'} = \langle \boldsymbol{a}_m, \boldsymbol{a}_{m'} \rangle$ be the elements of the kernel matrix over the attributes. Since $\mathbf{L}$ is computed directly from the attribute labels, it preserves the correlations among them and serves as the "perfect" target kernel for the transformed kernel $\widetilde{\mathbf{K}} = \mathbf{K}\mathbf{B}\mathbf{B}^\top\mathbf{K}$ to align to. The CKA is then computed by,

$$\rho(\widetilde{\mathbf{K}}, \mathbf{L}) = \mathrm{Tr}(\widetilde{\mathbf{K}}\mathbf{L}) / \left(\sqrt{\mathrm{Tr}(\widetilde{\mathbf{K}}\widetilde{\mathbf{K}})} \sqrt{\mathrm{Tr}(\mathbf{L}\mathbf{L})} \right) \tag{15.7}$$

where we abuse the notation $\mathbf{L}$ slightly to denote that it is centered [100].

We would like to integrate the kernel alignment with UDICA in a unified optimization problem. To this end, first, it is safe to drop $\mathrm{Tr}(\mathbf{LL})$ in Eq. (15.7) since it has nothing to do with the projection $\mathbf{B}$ we are learning. Moreover, note that the role of $\mathrm{Tr}(\widetilde{\mathbf{K}}\widetilde{\mathbf{K}})$ duplicates with the regularization in Eq. (15.6) to some extent, as it is mainly to avoid trivial solutions for the kernel alignment. We thus only add $\mathrm{Tr}(\widetilde{\mathbf{K}}\mathbf{L})$ to the nominator of UDICA,

$$\max_{\mathbf{B}} \; \frac{\mathrm{Tr}(\gamma \mathbf{B}^\top \mathbf{K}^2 \mathbf{B}/\mathsf{M} + (1-\gamma)\mathbf{B}^\top \mathbf{KLKB})}{\mathrm{Tr}(\mathbf{B}^\top \mathbf{KQKB} + \mathbf{B}^\top \mathbf{KB})}, \tag{15.8}$$

where $\gamma \in [0, 1]$ balances the data variance and the kernel alignment with the supervised attribute labeling information. We cross-validate γ in our experiments. We name this formulation **KDICA**, which couples the CKA and UDICA. The former closely tracks the attribute-discriminative information and the latter facilitates the cross-category generalization of the attribute detectors to be trained upon KDICA.

Optimization. By writing out the Lagrangian of the formalized problem (Eq. (15.8)) and then setting the derivative with respect to $\mathbf{B}$ to 0, we arrive at a generalized eigen-decomposition problem,

$$\left(\gamma \mathbf{K}^2/\mathsf{M} + (1-\gamma)\mathbf{KLK}\right)\mathbf{B} = \left(\mathbf{KQK} + \mathbf{K}\right)\mathbf{B}\boldsymbol{\Gamma}, \tag{15.9}$$

where $\boldsymbol{\Gamma}$ is a diagonal matrix containing all the eigenvalues (Lagrangian multipliers). We find the solution $\mathbf{B}$ as the Leading eigen-vectors. The number of eigen-vectors is cross-validated in our experiments. Again, we remind that $(\mathbf{KB})$ serves as the new feature representations of the images for training attribute detectors. Algorithm 9 sketches our proposed approach.

Algorithm 9 Kernel-alignment Domain-Invariant Component Analysis (KDICA).

Input: Parameters γ and $\mathsf{b} \ll \mathsf{M}$. Training data $\mathcal{S} = \{(\boldsymbol{x}_m, y_m, \boldsymbol{a}_m)\}_{m=1}^{\mathsf{M}}$
1: Calculate gram matrices $[K_{ij}] = k(\boldsymbol{x}_i, \boldsymbol{x}_j)$ and $[L_{ij}] = l(\boldsymbol{a}_i, \boldsymbol{a}_j)$
2: Solve $(\gamma \mathbf{K}^2/\mathsf{M} + (1-\gamma)\mathbf{KLK})\mathbf{B} = (\mathbf{KQK} + \mathbf{K})\mathbf{B}\boldsymbol{\Gamma}$.
3: Output $\mathbf{B}$ and $\widetilde{\mathbf{K}} \leftarrow \mathbf{KBB}^{\mathrm{T}}\mathbf{K}$
4: Use $(\mathbf{KB})$ as new data representations to train linear classifiers and $\widetilde{\mathbf{K}}$ for kernelized ones.
Output: Projection $\mathbf{B}_{\mathsf{M}\times\mathsf{b}}$

15.3 Experimental Results

This section presents our experimental results on four benchmark datasets. We test our approach for both the immediate task of attribute detection and another problem, zero-shot learning, which could benefit from high-quality attribute detectors.

Dataset. We use four datasets to validate the proposed approach; three of them contain images for object and scene recognition and the last one contains videos for action recognition. (a) The **Animal with attribute (AWA)** [287] dataset comprises of 30,475 images belonging to 50 animal classes. Each class is annotated with 85 attributes. Following, the standard split by the dataset, we divide the dataset into 40 classes (24,295 images) for training and 10 classes (6,180 images) for testing. (b) **Caltech-UCSD Birds 2011 (CUB)** [518] is a dataset with fine-grained objects. There are 11,788 images of 200 different bird classes in CUB. Each class is annotated with 312 binary attributes. We split the dataset as suggested in [7] to facilitate direct comparison (150 classes for training and 50 classes for testing). (c) **aPascal-aYahoo** [157] consists of two attribute datases: the aPASCAL dataset, which contains 12,695 images (6,340 for training and 6,355 for testing) collected for the Pascal VOC 2008 challenge, and aYahoo including 2,644 test images. Each image is annotated with 64 attributes. There are 20 object classes in aPascal and 12 in aYahoo and they are disjoint. Following the settings of [439, 568], we use the predefined training images in aPascal as the training set and test on aYahoo. (d) **UCF101 dataset** [451] is a large dateset for video action recognition. It contains 13,320 videos of 101 action classes. Each action class comes with 115 attributes. The videos are collected from YouTube with large variations in camera motion, object appearance, viewpoint, cluttered background, and illumination conditions. We run 10 rounds of experiments each with a random split of 81/20 classes for the training/testing sets, and then report the averaged results.

Features. For the first three image datasets, we use the Convolutional Neural Network (CNN) implementation provided by Caffe [255], particularly with the 19-layer network architecture and parameters from Oxford [443], to extract 4,096-dimensional CNN feature representations from images (i.e., the activations of the first fully connected layer fc6). For the UCF101 dataset, we use the 3D CNN (C3D) [492] pre-trained on the Sport 1M dataset [265] to construct video-clip features from both spatial and temporal dimensions. We then use average pooling to obtain the video-level representations. We ℓ_2 normalize the features.

Implementation details. We choose the Gaussian RBF kernel and fix the bandwidth parameter as 1 for our approach to learning new image representations. After that, to train the attribute detectors, we input the learned representations into standard linear SVM (see the empirical kernel map in Sect. 15.2.2). There are two free hyperparameters when we train the detectors using the representations learned through UDICA, the hyperparameter C in SVM and the number b of leading eigen-vectors in UDICA. We use fivefold cross-validation to choose the best values for C and b, respectively from $\{0.01, 0.1, 1, 10, 100\}$ and $\{30, 50, 70, 90, 110, 130, 150\}$. We use the same C and b for KDICA and only cross-validate γ in Eq. (15.9) from $\{0.2, 0.5, 0.8\}$ to learn the SVM based attribute detectors with KDICA.

Evaluation. We first test our approach to attribute detection on all the four datasets. To see how much the other tasks, which involve attributes, can gain from higher quality attribute detectors, we further conduct zero-shot learning [287, 353] experiments on AWA, CUB, and UCF101. We evaluate the results of attribute detection by the averaged Area Under ROC Curve (AUC), the higher the better, and the results of zero-shot learning by classification accuracy.

15.3.1 Attribute Prediction

Table 15.1 presents the attribute prediction performance of our approaches and several competitive baselines. In particular, we compare with four state-of-the-art attribute detection methods: Directly Attribute Prediction (DAP) [287], Indirectly Attribute Prediction (IAP) [287], Attribute Label Embedding (ALE) [7], and Hypergraph-regularized Attribute Predictors (HAP) [87]. Note that, we can directly contrast our methods with DAP to see the effectiveness of the learned new representations, because they share the same input and classifiers and only differ in that we learn the new attribute-discriminative and category-invariant feature representations. The IAP model first maps any input to the seen classes and then predicts the attributes on top of those. The ALE method unifies attribute prediction with object class prediction instead of directly optimizing with respect to attributes. We thus do not expect it to perform quite well on the attribute prediction task. HAP explores the correlations among attributes explicitly by hypergraphs, while we achieve this implicitly in the kernel alignment. Additionally, we also show the results of CSHAP_G and CSHAP_H, two variations of HAP to model class labels.

We include in Table 15.1 both the results of these methods reported in the original papers, when they are available, and those we obtained (marked by '*') by running the source code provided by the authors. We use the same features we extracted for the baselines and our approach.

Overall results. From Table 15.1, we can find that UDCIA and KDICA outperform all the baselines on all the four datasets. More specifically, the relative accuracy gains

Table 15.1 Average Attribute Prediction Accuracy (%, results evaluated by AUC). The results marked by * are obtained by us rerunning the code of the existing methods

Approcahes	AWA	CUB	aYahoo	UCF101
IAP [287]	74.0/79.2*	74.9*	–	–
ALE [7]	65.7	60.3	–	–
HAP [87]	74.0/79.1*	68.5/74.1*	58.2*	72.1 ± 1.1
CSHAP$_G$ [87]	74.3/79.4*	62.7/74.6*	58.2*	72.3 ± 1.0
CSHAP$_H$ [87]	74.0/79.0*	68.5/73.4*	65.2*	72.4 ± 1.1
DAP [287]	72.8/78.9*	61.8/72.1*	77.4*	71.8 ± 1.2
UDICA (Ours)	**83.9**	**76.0**	**82.3**	**74.3 ± 1.3**
KDICA (Ours)	**84.4**	**76.4**	**84.7**	**75.5 ± 1.1**

Fig. 15.3 Some attributes on which the proposed KDICA significantly outperforms DAP

of UDCIA over DAP are 6.3% on the AWA dataset and 5.4% on the CUB dateset, respectively, under the same feature and experimental settings. These clearly validate our assumption that blurring the category boundaries improves the generalizabilities of attribute detectors to previously unseen categories. The KDICA with CKA is slightly better than the UDICA approach by incorporating attribute discriminative signals into the new feature representations. Delving into the per-unseen-class attribute detection result, we find that our KDICA-based approach improves the results of DAP for 71 out of 85 attributes on AWA and 272 out of 312 on CUB.

When does domain generalization help? We give some qualitative analyses using Figs. 15.3 and 15.4 here. For the attributes in Fig. 15.3, the proposed KDICA significantly improves the performance of the DAP approach. Those attributes ("muscle," "domestic," etc.) appear in visually quite different object categories. It seems like breaking the category boundaries is necessary in this case in order to make the attribute detectors generalize to the unseen classes. On the other hand, Fig. 15.4 shows the attributes for which our approach can hardly improve DAP's performance. The attribute "yellow" is too trivial to detect with nearly 100% accuracy already by DAP. The attribute "swim" is actually shared by visually similar categories, leaving not much room for KDICA to play any role.

Fig. 15.4 Example attributes that KDICA could not improve the detection accuracy over the traditional DAP approach

Table 15.2 Zero-shot recognition performances (%, in accuracy). The results marked by * are obtained by us rerunning the source code provided by the authors

Approcahes	AWA	CUB	UCF101
ALE [7]	37.4	18.0	–
HLE [7]	39.0	12.1	–
AHLE [7]	43.5	17.0	–
DA [251]	30.6	–	–
MLA [172]	41.3	–	–
ZSRF [250]	48.7	–	–
SM [173]	66.0	–	–
Embedding [8]	60.1	29.9	–
IAP [287]	42.2/49.4*	4.6/34.9*	–
HAP [87]	45.0/55.6*	17.5/40.7*	–
CSHAP_G [87]	45.0/54.5*	17.5/38.7*	–
CSHAP_H [87]	45.6/53.3*	17.5/36.9*	–
DAP [287]	41.2/58.9*	10.5/39.8*	26.8 ± 1.1
UDICA (Ours)	**63.6**	**42.4**	**29.6 ± 1.2**
KDICA (Ours)	**73.8**	**43.7**	**31.1 ± 0.8**

15.3.2 Zero-Shot Learning Based on Detected Attributes

As the intermediate representations of images and videos, attributes are often used in high-level computer vision applications. In this section, we conduct experiments on zero-shot learning [287, 353] to examine whether the improved attribute detectors could also benefit this task.

Given our UDICA and KDICA-based attribute detection results, we simply input them to the second layer of the DAP model [287] to solve the zero-shot learning problem. We compare it with several well-known zero-shot recognition systems as shown in Table 15.2. We run our own experiments for some of them whose source code are provided by the authors. The corresponding results are marked by '*'.

We see that in Table 15.2 the proposed simple solution to zero-shot learning outperforms the other state-of-the-art methods on the AWA, CUB, and UCF101 datasets, especially its immediate rival DAP. In addition, we notice that our kernel alignment technique (KDICA) improves the zero-shot recognition results over UDICA significantly on AWA. The improvements over UDICA on the other two datasets are also more significant than the improvements for the attribute prediction task (see Sect. 15.3.1 and Table 15.1). This observation is interesting; it implies that increasing the quality of the attribute detectors is rewarding, because the increase will be magnified to even larger improvement for the zero-shot learning. Similar observation applies if we compare the differences between DAP and UDICA/KDICA respectively in Tables 15.1 and Table 15.2. Finally, we note that our main purpose is to investigate how better attribute detectors can benefit zero-shot learning—we do not expect to have a thorough comparison of the existing zero-shot learning methods.

15.4 Related Work

Our approach is related to two major research areas, attribute detection and domain adaptation/generalization. We unify them in this work.

Learning attributes. Earlier work on attribute detection mainly focused on modeling the correlations among attributes [70, 72, 75, 87, 244, 245, 251, 508], localizing some special part-related attributes (e.g., tails of mammals) [33, 35, 47, 133, 258, 410, 580], and the relationship between attributes and categories [245, 320, 359, 532]. Some recent work has applied deep models to attribute detection [79, 147, 316, 580]. None of these methods explicitly model the cross-category generalization of the attributes, except the one by Farhadi et al. [157], to the best of our knowledge, where the authors select features within each category to down-weight category-specific cues. Likely, due to the fact that the attribute and category cues are interplayed, their feature selection procedure only gives limited gain. We propose to overcome this challenge by investigating all categories together and employing nonlinear mapping functions.

Attributes possess versatile properties and benefit a wide range of challenging computer vision tasks. They serve as the basic building blocks for one to compose categories (e.g., different objects) [7, 156, 250, 263, 287, 353, 526, 569] and describe instances [157, 280, 360, 363, 522], enabling knowledge transfer between them. Attributes also reveal the rich structures underlying categories and are thus often employed to regulate machine learning models for visual recognition [177, 180, 246, 296, 433, 436, 462, 491]. Moreover, attributes offer a natural human–computer interaction channel for visual recognition with humans in the loop [50], relevance feedback in image retrieval [199, 272, 280, 360, 383, 414, 439, 476, 568], and active learning [39, 273, 283, 301, 361].

Domain generalization and adaptation. Domain generalization is still at its early developing stage. A feature projection-based algorithm, Domain-Invariant Component Analysis (DICA), was introduced in [339] to learn by minimizing the variance of the source domains. Recently, domain generation has been introduce into computer vision community for object recognition [190, 549] and video recognition [345].

We propose to gear multisource domain generalization techniques for the purpose of learning cross-category generalizable attribute detectors. Multisource domain adaptation [135, 197, 238, 323, 471] is related to our approach if we consider a transductive setting (i.e., the learner has access to the test data). While it assumes a single target domain, in attribute detection the test data are often sampled from more than one unseen domain.

15.5 Conclusion

We propose to reexamine the fundamental attribute detection problem, and learn a novel attribute-oriented feature representation by casting the problem as multisource domain generalization. The new feature representations enable one to conveniently apply off-shelf classifiers to obtain high-quality attribute detectors that are capable of breaking the boundaries of object categories and generalizing well to unseen classes. Extensive experiment on four datasets, and two tasks validate that our attribute representation not only improves the quality of attributes, but also benefits succeeding applications, for instance zero-shot recognition, as well as image retrieval included in our conference paper [179].

Acknowledgements This work was supported in part by NSF IIS-1566511. Chuang Gan was partially supported by the National Basic Research Program of China Grant 2011CBA00300, 2011CBA00301, the National Natural Science Foundation of China Grant 61033001, 61361136003. Tianbao Yang was partially supported by NSF IIS-1463988 and NSF IIS-1545995.

Chapter 16
Unifying Multi-domain Multitask Learning: Tensor and Neural Network Perspectives

Yongxin Yang and Timothy M. Hospedales

Abstract Multi-domain learning aims to benefit from simultaneously learning across several different but related domains. In this chapter, we propose a single framework that unifies multi-domain learning (MDL) and the related but better studied area of multitask learning (MTL). By exploiting the concept of a *semantic descriptor* we show how our framework encompasses various classic and recent MDL/MTL algorithms as special cases with different semantic descriptor encodings. As a second contribution, we present a higher order generalization of this framework, capable of simultaneous multitask-multi-domain learning. This generalization has two mathematically equivalent views in multilinear algebra and gated neural networks, respectively. Moreover, by exploiting the semantic descriptor, it provides neural networks the capability of zero-shot learning (ZSL), where a classifier is generated for an unseen class without any training data; as well as zero-shot domain adaptation (ZSDA), where a model is generated for an unseen domain without any training data. In practice, this framework provides a powerful yet easy to implement method that can be flexibly applied to MTL, MDL, ZSL, and ZSDA.

16.1 Introduction

The multi-domain setting arises when there is data about a task in several different but related domains. For example in visual recognition of an object when viewed with different camera types. Multi-domain learning (MDL) models [115, 131, 560] aim to learn a cross-domain parameter sharing strategy that reflects the domains' similarities and differences. Such selective parameter sharing aims to be robust to the differences in statistics across domains, while exploiting data from multiple domains to improve performance compared to learning each domain separately.

Y. Yang · T.M. Hospedales (✉)
Queen Mary, University of London, London, UK
e-mail: t.hospedales@qmul.ac.uk

Y. Yang
e-mail: yongxin.yang@qmul.ac.uk

G. Csurka (ed.), *Domain Adaptation in Computer Vision Applications*,
Advances in Computer Vision and Pattern Recognition,
DOI 10.1007/978-3-319-58347-1_16

In this chapter, we derive a general framework that encompasses MDL and MTL from both neural network and tensor factorization perspectives. Many classic and recent MDL/MTL algorithms can be understood by the assumptions about the cross-domain/task sharing structure encoded in their designs. E.g., the assumption that each task/domain's model is a linear combination of a global and a task-specific parameter vector [115, 149]. Our framework includes these as special cases corresponding to specific settings of a *semantic descriptor vector* parameterizing tasks/domains [560]. This vector can be used to recover existing models from our framework, but more generally it allows one to relax the often implicit assumption that domains are atomic/categorical entities, and exploit available *metadata* about tasks/domains to guide sharing structure for better MDL/MTL [560, 562]. For example, in surveillance video analysis, exploiting the knowledge of the time of day and day of week corresponding to each domain for better MDL. Finally, the idea of a semantic task/domain descriptor, allows our framework to go beyond the conventional MDL/MTL setting, and address both zero-shot learning [560] and zero-shot domain adaptation [560, 562]—where a model can be deployed for a new task/domain without any training data, solely by specifying the task/domain's semantic descriptor metadata.

Multi-domain versus Multitask Learning. The difference between domains and tasks can be subtle, and some multi-domain learning problems can be addressed by methods proposed for multitask learning and vice-versa. However, to better understand this work, it is useful to distinguish them clearly. Domains refer to multiple datasets addressing the same task, but with differing statistical bias. For example camera type for object recognition; time of day or year for surveillance video analysis; or more subtle human biases in data collection [489]. Tasks, on the other hand would refer to different object categories to recognize. In other words, a task change affects the output label space of a supervised learning problem, while a domain change does not.

A classic benchmark with multiple domains is the Office (OFF31) dataset [407]. It contains images of the same set of categories (e.g., mug, laptop, keyboard) from three data sources (Amazon website, webcam, and DSLR). In this context, multitask learning could improve performance by sharing information about how to recognize keyboard and laptop; while multi-domain learning could improve performance by sharing knowledge about how to recognize those classes in Amazon product versus webcam images. Some problems can be interpreted as either setting. E.g., in the School dataset [17] the goal is to predict students' exam scores based on their characteristics. This dataset is widely used to evaluate MTL algorithms, where students from different schools are grouped into different tasks. However, one can argue that school groupings are better interpreted as domains than tasks.

As a rule of thumb, multi-domain learning problems occur when a model from domain A could be directly applied to domain B albeit with reduced performance; while multitask learning problems occur where a model for task A can not meaningfully be applied to task B because their label-spaces are fundamentally different. In some problems, the multi-domain and multitask setting occur simultaneously. E.g., in the OFF31 dataset there are both multiple camera types, and multiple objects to recognize. Few existing methods can deal with this setting. MTL methods break a multi-class problem into multiple 1-v-all tasks and share information across tasks [17, 279], while MDL methods typically deal with a single output problem in multiple domains [115]. Our higher order generalization addresses simultaneous multi-domain multitask learning as required by problems such as the one posed by OFF31.

Relation to Domain Adaptation and Domain Generalization. Dataset bias/domain shift means that models trained on one domain often have weak performance when deployed in another domain. The community has proposed two different approaches to alleviate this: (i) Domain adaptation (DA): calibrating a pretrained model to a target domain using a limited amount of labeled data—supervised DA [407], or unlabeled data only—unsupervised DA [200], or both—semi-supervised DA [299]. (ii) Domain generalization (DG): to train a model that can is insensitive to domain bias, e.g., learning domain invariant features [339].

The objective of multi-domain learning is different from the mentioned domain adaptation and domain generalization. MDL can be seen as a bidirectional generalization of DA with each domain benefiting the others, so that all domains have maximal performance; rather than solely transferring knowledge from source → target domain as in DA. In its conventional form MDL does not overlap with DG, because it aims to improve the performance on the set of given domains, rather than address a held-out domain. However, our zero-shot domain adaptation extension of MDL, relates to DG insofar as aiming to address a held-out domain. The difference is that we require a semantic descriptor for the held-out domain, while DG does not. However, where such a descriptor exists, ZSDA is expected to outperform DG.

16.2 Methodology—Single Output Models

We start from the linear model assumption made by most popular MTL/MDL methods [17, 115, 253, 279]—i.e., that a domain/task corresponds to a univariate linear regression or binary classification problem. The case where a domain/task needs more than that (e.g., multi-class problem) will be discussed in Sect. 16.3. We also assume the domains/tasks are homogeneous, i.e., different domains/tasks have model representations and instance feature vectors of the same size.

16.2.1 Formulation: Vector-Matrix Inner Product

Assume we have M domains (tasks), and the ith domain has N_i instances. We denote the D-dimensional feature vector[1] of jth instance in ith domain (task) and

---

[1] All vectors (feature $\mathbf{x}$, weights $\mathbf{w}$, and domain descriptor $\mathbf{z}$) are by default column vectors.

its associated B-dimensional semantic descriptor[2] by the pair $\{\{\mathbf{x}_j^{(i)}, \mathbf{z}^{(i)}\}_{j=1}^{N_i}\}_{i=1}^{M}$ and the corresponding label $\{\{y_j^{(i)}\}_{j=1}^{N_i}\}_{i=1}^{M}$. All the weight vectors $\mathbf{w}^{(i)}$ for each domain (task) i can be stacked into a single weight matrix $\tilde{\mathbf{W}}$. Without loss of generality, we to minimize the empirical risk for all domains (tasks),

$$\arg\min_{\tilde{\mathbf{W}}} \frac{1}{M}\sum_{i=1}^{M}\left(\frac{1}{N_i}\sum_{j=1}^{N_i}\ell\left(\hat{y}_j^{(i)}, y_j^{(i)}\right)\right). \tag{16.1}$$

Here $\ell(\hat{y}, y)$ is a loss function depending on the predicted $\hat{y}$ and true label y. For the ith domain/task, the linear model $\mathbf{w}^{(i)}$ makes predictions as

$$\hat{y}_j^{(i)} = \mathbf{x}_j^{(i)} \cdot \mathbf{w}^{(i)} = \mathbf{x}_j^{(i)\top}\mathbf{w}^{(i)}. \tag{16.2}$$

Now we introduce a key idea in our work: rather than being learned directly, each task/domain's model $\mathbf{w}^{(i)}$ is *generated* by a linear function $f(\cdot)$ of its descriptor, termed the weight generating function,

$$\mathbf{w}^{(i)} = f(\mathbf{z}^{(i)}) = \mathbf{W}\mathbf{z}^{(i)}. \tag{16.3}$$

That is, the linear model for the ith domain/task is produced by its B-dimensional semantic descriptor hitting a $D \times B$ matrix $\mathbf{W}$. If all semantic descriptors are stacked (as columns) into matrix $\mathbf{Z}$, we have $\tilde{\mathbf{W}} = f(\mathbf{Z}) = \mathbf{W}\mathbf{Z}$.

Rather than learning the per-domain models $\tilde{\mathbf{W}}$ independently as in Eq. (16.1), we now learn the *weight generating function* parametrized by matrix $\mathbf{W}$ instead. By substituting Eq. (16.3) into Eq. (16.2), we can rewrite the prediction for the ith task/domain into a bilinear form,

$$\hat{y}_j^{(i)} = \mathbf{x}_j^{(i)\top}\mathbf{W}\mathbf{z}^{(i)}. \tag{16.4}$$

This general formulation encompasses many MTL/MDL methods. As we will see, the two key axes of design space on which existing MTL/MDL algorithms differ are the encoding of descriptors $\mathbf{z}$ and decomposition or regularization of matrix $\mathbf{W}$.

16.2.2 Semantic Descriptor Design

One-hot encoding z. In the simplest scenario $\mathbf{z}$ is a one-hot encoding vector that *indexes* domains (Fig. 16.1). The model generation function $f(\mathbf{z}^{(i)})$ then just *selects* one column from the matrix $\mathbf{W}$. For example, $\mathbf{z}^{(1)} = [1, 0, 0]^\top$, $\mathbf{z}^{(2)} = [0, 1, 0]^\top$,

[2]Note that, in any multi-domain or multitask learning problem, all instances are at least implicitly associated with a semantic descriptor indicating their domain (task).

$$Z = \begin{bmatrix} & \text{Domain-1} & \text{Domain-2} & \text{Domain-3} \\ \text{Index-1} & 1 & 0 & 0 \\ \text{Index-2} & 0 & 1 & 0 \\ \text{Index-3} & 0 & 0 & 1 \end{bmatrix} \qquad Z = \begin{bmatrix} & \text{Domain-1} & \text{Domain-2} & \text{Domain-3} \\ \text{Index-1} & 1 & 0 & 0 \\ \text{Index-2} & 0 & 1 & 0 \\ \text{Index-3} & 0 & 0 & 1 \\ \text{Shared} & 1 & 1 & 1 \end{bmatrix}$$

Fig. 16.1 Domain descriptor for categorical/atomic domains. One-hot encoding (*left*), and one-hot with constant encoding (*right*)

$$Z = \begin{bmatrix} & \text{Domain-1} & \text{Domain-2} & \text{Domain-3} & \text{Domain-4} \\ \text{A-1-B-1} & 1 & 0 & 0 & 0 \\ \text{A-1-B-2} & 0 & 1 & 0 & 0 \\ \text{A-2-B-1} & 0 & 0 & 1 & 0 \\ \text{A-2-B-2} & 0 & 0 & 0 & 1 \end{bmatrix} \qquad Z = \begin{bmatrix} & \text{Domain-1} & \text{Domain-2} & \text{Domain-3} & \text{Domain-4} \\ \text{A-1} & 1 & 1 & 0 & 0 \\ \text{A-2} & 0 & 0 & 1 & 1 \\ \text{B-1} & 1 & 0 & 1 & 0 \\ \text{B-2} & 0 & 1 & 0 & 1 \end{bmatrix}$$

Fig. 16.2 Example domain descriptor for domains with multiple factors. One-hot encoding (*left*). Distributed encoding (*right*)

$\mathbf{z}^{(3)} = [0, 0, 1]^\top$ if there are $M = 3$ domains/tasks. In this case, the length of the descriptor and the number of unique domains (tasks) are equal $B = M$, and the stack of all $\mathbf{z}^i$ vectors (denoted $\mathbf{Z} = [\mathbf{z}^{(1)}, \mathbf{z}^{(2)}, \ldots])$ is an $M \times M$ identity matrix. Learning the 'weight generating function' is then equivalent to independently learning per-domain weights.

One-hot encoding z with a constant. A drawback of one-hot encoding is that the $\mathbf{z}^i$ are orthogonal to each other, which suggests that all domains/tasks are independent—there is no cross-domain/task information sharing. To encode an expected sharing structure of an underlying commonality across all domains/tasks, an alternative approach to constructing $\mathbf{z}$ is to append a constant term after the one-hot encoding. For the case of $M = 3$, we might have $\mathbf{z}^{(1)} = [1, 0, 0, 1]^\top$, $\mathbf{z}^{(2)} = [0, 1, 0, 1]^\top$, $\mathbf{z}^{(3)} = [0, 0, 1, 1]^\top$. Figure 16.1 shows the resulting $B \times M$ matrix $\mathbf{Z}$ (in this case, $B = M + 1$). The prediction of task (domain) i is given as $\hat{y}^{(i)} = (\mathbf{x}^{(i)})^\top \mathbf{W}\mathbf{z}^{(i)} = (\mathbf{x}^{(i)})^\top(\mathbf{w}^{(i)} + \mathbf{w}^{(4)})$, i.e., the sum of a task/domain-specific and a globally shared prediction. Learning the weight generator corresponds to training both the local and shared predictors. This approach is implicitly used by some classic MDL/MTL algorithms [115, 149].

Distributed encoding z. In most studies of MDL/MTL, domain, or task is assumed to be an atomic category which can be effectively encoded by the above indexing approaches. However, more structured domain/task-metadata is often available, such that a domain (task) is indexed by multiple factors (e.g., time: day/night, and date: weekday/weekend, for batches of video surveillance data). Suppose two categorical variables (A, B) describe a domain, and each of them has two states (1, 2), then at most four distinct domains exist. Figure 16.2(left) illustrates the semantic descriptors for 1-hot encoding. However, this encoding does not exploit the sharing cues encoded in the metadata (e.g., in the surveillance example that day-weekday should be more

Table 16.1 Existing methods as special cases of our framework. Each column of the **Z** matrices corresponds to the assumed domain/task descriptor ($\mathbf{z}^{(i)}$) encoding. The notion used in the table is the same as the original paper, e.g., **P** here is analogous to L in [279]

	Z	**P**	Norm on **P**	**Q**	Norm on **Q**
RMTL [149] & FEDA [115]	$\begin{bmatrix}1&0&0\\0&1&0\\0&0&1\\1&1&1\end{bmatrix}$	Identity	None	$\begin{bmatrix}\mid&\mid&\mid&\mid\\\mathbf{v}_1&\mathbf{v}_2&\mathbf{v}_3&\mathbf{w}_0\\\mid&\mid&\mid&\mid\end{bmatrix}$	None
MTFL [17]	$\begin{bmatrix}1&0&0\\0&1&0\\0&0&1\end{bmatrix}$	Identity	None	**W**	$\ell_{2,1}$ Norm
TNMTL [253]	$\begin{bmatrix}1&0&0\\0&1&0\\0&0&1\end{bmatrix}$	Identity	None	**W**	Trace Norm
GO-MTL [279]	$\begin{bmatrix}1&0&0\\0&1&0\\0&0&1\end{bmatrix}$	L	Frobenius	S	Entry-wise ℓ_1

similar to day-weekend and night-weekday than to night-weekend). Thus we propose to use a distributed encoding of the task/domain descriptor (Fig. 16.2(right)). Now prediction weights are given by a linear combination of **W**'s columns given by the descriptor, and learning the weight generating function means learning weights for each factor (e.g., day, night, weekday, weekend). We will demonstrate that the ability to exploit structured domain/task descriptors where available, improves information sharing compared to existing MTL/MDL methods in later experiments.

16.2.3 Unification of Existing Algorithms

The key intuitions of various MDL/MTL methods are encoded in constraints on **W** in Eq. (16.3) and/or encodings of descriptors **z**. Besides enforcing local and shared components [115, 149] (which we interpret as a one-hot+constant descriptor) many studies achieve information sharing via enforcing low-rank structure on $\tilde{\mathbf{W}}$ (the $D \times T$ stack of weight vectors for each task). Popular choices for modeling $\tilde{\mathbf{W}}$ are: (i) add regularization that encourages $\tilde{\mathbf{W}}$ to be a low-rank matrix (ii) explicit low-rank factorization $\tilde{\mathbf{W}} = \tilde{\mathbf{P}}\tilde{\mathbf{Q}}$, and optionally placing some constraint(s) on $\tilde{\mathbf{P}}$ and/or $\tilde{\mathbf{Q}}$. We assume our weight generating function, the $D \times B$ matrix **W**, is replaced by the dot-product of two factor matrices **P** and **Q** ($D \times K$ and $K \times B$, respectively). Thus, Eq. (16.3) becomes

$$\mathbf{w}^{(i)} = f(\mathbf{z}^{(i)}) = \mathbf{P}\mathbf{Q}\mathbf{z}^{(i)} \tag{16.5}$$

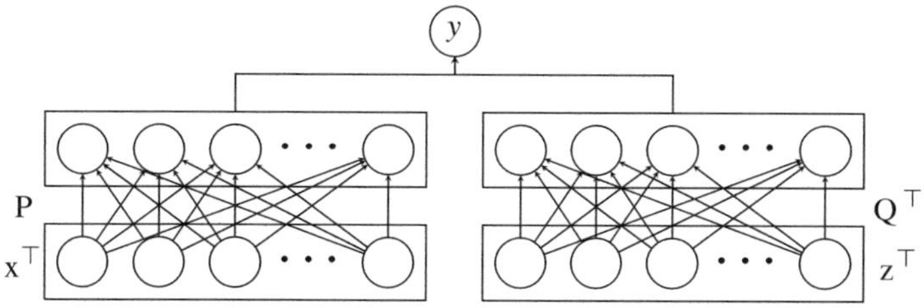

Fig. 16.3 Two-sided neural network for Multitask/Multi-domain learning

That is, we generate specific weights for prediction by combining the task/domain descriptor $\mathbf{z}^{(i)}$ with matrices $\mathbf{P}$ and $\mathbf{Q}$; and learning corresponds to fitting $\mathbf{P}$ and $\mathbf{Q}$.

A variety of existing algorithms[3] are then special cases of our general framework. We illustrate this via MDL/MTL with $M = 3$ domains/tasks. Observe that RMTL [149], FEDA [115], MTFL [17], TNMTL [253], and GO-MTL [279] correspond to asserting specific settings of $\mathbf{Z}$, $\mathbf{P}$ and $\mathbf{Q}$ as shown in Table 16.1.

16.2.4 A Two-Sided Network View

We now provide an alternative neural network view of the class of methods introduced above. By substituting Eq. (16.5) into Eq. (16.2), the prediction is given by

$$\hat{y}_j^{(i)} = (\mathbf{x}_j^{(i)})^{\top}\mathbf{P}\mathbf{Q}\mathbf{z}^{(i)} \tag{16.6}$$

A mathematically equivalent neural network model is illustrated in Fig. 16.3. The introduction of this NN leads to a better understanding of our framework and the set of methods it encompasses. The left-hand side can be understood as a global representation learning network—$\mathbf{x}^{\top}\mathbf{P}$, and the right-hand side can be seen as a network that generates a model (the weight vector $\mathbf{z}^{\top}\mathbf{Q}^{\top}$) for the task/domain encoded by $\mathbf{z}$. This interpretation allows existing MTL/MDL models to be implemented as neural networks—and conveniently optimized by standard neural network libraries—by setting inputs $\mathbf{z}$ appropriately, and activating appropriate weight regularization (Table 16.1). However, going beyond existing methods, we exploit the semantic descriptor as an input, which allows information sharing to be guided by domain metadata [560] where available. Moreover, as a NN, both sides can go arbitrarily deeper [561]. E.g., the representation learning network can be a full-sized CNN that extracts features from raw images and everything can be trained end-to-end with back propagation.

[3]RMTL: **R**egularized **M**ulti–**T**ask **L**earning, FEDA: **F**rustratingly **E**asy **D**omain **A**daptation, MTFL: **M**ulti–**T**ask **F**eature **L**earning, TNMTL: **T**race-**N**orm **M**ulti–**T**ask **L**earning, and GO-MTL: **G**rouping and **O**verlap for **M**ulti–**T**ask **L**earning.

16.2.5 Application to Zero-Shot Learning

Zero-Shot Recognition. Zero-Shot Learning (ZSL) aims to eliminate the need for training data for a particular task. It has been widely studied in areas such as character [289] and object recognition [287, 449]. Typically, for ZSL, the label space of training and test data are disjoint, so no data has been seen for test-time categories. Instead, test-time classifiers are constructed given some mid-level information. Most existing ZSL methods follow data flows that can be illustrated as either: $X \rightarrow Z \rightarrow Y$ [353] or $Z \rightarrow Y \leftarrow X$ [169, 289], where Z is some "semantic descriptor", e.g., attributes [287] or semantic word vectors [449]. In our framework, ZSL can be achieved via the latter pipeline, implemented by the network in Fig. 16.3 [560]. By presenting each novel semantic vector $\mathbf{z}^{(t)}$ (assuming testing category are indexed by t) in turn along with novel category instance $\mathbf{x}_*$. Zero-shot recognition for $\mathbf{x}_*$ then is given by: $\hat{t} = \arg\max_t \mathbf{x}_*^\top \mathbf{P}\mathbf{Q}z^{(t)}$. In this chapter we focus our experiments on zero-shot domain adaptation (parametrized domains), the interested reader can see [560] for experiments applying our framework to zero-shot recognition (parametrized tasks).

Zero-Shot Domain Adaptation. Going beyond conventional ZSL, we generalize the notion of zero-shot learning of tasks to zero-shot learning of domains. In this context, zero-shot means no training data has been seen for the target domain prior to testing. The challenge is to construct a good model for a novel test domain-based solely on its semantic descriptor [560, 562]. We denote this problem setting as Zero-Shot Domain Adaptation[4] (ZSDA)

ZSDA becomes possible with a distributed rather than one-hot encoded domain descriptor, as in practice only a subset of domains is necessary to effectively learn $\mathbf{Q}$. Thus, a model $\mathbf{w}^{(*)}$ suitable for an *unseen* domain can be constructed without any training data—by applying its semantic descriptor $\mathbf{z}^{(*)}$ to the model generation matrix $\mathbf{Q}$: $\mathbf{w}^{(*)} = \mathbf{Q}\mathbf{z}^{(*)}$. The generated domain-specific model—$\mathbf{w}^{(*)}$ – is then then used to make predictions for the re-represented input: $\mathbf{x}_*^\top \mathbf{P}\mathbf{w}^{(*)}$.

16.3 Methodology—Multiple Output Models

Thus far, the final output of each model is a scalar (single output). However for some practical applications, multiple outputs are desirable or required. For example, assume that we have $M = 2$ handwriting digit datasets (domains): MNIST and USPS. For any MNIST or USPS image, a D-dimensional feature vector is extracted. The task is to classify the image from 0 to 9 and thus we have $D \times C$ ($C = 10$) model parameters for each dataset. Therefore, the full model for all digits and datasets should contain $D \times C \times M$ parameters. We denote this setting of multiple domains,

---

[4]Note that despite the title, [41] actually considers unsupervised domain adaptation without target domain labels, but *with* target domain data.

each of which has multiple tasks, as multi-domain-multitask learning. In some recent literature [394] a similar setting is named multilinear multitask learning.

16.3.1 Formulation: Vector-Tensor Inner Product

The key idea in the previous section was to generate a model vector via a descriptor vector hitting a matrix (Eq. (16.3)). To adapt this idea for this new setting, we propose

$$W^{(i)} = f(\mathbf{z}^{(i)}) = \mathcal{W} \times_3 \mathbf{z}^{(i)} \tag{16.7}$$

where $\times_n$ indicates the n-mode product of a tensor and vector (this is also referred to as tensor contraction in some studies as it is a generalization of inner product for vectors and/or matrices). The generated model is now a weight *matrix* $\mathbf{W}^{(i)}$ rather than a *vector* $\mathbf{w}^{(i)}$. The weight generating function is now parametrized by a third-order tensor $\mathcal{W}$ of size $D \times C \times B$, and it synthesizes the model matrix for the ith domain by hitting the tensor with its B-dimensional semantic descriptor $\mathbf{z}^{(i)}$. This is a natural extension: if the required model is a vector (single output), the weight generating function is a matrix (second-order tensor) hits the semantic descriptor $\mathbf{z}$ (Eq. (16.3)); when the required model is a matrix (multiple outputs), the weight generating function is then $\mathbf{z}$ hits a third-order tensor.

Given one-hot encoding descriptors $\mathbf{z}^{(1)} = [1, 0]^\top$ and $\mathbf{z}^{(2)} = [0, 1]^\top$ indicating MNIST and USPS, respectively. Equation (16.7) would just *slice* an appropriate matrix from the tensor $\mathcal{W}$. However alternative and more powerful distributed encodings of $\mathbf{z}^{(i)}$ are also applicable. The model prediction from Eq. (16.4) is then generalized as

$$\hat{\mathbf{y}}_j^{(i)} = \mathcal{W} \times_1 \mathbf{x}_j^{(i)} \times_3 \mathbf{z}^{(i)} \tag{16.8}$$

where $\hat{\mathbf{y}}_j^{(i)}$ is now a C-dimensional vector instead of a scalar as in Eq. (16.4). Nevertheless, this method does not provide information sharing in the case of conventional categorical (1-hot encoded) domains. For this we turn to tensor factorization next.

16.3.2 Tensor (De)composition

Recall that the key intuition of many classic (matrix-based) multitask learning methods is to exploit the information sharing induced by the row-rank factorization $\tilde{\mathbf{W}} = \tilde{\mathbf{P}}\tilde{\mathbf{Q}}$. i.e., composing the weight matrix for all tasks $\tilde{\mathbf{W}}$ from factor matrices $\tilde{\mathbf{P}}$ and $\tilde{\mathbf{Q}}$. For MDL with multiple outputs, we aim to extend this idea to the factorization of the weight tensor $\mathcal{W}$. In contrast to the case with matrices, there are multiple approaches to factorizing tensors, including CP [234], Tucker [493], and Tensor-Train [351] Decompositions.

CP decomposition. For a third-order tensor $\mathcal{W}$ of size $D \times C \times B$, the rank-K CP decomposition is

$$\mathcal{W}_{d,c,b} = \sum_{k=1}^{K} \mathbf{U}^{(D)}_{k,d}\mathbf{U}^{(C)}_{k,c}\mathbf{U}^{(B)}_{k,b} \tag{16.9}$$

$$\mathcal{W} = \sum_{k=1}^{K} \mathbf{U}^{(D)}_{k,\cdot} \odot \mathbf{U}^{(C)}_{k,\cdot} \odot \mathbf{U}^{(B)}_{k,\cdot} \tag{16.10}$$

where $\odot$ is outer product. The factor matrices $\mathbf{U}^{(D)}$, $\mathbf{U}^{(C)}$, and $\mathbf{U}^{(B)}$ are of respective size $K \times D$, $K \times C$, and $K \times B$.

Given a data point $\mathbf{x}$ and its corresponding descriptor $\mathbf{z}$,[5] Eq. (16.8) will produce a C-dimensional vector $\mathbf{y}$ (e.g., $C = 10$ the scores of 10 digits for the MNIST/USPS example). By substituting Eq. (16.10) into Eq. (16.8) and some reorganizing, we obtain

$$\mathbf{y} = (\mathbf{U}^{(C)})^\top \left((\mathbf{U}^{(D)}\mathbf{x}) \circ (\mathbf{U}^{(B)}\mathbf{z})\right) \tag{16.11}$$

where $\circ$ is the element-wise product. It also can be written as

$$\mathbf{y} = (\mathbf{U}^{(C)})^\top \operatorname{diag}(\mathbf{U}^{(B)}\mathbf{z})\mathbf{U}^{(D)}\mathbf{x} \tag{16.12}$$

from which we obtain a specific form of the weight generating function in Eq. (16.7), which is motived by CP decomposition

$$\mathbf{W}^{(i)} = f(\mathbf{z}^{(i)}) = \mathcal{W} \times_3 \mathbf{z}^{(i)} = (\mathbf{U}^{(D)})^\top \operatorname{diag}(\mathbf{U}^{(B)}\mathbf{z})\mathbf{U}^{(C)} \tag{16.13}$$

It is worth mentioning that this formulation has been used in the context of gated neural networks [440], such as Gated Autoencoders [132]. However, [132] uses the technique to model the relationship between two inputs (images), while we exploit it for knowledge sharing in multitask/multi-domain learning.

Tucker decomposition. Given, the same sized tensor $\mathcal{W}$, Tucker decomposition outputs a core tensor $\mathcal{S}$ of size $K_D \times K_C \times K_B$, and 3 matrices $\mathbf{U}^{(D)}$ of size $K_D \times D$, $\mathbf{U}^{(C)}$ of size $K_C \times C$, and $\mathbf{U}^{(B)}$ of size $K_B \times B$, such that,

$$\mathcal{W}_{d,c,b} = \sum_{k_D=1}^{K_D}\sum_{k_C=1}^{K_C}\sum_{k_B=1}^{K_B} \mathcal{S}_{k_D,k_C,k_B}\mathbf{U}^{(D)}_{k_D,d}\mathbf{U}^{(C)}_{k_C,c}\mathbf{U}^{(B)}_{k_B,b} \tag{16.14}$$

$$\mathcal{W} = \mathcal{S}\times_1\mathbf{U}^{(D)}\times_2\mathbf{U}^{(C)}\times_3\mathbf{U}^{(B)} \tag{16.15}$$

Substituting Eq. (16.15) into Eq. (16.8), we get the prediction for instance $\mathbf{x}$ in domain/task $\mathbf{z}$

$$\mathbf{y} = \left((\mathbf{U}^{(D)}\mathbf{x}) \otimes (\mathbf{U}^{(B)}\mathbf{z})\right) \mathcal{S}_{(2)}^\top \mathbf{U}^{(C)} \tag{16.16}$$

---

[5] We omit the upper and lower scripts for clarity.

where $\otimes$ is Kronecker product. $\mathcal{S}_{(2)}$ is the mode-2 unfolding of $\mathcal{S}$ which is a $K_C \times K_D K_B$ matrix, and its transpose $\mathcal{S}_{(2)}^\top$ is a matrix of size $K_D K_B \times K_C$.

This formulation was used by studies of Gated Restricted Boltzmann Machines [330] for similar image-transformation purposes as [132]. The weight generating function (Eq. (16.7)) for Tucker decomposition is

$$\mathbf{W}^{(i)} = f(\mathbf{z}^{(i)}) = \mathcal{W} \times_3 \mathbf{z}^{(i)} = \mathcal{S} \times_1 \mathbf{U}^{(D)} \times_2 \mathbf{U}^{(C)} \times_3 (\mathbf{U}^{(B)} \mathbf{z}^{(i)}). \tag{16.17}$$

TT decomposition. Given the same sized tensor $\mathcal{W}$, Tensor-Train (TT) decomposition produces two matrices $\mathbf{U}^{(D)}$ of size $D \times K_D$ and $\mathbf{U}^{(B)}$ of size $K_B \times B$ and a third-order tensor $\mathcal{S}$ of size $K_D \times C \times K_B$, so that

$$\mathcal{W}_{d,c,b} = \sum_{k_D=1}^{K_D} \sum_{k_B=1}^{K_B} \mathbf{U}^{(D)}_{d,k_D} \mathcal{S}_{k_D,c,k_B} \mathbf{U}^{(B)}_{k_B,b}, \tag{16.18}$$

$$\mathcal{W} = \mathcal{S} \times_1 (\mathbf{U}^{(D)})^\top \times_3 \mathbf{U}^{(B)}. \tag{16.19}$$

Substituting Eq. (16.19) into Eq. (16.8), we obtain the MDL/MTL prediction

$$\mathbf{y} = \left((\mathbf{U}^{(D)})^\top \mathbf{x}) \otimes (\mathbf{U}^{(B)} \mathbf{z}) \right) \mathcal{S}_{(2)}^\top \tag{16.20}$$

where $\mathcal{S}_{(2)}$ is the mode-2 unfolding of $\mathcal{S}$ which is a $C \times K_D K_B$ matrix, and its transpose $\mathcal{S}_{(2)}^\top$ is a matrix of size $K_D K_B \times C$. The weight generating function (Eq. (16.7)) for Tensor-Train decomposition is

$$\mathbf{W}^{(i)} = f(\mathbf{z}^{(i)}) = \mathcal{W} \times_3 \mathbf{z}^{(i)} = \mathcal{S} \times_1 (\mathbf{U}^{(D)})^\top \times_3 (\mathbf{U}^{(B)} \mathbf{z}^{(i)}). \tag{16.21}$$

16.3.3 Gated Neural Network Architectures

We previously showed the connection between matrix factorization for single output models, and a two-sided neural network in Sect. 16.2.4. We will next draw the link between tensor factorization and gated neural network [440] architectures. First, we recap the factors used by different tensor (de)composition methods in Table 16.2.

To make the connection to neural networks, we need to introduce two new layers:

Hadamard Product Layer Takes as input two equal-length vectors $\mathbf{u}$ and $\mathbf{v}$ and outputs $[u_1 v_1, u_2 v_2, \cdots, u_K v_K]$. It is a deterministic layer that does Hadamard (element-wise) product, where the input size is $K + K$ and output size is K.

Kronecker Product Layer Takes as input two arbitrary-length vectors $\mathbf{u}$ and $\mathbf{v}$ and outputs $[u_1 v_1, u_2 v_1, \cdots, u_{K_u} v_1, u_1 v_2, \cdots, u_{K_u} v_{K_v}]$. It is a deterministic layer that takes input of size $K_u + K_v$ and returns the size $K_u K_v$ Kronecker product.

Table 16.2 Summary of factors used by different tensor (de)composition methods

Method	Factors (Shape)			
CP	$\mathbf{U}^{(D)}$ $(K \times D)$	$\mathbf{U}^{(C)}$ $(K \times C)$	$\mathbf{U}^{(B)}$ $(K \times B)$	
Tucker	$\mathbf{U}^{(D)}$ $(K_D \times D)$	$\mathbf{U}^{(C)}$ $(K_C \times C)$	$\mathbf{U}^{(B)}$ $(K_B \times B)$	$\mathcal{S}$ $(K_D \times K_C \times K_B)$
TT	$\mathbf{U}^{(D)}$ $(D \times K_D)$		$\mathbf{U}^{(B)}$ $(K_B \times B)$	$\mathcal{S}$ $(K_D \times C \times K_B)$

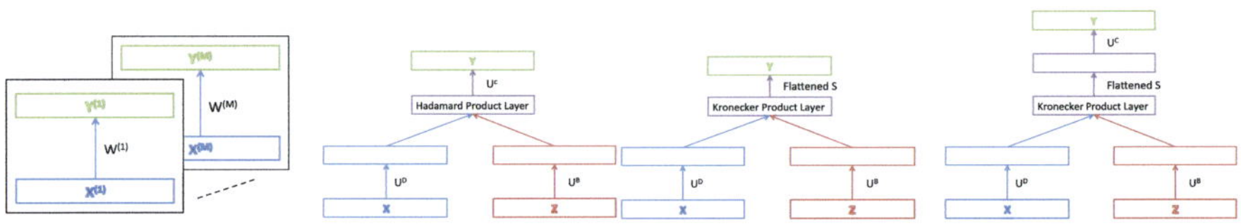

(a) Single domain learning (b) CP network (c) TT network (d) Tucker network

Fig. 16.4 Learning multiple domains independently, versus learning with parametrized neural networks encoding the factorization assumptions of various tensor decomposition methods

Figure 16.4 illustrates the approaches to multi-domain learning in terms of NNs. Single domain learning learning of M domains requires M single-layer NNs, each with a $D \times C$ weight matrix (Fig. 16.4a). Considering this set of weight matrices as the corresponding $D \times C \times M$ tensor, we can use the introduced layers to define gated networks (Figs. 16.4b–d) that model low-rank versions of this tensor with the corresponding tensor factorization assumptions in Eqs. (16.11), (16.16), and (16.20) and summarized in Table 16.2. Rather than maintaining a separate NN for each domain as in Fig. 16.4a, the networks in Figs. 16.4b–d maintain a single NN for all domains. The domain of each instance is signaled to the network via its corresponding descriptor, which the right-hand side of the network uses to synthesize the recognition weights accordingly.

We note that we can further unify all three designs, as well as the single output model proposed in Sect. 16.2.4, by casting them as special cases of the Tucker Network as shown in Table 16.3. Thus, we can understand all these factorization-based approaches by their connection to the idea of breaking down the stacked model parameters (matrix $\mathbf{W}$ or tensor $\mathcal{W}$) into a smaller number of parameters composing a domain-specific ($\mathbf{U}^{(B)}$), task-specific ($\mathbf{U}^{(C)}$) and shared components ($\mathbf{U}^{(D)}$). It is important to note however that, despite our model's *factorized representation assumption* in common with tensor decomposition, the way to train our model is not by training a set of models and decomposing them—in fact matrix/tensor *decomposition* is not used at all. Rather a single Tucker network of Fig. 16.4d is trained end-to-end with backpropagation to minimize the multi-domain/task loss. The network architecture enforces that backpropagation trains the individual factors (Table 16.2) such that their corresponding tensor *composition* solves the multi-domain-multitask problem. In summary, our framework can be seen as 'discriminatively trained' tensor

Table 16.3 Tensor and the matrix-factorization-based single output (Sect. 16.2.4, [560]) networks as special cases of the Tucker Network. Underlined variables are constant rather than learned parameters

Method/Factors	$\mathbf{U}^{(D)}$	$\mathbf{U}^{(C)}$	$\mathbf{U}^{(B)}$	$\mathcal{S}$
Tucker	$\mathbf{U}^{(D)}$	$\mathbf{U}^{(C)}$	$\mathbf{U}^{(B)}$	$\mathcal{S}$
CP	$\mathbf{U}^{(D)}$	$\mathbf{U}^{(C)}$	$\mathbf{U}^{(B)}$	$\underline{K \times K \times K \text{IdentityTensor}}$
TT	$(\mathbf{U}^{(D)})^\top$	$\underline{C \times C}$ Identity Matrix	$\mathbf{U}^{(B)}$	$\mathcal{S}$
Single Output	$\mathbf{P}^\top$	$\underline{K \times 1}$ All-ones Vector	$\mathbf{Q}$	$\underline{K \times K \times K}$ Identity Tensor

factorization, or as a gated neural network, where the NN's weights are dynamically *parametrized* by a second input, the descriptor $\mathbf{z}$.

16.4 Experiments

We explore three sets of experiments on object recognition (Sect. 16.4.1), surveillance image analysis (Sect. 16.4.2), and person recognition/soft-biometrics (Sect. 16.4.3). The first recognition experiment follows the conventional setting of domains/tasks as atomic entities, and the latter experiments explore the potential benefits of informative domain descriptors, including zero-shot domain adaptation.

Implementation. We implement our framework with TensorFlow [1], taking the neural network interpretation of each method, thus allowing easy optimization with SGD-based backpropagation. We use hinge loss for the binary classification problems and (categorical) cross-entropy loss for the multi-class classification problems.

16.4.1 Multi-domain Multitask Object Recognition

In this section, we assume conventional atomic domains (so domain descriptors are simply indicators rather than distributed codes), but explore a multi-domain multitask (MDMTL) setting. Thus there is a multi-class problem within each domain, and our method (Sect. 16.3) exploits information sharing across both domains and tasks. To deal with multi-class recognition within each domain, it generalizes existing vector-valued MTL/MDL methods, and implements a matrix-valued weight generating function parametrized by a low-rank tensor (Fig. 16.4).

Datasets. We first evaluate the multi-domain multitask setting using the well-known Office-Caltech (OC10) dataset [200] described in Chap. 3 (see Fig. 16.5 for an illustration). The features used are the provided 800-dimensional SURFBOV features

Fig. 16.5 An image of a backpack collected from four different sources in the OC10 dataset

that were preprocessed by normalizing the sum of each instance's feature vector to one then applying a z-score function as suggested by [200].

Settings. We compare the three proposed method variants: CP, Tucker, and TT-Networks with two baselines. **SDL:** training each domain independently and **Aggregation**: ignoring domains and training an aggregate model for all data. For these two baselines, we use a vanilla feed-forward neural network without hidden layers thus there are no hyperparameters to tune. For our methods, the tensor rank(s), i.e., K for CP-Network, (K_D, K_C, K_B) for Tucker Network, and (K_D, K_B) for TT-network are chosen by tenfold cross validation. The grids of K_D, K_C, and K_B are respectively $[16, 64, 256]$, $[2, 4, 8]$, and $[2, 4]$. The multi-class recognition error rate at 9 increasing training-testing-ratios $(10\%, 20\% \ldots 90\%)$ is computed, and for each training-testing-ratio, we repeat the experiment 10 times with random splits.

Results and Analysis. The result is shown in Fig. 16.6. We can see that the proposed methods perform well compared to *SDL*. When the training data is extremely small, *Aggregation* is a reasonably good choice as the benefit of more data outweighs the drawback of mixing domains. However, the existence of domain bias eventually prevents a single model from working well for all domains. Our proposed methods can produce different models for the various domains so they generally outperform the baselines. Tucker and TT-Network are better than CP-Network because of their greater flexibility on choosing more than one tensor rank. However as a drawback, this also introduces more hyperparameters to tune.

16.4.2 Surveillance Image Classification

In surveillance video analysis, there are many covariates, such as season, workday/holiday, and day/night. Each of these affects the distribution of image features, and thus introduces domain shift. Collecting the potentially years of training data required to train a single general model is both expensive and suboptimal (due to ignoring domain shift, and treating all data as a single domain). Thus in this section we explore the potential for multi-domain learning with distributed domain descrip-

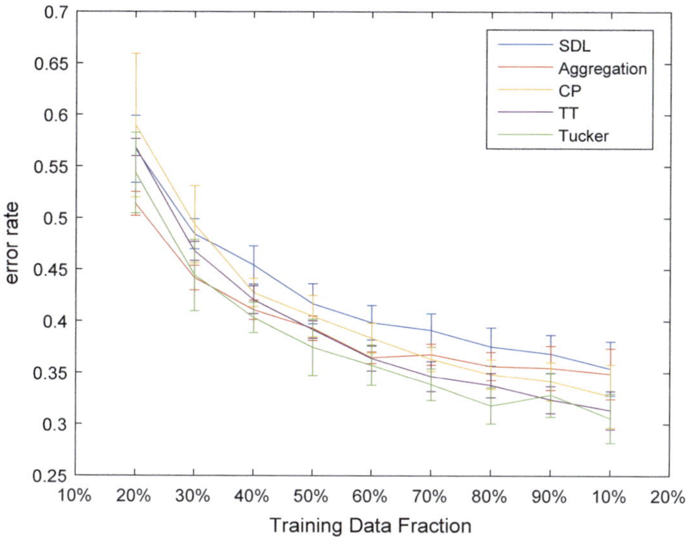

Fig. 16.6 Office Dataset: Error mean and standard deviation recognizing $C = 10$ classes across $M = 4$ domains. Comparison of three parametrized neural networks with SDL and Aggregation baselines

tors (Sect. 16.2) to improve performance by modeling the factorial structure in the domain shift. Furthermore, we demonstrate the potential of ZSDA to adapt a system to apply in a new set of conditions for which no training data exists.

Data. We consider the surveillance image classification task proposed by [235]. This is a binary classification of each frame in a 12-day surveillance stream as being empty or containing cars. Originally, [235] investigated continuous domains (which can be seen as a one-dimensional domain descriptor containing time-stamp). To explore a richer domain descriptor, we use a slightly different definition of domains, considering instead weekday/weekend and day/night as domain factors, generating $2 \times 2 = 4$ distinct domains, each encoded by a 2-of-4 binary domain descriptor. Figure 16.7(top) illustrates the more obvious domain factor: day/night. This domain shift induces a larger image change than the task-relevant presence or absence of a car.

Settings. We use the 512 dimensional GIST feature for each frame provided by [235]. We perform two experiments: *Multi-domain learning*, and *zero-shot domain adaptation*. For MDL, we split all domains' data into half training and half testing, and repeat for 10 random splits. We use our single output network (Fig. 16.3, Table 16.3 bottom row) with a distributed domain descriptor for two categories with two states (i.e., same descriptor as Fig. 16.2, right). The baselines are: (i) **SDL**: train an independent model for each domain (ii) **Aggregation**: to train a single model covering all domains (ii) **Multi-Domain I**: a multi-domain model with low-rank factorization of $\tilde{\mathbf{W}}$ and one-hot encoding of domain descriptor (in this case, $\mathbf{Z}$ is an identity matrix

Fig. 16.7 Illustration of domain factors in surveillance car recognition task. *Above*: Example frames illustrating day/night domain factor. (*Left*: With car. *Middle* and *right*: No cars.) *Below*: Activity map illustration of weekday/weekend domain factor. (*Left*: Weekday, *Middle*: Weekend: *Right*: Weekday–Weekend difference.)

thus $\tilde{\mathbf{W}} = \mathbf{WZ} = \mathbf{W}$—this roughly corresponds to our reimplementation of [279]), and (iv) **Multi-Domain II**: a factorized multi-domain model with one-hot + constant term encoding (this is in fact the combination the sharing structure and factorization proposed in [149] and [279] respectively).

For ZSDA, we do leave-one-domain-out cross-validation: holding out one of the four domains for testing, and using the observed three domains' data for training. Although the train/test splits are not random, we still repeat the procedure 10 times to reduce randomness of the SGD optimization. Our model is constructed on the fly for the held-out domain based on its semantic descriptor. As a baseline, we train an aggregated model from all observed domains' data, and apply it directly to the held-out domain (denoted as **Direct**). We set our rank hyperparameter via the heuristic $K = \frac{D}{\log(D)}$. We evaluate the the mean and standard deviation of error rate.

Results and Analysis. The results shown in Table 16.4 demonstrate that our proposed method outperforms alternatives in both MDL and ZSDA settings. For MDL we see that training a per-domain model and ignoring domains altogether perform similarly (SDL vs Aggregation). By introducing more sharing structure, e.g., Multi-Domain I is built with low-rank assumption, and multi-domain II further assumes that there is a globally shared factor, the multi-domain models clearly improve performance. Finally, our full method performs notably better than the others because it can benefits from both low-rank modeling and also exploiting the structured information in the distributed encoding of domain semantic descriptor.

Table 16.4 Surveillance image classification. Mean error rate (%) and standard deviation

MDL Experiment	SDL	Aggregation	Multi-Domain I	Multi-Domain II	Parametrized NN
Err. Rate	10.82 ± 3.90	11.05 ± 2.73	10.00 ± 0.90	8.86 ± 0.79	$\mathbf{8.61 \pm 0.51}$

ZSDA Experiment	Direct	Parametrized NN
Err. Rate	12.04 ± 0.11	$\mathbf{9.72 \pm 0.08}$

In ZSDA, our proposed method also clearly outperforms the baseline of directly training on all the source domains. What information is our model able to exploit to achieve this? One cue is that various directions including right turn are common on weekends and weekdays are primarily going straight (illustrated in Fig. 16.7(below) by way of an activity map). This can, e.g., be learned from the weekend-day domain, and transferred to the held-out weekend-night domain because the domain factors inform us that those two domains have the weekend factor in common.

16.4.3 Gait-Based Soft-Biometrics and Recognition

Gait-based person and soft biometric recognition are desirable capabilities due to not requiring subject cooperation [585]. However, they are challenging especially where there are multiple covariates such as viewing angle and accessory status (e.g., object carrying). Again training a model for every covariate combination is infeasible, and conventional domain adaptation is not scalable as the number of resulting domains grows exponentially with independent domain factors. In contrast, zero-shot domain adaptation could facilitate deploying a camera with a calibration step to specify covariates such as view angle, but no data collection or retraining.

Data. We investigate applying our framework to this setting using the CASIA gait analysis dataset [585] with data from 124 individuals under 11 viewing angles. Each person has three situations: normal ('nm'), wearing overcoat ('cl') and carrying a bag ('bg'). This naturally forms $3 \times 11 = 33$ domains. We extract Gait Energy Image (GEI) features, followed by PCA reduction to 300 dimensions.

Settings. We consider two gait analysis problems: (i) Soft-biometrics: Female/Male classification and (ii) Person verification/matching. For matching each image pair $\mathbf{x}_i$ and $\mathbf{x}_j$, generates a pairwise feature vector by $\mathbf{x}_{ij} = |\mathbf{x}_i - \mathbf{x}_j|$. The objective is to learn a binary verification classifier on $\mathbf{x}_{ij}$ to predict if two images are the same person or not. All experiment settings (baseline methods, training/testing splits, experiments repeats, and the choice of hyperparameter) are the same as in Sect. 16.4.2, except that for the verification problem we build a balanced (training and testing) set of positive/negative pairs by down-sampling negative pairs.

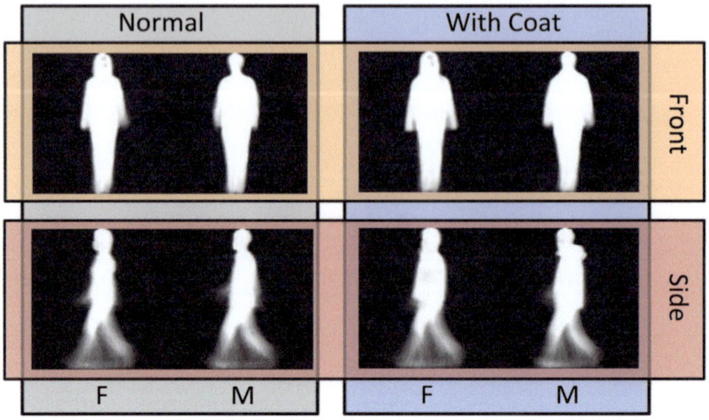

Fig. 16.8 Example gait images illustrating independent domain factors

Table 16.5 Gait: Male/Female biometrics. Error rate (%) and standard deviation

MDL Experiment	SDL	Aggregation	Multi-domain I	Multi-domain II	Parametrized NN
Err. Rate	2.35 (±0.20)	2.62 (±0.18)	2.25 (±0.20)	2.07 (± 0.15)	**1.64(±0.14)**

ZSDA Experiment	Direct	Parametrized NN
Err. Rate	3.01 (±0.08)	**2.19 (±0.05)**

Table 16.6 Gait: Person verification. Error rate(%) and standard deviation

MDL experiment	SDL	Aggregation	Multi-domain I	Multi-domain II	Parametrized NN
Err. Rate	23.30 (±0.28)	24.62 (±0.32)	22.18 (±0.25)	21.15 (± 0.13)	**19.36(±0.09)**

ZSDA Experiment	Direct	Parametrized NN
Err. Rate	26.93 (±0.10)	**23.67 (±0.11)**

Results and Analysis. Figure 16.8 illustrates the nature of the domain factors here, where the cross-domain variability is again large compared to the cross-class variability. Our framework uniquely models the fact that each domain factor (e.g., view angle and accessory status) can occur independently. The results shown in Tables 16.5 and 16.6 demonstrate the same conclusions—that explicitly modeling MDL structure improves performance (Multi-domain I and II improve on SDL and Aggregation), with our most general method performing best overall.

16.5 Conclusion

In this chapter, we discussed multi-domain learning, a bi-directional generalization of domain adaptation and zero-shot domain adaptation, an alternative to domain-generalization approaches. We introduced a semantic domain/task descriptor to unify various existing multitask/multi-domain algorithms within a single matrix factorization framework. To go beyond the single output problems considered by prior methods, we generalized this framework to tensor factorization, which allows knowledge sharing for methods parametrized by matrices rather than vectors. This allows multi-domain learning for multi-output problems or simultaneous multitask-multi-domain learning. All these approaches turn out to have equivalent interpretations as neural networks, which allow easy implementation and optimization with existing toolboxes. Promising lines of future inquiry include extending this framework for end-to-end learning in convolutional neural networks [561], tensor rank-based regularization [563], and applying these ideas to solve practical computer vision problems.

References

1. Martín Abadi, Ashish Agarwal, Paul Barham, Eugeneo Brevd, Zhifeng Chen, Craig Citro, Greg S. Corrado, Andy Davis, Jeffrey Dean, Matthieu Devin, Sanjay Ghemawat, Ian Goodfellow, Andrew Harp, Geoffrey Irving, Michael Isard, Yangqing Jia, Rafal Jozefowicz, Lukasz Kaiser, Manjunath Kudlur, Josh Levenberg, Dan Mané, Rajat Monga, Sherry Moore, Derek Murray, Chris Olah, Mike Schuster, Jonathon Shlens, Benoit Steiner, Ilya Sutskever, Kunal Talwar, Paul Tucker, Vincent Vanhoucke, Vijay Vasudevan, Fernanda Viégas, Oriol Vinyals, Pete Warden, Martin Wattenberg, Martin Wicke, Yuan Yu, and Xiaoqiang Zheng. TensorFlow: Large-scale machine learning on heterogeneous systems, 2015. Software available from www.tensorflow.org.
2. P-A Absil, Robert Mahony, and Rodolphe Sepulchre. *Optimization Algorithms on Matrix Manifolds*. Princeton University Press, 2008.
3. Ayan Acharya, Eduardo R. Hruschka, Joydeep Ghosh, and Sreangsu Acharyya. Transfer learning with cluster ensembles. In *ICML Workshop on Unsupervised and Transfer Learning (WUTL)*, 2012.
4. Ankur Agarwal and Bill Triggs. A local basis representation for estimating human pose from cluttered images. In *Asian Conference on Computer Vision (ACCV)*, 2006.
5. Pulkit Agrawal, Ross Girshick, and Jitendra Malik. Analyzing the performance of multilayer neural networks for object recognition. In *European Conference on Computer Vision (ECCV)*, 2014.
6. Julien Ah-Pine, Marco Bressan, Stéphane Clinchant, Gabriela Csurka, Yves Hoppenot, and Jean-Michel Renders. Crossing textual and visual content in different application scenarios. *Multimedia Tools and Applications*, 42(1):31–56, 2009.
7. Zeynep Akata, Florent Perronnin, Zaid Harchaoui, and Cordelia Schmid. Label-embedding for attribute-based classification. In *IEEE Conference on Computer Vision and Pattern Recognition (CVPR)*, 2013.
8. Zeynep Akata, Scott Reed, Daniel Walter, Honglak Lee, and Bernt Schiele. Evaluation of output embeddings for fine-grained image classification. In *IEEE Conference on Computer Vision and Pattern Recognition (CVPR)*, 2015.
9. Samir Al-Stouhi and Chandan K. Reddy. Adaptive boosting for transfer learning using dynamic updates. In *Joint European Conference on Machine Learning and Knowledge Discovery in Databases (ECML PKDD)*, 2011.
10. Rahaf Aljundi, R'emi Emonet, Damien Muselet, and Marc Sebban. Landmarks-based kernelized subspace alignment for unsupervised domain adaptation. In *IEEE Conference on Computer Vision and Pattern Recognition (CVPR)*, 2015.
11. Rahaf Aljundi and Tinne Tuytelaars. Lightweight unsupervised domain adaptation by convolutional filter reconstruction. In *ECCV Workshop on Transferring and Adapting Source Knowledge in Computer Vision (TASK-CV)*, 2016.

G. Csurka (ed.), *Domain Adaptation in Computer Vision Applications*,
Advances in Computer Vision and Pattern Recognition,
DOI 10.1007/978-3-319-58347-1

12. Shun-ichi Amari and Hiroshi Nagaoka. *Methods of information geometry*, volume 191. American Mathematical Soc., 2007.
13. Rie Kubota Ando and Tong Zhang. A framework for learning predictive structures from multiple tasks and unlabeled data. *Journal of Machine Learning Research*, 6:1817–1853, 2005.
14. Christophe Andrieu, Nando de Freitas, Arnaud Doucet, and Michael I. Jordan. An introduction to mcmc for machine learning. *Machine Learning*, 50(1):5–43, 2003.
15. Relja Arandjelovic and Andrew Zisserman. All about VLAD. In *IEEE Conference on Computer Vision and Pattern Recognition (CVPR)*, 2013.
16. Pablo Arbelaez, Michael Maire, Charless Fowlkes, and Jitendra Malik. Contour detection and hierarchical image segmentation. *Transactions on Pattern Analysis and Machine Intelligence (PAMI)*, 33(5):898–916, 2011.
17. Andreas Argyriou, Theodoros Evgeniou, and Massimiliano Pontil. Convex multi-task feature learning. *Machine Learning*, 73(3):243–272, 2008.
18. Andrew Arnold, Ramesh Nallapati, and William Cohen. A comparative study of methods for transductive transfer learning. In *ICDM Workshop (ICDMW)*, 2007.
19. Mathieu Aubry, Daniel Maturana, Alexei Efros, Bryan Russell, and Josef Sivic. Seeing 3d chairs: exemplar part-based 2d-3d alignment using a large dataset of CAD models. In *IEEE Conference on Computer Vision and Pattern Recognition (CVPR)*, 2014.
20. Mathieu Aubry and Bryan C. Russell. Understanding deep features with computer-generated imagery. In *IEEE International Conference on Computer Vision (ICCV)*, 2015.
21. Yusuf Aytar and Andrew Zisserman. Tabula rasa: Model transfer for object category detection. In *IEEE International Conference on Computer Vision (ICCV)*, 2011.
22. Jimmy Ba and Rich Caruana. Do deep nets really need to be deep? In *Annual Conference on Neural Information Processing Systems (NIPS)*, 2014.
23. Artem Babenko, Anton Slesarev, Alexandr Chigorin, and Victor S. Lempitsky. Neural codes for image retrieval. In *European Conference on Computer Vision (ECCV)*, 2014.
24. Vijay Badrinarayanan, Alex Handa, and Roberto Cipolla. SegNet: A deep convolutional encoder-decoder architecture for robust semantic pixel-wise labelling. *CoRR*, arXiv:1505.07293, 2015.
25. Mahsa Baktashmotlagh, Mehrtash Harandi, Brian Lovell, and Mathieu Salzmann. Unsupervised domain adaptation by domain invariant projection. In *IEEE International Conference on Computer Vision (ICCV)*, 2013.
26. Mahsa Baktashmotlagh, Mehrtash Harandi, Brian Lovell, and Mathieu Salzmann. Domain adaptation on the statistical manifold. In *IEEE Conference on Computer Vision and Pattern Recognition (CVPR)*, 2014.
27. Mahsa Baktashmotlagh, Mehrtash Harandi, and Mathieu Salzmann. Distribution-matching embedding for visual domain adaptation. *Journal of Machine Learning Research*, 2:1–30, 2016.
28. Evgeniy Bart and Shimon Ullman. Cross-generalization: Learning novel classes from a single example by feature replacement. In *IEEE Conference on Computer Vision and Pattern Recognition (CVPR)*, 2005.
29. Herbert Bay, Tinne Tuytelaars, and Luc Van Gool. Surf: Speeded up robust features. In *European Conference on Computer Vision (ECCV)*, 2006.
30. Shai Ben-David, John Blitzer, Koby Crammer, Alex Kulesza, Fernando Pereira, and Jennifer Wortman Vaughan. A theory of learning from different domains. *Machine Learning*, 20(3):151–175, 2010.
31. Shai Ben-David, John Blitzer, Koby Crammer, and Fernando Pereira. Analysis of representations for domain adaptation. In *Annual Conference on Neural Information Processing Systems (NIPS)*, 2006.
32. Yoshua Bengio, Aaron Courville, and Pascal Vincent. Representation learning: A review and new perspectives. *Transactions on Pattern Analysis and Machine Intelligence (PAMI)*, 35(8):1798–1828, 2013.

33. Tamara L. Berg, Alexander C. Berg, and Jonathan Shih. Automatic attribute discovery and characterization from noisy web data. In *European Conference on Computer Vision (ECCV)*, 2010.
34. Tamara L. Berg, Alexander Sorokin, Gang Wang, David A. Forsyth, Derek Hoiem, Ian Endres, and Ali Farhadi. It's all about the data. *Proceedings of the IEEE*, 98(8):1434–1452, 2010.
35. Thomas Berg and Peter Belhumeur. Poof: Part-based one-vs.-one features for fine-grained categorization, face verification, and attribute estimation. In *IEEE Conference on Computer Vision and Pattern Recognition (CVPR)*, 2013.
36. Alessandro Bergamo and Lorenzo Torresani. Exploiting weakly-labeled web images to improve object classification: a domain adaptation approach. In *Annual Conference on Neural Information Processing Systems (NIPS)*, 2010.
37. Stanely Bileschi. CBCL StreetScenes challenge framework, 2007.
38. Jeff A. Bilmes. A gentle tutorial of the EM algorithm and its application to parameter estimation for Gaussian mixture and hidden Markov models. Technical report, International Computer Science Institute, 1998.
39. Arijit Biswas and Devi Parikh. Simultaneous active learning of classifiers & attributes via relative feedback. In *IEEE Conference on Computer Vision and Pattern Recognition (CVPR)*, 2013.
40. John Blitzer, Mark Dredze, and Fernando Pereira. Biographies, bolly-wood, boomboxes and blenders: Domain adaptation for sentiment classification. In *Annual Meeting of the Association for Computational Linguistics (ACL)*, 2007.
41. John Blitzer, Dean P. Foster, and Sham M. Kakade. Zero-shot domain adaptation: A multi-view approach. Technical report, University of California, Berkeley, 2009.
42. John Blitzer, Sham Kakade, and Dean P. Foster. Domain adaptation with coupled subspaces. In *International Conference on Artificial Intelligence and Statistics (AISTATS)*, 2011.
43. John Blitzer, Ryan McDonald, and Fernando Pereira. Domain adaptation with structural correspondence learning. In *International Conference on Empirical Methods in Natural Language Processing (EMNLP)*, 2006.
44. Erik Bochinski, Volker Eiselein, and Thomas Sikora. Training a convolutional neural network for multi-class object detection using solely virtualworld data. In *IEEE International Conference on Advanced Video and Signal-based Surveillance (AVSS)*, 2016.
45. Karsten M. Borgwardt, Arthur Gretton, Malte J. Rasch, Hans-Peter Kriegel, Bernhard Schölkopf, and Alex J. Smola. Integrating structured biological data by kernel maximum mean discrepancy. *Bioinformatics*, 22:49–57, 2006.
46. Léon Bottou. *Online Algorithms and Stochastic Approximations*. Cambridge University Press, 1998.
47. Lubomir Bourdev, Subhransu Maji, and Jitendra Malik. Describing people: A poselet-based approach to attribute classification. In *IEEE International Conference on Computer Vision (ICCV)*, 2011.
48. Konstantinos Bousmalis, Nathan Silberman, David Dohan, Dumitru Erhan, and Dilip Krishnan. Unsupervised pixel-level domain adaptation with generative adversarial networks. *CoRR*, arXiv:1612.05424, 2016.
49. Konstantinos Bousmalis, George Trigeorgis, Nathan Silberman, Dumitru Erhan, and Dilip Krishnan. Domain separation networks. In *Annual Conference on Neural Information Processing Systems (NIPS)*, 2016.
50. Steve Branson, Catherine Wah, Florian Schroff, Boris Babenko, Peter Welinder, Pietro Perona, and Serge Belongie. Visual recognition with humans in the loop. In *European Conference on Computer Vision (ECCV)*, 2010.
51. Michael D. Breitenstein, Fabian Reichlin, Esther Koller-Meier, Bastien Leibe, and Luc Van Gool. Online multi-person tracking-by-detection from a single, uncalibrated camera. *Transactions on Pattern Analysis and Machine Intelligence (PAMI)*, 31(9):1820–1833, 2011.
52. Jane Bromley, James W Bentz, Léon Bottou, Isabelle Guyon, Yann LeCun, Cliff Moore, Eduard Säckinger, and Roopak Shah. Signature verification using a "siamese" time delay neural network. *International Journal of Pattern Recognition and Artificial Intelligence*, 7(04):669–688, 1993.

53. Gabriel J. Brostow, Julie Fauqueur, and Roberto Cipolla. Semantic object classes in video: A high-definition ground truth database. *Pattern Recognition Letters*, 30(2):88–89, 2009.
54. Gabriel J. Brostow, Jamie Shotton, and Roberto Cipolla. Segmentation and recognition using structure from motion point clouds. In *European Conference on Computer Vision (ECCV)*, 2008.
55. Lorenzo Bruzzone and Mattia Marconcini. Domain adaptation problems: A dasvm classification technique and a circular validation strategy. *Transactions on Pattern Analysis and Machine Intelligence (PAMI)*, 32:770–787, 2010.
56. Daniel J. Butler, Jonas Wulff, Garrett B. Stanley, and Michael J. Black. A naturalistic open source movie for optical flow evaluation. In *European Conference on Computer Vision (ECCV)*, 2012.
57. Deng Cai, Xiaofei He, and Jiawei Han. Efficient kernel discriminant analysis via spectral regression. In *IEEE International Conference on Data Mining (ICDM)*, 2007.
58. Jian-Feng Cai, Emmanuel J. Candés, and Zuowei Shen. A singular value thresholding algorithm for matrix completion. *Journal on Optimization*, 20(4):1956–1982, 2010.
59. Guanqun Cao, Alexandros Iosifidis, Ke Chen, and Moncef Gabbouj. Generalized multi-view embedding for visual recognition and cross-modal retrieval. *CoRR*, arXiv:1605.09696, 2016.
60. Kevin M. Carter. *Dimensionality reduction on statistical manifolds*. ProQuest, 2009.
61. Rich Caruana. Multitask learning: A knowledge-based source of inductive bias. *Machine Learning*, 28:41–75, 1997.
62. Rui Caseiro, Joao F. Henriques, Pedro Martins, and Jorge Batista. Beyond the shortest path: Unsupervised domain adaptation by sampling subspaces along the spline flow. In *IEEE Conference on Computer Vision and Pattern Recognition (CVPR)*, 2015.
63. Lluís Castrejón, Yusuf Aytar, Carl Vondrick, Hamed Pirsiavash, and Antonio Torralba. Learning aligned cross-modal representations from weakly aligned data. In *IEEE Conference on Computer Vision and Pattern Recognition (CVPR)*, 2016.
64. Yee Seng Chan and Hwee Tou Ng. Domain adaptation with active learning for word sense disambiguation. In *Annual Meeting of the Association for Computational Linguistics (ACL)*, 2007.
65. Olivier Chapelle, Bernhard Schlkopf, and Alexander Zien. *Semi-supervised learning*. MIT Press, 2006.
66. Ken Chatfield, Karen Simonyan, Andrea Vedaldi, and Andrew Zisserman. Return of the devil in the details: Delving deep into convolutional nets. In *BMVA British Machine Vision Conference (BMVC)*, 2014.
67. Ratthachat Chatpatanasiri, Teesid Korsrilabutr, Pasakorn Tangchanachaianan, and Boonserm Kijsirikul. A new kernelization framework for mahalanobis distance learning algorithms. *Neurocomputing*, 73(10):1570–1579, 2010.
68. Rita Chattopadhyay, Jieping Ye, Sethuraman Panchanathan, Wei Fan, and Ian Davidson. Multi-source domain adaptation and its application to early detection of fatigue. In *ACM SIGKDD Conference on Knowledge Discovery and Data Mining (SIGKDD)*, 2011.
69. Kamalika Chaudhuri, Sham M. Kakade, Karen Livescu, and Karthik Sridharan Sridharan. Multi-view clustering via canonical correlation analysis. In *International Conference on Machine Learning (ICML)*, 2009.
70. Chao-Yeh Chen and Kristen Grauman. Inferring analogous attributes. In *IEEE Conference on Computer Vision and Pattern Recognition (CVPR)*, 2014.
71. Chenyi Chen, Ari Seff, Alain L. Kornhauser, and Jianxiong Xiao. DeepDriving: Learning affordance for direct perception in autonomous driving. In *IEEE International Conference on Computer Vision (ICCV)*, 2015.
72. Huizhong Chen, Andrew Gallagher, and Bernd Girod. Describing clothing by semantic attributes. In *European Conference on Computer Vision (ECCV)*, 2012.
73. Liang-Chieh Chen, Sanja Fidler, and Raquel Yuille, Alan L. Urtasun. Beat the MTurkers: Automatic image labeling from weak 3D supervision. In *IEEE Conference on Computer Vision and Pattern Recognition (CVPR)*, 2014.

74. Lin Chen, Wen Li, and Dong Xu. Recognizing rgb images by learning from rgb-d data. In *IEEE Conference on Computer Vision and Pattern Recognition (CVPR)*, 2014.
75. Lin Chen, Qiang Zhang, and Baoxin Li. Predicting multiple attributes via relative multi-task learning. In *IEEE Conference on Computer Vision and Pattern Recognition (CVPR)*, 2014.
76. Minmin Chen, Kilian Q. Weinberger, and John Blitzer. Co-training for domain adaptation. In *Annual Conference on Neural Information Processing Systems (NIPS)*, 2011.
77. Minmin Chen, Zhixiang Xu, Kilian Q. Weinberger, and Fei Sha. Marginalized denoising autoencoders for domain adaptation. In *International Conference on Machine Learning (ICML)*, 2012.
78. Ning Chen, Jun Zhu, Jianfei Chen, and Bo Zhang. Dropout training for support vector machines. In *AAAI Conference on Artificial Intelligence (AAAI)*, 2014.
79. Qiang Chen, Junshi Huang, Rogerio Feris, Lisa M Brown, Jian Dong, and Shuicheng Yan. Deep domain adaptation for describing people based on fine-grained clothing attributes. In *IEEE Conference on Computer Vision and Pattern Recognition (CVPR)*, 2015.
80. Wei-Yu Chen, Tzu-Ming Harry Hsu, and Yao-Hung Hubert Tsai. Transfer neural trees for heterogeneous domain adaptation. In *European Conference on Computer Vision (ECCV)*, 2016.
81. Xianjie Chen, Roozbeh Mottaghi, Xiaobai Liu, Sanja Fidler, Raquel Urtasun, and Alan Yuille. Detect what you can: Detecting and representing objects using holistic models and body parts. In *IEEE Conference on Computer Vision and Pattern Recognition (CVPR)*, 2014.
82. Xinlei Chen and Abhinav Gupta. Webly supervised learning of convolutional networks. In *IEEE International Conference on Computer Vision (ICCV)*, 2015.
83. Yisong Chen, Guoping Wang, and Shihai Dong. Learning with progressive transductive support vector machine. *Pattern Recognition Letters*, 24(12):845–855, 2003.
84. Haibin Cheng, Pang-Ning Tan, and Rong Jin. Localized support vector machine and its efficient algorithm. In *SIAM International Conference on Data Mining (SDM)*, 2007.
85. Boris Chidlovskii, Stéphane Clinchant, and Gabriela Csurka. Domain adaptation in the absence of source domain data. In *Joint European Conference on Machine Learning and Knowledge Discovery in Databases (ECML PKDD)*, 2016.
86. Boris Chidlovskii, Gabriela Csurka, and Shalini Gangwar. Assembling heterogeneous domain adaptation methods for image classification. In *CLEF online Working Notes*, 2014.
87. Sun-Wook Choi, Chong Ho Lee, and In Kyu Park. Scene classification via hypergraph-based semantic attributes subnetworks identification. In *European Conference on Computer Vision (ECCV)*, 2014.
88. Sumit Chopra, Suhrid Balakrishnan, and Raghuraman Gopalan. DLID: Deep learning for domain adaptation by interpolating between domains. In *ICML Workshop on Challenges in Representation Learning (WREPL)*, 2013.
89. Sumit Chopra, Raia Hadsell, and Yann LeCun. Learning a similarity metric discriminatively, with application to face verification. In *IEEE Conference on Computer Vision and Pattern Recognition (CVPR)*, 2005.
90. Brian Chu, Vashisht Madhavan, Oscar Beijbom, Judy Hoffman, and Trevor Darrell. Best practices for fine-tuning visual classifiers to new domains. In *ECCV Workshop on Transferring and Adapting Source Knowledge in Computer Vision (TASK-CV)*, 2016.
91. Wen-Sheng Chu, Fernando De la Torre, and Jeffery F. Cohn. Selective transfer machine for personalized facial action unit detection. In *IEEE Conference on Computer Vision and Pattern Recognition (CVPR)*, 2013.
92. Mircea Cimpoi, Subhransu Maji, and Andrea Vedaldi. Deep filter banks for texture recognition and segmentation. In *IEEE Conference on Computer Vision and Pattern Recognition (CVPR)*, 2015.
93. Dan Cireşan, Ueli Meier, Jonathan Masci, and Jürgen Schmidhuber. Multi-column deep neural network for traffic sign classification. *Neural Networks*, 32:333–338, 2012.
94. Stéphane Clinchant, Gabriela Csurka, and Boris Chidlovskii. Transductive adaptation of black box predictions. In *Annual Meeting of the Association for Computational Linguistics (ACL)*, 2016.

95. David Cohn, Les Atlas, and Richard Ladner. Improving generalization with active learning. *Machine Learning*, 15(2):201–221, 1994.
96. Brendan Collins, Jia Deng, Kai Li, and Li Fei-Fei. Towards scalable dataset construction: An active learning approach. In *European Conference on Computer Vision (ECCV)*, 2008.
97. Marius Cordts, Mohamed Omran, Sebastian Ramos, Timo Rehfeld, Markus Enzweiler, Rodrigo Benenson, Uwe Franke, Stefan Roth, and Bernt Schiele. The Cityscapes dataset for semantic urban scene understanding. In *IEEE Conference on Computer Vision and Pattern Recognition (CVPR)*, 2016.
98. Marius Cordts, Mohamed Omran, Sebastian Ramos, Timo Scharwächter, Markus Enzweiler, Rodrigo Benenson, Uwe Franke, Stefan Roth, and Bernt Schiele. The cityscapes dataset. In *CVPR Workshop on The Future of Datasets in Vision (FCV)*, 2015.
99. C. Cortes, M. Mohri, M. Riley, and A. Rostamizadeh. Sample selection bias correction theory. In *Proceedings of the 19th international conference on Algorithmic Learning Theory*, ALT'08, pages 38–53, Berlin, Heidelberg, 2008. Springer-Verlag.
100. Corinna Cortes, Mehryar Mohri, and Afshin Rostamizadeh. Algorithms for learning kernels based on centered alignment. *Journal of Machine Learning Research*, 13(1):795–828, 2012.
101. Nicolas Courty, Rémi Flamary, Devis Tuia, and Alain Rakotomamonjy. Optimal transport for domain adaptation. *CoRR*, arXiv:1507.00504, 2015.
102. Elliot J. Crowley and Andrew Zisserman. In search of art. In *ECCV Workshop on Computer Vision for Art Analysis*, 2014.
103. Elliot J. Crowley and Andrew Zisserman. The state of the art: Object retrieval in paintings using discriminative regions. In *BMVA British Machine Vision Conference (BMVC)*, 2014.
104. Elliot J. Crowley and Andrew Zisserman. The art of detection. In *ECCV Workshop on Computer Vision for Art Analysis, (CVAA)*, 2016.
105. Gabriela Csurka, Boris Chidlovskii, and Stéphane Clinchant. Adapted domain specific class means. In *ICCV workshop on Transferring and Adapting Source Knowledge in Computer Vision (TASK-CV)*, 2015.
106. Gabriela Csurka, Boris Chidlovskii, Stéphane Clinchant, and Sophia Michel. Unsupervised domain adaptation with regularized domain instance denoising. In *ECCV workshop on Transferring and Adapting Source Knowledge in Computer Vision (TASK-CV)*, 2016.
107. Gabriela Csurka, Boris Chidlovskii, and Florent Perronnin. Domain adaptation with a domain specific class means classifier. In *ECCV Workshop on Transferring and Adapting Source Knowledge in Computer Vision (TASK-CV)*, 2014.
108. Gabriela Csurka, Christopher Dance, Lixin Fan, Jutta Willamowski, and Cédric Bray. Visual categorization with bags of keypoints. In *ECCV Workshop on Statistical learning in computer vision (SLCV)*, 2004.
109. Gabriela Csurka, Diane Larlus, Albert Gordo, and Jon Almazan. What is the right way to represent document images? *CoRR*, arXiv:1603.01076, 2016.
110. Yan Le Cun, B. Boser, J. S. Denker, R. E. Howard, W. Habbard, L. D. Jackel, and D. Henderson. Handwritten digit recognition with a back-propagation network. In *Annual Conference on Neural Information Processing Systems (NIPS)*, 1990.
111. Wenyuan Dai, Yuqiang Chen, Gui-rong Xue, Qiang Yang, and Yong Yu. Translated learning: Transfer learning across different feature spaces. In *Annual Conference on Neural Information Processing Systems (NIPS)*, 2008.
112. Wenyuan Dai, Qiang Yang, Giu-Rong Xue, and Yong Yu. Boosting for transfer learning. In *International Conference on Machine Learning (ICML)*, 2007.
113. Wenyuan Dai, Qiang Yang, Gui-Rong Xue, and Yong Yu. Self-taught clustering. In *International Conference on Machine Learning (ICML)*, 2008.
114. Navneet Dalal and Bill Triggs. Histograms of oriented gradients for human detection. In *IEEE Conference on Computer Vision and Pattern Recognition (CVPR)*, 2005.
115. Hal Daumé III. Frustratingly easy domain adaptation. In *Annual Meeting of the Association for Computational Linguistics (ACL)*, 2007.
116. Hal Daumé III. Frustratingly easy domain adaptation. *CoRR*, arXiv:0907.1815, 2009.

117. Hal Daumé III, Abhishek Kumar, and Avishek Saha. Co-regularization based semi-supervised domain adaptation. In *Annual Conference on Neural Information Processing Systems (NIPS)*, 2010.
118. Hal Daumé III and Daniel Marcu. Domain adaptation for statistical classifiers. *Journal of Artificial Intelligence Research*, 26(1):101–126, 2006.
119. Jason V. Davis, Brian Kulis, Prateek Jain, Suvrit Sra, and Inderjit S. Dhillon. Information-theoretic metric learning. In *International Conference on Machine Learning (ICML)*, 2007.
120. Jia Deng, Wei Dong, Richard Socher, Li-Jia Li, Kai Li, and Li Fei-Fei. Imagenet: A large-scale hierarchical image database. In *IEEE Conference on Computer Vision and Pattern Recognition (CVPR)*, 2009.
121. Thomas Deselaers, Bogdan Alexe, and Vittorio Ferrari. Localizing objects while learning their appearance. In *European Conference on Computer Vision (ECCV)*, 2010.
122. Chris Ding, Tao Li, Wei Peng, and Haesun Park. Orthogonal nonnegative matrix tri-factorizations for clustering. In *ACM SIGKDD Conference on Knowledge Discovery and Data Mining (SIGKDD)*, 2005.
123. Santosh Divvala, Ali Farhadi, and Carlos Guestrin. Learning everything about anything: Webly-supervised visual concept learning. In *IEEE Conference on Computer Vision and Pattern Recognition (CVPR)*, 2014.
124. Piotr Dollár, Christian Wojek, Bernt Schiele, and Pietro Perona. Pedestrian detection: a benchmark. In *IEEE Conference on Computer Vision and Pattern Recognition (CVPR)*, 2009.
125. Piotr Dollár, Christian Wojek, Bernt Schiele, and Pietro Perona. Pedestrian detection: an evaluation of the state of the art. *Transactions on Pattern Analysis and Machine Intelligence (PAMI)*, 34(4):743–761, 2012.
126. Jeff Donahue, Judy Hoffman, Erik Rodner, Kate Saenko, and Trevor Darrell. Semi-supervised domain adaptation with instance constraints. In *IEEE Conference on Computer Vision and Pattern Recognition (CVPR)*, 2013.
127. Jeff Donahue, Yangqing Jia, Oriol Vinyals, Judy Hoffman, Ning Zhang, Eric Tzeng, and Trevor Darrell. Decaf: A deep convolutional activation feature for generic visual recognition. *CoRR*, arXiv:1310.1531, 2013.
128. Jeff Donahue, Yangqing Jia, Oriol Vinyals, Judy Hoffman, Ning Zhang, Eric Tzeng, and Trevor Darrell. Decaf: A deep convolutional activation feature for generic visual recognition. In *International Conference on Machine Learning (ICML)*, 2014.
129. David L. Donoho. Compressed sensing. *Transactions on Information Theory*, 52:1289–1306, 2006.
130. Mark Dredze and Koby Crammer. Online methods for multi-domain learning and adaptation. In *International Conference on Empirical Methods in Natural Language Processing (EMNLP)*, 2008.
131. Mark Dredze, Alex Kulesza, and Koby Crammer. Multi-domain learning by confidence-weighted parameter combination. *Machine Learning*, 79(1):123–149, 2010.
132. Alain Droniou and Olivier Sigaud. Gated autoencoders with tied input weights. In *International Conference on Machine Learning (ICML)*, 2013.
133. Kun Duan, Devi Parikh, David Crandall, and Kristen Grauman. Discovering localized attributes for fine-grained recognition. In *IEEE Conference on Computer Vision and Pattern Recognition (CVPR)*, 2012.
134. Lixin Duan, Ivor W. Tsang, and Dong Xu. Domain transfer multiple kernel learning. *Transactions on Pattern Analysis and Machine Intelligence (PAMI)*, 34(3):465–479, 2012.
135. Lixin Duan, Ivor W. Tsang, Dong Xu, and Tat-Seng Chua. Domain adaptation from multiple sources via auxiliary classifiers. In *International Conference on Machine Learning (ICML)*, 2009.
136. Lixin Duan, Ivor W. Tsang, Dong Xu, and Steve J. Maybank. Domain Transfer SVM for video concept detection. In *IEEE Conference on Computer Vision and Pattern Recognition (CVPR)*, 2009.
137. Lixin Duan, Dong Xu, and Shih-Fu Chang. Exploiting web images for event recognition in consumer videos: A multiple source domain adaptation approach. In *IEEE Conference on Computer Vision and Pattern Recognition (CVPR)*, 2012.

138. Lixin Duan, Dong Xu, and Ivor W. Tsang. Domain adaptation from multiple sources: A domain-dependent regularization approach. *Transactions on Neural Networks and Learning Systems*, 23(3):504–518, 2012.
139. Lixin Duan, Dong Xu, and Ivor W Tsang. Learning with augmented features for heterogeneous domain adaptation. *Transactions on Pattern Analysis and Machine Intelligence (PAMI)*, 36(6):1134–1148, 2012.
140. Lixin Duan, Dong Xu, Ivor W Tsang, and Jiebo Luo. Visual event recognition in videos by learning from web data. *Transactions on Pattern Analysis and Machine Intelligence (PAMI)*, 34(9):1667–1680, 2012.
141. John Duchi, Elad Hazan, and Yoram Singer. Adaptive subgradient methods for online learning and stochastic optimization. Technical report, EECS Department, University of California, Berkeley, 2010.
142. Miroslav Dudík, Robert E. Schapire, and Steven J. Phillips. Correcting sample selection bias in maximum entropy density estimation. In *Annual Conference on Neural Information Processing Systems (NIPS)*, 2005.
143. Alan Edelman, Tomás A. Arias, and Steven T. Smith. The geometry of algorithms with orthogonality constraints. *Journal of Matrix Analysis and Applications*, 20(2):303–353, 1998.
144. David Eigen, Christian Puhrsch, and Rob Fergus. Depth map prediction from a single image using a multi-scale deep network. In *Annual Conference on Neural Information Processing Systems (NIPS)*, 2014.
145. Ian Endres, Vivek Srikumar, Ming-Wei Chang, and Derek Hoiem. Learning shared body plans. In *IEEE Conference on Computer Vision and Pattern Recognition (CVPR)*, 2012.
146. Markus Enzweiler and Dariu M. Gavrila. Monocular pedestrian detection: Survey and experiments. *Transactions on Pattern Analysis and Machine Intelligence (PAMI)*, 31(12):2179–2195, 2009.
147. Victor Escorcia, Juan Carlos Niebles, and Bernard Ghanem. On the relationship between visual attributes and convolutional networks. In *IEEE Conference on Computer Vision and Pattern Recognition (CVPR)*, 2015.
148. Marc Everingham, Luc Van Gool, Chris Williams, John Winn, and Andrew. Zisserman. The pascal visual object classes (voc) challenge. *International Journal of Computer Vision*, 88(2):303–338, 2010.
149. Theodoros Evgeniou and Massimiliano Pontil. Regularized multi-task learning. In *ACM SIGKDD Conference on Knowledge Discovery and Data Mining (SIGKDD)*, 2004.
150. Rong-En Fan, Kai-Wei Chang, Cho-Jui Hsieh, Xiang-Rui Wang, and Chih-Jen Lin. LIBLINEAR: A library for large linear classification. *Journal of Machine Learning Research*, 9, 2008.
151. Chen Fang, Ye Xu, and Daniel N. Rockmore. Unbiased metric learning: On the utilization of multiple datasets and web images for softening bias. In *IEEE International Conference on Computer Vision (ICCV)*, 2013.
152. Nazli FarajiDavar, Teofilo deCampos, and Josef Kittler. Adaptive transductive transfer machines. In *BMVA British Machine Vision Conference (BMVC)*, 2014.
153. Nazli FarajiDavar, Teofilo deCampos, and Josef Kittler. Transductive transfer machines. In *Asian Conference on Computer Vision (ACCV)*, 2014.
154. Nazli FarajiDavar, Teofilo deCampos, Josef Kittler, and Fei Yang. Transductive transfer learning for action recognition in tennis games. In *IEEE International Conference on Computer Vision (ICCV)*, 2011.
155. Nazli FarajiDavar, Teofilo deCampos, David Windridge, Josef Kittler, and William Christmas. Domain adaptation in the context of sport video action recognition. In *BMVA British Machine Vision Conference (BMVC)*, 2012.
156. Ali Farhadi, Ian Endres, and Derek Hoiem. Attribute-centric recognition for cross-category generalization. In *IEEE Conference on Computer Vision and Pattern Recognition (CVPR)*, 2010.
157. Ali Farhadi, Ian Endres, Derek Hoiem, and David Forsyth. Describing objects by their attributes. In *IEEE Conference on Computer Vision and Pattern Recognition (CVPR)*, 2009.

158. Manaal Faruqui and Chris Dyer. Improving vector space word representations using multilingual correlation. In *Conference of the European Chapter of the Association for Computational Linguistics (EACL)*, 2014.
159. Li Fei-Fei, Rob Fergus, and Pietro Perona. One-shot learning of object categories. *Transactions on Pattern Analysis and Machine Intelligence (PAMI)*, 28(4):594–611, 2006.
160. Li Fei-Fei, Rob Fergus, and Pietro Perona. Learning generative visual models from few training examples: An incremental bayesian approach tested on 101 object categories. *Computer Vision and Image Understanding*, 106(1):57–70, 2007.
161. Christiane Fellbaum. *WordNet: An Electronic Lexical Database*. Bradford Books, 1998.
162. Pedro F Felzenszwalb, Ross B Girshick, David McAllester, and Deva Ramanan. Object detection with discriminatively trained part-based models. *Transactions on Pattern Analysis and Machine Intelligence (PAMI)*, 32(9):1627–1645, 2010.
163. Robert Fergus, Li Fei-Fei, Pietro Perona, and Andrew Zisserman. Learning object categories from google's image search. In *IEEE International Conference on Computer Vision (ICCV)*, 2005.
164. Basura Fernando, Amaury Habrard, Marc Sebban, and Tinne Tuytelaars. Unsupervised visual domain adaptation using subspace alignment. In *IEEE International Conference on Computer Vision (ICCV)*, 2013.
165. Basura Fernando, Amaury Habrard, Marc Sebban, and Tinne Tuytelaars. Subspace alignment for domain adaptation. *CoRR*, arXiv:1409.5241, 2014.
166. Vittorio Ferrari and Andrew Zisserman. Learning visual attributes. In *Annual Conference on Neural Information Processing Systems (NIPS)*, 2007.
167. Michael Fink. Object classification from a single example utilizing class relevance pseudo-metrics. In *Annual Conference on Neural Information Processing Systems (NIPS)*, 2004.
168. Yoav Freund and Robert Schapire. A decision-theoretic generalization of on-line learning and an application to boosting. *Journal of Computer and System Sciences*, 55(1):119–139, 1997.
169. Andrea Frome, Greg S. Corrado, Jon Shlens, Samy Bengio, Jeff Dean, Marc'Aurelio Ranzato, and Tomas Mikolov. Devise: A deep visual-semantic embedding model. In *Annual Conference on Neural Information Processing Systems (NIPS)*, 2013.
170. Yanwei Fu, Timothy M. Hospedales, Tao Xiang, Zhengyong Fu, and Shaogang Gong. Transductive multi-view embedding for zero-shot recognition and annotation. In *European Conference on Computer Vision (ECCV)*, 2014.
171. Yanwei Fu, Timothy M. Hospedales, Tao Xiang, and Shaogang Gong. Learning multimodal latent attributes. *Transactions on Pattern Analysis and Machine Intelligence (PAMI)*, 36(2):303–316, 2014.
172. Yanwei Fu, Timothy M. Hospedales, Tao Xiang, and Shaogang Gong. Learning multimodal latent attributes. *Transactions on Pattern Analysis and Machine Intelligence (PAMI)*, 36(2):303–316, 2014.
173. Zhenyong Fu, Tao Xiang, Elyor Kodirov, and Shaogang Gong. Zero-shot object recognition by semantic manifold distance. In *IEEE Conference on Computer Vision and Pattern Recognition (CVPR)*, 2015.
174. Adrien Gaidon and Eleonora Vig. Online domain adaptation for multi-object tracking. In *BMVA British Machine Vision Conference (BMVC)*, 2015.
175. Adrien Gaidon, Qiao Wang, Yohann Cabon, and Eleonora Vig. Virtual worlds as proxy for multi-object tracking analysis. In *IEEE Conference on Computer Vision and Pattern Recognition (CVPR)*, 2016.
176. Adrien Gaidon, Gloria Zen, and José A. Rodriguez-Serrano. Self-learning camera: Autonomous adaptation of object detectors to unlabeled video streams. *CoRR*, arXiv:1406.4296, 2014.
177. Chuang Gan, Ming Lin, Yi Yang, Yueting Zhuang, and Alexander G. Hauptmann. Exploring semantic inter-class relationships (SIR) for zero-shot action recognition. In *AAAI Conference on Artificial Intelligence (AAAI)*, 2015.
178. Chuang Gan, Chen Sun, Lixin Duan, and Boqing Gong. Webly-supervised video recognition by mutually voting for relevant web images and web video frames. In *European Conference on Computer Vision (ECCV)*, 2016.

179. Chuang Gan, Tianbao Yang, and Boqing Gong. Learning attributes equals multi-source domain generalization. In *IEEE Conference on Computer Vision and Pattern Recognition (CVPR)*, 2016.
180. Chuang Gan, Yi Yang, Linchao Zhu, Deli Zhao, and Yueting Zhuang. Recognizing an action using its name: A knowledge-based approach. *International Journal of Computer Vision*, pages 1–17, 2016.
181. Yaroslav Ganin and Victor Lempitsky. Unsupervised domain adaptation by backpropagation. *CoRR*, arXiv:1409.7495, 2014.
182. Yaroslav Ganin and Victor Lempitsky. Unsupervised domain adaptation by backpropagation. In *International Conference on Machine Learning (ICML)*, 2015.
183. Yaroslav Ganin, Evgeniya Ustinova, Hana Ajakan, Pascal Germain, Hugo Larochelle, François Laviolette, Mario Marchand, and Victor S. Lempitsky. Domain-adversarial training of neural networks. *Journal of Machine Learning Research*, 2016.
184. Jean-Luc Gauvain and Chin-Hui Lee. Maximum a posteriori estimation for multivariate gaussian mixture observations of markov chain. *Transactions on Speech and Audio Processing*, 2(2):291–298, 1994.
185. Liang Ge, Jing Gao, Hung Ngo, Kang Li, and Aidong Zhang. On handling negative transfer and imbalanced distributions in multiple source transfer learning. In *SIAM International Conference on Data Mining (SDM)*, 2013.
186. Andreas Geiger, Philip Lenz, Christoph Stiller, and Raquel Urtasun. Vision meets robotics: The KITTI dataset. *International Journal of Robotics Research*, 32:1231–1237, 2013.
187. Andreas Geiger, Philip Lenz, and Raquel Urtasun. Are we ready for autonomous driving? the KITTI vision benchmark suite. In *IEEE Conference on Computer Vision and Pattern Recognition (CVPR)*, 2012.
188. Pascal Germain, Amaury Habrard, François Laviolette, and Emilie Morvant. A PAC-Bayesian approach for domain adaptation with specialization to linear classifiers. In *International Conference on Machine Learning (ICML)*, 2013.
189. Muhammad Ghifary, W. Bastiaan Kleijn, and Mengjie Zhang. Domain adaptive neural networks for object recognition. *CoRR*, arXiv:1409.6041, 2014.
190. Muhammad Ghifary, W. Bastiaan Kleijn, Mengjie Zhang, and David Balduzzi. Domain generalization for object recognition with multi-task autoencoders. In *IEEE International Conference on Computer Vision (ICCV)*, 2015.
191. Muhammad Ghifary, W Bastiaan Kleijn, Mengjie Zhang, and David Balduzzi. Deep reconstruction-classification networks for unsupervised domain adaptation. In *European Conference on Computer Vision (ECCV)*, 2016.
192. Ross Girshick, Jeff Donahue, Trevor Darrell, and Jagannath Malik. Rich feature hierarchies for accurate object detection and semantic segmentation. In *IEEE Conference on Computer Vision and Pattern Recognition (CVPR)*, 2014.
193. Ross Girshick, Forrest Iandola, Trevor Darrell, and Jitendra Malik. Deformable part models are convolutional neural networks. In *IEEE Conference on Computer Vision and Pattern Recognition (CVPR)*, 2015.
194. Xavier Glorot, Antoine Bordes, and Yoshua Bengio. Domain adaptation for large-scale sentiment classification: A deep learning approach. In *International Conference on Machine Learning (ICML)*, 2011.
195. Daniel Goehring, Judy Hoffman, Erik Rodner, Kate Saenko, and Trevor Darrell. Interactive adaptation of real-time object detectors. In *International Conference on Robotics and Automation (ICRA)*, 2014.
196. Boqing Gong, Kristen Grauman, and Fei Sha. Connecting the dots with landmarks: Discriminatively learning domain invariant features for unsupervised domain adaptation. In *International Conference on Machine Learning (ICML)*, 2013.
197. Boqing Gong, Kristen Grauman, and Fei Sha. Reshaping visual datasets for domain adaptation. In *Annual Conference on Neural Information Processing Systems (NIPS)*, 2013.
198. Boqing Gong, Kristen Grauman, and Fei Sha. Learning kernels for unsupervised domain adaptation with applications to visual object recognition. *International Journal of Computer Vision*, 109(1):3–27, 2014.

199. Boqing Gong, Jianzhuang Liu, Xiaogang Wang, and Xiaoou Tang. Learning semantic signatures for 3d object retrieval. *Transactions on Multimedia*, 15(2):369–377, 2013.
200. Boqing Gong, Yuan Shi, Fei Sha, and Kristen Grauman. Geodesic flow kernel for unsupervised domain adaptation. In *IEEE Conference on Computer Vision and Pattern Recognition (CVPR)*, 2012.
201. Shaogang Gong, Marco Cristani, Shuicheng Yan, and Chen Change Loy. *Person re-identification*. Springer, 2014.
202. Yunchao Gong, Qifa Ke, Michael Isard, and Svetlana Lazebnik. A multi-view embedding space for modeling internet images, tags, and their semantics. *International Journal of Computer Vision*, 106(2):210–233, 2014.
203. Yunchao Gong, Liwei Wang, Ruiqi Guo, and Svetlana Lazebnik. Multi-scale orderless pooling of deep convolutional activation features. In *European Conference on Computer Vision (ECCV)*, 2014.
204. Ian Goodfellow, Jean Pouget-Abadie, Mehdi Mirza, Bing Xu, David Warde-Farley, Sherjil Ozair, Aaron Courville, and Yoshua Bengio. Generative adversarial nets. In *Annual Conference on Neural Information Processing Systems (NIPS)*, 2014.
205. Raghuraman Gopalan. Learning cross-domain information transfer for location recognition and clustering. In *IEEE Conference on Computer Vision and Pattern Recognition (CVPR)*, 2013.
206. Raghuraman Gopalan, Ruonan Li, and Rama Chellappa. Domain adaptation for object recognition: An unsupervised approach. In *IEEE International Conference on Computer Vision (ICCV)*, 2011.
207. Raghuraman Gopalan, Ruonan Li, and Rama Chellappa. Unsupervised adaptation across domain shifts by generating intermediate data representations. *Transactions on Pattern Analysis and Machine Intelligence (PAMI)*, 36(11), 2014.
208. Albert Gordo, Jon Almazán, Jerome Revaud, and Diane Larlus. Deep image retrieval: Learning global representations for image search. In *European Conference on Computer Vision (ECCV)*, 2016.
209. Philippe-Henri Gosselin, Naila Murray, Hervé Jégou, and Florent Perronnin. Revisiting the Fisher vector for fine-grained classification. *Pattern Recognition Letters*, 49(11):92–98, 2014.
210. Kristen Grauman, Gregory Shakhnarovich, and Trevor Darrell. Inferring 3D structure with a statistical image-based shape model. In *IEEE International Conference on Computer Vision (ICCV)*, 2003.
211. Doug Gray, Shane Brennan, and Hai Tao. Evaluating appearance models for recognition, reacquisition, and tracking. In *International Workshop on Performance Evaluation of Tracking and Surveillance (PETS)*, 2007.
212. Arthur Gretton, Karsten M Borgwardt, Malte J Rasch, Bernhard Schölkopf, and Alexander Smola. A kernel two-sample test. *Journal of Machine Learning Research*, 13(1):723–773, 2012.
213. Arthur Gretton, Karsten M. Borgwardt, Malte J Rasch, Bernhard Schlkopf, and Alex J. Smola. A kernel method for the two sample problem. In *Annual Conference on Neural Information Processing Systems (NIPS)*, 2007.
214. Arthur Gretton, Alex Smola, Jiayuan Huang, Marcel Schmittfull, Karsten Borgwardt, and Bernhard Schölkopf. Covariate shift by kernel mean matching. In Joaquin Quiñonero Candela, Masashi Sugiyama, Anton Schwaighofer, and Neil D. Lawrence, editors, *Dataset Shift in Machine Learning*. The MIT Press, 2009.
215. Gregory Griffin, Alex Holub, and Pietro Perona. Caltech-256 object category dataset. Technical report, Californian Institute of Technologie, 2007.
216. Matthieu Guillaumin, Daniel Küttel, and Vittorio Ferrari. Imagenet auto-annotation with segmentation propagation. *International Journal of Computer Vision*, 110(3):328–348, 2014.
217. Ralf Haeusler and Daniel Kondermann. Synthesizing real world stereo challenges. In *German Conference on Pattern Recognition (GCPR)*, 2013.
218. Haltakov Haltakov, Christian Unger, and Slobodan Ilic. Framework for generation of synthetic ground truth data for driver assistance applications. In *German Conference on Pattern Recognition (GCPR)*, 2013.

219. Jihun Ham, Daniel D Lee, Sebastian Mika, and Bernhard Schölkopf. A kernel view of the dimensionality reduction of manifolds. In *International Conference on Machine Learning (ICML)*, 2004.
220. David J. Hand. Classifier technology and the illusion of progress. *Statistical Science*, 21:1–15, 2006.
221. Ankur Handa, Viorica Patraucean, Vijay Badrinarayanan, Simon Stent, and Roberto Cipolla. Synthcam3d: Semantic understanding with synthetic indoor scenes. *CoRR*, arXiv:1505.00171, 2015.
222. Ankur Handa, Viorica Patraucean, Vijay Badrinarayanan, Simon Stent, and Roberto Cipolla. Understanding real world indoor scenes with synthetic data. In *IEEE Conference on Computer Vision and Pattern Recognition (CVPR)*, 2016.
223. David R. Hardoon, Sandor Szedmak, and John Shawe-Taylor. Canonical correlation analysis: An overview with application to learning methods. *Neurocomputing*, 16(12):2639–2664, 2004.
224. Maayan Harel and Shie Mannor. Learning from multiple outlooks. In *International Conference on Machine Learning (ICML)*, 2011.
225. Bharath Hariharan, Jitendra Malik, and Deva Ramanan. Discriminative decorrelation for clustering and classification. In *European Conference on Computer Vision (ECCV)*, 2012.
226. Adam W. Harley, Alex Ufkes, and Konstantinos G. Derpanis. Evaluation of deep convolutional nets for document image classification and retrieval. In *International Conference on Document Analysis and Recognition (ICDAR)*, 2015.
227. Richard Hartley, Jochen Trumpf, Yuchao Dai, and Hongdong Li. Rotation averaging. *International Journal of Computer Vision*, 103(3):267–305, 2013.
228. Trevor Hastie, Robert Tibshirani, and Jerome Friedman. *The Elements of Statistical Learning: Data Mining, Inference, and Prediction*. Springer, 2009.
229. Hironori Hattori, Vishnu Naresh Boddeti, Kris M. Kitani, and Takeo Kanade. Learning scene-specific pedestrian detectors without real data. In *IEEE Conference on Computer Vision and Pattern Recognition (CVPR)*, 2015.
230. Kaiming He, Xiangyu Zhang, Shaoqing Ren, and Jian Sun. Deep residual learning for image recognition. *CoRR*, arXiv:1512.03385, 2015.
231. Kaiming He, Xiangyu Zhang, Shaoqing Ren, and Jian Sun. Delving deep into rectifiers: Surpassing human-level performance on imagenet classification. In *IEEE International Conference on Computer Vision (ICCV)*, 2015.
232. Geoffrey E. Hinton, Oriol Vinyals, and Jeff Dean. Distilling the knowledge in a neural network. In *NIPS Workshop on Deep Learning and Representation Learning*, 2014.
233. Martin Hirzer, Csaba Beleznai, Peter M. Roth, and Horst Bischof. Person re-identification by descriptive and discriminative classification. In *Scandinavian Conference (SCIA)*, 2011.
234. Frank Lauren Hitchcock. The expression of a tensor or a polyadic as a sum of products. *Journal of Mathematics and Physics*, 6(1):164–189, 1927.
235. Judy Hoffman, Trevor Darrell, and Kate Saenko. Continuous manifold based adaptation for evolving visual domains. In *IEEE Conference on Computer Vision and Pattern Recognition (CVPR)*, 2014.
236. Judy Hoffman, Sergio Guadarrama, Eric S. Tzeng, Ronghang Hu, Jeff Donahue, Ross Girshick, Trevor Darrell, and Kate Saenko. LSDA: Large scale detection through adaptation. In *Annual Conference on Neural Information Processing Systems (NIPS)*, 2014.
237. Judy Hoffman, Saurabh Gupta, and Trevor Darrell. Learning with side information through modality hallucination. In *IEEE Conference on Computer Vision and Pattern Recognition (CVPR)*, 2016.
238. Judy Hoffman, Brian Kulis, Trevor Darrell, and Kate Saenko. Discovering latent domains for multisource domain adaptation. In *European Conference on Computer Vision (ECCV)*, 2012.
239. Judy Hoffman, Erik Rodner, Jeff Donahue, Trevor Darrell, and Kate Saenko. Efficient learning of domain-invariant image representations. In *International Conference on Learning representations (ICLR)*, 2013.

240. Judy Hoffman, Eric Tzeng, Jeff Donahue, Yangqing Jia, Kate Saenko, and Trevor Darrell. One-shot adaptation of supervised deep convolutional models. *CoRR*, arXiv:1312.6204, 2013.
241. Judy Hoffman, Eric Tzeng, Jeff Donahue, Yangqing Jia, Kate Saenko, and Trevor Darrell. One-shot adaptation of supervised deep convolutional models. In *International Conference on Learning representations (ICLR)*, 2014.
242. Alex Holub, Pietro Perona, and Michael C. Burl. Entropy-based active learning for object recognition. In *CVPR Workshop on Online Learning for Classification (OLC)*, 2008.
243. Jiayuan Huang, Alex Smola, Arthur Gretton, Karsten Borgwardt, and Bernhard Schölkopf. Correcting sample selection bias by unlabeled data. In *Annual Conference on Neural Information Processing Systems (NIPS)*, 2007.
244. Sheng Huang, Mohamed Elhoseiny, Ahmed Elgammal, and Dan Yang. Learning hypergraph-regularized attribute predictors. In *IEEE Conference on Computer Vision and Pattern Recognition (CVPR)*, 2015.
245. Sung Ju Hwang, Fei Sha, and Kristen Grauman. Sharing features between objects and their attributes. In *IEEE Conference on Computer Vision and Pattern Recognition (CVPR)*, 2011.
246. Sung Ju Hwang and Leonid Sigal. A unified semantic embedding: Relating taxonomies and attributes. In *Annual Conference on Neural Information Processing Systems (NIPS)*, 2014.
247. Sergey Ioffe and Christian Szegedy. Batch normalization: Accelerating deep network training by reducing internal covariate shift. In *International Conference on Machine Learning (ICML)*, 2015.
248. Vidit Jain and Eric Learned-Miller. Online domain adaptation of a pre-trained cascade of classifiers. In *IEEE Conference on Computer Vision and Pattern Recognition (CVPR)*, 2011.
249. Omar Javed, Saad Ali, and Mubarak Shah. Online detection and classification of moving objects using progressively improving detectors. In *IEEE Conference on Computer Vision and Pattern Recognition (CVPR)*, 2005.
250. Dinesh Jayaraman and Kristen Grauman. Zero-shot recognition with unreliable attributes. In *Annual Conference on Neural Information Processing Systems (NIPS)*, 2014.
251. Dinesh Jayaraman, Fei Sha, and Kristen Grauman. Decorrelating semantic visual attributes by resisting the urge to share. In *IEEE Conference on Computer Vision and Pattern Recognition (CVPR)*, 2014.
252. I-Hong Jhuo, Dong Liu, D.T. Lee, and Shih.-Fu. Chang. Robust visual domain adaptation with low-rank reconstruction. In *IEEE Conference on Computer Vision and Pattern Recognition (CVPR)*, 2012.
253. Shuiwang Ji and Jieping Ye. An accelerated gradient method for trace norm minimization. In *International Conference on Machine Learning (ICML)*, 2009.
254. Yangqing Jia, Mathieu Salzmann, and Trevor Darrell. Learning cross-modality similarity for multinomial data. In *IEEE International Conference on Computer Vision (ICCV)*, 2011.
255. Yangqing Jia, Evan Shelhamer, Jeff Donahue, Sergey Karayev, Jonathan Long, Ross Girshick, Sergio Guadarrama, and Trevor Darrell. Caffe: Convolutional architecture for fast feature embedding. *CoRR*, arXiv:1408.5093, 2014.
256. Wei Jiang, Eric Zavesky, Shih-Fu Chang, and Alex Loui. Cross-domain learning methods for high-level visual concept classification. In *International Conference on Image Processing (ICIP)*, 2008.
257. Thorsten Joachims. Transductive inference for text classification using support vector machines. In *International Conference on Machine Learning (ICML)*, 1999.
258. Jungseock Joo, Shuo Wang, and Song-Chun Zhu. Human attribute recognition by rich appearance dictionary. In *IEEE International Conference on Computer Vision (ICCV)*, 2013.
259. Ajay J Joshi, Fatih Porikli, and Nikolaos Papanikolopoulos. Multi-class active learning for image classification. In *IEEE Conference on Computer Vision and Pattern Recognition (CVPR)*, 2009.
260. Toshihiro Kamishima, Masahiro Hamasaki, and Shotaro Akaho. Trbagg: A simple transfer learning method and its application to personalization in collaborative tagging. In *IEEE International Conference on Data Mining (ICDM)*, 2009.

261. Takafumi Kanamori, Shohei Hido, and Masashi Sugiyama. Efficient direct density ratio estimation for non-stationarity adaptation and outlier detection. *Journal of Machine Learning Research*, 10:1391–1445, 2009.
262. Biliana Kaneva, Antonio Torralba, and William T. Freeman. Evaluating image features using a photorealistic virtual world. In *IEEE International Conference on Computer Vision (ICCV)*, pages 2282–2289, 2011.
263. Pichai Kankuekul, Aram Kawewong, Sirinart Tangruamsub, and Osamu Hasegawa. Online incremental attribute-based zero-shot learning. In *IEEE Conference on Computer Vision and Pattern Recognition (CVPR)*, 2012.
264. Ashish Kapoor, Kristen Grauman, Raquel Urtasun, and Trevor Darrell. Active learning with gaussian processes for object categorization. In *IEEE International Conference on Computer Vision (ICCV)*, 2007.
265. Andrej Karpathy, George Toderici, Sanketh Shetty, Thomas Leung, Rahul Sukthankar, and Li Fei-Fei. Large-scale video classification with convolutional neural networks. In *IEEE Conference on Computer Vision and Pattern Recognition (CVPR)*, 2014.
266. Robert E Kass and Paul W Vos. *Geometrical foundations of asymptotic inference*. Wiley. com, 2011.
267. Koray Kavukcuoglu, Marc'Aurelio Ranzato, and Yann LeCun. Fast inference in sparse coding algorithms with applications to object recognition. *CoRR*, arXiv:1010.3467, 2010.
268. Aditya Khosla, Tinghui Zhou, Tomasz Malisiewicz, Alexei A. Efros, and Antonio Torralba. Undoing the damage of dataset bias. In *European Conference on Computer Vision (ECCV)*, 2012.
269. Daniel Kifer, Shai Ben-David, and Johannes Gehrke. Detecting change in data streams. In *International Conference on Very large Data Bases (VLDB)*, 2004.
270. Diederik P. Kingma and Jimmy Ba. Adam: A method for stochastic optimization. In *International Conference on Learning representations (ICLR)*, 2015.
271. Brendan F. Klare, Serhat S. Bucak, Anil K. Jain, and Tayfun Akgul. Towards automated caricature recognition. In *International Conference on Biometrics (ICB)*, 2012.
272. Adriana Kovashka, Devi Parikh, and Kristen Grauman. Whittlesearch: Image search with relative attribute feedback. In *IEEE Conference on Computer Vision and Pattern Recognition (CVPR)*, 2012.
273. Adriana Kovashka, Sudheendra Vijayanarasimhan, and Kristen Grauman. Actively selecting annotations among objects and attributes. In *IEEE International Conference on Computer Vision (ICCV)*, 2011.
274. Ranjay Krishna, Yuke Zhu, Oliver Groth, Justin Johnson, Kenji Hata, Joshua Kravitz, Stephanie Chen, Yannis Kalantidis, Li-Jia Li, David A Shamma, Michael Bernstein, and Li Fei-Fei. Visual genome: Connecting language and vision using crowdsourced dense image annotations. *CoRR*, arXiv:1602:07332, 2016.
275. Alex Krizhevsky, Ilya Sutskever, and Geoffrey E. Hinton. ImageNet classification with deep Convolutional Neural Networks. In *Annual Conference on Neural Information Processing Systems (NIPS)*, 2012.
276. Anders Krogh and Jesper Vedelsby. Neural network ensembles, cross validation, and active learning. In *Annual Conference on Neural Information Processing Systems (NIPS)*, 1995.
277. Roland Kuhn, Jean-Claude Junqua, Patrick Nguyenand, and Nancy Niedzielski. Rapid speaker adaptation in eigenvoice space. *Transactions on Speech and Audio Processing*, 8(6):695–707, 2000.
278. Brian Kulis, Kate Saenko, and Trevor Darrell. What you saw is not what you get: Domain adaptation using asymmetric kernel transforms. In *IEEE Conference on Computer Vision and Pattern Recognition (CVPR)*, 2011.
279. Abhishek Kumar and Hal Daumé III. Learning task grouping and overlap in multi-task learning. In *International Conference on Machine Learning (ICML)*, 2012.
280. Neeraj Kumar, Alexander C. Berg, Peter N. Belhumeur, and Shree K. Nayar. Attribute and simile classifiers for face verification. In *IEEE International Conference on Computer Vision (ICCV)*, 2009.

281. Abhijit Kundu, Yin F. Li, Daellert, Fuxin Li, and James M. Rehg. Joint semantic segmentation and 3D reconstruction from monocular video. In *European Conference on Computer Vision (ECCV)*, 2014.
282. Daniel Küttel and Vittorio Ferrari. Figure-ground segmentation by transferring window masks. In *IEEE Conference on Computer Vision and Pattern Recognition (CVPR)*, 2012.
283. Shrenik Lad and Devi Parikh. Interactively guiding semi-supervised clustering via attribute-based explanations. In *European Conference on Computer Vision (ECCV)*, 2014.
284. Kevin Lai, Liefeng Bo, Xiaofeng Ren, and Dieter Fox. A large-scale hierarchical multi-view rgb-d object dataset. In *International Conference on Robotics and Automation (ICRA)*, 2011.
285. Kevin Lai and Dieter Fox. 3D laser scan classification using web data and domain adaptation. In *Robotics: Science and Systems Conference (RSS)*, 2009.
286. Kevin Lai and Dieter Fox. Object recognition in 3D point clouds using web data and domain adaptation. *International Journal of Robotics Research*, 29(8):1019–1037, 2010.
287. Christoph H. Lampert, Hannes Nickisch, and Stefan Harmeling. Learning to detect unseen object classes by between-class attribute transfer. In *IEEE Conference on Computer Vision and Pattern Recognition (CVPR)*, 2009.
288. Gert Lanckriet, Nello Cristianini, Peter Bartlett, Laurent El Ghaoui, and Michael I. Jordan. Learning the kernel matrix with semidefinite programming. *Journal of Machine Learning Research*, 5:27–72, 2004.
289. Hugo Larochelle, Dumitru Erhan, and Yoshua Bengio. Zero-data learning of new tasks. In *AAAI Conference on Artificial Intelligence (AAAI)*, 2008.
290. Ryan Layne, Timothy M. Hospedales, and Shaogang Gong. Re-id: Hunting attributes in the wild. In *BMVA British Machine Vision Conference (BMVC)*, 2014.
291. Yann LeCun, Léon Bottou, Yoshua Bengio, and Patrick Haffner. Gradient-based learning applied to document recognition. *Proceedings of the IEEE*, 86(11):2278–2324, 1998.
292. Christopher J. Leggetter and Philip C. Woodland. Maximum likelihood linear regression for speaker adaptation of continuous density hidden markov models. *Computer Speech and Language*, 9(2):171–185, 1995.
293. Bastian Leibe and Bernt Schiele. Analyzing appearance and contour based methods for object categorization. In *IEEE Conference on Computer Vision and Pattern Recognition (CVPR)*, 2003.
294. Anat Levin, Paul Viola, and Yoav Freund. Unsupervised improvement of visual detectors using co-training. In *IEEE International Conference on Computer Vision (ICCV)*, 2013.
295. Elizaveta Levina and Peter J. Bickel. Maximum likelihood estimation of intrinsic dimension. In *Annual Conference on Neural Information Processing Systems (NIPS)*, 2004.
296. Li-Jia Li, Hao Su, Li Fei-Fei, and Eric P Xing. Object bank: A high-level image representation for scene classification & semantic feature sparsification. In *Annual Conference on Neural Information Processing Systems (NIPS)*, 2010.
297. Ruonan Li and Todd Zickler. Discriminative virtual views for cross-view action recognition. In *IEEE Conference on Computer Vision and Pattern Recognition (CVPR)*, 2012.
298. Wei Li and Xiaogang Wang. Locally aligned feature transforms across views. In *IEEE Conference on Computer Vision and Pattern Recognition (CVPR)*, 2013.
299. Wen Li, Lixin Duan, Dong Xu, and Iwor W. Tsang. Learning with augmented features for supervised and semi-supervised heterogeneous domain adaptation. *Transactions on Pattern Analysis and Machine Intelligence (PAMI)*, 36(6):1134–1148, 2014.
300. Wenbin Li and Mario Fritz. Recognizing materials from virtual examples. In *European Conference on Computer Vision (ECCV)*, 2012.
301. Liang Liang and Kristen Grauman. Beyond comparing image pairs: Setwise active learning for relative attributes. In *IEEE Conference on Computer Vision and Pattern Recognition (CVPR)*, 2014.
302. Xuejun Liao, Ya Xue, and Lawrence Carin. Logistic regression with an auxiliary data source. In *International Conference on Machine Learning (ICML)*, 2005.
303. Tsung-Yi Lin, Michael Maire, Serge Belongie, James Hays, Pietro Perona, Deva Ramanan, Piotr Dollár, and C.Lawrence Zitnick. Microsoft COCO: Common objects in context. In *European Conference on Computer Vision (ECCV)*, 2014.

304. Ming-Yu Liu and Oncel Tuzel. Coupled generative adversarial networks. In *Annual Conference on Neural Information Processing Systems (NIPS)*, 2016.
305. Xiuwen Liu, Anuj Srivastava, and Kyle Gallivan. Optimal linear representations of images for object recognition. *Transactions on Pattern Analysis and Machine Intelligence (PAMI)*, 26:662–666, 2004.
306. Joan M. Llargues, Juan Peralta, Raul Arrabales, Manuel González, Paulo Cortez, and Antonio M. López. Artificial intelligence approaches for the generation and assessment of believable human-like behaviour in virtual characters. *Expert Systems With Applications*, 41(16):7281–7290, 2014.
307. Jonathan Long, Evan Shelhamer, and Trevor Darrell. Fully convolutional networks for semantic segmentation. In *IEEE International Conference on Computer Vision (ICCV)*, 2015.
308. Jonathan L. Long, Ning Zhang, and Trevor Darrell. Do convnets learn correspondence? In *Annual Conference on Neural Information Processing Systems (NIPS)*, 2014.
309. Mingsheng Long, Yue Cao, Jianmin Wang, and Michael I. Jordan. Learning transferable features with deep adaptation networks. In *International Conference on Machine Learning (ICML)*, 2015.
310. Mingsheng Long, Guiguang Ding, Jianmin Wang, Jiaguang Sun, Yuchen Guo, and Philip S. Yu. Transfer sparse coding for robust image representation. In *IEEE Conference on Computer Vision and Pattern Recognition (CVPR)*, 2013.
311. Mingsheng Long, Jianmin Wang, Guiguang Ding, Sinno Jialin Pan, and Philip S. Yu. Adaptation regularization: a general framework for transfer learning. *Transactions on Knowledge and Data Engineering*, 5(26):1076–1089, 2014.
312. Mingsheng Long, Jianmin Wang, Guiguang Ding, Jiaguang Sun, and Philip S. Yu. Transfer feature learning with joint distribution adaptation. In *IEEE International Conference on Computer Vision (ICCV)*, 2013.
313. Mingsheng Long, Jianmin Wang, Guiguang Ding, Jiaguang Sun, and Philip S. Yu. Transfer joint matching for unsupervised domain adaptation. In *IEEE Conference on Computer Vision and Pattern Recognition (CVPR)*, 2014.
314. Mingsheng Long, Jianmin Wang, and Michael I. Jordan. Deep transfer learning with joint adaptation networks. *CoRR*, arXiv:1605.06636, 2016.
315. David G Lowe. Distinctive image features from scale-invariant keypoints. *International Journal of Computer Vision*, 60(2):91–110, 2004.
316. Ping Luo, Xiaogang Wang, and Xiaoou Tang. A deep sum-product architecture for robust facial attributes analysis. In *IEEE International Conference on Computer Vision (ICCV)*, 2013.
317. Andy Jinhua Ma, Jiawei Li, Pong C. Yuen, and Ping Li. Cross-domain person reidentification using domain adaptation ranking svms. *Transactions on Image Processing*, 24(5):1599–1613, 2015.
318. Bingpeng Ma, Yu Su, and Frédéric Jurie. Local descriptors encoded by Fisher vectors for person re-identification. In *ECCV Workshop on Re-Identification (Re-Id)*, 2012.
319. Laurens van der Maaten, Minmin Chen, Stephen Tyree, and Kilian Weinberger. Learning with marginalized corrupted features. In *International Conference on Machine Learning (ICML)*, 2013.
320. Dhruv Mahajan, Sundararajan Sellamanickam, and Vinod Nair. A joint learning framework for attribute models and object descriptions. In *IEEE International Conference on Computer Vision (ICCV)*, 2011.
321. Tomasz Malisiewicz, Abhinav Gupta, and Alexei A Efros. Ensemble of exemplar-svms for object detection and beyond. In *IEEE International Conference on Computer Vision (ICCV)*, 2011.
322. Yishay Mansour, Mehryar Mohri, and Afshin Rostamizadeh. Domain adaptation: Learning bounds and algorithms. In *Annual Conference on Learning Theory (COLT)*, 2009.
323. Yishay Mansour, Mehryar Mohri, and Afshin Rostamizadeh. Domain adaptation with multiple sources. In *Annual Conference on Neural Information Processing Systems (NIPS)*, 2009.

324. Yishay Mansour, Mehryar Mohri, and Afshin Rostamizadeh. Multiple source adaptation and the Rényi divergence. In *Conference on Uncertainty in Artificial Intelligence (UAI)*, 2009.
325. Javier Marín, David Vázquez, David Gerónimo, and Antonio M. López, López. Learning appearance in virtual scenarios for pedestrian detection. In *IEEE Conference on Computer Vision and Pattern Recognition (CVPR)*, 2010.
326. Francisco Massa, Bryan C. Russell, and Mathieu Aubry. Deep exemplar 2D-3D detection by adapting from real to rendered views. In *IEEE Conference on Computer Vision and Pattern Recognition (CVPR)*, 2016.
327. Giona Matasci, Michele Volpi, Mikhail Kanevski, Lorenzo Bruzzone, and Devis Tuia. Semi-supervised transfer component analysis for domain adaptation in remote sensing image classification. *Transactions on Geoscience and Remote Sensing*, 53(7):3550–3564, 2015.
328. Nikolaus Mayer, Eddy Ilg, Philip Hausser, Philipp Fischer, Daniel Cremers, Alexey Dosovitskiy, and Thomas Brox. A large dataset to train convolutional networks for disparity, optical flow, and scene flow estimation. In *IEEE Conference on Computer Vision and Pattern Recognition (CVPR)*, 2016.
329. Stephan Meister and Daniel Kondermann. Real versus realistically rendered scenes for optical flow evaluation. In *ITG Conference on Electronic Media Technology (CEMT)*, 2011.
330. Roland Memisevic and Geoffrey E. Hinton. Unsupervised learning of image transformations. In *IEEE Conference on Computer Vision and Pattern Recognition (CVPR)*, 2007.
331. Microsoft. Microsoft Research Cambridge Object Recognition Image Database. http://research.microsoft.com/en-us/downloads/b94de342-60dc-45d0-830b-9f6eff91b301/default.aspx, 2005.
332. Stephen Milborrow, John Morkel, and Fred Nicolls. The MUCT Landmarked Face Database. In *Annual Symposium of the Pattern Recognition Association of South Africa*, 2010. http://www.milbo.org/muct.
333. Erik G. Miller, Nicholas E. Matsakis, and Paul A. Viola. Learning from one example through shared densities on transforms. In *IEEE Conference on Computer Vision and Pattern Recognition (CVPR)*, 2010.
334. Fatemeh Mirrashed, Vlad I. Morariu, Behjat Siddiquie, Rogerio S. Feris, and Larry S. Davis. Domain adaptive object detection. In *Workshops on Application of Computer Vision (WACV)*, 2013.
335. Volodymyr Mnih, Koray Kavukcuoglu, David Silver, Alex Graves, Ioannis Antonoglou, Daan Wierstra, and Martin Riedmiller. Playing Atari with deep reinforcement learning. In *NIPS Workshop on Deep Learning*, 2013.
336. Roozbeh Mottaghi, Xianjie Chen, Xiaobai Liu, Nam-Gyu Cho, Seong-Whan Lee, Sanja Fidler, Raquel Urtasun, and Alan Yuille. The role of context for object detection and semantic segmentation in the wild. In *IEEE Conference on Computer Vision and Pattern Recognition (CVPR)*, 2014.
337. Yair Movshovitz-Attias, Takeo Kanade, and Yaser Sheikh. How useful is photo-realistic rendering for visual learning? *CoRR*, arXiv:1603.08152, 2016.
338. Damian Mrowca, Marcus Rohrbach, Judy Hoffman, Ronghang Hu, Kate Saenko, and Trevor Darrell. Spatial semantic regularisation for large scale object detection. In *IEEE International Conference on Computer Vision (ICCV)*, 2015.
339. Krikamol Muandet, David Balduzzi, and Bernhard Schölkopf. Domain generalization via invariant feature representation. In *International Conference on Machine Learning (ICML)*, 2013.
340. Kevin Murphy, Antonio Torralba, and William T. Freeman. Using the forest to see the trees: a graphical model relating features, objects, and scenes. In *Annual Conference on Neural Information Processing Systems (NIPS)*, 2003.
341. S. A. Nene, S. K. Nayar, and H. Murase. Columbia Object Image Library (COIL-20). Technical report, CUCS-005-96, February 1996.
342. Yuval Netzer, Tao Wang, Adam Coates, Alessandro Bissacco, Bo Wu, and Andrew Y. Ng. Reading digits in natural images with unsupervised feature learning. In *NIPS Workshop on Deep Learning and Unsupervised Feature Learning (DLUFL)*, 2011.

343. Jiquan Ngiam, Aditya Khosla, Mingyu Kim, Juhan Nam, Honglak Lee, and Andrew Y Ng. Multimodal deep learning. In *International Conference on Machine Learning (ICML)*, 2011.
344. Jie Ni, Qiang Qiu, and Rama Chellappa. Subspace interpolation via dictionary learning for unsupervised domain sadaptation. In *IEEE International Conference on Computer Vision (ICCV)*, 2013.
345. Li Niu, Wen Li, and Dong Xu. Visual recognition by learning from web data: A weakly supervised domain generalization approach. In *IEEE Conference on Computer Vision and Pattern Recognition (CVPR)*, 2015.
346. Hyeonwoo Noh, Seunghoon Hong, and Bohyung Han. Learning deconvolution network for semantic segmentation. In *IEEE International Conference on Computer Vision (ICCV)*, 2015.
347. David Novotny, Diane Larlus, and Andrea Vedaldi. I have seen enough: Transferring parts across categories. In *BMVA British Machine Vision Conference (BMVC)*, 2016.
348. Naveen Onkarappa and Angel D. Sappa. Synthetic sequences and ground-truth flow field generation for algorithm validation. *Multimedia Tools and Applications*, 74(9):3121–3135, 2015.
349. Maxime Oquab, Léon Bottou, Ivan Laptev, and Josef Sivic. Learning and transferring mid-level image representations using convolutional neural networks. In *IEEE Conference on Computer Vision and Pattern Recognition (CVPR)*, 2014.
350. Vicente Ordonez, Jia Deng, Yejin Choi, Alexander C. Berg, and Tamara L. Berg. From large scale image categorization to entry-level categories. In *IEEE International Conference on Computer Vision (ICCV)*, 2013.
351. Ivan V. Oseledets. Tensor-train decomposition. *Journal on Scientific Computing*, 33(5):2295–2317, 2011.
352. Sakrapee Paisitkriangkrai, Chunhua Shen, and Anton van den Hengel. Learning to rank in person re-identification with metric ensembles. *CoRR*, arXiv:1503.01543, 2015.
353. Mark Palatucci, Dean Pomerleau, Geoffrey E. Hinton, and Tom M. Mitchell. Zero-shot learning with semantic output codes. In *Annual Conference on Neural Information Processing Systems (NIPS)*, 2009.
354. Sinno J. Pan, James T. Tsang, Ivor W.and Kwok, and Qiang Yang. Domain adaptation via transfer component analysis. *Transactions on Neural Networks*, 22(2):199–210, 2011.
355. Sinno J. Pan and Qiang Yang. A survey on transfer learning. *Transactions on Knowledge and Data Engineering*, 22(10):1345–1359, 2010.
356. Sinno Jialin Pan, Xiaochuan Ni, Jian-Tao Sun, Qiang Yang, and Zheng Chen. Cross-domain sentiment classification via spectral feature alignment. In *International Conference on World Wide Web (WWW)*, 2010.
357. Pau Panareda-Busto, Joerg Liebelt, and Juergen Gall. Adaptation of synthetic data for coarse-to-fine viewpoint refinement. In *BMVA British Machine Vision Conference (BMVC)*, 2015.
358. Jeremie Papon and Markus Schoeler. Semantic pose using deep networks trained on synthetic RGB-D. In *IEEE International Conference on Computer Vision (ICCV)*, 2015.
359. Devi Parikh and Kristen Grauman. Interactively building a discriminative vocabulary of nameable attributes. In *IEEE Conference on Computer Vision and Pattern Recognition (CVPR)*, 2011.
360. Devi Parikh and Kristen Grauman. Relative attributes. In *IEEE International Conference on Computer Vision (ICCV)*, 2011.
361. Amar Parkash and Devi Parikh. Attributes for classifier feedback. In *European Conference on Computer Vision (ECCV)*, 2012.
362. Novi Patricia and Barbara Caputo. Learning to learn, from transfer learning to domain adaptation: A unifying perspective. In *IEEE Conference on Computer Vision and Pattern Recognition (CVPR)*, 2014.
363. Genevieve Patterson and James Hays. SUN attribute database: Discovering, annotating, and recognizing scene attributes. In *IEEE Conference on Computer Vision and Pattern Recognition (CVPR)*, 2012.
364. Xingchao Peng, Baochen Sun, Karim Ali, and Kate Saenko. Learning deep object detectors from 3D models. In *IEEE International Conference on Computer Vision (ICCV)*, 2015.

365. Bojan Pepik, Michael Stark, Peter Gehler, and Bernt Schiele. Teaching 3D geometry to deformable part models. In *IEEE Conference on Computer Vision and Pattern Recognition (CVPR)*, 2012.
366. Florent Perronnin, Christopher Dance, Gabriela Csurka, and Marco Bressan. Adapted vocabularies for generic visual categorization. In *European Conference on Computer Vision (ECCV)*, 2006.
367. Florent Perronnin, Yan Liu, Jorge Sánchez, and Hervé Poirier. Large-scale image retrieval with compressed Fisher vectors. In *IEEE Conference on Computer Vision and Pattern Recognition (CVPR)*, 2010.
368. Florent Perronnin, Jorge Sánchez, and Yan Liu. Large-scale image categorization with explicit data embedding. In *IEEE Conference on Computer Vision and Pattern Recognition (CVPR)*, 2010.
369. Florent Perronnin, Jorge Sánchez, and Thomas Mensink. Improving the fisher kernel for large-scale image classification. In *European Conference on Computer Vision (ECCV)*, 2010.
370. Leonid Pishchulin, Arjun Jain, Mykhaylo Andriluka, Thorsten Thormahlen, and Bernt Schiele. Articulated people detection and pose estimation: reshaping the future. In *IEEE Conference on Computer Vision and Pattern Recognition (CVPR)*, 2012.
371. Leonid Pishchulin, Arjun Jain, Christian Wojek, Mykhaylo Andriluka, Thorsten Thormählen, and Bernt Schiele. Learning people detection models from few training samples. In *IEEE Conference on Computer Vision and Pattern Recognition (CVPR)*, 2011.
372. Peter Prettenhofer and Benno Stein. Cross-language text classification using structural correspondence learning. In *Annual Meeting of the Association for Computational Linguistics(ACL)*, 2010.
373. Amazon Mechanical Turk. http://www.mturk.com.
374. Guo-Jun Qi, Charu Aggarwal, and Thomas Huang. Towards semantic knowledge propagation from text corpus to web images. In *International Conference on World Wide Web (WWW)*, 2011.
375. Guo-Jun Qi, Charu Aggarwal, Yong Rui, Qi Tian, Shiyu Chang, and Thomas Huang. Towards cross-category knowledge propagation for learning visual concepts. In *IEEE Conference on Computer Vision and Pattern Recognition (CVPR)*, 2011.
376. Guo-Jun Qi, Xian-Sheng Hua, Yong Rui, Jinhui Tang, and Hong-Jiang Zhang. Two-dimensional active learning for image classification. In *IEEE Conference on Computer Vision and Pattern Recognition (CVPR)*, 2008.
377. Qiang Qiu, Vishal M. Patel, Pavan Turaga, and Rama Chellappa. Domain adaptive dictionary learning. In *European Conference on Computer Vision (ECCV)*, 2012.
378. Brian Quanz, Jun Huan, and Meenakshi Mishra. Knowledge transfer with low-quality data: A feature extraction issue. *Transactions on Knowledge and Data Engineering*, 24(10):1789–1802, 2012.
379. Piyush Rai, Avishek Saha, Hal Daumé III, and Suresh Venkatasubramanian. Domain adaptation meets active learning. In *ACL Workshop on Active Learning for Natural Language Processing (ALNLP)*, 2010.
380. Rajat Raina, Alexis Battle, Honglak Lee, Benjamin Packer, and Andrew Y. Ng. Self-taught learning: transfer learning from unlabeled data. In *International Conference on Machine Learning (ICML)*, 2007.
381. Anant Raj, Vinay P. Namboodiri Namboodiri, and Tinne Tuytelaars. Subspace alignment based domain adaptation for rcnn detector. In *BMVA British Machine Vision Conference (BMVC)*, 2015.
382. Nikhil Rasiwasia, Jose Costa Pereira, Emanuele Coviello, Gabriel Doyle, Gert R. G. Lanckriet, Roger Levy, and Nuno Vasconcelos. A new approach to cross-modal multimedia retrieval. In *ACM Multimedia*, 2010.
383. Mohammad Rastegari, Abdou Diba, Devi Parikh, and Alireza Farhadi. Multi-attribute queries: To merge or not to merge? In *IEEE Conference on Computer Vision and Pattern Recognition (CVPR)*, 2013.

384. Ali Sharif Razavian, Hossein Azizpour, Josephine Sullivan, and Stefan Carlsson. CNN Features off-the-shelf: an Astounding Baseline for Recognition. *CoRR*, arXiv:1403.6382, 2014.
385. Douglas A. Reynolds, Thomas F. Quatieri, and Robert B. Dunn. Speaker verification using adapted Gaussian Mixture Models. *Digital Signal Processing*, 10(1):19–41, 2000.
386. Stephan R. Richter, Vibhav Vineet, Stefan Roth, and Vladlen Koltun. Playing for data: Ground truth from computer games. In *European Conference on Computer Vision (ECCV)*, 2016.
387. Stephan R. Richter, Vibhav Vineet, Stefan Roth, and Koltun Vladlen. Playing for data: Ground truth from computer games. In *European Conference on Computer Vision (ECCV)*, 2016.
388. Erik Rodner and Joachim Denzler. Learning with few examples by transferring feature relevance. In *BMVA British Machine Vision Conference (BMVC)*, 2009.
389. Erik Rodner, Judy Hoffman, Jeff Donahue, Trevor Darrell, and Kate Saenko. Towards adapting imagenet to reality: Scalable domain adaptation with implicit low-rank transformations. *CoRR*, arXiv:1308.4200, 2013.
390. José A. Rodríguez-Serrano, Harsimrat Sandhawalia, Raja Bala, Florent Perronnin, and Craig Saunders. Data-driven vehicle identification by image matching. In *ECCV Workshop on Computer Vision in Vehicle Technologies: From Earth to Mars (CVVT)*, 2012.
391. José A. Rodríguez-Serrano, Florent Perronnin, Gemma Sánchez, and Josep Lladós. Unsupervised writer adaptation of whole-word HMMs with application to word-spotting. *Pattern Recognition Letters*, 31(8):742–749, 2010.
392. Marcus Rohrbach, Sandra Ebert, and Bernt Schiele. Transfer learning in a transductive setting. In *Annual Conference on Neural Information Processing Systems (NIPS)*, 2013.
393. Marcus Rohrbach, Michael Stark, György Szarvas, Iryna Gurevych, and Bernt Schiele. What helps where – and why? semantic relatedness for knowledge transfer. In *IEEE Conference on Computer Vision and Pattern Recognition (CVPR)*, 2010.
394. Bernardino Romera-Paredes, Hane Aung, Nadia Bianchi-Berthouze, and Massimiliano Pontil. Multilinear multitask learning. In *International Conference on Machine Learning (ICML)*, 2013.
395. German Ros, Sebastian Ramos, Manuel Granados, Amir H. Bakhtiary, David Vázquez, and Antonio M. López. Vision-based offline-online perception paradigm for autonomous driving. In *Winter Conference on Applications of Computer Vision (WACV)*, 2015.
396. German Ros, Laura Sellart, Joanna Materzyńska, David Vázquez, and Antonio M. López. The SYNTHIA dataset: A large collection of synthetic images for semantic segmentation of urban scenes. In *IEEE Conference on Computer Vision and Pattern Recognition (CVPR)*, 2016.
397. German Ros, Simon Stent, Pablo F. Alcantarilla, and Tomoki Watanabe. Training constrained deconvolutional networks for road scene semantic segmentation. *CoRR*, arXiv:1604.01545, 2016.
398. Chuck Rosenberg, Martial Hebert, and Henry Schneiderman. Semisupervised self-training of object detection models. In *Workshops on Application of Computer Vision (WACV/MOTION)*, 2005.
399. Peter M. Roth, Sabine Sternig, Helmut Grabner, and Horst Bischof. Classifier grids for robust adaptive object detection. In *IEEE Conference on Computer Vision and Pattern Recognition (CVPR)*, 2009.
400. Sam T Roweis and Lawrence K Saul. Nonlinear dimensionality reduction by locally linear embedding. *Science*, 290(5500):2323–2326, 2000.
401. Artem Rozantsev, Vincent Lepetit, and Pascal Fua. On rendering synthetic images for training an object detector. *Computer Vision and Image Understanding*, 137:24–37, 2015.
402. Artem Rozantsev, Mathieu Salzmann, and Pascal Fua. Beyond sharing weights for deep domain adaptation. *CoRR*, arXiv:1603.06432, 2016.
403. Evgenia Rubinshtein and Anuj Srivastava. Optimal linear projections for enhancing desired data statistics. *Statistics Computing*, 20(3):267–282, 2010.
404. Olga Russakovsky, Jia Deng, Hao Su, Jonathan Krause, Sanjeev Satheesh, Sean Ma, Zhiheng Huang, Andrej Karpathy, Aditya Khosla, Michael Bernstein, Alexander C. Berg, and Li Fei-Fei. Imagenet large scale visual recognition challenge. *International Journal of Computer Vision*, 115(3):211–252, 2015.

405. Olga Russakovsky, Li-Jia Li, and Li Fei-Fei. Best of both worlds: human-machine collaboration for object annotation. In *IEEE Conference on Computer Vision and Pattern Recognition (CVPR)*, 2015.
406. Bryan C. Russell, Antonio Torralba, Kevin P. Murphy, and William T. Freeman. LabelMe: a database and web-based tool for image annotation. *International Journal of Computer Vision*, 77:157–173, 2008.
407. Kate Saenko, Brian Kulis, Mario Fritz, and Trevor Darrell. Adapting visual category models to new domains. In *European Conference on Computer Vision (ECCV)*, 2010.
408. Avishek Saha, Piyush Rai, Hal Daumé III, Suresh Venkatasubramanian, and Scott L. DuVall. Active supervised domain adaptation. In *Joint European Conference on Machine Learning and Knowledge Discovery in Databases (ECML PKDD)*, 2011.
409. Jorge Sánchez, Florent Perronnin, Thomas Mensink, and Jakob Verbeek. Image classification with the Fisher Vector: Theory and practice. *International Journal of Computer Vision*, 105(3):222–245, 2013.
410. Ramachandruni N. Sandeep, Yashaswi Verma, and C. V. Jawahar. Relative parts: Distinctive parts for learning relative attributes. In *IEEE Conference on Computer Vision and Pattern Recognition (CVPR)*, 2014.
411. Scott Satkin, Jason Lin, and Martial Hebert. Data-driven scene understanding from 3D models. In *BMVA British Machine Vision Conference (BMVC)*, 2012.
412. Shreyas Saxena and Jakob Verbeek. Heterogeneous face recognition with cnns. In *ECCV Workshop on Transferring and Adapting Source Knowledge in Computer Vision (TASK-CV)*, 2016.
413. Timo Scharwächter, Markus Enzweiler, Uwe Franke, and Stefan Roth. Efficient multi-cue scene segmentation. In *German Conference on Pattern Recognition (GCPR)*, 2013.
414. Walter J Scheirer, Neeraj Kumar, Peter N Belhumeur, and Terrance E Boult. Multi-attribute spaces: Calibration for attribute fusion and similarity search. In *IEEE Conference on Computer Vision and Pattern Recognition (CVPR)*, 2012.
415. Johannes Schels, Jörg Liebelt, Klaus Schertler, and Rainer Lienhart. Synthetically trained multi-view object class and viewpoint detection for advanced image retrieval. In *International Conference on Multimedia Retrieval (ICMR)*, 2011.
416. Bernhard Schölkopf, Alexander Smola, and Klaus-Robert Müller. Kernel principal component analysis. In *Annual Conference on Neural Information Processing Systems (NIPS)*, 1997.
417. Florian Schroff, Antonio Criminisi, and Andrew Zisserman. Harvesting image databases from the web. In *IEEE International Conference on Computer Vision (ICCV)*, 2007.
418. Pierre Sermanet, David Eigen, Xiang Zhang, Michaël Mathieu, Rob Fergus, and Yann LeCun. Overfeat: Integrated recognition, localization and detection using convolutional networks. *CoRR*, arXiv:1312.6229, 2013.
419. Burr Settles. active learning literature survey. Technical Report Computer Sciences Technical Report 1648, University of Wisconsin-Madison, 2010.
420. H. Sebastian Seung, Manfred Opper, and Haim Sompolinsky. Query by committee. In *Annual ACM workshop on Computational Learning Theory (CLT)*, 1992.
421. Alireza Shafaei, James J. Little, and Mark Schmidt. Play and learn: Using video games to train computer vision models. In *BMVA British Machine Vision Conference (BMVC)*, 2016.
422. Shai Shalev-Shwartz. *Online Learning: Theory, Algorithms, and Applications*. PhD thesis, Hebrew University, 7 2007.
423. Shai Shalev-Shwartz. Online learning and online convex optimization. *Foundations and Trends in Machine Learning*, 4(2):107–194, 2011.
424. Abhishek Sharma and David W. Jacobs. Bypassing synthesis: PLS for face recognition with pose, low-resolution and sketch. In *IEEE Conference on Computer Vision and Pattern Recognition (CVPR)*, 2011.
425. Abhishek Sharma, Abhishek Kumar, Hal Daumé III, and David W. Jacobs. Generalized multiview analysis: A discriminative latent space. In *IEEE Conference on Computer Vision and Pattern Recognition (CVPR)*, 2012.

426. Pramod Sharma, Chang Huang, and Ram Nevatia. Unsupervised incremental learning for improved object detection in a video. In *IEEE Conference on Computer Vision and Pattern Recognition (CVPR)*, 2012.
427. Pramod Sharma and Ram Nevatia. Efficient detector adaptation for object detection in a video. In *IEEE Conference on Computer Vision and Pattern Recognition (CVPR)*, 2013.
428. Viktoriia Sharmanska, Novi Quadrianto, and Christoph H. Lampert. Augmented attribute representations. In *European Conference on Computer Vision (ECCV)*, 2012.
429. Sumit Shekhar, Vishal M. Patel, Hien V. Nguyen, and Rama Chellappa. Generalized domain-adaptive dictionaries. In *IEEE Conference on Computer Vision and Pattern Recognition (CVPR)*, 2013.
430. Haoquan Shen, Shoou-I Yu, Yi Yang, Deyu Meng, and Alex Hauptmann. Unsupervised video adaptation for parsing human motion. In *European Conference on Computer Vision (ECCV)*, 2014.
431. Xiaoxiao Shi, Wei Fan, and Jiangtao Ren. Actively transfer domain knowledge. In *Joint European Conference on Machine Learning and Knowledge Discovery in Databases (ECML PKDD)*, 2008.
432. Xiaoxiao Shi, Qi Liu, Wei Fan, Philip S. Yu, and Ruixin Zhu. Transfer learning on heterogeneous feature spaces via spectral transformation. In *IEEE International Conference on Data Mining (ICDM)*, 2010.
433. Zhiyuan Shi, Yongxin Yang, Timothy M Hospedales, and Tao Xiang. Weakly supervised learning of objects, attributes and their associations. In *European Conference on Computer Vision (ECCV)*, 2014.
434. Hidetoshi Shimodaira. Improving predictive inference under covariate shift by weighting the log-likelihood function. *Journal of Statistical Planning and Inference*, 90(2):227–244, 2000.
435. Jamie Shotton, Andrew Fitzgibbon, Mat Cook, Toby Sharp, Mark Finocchio, Richard Moore, Alex Kipman, and Andrew Blake. Real-time human pose recognition in parts from single depth images. In *IEEE Conference on Computer Vision and Pattern Recognition (CVPR)*, 2011.
436. Abhinav Shrivastava, Saurabh Singh, and Abhinav Gupta. Constrained semi-supervised learning using attributes and comparative attributes. In *European Conference on Computer Vision (ECCV)*, 2012.
437. Xiangbo Shu, Guo-Jun Qi, Jinhui Tang, and Wang Jingdong. Weakly-shared deep transfer networks for heterogeneous-domain knowledge propagation. In *ACM Multimedia*, 2015.
438. Si Si, Dacheng Tao, and Bo B. Geng. Bregman divergence-based regularization for transfer subspace learning. *Transactions on Knowledge and Data Engineering*, 22(7):929 –942, 2010.
439. Behjat Siddiquie, Rogerio S Feris, and Larry S Davis. Image ranking and retrieval based on multi-attribute queries. In *IEEE Conference on Computer Vision and Pattern Recognition (CVPR)*, 2011.
440. Olivier Sigaud, Clment Masson, David Filliat, and Freek Stulp. Gated networks: an inventory. *CoRR*, arXiv:1512.03201, 2015.
441. Nathan Silberman, Derek Hoiem, Pushmeet Kohli, and Rob Fergus. Indoor segmentation and support inference from rgbd images. In *European Conference on Computer Vision (ECCV)*, 2012.
442. Karen Simonyan and Andrew Zisserman. Two-stream convolutional networks for action recognition in videos. In *Annual Conference on Neural Information Processing Systems (NIPS)*, 2014.
443. Karen Simonyan and Andrew Zisserman. Very deep convolutional networks for large-scale image recognition. *CoRR*, arXiv:1409.1556, 2014.
444. Ajit Singh, Paul Singh, and Geoffrey J. Gordon. Relational learning via collective matrix factorization. In *ACM SIGKDD Conference on Knowledge Discovery and Data Mining (SIGKDD)*, 2008.
445. Josef Sivic, and Andrew Zisserman. Video google: A text retrieval approach to object matching in videos. In *IEEE International Conference on Computer Vision (ICCV)*, 2003.

446. Brandon Smith and Li Zhang. Collaborative facial landmark localization for transferring annotations across datasets. In *European Conference on Computer Vision (ECCV)*, 2014.
447. Alex Smola, Arthur Gretton, Le Song, and Bernhard Schölkopf. A hilbert space embedding for distributions. In *Algorithmic Learning Theory*, 2007.
448. Yainuvis Socarras, Sebastian Ramos, David Vázquez, Antonio M. López, and Theo Gevers. Adapting pedestrian detection from synthetic to far infrared images. In *ICCV Workshop on Visual Domain Adaptation and Dataset Bias (VisDA)*, 2013.
449. Richard Socher, Milind Ganjoo, Christopher D. Manning, and Andrew Y. Ng. Zero-shot learning through cross-modal transfer. In *Annual Conference on Neural Information Processing Systems (NIPS)*, 2013.
450. Richard Socher and Fei-Fei Li. Connecting modalities: Semi-supervised segmentation and annotation of images using unaligned text corpora. In *IEEE Conference on Computer Vision and Pattern Recognition (CVPR)*, 2010.
451. Khurram Soomro, Amir Roshan Zamir, and Mubarak Shah. UCF101: A dataset of 101 human actions classes from videos in the wild. *CoRR*, arXiv:1212.0402, 2012.
452. César De Souza, Adrien Gaidon, Yohann Cabon, and Antonio M. López. Procedural generation of videos to train deep action recognition networks. *CoRR*, arXiv:1612.00881, 2016.
453. Bharath K Sriperumbudur, Arthur Gretton, Kenji Fukumizu, Bernhard Schölkopf, and Gert RG Lanckriet. Hilbert space embeddings and metrics on probability measures. *Journal of Machine Learning Research*, 11:1517–1561, 2010.
454. Anuj Srivastava and Xiuwen Liu. Tools for application-driven linear dimension reduction. *Neurocomputing*, 67:136–160, 2005.
455. Nitish Srivastava, Geoffrey E. Hinton, Alex Krizhevsky, Ilya Sutskever, and Ruslan Salakhutdinov. Dropout: A simple way to prevent neural networks from overfitting. *Journal of Machine Learning Research*, 2014.
456. Severin Stalder, Helmut Grabner, and Luc Van Gool. Exploring context to learn scene specific object detectors. In *International Workshop on Performance Evaluation of Tracking and Surveillance (PETS)*, 2009.
457. Michael Stark, Michael Goesele, and Bernt Schiele. A shape-based object class model for knowledge transfer. In *IEEE International Conference on Computer Vision (ICCV)*, 2009.
458. Michael Stark, Michael Goesele, and Bernt Schiele. Back to the future: Learning shape models from 3D CAD data. In *BMVA British Machine Vision Conference (BMVC)*, 2010.
459. Ingo Steinwart. On the influence of the kernel on the consistency of support vector machines. *Journal of Machine Learning Research*, 2:67–93, 2002.
460. Hao Su, Charles R. Qi, Yangyan Yi, and Leonidas Guibas. Render for CNN: viewpoint estimation in images using CNNs trained with rendered 3D model views. In *IEEE International Conference on Computer Vision (ICCV)*, 2015.
461. Hao Su, Fan Wang, Yangyan Yi, and Leonidas Guibas. 3D-assisted feature synthesis for novel views of an object. In *IEEE International Conference on Computer Vision (ICCV)*, 2015.
462. Yu Su, Moray Allan, and Frédéric Jurie. Improving object classification using semantic attributes. In *BMVA British Machine Vision Conference (BMVC)*, 2010.
463. Masashi Sugiyama, Shinichi Nakajima, Hisashi Kashima, Paul von. Buenau, and Motoaki Kawanabe. Direct importance estimation with model selection and its application to covariate shift adaptation. In *Annual Conference on Neural Information Processing Systems (NIPS)*, 2008.
464. Baochen Sun. *Correlation Alignment for Domain Adaptation*. PhD thesis, University of Massachusetts Lowell, 8 2016.
465. Baochen Sun, Jiashi Feng, and Kate Saenko. Return of frustratingly easy domain adaptation. In *AAAI Conference on Artificial Intelligence (AAAI)*, 2016.
466. Baochen Sun, Xingchao Peng, and Kate Saenko. Generating large scale image datasets from 3d cad models. In *CVPR Workshop on The Future of Datasets in Vision (FDV)*, 2015.
467. Baochen Sun and Kate Saenko. From virtual to reality: Fast adaptation of virtual object detectors to real domains. In *BMVA British Machine Vision Conference (BMVC)*, 2014.

468. Baochen Sun and Kate Saenko. Deep coral: Correlation Alignment for deep domain adaptation. In *ECCV Workshop on Transferring and Adapting Source Knowledge in Computer Vision (TASK-CV)*, 2016.
469. Chen Sun, Chuang Gan, and Ram Nevatia. Automatic concept discovery from parallel text and visual corpora. In *IEEE International Conference on Computer Vision (ICCV)*, 2015.
470. Chen Sun, Sanketh Shetty, Rahul Sukthankar, and Ram Nevatia. Temporal localization of fine-grained actions in videos by domain transfer from web images. In *ACM Multimedia*, 2015.
471. Qian Sun, Rita Chattopadhyay, Sethuraman Panchanathan, and Jieping Ye. A two-stage weighting framework for multi-source domain adaptation. In *Annual Conference on Neural Information Processing Systems (NIPS)*, 2011.
472. Christian Szegedy, Wei Liu, Yangqing Jia, Pierre Sermanet, Scott Reed, Dragomir Anguelov, Dumitru Erhan, Vincent Vanhoucke, and Andrew Rabinovich. Going deeper with convolutions. In *IEEE Conference on Computer Vision and Pattern Recognition (CVPR)*, 2015.
473. ben Tan, Yangqiu Song, Erheng Zhong, and Qiang Yang. Transitive transfer learning. In *ACM SIGKDD Conference on Knowledge Discovery and Data Mining (SIGKDD)*, 2015.
474. Ben Tan, Erheng Zhong, Michael Ng, and K. Qiang Yang. Mixed-transfer: Transfer learning over mixed graphs. In *SIAM International Conference on Data Mining (SDM)*, 2014.
475. Kevin Tang, Vignesh Ramanathan, Li Fei-Fei, and Daphne Koller. Shifting weights: Adapting object detectors from image to video. In *Annual Conference on Neural Information Processing Systems (NIPS)*, 2012.
476. Ran Tao, Arnold WM Smeulders, and Shih-Fu Chang. Attributes and categories for generic instance search from one example. In *IEEE Conference on Computer Vision and Pattern Recognition (CVPR)*, 2015.
477. Geoffrey R. Taylor, Andrew J. Chosak, and Paul C. Brewer. OVVV: Using virtual worlds to design and evaluate surveillance systems. In *IEEE Conference on Computer Vision and Pattern Recognition (CVPR)*, 2007.
478. Unity Technologies. Unity Development Platform.
479. George R. Terrell. The maximal smoothing principle in density estimation. *Journal of the American Statistical Association*, 85(410):470–477, 1990.
480. Giorgos Tolias, Ronan Sicre, and Hervé Jégou. Particular object retrieval with integral max-pooling of CNN activations. In *International Conference on Machine Learning (ICML)*, 2016.
481. Tatiana Tommasi and Barbara Caputo. The more you know, the less you learn: from knowledge transfer to one-shot learning of object categories. In *BMVA British Machine Vision Conference (BMVC)*, 2009.
482. Tatiana Tommasi and Barbara Caputo. Safety in numbers: learning categories from few examples with multi model knowledge transfer. In *IEEE Conference on Computer Vision and Pattern Recognition (CVPR)*, 2010.
483. Tatiana Tommasi and Barbara Caputo. Frustratingly easy NBNN domain adaptation. In *IEEE International Conference on Computer Vision (ICCV)*, 2013.
484. Tatiana Tommasi, Novi Patricia, Barbara Caputo, and Tinne Tuytelaars. A deeper look at dataset bias. In *German Conference on Pattern Recognition (GCPR)*, 2015.
485. Tatiana Tommasi, Novi Quadrianto, Barbara Caputo, and Christoph H. Lampert. Beyond dataset bias: Multi-task unaligned shared knowledge transfer. In *Asian Conference on Computer Vision (ACCV)*, 2012.
486. Tatiana Tommasi and Tinne Tuytelaars. A testbed for cross-dataset analysis. In *ECCV Workshop on Transferring and Adapting Source Knowledge in Computer Vision (TASK-CV)*, 2014.
487. Jonathan J Tompson, Arjun Jain, Yann LeCun, and Christoph Bregler. Joint training of a convolutional network and a graphical model for human pose estimation. In *Annual Conference on Neural Information Processing Systems (NIPS)*, 2014.
488. Simon Tong and Daphne Koller. Support vector machine active learning with applications to text classification. *Journal of Machine Learning Research*, 2:45–66, 2002.
489. Antonio Torralba and Alexei A. Efros. Unbiased look at dataset bias. In *IEEE Conference on Computer Vision and Pattern Recognition (CVPR)*, 2011.

490. Antonio Torralba, Kevin P. Murphy, and William T. Freeman. Sharing visual features for multiclass and multiview object detection. *Transactions on Pattern Analysis and Machine Intelligence (PAMI)*, 29(5):854–869, 2007.
491. Lorenzo Torresani, Martin Szummer, and Andrew Fitzgibbon. Efficient object category recognition using classemes. In *European Conference on Computer Vision (ECCV)*, 2010.
492. Du Tran, Lubomir Bourdev, Rob Fergus, Lorenzo Torresani, and Manohar Paluri. C3d: Generic features for video analysis. *IEEE International Conference on Computer Vision (ICCV)*, 2015.
493. Ledyard R. Tucker. Some mathematical notes on three-mode factor analysis. *Psychometrika*, 31(3):279–311, 1966.
494. Shubham Tulsiani, João Carreira, and Jitendra Malik. Pose induction for novel object categories. In *IEEE International Conference on Computer Vision (ICCV)*, 2015.
495. Shubham Tulsiani and Jitendra Malik. Viewpoints and keypoints. In *IEEE Conference on Computer Vision and Pattern Recognition (CVPR)*, 2015.
496. Eric Tzeng, Coline Devin, Judy Hoffman, Chelsea Finn, Xingchao Peng, Sergey Levine, Kate Saenko, and Trevor Darrell. Towards adapting deep visuomotor representations from simulated to real environments. *CoRR*, arXiv:1511.07111, 2015.
497. Eric Tzeng, Judy Hoffman, Trevor Darrell, and Kate Saenko. Simultaneous deep transfer across domains and tasks. In *IEEE International Conference on Computer Vision (ICCV)*, 2015.
498. Eric Tzeng, Judy Hoffman, Kate Saenko, and Trevor Darrell. Adversarial discriminative domain adaptation. In *NIPS Workshop on Adversarial Training, (WAT)*, 2016.
499. Eric Tzeng, Judy Hoffman, Ning Zhang, Kate Saenko, and Trevor Darrell. Deep domain confusion: Maximizing for domain invariance. *CoRR*, arXiv:1412.3474, 2014.
500. Jasper R.R. Uijlings, Koen E.A. van de Sande, Theo Gevers, and Arnold W.M. Smeulders. Selective search for object recognition. *International Journal of Computer Vision*, 104(2):154–171, 2013.
501. Laurens van der Maaten. Barnes-Hut-SNE. *CoRR*, arXiv:1301.3342, 2013.
502. Manik Varma and Andrew Zisserman. A statistical approach to material classification using image patch exemplars. *Transactions on Pattern Analysis and Machine Intelligence (PAMI)*, 31(11):2032–2047, 2009.
503. David Vazquez, Antonio M. López, Javier Marín, Daniel Ponsa, and David Gerónimo. Virtual and real world adaptation for pedestrian detection. *Transactions on Pattern Analysis and Machine Intelligence (PAMI)*, 36(4):797–809, 2014.
504. David Vázquez, Antonio M. López, Daniel Ponsa, and David Gerónimo. Interactive training of human detectors. In Angel D. Sappa and Jordi Vitrià, editors, *Multimodal Interaction in Image and Video Applications Intelligent Systems*, pages 169–184. Springer, 2013.
505. David Vázquez, Antonio M. López, Daniel Ponsa, and Javier Marín. Cool world: domain adaptation of virtual and real worlds for human detection using active learning. In *NIPS Workshop on Domain Adaptation: Theory and Applications (DATA)*, 2011.
506. David Vázquez, Antonio M. López, Daniel Ponsa, and Javier Marín. Virtual worlds and active learning for human detection. In *International Conference on Multimodal Interaction (ICMI)*, 2011.
507. Andrea Vedaldi, Varun Gulshan, Manik Varma, and Andrew Zisserman. Multiple kernels for object detection. In *IEEE International Conference on Computer Vision (ICCV)*, 2009.
508. Andrea Vedaldi, Siddarth Mahendran, Stavros Tsogkas, Subhrajyoti Maji, Ross Girshick, Juho Kannala, Esa Rahtu, Iasonas Kokkinos, Matthew B Blaschko, Daniel Weiss, Ben Taskar, Karen Simonyan, Naomi Saphra, and Sammy Mohamed. Understanding objects in detail with fine-grained attributes. In *IEEE Conference on Computer Vision and Pattern Recognition (CVPR)*, 2014.
509. Ramakrishna Vedantam, Xiao Lin, Tanmay Batra, C. Lawrence Zitnick, and Devi Parikh. Learning common sense through visual abstraction. In *IEEE International Conference on Computer Vision (ICCV)*, 2015.

510. V.S.R. Veeravasarapu, Rudra Narayan Hota, Constantin Rothkopf, and Ramesh Visvanathan. Model validation for vision systems via graphics simulation. *CoRR*, arXiv:1512.01401, 2015.
511. V.S.R. Veeravasarapu, Rudra Narayan Hota, Constantin Rothkopf, and Ramesh Visvanathan. Simulations for validation of vision systems. *CoRR*, arXiv:1512.01030, 2015.
512. V.S.R. Veeravasarapu, Constantin Rothkopf, and Ramesh Visvanathan. Model-driven simulations for deep convolutional neural networks. *CoRR*, arXiv:1605.09582, 2016.
513. Sudheendra Vijayanarasimhan and Kristen Grauman. What's it going to cost you?: Predicting effort vs. informativeness for multi-label image annotations. In *IEEE Conference on Computer Vision and Pattern Recognition (CVPR)*, 2009.
514. Pascal Vincent, Hugo Larochelle, Yoshua Bengio, and Pierre-Antoine Manzagol. Extracting and composing robust features with denoising autoencoders. In *International Conference on Machine Learning (ICML)*, 2008.
515. Alexei Vinokourov, Nello Cristianini, and John Shawe-Taylor. Inferring a semantic representation of text via cross-language correlation analysis. In *Annual Conference on Neural Information Processing Systems (NIPS)*, 2003.
516. Paul Viola and Michael Jones. Rapid object detection using a boosted cascade of simple features. In *IEEE Conference on Computer Vision and Pattern Recognition (CVPR)*, 2001.
517. Catherine Wah, Steve Branson, Pietro Perona, and Serge Belongie. Multiclass recognition and part localization with humans in the loop. In *IEEE International Conference on Computer Vision (ICCV)*, 2011.
518. Catherine Wah, Steve Branson, Peter Welinder, Pietro Perona, and Serge Belongie. The Caltech-UCSD birds-200-2011 dataset. Technical Report CNS-TR-2011-001, California Institute of Technology, 2011.
519. Chang Wang and Sridhar Mahadevan. Manifold alignment without correspondence. In *AAAI International Joint Conference on Artificial Intelligence (IJCAI)*, 2009.
520. Chang Wang and Sridhar Mahadevan. Heterogeneous domain adaptation using manifold alignment. In *AAAI International Joint Conference on Artificial Intelligence (IJCAI)*, 2011.
521. Heng Wang, Muhammad Muneeb Ullah, Alexander Kläser, Ivan Laptev, and Cordelia Schmid. Evaluation of local spatio-temporal features for action recognition. In *BMVA British Machine Vision Conference (BMVC)*, 2009.
522. LiMin Wang, Yu Qiao, and Xiaoou Tang. Motionlets: Mid-level 3d parts for human motion recognition. In *IEEE Conference on Computer Vision and Pattern Recognition (CVPR)*, 2013.
523. Liwei Wang, Yin Li, and Svetlana Lazebnik. Learning deep structure-preserving image-text embeddings. In *IEEE Conference on Computer Vision and Pattern Recognition (CVPR)*, 2016.
524. Meng Wang and Xiaogang Wang. Automatic adaptation of a generic pedestrian detector to a specific traffic scene. In *IEEE Conference on Computer Vision and Pattern Recognition (CVPR)*, 2011.
525. Weiran Wang, Raman Arora, Karen Livescu, and Jeff Bilmes. On deep multi-view representation learning. In *International Conference on Machine Learning (ICML)*, 2015.
526. Xiaoyang Wang and Qiang Ji. A unified probabilistic approach modeling relationships between attributes and objects. In *IEEE International Conference on Computer Vision (ICCV)*, 2013.
527. Xiaoyu Wang, Gang Hua, and Tony X. han. Detection by detections: Non-parametric detector adaptation for a video. In *IEEE Conference on Computer Vision and Pattern Recognition (CVPR)*, 2012.
528. Xiaoyu Wang, Ming Yang, Shenghuo Zhu, and Yuanqing Lin. Regionlets for generic object detection. In *IEEE International Conference on Computer Vision (ICCV)*, 2013.
529. Xin-Jing Wang, Lei Zhang, Xirong Li, and Wei-Ying Ma. Annotating images by mining image search results. *Transactions on Pattern Analysis and Machine Intelligence (PAMI)*, 30:1919–1932, 2008.
530. Xuezhi Wang, Tzu-Kuo Huang, and Jeff Schneider. Active transfer learning under model shift. In *International Conference on Machine Learning (ICML)*, 2014.
531. Xuezhi Wang and Jeff Schneider. Flexible transfer learning under support and model shift. In *Annual Conference on Neural Information Processing Systems (NIPS)*, 2014.

532. Yang Wang and Greg Mori. A discriminative latent model of object classes and attributes. In *European Conference on Computer Vision (ECCV)*, 2010.
533. Kilian Q Weinberger and Lawrence K Saul. Unsupervised learning of image manifolds by semidefinite programming. *International Journal of Computer Vision*, 70(1):77–90, 2006.
534. Kilian Q. Weinberger and Lawrence K. Saul. Distance metric learning for large margin nearest neighbor classification. *Journal of Machine Learning Research*, 10:207–244, 2009.
535. Karl Weiss, Taghi M. Khoshgoftaar, and DingDing Wang. A survey of transfer learning. *Journal of Big Data*, 9(3), 2016.
536. Jason Weston, Samy Bengio, and Nicolas Usunier. Large scale image annotation: learning to rank with joint word-image embeddings. *Machine Learning*, 81(1):21–35, 2010.
537. Zheng Whang, Yangqiu Song, and Changshui Zhang. Transferred dimensionality reduction. In *Joint European Conference on Machine Learning and Knowledge Discovery in Databases (ECML PKDD)*, 2008.
538. Lieve Van Woensel, Geoff Archer Archer, and Darja Panades-Estruch, Laura abd Vrscaj. Ten technologies which could change our lives. Technical report, EPRS - European Parlimentary Research Service, January 2015.
539. Phil C. Woodland. Speaker adaptation: techniques and challenges. In *IEEE Workshop on Automatic Speech Recognition and Understanding (ASRU)*, 1999.
540. Bo Wu and Ram Nevatia. Improving part based object detection by unsupervised, online boosting. In *IEEE Conference on Computer Vision and Pattern Recognition (CVPR)*, 2007.
541. Jianxiong Xiao, James Hays, Krista A. Ehinger, Aude Oliva, and Antonio Torralba. Sun database: Large-scale scene recognition from abbey to zoo. In *IEEE Conference on Computer Vision and Pattern Recognition (CVPR)*, 2010.
542. Min Xiao and Yuhong Guo. Semi-supervised subspace co-projection for multi-class heterogeneous domain adaptation. In *Joint European Conference on Machine Learning and Knowledge Discovery in Databases (ECML PKDD)*, 2015.
543. Chang Xu, Dacheng Tao, and Chao Xu. A survey on multi-view learning. *CoRR*, arXiv:1304.5634, 2013.
544. Jiaolong Xu, Sebastian Ramos, David Vázquez, and Antonio M. López. Domain adaptation of deformable part-based models. *Transactions on Pattern Analysis and Machine Intelligence (PAMI)*, 36(12):2367–2380, 2014.
545. Jiaolong Xu, Sebastian Ramos, David Vázquez, and Antonio M. López. Hierarchical adaptive structural SVM for domain adaptation. *International Journal of Computer Vision*, 119(2):159–178, 2016.
546. Jiaolong Xu, David Vázquez, Antonio M. López, Javier Marín, and Daniel Ponsa. Learning a part-based pedestrian detector in a virtual world. *Transactions on Intelligent Transportation Systems*, 15(5):2121–2131, 2014.
547. Jiaolong Xu, David Vázquez, Krystian Mikolajczyk, and Antonio M. López. Hierarchical online domain adaptation of deformable part-based models. In *International Conference on Robotics and Automation (ICRA)*, 2016.
548. Xiang Xu, Shaogang Gong, and Timothy M. Hospedales. Cross-domain traffic scene understanding by motion model transfer. In *International Workshop on Analysis and Retrieval of Tracked Events and Motion in Imagery Stream (ARTEMIS)*, 2013.
549. Zheng Xu, Wen Li, Li Niu, and Dong Xu. Exploiting low-rank structure from latent domains for domain generalization. In *European Conference on Computer Vision (ECCV)*, 2014.
550. Zhijie Xu and Shiliang Sun. Multi-source transfer learning with multi-view adaboost. In *Annual Conference on Neural Information Processing Systems (NIPS)*, 2010.
551. Makoto Yamada, Leonid Sigal, and Michalis Raptis. No bias left behind: Covariate shift adaptation for discriminative 3d pose estimation. In *European Conference on Computer Vision (ECCV)*, 2012.
552. Fei Yan and Krystian Mikolajczyk. Deep correlation for matching images and text. In *IEEE Conference on Computer Vision and Pattern Recognition (CVPR)*, 2015.
553. Yuguang Yan, Qingyao Wu, Mingkui Tan, and Huaqing Min. Online heterogeneous transfer learning by weighted offline and online classifiers. In *ECCV Workshop on Transferring and Adapting Source Knowledge in Computer Vision (TASK-CV)*, 2016.

554. Jun Yang, Rong Yan, and Alexander G. Hauptmann. Cross-domain video concept detection using adaptive SVMs. In *ACM Multimedia*, 2007.
555. Jun Yang, Rong Yan, and Alexander G. Hauptmann. Cross-domain video concept detection using adaptive svms. In *IEEE International Conference on Computer Vision (ICCV)*, 2013.
556. Liu Yang, Liping Jing, Jian Yu, and Michael K. Ng. Learning transferred weights from co-occurrence data for heterogeneous transfer learning. *Transactions on Neural Networks and Learning Systems*, 27(11):2187–2200, 2015.
557. Meng Yang, Lei Zhang, Xiangchu Feng, and David Zhang. Fisher discrimination dictionary learning for sparse representation. In *IEEE International Conference on Computer Vision (ICCV)*, 2011.
558. Qiang Yang, Yuqiang Chen, Gui-Rong Xue, Wenyuan Dai, and Yu. Yong. Heterogeneous transfer learning for image clustering via the socialweb. In *Annual Meeting of the Association for Computational Linguistics(ACL)*, 2009.
559. Yi Yang and Deva Ramanan. Articulated human detection with flexible mixtures of parts. *Transactions on Pattern Analysis and Machine Intelligence (PAMI)*, 35(12):2878–2890, 2013.
560. Yongxin Yang and Timothy M. Hospedales. A unified perspective on multi-domain and multi-task learning. In *International Conference on Learning representations (ICLR)*, 2015.
561. Yongxin Yang and Timothy M. Hospedales. Deep multi-task representation learning: A tensor factorisation approach. In *ICLR*, 2016.
562. Yongxin Yang and Timothy M. Hospedales. Multivariate regression on the grassmannian for predicting novel domains. In *IEEE Conference on Computer Vision and Pattern Recognition (CVPR)*, 2016.
563. Yongxin Yang and Timothy M. Hospedales. Trace norm regularised deep multi-task learning. *CoRR*, arXiv:1606.04038, 2016.
564. Ting Yao, Yingwei Pan, Chong-Wah Ngo, Houqiang Li, and Tao Mei. Semi-supervised domain adaptation with subspace learning for visual recognition. In *IEEE Conference on Computer Vision and Pattern Recognition (CVPR)*, 2015.
565. Yi Yao and Gianfranco Doretto. Boosting for transfer learning with multiple sources. In *IEEE Conference on Computer Vision and Pattern Recognition (CVPR)*, 2010.
566. Dong Yi, Zhen Lei, and Stan Z. Li. Deep metric learning for practical person re-identification. *CoRR*, arXiv:1407.4979, 2014.
567. Jason Yosinski, Jeff Clune, Yoshua Bengio, and Hod Lipson. How transferable are features in deep neural networks? In *Annual Conference on Neural Information Processing Systems (NIPS)*, 2014.
568. Felix X. Yu, Rongrong Ji, Ming-Hen Tsai, Guangnan Ye, and Shih-Fu Chang. Weak attributes for large-scale image retrieval. In *IEEE Conference on Computer Vision and Pattern Recognition (CVPR)*, 2012.
569. Xiaodong Yu and Yiannis Aloimonos. Attribute-based transfer learning for object categorization with zero/one training example. In *European Conference on Computer Vision (ECCV)*, 2010.
570. Bianca Zadrozny. Learning and evaluating classifiers under sample selection bias. In *International Conference on Machine Learning (ICML)*, 2004.
571. Matthew D. Zeiler. ADADELTA: an adaptive learning rate method. *CoRR*, arXiv:1212.5701, 2012.
572. Matthew D. Zeiler and Rob Fergus. Visualizing and understanding convolutional networks. *CoRR*, arXiv:1311.2901, 2013.
573. Matthew D. Zeiler and Rob Fergus. Visualizing and understanding convolutional networks. In *European Conference on Computer Vision (ECCV)*, 2014.
574. Matthew D. Zeiler, Dilip Krishnan, Graham W. Taylor, and Rob Fergus. Deconvolutional networks. In *IEEE Conference on Computer Vision and Pattern Recognition (CVPR)*, 2010.
575. Zheng-Jun Zha, tao Mei, Meng Wang, Zengfu Wang, and Xian-Sheng Hua. Robust distance metric learning with auxiliary knowledge. In *AAAI International Joint Conference on Artificial Intelligence (IJCAI)*, 2009.

576. Deming Zhai, Bo Li, Hong Chang, Shiguang Shan, Xilin Chen, and Wen Gao. Manifold alignment via corresponding projections. In *BMVA British Machine Vision Conference (BMVC)*, 2010.
577. Cha Zhang, Raffay Hammid, and Zhengyou Zhang. Taylor expansion based classifier adaptation: Application to person detection. In *IEEE Conference on Computer Vision and Pattern Recognition (CVPR)*, 2008.
578. Kun Zhang, Bernhard Schölkopf, Krikamol Muandet, and Zhikun Wang. Domain adaptation under target and conditional shift. *Journal of Machine Learning Research*, 28(3):819–827, 2013.
579. Ning Zhang, Jeff Donahue, Ross Girshick, and Trevor Darrell. Part-based R-CNNs for fine-grained category detection. In *European Conference on Computer Vision (ECCV)*, 2014.
580. Ning Zhang, Manohar Paluri, Marc'Aurelio Ranzato, Trevor Darrell, and Lubomir Bourdev. Panda: Pose aligned networks for deep attribute modeling. In *IEEE Conference on Computer Vision and Pattern Recognition (CVPR)*, 2014.
581. Yu Zhang and Dit-Yan Yeung. Transfer metric learning by learning task relationships. In *ACM SIGKDD Conference on Knowledge Discovery and Data Mining (SIGKDD)*, 2010.
582. Zhanpeng Zhang, Ping Luo, Chen Change Loy, and Xiaoou Tang. Facial landmark detection by deep multi-task learning. In *European Conference on Computer Vision (ECCV)*, 2014.
583. Ziming Zhang and Venkatesh Saligrama. Person re-identification via structured prediction. *CoRR*, arXiv:1406.4444, 2014.
584. Rui Zhao, Wanli Ouyang, and Xiaogang Wang. Person re-identificationby saliency learning. *CoRR*, arXiv:1412.1908, 2014.
585. Shuai Zheng, Junge Zhang, Kaiqi Huang, Ran He, and Tieniu Tan. Robust view transformation model for gait recognition. In *International Conference on Image Processing (ICIP)*, 2011.
586. Erheng Zhong, Wei Fan, Jing Peng, Kun Zhang, Jiangtao Ren, Deepak Turaga, and Olivier Verscheure. Cross domain distribution adaptation via kernel mapping. In *ACM SIGKDD Conference on Knowledge Discovery and Data Mining (SIGKDD)*, 2009.
587. Joey Tianyi Zhou, Sinno Jialin Pan, Ivor W. Tsang, and Yan Yan. Hybrid heterogeneous transfer learning through deep learning. In *AAAI Conference on Artificial Intelligence (AAAI)*, 2014.
588. Joey Tianyi Zhou, Ivor W. Tsang, Sinno Jialin Pan, and Mingkui Tan. Heterogeneous domain adaptation for multiple classes. In *International Conference on Artificial Intelligence and Statistics (AISTATS)*, 2014.
589. Mianwei Zhou and Kevin C. Chang. Unifying learning to rank and domain adaptation: Enabling cross-task document scoring. In *ACM SIGKDD Conference on Knowledge Discovery and Data Mining (SIGKDD)*, 2014.
590. Fan Zhu and Ling Shao. Enhancing action recognition by cross-domain dictionary learning. In *BMVA British Machine Vision Conference (BMVC)*, 2013.
591. Xiangxin Zhu, Carl Vondrick, Charles C. Fowlkes, and Deva Ramanan. Do we need more training data? *International Journal of Computer Vision*, 119(1):76–92, 2016.
592. Xiaojin Zhu, Andrew B. Goldberg, Ronald Brachman, and Thomas Dietterich. *Introduction to semi-supervised learning*. Morgan & Claypool Publishers, 2009.
593. Yin Zhu, Yuqiang Chen, Zhongqi Lu, Sinno J. Pan, Gui-Rong Xue, Yong Yu, and Qiang Yang. Heterogeneous transfer learning for image classification. In *AAAI Conference on Artificial Intelligence (AAAI)*, 2011.
594. Yuke Zhu, Roozbeh Mottaghi, Eric Kolve, Joseph J. Lim, and Abhinav Gupta. Target-driven visual navigation in indoor scenes using deep reinforcement learning. *CoRR*, arXiv:1609.05143, 2016.

595. C. Lawrence Zitnick and Piotr Dollár. Edge boxes: Locating object proposals from edges. In *European Conference on Computer Vision (ECCV)*, 2014.
596. C. Lawrence Zitnick, Ramakrishna Vedantam, and Devi Parikh. Adopting abstract images for semantic scene understanding. *Transactions on Pattern Analysis and Machine Intelligence (PAMI)*, 38(4):627–638, 2016.
597. Laurent Zwald and Gilles Blanchard. On the convergence of eigenspaces in kernel principal component analysis. In *Annual Conference on Neural Information Processing Systems (NIPS)*, 2005.

Index

G. Csurka (ed.), *Domain Adaptation in Computer Vision Applications*, Advances in Computer Vision and Pattern Recognition, DOI 10.1007/978-3-319-58347-1

MIX
Papier aus verantwortungsvollen Quellen
Paper from responsible sources
FSC® C105338
FSC
www.fsc.org

If you have any concerns about our products,
you can contact us on
ProductSafety@springernature.com

In case Publisher is established outside the EU,
the EU authorized representative is:
Springer Nature Customer Service Center GmbH
Europaplatz 3, 69115 Heidelberg, Germany

Printed by Libri Plureos GmbH
in Hamburg, Germany